The New Silk Roads: Transport and Trade in Greater Central Asia

S. Frederick Starr, Editor

Johns Hopkins University-SAIS, 1619 Massachusetts Ave. NW, Washington, D.C. 20036
Uppsala University, Box 514, 75120 Uppsala, Sweden
www.silkroadstudies.org

"The New Silk Roads: Transport and Trade in Greater Central Asia" is a monograph produced by the Central Asia-Caucasus Institute & Silk Road Studies Program.

The Central Asia-Caucasus Institute and Silk Road Studies Program is a joint transatlantic independent and externally funded research and policy center. The Joint Center has offices in Washington and Uppsala, and is affiliated with the Paul H. Nitze School of Advanced International Studies of Johns Hopkins University and the Department of Eurasian Studies of Uppsala University. The Joint Center is the first of its kind and is today firmly established as a leading focus of research and policy worldwide, serving a large and diverse community of analysts, scholars, policy-watchers, business leaders and journalists. The Joint Center aims to be at the forefront of research on issues of conflict, security and development in the region; and to function as a focal point for academic, policy, and public discussion of the region through its applied research, its publications, teaching, research cooperation, public lectures and seminars.

ISBN: 91-85473-35-9

Printed in the United States of America

Cover photo credits: Upper right, the American funded bridge over the Pyanj river connecting Tajikistan and Afghanistan, photographed from the Tajik side. Photo courtesy of U.S. Army Corps of Engineers. Left and center pictures, courtesy of Hermine Dreyfuss, Washington, DC.

Distributed in North America by:

The Central Asia-Caucasus Institute
Paul H. Nitze School of Advanced International Studies
1619 Massachusetts Ave. NW, Washington, D.C. 20036
Tel. +1-202-663-7723; Fax. +1-202-663-7785
E-mail: caci2@jhu.edu

Distributed in Europe by:

The Silk Road Studies Program
Uppsala University
Box 514, SE-75120 Uppsala
Sweden
Tel. +46-18-471-2217; Fax. +46-18-106397
E-mail: info@silkroadstudies.org

Editorial correspondence should be addressed to Svante E. Cornell, Research and Publications Director, at either of the addresses above. (preferably by e-mail)

Table of Contents

Introduction

S. Frederick Starr

It has been centuries since the last discovery of a new continent. Yet something like this is happening today. Long before the voyages of exploration that began in the fifteenth century it was customary to speak of Europe and Asia as separate places divided from each other by a huge and forbidding territory. The camel caravans that traversed this middle zone were too few and too infrequent to provide a permanent economic link between them, let alone to enable Asians or Europeans to recognize their regions as complementary parts of a single land mass or continent. Even when seafarers discovered faster sea routes, geographers continued to speak of Europe and Asia as if they were separate continents.

This is now changing. Thanks to the collapse of the USSR, whose closed border stood like a wall across the heart of Eurasia, to China's decision to open trade across its western border, and to the gradual return of Afghanistan to the community of nations, continental trade spanning the entire Eurasian land mass is again becoming possible. Western Europe, China, the Middle East, and the Indian sub-continent can, in time, connect with one another and with the lands between by means of direct roads, railroads, and technologies for transporting gas, oil, and hydroelectric power. These "new Silk Roads" have enormous potential for the entire Eurasian continent, and especially for the countries of "Greater Central Asia" which they must traverse.

This book reviews the state of the links of transport and trade that are bringing about this fundamental change on the world's largest continent. It explores the potential of such interchange for fifteen of the countries most directly affected by it. It identifies some of the many impediments to the full realization of this epochal project. And it suggests a few steps that might be taken to ameliorate or remove these impediments.

The studies upon which these conclusions are based were prepared by a group of eminent scholars from sixteen countries who gathered in Kabul, Afghanistan, in April, 2006. A report on this conference has been published as "First Kabul Conference on Partnership, Trade and Development in Greater Central Asia." and is available on line at cacianalyst.org. The conference and this resulting book were a joint undertaking of the Kazakhstan Institute of Strategic Studies and the Central Asia-Caucasus Institute of Johns Hopkins University's School of Advanced International Studies. Both of the keynote speakers, Hon. Kassymzhomart Tokaev, Foreign Minister of Kazakhstan, and Hon. Richard A. Boucher, U.S. Assistant Secretary of State for South and Central Asia, welcomed the emergence of this new continental transport and trade as a development that can, if prudently managed, benefit the economic life and security of all countries involved. Both saw it as a potential "win-win" situation that is directed against no one. Equally important, they viewed the emergence of transport and trade-oriented countries in "Greater Central Asia" as a natural and inevitable process driven by the forces of the modern global economy and not by mere geopolitics.

In light of the many and complex factors impeding the emergence of these new continent-wide transport routes, this last claim may at first seem exaggerated. Yet as the authors of the paper on Kyrgyzstan argue, the only global change that might short-circuit this process is the shrinking of the globe's northern ice-cap. This could open a year-round northern seaway between Europe and East Asia that would reduce the sea route from Europe to Japan and China by half and cut the cost of transport by 1.6 times. Whether this becomes a reality will probably be known within a decade. Meanwhile, the single most likely means of improving the efficiency and reducing the cost of continental transport of goods and energy across Eurasia involves land routes through Central Asia.

Continental and Regional Trade: Central Asia's Potential Money Machine

To date, there is no commonly accepted methodology for estimating the scale and value of trade that will develop with the opening of the main road and railroad routes across the heart of Central Asia (including Afghanistan). However, the papers in this volume offer many intriguing if partial indications. For example, experts in Azerbaijan confidently predict that the volume of inland transportation, especially the container trade, will double in size between 2002 and 2015. Almost all of the growth will come from containers that might otherwise be transported by sea via the Suez Canal. Turning to the eastern end of the Europe-China trade, the authors of the chapter on China focus on the overland route running from Lianyungang on China's East-Coast via Xinjiang and Central Asia to Rotterdam. They argue that this route will cut the transport time from China to Europe from 20-40 days along current sea-borne routes to a mere eleven days. Even the continental route via Russia is 1300km longer than this new Central Asian variant. If the so-called "second Euro-Asia land bridge were opened through Central Asia it could reduce the transit costs from $167/ton by sea to $111 by land". While the authors do not estimate the volume of goods likely to be transported over this quicker route, it is bound to be very large, especially for high-value items. Taleh Ziyadov, in his chapter on Azerbaijan, predicts a growth of 2 million tons through his country in the first two years, with an addition 6-8 million tons in the following three years.

If Central Asia were to carry out basic improvements in transport systems heading south to Afghanistan, the Asian Development Bank (ADB) predicts that overall trade would increase by up to $12 billion, a growth of 80%.

Continuing on to India, we see that even during the last three years that country's trade with Afghanistan and the rest of Central Asia has grown on average by about 49% annually. Its total foreign trade as well as trade with Europe, CIS plus Iran, Afghanistan and Pakistan has grown at about 26 % annually, a figure that is sure to increase in the coming years. In his chapter, Gulshan Sachdeva uses the lower figure of 26% to predict a total Indian trade with Europe, Russia, Central Asia, Iran, and Pakistan by 2014-15 of $500 billion annually. If only 10% of this trade is carried overland via the emerging Greater Central Asian corridors the value would be $50 billion.

A separate estimate by the Asian Development Bank found that new roads expected to be completed by 2010 should boost total regional trade among the countries adjoining Afghanistan by 160% and transit trade through that country by 113%. ADB concludes that even during the coming half decade these changes will boost exports from Afghanistan and its neighbors by 14% or $5.8 billion and imports by 16% or $6.7 billion. For Afghanistan alone total incremental exports are projected to increase by 202% and imports by 54% for the five year horizon. Masood Aziz, viewing these developments, believes that Afghanistan and neighboring countries in Greater Central Asia will quickly be able to boost their two-way trade with China, India, Russia, Turkey/Europe by as much as 50%.

The impact of expanded trade across the emerging transit corridors will affect each country differently. Thus, the new roads will enable China, Europe, India, and Russia to exchange high value goods more efficiently than is possible with ship or even rail transit, which place a premium on bulk shipment. Europe will finally achieve the benefits it projected when it launched its TRACECA east-west transport program (Transport Corridor Europe-Caucasus-Asia). Russia's economically backward Urals region and West Siberia will gain access to efficient trade corridors to India, Southeast Asia, and the Middle East. Turkey and Azerbaijan will become key transit countries on east-west routes crossing both Central Asia and Iran, and at the same time will be drawn closer to European trading partners. This will enable Turkey to increase its trade with Central Asia from the present low figure of only 1% of its total trade. Azerbaijan will also become the key link in a new north-south route linking Iran and Russia.

Kazakhstan and Uzbekistan both stand to benefit from the expansion of north-south routes linking northern Europe and Russia with the Persian Gulf and Arabian Sea, even as they compete to see which will become the pre-eminent transit country for east-west trade over the emerging road and railroad systems.

Producers of gas and oil in the Caspian region are already discovering the benefits to both their economies and security that arise from multiple pipelines. New long-distance electric lines will soon enable Tajikistan and the Kyrgyz Republic, potentially among the largest world's producers of hydroelectric energy, to gain access to eager markets in Pakistan. In a development with close parallels to the efficient marketing of hydrocarbons and electricity, Uzbekistan, Turkmenistan, and Tajikistan will be able to export their most valuable crop, cotton, directly to nearby markets in South Asia, rather than exclusively through Russia and the Baltic, 7,000 km. away. This will break the export monopoly that Russia has successfully imposed on them for a century and establish instead a market regimen. Turkmenistan, too, will gain access to multiple buyers of its gas and oil, as well as cotton.

Afghanistan, like all countries in the region, will benefit from the payment of transit fees and duties. Its neighbour Iran will be able to reclaim its traditional vocation as a moderate trading state looking eastward as opposed to its present role as a militant Shii'a state fighting for influence in the Arab lands to its West. And the reopening of ancient east-west trade corridors across Pakistan and the expansion of new ones coming south from China will break the isolation that has been Pakistan's fate since its founding and return the Indus valley to its ancient status as an entrepot for trade in all directions.

Besides these and other gains that will be specific to each country, some general benefits should be noted. It is all but certain that the emergence of continental overland trade in Eurasia will benefit the GDP of all countries involved. A report by the United Nations estimates that GDP will be 50% higher across all Central Asia within a decade if the countries cooperate with one another in fostering trade. The ADB expects export and continental trade along corridors now under construction to boost Afghanistan's annual rate of GDP growth from 8.8% to 12.7%, which translates into the creation of 771,000 full-time jobs. The authors of the China paper presented in this volume believe that such trade will increase GDP in the politically sensitive Turkic province of Xinjiang by as much as 2-3%, and will also boost income in the relatively backward western provinces along the route from China's east coast to Xinjiang .

No less important is the new governmental revenue that will accrue everywhere from the duties and transit fees levied on road, rail, pipeline, and electric line use. This is no trivial matter in countries like Afghanistan, Tajikistan, Uzbekistan and the Kyrgyz Republic, where the chronic underfunding of governments cripples the delivery of such basic services as medicine and education, undermines security, and invites underpaid local officials to engage in corruption, including drug trafficking. It should be remembered that in Afghanistan at present the U.S. government is paying the wages of nearly all local civil servants. This will not change until the government in Kabul has a reliable income stream, and the best prospect for creating one are the duties and tariffs on trade. The situation in Afghanistan is admittedly extreme, but it differs from the Kyrgyz Republic, Tajikistan, and even Uzbekistan more in degree than in kind. It is no exaggeration to say that transport and trade are matters of life and death to many of the countries of the wider Central Asian region.

Overall, the opening (or reopening) of the great continental trade routes linking China, India, Europe, Russia, and the Middle East will have a stunning impact on all countries of Greater Central Asia that these routes traverse. Without exception, these countries are landlocked, even "double-landlocked." As Masood Aziz notes in his chapter, shipping costs for landlocked countries are more than half again greater than for coastal countries, which reduces trade by 80% and forces down wages accordingly. The opening of efficient new transit corridors does not remove this "distance tariff" but it ameliorates it, and goes far towards freeing affected countries from its onerous effects.

Is it any wonder, then, that the Asia Development Bank, World Bank, European Bank for Reconstruction and Development, Economic Cooperation Organization, Shanghai Cooperation Organization, and Organization for Security and Cooperation in Europe all support programs to rebuild transit routes and corridors of trade linking the Asian and European fringes of Eurasia? Is it any wonder that the United States' State Department has reorganized its European and Asian bureaus to facilitate such redevelopment, and has even appointed a Special Ambassador for Trade in Greater Central Asia? These and many other states, notably China and Japan, have embraced the expansion of free trade across the emerging Eurasian continent as an effective engine for development, an efficient means of creating jobs, and a reliable method of generating governmental income on a continent-wide basis. Moreover, all these entities understand that open transport and free trade are not against anyone, and stand to benefit all, notwithstanding any short-term dislocations they may cause as protectionism, rent-seeking, and other barriers to trade are being cut back.

If Continental Trade is So Good an Idea, Why Does it Not Exist?

With so many powerful institutions championing continental trade, and with so many of the key states committed to its development, why does Eurasia-wide continental trade not already exist? Or, on a more modest level, when such evident economic benefits are to be reaped even from intra-regional trade, why has it been so slow to develop in Central Asia and the broader zone of which it is a part? What forces are holding back the development of land-based trade in Eurasia?

Since successful modern trade involves so many separate elements, any one of which can, by its absence, retard the broader process, one must be wary of simple explanations. Legal, economic, tax, organizational, banking, managerial, technological, human resource, security, communications, and personal issues all play a part. Given this welter of separate elements, each of which must be coordinated with the others, it may be more pertinent to ask how Eurasian trade has managed to develop as quickly as it has, rather than why it is not evolving at a yet faster clip.

Assuming that the pace could nonetheless be swifter, why have so many powerful nations and international institutions been unable to move the process forward faster? One important reason traces back to the question of complexity. A smoothly-running regimen for international trade requires the coordination of many discrete elements, and no one institution is in control of more than a couple of the many variables. An international financial institution can draft new tariff policies or design a computerized information system for tax collection, but it cannot command their acceptance by the governments of sovereign states. A national president may command the resources to rebuild a road or set up an efficient border post but this does not mean that the president of the neighboring country will do so as well.

Given this situation, it is understandable that while the promotion of regional and continental trade is a high priority for everyone, it is the *top* priority for none. With the sole exception of the Asia Development Bank, which has consistently championed the expansion of trade and even been willing to stake its reputation on progress in this area, no country or international institution has "gone to the mat" over Eurasian trade.

But perhaps the measured pace at which transport and trade are developing is a result of the great costs involved? It is true, of course, that the Tajik government is unlikely to have covered the cost of building the bridge across the Panzh River at the Tajik-Afghan border that was eventually funded by the United States, or the Chinese-built tunnel further north on that same road. Nor could the government of Azerbaijan have paid for the Baku-Ceyhan pipeline which, like many railroad projects since the 1840s, required international financing.

Yet one must question whether cost considerations are the main brake on transport development. Thus, the cost of rebuilding the "Ring Road" linking the Afghan cities of Kabul, Kandahar, and Herat, as well as the main arteries connecting this road with major international routes, is estimated at $5.6 billion. Yet this sum is less than 5% of the combined projected national investments in Afghanistan of the main participating countries. Similarly, different track sizes between China and Kazakhstan require that all cargoes be off-loaded at the border, causing delays of three days on most shipments. China has introduced a faster process but Kazakhstan has yet to do so, even though the costs are no insurmountable. And compared with security budgets, for example, the total cost of all major transport infrastructure projects in Greater Central Asia is modest indeed, and easily within the power of regional governments to assemble, were they to work together and with international donors.

Unfortunately, this discussion may overestimate the degree to which key national and international political figures really understand the potential gains to be reaped from the expansion of transport and trade. In the former Soviet states, three-quarters of a century of national autarky have left older leaders unable fully to grasp the benefits their countries might deride from freer trade. It is one thing for them to affirm free trade as an abstraction and quite another to risk alienating powerful domestic interests to advance it. The fact that Soviet citizens were long accustomed to view Afghanistan and Pakistan as primitive and unstable backwaters makes it all the harder for them to embrace the possibility that their own future prosperity might depend on them.

The hold of old habits is equally strong in most other countries. Afghan leaders have had little contact until recently with countries to their north, while Pakistan's government embraced transport and trade in the early 1990s and then backed away from them. Nor are Europeans and Indians much better at conceiving something that flies in the face of commonly accepted belief that the age of land-bound Marco Polos is past and that water transport is always cheaper.

To sum up, a major force stifling policies that might foster continent-wide transport and trade is a poverty of strategic imagination in many quarters.

Lacking the capacity to frame and embrace the bigger picture, many leaders and policy-makers are glad to content themselves with a plethora of *ad hoc* measures that are not without value but which lack any clear relationship to a broader strategy.

Those governments with anything approaching a strategy in this regard, notably China but also, to a lesser extent, Russia, tend to have highly centralized and governmentalized systems of rule that do not need to respond to the immediate concerns of their electorates. In the case of Russia, which has taken a strategic approach to transport and trade, it persists in seeing the issue in terms of nineteenth-century mercantilism and the "zero sum" thinking to which it naturally gives rise. By contrast, India, the EU, Japan, and the US, all suffer from the common problem of democratic states, namely, a preoccupation with tactical and short-term concerns at the expense of the strategic and long-term.

By no means all the factors inhibiting the expansion of transport and trade across the Eurasian continent are so conceptual and abstract in nature. A far greater number arise from the realities of daily life and the interplay of real-life interests within the many countries involved. A review of several of the more obvious practical impediments to the development of trade and commerce confirms this point, and gives relevance and poignancy to the adage, coined by U.S. Congressman "Tip" O'Neill, that "All politics are local."

A simple example of this is the unwillingness of most regional states to reckon with the vast networks of illegal and untaxed shuttle traders whose activities undermine legitimate cross-border commerce and rob the state of revenue. Thus, the Kazakh Customs Committee estimates that shuttle trade between China and Kazakhstan at US$2-3.5 billion per annum, making it comparable to the official bilateral trade. Unfortunately, such traders supply a regular flow of bribes and favors to local officials and customs officers, i.e., to the very officials on whom the state relies to thwart shuttle trading.

The most egregious example of how illegal cross-border trading can protect itself from reform is the drug trade from Afghanistan. Demand driven and feeding supply chains that stretch to the main European capitals, this commerce accounts for more than 95% of all Afghan exports. Through generous bribes to officials in every transit countries, the main trafficking organizations (which are based in Russia, Turkey, and the Balkans) are able to protect themselves against would-be reformers and also to maintain in office officials at all levels who are ready to protect them.

The mountains of paperwork required at all regional border crossings do much to promote illegal trade. Surveys of truck drivers indicate that the slow processing of vehicles at border crossings are a far more significant brake on legal transit than poor security or bad roads. Tajik government surveys indicate that a trucker passing between Uzbekistan and Tajikistan must produce seventy documents, while 31 signatures are required on the Kyrgyz border. Evidence presented in the Afghanistan chapter indicates hat the situation is no better elsewhere, with 57 signatures required for imports to Afghanistan, 45 for Iran, and 27 for Kyrgyzstan.

In some instances these procedures are defended as a means of protecting the transited country from corruption. Thus, several regional states require that truckers shipping alcoholic beverages through their territory deposit in the state bank the full value of the shipment, to be repaid only when the cargo passes into a third country. The effect of such laws is to drive liquor transit into the illegal shuttle sector, which denies duties to the state and decreases trade overall.

Further slowing the transit of goods and adding to the cost is the near-universal practice of local police setting up unofficial checkpoints at which they extort payments from international truckers. A secret Tajik survey found that a truck passing between Jambul and Karaganda in Kazakhstan had to make payments at nine such stops, increasing the cost of trade by 2-3%. An additional illegal fee was charged for the unofficial police "escorts" who accompanied the foreign truck across their territory. Kazakhstan, it must be said, is by no means the worst offender in this regard. Again, since this system of peculation is deeply entrenched among underpaid and under-professionalized civil servants, any effort to rout it out faces formidable obstacles.

A more fundamental retardant of cross-border trade of all sorts across Central Asia is the urge to protectionism. No country is immune from this seductive policy. Kyrgyzstan's decision to join the World Trade Organization (WTO) in 1998 was supposed to have proclaimed the benefits of free trade to all its regional neighbors. Instead, the resulting flood of Chinese goods on the Bishkek market convinced Uzbekistan and others that, without protection, domestic manufactures would quickly die under the pressure of cheaper foreign products.

Trade imbalances are a problem that can impede regional and continental trade. Pakistan's sales to Afghanistan far surpass Afghanistan's to Pakistan, while Tajik sales to Kazakhstan are a pittance compared with the value of the reverse traffic. And across Central Asia the trade imbalance with China is extremely lopsided, reaching 3:1 in Kyrgyzstan and 9:1 ratio in Tajikistan. If unofficial trade is added, the figures would be yet more lopsided. It is difficult to make the case that in the long run this problem is most effectively addressed through more international trade in all directions, rather than less. Politicians sensitive to the short-term impact of their actions on local publics cannot afford the luxury of a long-term view.

Closely related to the problem of trade imbalances are the unpredictable and often destabilizing fluctuations to which international trade is subject. Tajikistan and the Kyrgyz Republic, for example, both opened their doors to cross-border trade in the expectation that it would be a steadily rising tide. Instead, it has ebbed and flowed in ways that local planners find extremely upsetting. For example, the Russian economic crisis of 1997 wreaked havoc on Central Asian economies, and led to many damaging secondary effects, including a 50% drop in imports of building materials and other critical products from Turkey.

These and other unwelcome consequences of cross-border trade have encouraged protectionist sentiment across the region. When the Soviet-era Dushanbe Cement plant finally went back into operation, Tajiks welcomed it as a chance to cut off cement imports from Uzbekistan and curtail the "mafias" associated with them. Felt even in the Kyrgyz Republic, a WTO member, protectionism has found its most sympathetic home in Turkmenistan and especially in Uzbekistan. Beginning in the mid-1990s Uzbekistan has pursued a policy of grain self-sufficiency, and in recent years has extended this protection to many consumer products. This has curtailed bilateral trade with China and, if continued, will equally discourage interchange with Europe, India, and Russia.

More serious, Uzbekistan's protectionist impulse has combined with the government's concerns over security threats arising from the territories of its neighbors to justify a strict border regimen that effectively thwarts trade throughout the region.

The inevitable response to such actions is for self-identified "global thinkers" to call for more reform in the countries of Greater Central Asia. While this may indeed be the most productive path, doubters in the region can point to much that feeds their skepticism. Bluntly, many "reforms" have brought unwelcome consequences.

The negative consequences of Kyrgyzstan's WTO entry have been noted. In the same spirit, many reformers call for Central Asian countries to join the Transports International Routiers (TIR) convention that governs continental road transport. China is currently working to do so and its neighbors to the West are under pressure to follow suit. Similar pressures come from Europe, and in due course will come from India, Turkey, and Iran---all with good reason. Cargos transported under TIR are exempt from customs inspection, which is essential if goods are ever to be transported smoothly between the great economies of western and eastern Eurasia. In fact, it is probably only the pressure of TIR that will cut back the present border delays that can ground a truck for up to a month.

Yet TIR costs money. Its strict emissions requirements will force the retirement of the entire Soviet and Russian-built truck fleet that is the backbone of Central Asian and even Afghan road transport. Vehicles meeting TIR standards are far more expensive---up to $100,000 each, a figure that is far beyond the capacities of most Central Asian shippers. Until they gain access to credit for new trucks, this means that the very trucking firms which should benefit from their central position on the Eurasian continent may be sidelined as Chinese, European, and eventually Indian and Turkish truckers dominate the field.

Thanks to the bitter experience of the past, even proposals to establish customs unions and free trade zones are viewed in Central Asia with suspicion. The Economic Cooperation Organization (ECO) and Commonwealth of Independent States (CIS) both long championed free trade zones, but failed to overcome the skepticism of some of their members. More recently, Russia has promoted the Eurasian Economic Community (EAEC or EURASEC) as a customs union that would combine Russia, Belarus, Kazakhstan, the Kyrgyz Republic, Tajikistan, and Uzbekistan in a free trade zone. Kyrgyz experts, however, calculate that EURASEC will likely have a sharply adverse impact on their country and Tajikistan. The Asian Development Bank reached similar conclusions even for Kazakhstan which, it argues, would suffer a $10 billion loss and slow-down in GDP growth if this project were to be implemented as planned.

Beyond these many practical issues inhibiting continental and regional trade in Central Asia are various political disputes that find expression at the region's border stations. For example, political tensions between Tajikistan and Uzbekistan have led to extremely slow border crossings between those countries. Many Kazakh, Russian and Uzbek shippers therefore choose to avoid these by proceeding instead through the Kyrgyz city of Osh and thence to Irkeshtam. Crossings along the Uzbek-Turkmen border are similarly slow. Chinese concerns over Islamic and secessionist activists have caused the processing of trucks at the border between Xinjiang and Pakistan atop the Karakuram Highway to slow nearly to a halt for long periods.

In spite of these persisting problems, political problems today are far less serious an impediment to continental and regional trade than a decade ago.

Not only has China opened up its western border in way that encourages neighboring countries to do likewise, but Afghanistan, which had been an impassible barrier to both east-west and north-south transit headed towards Pakistan and the Indian sub-continent, has emerged with a normal government committed to expanding trade in every direction. This development has done more than anything since 1991 to raise hopes about the renewal of continental transport.

The great exception to this positive trend is the on-going conflict between India and Pakistan over Kashmir. It is above all for this reason that total two-way trade between India and Central Asia is a mere $200 million, a pittance compared with Turkey's figure of $2 billion, which itself reflects undertrading, or that Turkish imports from India are a mere $1.2 billion. To appreciate the importance of this impediment, it is necessary to recall the region's history.

For 2,500 years trade between West and East meant trade between the Mediterranean world (including Europe) and both China and India. In many ways the Indian courts were more open to such interchange than their counterparts in China. The so-called "Silk Roads" headed equally to India and China. Even Marco Polo began his trip as if he was intending to go to India and only at some point three quarters of the way across Afghanistan did he take the left turn up the Vakhan Corridor towards China rather than continuing straight to the Indus valley.

Indians, unlike Chinese, participated actively in continental trade. Whereas Chinese left transport along the "Silk Roads" mainly to Central Asians and Persians, Indians themselves established mercantile centers in all the major cities of Greater Central Asia. Called "Hindus" but in actuality including both Hindus and Muslims, the Indian trading houses were among the best-organized commercial presences throughout Central Asia, Iran, and even in the Caucasus.

In light of this, it is all the more astonishing that the reopening of Afghanistan did not unleash a flood of overland transit and trade extending clear across the Indian sub-continent to Southeast Asia and, in the West, to the Middle East, Europe, and Russia. But it did not, and the main reason has not been the many impediments discussed above, but the conflict over

Kashmir. Because of this, what should be one of the main trade corridors on earth does not function at all. The economic cost of this stand-off to both India and Pakistan is far greater than either country has acknowledged, for their calculations fail to include estimates of lost opportunities.

Gulshan Sachdeva, in his insightful paper on India, enumerates a number of positive developments that have occurred recently. Looking hopefully to the future, India has even set up bilateral trade commissions with all the countries of Central Asia. But when a series of terrorist bombs exploded in Bombay in 2006 were traced to activists from Kashmir, it understandably hardened India's resolve to address this issue before opening its western door to trade through Pakistan.

One thing is certain: when these trade portals are finally opened, both countries will begin a new era of land-based trade with the West and with China. While the scale of this activity may pale in comparison with the Indian economy as a whole, it will have a transforming effect on Pakistan, returning the Indus valley to the status of continental entrepot it enjoyed from the Mohanjo-Daro age four millennia ago. And the impact on all other countries on Eurasia will be equally great.

"Undertrading" and Opportunity Cost

Economics being a practical field, it does not tend to dwell on what does not exist. Nonetheless, it acknowledges that in the modern world, certain levels of trade between neighboring countries can be considered "normal," the actual level being based on a series of economic performance indicators on the two countries in question. Those paired countries that fall under this norm can be said to be "undertrading." By any such measure, undertrading is the universal pathology of the economies of Greater Central Asia. Due to such undertrading, the ranking of trading partners among most countries of the region is the same today as fifteen years ago, just after the Soviet collapse. The papers in this volume are a record of this undertrading, and a kind of Linnean inventory of the forms that undertrading can take.

Economics also recognizes that every opportunity foregone is a cost incurred. This foregone benefit is called the "opportunity cost," and for many situations this cost can be estimated. We do not know the total volume of undertrading across the many countries of Greater Central Asia. Hence we cannot calculate the opportunity cost that is foregone each year that the Eurasian states and their partners further afield fail to develop continental trade. However, it is clear that the opportunity cost is huge, an enormous figure for any country but a staggering sum for the emerging economies of Central Asia. More to the point, the sums involved are grossly incommensurate with the modest scale of the many practical problems that to date have impeded the development of this trade. One might reasonably argue that, with the exception of the Kashmir issue, all the various impediments would long since have been swept away if the bureaucrats responsible for them had ever paused to reckon the opportunity cost of inaction.

What is Being Done?

What, if anything, is being done to narrow the yawning gap between reality and potential in continental trade across Eurasia? Had this issue been raised a mere decade ago the answer would have been "close to nothing." The Central Asian states had by 1996 launched and abandoned two different attempts to bring about a customs union. The Economic Cooperation Organization had set forth ringing goals but done nothing to achieve them, and the European Union had launched its TRACECA program with far more fanfare than action. Today the situation has changed dramatically for the better, as is evident from a quick review of the major emerging corridors of trade.

East-West Transit

East-West transit is on the eve of a boom. The opening of the Baku-Ceyhan pipeline and pressures by Russia's Gazprom on western consumers have revived prospects of gas and oil being shipped across the Caspian by pipeline. EU countries are finally acknowledging their strategic interest in the Caspian region and two EU presidencies, Finland and Slovenia, have proposed to translate that recognition into action. Kazakhstan has already committed to the trans-Caspian project, and Turkey is pushing its related Nakubo project to transfer energy onward to Austria and the heart of Europe.

Parallel with this, China and Kazakhstan are working on a major pipeline to transmit Kazakh gas to the heart of China, and both Uzbekistan and

Turkmenistan are also planning to send gas eastward to Xinjiang. The Kyrgyz Republic has found in neighboring China a new customer for electricity from its Toktogul hydroelectric plant. This activity has in turn revived plans for completing an East-West railroad from China to Europe via Central Asia and the Caucasus. This 7077 km. undertaking calls for an as yet unbuilt railroad across the breadth of Kazakhstan (or, as Tashkent would prefer, Uzbekistan), as well as a reconstructed rail line from Baku to Batumi or Poti on the Black Sea. A related project would link the above railroad at Tbilisi with the Turkish railhead at Kars, opening the possibility of direct rail shipment from China to Istanbul and beyond.

Ill-founded Armenian resistence to this phase of the project is holding up the link to Kars but is unlikely to prevail for long against an undertaking grounded in such powerful commercial logic. Meanwhile, old hopes for the construction of a Europe-Asian highway through Central Asia are being pushed from both ends of the Eurasian continent. While progress has been slow, the unacknowledged but real competition between Uzbekistan and Kazakhstan to serve as the Central Asian link of this project attests to the growing expectation that it will be realized.

Absent so far is any comprehensive plan for more southerly east-west railroads and highways from the Middle East to India. Political problems plague such a project at both ends (the Iran-Iraq border and Kashmir) and in the middle (blockades against Iran). The only concrete proposal utilizing this southern route was for a gas pipeline from Iran to India via Pakistan. Announced with much publicity in 2006, this project has been judged unfundable and appears to be stillborn.

North-South Transit

For many years, both of the two main projects for north-south transport across the belt of the Eurasian continent deliberately avoided Afghanistan. Historically, the first of these was China's plan to build a highway connecting its western province of Xinjiang and the Arabian Sea via Pakistan's Indus valley and Islamabad. The Karakuram Highway was built over twenty years beginning after the Soviet-Chinese conflict of the 1960s. After years of neglect, the deeply rutted roadway of the Pakistani section of the highway is being reconstructed and extended southward. Its terminus is the new Pakistani port at Gwadar, which is being built with Chinese support.

The second of these is Russia's scheme to build a a road and railroad connection between Russia and the Persian Gulf, crosses Kazakhstan, Turkmenistan, and Iran, culminating at the port of Chahbahar. India has joined as a sponsor, and many other countries have associated themselves with the project, officially called the International North-South Transport Corridor. Related north-south routes are the railroad being built by Azerbaijan, Iran, and Russia across Azerbaijan and Russia's large investment in its Volga/Caspian port of Astrakhan.

These two projects are both complementary and competitive with one another. The opening of Afghanistan has increased the competitive element, for both Chahbahar and Gwadar aspire to become the main southern port for Central Asia as a whole and for routes crossing Afghanistan. There is surely a place for both, however, since geography favors Chahbahar for shipments to the Gulf states and Africa, and Gwadar as the main port leading to India and southeast Asia. The fact that India has invested in Chahbahar even though the shortest route to Central Asia and the West would be through Gwadar or Karachi testifies further to the opportunity cost of the conflict over Kashmir.

Since these projects were inaugurated, Afghanistan has opened up to transit trade, leading to a rush of interest in more traditional routes through Uzbekistan, Tajikistan, and Turkmenistan. Usually grouped under the heading "north-south routes," these are also continuations of transport corridors beginning in both Europe and China. The principal routes today, as in the past, cross the Panzh River either through Termez in Uzbekistan, where the Soviet era bridge remains, or at the Tajik-Afghan border, where the United States has costructed a new bridge. New tunnels speed transport northward on the route acrosss Tajikistan, while an alternative highway is now open to the northeast to China via Khorog and the Kulma Pass. Since the processing of shipments on the Uzbek-Tajik border is slowed by political blockage, much of the traffic north to Kazakhstan and Russia has shifted eastward through Khorog and Osh to Bishkek, or westward through Uzbekistan.

Further routes from Afghanistan run directly west from Herat to Mashad in Iran via a highway newly reconstructed by Iran, or northwest to Turkmenistan. India has financed the construction of a southwestern road connecting the Afghan Ring Road with the new port at Chahbahar, but the analogous southeastern link between the Ring Road and the new port at Gwadar in Pakistan is being held up by political disputes between Pakistan and Afghanistan. The continuing failure of Pakistan to reach accord on this project will effectively cancel out the large investment which that country and China have made in the facilities at the new port.

The same political stand-off between Pakistan and Afghanistan that is holding back this project is thwarting the rapid expansion of transport over existing roads through Afghanistan. A Pakistani trucking company with links to the military long prevented Afghan drivers from delivering goods to the Karachi port. Afghanistan, citing drug smuggling and tax evasion, prevents Pakistani drivers from passing through Afghanistan. The result is a bizarre system of off-loading and on-loading at the Afghan borders that costs both countries an estimated 5% of the value of products shipped. Interestingly, truckers themselves are cooperating effectively even when their governments are not!

Whatever the timing of the above north-south corridors through Afghanistan, it is probable that in time all of them will be built. Support from the Asia Development Bank, Islamic Development Bank, World Bank, India, Iran, Japan, Kuwait, and Pakistan, as well as Tajikistan, Turkmenistan, and Uzbekistan, makes this outcome more than likely.

These highway corridors are not yet being supplemented by any planned rail line across Afghanistan. The absence of such a project leaves a significant gap in an otherwise rapidly developing transport system. Such a project has not yet been taken up by the Central-South Asian Transport and Trade Forum (CSATTF), an ADB-assisted entity for exchanging information on new transport corridors across Central and South Asia. However, the construction of a much-discussed gas pipeline from Turkmenistan across Afghanistan to Pakistan and eventually India could provide the necessary stimulus for constructing a rail corridor as well.

The 1,700 km. trans-Afghan gas pipeline project was stuck in limbo while a new government was being formed in Kabul but is now under active consideration once more, this time with strong support from the ADB. The Turkmen government claims that studies it has commissioned from an American firm lay to rest accusations by Russia's Gazprom that southeastern Turkmenistan lacked the gas to justify such a project. Moreover, India, having earlier been committed to the Iran-Pakistan-India route mentioned above, has not only joined the project but proposed that it be expanded to include an oil pipeline as well.

Yet another emerging north-south transport corridor are the long electric lines that will bring hydroelectric power from Tajikistan to Afghanistan and on to Pakistan. Built with American assistance, these lines will provide a much-needed income stream to the Tajik government. It remains to be seen whether and how the Kyrgyz Republic and Uzbekistan will join in this emerging industry. Turkmenistan, though, is already sending electric power across the border to Afghanistan.

The fact that India bid (albeit unsuccessfully, losing out to China) for Kazakhstan's Petrokazakhstan firm indicates that one way or another India is determined to import gas and oil from the Central Asian region in the coming years.

However, this, too, remains subject to the unresolved Kashmir problem. Until this "Rubic's cube" is either solved or Pakistan and India are willing to segregate the transport of goods and energy across their common border from their outstanding unresolved issues, the obstacle will remain. As noted earlier, the negative effects of this blockage are to be felt clear to Europe and China.

Does the Necessary National and International Resolve Exist?

The establishment of Eurasia-wide corridors for transport and trade involves a bewildering array of separate projects, many of them linked to one another in sequences that are by no means obvious. In the words of Robert S. Deutsch, the American official responsible for fostering transport across Greater Central Asia,

"There are many eggs and many chickens." During the 1990s, the opening of Central Asian trade routes was seen principally as a regional affair and therefore left mainly to the countries themselves to achieve. Not only did they fail to do so, but they allowed many old Soviet-era routes and corridors to fall into decay. Today this is generally understood to be a global project, requiring close cooperation among regional states and between those states and the world's major economic powers and financial institutions. However, all of these countries and institutions face other concerns besides reopening the "Silk Roads" of Greater Central Asia. It is therefore pertinent to ask, "Does there exist the political will that will be required to reopen continental trade across Eurasia?"

Any answer to this question must begin with the regional states themselves. Surveying governments across Central Asia, Afghanistan and the Caucasus, it is clear that their understanding of the issues has increased enormously, as has their level of interest in addressing them. Basic geopolitical concepts have begun to shift as Soviet borders fade into history and new relationships based on economic and geographical reality begin to emerge. It would be too optimistic to claim that regional leaders adequately understand the opportunity cost of inaction, but they are increasingly aware that progress in this area will produce measurable gains for their countries. At the same time, all of the local interests that have thwarted continental trade in the past are still present and must be faced.

The country that has come furthest in championing continental trade across Greater Central Asia is Kazakhstan, which is now the clear regional leader in this regard. By promoting the International Transport Consortium and a Common Transport Policy it hopes to bring about a united regional voice on the modernization of transportation infrastructure and to coordinate that voice with all Eurasian powers.

Overall, regional leaders are ready to act on transport and trade if other leaders do so, and if they are backed up by major powers and international organizations. Even Uzbekistan, with its history of protectionism, may be ready for change, since its policy of autarky has failed to sustain the GDP gains that were achieved throughout the 1990s. But this will happen only when the international environment makes change unavoidable.

What, then, of the main Eurasian economic powers whose economies will drive the growth of transport and trade along the emerging corridors? Do they grasp the potential and are they translating that understanding into constructive programs?

China, for one, clearly perceives the importance of continental trade and has moved in a purposeful manner to promote it. Its main failure to date is to drive its Gwadar project to completion and to engage Pakistan in the development of access roads from central Pakistan and Afghanistan.

Russia, too, perceives the trend towards continental trade and has moved decisively on two fronts: first, to oppose all east-west transport routes (roads, railroads, and energy) not running through its own territory, and, second, to promote its own North-South corridor to Iran while at the same time discouraging former Soviet states of Central Asia and Afghanistan from opening direct links with Pakistan and India. On the first front Moscow has largely failed, while its North-South link is fast becoming a reality, with some twenty nations now committed to participate. Meanwhile, Russia has been unable to slow the formation of transport ties between India, Pakistan, Afghanistan and Central Asia.

For a decade the European Union's commitment to continental trade was more rhetorical than operation. Now that it recognizes that its interests are clearly at stake in the Caspian energy sector, it is working to find a new role for itself. Cooperation with the United States in this area looks more likely than ever, and holds much promise.

India, a late-comer to these issues, is running hard to catch up, having signed bi-lateral agreements with all regional countries in support of regional and continental trade. For the time being, India is supporting Russia's north-south corridor but in the long run its interests in road, rail, and energy transport clearly lie with the more direct routes across Pakistan and Afghanistan. These corridors, however, remain hostage to the on-going disagreements with Pakistan over Kashmir.

Japan has demonstrated a subtle understanding of the economic and geopolitical issues relating to continental transport and trade and has moved deftly to advance its interests in this area. Japan has sponsored major road construction projects in Afghanistan and developed its "Japan Plus Central Asia" initiative as a forum for addressing future joint activities in trade and transport, as well as other areas.

During the 1990s the United States concentrated mainly on intra-regional trade in Central Asia. With its decisive intervention in Afghanistan, however, it opened the door to continental trade. After first insisting that its interests in the region were confined to its anti-terrorism project and were therefore temporary, it then acknowledged its long-term interests there. This is affirmed by Congress in a new Silk Road II Act and has been given institutional reality by the reorganization of the State Department to bring Central and South Asia together under a new combined bureau and by the appointment of a special ambassador for transport and trade issues in Central Asia and Afghanistan. U.S. assistance has been crucial in major infrastructure projects in Afghanistan and Tajikistan.

No less than the major countries, international agencies and financial institutions play a central role in advancing a continental trade regimen across Greater Central Asia. Funded by national governments, these bodies are able to stand above national interest in a way that is difficult, if not impossible, for their sponsors.

Among international agencies, none has come close to the Asia Development Bank in its clear and sustained grasp of the issues affecting continental trade and in the range and effectiveness of its programs to address them. Sponsored mainly by Japan, the ADB has founded the six-nation Central Asia Regional Economic Cooperation (CAREC) and within CAREC a Trade Facilitation Program that is working to develop a common systems of customs across Greater Central Asia. Agreements signed by the participating countries will, if implemented, bring about the standardization and simplification of customs practices.

The World Bank has carried out important research on the status and prospects for regional trade within Central Asia. Its many programs emphasize more the revitalization of important infrastructure and trade links with the Russia that lapsed after 1991 than the creation *de novo* of new continental corridors, yet its field of vision has steadily broadened to embrace longer routes as well.

The World Trade Organization is arguably the single most important framework organization for the countries of Central Asia and their prospective continental trading partners. China's accession and Russia's likely future accession leaves Central Asian countries (other than Kyrgyzstan, which joined in 1998) isolated as non-members between four major poles of members, China, Europe, India, and Russia. As Sanat Kushkumbaev states in his chapter on Kazakhstan, "WTO membership will provide a base to these countries to establish a realistic mechanism to overcome their trade related problems."

Until recently, the South Asian Association for Regional Cooperation (SAARC) has been oriented towards trade from India to Southeast Asia rather than towards Afghanistan and the North. When SAARC approved Afghanistan for membership in 2005 the organization became a significant presence in the promotion of continental trade, not least through its 2004 Agreement on South Asia Free Trade Area (SAFTA). As Gulshan Sachdeva observes in his paper, "Afghanistan's membership to SAARC has the potential to fundamentally change and rejuvenate regional economic linkages between the South Asian and greater Central Asian regions."

The Economic Cooperation Organization is an old organization (founded 1985) that has expanded to include all countries of Central Asia, along with Afghanistan, Iran, Pakistan, and Turkey. As such, it has important long-term prospects for playing a role in the opening of a southern east-west route from Turkey to India across Iran, Afghanistan and Pakistan, as well as in the improvement of Central Asian links across Afghanistan and Turkmenistan to Iran. To now, though, ECO has been a passive force, impeded by internal organizational issues and regional politics from fulfilling this larger mission.

The Eurasian Economic Community initiated by Russia and involving four states of Central Asia (Kazakhstan, the Kyrgyz Republic, Tajikistan and Uzbekistan) along with Belarus, is the economic successor to the Commonwealth of Independent States, and also to the locally-based Central Asian Economic Community, which it absorbed. Besides the likelihood that the implementation of its programs might harm the Central Asian economies, it is not clear that this project can survive the entry of member states into the WTO. Under any circumstances, its rise leaves open the possibility of Central Asian governments establishing a purely Central Asian economic organization, for which the presidents of both Kazakhstan and Uzbekistan have called.

The Shanghai Cooperation Organization began in 2001 with a focus on security issues but has since broadened its purview to include transport and trade. At the same time it has expanded its original membership to include Uzbekistan, with Afghanistan, Iran, and Pakistan as possible future additions. While SCO can certainly play a constructive role in improving the basis for continental transport, it remains unclear what its specific mission in this sphere might be, given the existing high level of activity of its chief sponsors, China and Russia, and the plethora of other entities already active.

The Organization of Security and Cooperation in Europe may seem an unlikely player in transportation and trade issues in Greater Central Asia. Nonetheless, it has hosted successful conferences in Dushanbe and Istanbul on continental trade and intends to use its convening power further to promote investment and transport.

Finally, the United Nations figures at least marginally in the skein of institutions fostering continental interchange across Eurasia. In 2003 it organized a major conference of landlocked developing countries in Almaty, Kazakhstan, at which ministers and experts from seventy five countries adopted an "Almaty Action Plan." The aims of this document are expansive, embracing infrastructure, the simplification of trade, and technical assistance. More important in the long run is the UN's active role (through the United Nations Drug Control Program) in the struggle against illegal trafficking in narcotics. Since drug trafficking remains the one Central Asian industry besides oil and gas that is thoroughly integrated on a continental basis, and since it is also the region's most lucrative export (even though the profits mainly go elsewhere), the UN's paramount role in fighting it is all the more critical.

Conclusion

These many states and diverse international institutions are but a sampling of the many entities actively involved in the development of continental trade across Eurasia. Numerous other bodies are involved in the most direct way. Many are private. Among these are the professional shippers in eastern Turkey, the Russian Urals, or Pakastani Punjab who see an opportunity in forwarding cargoes across the vast continent; the cotton farmer in Turkmenistan who borrows a truck from his cooperative to try to deliver a load to a Karachi spinning mill; the cement maker in Dushanbe who discovers a market in southern Tajikistan; the European manufacturer of fuel additives who wants to market his product in Kazakhstan; or the Indian or Chinese appliance manufacturer with an eye on markets in eastern Europe.

Taking into account all these diverse agents of change, it is hard to conclude that the process as a whole is not extremely chaotic. It abounds in grandiose ambitions, crashing failures, overlapping initiatives, false starts, and on major issues a near-total lack of coordination. Above all, it abounds with competition among diverse nations, businesses, and even public agencies that claim to serve the common good.

Yet the fact that the process is chaotic and shot through with competing interests in no way signifies that there is insufficient will to see the task through to a successful conclusion. On the contrary, it is precisely in this chaos and competition that one can discern the will that will be essential in achieving ultimate success. More than one of our authors regrets the absence of a single grand regional coordinating body to oversee the process. However, one might instead argue that the chaotic pluralism that now exists is far better. On the one hand it prevents any single state or grouping of states from controlling the development of continental trade in a way that would inevitably serve their particular interest. On the other, it moderates the pretensions of politicians and increases their exposure to the austere discipline of market forces.

This in turn strengthens the sovereignty and independence of the countries in Greater Central Asia that form the hub of the emerging trade networks. Working with diverse partner countries and international agencies, they can play them off against each other in ways that ultimately benefit the transport system as a whole, and the region. By such a process, Central Asian countries can pursue the multi-directional foreign policies that will be essential to their long-term viability as states and to their prosperity as peoples.

To say that the best strategic and operational decisions are those that are tested by competition and market realities in no way minimizes the importance of the several political problems that are impeding the opening of the "New Silk Roads."

The India-Pakistan conflict over Kashmir is like a cork that is bottling up continental trade to the Southeast. Unresolved issues between Pakistan and Afghanistan have a similar effect. In the South Caucasus, the unresolved Karabakh conflict exerts a negative influence on both highway and rail projects through that critical corridor. Similarly, Uzbek protectionism and Afghan hostilities to foreign truckers damage prospects for trade across those countries.

Acknowledging this, the best way forward is to pursue whatever options make the best market sense under the circumstances. If one channel is blocked, let trade flow through others. This process will encourage, even force, those countries responsible for the main political blockages to calculate the *opportunity cost* to themselves of their own policies. They will see that the opening of continental trade is an elemental process that can be thwarted in one dimension but will quickly find a productive outlet in another. They will see how opportunities can quickly slip from their grasp and into the hands of others who are more receptive to the process as a whole and more committed to its success. For the first time in centuries, new Silk Roads across the Eurasian continent are on the cutting edge of change, rather than its victim.

Afghanistan

Masood Aziz

The Problem in its Historical Context

Afghanistan once occupied a coveted place at the center of the world's richest pathways to prosperity and civilization. This historic and geopolitical role was well established over two thousand years ago. Afghanistan was then at the center of the global exchange of ideas, art and culture, and of long-distance trade, as it was located between China and India in the East and a fast growing Europe in the West. The flow of trade, artisans, techniques, tools and innovations along the legendary Silk Road, allowed the flourishing of ideas and the growth of the great ancient cities of Central Asia, enabling them to spread their influence far beyond the region.

Following the past quarter-century of turmoil, war and instability, Afghanistan is working to rebuild a secure environment for its people and to re-establish a new Silk Road. The hope and potential for these new silk roads is that they will allow Central Asia once more to interact with South Asia, China and the Far East and to re-engage with Europe and beyond.

Economic Conditions for Trade in Afghanistan and the Region

The United Nations classifies Afghanistan as a "least developed country" with some of the world's lowest rankings in basic development indicators. Afghanistan's economy and physical infrastructure has been devastated. The damaging impact of the Soviet invasion and occupation, the ensuing civil war, and the brutally repressive Taliban regime all contributed to the underdevelopment of the country.

Since the ousting of the Taliban, Afghanistan, with the help of the international community, has made significant progress on many fronts including enacting a constitution, holding elections, building its institutions, and reviving education and health services. Since the fall of the Taliban in 2001, there has been keen interest in developing Afghanistan as a potential regional partner for trade and security in Central Asia.

International donors and their Afghan partners have produced strategies to improve old transit routes and to create new roads connecting Afghanistan to its neighbors. This will allow Central Asian countries to connect with Pakistan and India, and China to connect with Iran and beyond, all with Afghanistan as the central landbridge between them. These strategies have the potential of creating significant economic growth and at the same time contributing greatly to the establishment of peace and security throughout the region.

For the purpose of this paper all references to "Greater Central Asia" should be understood to include Afghanistan, India, Iran, Kazakhstan, the Kyrgyz Republic, Pakistan, Tajikistan, Turkmenistan, and Uzbekistan. The inclusion of Pakistan and Iran is essential because of their proximity and territorial ties but the inclusion of India is of yet greater importance because of its significant presence in all aspect of regional life. In addition to the greater Central Asian region, a second group of relevant countries and regions include China, Russia, as well as the Middle East, Europe, Japan and the United States.

The countries in the Greater Central Asia region share many common economic characteristics such as difficult topography and lack of direct access to the seas. They are also characterized by underdeveloped transport infrastructure and commodity-oriented economies. However, many of the countries also share significant cultural, social, and ethnic bonds which make the further development of ties quite natural.

Despite many common characteristics, trade among countries of Greater Central Asia constitutes only a fraction of the region's total trade. Moreover, Central Asian countries are under-trading with Western Europe and South and East Asia compared to their potential. Economists use the so-called "gravity model" to assess trade potential.[1] This estimates potential bilateral trade using a simple model that takes into account two countries' relative economic size and the distance between them. The results of such estimates can then be compared to actual trade flows to provide estimates of lost trade. For example, Babetskii finds that Kazakhstan, Kyrgyzstan, Turkmenistan and Uzbekistan traded much less from 1997 to 2002 than the countries of the European Union (EU), accounting for relative size, GDP, and distance from trading partners.[2] Further, Elborgh-Woytek finds that the countries of the Commonwealth of Independent States (CIS) sharply under-trade with the EU.[3] In particular, the study found that the ratio of actual to potential trade in 2001 was only about 0.3.

The European Bank for Reconstruction and Development (EBRD)[4] compared actual and predicted levels of trade and found that Kyrgyzstan's and Uzbekistan's trade was considerably lower than their potential. The reasons for this "undertrading" are explained in terms of Central Asia's landlocked states, lack of adequate physical infrastructure, poor trade facilitation mechanisms, onerous trade restrictions, and governance issues affecting customs and transport services.

Our understanding of the existence of "undertrading" in the region compels us to examine its causes. Such an examination leads to the important realization that closer coordination and better trade policies will unlock significant, yet existing potentials and pave the way for regional and indeed continental trade to increase substantially.

---

[1] For more on the "gravity model", see Babetskii, Ian., Babetskaia-Kukharchuk, Oxana., Raiser, Martin. "How deep is your trade? Transition and international integration in Eastern Europe and the former Soviet Union," Working paper No. 83. European Bank for Reconstruction and Development, London, 2003.

[2] Ibid.

[3] Elborgh-Woytek, Katrin, "Of Openness and Distance: Trade Developments in the Commonwealth of Independent States, 1993-2002," IMF Working Paper No. 03/207. International Monetary Fund, Washington, DC. 2003, pp. 9-17.

[4] See the EBRD report, "Transition Report 2003: Integration and Regional Cooperation," European Bank for Reconstruction and Development (EBRD), London. 2003, pp. 113-116.

Regional and Transcontinental Potential

Central Asian countries could benefit greatly from closer cooperation at the regional and continental levels. As mentioned, empirical studies indicate that landlocked countries are at a great natural disadvantage in achieving growth, which makes a liberal trading process and effective regional cooperation all the more important. Over the period 1960-92 landlocked developing countries grew at an average of 1.5 percent per year slower than countries that were not landlocked.[5] Over a span of decades this weak growth adds up to a significant loss of opportunity for these developing and impoverished countries.

Thus, examining alternatives become a requisite. Indeed, in a study of human development factors in Central Asian countries, the United Nations found that the largest aggregate economic gains come from reductions in the cost of trade, and the largest losses comes from civil war. This study reported that over ten years, the GDPs of Central Asian countries could be *50 percent higher* as a result of comprehensive and continuous regional cooperation![6]

It follows that the growth and sustainability of the entire region is largely and directly dependent on strong and effective cooperation for genuine regional trade integration. In this regard, Afghanistan becomes particularly central to this endeavor as it has the potential of connecting traffic between Central and South Asia and of linking China to the Arabian Sea and beyond.

The Potential for Trade in Greater Central Asia

Trade engenders and deepens specialization and specialization in turn assures economies of scale, especially for those countries with relatively modest domestic economies. Through increased economic integration with the world beyond their regional borders, trading economies can acquire and diffuse new technologies from more advanced countries and help reduce poverty.

---

[5] MacKellar, Landis; Woergoetter, Andreas and Woerz, Julia. "Economic Development Problems of Landlocked Countries," Transition Economics Series 14. Institute for Advanced Studies, Austria. 2000, p. 15.

[6] United Nations Central Asia Human Development Report 2005. United Nations Development Programme, New York. 2005, pp. 205-212.

Recent studies show that over fifteen years, global free trade could save 440 million people from poverty.[7] Global free trade would create welfare gains estimated at $203 billion annually for developing countries, or 3.2 percent of GDP. Note that global concessional assistance going from industrialized countries to developing countries is about $50 billion annually. Interestingly, the total welfare gains of $203 billion produced from global free trade would amount to about four times the size of the concessional assistance figure.

Exploiting Afghanistan's position as a land bridge between Central and South Asia and the other neighboring economies can be a significant source of regional economic growth. The Asian Development Bank (ADB) and other recent studies point to substantial economic benefits over the next five to ten years from the development of road corridors connecting Central Asia and South Asia. A study by Ojala estimates that improved road corridors can increase export and import prices in Central Asia between 7% and 10%.[8]

Studying the potential benefits of North-South corridors, the ADB found that overall trade can increase by as much as 15%, or $12 billion, for the Greater Central Asia region as a whole if transportation and trade facilitation are improved.[9]

The Impact of the Central-South Asia Corridors in Regional and Continental Trade

In 2003 the ADB sponsored a "Ministerial Conference on Transport and Trade in Central and South Asia" where a "Central and South Asia Trade and Transport Forum (CSATTF)" was established. As part of this initiative, studies were conducted to assess the benefits of regional trade via the development specific road corridors.

The related ADB study identified 52 potential road corridors through Afghanistan connecting Tajikistan, Uzbekistan, and Turkmenistan with five

---

[7] Cline, William R, *Trade Policy and Global Poverty*. Center for Global Development, Institute for International Economics, Washington DC, 2004, pp.227-261.

[8] Byrd, William, "Prospects for Regional Development and Economic Cooperation in the Wider Central Asia Region," Paper prepared for the Kabul Conference on Regional Economic Cooperation, December 3-5, 2005. World Bank. Washington DC. January 2006, p.55.

[9] Ibid.

seaports in Pakistan and Iran. Thirty-one of these roads would link to Pakistan ports and the other twenty-one to ports in Iran (figures 1 and 2).

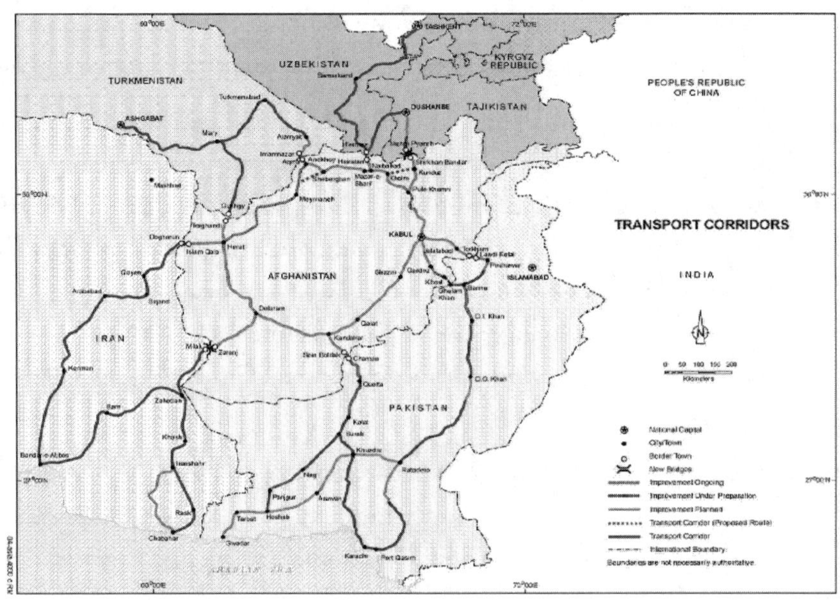

Figure 1: Regional Corridor Map: Afghanistan as a Landbridge[10]

The total distance of the combined corridors is about 13,586 kilometers or 8,444 miles. It is assumed that the corridors are to originate in Dushanbe for Tajikistan, Tashkent for Uzbekistan, and Ashgabat for Turkmenistan and then enter Afghanistan from Tajikistan at Shirkhan Bandar (or Hairatan), from Uzbekistan at Hairatan and from Turkmenistan at Aqina (or Torghandi). The corridors exit Afghanistan from Nangargar province to Pakistan's ports at Torkham (leading to Karachi/Port Qasim) or via Afghanistan's Kandahar province at Spin Boldak (leading to Karachi or Gwadar). In addition, the corridors would lead to Iranian ports via the

[10] Source: Alamgir, Mohiuddin, "Report on the E[illegible]onomic Impact of Central-South Asian Road Corridors." Central and South Asia [illegible]nsport and Trade Forum. Report prepared for the Second Ministerial Conference on Transport and Trade in Central and South Asia. Asian Development Bank, Manila, Philippines, March 3 and 4, 2005.p.8.

Afghanistan exit points at Zaranz going towards Bandar e-Abbas (or Chabahar) and via the exit point of Islam Qala going towards Bandar e-Abbas.

Figure 2: Afghanistan Primary Road Network[II]

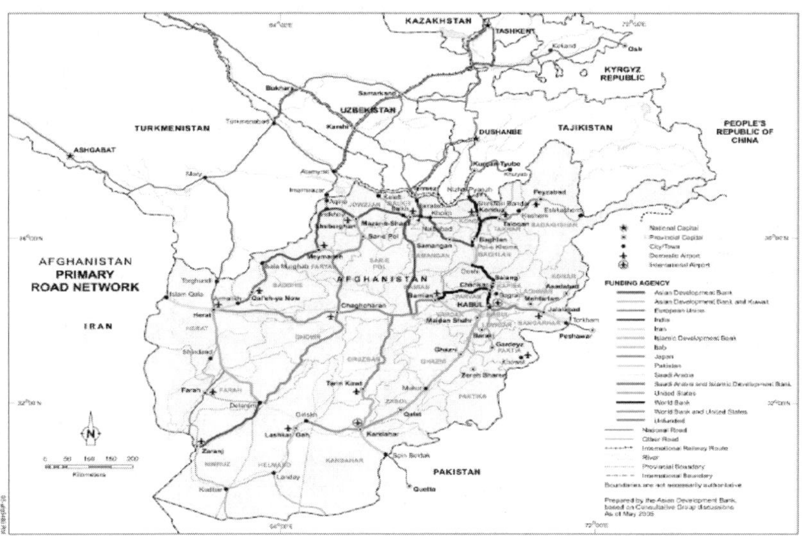

The above development would offer a large number of options for private transport through Afghanistan. For example, as many as fourteen routes connect Tajikistan and Pakistan via Kabul to the exit point at Torkham. Other entry/exit points allow for seven routes linking Uzbekistan and Pakistan and five between Uzbekistan and Iran. In addition, ten routes connect Tajikistan to Iran via various alternatives in Afghanistan and six alternative routes between Turkmenistan and Pakistan, along with ten routes connecting Turkmenistan and Iran all via Afghanistan.

It is important to note that these corridors not only link Central Asia to sea ports in the South but also open up routes to Kazakhstan, Kyrgyzstan, and, importantly, China. Tables 1, 2 and 3, below list the ten longest road corridors ranked by to sea ports.

[II] Source: Van Zant, Eric, "Reconnecting Afghanistan," Asia Development Bank Review. Asia Development Bank. Manila, Philippines, December 2005, p. 6.

Tables 1, 2 and 3: Central-South Asian Road Corridors

Table 1: From Tajikistan (Dushanbe) to Pakistan and Iran Ports

Corridor Number	Road Corridor/Road Section	Distance (km)	Rank
1	Via Nizhni Pyanzh/Kabul/Spin Boldak/Karachi	1990	1
2	Via Termez/Kabul/Spin Boldak/Karachi	2095	2
7	Via Nizhni Pyanzh/Kabul/Spin Boldak/Surab/Gwadar	2246	3
3	Via Nizhni Pyanzh/Kabul/Torkham/Karachi	2251	4
8	Via Nizhni Pyanzh/Kabul/Spin Boldak/Khuzdar/Gwadar	2261	5
47	Via Gushgy/Zaranj/Chahbahar	2304	6
25	Via Gushgy/Herat and Spin Boldak/Karachi	2309	7
9	Via Termez/Kabul/Spin Boldak/Surab/Gwadar	2351	8
4	Via Termez/Kabul/Torkham/Karachi	2356	9
10	Via Termez/Kabul/Spin Boldak/Khuzdar/Gwadar	2366	10

Table 2: From Uzbekistan (Tashkent) to Pakistan and Iran Ports

Corridor Number	Road Corridor/Road Section	Distance (km)	Rank
35	Via Termez/Kabul/Zaranj/Chahbahar	2564	1
30	Via Gushgy/Herat/Spin Boldak/Surab/Gwadar	2565	2
33	Via Termez/Herat/Zaranj/Chahbahar	2569	3
	Via Termez/Herat/Spin Boldak/Karachi	2574	4
31	Via Gushgy/Herat/Spin Boldak/Khuzdar/Gwadar	2580	5
41	Via Termez/Kabul and Zaranj/Bandar Abbas	2632	6
37	Via Termez/Herat and Zaranj/Bandar Abbas	2637	7
52	Via Imamnazar/Islam Qala/Bandar Abbas	3123	8
46	Via Termez/Kabul/Zaranj/Bandar Abbas	3178	9
44	Via Termez/Herat and Zaranj/Bandar Abbas	3183	10

Table 3: From Turkmenistan (Ashgabat) to Pakistan and Iran Ports

Corridor Number	Road Corridor/Road Section	Distance (km)	Rank
15	Via Termez/Kabul and Spin Boldak/Karachi	2641	1
39	Via Termez/Herat and Islam Qala/Bandar Abbas	2666	2
32	Via Nizhni Pyanz/Herat/Zaranj/Chahbahar	2667	3
5	Via Nizhni Pyanzh/Kunduz/Herat/Spin Boldak/Karachi	2672	4
36	Via Nizhni Pyanzh/Herat and Zaranj/Bandar Abbas	2735	5
38	Via Nizhni Pyanzh/Herat and Islam Qala/Bandar Abbas	2764	6
13	Via Termez/Herat/Spin Boldak/Surab/Gwadar	2830	7
14	Via Termez/Herat/Spin Boldak/Khuzdar/Gwadar	2845	8
18	Via Termez/Kabul/Spin Boldak/Surab/Gwadar	2897	9
16	Via Termez/Kabul and Torkham/Karachi	2902	10

Source: Alamgir, Mohiuddin, "Report on the Economic Impact of Central-South Asian Road Corridors." Central and South Asia Transport and Trade Forum. Report prepared for the Second Ministerial Conference on Transport and Trade in Central and South Asia. Asian Development Bank, Manila, Philippines, March 3 and 4, 2005. pp. 15-16.

Regional Benefits and Impact of the Road Corridors

The benefits from developing Central Asian transport corridors are significant for the greater Central Asian countries as well as for neighboring regions. However, the benefits of regional corridors only materialize when participating countries cooperate with one another. The ADB found that once the corridors are built total regional trade will increase by 160% and combined transit trade will grow by 113%. Total exports among the participating countries by 2010 will increase by 14% (or $5.8 billion) and total imports will grow by 16% (or $6.7 billion). The impact on GDP as a result of trade via the corridors is also noteworthy. The ADB estimates that the combined GDP of the participant countries in the region will increase by over 5% per year during the next five years, for a total growth of $5.9 billion. These benefits come at a relatively low cost as the corridors require a total investment of about $5 billion for the entire region. This level of investment represents less than 5% of the combined projected total national investments by participating countries over the same period.

Participating countries will also benefit from increased employment as a result of trade. The corridors are estimated to increase full-time employment in the region by 1.8 million jobs. In addition, the constructions of the road corridor itself will add 12 million person-days of temporary employment for the duration of construction and 15 million person-days of permanent employment for ongoing road and infrastructure maintenance. The creation of jobs is significant for the Central Asia countries given current levels of unemployment and underemployment.

Impact of Road Corridors on Afghanistan

With about 652,000 square kilometers, Afghanistan is a relatively large country and roads are its principal means of transport. Afghanistan's road network comprises about 6,100 km of national roads, 15,000 km of provincial roads, 15,000 to 20,000 km of rural roads, and 3,000 km of urban roads, including 1,060 km in Kabul.[12] The national highways add up to about 3,300

[12] Pyo, D.S.; Alam, M. and Gupta, M.D. "Report and Recommendation of the President to the Board of Directors a Proposed Loan to the Islamic Republic of Afghanistan for the Qaisar-Bala Murghab Road Project," Asia Development Bank.

km, the largest part of which– 2,300 km –is the ring road that connects Afghanistan's major regional centers of Herat, Kandahar, Maimana, Mazar-e-Sharif, Sheberghan and Kabul. These roads are also the main connectors to neighboring countries. With donor support, Afghanistan is now undertaking a massive infrastructure investment effort to rebuild this ring road. The target is to double the amount of paved road in the country to 32% of the total by 2010.

Table 4: Key Economic Impact of the Road Corridors on the Region[13]

Economic Impact on Regional Trade	Figures
Combined incremental regional trade growth 2002-2010 (in percent)	160
Combined incremental regional transit trade growth 2002-2010 (in percent)	111
Corridor investment cost (in million dollars)	5639
Corridor investment as % of total investment	4.55
Annual travel cost saving/$ of investment 2010 (in dollars)	0.31
Incremental annual GDP growth rate 2005-2010 (in percent)	0.43
Incremental annual GDP/$ of investment 2010 (in dollars)	1.05
Incremental annual full time employment in 2010 (million)	1.86
Total incremental export growth 2002-2010 (in percent)	14
Total incremental import growth 2002-2010 (in percent)	16
Incremental revenue in 2010 (in million dollars)	910

As part of the development of road corridors running through Central Asia, connecting North to South and East to West, the emergence of new alternative routes will offer Afghanistan unique prospects to revive its

---

July 2005, p. 10. Available at http://www.adb.org/Documents/RRPs/AFG/rrp-afg-37075-02.pdf.

[13] Source: Alamgir, Mohiuddin, "Report on the Economic Impact of Central-South Asian Road Corridors." Central and South Asia Transport and Trade Forum. Report prepared for the Second Ministerial Conference on Transport and Trade in Central and South Asia. Asian Development Bank, Manila, Philippines, March 3 and 4, 2005. p. iii.

central role as the facilitator of regional economic cooperation and growth. In this sense, all "roads [could] lead to Kabul".

- Trade Growth

Out of the total 13,586 kilometers of roads that are needed for regional trade, 3,657 are to be built in Afghanistan. Their benefit to the country will be significant. The ADB estimates that Afghanistan's exports will increase by 202% and imports will increase by 54% over the next five years. This translates into the addition of $592 million in exports and $1,318 million in imports.

- GDP Growth

In terms of the economic impact of the road corridors, the ADB estimates that by 2010 Afghanistan will add $1.8 billion to its GDP. The annual projected rate of GDP growth is estimated to be 12.7%, as opposed to 8.8% without the road corridors. This is a net annual incremental increase of 3.9% in GDP for Afghanistan over the same period. Afghanistan's per capita GDP has been very low - a mere $122 in 2001/2002. Given this, and due to the road corridors, an increase per capita of 36% is of a huge importance. Key measures of the economic impact of the road corridors are listed in the Table 5 below, along with other participating countries in the region.

- Job Creation and Long-Term Employment

Another essential factor in the need for regional cooperation is the creation of jobs and job security via increased trade. As many of the road segments will pass through poorer regions trade will spur more sustained and balanced regional development. Rural areas along both North-South and East-West corridors will gain from the construction of the roads, but more important, market access will expand as transport time and costs are reduced. The issue of job creation is also vital for Afghanistan's long-term sustainability and its regional security implications. According to the ADB, the development of regional road corridors will add a total of 771,000 full-time jobs in Afghanistan's economy out of a total of 1.8 million for the region. The added jobs in Afghanistan represent about 41% of the total job increase projected for the region as a whole as a result of the transport corridors. In addition to the creation of full time jobs, road construction and maintenance will create additional employment in Afghanistan. Thus, Afghanistan will add 4.6 million person days during the 5 year construction period, 38% of the total 12 million jobs creation projected for the region. In addition, and perhaps more significantly, as the road corridors need to be maintained, this will entail the creation of an addition 4.1 million permanent jobs. These job creations are of vital importance to both the security and stability of Afghanistan as it is an additional opportunity to rehabilitate and re-integrate ex-combatants into the economic life of the nation and is a basis for creating wider sustained economic benefits and assuring stability.

- Increase in Freight

The flow of trade will increase with the development of the fifty-two corridors. The ADB estimates that by 2010, the annual increase in two-way freight will be 4.594 million tons for the two Afghanistan-Pakistan crossings (Spin Boldak and Torkham). In addition, freight will increase by 923 thousand tons at the Uzbekistan-Afghanistan crossing point and 740 thousand tons for the Turkmenistan-Afghanistan point.

- Travel Time and Travel Costs Savings

A total of 139 hours will be saved in travel time as a result of the new corridors, and Afghanistan will stand to gain the most from this improvement. Total savings in travel time in Afghanistan will be 71 hours. This is about half the total travel time savings for the entire region. As the road corridors are built, total savings in overall travel costs will be $1.728 billion for the all participating countries. Again, Afghanistan stands to gain the most from the new road corridors with a total savings in travel costs of $746 million, which is 43% of the total savings for the region. It is important to note that among some of the more challenging impediments to trade are travel costs and travel time. With improvements in both of these, as described above, regional economic growth has a concrete chance of reaching its potential in Central Asia.

o Impact on State Revenues

Increases in regional trade resulting from the new road corridors will cause governmental revenues to increase substantially. According to the 2005 ADB study, revenue increases based on current tariffs and transit fees will reach $910 million for the participating countries of the projected eight years to 2010. Afghanistan will stand to gain relatively significantly as its revenues will increase by $208 million or about 23% of the region's total.

Economic Diversification – Central Asia Countries as a Special Case

Central Asian countries, because of their legacies from the former Soviet-run economies, continue to have dominance of primary commodities and low value-added manufactured products in their exports. Massive reliance on shipments by rail, coupled with the high cost of road transport, has led to a distorted export structure in Central Asia. A study by Raballand[14] confirms that the exports of Central Asian countries are concentrated in bulk commodities with relatively low value-added manufactured products. This serves to reinforce production structures established by central planning in the Soviet era. The development of road corridors will open new types of trade flows which, in turn, will foster economic diversification for Central Asia and to the further benefit of the entire region.

---

[14] Raballand, Gaël; Antoine Kunth, and Richard Auty (2005). "Central Asia's Transport Cost Burden and Its Impact on Trade," *Economic Systems* 29(1). Munich. March 2005, pp. 6-31.

Table 5: Economic Impact on Afghanistan and the Region

Economic Impact Measure	Afghanistan	Total for Region	Afghanistan's share compared to the Region
Total road distances (km)	3,657	13,586	
Total travel time and cost impact			
Total time saving (hours)	71	139	51%
Time saved per km (hours)	0.019	0.010	
Total travel cost savings ($ million)	745.7	1728.3	43%
Total freight impact (000 tons)			
Tajikistan-Afghanistan border (Nizhni Pyanzh-Shirkhan Bndr)		222	
Afghanistan-Pakistan border (Spin Boldak-Chaman)		2,061	
Afghanistan-Pakistan border (Torkham)		2,533	
Uzbekistan-Afghanistan border (Termez-Hairatan)		923	
Turkmenistan-Afghanistan border (Imamnazar-Aquina)		252	
Turkmenistan-Afghanistan border (Gushgy-Torghandi)		488	
Afghanistan-Iran border (Zaranz-Milak)		848	
Afghanistan-Iran border (Islam Qala-Dogharun)		123	
Employment impact			
Total full time employment	771,000	1.863	41%
Temporary emplymt/road rehabilitation (million person days)	4.59	12.18	38%
Permanent emplymt/road maintenance (million person days)	4.02	14.99	27%
GDP impact			
Increase in GDP 2005-2010 ($ million)	1,827	5,927	31%
Annual real GDP growth/2005-2010 without corridor(%)	8.75	4.60	
Annual real GDP growth/2005-2010 with corridor (%)	12.68	5.03	
Difference in annual GDP growth with corridor (%)	3.93	0.43	
Export impact			
Increase in annual exports with corridor ($ million)	592	5768	10%
Import impact			
Increase in annual imports with corridor ($ million)	1,318	6,720	20%
Regional trade impact			
Increase in annual intraregional exports with corridor ($ million	553	2,847	19%
State Revenue impact			
Annual increase in state revenue ($ million)	208	910	23%
Total cost of corridor construction ($ million)	1,932	5,639	34%
Corridor investment as % of total investments (2002-2010)	6.36	4.55	

Source: Alamgir, "Report on the Economic Impact of Central-South Asian Road Corridors", p. 47.

Opportunities and Impediments to Regional Trade

Its landlocked geography leaves the Central Asia region profoundly dependent on its immediate neighbors for access to the rest of the world. With the break-up of the Soviet Union, the emergence of independent states in Central Asia, and the defeat of the Taliban in Afghanistan, new and hopeful opportunities have opened for greater regional cooperation.

Yet in spite of a number of successful meetings of the interested countries and both regional and bilateral agreements, overall progress has been slow. Against this background, the opening of the North-South and East-West corridors via Afghanistan offers new hope for substantial long-term development in the region.

Impediments to regional trade are numerous, and the challenges seem at times insurmountable (see table 6 below). These challenges fall into two very different groups, the first pertaining to the economic and social environment as a whole and the second consisting of specific and more limited issues that are subject to shorter-term solutions.

The first group includes legacies reflective of historic and geopolitical factors. Prominent among them are regional insecurity, terrorism and narcotics trafficking and production. These challenges greatly impede normal economic growth and hinder social betterment, but will only be resolved with large expenditures over time.

More immediate obstacles to trade include infrastructure costs, and costs arising from the lack of proper legal and regulatory systems, restrictive trade policies, poor border management, and the absence of effective transport facilitation. They also include inadequately harmonized trade and customs procedures, lack of transparency, high levels of corruption, a large informal or illegal sector, a weak private sector, and the absence of vital services such as trade finance, banking, insurance, bonding, and telecommunication facilities. This second layer of obstacles can be resolved relatively quicker but requires a strong sense of cooperation among regional players and within each country. More importantly, these challenges, once addressed, can pave the way to resolving the more daunting first layer obstacles which have held back growth and stability.

Impediments to Trade

Numerous studies show that being landlocked is a significant impediment to economic growth. One study found that based on shipping company information, landlocked country's shipping costs are more than 50 percent higher compared to costs of coastal countries. The same study found that more than 70 percent of the variation in per capita income can be explained by the proximity of a country to important markets.[15] Landlocked countries, because they incur greater transport costs, keep their wages lower to remain competitive. Further, another study, looking at Central Asian countries specifically has concluded that being landlocked is estimated to reduce trade by more then 80%.[16] This drastic reduction in trade was mainly due to various costs related to crossing many borders and due to navigating via land through neighboring countries where trade is subject to additional administrative restrictions and rigid procedures rather than due to geographical distance to destination markets per se.

Given the above, Central Asia countries, even though they cannot reduce physical distances per se, they can gain significantly from reducing the cost of trade and transit. In focusing on cost reduction, they can benefit by focusing on a flexible and suitable transport infrastructure investment strategy, and even more importantly, by designing and implementing a cooperative approach to a well-crafted transport and trade facilitation and logistics strategy among partner countries.

---

[15] Molnar, Eva, and Ojala, Lauri, 'Transport and Trade Facilitation Issues in the CIS-7 Countries, Kazakhstan, and Turkmenistan', Paper prepared for the Lucerne Conference of the CIS-7 Initiative, 20th-22nd January 2003, p.39. Available at http://www.cis7.org/.

[16] Raballand, Gaël, "Determinants of the Negative Impact of Being Landlocked on Trade: An Empirical Investigation Through the Central Asian Case," *Comparative Economic Studies*, December 2003, Volume 45, Number 4, pp. 520-536.

Table 6: Key Trade and Transit impediment[17]

Trade Policy	▪ Differences in tariff rates ▪ Different stages in the WTO accession process ▪ Overlapping, sometimes inconsistent regional trade preferences ▪ Non-tariff tax barriers such as excise taxes on imports, labeling requirements, import licenses
Border Management	▪ Lack of harmonized customs procedures, leading to detailed checks at borders ▪ Numerous and cumbersome documentation requirements ▪ Lack of recognition of TIR seals and high cost of transit convoys ▪ Lengthy transshipment procedures and lack of adequate logistics ▪ High levels of corruption of customs officials and other inspection agencies
Transport Sector	▪ Visa restrictions on entry of foreign truckers ▪ Truck entry fees ▪ Trucking cartels to guarantee safe passage ▪ Lack of modern (TIR compatible) trucking fleet ▪ Slow speed of rail cargo leading to lack of competitiveness ▪ Lack of freight forwarding firms offering smaller tonnage freights on rail cargo

Opportunities in Facilitating Trade

- The Importance of Local and Regional Development for Generating Continental Trade

Due to Central Asia's landlocked character, when promoting long distance and continental trade one must focus on development of ports. Most of Afghanistan's trade is now conducted via Pakistan mainly through Karachi. However, as an ADB study points out, Karachi and its nearby sister port Qasim have a total of forty berths between them, which are largely underutilized. This capacity is largely underutilized and is available for trade involving Afghanistan, the Central Asian republics, and the more distant trading partners.

In addition to these two ports, the new deep-water port at Gwadar in Pakistan is also coming on line. According to the Economic Cooperation Organization (ECO), part of the trade from Central Asia and beyond, could

[17] Source: Byrd, William, "Prospects for Regional Development and Economic Cooperation in the Wider Central Asia Region." Paper prepared for the Kabul Conference on Regional Economic Cooperation, December 3-5, 2005. World Bank. Washington DC, January 2006, p.17.

transit via Gwadar. The ECO study shows that as much as 40 percent of total transit can be channeled in this way.[18] Further, Iran's new port at Chabahar has four berths and Bandar e-Abbas another twenty six. With further increases in efficiencies and better trade facilitation, the capacity of both ports could be enhanced, thereby creating no less than four significant regionally competitive outlets for third country or longer-distance trade.

The Asian Development Bank studied long distance and third country transit trade entering the region through the warm water ports mentioned above[19]. It estimated the current level of transit trade to be about $2.5 billion for the countries in the region of the road corridors discussed above. If the further road corridors are built by 2010 however, transit trade could grow to $6.3 billion from the current $2.8 billion, a substantial increase of 80 percent.

Thus, the development of local ports can unlock the potential of the entire region. This will draw longer-distance partners, including China, Russia and India, on the one hand, and the Middle East and Europe on the other. The development of continental trade starts by developing local port capacity, improving efficiency, and implementing better trade facilitation strategies.

o Effective Trade Facilitation & Its Regional Benefits

Strategies in trade coordination and facilitation have the singular potential to make a significant difference in spurring economic growth. In this regard, there are practical areas where quick gains can be achieved and where investments can show adequate and fast returns. To explore these, let us focus on (1) the costs of trade facilitation; (2) customs transit and border management issues; (3) the role of the private sector, and (4) the importance of the informal sector, including the informal banking sector. We will also touch on such key related aspects such as the development of the insurance

---

[18] Alamgir, Mohiuddin, "Report on the Economic Impact of Central-South Asian Road Corridors," Central and South Asia Transport and Trade Forum (CSATTF). Report prepared for the Second Ministerial Conference on Transport and Trade in Central and South Asia. Asian Development Bank, Manila, Philippines, March 3 and 4, 2005, p.28.

[19] Ibid.

industry, the role of the international community, regional trade and policy harmonization, and the need for a regional funding mechanism

o The Costs of Trade Logistics in Facilitation

The benefits of the new road corridors depend greatly on achieving successful cooperation in trade and transit facilitation measures including trade logistics. In addition, improvements in trade facilitation is a quick and concrete way of demonstrating the benefits from the required investments in large physical infrastructure, trade logistics costs are part and parcel of the trading activity. Molnar and Ojala argue that in a well functioning market economy logistics costs are usually less than 10 percent of the sale price of manufactured goods.[20] But over long distances freight costs alone can use up to 50 percent of the sales price. This helps explain why the trade volumes of landlocked countries are 60 percent lower than representative coastal economies. Under such circumstances, trade logistics can become as decisive a function as purchasing, production, distribution and marketing. (See table 7).

Table 7: Trade Logistics Costs[21]

	Direct Logistics Costs	**Indirect Logistics Costs**
Overhead or Opportunity costs	- Inventory costs - Value of time - Technology/IT costs	- Cost of lost sales - Customer service costs - Obsolescence - IT maintenance
Activity / Function related costs	- Transport/Freight costs - Cargo handling - Warehousing/storage - Insurance - Documentation - Telecommunications	- Packaging - IT personnel - Cost of capital in logistics equipment - Administration

[20] Molnar, Eva, and Ojala, Lauri, "Transport and Trade Facilitation Issues in the CIS-7 Countries, Kazakhstan, and Turkmenistan," Paper prepared for the Lucerne conference of the CIS-7 Initiative, 20th-22nd January 2003, pp. 9-12. Available at http://www.cis7.org.

[21] Source: Molnar, Eva, and Ojala, Lauri, 'Transport and Trade Facilitation Issues in the CIS-7 Countries, Kazakhstan, and Turkmenistan.' Paper prepared for the Lucerne Conference of the CIS-7 Initiative, 20th-22nd January 2003, p.11.

o Customs, Transit and Border Management

A key impediment to trade is the endless procedures at border and custom posts. Burdensome documentation, rigid procedures, and the lack of harmonized laws prevent commercial traffic from reaching its potential. As shown in Table 8, fifty-seven signatures for imports are required for Afghanistan, forty-five for Iran, and twenty-two for both India and the Kyrgyz Republic, while average for the OECD countries is only three. The number of documents required to export is eighteen for Uzbekistan and 15 for India, compared with only six for the OECD countries. Finally, the average delay on imports is a staggering 139 days for Uzbekistan, 97 for Afghanistan and 87 for Kazakhstan, against fourteen in OECD countries.

Table 8: Cross Border Trading Costs: Procedures and Documentation[22]

Country or Region	Documents for export (number)	Signatures for export (number)	Time for export (days)	Documents for import (number)	Signatures for import (number)	Time for import (days)
OECD - High Income	5.3	3.2	12.6	6.9	3.3	14
Afghanistan	..	..	..	10	57	97
Kazakhstan	14	15	93	18	17	87
Kyrgyz Republic	..	..	..	18	27	127
Uzbekistan	..	..	..	18	32	139
Iran	11	30	45	11	45	51
India	10	22	36	15	27	43
Pakistan	8	10	33	12	15	39
Turkey	9	10	20	13	20	25
Russian Federation	8	8	29	8	10	35
Germany	4	1	6	4	1	6
United States	6	5	9	5	4	9

The transformation of laws and customs procedures cannot be accomplished overnight, in part because they in turn lead to to such broader changes as the reduction of rigid cultures of control and a renewed focus on the elimination of corruption. All this assumes higher levels of bilateral and regional cooperation, especially in such key areas as the reform of existing bilateral agreements; negotiation of transport accessibility agreements; development

[22] Source: See online report by the World Bank, "Doing Business, Get Full Date," Afghanistan, Trading Across Borders, World Bank. Washington DC. Available at http://www.doingbusiness.org/CustomQuery/.

of transshipment arrangements; piloting of joint processing; and development of IT interfaces.

A key constraint to efficient trade flows through Afghanistan is the need to trans-ship cargo—the unloading and re-loading from one truck to another or from rails to trucks, etc. at crossing points between countries. *The high level of truck-to-truck trans-shipment at the borders of Afghanistan may be unique in international transit systems.*[23] For example, a great amount of cargo going to Kabul via Pakistan is trans-shipped in Peshawar, Quetta or Spin Boldak. The same occurs at the Iran/Afghanistan border points. The reluctance to allow Pakistani drivers through Afghanistan and concerns about drug smuggling play a part in this problem. Trans-shipment increases handling costs and transit times and causes damaged and lost cargo. Inadequate training and poor working conditions for personnel at customs points adds further to the costs. The World Bank found in 2005 that cargoes to and from Afghanistan lose an average of 5 percent of their value to spoilage and loss, and that in some cases the losses reach 30 to 50 percent.[24] Any solution to this issue will take some time to implement, as security concerns and infrastructure development take priority in the short-term. One "quick-win" solution is to allow for trans-shipment to take place away from the border or in a neighboring country where both examination and trans-shipment can be carried out.

Uzbekistan has an opportunity to help ease trans-shipment by lifting some of the restrictions at Hayratan. This will support the World Bank's development efforts on the Afghan side of the border. Related measures would be for Turkmenistan and the Iranian governments to upgrade the facilities on their sides of the border. Also important would be to modernize

---

[23] See the World Bank report, "Trade and Regional Cooperation between Afghanistan and its Neighbors," Report No. 26769. Poverty Reduction and Economic Management Sector Unit South Asia Region. Washington DC, February 18, 2004, p.31. Available at http://www.worldbank.org/transport/learning/learning%20week/trade_facil_2005/Regional%20and%20Country%20Report/World%20Bank%20(2004b)%20Afghanistan.pdf.

[24] See the World Bank report, "The Investment Climate in Afghanistan," Washington DC, December 2005, p. ix. Available at www.ipanet.net/investmenthorizons_afghanistan.

the Afghanistan Transit Trade Agreement (ATTA) agreement with Pakistan, as well as to open greater access to Pakistan for Afghan vehicles.

The streamlining of border procedures should also be given high priority, preferably by reducing them to a single document. Afghan authorities have already introduced new customs declaration forms with the adoption of the Afghan Customs Clearance Declaration (ACCD). While these are a significant improvement over the previous document, the new process still fails to conform to international formats. As such, going forward with the standard Single Administrative Document (SAD) as part of the modernization process and the ASYCUDA[25] computer system is highly desirable to help facilitate the growth of trade at the border.

o The Role of the Private Sector

Some 38 percent of the exporters surveyed by the World Bank identified the cost of transport as either a major or very severe obstacle to trade in Afghanistan.[26] It is vital to recognize the role of the private sector in reducing these costs. The first step is to have an inclusive approach in the process of evaluation and implementation of reforms by seeking and encouraging direct private sector participation and input. In doing so, there are a number of key areas for cooperation where that sector can make a successful contribution to the expansion of trade.

Associations of private transport operators are useful in engaging the private sector. The United Nations Conference on Trade and Development (UNCTAD), the Asian Development Bank, and the World Bank have all proposed the creation of such forums as a Trade and Transport Facilitation Committee. These associations should include truckers, freight forwarders and freight brokers as well as transport insurance companies, etc. They could develop recommendations for streamlining border controls and reducing entry barriers for private investors, and also propose policies to stimulate private sector activity.

---

[25] ASYCUDA: Automated Issues under discussion. A system for customs data.

[26] See the World Bank report, "The Investment Climate in Afghanistan," Washington DC, December 2005, pp. 29-30. Available at www.ipanet.net/investmenthorizons_afghanistan.

Politicians and donors often find it easier to commit resources if a problem can be quantified and if the results of their interventions can be concretely measured. The World Bank has gained experience in developing performance measurements on the facilitation of trade. These involve regularly checking border crossing times, the number of irregularities discovered during inspections, incidents of corruption, etc. The information is collected from public agencies and the trucking businesses and transformed into electronic format to be entered into a computer system. With the assistance of the private sector, the World Bank is developing such a system for nine corridors in Central Asia, and is working along the same lines on customs projects in Afghanistan and Pakistan.[27]

The new Customs Law introduced in Afghanistan is largely compatible with international standards. However, the Asian Development Bank has pointed to a few problems.[28] Thus, there is no provision for a user fee, as required for future World Trade Organization (WTO) membership; it is an obligation to use a Customs broker for every operation, which is contrary to WTO regulations; Customs is unable to carry out a large number of investigations; and has significant limitations in enforcement. It is also important to point out that sudden or erratic introduction of trade legislation can be a hindrance to the efficient flow of trade at the border and costly to the private sector. In this regard, maintaining a stable customs legislative environment is vital as a risk mitigation strategy and as an important factor in the promotion of trade. Direct input from the business community will be highly valuable in reducing one of the key impediments that make trade costly.

---

[27] Byrd, William, "Prospects for Regional Development and Economic Cooperation in the Wider Central Asia Region," Paper prepared for the Kabul Conference on Regional Economic Cooperation, December 3-5, 2005. World Bank. Washington DC. January 2006, p.56.

[28] Bayley, Anthony, "Report On Border And Customs Related Facilities And Procedures In Afghanistan," Paper prepared for the Second Meeting of the Trade and Customs Working Group Bangkok 13-14, Central and South Asia Transport and Trade Forum (CSATTF). Asia Development Bank, Manila, Philippines. December 2005, p. 49.

o The Importance of the Informal Sector

According to official data, trade flows between Afghanistan and its neighbors comprise only 10 to 12 percent of all Afghan exports.[29] However, if data on the vibrant informal economy were added, the percentage would rise sharply. The informal economy in Afghanistan, inclusive of drugs, accounts for some 80 to 90 percent of the total economy.[30] Thus, informal and illegal trade far exceeds official trade. Surveys conducted in Central Asia by the United Nations Development Program (UNDP) found that much of the informal trading is conducted by small-scale "shuttle traders" who are subject to the highest level of restrictions at borders. In the case of Afghanistan—as in many other cases—informal trading has allowed Afghans to survive during the years of conflict via a flexible and inherently dynamic set of mechanisms.

However, the informal sector constrains long-term growth. It hinders revenue distribution and mobilization and jeopardizes state building, sustainability, and security. It is therefore vital to not only develop the institutions that can allow and encourage the informal sector to become formal but to also devise short-term approaches towards specific solutions which can galvanize the participation of both small-scale and larger scale informal traders.

Restrictive policies can often push traders even further into the informal sector. This type of growth in the informal economy has the potential of spilling over to neighboring countries, especially in and around Afghanistan creating additional and persistent security issues in the region. There is an opportunity here to cooperate in this particular area so that the impact of the informal sector on each neighbor is understood and where significant improvements can be achieved both in the economic and security sectors. Some, including the World Bank, have suggested the creation of border trading zones that would help traders transfer their activities from the

---

[29] See the World Bank report, "State Building, Sustaining Growth, and Reducing Poverty: a Country Economic Report," Washington DC, 2005, p. xxi. Available http://siteresources.worldbank.org/INTAFGHANISTAN/Resources/0821360957_Afghanistan--State_Building.pdf.

[30] Ibid., p. 5.

informal and illegal sectors to the legal sector.[31] Traders operating in the informal sector could be offered access to certain restricted markets in exchange for an entry fee. This scheme has the potential to separate informal trade from narcotics products. Border trading zones can also generate substantial revenue for the state, at the same time allowing control over the movements of goods and reducing smuggling. The World Bank points to the example of bazaars in Pakistan that allow informal trading from Afghanistan. Similar but better regulated zones could be set up in other countries neighboring Afghanistan.

Business in Afghanistan still relies on the centuries-old "*hawala*" system for transferring funds and payments, and for short-term loans. The hawala networks are based on an honor system for payments and commissions. It is cash-based and paperless, and thus does not lend itself to modern banking and accounting practices. A World Bank survey reports that only about 30 percent of businesses in Afghanistan maintain bank accounts.[32] The same survey found that 21 percent of firms have obtained loans from the *hawaladars*, and 14 percent of exporters received payments through hawala transfers. Abolishing or heavily regulating the hawala system is not a feasible solution for Afghanistan as it could push hawaladars farther out of reach of the more formal sector and thus dampen trade. Moreover, the system is quite effective. Table 9 shows that hawala transfers are as efficient as formal transfers, while the length of time to clear a hawala transfer is very close to that required for a bank draft.

However, despite the efficiency and resilience of the hawala system, the informal banking system cannot sustain the further development of trade among the countries in the region, let alone continental trade. It perpetuates money laundering and further complicates the fight against terrorism.

---

[31] Byrd, William, "Prospects for Regional Development and Economic Cooperation in the Wider Central Asia Region," Paper prepared for the Kabul Conference on Regional Economic Cooperation, December 3-5, 2005. World Bank. Washington DC, January 2006, p.58.

[32] See the World Bank report, "The Investment Climate in Afghanistan," Washington DC, December 2005, p. vi. Available at www.ipanet.net/investmenthorizons_afghanistan.

Beyond this, it hinders the Central Bank's ability to manage monetary policy, thus further thwarting long-term economic growth.

To address this problem Afghanistan should work towards the implementation of a self-regulatory financial services system, instead of building a traditional regulatory banking regimen. As an example, the World Bank had proposed a staged approach for transforming the informal banking sector into a more formalized one.[33] The following measures are suggested:

- The government, through the Central Bank, should engage the private sector and the hawaladars in direct dialogue, working with the informal Money Exchange Dealers Association to devise a self-regulatory and supervisory framework as an interim solution. The dealers are the only entities that can elucidate the current types of hawala and would be best placed to develop self-regulatory mechanism if sufficient incentives are offered them.
- Authorities should encourage applications for money service businesses from large money exchange dealers who could meet legal licensing requirements.
- The Central Bank could then consider licensing compliant money service businesses as non-banking financial institutions and sanction their participation in a wider range of formally regulated financial activities.
- As a final step, authorities might consider the transformation of some of the larger money exchange dealers into full fledged banks engaging in rural finance, trade finance, insurance and financial services. This would fuel the growth of trade and promote sustainability in the economy.

---

[33] Ibid., pp. 49-54.

Table 9: Comparing the Hawaladars with Banks[34]	
% of firms with a loan from a *hawaladars*	21
% of firms with some form of bank credit	0.9
% of domestic firms that primarily pay by *hawala* transfer	10
% of domestic firms that primarily pay by bank transfer, check, or bank draft	11
% of exporting firms that primarily pay by *hawala* transfer	14
% of exporting firms that primarily pay by bank transfer, check, or bank draft	30
Average time to clear *hawala* transfer from domestic customer	28 days
Average time to clear a bank draft from domestic customer	7.3 days
Average time to clear *hawala* transfer from export customer	9.2 days
Average time to clear a bank draft from export customer	7.2 days

- Developing the Insurance Industry

The lack of trade and business insurance impedes trade in Afghanistan. Businesses and potential investors have cited this weakness as a major reason for their reluctance to make investments. A World Bank[35] survey found that 32 percent of business respondents cited the lack of shipping insurance as a major or severe impediment to their export activity. Because it is nearly impossible to get good local insurance for the transport of goods, truckers raise their rates to cover their potential losses or, worse, they get no coverage and thus are left subject to catastrophic loss. Under such circumstances, most international shipping lines do not allow their containers into the country.

Without transit insurance, Afghanistan's trade will remain underdeveloped. International donors have recently developed programs that address political risk, but general liability, product liability, and transit and trade insurance are not available. Nor is the private sector fully engaged in creating an adequate insurance marketplace.

The only path forward is to open the insurance sector to private competition and to allow the participation of foreign insurance companies with

---

[34] Source: See the World Bank report, "The Investment Climate in Afghanistan", December 2005, p. 23. Washington DC. Available at www.ipanet.net/investmenthorizons_Afghanistan.

[35] Ibid., p. 29.

experience in transport insurance. A thorough assessment of the legal environment for an insurance industry is also needed. The authorities would need to directly engage private investors and the international and regional insurance providers. In this sense, close cooperation with neighboring countries would allow for the development of regional sectors with their particular expertise. Insurance being vital to trade, the only sure way of developing it, is to engage with the private sector so that the creation of basic insurance for trade, transit, and freight forwarding is assured.

- The Role of the International Community

International donors will continue to be essential if the Afghan trade is to develop. International organizations also have a role to play. A number of recent developments in regional cooperation support Afghanistan's potential role as a land bridge. Afghanistan joined the Central Asia Regional Economic Cooperation (CAREC) which fosters integrated initiatives to link Central Asia economies, streamlining finances and developing common approaches to technical assistance. In November, 2005, the South Asian Association for Regional Cooperation (SAARC) admitted Afghanistan to membership. Also, Afghanistan has observer status in the Shanghai Cooperation Organization (SCO) and started accession talks with the World Trade Organization (WTO). WTO accession is vital for Afghanistan's full interaction with the world's major economies.

Acknowledging this, the intricate web of rules and agreements created by overlapping integrative organizations can often delay real progress. As can be seen in the figure below, overlapping agreements have already resulted in a spaghetti bowl of conflicting trade rules. The best way to extricate Afghanistan and the region from this web is for all parties in the region to join the WTO. This would integrate disparate policy processes into a more cohesive strategy of regional and global cooperation.

Figure 3: Spaghetti Bowl: Regional Agreements

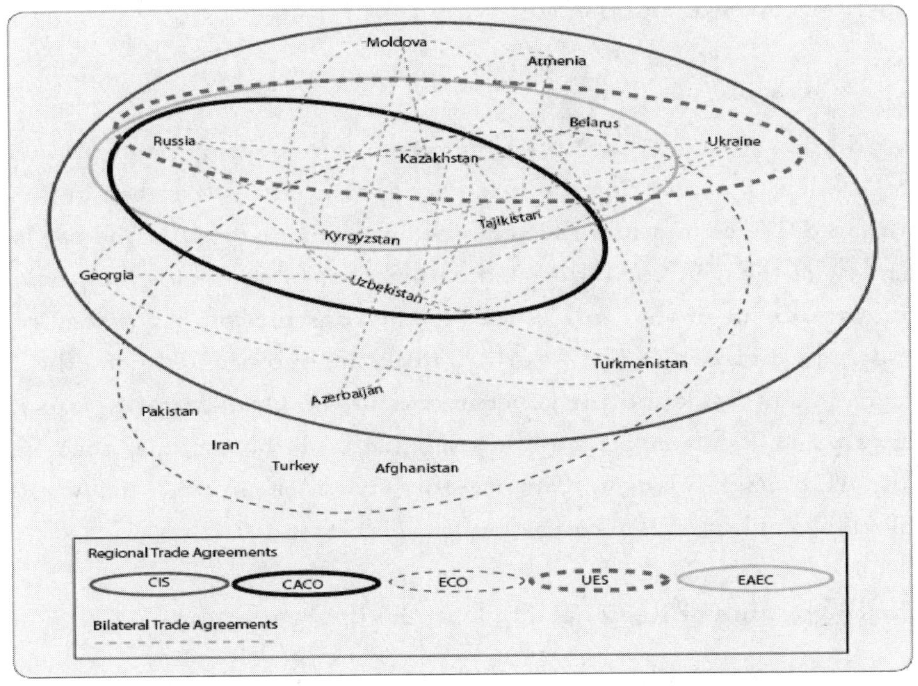

Source: United Nations Central Asia Human Development Report 2005. United Nations Development Programme, New York. 2005. p. 57.

One of the impediments to regional development in the area is the lack of dedicated regional funding mechanisms. The development of Afghanistan can be used as a spring board to establish such a mechanism. This initiative would look at the reconstruction of Afghanistan as an integral part of the development of a regional program and thus would establish a funding mechanism via the creation of a special trust fund. The World Bank[36] has a similar proposal specifically to support the modernization of the trucking fleet in Central Asia via a regional trust fund. Funding could be directed in such a way where both private and public sector operators could benefit, and at the same time. Governments would be incentivised to reduce entry barriers and assure the implementation of international standards such as the

---

36 Byrd, William, "Prospects for Regional Development and Economic Cooperation in the Wider Central Asia Region," Paper prepared for the Kabul Conference on Regional Economic Cooperation, December 3-5, 2005. World Bank. Washington DC. January 2006, p.59.

TIR (Transport International Routière) convention, freight load limits, emission standards and the like.

- Investing in Road Corridors

In addition, donors can promote economic development and regional cooperation by supporting the road corridor initiative described in this paper. In the ADB's estimation, the required investment to build the roads is less than 5% of the combined projected national investments for the participating countries. Some of the work related to the construction of the road corridors is already underway. The World Bank, the European Union, the Islamic Development Bank and the governments of the United States, Japan, India, Kuwait and Pakistan are building segments of the regional road network. The ADB itself plans to finance road corridor projects in Afghanistan, Pakistan, Tajikistan, Turkmenistan and Uzbekistan.[37]

The Importance of Regional Trade in the Energy Sector

Trade and Transportation Benefits of Oil and Gas

Afghanistan is crucial in linking South Asia to the natural resources of Central Asia and unlocking the enormous benefits to the entire region from the trade of oil and gas. The economies of China and India are growing at an explosive pace; with the combined GDP of the two countries projected to be almost double that of the United States by 2030.

The sheer size of these two economies creates gigantic appetites for energy. According to the U.S. Department of Energy, while world energy consumption is expected to increase by 2.6% annually from current levels to 2030; India's energy consumption will increase by 3.8% and China's by 5.0%

[37]Alamgir, Mohiuddin, "Report on the Economic Impact of Central-South Asian Road Corridors," Central and South Asia Transport and Trade Forum (CSATTF). Report prepared for the Second Ministerial Conference on Transport and Trade in Central and South Asia. Asian Development Bank, Manila, Philippines, March 3 and 4, 2005.

over the same period. This compares to a projected annual increase of only 1.3% for all OECD countries over the same period.[38]

By 2025 China will need 14.2 million barrels of oil a day to sustain its growth –double the amount in 2005. India's projected needs are greater still. India's oil imports stand at about 1.4 million barrels a day but, in order to address its economic growth, imports are projected to rise to about 5 million barrels a day by 2020, an increase of 360%.[39] In addition, India's natural gas consumption is projected to increase to about 6.8 billion cubic feet per day within 10 years, and to increase six-fold within 20 years, resulting in a need for about 400 million metric standard cubic meters per day of natural gas.[40]

Beyond the purely political or security related issues, the economic reasons that naturally link Central Asia's gas and oil resources to the needs of South Asia are overwhelmingly significant. These include the need to sustain the phenomenal economic growth of South Asia, the need for Central Asian countries to diversify their economies by directly benefiting from global market prices, and the unique opportunity to support Afghanistan's role as an energy transport corridor achieving stability and prosperity in the regional as a whole.

Most of northern India and Pakistan are devoid of energy resources. Accounting for half of South Asia's GDP, this region has perhaps the scantiest endowment of hydrocarbons of any important economic zone on earth. In sharp contrast, just a few hundred kilometers away, the plains of Central Asia consisting of Turkmenistan and Uzbekistan and the northern regions of Afghanistan may hold as much as over 217 tcf (trillion cubic feet) of gas reserves, more than the estimates for Saudi Arabia's reserves. *Clearly, these two regions need to find each other.* This is even more urgent as global fuel prices have jumped by 210% since 2002.[41] Failing to access Central Asian

---

[38] See "International Energy Outlook 2006," U.S. Department of Energy, p.101. Available at http://www.eia.doe.gov/oiaf/ieo/index.html.

[39] Bush, Jason, "China and India: A Rage for Oil," *Businessweek*, September 5, 2005.

[40] "India In-Depth," Rigzone.com, May 4, 2006. Available at http://www.rigzone.com/analysis/rigs/insight.asp?i_id=211.

[41] Bloomberg.com, Market Data, Jul 13, 2006. See internet reference of http://www.bloomberg.com/markets/commodities/energyprices.html.

energy will endanger the economies of India and Pakistan at a time when neither can afford a pause in their growth.

How is the South Asia region going to connect to Central Asia and solve its energy needs to support its massive growth? Two alternatives have been advanced: the Turkmenistan-Afghanistan-Pakistan-India (TAPI) pipeline and the Termez-Kabul-Peshawar-India (TKPI) pipeline (See Appendix A for a map of the Pipeline Routes).

The Amu Darya basin of Uzbekistan contains significant reserves of natural gas. Adjacent areas of Afghanistan and Tajikistan remain less explored and have smaller proven natural gas reserves. However, estimates from Soviet times indicated that Afghanistan's Northern region may hold about 5 tcf of natural gas. These estimates were updated in 2006 by the U.S. Geological Survey, (USGS),[42] which showed that Northern Afghanistan holds 18 times the oil and triple the natural gas resources previously thought. This 2006 Survey by the USGS confirmed over 15.6 tcf of natural gas (possibly up to 36.5 tcf) and about 1.6 billion barrels of oil (possibly up to 3.6 bbo) in the Amu Darya Basin not even counting the vast reserves of Turkmenistan. USGS has not yet assessed all areas in the basin and may well discover additional reserves.

With the exception of a relatively small Turkmen pipeline to Iran, neither gas nor oil pipelines connect Central Asia to South Asia. Gas has been transported north to Russia by means of the Russian energy monopoly Gazprom. Finding alternatives to the Russian route is a compelling challenge if the landlocked Central Asian countries are to create anything matching the rates of economic growth that South East Asian countries have experienced.

The idea of building a gas and oil pipeline from Central Asia to South Asia has existed for some time. The original Trans-Afghan Pipeline was conceived in the early 1990s when international gas and oil corporations, along with the government of Turkmenistan sought to negotiate their way through very challenging security and political challenges, but to no avail.

---

[42] United States Geological Survey, "USGS Assessment Significantly Increases Afghanistan Petroleum Resource Base," Release of March 14, 2006. Reston, VA. Available at http://pubs.usgs.gov/fs/2006/3031/

With the fall of the Taliban and improved security, the project was resuscitated. The Asian Development Bank supported a feasibility study to establish the Turkmenistan-Afghanistan-Pakistan-India (TAPI) pipeline. In May 2002, the heads of state of Afghanistan, Pakistan, and Turkmenistan met in Islamabad to restart the Natural Gas Pipeline Project. A ministerial level steering committee was formed later in the same year. The project aims to construct natural-gas transmission pipeline of 1,700 kilometers to transport 30 billion cubic meters of gas per year from Turkmenistan's Dauletabad gas fields to Afghanistan, Pakistan, and possibly to India. The route proposed is from Dauletabad to the Afghan cities of Herat and Khandahar and then to Multan in Pakistan. The ADB estimates the cost of the project to be $3.3 billion and projects that its implementation will take five years. The TAPI project, if constructed as planned will enable Afghanistan to reclaim its status as the landbridge between Central and South Asia.

The Turkmenistan-Afghanistan-Pakistan-India pipeline has been proposed to follow the route Dauletabad -Kandahar- Multan. However, there is an alternative route to connect the energy fields of Central Asia with the needs of South Asia: the Termez-Kabul-Peshawar-India route (TKPI). This pipeline would connect the southernmost city in Uzbekistan, Termez, to Kabul via the Mazar-i-Sharif and then would run from Kabul to Islamabad. Termez is 300 km from Kabul and Kabul is 200 km from Peshawar, which in turn is about 250 km from Islamabad. Extending this route to India would only require about 250 km via Lahore, the major economic center of Lahore-Amritsar. The distance of the TKPI route is only half of TAPI's 1,700 km. It will take the pipeline through much more populated areas but still reach the same destinations in Pakistan and India. Notably, it will also go through Kabul, brining additional benefits to Afghanistan's energy starved capital.

Benefits of Energy Corridors between Central and South Asia

No matter which route the pipelines take, it is obvious that Turkmenistan, Uzbekistan and the Northern territories of Afghanistan will help meet the growing thirst of South Asia for gas and oil. The cascading benefits of unlocking potentials in this manner should not be underestimated in terms of their actual economic, social and political impact. Pipelines will foster and help create regional stability and security in a region that is much in need of both.

Both Turkmenistan and Uzbekistan will be able to demand from Pakistan and India higher prices for their gas and oil than they now get from Russia's Gazprom. Russia's monopoly over Central Asian exports of oil and gas has thwarted the region's economic growth. The combined Kazakh, Turkmen and Uzbek production of oil can double over the next 10 years; if even part of this crosses Uzbekistan to Pakistan and India, all will benefit.[43]

The recently discovered gas reserves in northern Afghanistan are of great significance to the country's future. The U.S. government's assessment concluded that the unit cost of producing gas from the Afghan plains would be very low. The only local market for this gas is Kabul, which is too small. However, the major energy firms would be interested in developing local Afghan pipelines if they could also be linked with the Uzbek gas reserves and with lucrative markets in Pakistan and India. Tariffs on such a pipeline to South Asia could pay for the pipeline, resulting in a costless delivery of gas to Kabul and Pakistan.

The construction of the gas pipelines could create substantial revenues for Afghanistan. It is estimated that if the pipeline to Pakistan existed today, and if Afghanistan charged world prices for transport of gas through its country, it would be earning about $1 billion to $1.5 billion in annual revenues from the gas pipeline tax alone. The Afghan Government could reap another $0.5 billion in revenues on the transport of oil from Central Asia to South Asia.[44] Pakistan would benefit too because it is not able to sustain the current demand in its domestic market and because it is transporting gas and oil thousand of kilometers inland from its ports. Further, India would find an additional source of energy and would diversify its ability to bargain for its growing needs.

---

43 Cassam, Mohamed, "The Termez-Kabul-Peshawar Energy Corridor," Prepared for the Afghan Minister of Finance, H.E. Hedayat Amin Arsala. Courtesy of the author. January 2, 2005, p. 7.

44 Kaufmann, Klaus-Dieter and Feizlmayr, Adolf H. "Analysis pegs pipeline ahead of LNG for Caspian area to China," *Oil and Gas Journal*, 102(10), March 8, 2004, p. 58.

The proposed pipelines will also bring significant indirect economic benefits. They would create jobs, promote the construction of new and improved infrastructure, and increase the availability of electricity, gas, and oil to regional industries. Households along the length of the energy corridor from the Uzbek border to Pakistan would see their incomes rise. The pipelines represent an opportunity to have locals privately own small community power stations which can act as small energy generators providing the local populations not only with jobs but with cheap energy.

Winter heating is a particularly severe problem in Afghanistan. Existing diesel generators producing electricity could easily be converted to gas if gas were to become reasonably available. Such generators can double as space heaters. This space heating would come at zero cost by utilizing the otherwise wasted heat created by the generator. This use of heat from power generation is called "distributive energy". Distributive energy achieves a 60% to 70% rate of efficiency as compared with only 30% to 40% for central power plants.[45] Because of the severe winters in Afghanistan and the mountainous regions of Pakistan and India, this seemingly free source of energy can be promoted as an important benefit to the local population and as a result of the new pipelines.

Finally, high-speed fiber optic cables can be installed inside the pipelines. These cables are part of a high capacity telecommunication SCADA[46] backbone system that can modernize the region's communication systems, provide a mechanism for developing regional telecom "hubs", and be a source of revenue not only for the governments but for local and regional businesses.

Each of the routes discussed has economic and political advantages. For example, although the Termez-Kabul-Pesahwar pipeline (TKP) would only be half the length of the Dauletabad-Herat-Kandahar (DHK) route, it would not have access to the large Turkmen gas fields. Other factors make all of these projects demanding indeed. Security issues are prominent,

---

[45] Cassam, Mohamed, "The Termez-Kabul-Peshawar Energy Corridor," Prepared for the Afghan Minister of Finance, H.E. Hedayat Amin Arsala. Courtesy of the author. January 2, 2005, p. 19.
[46] SCADA: Supervisory Control And Data Acquisition.

because either pipeline would traverse territories not yet fully stable and secured. In the DHK route, the pipeline would traverse mostly deserted regions in Afghanistan. Once the TKP route reaches Pakistan, it must traverse Baluchistan, which has been mired in local instability.

However, despite the known security issues, some concerns are overstated. Assuming wise revenue-sharing on the part of central governments, all local areas, whether in Afghanistan or Pakistan, would have a stake in the success of the pipelines. The pipelines and energy corridors as important sources of revenue, can be a considerable counterbalance to the scourge of drug trafficking affecting not only the region but the rest of world. The local, mostly very poor populations will see important improvements to their daily lives. A true economic alternative that can help in generating income for the poor, spur the development of small businesses and increase the central governments' revenues is of great value and needs to be pursued with zeal by all key participants. Such an important source of income would also greatly alleviate the cost of reconstruction assisting donors in establishing more economically sustainable solutions.

As a regional and global power, India especially has an important stake in assuring the development of such pipelines. However, India is also concerned about the security of gas and oil supplies emanating from routes through Pakistan. Pakistan and India are in the same camp when it comes to their deficient energy resources. Additional safeguards can be established to assure India further. This could come in the form of agreements among all parties, including Pakistan that the supply of energy from Uzbekistan or Turkmenistan can be stopped if there were an interruption of the flow of gas or oil to India from Pakistan. In addition, India and Pakistan could trade other forms of energy such as electricity where India generates and exports electricity to Pakistan. This way India would retain a bargaining power in terms of reducing the flow of electricity if other agreements are not sustained by Pakistan.

Benefits of Regional Trade in Electric Power

Central Asia is endowed with huge hydroelectric potential, while Pakistan and India both suffer from electricity shortages. Even Kazakhstan, traditionally a supplier of electricity, is expected to turn into a net importer by the year 2020. The transport of electricity between suppliers and consumers in the region may also provide a catalyst to related development in the overall use of water resources.

At present, over 90% of the Afghan population does not have access to electricity. The little access that is available is sporadic and unreliable. The country lacks a national electricity grid and existing equipment is of poor quality. About 475 megawatts (MW) of electrical generating capacity existed before the Soviet invasion in 1979, while today only about 270 MW is available.[47] The need to re-build capacity is undeniable but it is also important to import more electricity from Afghanistan's neighbors to the north. Unfortunately the badly damaged transmission and distribution networks prevent this. The problem is acute in all Afghanistan's electricity-producing neighbors, as well as in Afghanistan itself. The recurring losses (called "technical losses") are in the range of about 18% to 22% of total revenues from energy for Uzbekistan, Tajikistan, Kazakhstan and Kyrgyzstan. In addition, non-technical losses (delivered but unbilled consumption and uncollected bills) can reach up to 18% for the same countries.[48] For Afghanistan, technical losses were estimated at about 25% in 2002 and non-technical losses had reached about 20%. Thus, over 45% of all electricity produced in the region is either lost or goes unbilled, a significant loss to the development of all countries involved.

In fact, Afghanistan has the potential to link key suppliers of electricity with key consumers in the region due to its vital geographic location and at the same time creating benefits to its own population. At a June 2006 meeting in Turkey, representatives of Tajikistan, Kyrgyzstan, Afghanistan and Pakistan signed an agreement to supply power from Tajikistan and Kyrgyzstan to

---

[47] Breckon, Michael, "Afghanistan: Preparing the National Power Transmission Grid Project," Asia Development Bank. Project Number: 37118-01. Manila, Philippines. January 2006, p. 9. Available at http://www.adb.org/Documents/Reports/Consultant/37118-AFG/final-report.pdf.

[48] See the World Bank report "Regional Electricity Export Potential Study," Europe and Central Asia Region. Washington, D.C. December 2004, p. vi and pp. 38-39. Available at http://www.adb.org/Documents/Reports/CAREC/Energy/CA-REEPS.pdf.

Pakistan via Afghanistan.[49] However, the parties have yet to find the necessary financing, not to mention participants from the private sector. Problems also arise from the less than robust cooperation at the working level between the countries involved.

Today 35 percent of Kabul's electricity and 100 percent of Kandahar's emergency electricity is supplied by diesel generators.[50] This makes the capital of Afghanistan—one of the poorest countries—amongst the most expensive electricity per kilowatt city in the world. Better coordination among suppliers and consumers of electricity can contribute greatly to reducing the level of poverty in Afghanistan. At the same time it will offer alternatives to poppy production, thus helping stabilize the region. Nor would the stabilizing effect of Tajik and Kyrgz hydroelectric power be limited to Afghanistan. On 24 September, 2006, a power outage plunged Pakistan into darkness, leaving the entire country disconnected from its national electricity transmission system and revealing the vulnerability of its electrical networks. News reports confirmed that about 90 percent of Pakistan was affected by the power outage.[51]

In the near future it will be possible to speak of electricity corridors the way we speak today of road corridors. One example of such a corridor would originate with Kazakhstan's electric grid, cross the border with Kyrgyzstan, and then to Pakistan's grid through Afghanistan. Another example is the development of up to 1,000 MW of hydro-electricity potentially available in Tajikistan to export to Afghanistan and Pakistan. As one country uses excess supply to address energy shortages in a neighboring country, it will establish strong bonds of mutual support, to the ultimate advantage of their populations. It is estimated that the cost of power shortages to the industrial

---

[49] "Agreement on power supply project from Tajikistan, Kyrgyzstan to Pakistan signed," PakTribune, June 16, 2006. Available at http://www.paktribune.com/news/index.shtml?147111.

[50] Paterson, Anna, "Understanding Markets in Afghanistan, A Study of the Market for Petroleum Fuels," Afghanistan Research and Evaluation Unit, October 2005, p. 4. Available at http://www.areu.org.af/index.php?option=com_content&task=view&id=32&Itemid=37.

[51] "Worst ever power outage hits country," Pakistan Observer, Islamabad, Pakistan. September 25, 2006. Available at http://archive.pakobserver.net/200609/25/.

sectors of India and Pakistan is an astounding 1.5% and 1.8% of GDP, respectively. Further, it is estimated that every unit of electricity from an outage results in an economic loss of five to ten times the cost of the electricity generated, due to wastage in material, labor and lost of production.[52] This economic cost results in perpetuating the effects of poverty and holds down the human development index for theses countries. However, via trading electricity, both countries would benefit greatly. If Pakistan were to sell about 3,000 MW of power to India, it would generate annual net earnings in the order of $160 million. It could also lead to a 10 percent decrease in Pakistan's defense expenditure, with an additional saving of $300 million. Thus, electricity sales could benefit Pakistan's coffers by up to $460 million a year.[53] These are significant savings that can be used to improve education and the health sector as well as in creating a more promising investment climate for Pakistan where Indian businesses can invest. Ultimately, the fruits of such cooperation are even greater as they have the potential of easing tensions between these two neighbors and would contribute to regional stability in this imminently important part of the world.

Conclusions

As described in this report, the landlocked — in some cases doubly landlocked — character of Central Asian countries has thwarted their economic development. High transportation cost, reduced competition, and long travel times create unemployment and stagnant living standards. Shipping costs for these countries are 50 percent higher than for coastal states, which reduce their trade by more than 80 percent.

---

[52] Lama, Mahendra P, "Reforms and Power Sector in South Asia: Scope and Challenges for Cross Border Trade," Jawaharlal Nehru University, New Delhi, India. October 2002. p.17. Available at http://www.saneinetwork.net/pdf/SANEI_II/Reforms_and_PowerSector_in_SouthAsia.pdf.

[53] See the USAID report, "Economic and Social Benefits of Power Trade Between India and Pakistan," South Asia Regional Initiative for Energy Cooperation and Development. New Delhi. 2005. Available at http://www.sari-energy.org/initiatives.html.

At the same time, the benefits from increased trade, both regionally and globally are significant. Cline estimated that over fifteen years, global free trade could reduce the number of those living in poverty by 440 million people.[54] For Central Asian countries alone the United Nations argues that GDP could be 50 *percent* higher after 10 years of continuous and comprehensive regional cooperation.[55] Inter-regional trade among these countries is relatively small. However, once the major regional economic powers of China, Iran, India, and Pakistan are added, intra-regional trade will also grow, to the point that it could reach more than half of total trading volume. *This particular characteristic is now recognized as unlike any other developing region and makes this geographic area quite unique.* There lies the exceptional opportunity to engage in closer regional cooperation to increase trade both within the region and with the major more distant partners via continental trade corridors.

Even though the landlocked countries of Central Asia cannot eliminate physical distances, they can gain significantly from reducing trade and transit costs. By coming together to reduce costs, partner countries can benefit at the same time by developing suitable transport infrastructures and investment strategies, and by working out common programs for facilitating trade. Emphasis must be placed on effective trade logistics and trade facilitation; customs and border management; and on directly engaging the private sector as a key partner in regional trade facilitation. In addition, it is crucial to engage the informal sector by promoting self-regulation of the hawala system, as one key catalyst, so that the hawaladars over time can participate in a wider range of more formalized financial activities, at the same time increasing their services to a wider population and helping to fuel an expanding trade-based economy.

As Afghanistan realizes its potential as a land-bridge to Greater Central Asia it will stimulate numerous investment projects in the region. Thus, the reconstruction of Afghanistan would become an integral part of a successful

---

[54] Cline, William R. *Trade Policy and Global Poverty*. Center for Global Development, Institute for International Economics, 2004. Washington DC, pp.227-261.
[55] *United Nations Central Asia Human Development Report 2005*. United Nations Development Programme, New York, 2005, pp 205-212. Available at UNDP.org.

regional development strategy. The creation of a special trust fund dedicated to the development of regional initiatives with Afghanistan as a central focus but with direct and measurable benefits to regional players could greatly promote this end.

Our examination of the benefits from trade in the energy sector also demonstrates that Central Asia and South Asia can help to fulfill each other's needs. The proximity of supplier and consumer countries, the seasonal nature of hydroelectric power production, and the huge pull from the explosive economic growth in India and Pakistan, all set the stage for successful region wide trade in gas, oil and electrical energy. Impoverished populations in Afghanistan and Pakistan will benefit immediately. In particular in Afghanistan, where energy costs are among the highest of any country, the energy programs would not only create economic corridors and sustainable alternative sources of income against the threat from drug trafficking but also add much needed revenue streams for the state.

Finally, the development of road corridors will bring concrete benefits to all. Our examination of the ADB study showed that, with Afghanistan the central hub, the construction of North-South corridors to and from Central Asia can increase trade by as much as 15% or $12 billion if the new roads are matched by efforts to facilitate trade.[56] Employment in the region could increase by 1.8 million jobs, in addition to the creation of 15 million person-days of permanent employment for ongoing road and infrastructure maintenance. Reduced travel time will bring participating countries annual savings of over $1.7 billion and continental trade through new southern ports can be expected to increase by 80%, to $6.3 billion. As the benefits of the trade corridors are extensive and long-term relative to the total investment of only about $5.6 billion, the initiative has an undeniably compelling investment return. Donors and participant countries have an unprecedented opportunity to decisively engage in closer cooperation as it is a small price to pay for

---

[56] Alamgir, Mohiuddin, "Report on the Economic Impact of Central-South Asian Road Corridors," Central and South Asia Transport and Trade Forum (CSATTF). Report prepared for the Second Ministerial Conference on Transport and Trade in Central and South Asia. Asian Development Bank, Manila, Philippines, March 3 and 4, 2005.

regional prosperity and for the creation of closer ties among nations leading to significant economic expansion, sustained stability and regional security.

Appendix A: Pipeline Routes Through Afghanistan[57]

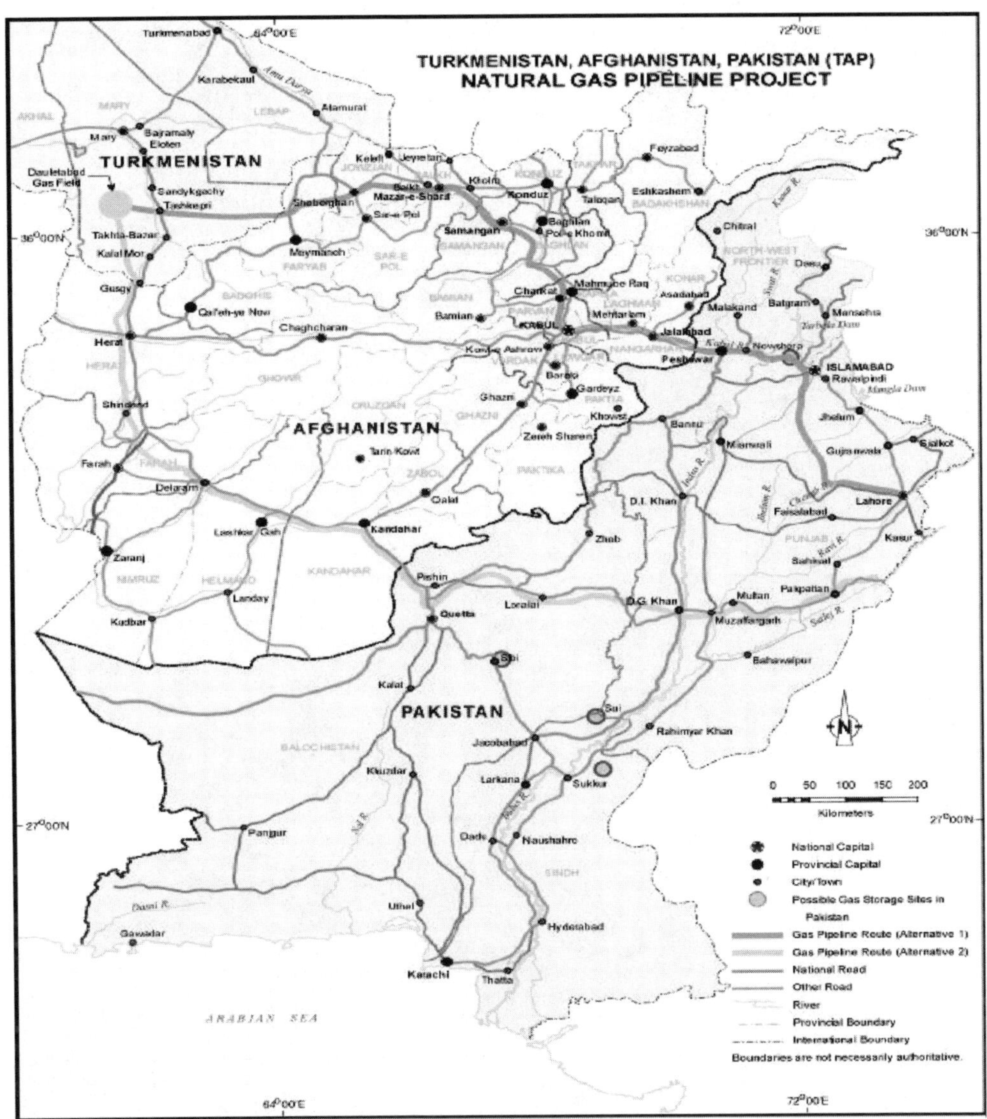

---

[57] Source: Chander, S., "Technical Assistance for the Feasibility Studies of the Turkmenistan – Afghanistan – Pakistan Natural Gas Pipeline Project," Asia Development Bank. Manila, Philippines, December 2002, p.3.

Pakistan

Aftab Kazi*

Background

Political orders can shape socioeconomic and cultural development by conquests and migrations, through economic or military disasters and civil wars, or simply by their collapse and the creation of power vacuums. The construction of new political orders can take decades. The power vacuum following the fall of the Soviet Union initiated the emergence of a new political order, which, among other things, must somehow determine how landlocked Central Asian countries—including Afghanistan, but also the Caucasus—can reconnect with the world economy via cost-effective transportation routes in Southwest Asia. Today these states are dependent upon old Soviet routes to the north. Constant civil unrest in Afghanistan continues to hamper efforts to create the commercial regime needed to restart Central Asia's long-stalled economic and new political links with its southern neighbors. In spite of this, there are ample geographic, political and economic reasons to believe that alternative transportation routes originating at the warm waters of the Arabian Sea and continuing to Central Asia's historic land outlets can stimulate regional and cross-continental trade,

---

* The Author is grateful to officials at the U.S. Department of Commerce, Washington, DC and Ministries of Commerce, Communications, Ports and Shipping, and Foreign Affairs, Government of Pakistan, Islamabad for sharing their viewpoints and for providing appropriate documentation to substantiate various themes developed in this paper. The author is also grateful to Ambassador M. Alam Brohi and his staff at the Embassy of Pakistan, Bishkek, Kyrgyz Republic for arranging several high level meetings in Islamabad. The assistance of my students and research assistants Selbi Hanova and Ailar Saparova is also greatly appreciated.

advance the ongoing economic and political transitions, and foster regional stability.

Approximately seventeen years of international effort to invigorate the economies of the Central Asian states has yet to yield substantial results, except in Kazakhstan. Attempts to create regional economic unions akin to the Economic Cooperation Organization (ECO) or the Central Asian Common Market have failed to integrate Central Asian republics (CARs) with one another or with the world economy. These states are hindered by dependency-oriented, unidirectional Soviet transportation infrastructures and the lack even of international awareness of the possibility of renewing traditional communication routes through Southwest Asian ports in Pakistan and Iran. The Greater Central Asia Partnership (GCAP) conceptualized by Professor S. Frederick Starr[1] is the first major attempt in the United States to craft a regional development strategy to reintegrate Central Asian trade cross-continentally via traditional transportation routes. The goal is to create modern rail, road and maritime trade infrastructures where formerly there were camel and horse caravan routes. This North-South corridor strategy promises to reintegrate efficiently Central Asia and Caucasus with the broad-based world economy. This in turn will further regional economic, social and political development in the region.

Conceptual Justification

GCAP is a gradually evolved geographic, political, and economic concept related to transit route politics. It is derived from earlier concepts in geopolitics and economics. Halford Mackinder's early twentieth century "heartland" theory of global politics depicted modern Central Asia and the surrounding regions as the center of competition among world powers. The "heartland" theory aroused interest within the area and was also applied to the strategic doctrines and defense policies of all the major powers. By the middle of the twentieth century Nicholas Spykman's "rimland" offered a plan by which heartland expansionism could be restricted. During the Cold War both the heartland and rimland theories were reflected in the defense

---

[1] S. Fredrick Starr, "Greater Central Asia Partnership: Afghanistan and its Neighbors," *Foreign Affairs*, July/August 2005, pp.168-174.

and foreign policies of the competing superpowers, whether in conflicts between the heartland and rimland spheres, or in the cooperative alliances that were formed within each power's respective area of influence.

GCAP proposes simultaneous cooperation between heartlands and rimlands by effecting an insertion between geopolitics and economics. The aim is to spur a new geographic, political and economic regime in Central and South Asia and surrounding regions, providing a mechanism for regional economic integration and cross-continental trade. GCAP's focus is to re-link Central Asia with the world economy through traditional Southwest Asian commercial transit routes via Afghanistan and through the Karakuram Mountains. This new geographical, political and economic realism is derived from the reality of extensive regional and cross-continental commerce between Europe and East, Central and South Asia across centuries. It is worth noting that for centuries on end the southern Indus river port of Barbarikon[2] in present day Pakistan served Central Asia as a trade node, as well as a nexus of economic and political socialization, within a network of land and sea "silk-routes."

The Indus River Basin served as a natural boundary between historic India or Hindustan (modern Pakistan) and Bharat (modern India). The Indus River Basin played a significant role in mediating and shaping intercultural and international relationships between Central and South Asia, including modern Afghanistan and Iran. Focusing upon transit routes as a requisite for trade growth, the strategic doctrine of GCAP requires cooperation between the heartland and the rimland. The Indus Basin state—modern Pakistan—plays a pivotal role in this configuration. Pakistan has much of the necessary rail, road and maritime infrastructures for trade, and can participate in prospective alternative oil and gas pipeline projects involving Europe,

---

[2] Barbarikon may be the port on the Indus that Alexander of Macedonia established in 332 B.C. to ship his war booty to Babylon by sea, while personally taking the harsh route through Gedrosia (modern Pakistani Baluchistan). All historians of Alexander describe this, yet the origins of Barbarikon/Bhambhor remain a mystery, and the pronunciation of the word Barbarikon resembles the localized term Bhambhor, just as the Greek word Indus is locally pronounced as Sindh, Hind by Persians and Al-Hind by Arabs. The Barbarikon port on the Indus is shown on the territorial map D of the Kushan Empire.

Central, South, Southeast and East Asia. Pakistani road and rail networks and port facilities can provide critical aid to the hitherto handicapped economic and political development processes in Central Asia. Justification for GCAP can be traced to various ancient, medieval and modern historical epochs. As a mechanism for modern-day cooperation it can help bridge the gap between conflicting political interests and regional interdependence arising from energy pipelines and trade routes. In the process it promises to forge new political trends, both regionally and internationally.

Critics of GCAP[3] oppose the idea of using traditional Southern transportation routes as main transportation routes but are unable to offer alternative solutions to the problems arising from Central Asia's landlocked condition. This paper demonstrates that alternative transportation routes through Pakistan, once fully functional, will facilitate the commercial transactions needed to strengthen economic and political linkages in Central and South Asia, the surrounding regions of China, Mongolia, Central Russia, the Middle East, as well as with the East Asian, European, American and African markets. GCAP focuses on transit-root corridors to aid the hitherto stunted process of political reordering in Central and South Eurasia.

GCAP's Historical Significance

Geopolitical orders often resemble previous epochs when analyzed across time periods and generations. Trade between the Indus Basin and Egypt, Mesopotamia, and Europe dates back to 3000 B.C. Early internal migrations within the Indus Basin occurred largely through the northern Khunjerab Pass in the Karakurams. [4] This pass contrasts historically with the Khyber, Golan

---

[3] Омаров М. Н, Новая Большая Игра В Центральной Азии. Мифы И Реальность. (Бишкек: «Салам», 2005). [Omarov, M.N (ed.) New Great Game in Central Asia: Myths and Reality. (Bishkek: Salam, 2005].

[4] Historical information provided in this paper is from several books, including the Encyclopedia Britannica. Several publications in Farsi on historic India, Sindh and Hindustan and Muslim rule in the subcontinent were also used as sources for historical information. References in English and Sindhi include: M.H. Panhwar, *Chronological Dictionary of Sindh* (Jamshoro, Pakistan: Institute of Sindhology, 1983); Eraly, Abraham, *The Mughal Throne: The Saga of India's Great Emperors* (London: Orion Books Ltd., 2004); Olmstead, A.T., *History of the Persian Empire* (Chicago: Phoenix Books, University of Chicago Press, 1948); Yunus, Mohammed and Parmar, Ardhana, *South*

and Bolan passes in Central Pakistan, all of which were largely used by conquerors. From Darius of Persia and Alexander of Macedonia to Muhammad bin Qasim and Mahmud of Ghazna, only one conqueror ever attempted to cross the eastern banks of the Indus inside the Bharatan hinterlands until the eleventh century A.D. The sole exception was Emperor Kanishka of the Kushan dynasty. From his capital in modern Peshawar, Kanishka in ca. 238 A.D. also penetrated the Eastern Punjab up to Mathura region in Bharat. At least until the mid eleventh century, dynasties of the Lodhis, Khiljis and their successors from Central Asia all penetrated into Eastern Punjab. On the Bharatan lands this established the foundations of the Muslim Empire in Delhi.

Although modern Western accounts of the region's history often describe the entire South Asian subcontinent as India, Central Asian and European records until the rise of British power in the eighteenth century applied the name Indostan or Hindustan mainly to territories of the Indus Basin and its tributaries in Punjab, Sindh and surrounding regions. After the establishment of Mughul rule in Delhi, Bharatan territory beyond the Indus Basin was also called Hindustan, as shown in Map A.

The annexation of the Indus Basin into Bharat by the Maurya dynasty in 327 B.C occurred not by conquest but through negotiations between the Greek General Seleucus and the Bharatan ruler Chandra Gupta Maurya.

Asia: A Historical Narrative (Karachi: Oxford University Press, 2003); Dani, Ahmad Hassan, *New Light on Central Asia* (Lahore: Sang-e-Meel Publications, 1993); Dr. Baloch, N.A., *Sindh: Studies in History, Vol. I* (Karachi: Kalhora Seminar Committee, 1996), and a publication in Sindhi: Shamsudin Rukandin Quraishi, *Aina-e-Qadeem Sindh* [*A Mirror of Ancient Sindh*] (Hyderabad Sindh: R.H. & Ahmed Brothers Publishers, 1956). Over 20 additional publications on the ancient and medieval history of Central and South Asia translated from Persian into the Sindhi and Urdu languages could be cited.

Map A.[5]

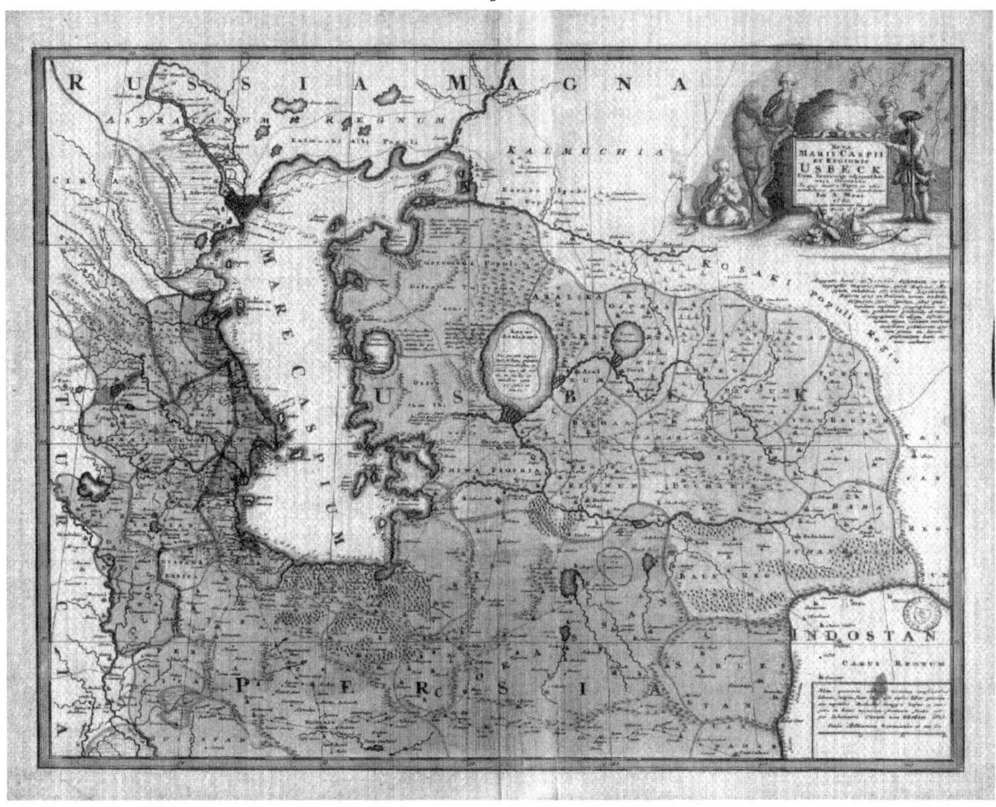

Seleucus came under pressure from local rivalries after Alexander the Great named him to rule over that largest part of Alexander's vast empire stretching from the Mediterranean to the Indus. Seleucus negotiated with Chandra Gupta an exchange of the Eastern Indus regions for peace on the eastern borders of his domain, in the territory that is now Pakistan. The fall of the Maurya dynasty reopened the Indus Basin's political links with Central Asia and Persia. The Gupta dynasty, which succeeded the Mauryas, ruled Eastern Punjab and parts of Sindh that are now within modern India, although not the entire Sindhu (Indus) Basin. Although the Lodhis of

[5] A Greco-Latin map of Central Asia, University of Leiden 1731 A.D.

Central Asia conquered Punjabi parts of the central Indus Basin during the eleventh century A.D., the entire Indus Basin was not formally annexed by an Indian –based dynasty until the seventeenth century, when the Mughul Emperor Akbar integrated it into his Empire. During the conquest by Arab General Muhammad bin Qasim in 610 A.D., Sindh state stretched from modern Kashmir to Karachi on the Arabian Sea coast, territory roughly equivalent to present day Pakistan. (See map B)

Map B[6]

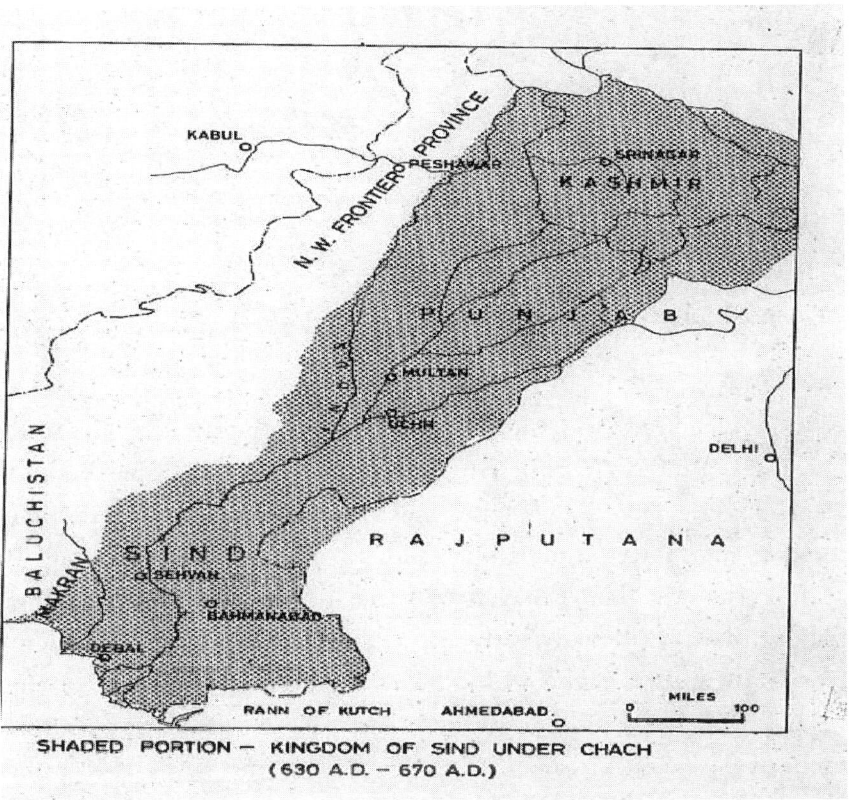

SHADED PORTION — KINGDOM OF SIND UNDER CHACH (630 A.D. – 670 A.D.)

[6] Source: Pithwala, Maneck, *Historical Geography of Sind*, Institute of Sindology Publication #53, Karachi, Pakistan, 1978.

Map C[7]

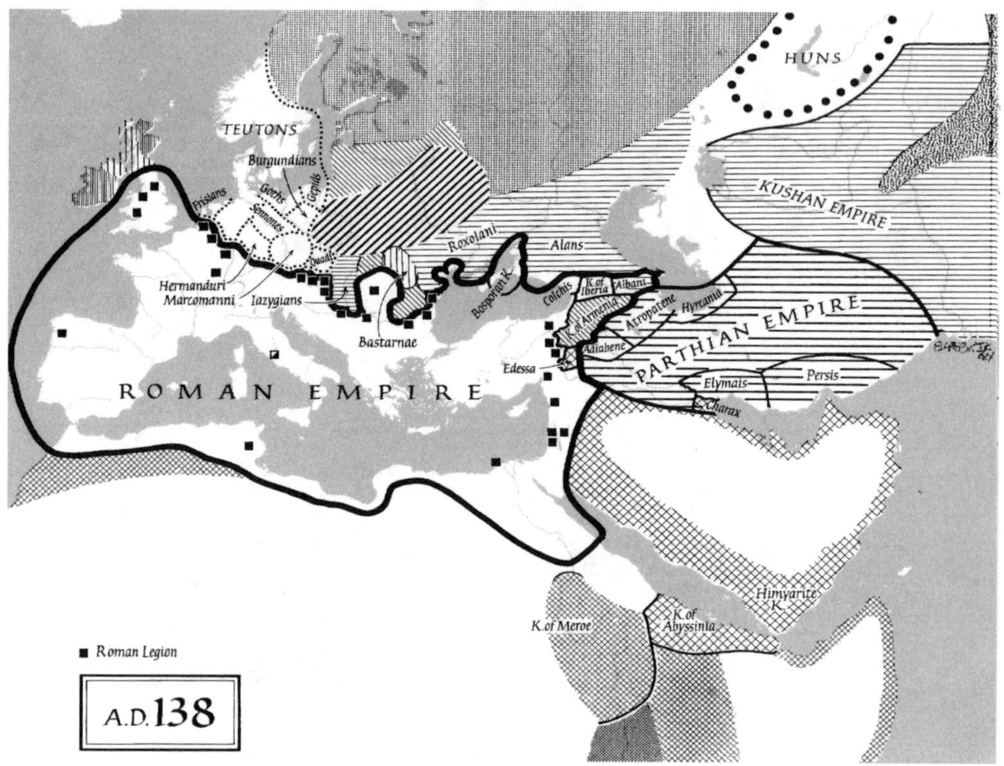

Around 500 A.D., not long before the Arab conquest, the Great Kushans ruled the Indus State. The Kushan Empire roughly encompassed the region of modern Central Asia, including Afghanistan and Pakistan—areas considered essential regional trade hubs in the GCAP concept. Political orders after the Kushan Empire adhered to a variety of ideologies yet followed similar territorial patterns. The Sasanids of Persia cultivated considerable influence in the Indus Basin until the beginnings of the Arab-Muslim era in Central and Southwest Asia. The Kushan Empire stretched from modern-day Uzbekistan through Tajikistan and parts of Kyrgyzstan to Afghanistan and from North-Central Pakistan to the Arabian Sea.

---

[7] Source: McEvedy, Colin, *The Penguin Atlas of Ancient History*, Penguin Books, 1988.

Maps D & E: Boundaries of the Kushan Empire

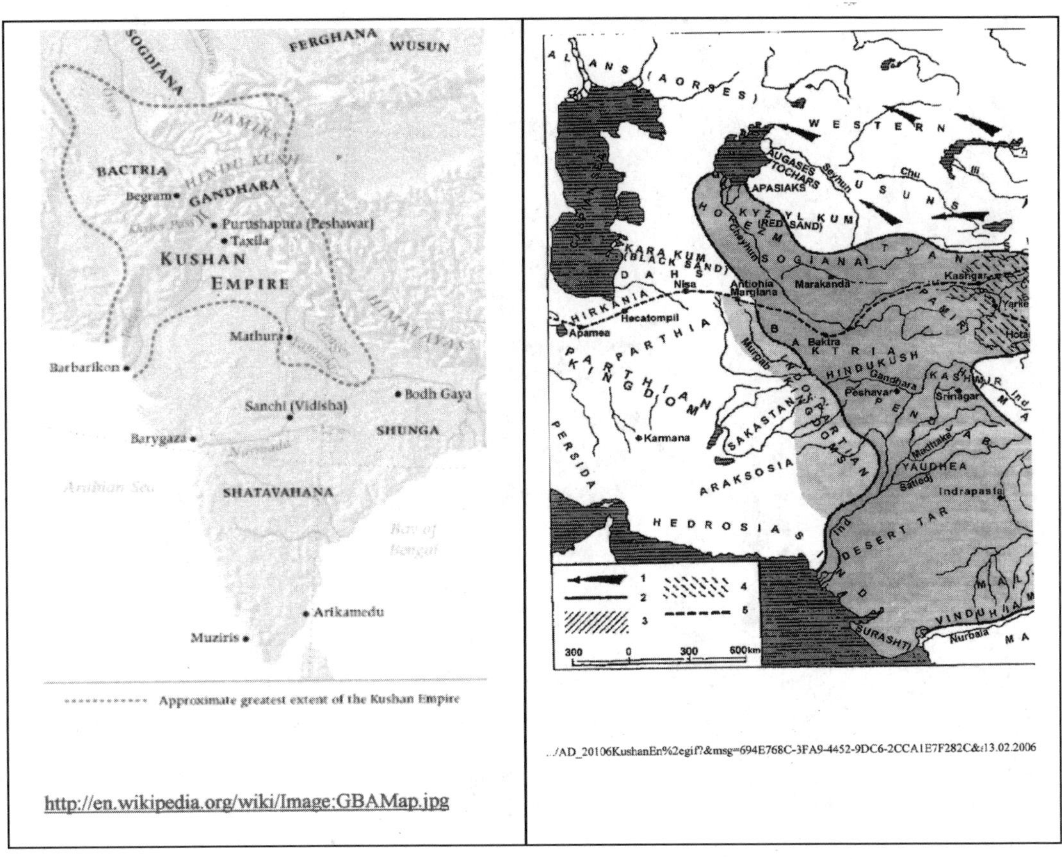

http://en.wikipedia.org/wiki/Image:GBAMap.jpg

.../AD_20106KushanEn%2egif?&msg=694E768C-3FA9-4452-9DC6-2CCA1E7F282C&:13.02.2006

The Indus coastal harbor of Barbarikon—some sixty km from Karachi—served as a route from the Arabian Sea into what is now Pakistan. Cross-continental trade between Rome, the Kushans and China was carried along this route.

Maps A, B and C show the resemblance between the Kushan Empire territory and the GCAP trade regions, with transportation corridors largely running through the coastal regions of what is now modern Pakistan.

Map F.

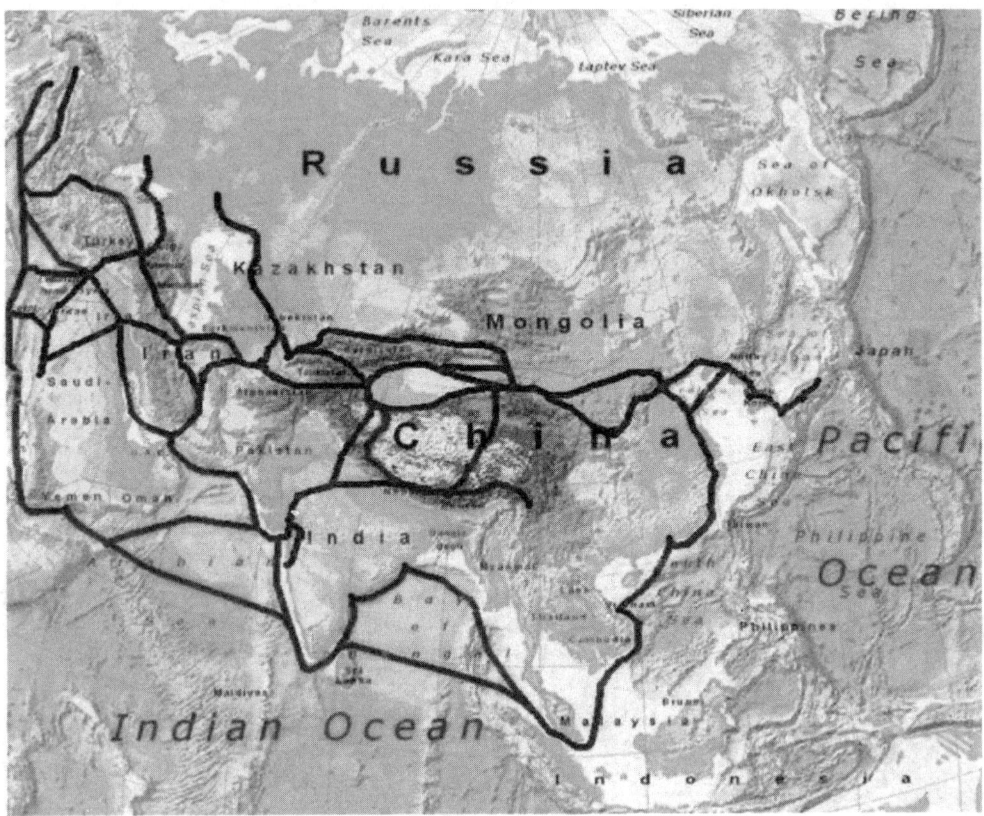

http://en.wikipedia.org/wiki/Image:Silkroutes.jpg

Contrary to the conclusions of the 1968 Dushanbe Conference on the 'Kushan Period' that examined India-Central Asia commercial and cultural interactions,[8] the name "India" referred to regions of modern Pakistan whence Kushan commercial and cultural influences (in the form of Hellenistic Gandharan arts) extended to Bharat.

---

[8]Cited by Ahmar, Moonis, "India and its Role in the New Central Asia," *Pakistan Horizon*, vol. 45, no.3, July 1992, p. 59, from Khilnani, Niranjan M., *Realities of Indian Foreign Policy* (New Delhi: ABC Publishing House, 1984), pp. 167-168.

Map G.[9]

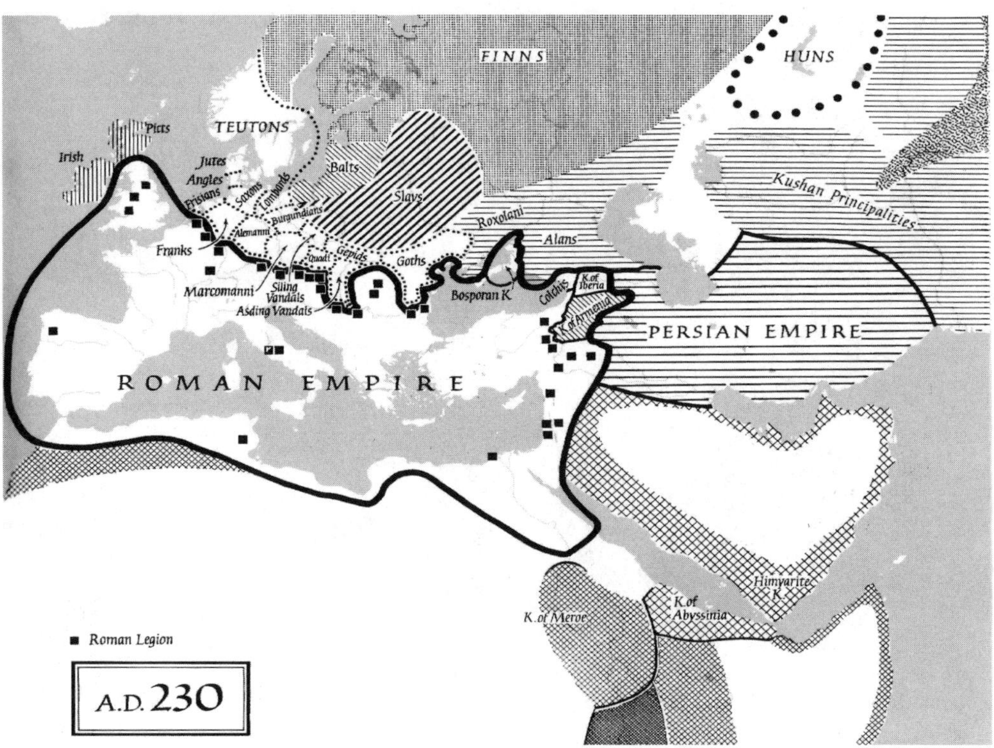

Thus, the GCAP proposal of regional partnerships resembles the trade patterns under the Kushans with their gold and silver currencies.

Moreover, transportation corridors used by the Kushans strikingly resemble trade routes currently planned by the Pakistan government. Modern technology has facilitated connections between Pakistan national highways, railways, and the port facilities of Karachi, Port Qasim and Gwadar. Newly planned roads include connecting points with Afghanistan at various junctions, among them Jalalabad, the Wakhan border, and Western China through the northern Karakuram Highway. Chinese roads connected to Kyrgyzstan and Kazakhstan provide a North-South alternative transit route (see map 1). Under a $200 million contract, China will refurbish the Karakuram highway with five to six bridges, making it a year-round

[9] Source: McEvedy, Colin, *The Penguin Atlas of Ancient History*, Penguin Books, 1988.

weather-fair road.[10] Pakistani transit routes connecting to India already exist, but their effectiveness largely depends upon long-term transit-related negotiations between the two countries.

Map H.[11]

The Geography, Politics and Economics of Transit Routes:

Pakistan's location allows it to provide convenient and modern rail and roadways with relatively short distances. Table 1 provides a comparative overview of distances between Islamabad and Karachi, the capital cities of Central Asia, and Soviet-era Russian port facilities.

---

[10] Conversations at the Ministry of Communications, Government of Pakistan, Islamabad, February 27, 2006.

[11] Source: McEvedy, Colin, *The Penguin Atlas of Ancient History*, Penguin Books, 1988.

Table 1: Distances Between Destinations in Pakistan, Russia and Central Asia[12]

From	To	Distance	From	To	Distance
Islamabad	Tashkent	800 km	Karachi	Dushanbe	2720 km
Islamabad	Dushanbe	640 km	Abadan	Dushanbe	3200 km
Islamabad	Alma Ata	1040 km	Bandar Abbas	Dushanbe	3440 km
Islamabad	Bishkek	960 km	Odessa	Dushanbe	3400 km
Tashkent	Chaman	1292 km	Vladivostok	Dushanbe	9500 km
Karachi	Lahore	1292 km	Gwadar	Karachi	489 km

Map I[13]

Pakistan expressed interest in being a major transit-route corridor for Central Asian states at the time of their independence in the 1990s. In 1995, the Pakistani government estimated distances to prospective port facilities and considered constructing more ports, in addition to Karachi and Port Qasim.

[12] Table prepared from the article by Shameem Akhtar, "Strategic Significance of Central Asia", *Pakistan Horizon*, Vol.45, No.3, July 1992, pp.29-56. Routes remain same since this publication.

[13] Source: Ministry of Communications, Government of Pakistan, Islamabad, 2006.

The new Gwadar deep-sea port on the Baluchistan coast and the highways connecting it to Afghanistan reduce the distances of Pakistan-Central Asia traffic by about 500 km. During a summer 2005 visit to the United States, Afghan President Hamid Karzai, in a speech at the Central Asia-Caucasus Institute, emphasized the 32 hour-long travel time by road from Karachi to Tashkent via Afghanistan. The distance between Karachi to Chaman is relatively longer than traveling from Chaman to Dushanbe via Afghanistan; the Gwadar port reduces travel time from five to ten hours, depending upon where the journey started.

The value of Afghanistan-Pakistan trade from 2004 to 2006 has fluctuated between $1 to 2 billion.[14] According to officials at Pakistan's Ministry of Foreign Affairs, "By early 2006, the Afghan-Pak trade has already reached US$1.2 billion as contrasted to the $3 million trade between India and Pakistan."[15] Pakistan shares a border of approximately 2500 km with Afghanistan and offers it key trade facilities. Trade volume between Afghanistan and Pakistan has continued to rise, despite some disagreements over tariffs on electrical supplies from Dubai, which is often smuggled back to Pakistan. Afghan government officials have complained about the length of time needed to clear cargo at Karachi and Port Qasim, yet recent port modernization and reformed customs rules and technology have reduced delays from twelve to four days.

Recent reports indicate that the value of trade between India and Pakistan may soon reach $1 billion[16], while Pakistan-Central Asian trade volumes remain similar to those of the mid-1990s. India-Afghanistan trade, much of it reconstruction assistance, moves through Pakistan on Afghani/Pakistani vehicles traveling between Karachi and Kabul. Direct transit for India through Pakistan is part of the compound package of confidence-building measures tied to the détente process between these two countries. Progress has been achieved, although far less than would be desirable.

---

[14] "Trade with Kabul to rise to $1 bn," Daily Dawn (Karachi), January 19, 2004.

[15] Personal meetings with top officials at the Ministry of Foreign Affairs, Government of Pakistan, Islamabad, February 28, 2006.

[16] "India Pakistan trade on the rise," Daily Dawn (Karachi), March 20, 2006.

Trade between Pakistan and the Central Asian states will likely increase thanks to new bilateral agreements on commercial mechanisms, and as transit security in Afghanistan is improved. Tajikistan, Afghanistan and Pakistan have agreed to construct jointly a key 20 km-long road through Wakhan border to facilitate trilateral trade; parallel to the road will be an electricity transmission line that will allow Pakistan to import electricity from Tajikistan, with the further possibility of exporting it to India.[17] Pakistan has also welcomed President Karzai's suggestion that electricity bound for Pakistan could be routed through Kabul, as opposed to traversing the remote Wakhan border route.

Pakistan's initiatives over the past seven years have improved its relations with the Central Asian states. Pakistan and Uzbekistan signed an extradition treaty in January 2002, and the Pakistani government waived a $10 million loan to Kyrgyzstan. The Almaty-Karachi road via the Karakuram Mountains (the Almaty-Bishkek-Kashgar-Karakuram-Islamabad-Karachi network) is functioning, although it transports a low volume of trade; trade volume will likely grow once the construction of the Gwadar port is complete. The development of Gwadar will open new opportunities for foreign direct investment in both Central and Southwest Asia. The Pakistani government has reservations about Tajikistan's decision to lease a military airbase to India, yet the Tajik government seems attentive to Pakistani concerns.[18] Other promising developments include the positive tone of Uzbek President Islam Karimov's May 2005 visit to Pakistan, and the revival of plans for a Turkmenistan-Afghanistan-Pakistan gas pipeline after Turkmenistan certified the size of the reserves in the Daulatabad gas fields.[19] Besides the historic ethnocultural relationship—the majority of the Pakistani people and their culture trace to the Ferghana and Zarafshan valleys of Central Asia — most Central Asian governments now acknowledge Pakistan's importance as a southern transit route, providing an outlet for their landlocked economies.

Pakistan has an edge over other transit routes because it offers three major seaports along the Arabian Sea. The planned Iranian port of Chahbahar at

---

[17] Meetings at the Ministry of Foreign Affairs, Islamabad, February 28, 2006.

[18] Meetings at the Ministry of Foreign Affairs, Islamabad, February 27, 2006.

[19] Ibid.

the mouth of the Persian Gulf is only 200 km away from Gwadar and is being built with Indian assistance. But Chahbahar will not be directly competitive with Gwadar for two reasons. First, Chabahar's scope will be limited since it is near the Strait of Hormuz and is constrained by the relatively shallow waters of the Persian Gulf. Second, regional commerce may grow to the point that existing port facilities may no longer be sufficient. Once the GCAP-proposed southern routes are developed, the construction of additional ports may be necessary, and these will likely be in Pakistan.

Let us now turn to the Pakistani government's plans to build rail and road networks to channel Central Asian traffic through Pakistan's national highways and to connect Afghanistan, Tajikistan, Kyrgyzstan and eastern Kazakhstan via the Karakuram mountains through the western China road network. The proposed gas pipeline from Turkmenistan to Pakistan via Afghanistan will also be considered in greater detail.

Rail and Road Network

Although the Karakuram Highway and Pakistan's national highway system already constitute an important North-South transit corridor, new internal bypasses, motorways and expressways that will facilitate Central Asian trade are now under construction or have been completed. Map 1 shows these routes. Pakistani officials believe that the addressing of underdevelopment, poverty and instability within Pakistan and nearby regions requires a formal network of commercial communication; official Pakistani investments in the transit sector reflect this concern. Table 2 provides an overview of planned rail and road infrastructure that will aid Central Asian trade. Pakistani roads carry 89 percent of the country's passenger traffic and 96 percent of all inbound and outbound freight traffic. This reliance has made the development of road infrastructure a top priority. N-5, the main national highway, connects Karachi in the south with Torkham at the Afghan border in the north; an additional Torkham-Jalalabad link with Afghanistan is nearing completion.

Table 2: Road Infrastructure in Pakistan

Roads	Purpose	From	To	Size	Bridges/Tunnels	Status
N-35 Karakuram Highway	Weather-fair year-long	Gilgit	Khunjrab Pass/Chinese Karakurams	Not Available	5 to 6 bridges	Existing. Weather-fair Cosigned with China
Motorway	Internal connection	Mansehra	Naran	124 km	No	Operational
N-15	National Highway	Naran	Jhakhand	48 km	No	Operational
N-75	National Highway	Islamabad	Murree	43 km	Yes, at Azad Pattan	Operational
M-1 Sec. I	Motorway	Mansehra	Nowshera	37 km	No	Planned
M-1 Sec. III	Motorway	Mansehra	Rawalpindi	23 km	No	Planned
	Nowshera Flyover	Chalbat	Nowshera	71 km	No	Operational
N-80	National Highway	Kohat	Bannu	1.9 km	Tunnel	Operational
M-2	Motorway	Rawalpindi	Lahore	359 km	No. Faizpur interchange	Operational
M-3	Motorway	Lahore	Faisalabad	52.5 km	No	Operational
M-5 & M-6	Motorways	Faisalabad	Karachi via D.I.G. Khan	Unknown	May be	Planned
M-8	Motorway	Gawadar-Turbat	Khuzdar	Unknown	Maybe	Planned
M-8	Motorway	Khuzdar	Ratodero-Wangu hills Reach	35 km	No	Planned
N-10	National Highway	Karachi	Gawadar-Giwani	500+ km	May be	Operational

(Table prepared from the Ministry of Communication, Islamabad Map, 2006. The author apologizes for inadvertent discrepancies in his interpretation of the map.)

The second North-South corridor in Pakistan, the Indus Highway, has been updated to meet international standards; it is expected that the entire highway will have been revamped by 2008. These highways, together with new roads, the Karachi-Gwadar highway, and other connecting routes in north-central Pakistan, have reduced the overall distance for Afghanistan and Central Asian trade from Pakistan by 500 km.[20]

Additional Roads

Direct rail and roads from Gwadar to Chaman are being planned with assistance from the Asian Development Bank (ADB); while the new port at Gwadar is already linked with Chaman via the coastal highway (N-10) and ECO Highway (N-25). Additional roads are being planned, along with the upgrade of the road from Gwadar Basima and Sorab, via Hoshab, Panjur, and Nag, at a total investment of $59 million. Construction of a new road to Pangur and beyond is a priority in order to facilitate trade with Afghanistan and Central Asia.[21]

The Liari-Gwadar road has been completed, and the Gwadar-Jiwani-Gabad road that will facilitate trade with Iran should be completed by 2009. It is reported that 57 percent of the Gwadar-Hoshab project is already completed with the rest to be finished by 2007. In addition, the Basima-Khuzdar road will be done by 2009, and 60 percent of the Khori-Wangu project has been completed; the remaining portion from Qubo Saeed Khan to the Wangu hills is expected to be finished within three years. The Qalat-Quetta-Chamman road contract has been awarded along with an ADB financial package, and the road is expected to complete within three years.[22]

The Pakistan North Western Railways network that serves the region from Karachi to Peshawar and points in between is being modernized thanks to an

---

[20] "Trade and Transport Facilitation in Pakistan: Prospects for Increasing Trade Volume," brief by the Ministry of Shipping and Ports, Government of Pakistan, Islamabad, February 27, 2006 (hereafter "Trade and Transport Facilitation in Pakistan").

[21] "Gwadar link roads to cost Rs. 35bn: PM," *Daily News* (Islamabad), March 21, 2006.

[22] Ibid.

agreement with China. The ADB has offered to assist the construction of a Gwadar-Chaman rail line that will extend to Kandahar, Kabul and Herat, with additional extensions to the north and west. This will allow travel to Daulatabad/Ashkgabat in Turkmenistan, Termez in Uzbekistan, and to Tajik Badakhshan via in-country railway connections.

The Pakistani road network is to be completed in the next three years with additional planned rail and road infrastructure to be completed over the coming decade. Pakistan is revitalizing its national highways with two-way double traffic lines; approximately 87 percent of this revitalization is now complete. The traffic on Pakistani national highways has almost doubled since the independence of the Central Asian states and the start of reconstruction in Afghanistan. This increase has generated a need for improvements and repairs to Pakistan's domestic rail and road network. In addition, China and Pakistan are exploring the possibility of developing a rail line and an oil pipeline from Gwadar north to the Karakuram mountain region on the border with Xinjiang.

The Gwadar Deep-Sea Port

Continuing instability in the Persian Gulf has led the ADB to consider the strategically located port of Gwadar as an alternative to Persian Gulf ports.[23] Despite having been refurbished to accommodate large cargos, the existing Pakistani ports of Karachi and Port Qasim were found unattractive due to their distance from main highways and shipping routes and their limitations in handling large mother ships and oil tankers. The construction of the Gwadar deep-sea port is therefore an important component of Pakistan's overall initiative to facilitate trade with the landlocked states of Central Asia.

Gwadar is near the mouth of the Persian Gulf, about 489 km from Karachi. Plans to develop the Gwadar port were initiated in the early 1990s, and the first phase of construction began in 2002 with Chinese assistance. In the early 1980s, during the Soviet-Afghan war, the United States also expressed

---

[23] "Gwadar," Board of Investment (BIO), Government of Pakistan, accessed November 15, 2004 via http://www.pakboi.gov.pkNews_event/Gwadar.html.

interest in helping to develop the Gwadar port facilities, but U.S. interest waned soon after the Geneva Agreement on Afghanistan was signed in 1985. The collapse of the Soviet Union, the growing importance of the Central Asian states and China's rising need for energy from the Persian Gulf all played a role in Beijing's decision to assist Pakistan with this initiative.

The first phase of construction cost $248 million, with $198 million coming from China and $50 million from Pakistan. This phase included three multipurpose berths of 200 meters each with 350 meters backup area and related ancillary facilities; a 5 km Approach Channel dredged to accommodate vessels up to 30,000 dwt [deadweight tonnage] and with up to 11.5 meters of draft, as well as cargo handling equation and operational craft.[24] The second phase, estimated to cost $524 million, will add seven 300-meter berths and two oil piers to accommodate oil tankers up to 200,000 dwt, bulk carriers up to 1000,000 dwt, general cargo vessels up to 100,000 dwt, and fourth generation container ships drawing 15.6 to 20 meters draft. The Phase One construction plans were revised in February 2005 to add an additional $39.8 million to dredge the port channel to 14.5 meters, which will help accommodate mother ships used for transshipment. This dredging has been scheduled to be complete by the end of 2006.[25]

The first phase of construction at Gwadar was completed ahead of schedule in November 2005. But inauguration of the first phase development was postponed following terrorist attacks in Baluchistan. These attacks were allegedly carried out by forces opposed to stability in Afghanistan and to alternative transportation routes for Central Asia. In spite of this setback, second phase construction is underway, and the inauguration of the first phase work will likely occur in 2007. In January 2007, the government of Pakistan invited all foreign ambassadors and heads of international financial institutions for a good will trip to the completed Gwadar port facilities. In addition to port construction, planned civilian structures will transform Gwadar into a modern port city capable of attracting foreign investment. Oman is planning to invest approximately $100 million in the city's

[24] "A Brief on Gwadar Port Project," Ministry of Shipping and Ports, Government of Pakistan, Islamabad, February 27, 2006.
[25] Ibid.

infrastructure and several Polish companies have expressed interest in performing the required engineering work.[26]

The coastal highways connecting Port Qasim and Karachi to Gwadar are complete, and the ADB is providing assistance to construct road and rail networks from Gwadar to Chaman, with links to the Afghan cities of Kandahar, Herat and Kabul. These links will in turn connect to border posts in Iran, Tajikistan, Turkmenistan and Uzbekistan, and will eventually extend to Europe via Turkmenistan and Turkey. Approximately 97 percent of Pakistani imports and exports pass through Karachi and Port Qasim. The new Gwadar deep-sea port will serve the specific needs of Central Asian trade, in addition to being a regional transit and transshipment hub.[27]

The Gwadar port was recently leased to Singapore Port Authority for operations, and the Pakistani government is pursuing reforms to streamline and secure the import-export process. A 40-year agreement between the Gwadar Port Authority (GPA) and the Concession Holding Company (CHC) — a subsidiary of the Singapore Port Authority was signed in January 2007 for operating and managing the port. The road network supporting Gwadar is being developed in accordance with the Asian Highway Network Agreement, ECO's Decade Program of Action on Transport and Communication, and ECO's Transit Transport Framework Agreement on the development of the New Silk Route linking China with Europe.[28] The Pakistani customs administration has undergone massive reforms to ensure transparency and provide a user-friendly automated clearance system that will reduce the time needed to clear goods. Tariffs at Gwadar will be as low as 5 percent on raw materials and foreign-made machinery. These reforms have been initiated under bilateral agreements with Iran, Turkey and China. Under the new rules, most cargo will be cleared in four days, instead of the usual 12 or more days. In addition, the

---

[26] "Polish Companies Interested in Gwadar Development," *Pak Tribune*, accessed November 15, 2004 via <http://www.paktribune.co./news/print.php?id=61615&PHPSESSID=56818006188776b>.

[27] "Trade and Transport Facilitation in Pakistan".

[28] Ibid.

Code of International Ship and Port Facility Security of the International Maritime Organization has been implemented by the Pakistani ministry responsible for ports and shipping, and the UN-sponsored Customs Trade Partnership against Terrorism has been voluntarily applied. The Pakistani National Logistic Cell will install container scanners at all border crossings, under the Container Security Initiative of the United States Department of Homeland Security.

Regional Trade Forecast

Pakistan's sea-borne trade in 2000 was 42 million tons. This is expected to rise to 78 million tons by 2015. Future trade estimates envisage substantial cargo from China, the Central Asian states, and Afghanistan. Gwadar will be the closest and most viable port for western China, Kyrgyzstan, eastern Kazakhstan and central Russia and Mongolia. This will be possible by using the Karakuram Highway, Indus Highway, and proposed linkages through Ratodero, Khuzdar, and Khairpur to Dadu, as well as links to Uzbekistan, Tajikistan and eastern Turkmenistan via Afghanistan. Table 3 displays estimated cargo figures for Gwadar.

The value of Pakistani trade has grown considerably. Exports have increased from $8 billion to over $14 billion in the past five years. Pakistan-Afghanistan trade has increased five-fold, and trade between India and Pakistan is experiencing similar growth.[29] Among Pakistani exports, cotton and textiles are prominent.[30] Pakistan's economic interaction with Central Asia remains minimal, and is limited to certain minerals, leather products, banking, services, training, and hotels. But projected energy transit and land-to-sea trade through Pakistani infrastructure will likely increase revenue from transit fees and tariffs in the upcoming years. Revenue estimates based on the gradual development of trade are about $1,000,000 per year, with Afghanistan benefiting from transit fees. Pakistani officials hope that new

---

[29] Conversations at the Ministry of Commerce, Government of Pakistan, Islamabad, February 27, 2006.

[30] "Monetary Policy Implications for Trade," a document published by the Ministry of Commerce, Government of Pakistan, Islamabad, 2006. Also discussed in conversations with high officials at the ministry.

projects to expand trade between Afghanistan, Pakistan and Central Asia will further boost state revenue.

Table 3: Estimated Cargo Trade Volume[31]

Description	Year		
	2005	2010	2015
Dry Cargo (million tons)	3.96	4.74	5.77
Liquid Cargo (million tons)	16.62	17.74	18.77
Container (1000 TEU*)	200	241	295
Trans-shipment (1000 TEU)	200	250	300

**Twenty-foot equivalent units*

Cross-Continental Trade

It is too early to estimate Central Asia's future continental trade, but feasible transit routes and uniform tariff policy between Central and South Asia, including Afghanistan, create the potential for increased continental trade in energy, cotton, textiles, minerals and other goods. Previous regional initiatives to expand continental trade have not been successful. However, the Central Asia Regional Economic Cooperation (CAREC), a multilateral network of national and international institutions, can help integrate the Central Asian countries into the international trading system. According to an ADB report, alternative transit routes through Southwest Asia, together with "reciprocal trade liberalization under regional trade agreements, can help liberalize trade policy at relatively low costs, reduce the risks of protectionist measures by trading partners, create new trade, and improve social welfare."[32] Yet the report warns that integrating the countries of Central Asia into the world economy without a regional trade agreement could divert existing trade and harm social welfare. Sound trade policy is therefore key, since "...improvements in transport infrastructure and transit

[31] Source: Ministry of Ports and Shipping, Government of Pakistan, 2006.

[32] Asian Development Bank (ADB), Central Asia: Increasing Gains from Trade Through Regional Cooperation in Trade Policy, Transport and Customs Transit (Manila: Asian Development Bank, 2006), p. ix.

systems in neighboring countries will do little to integrate a Central Asian country into the international trading system if its trade policy remains restrictive. If combined, however, regional cooperation in trade policy, transport, and customs transit can make a major contribution to the expansion of trade...."[33] The North-South alternative routes through Pakistan and Iran via Afghanistan, and through China and the Karakuram region of Pakistan, are being planned within this context.

The modest impact of Kyrgyzstan's relatively speedy economic liberalization and its membership in the World Trade Organization (WTO) demonstrates that without alternative routes of transportation, continental trade is impossible. Access to transit routes cannot alone guarantee appreciable trade growth, and neither regional nor continental trade can develop without a region-wide standardized tariff policy. Central Asia's ability to trade energy, minerals, agriculture and textiles with distant countries will depend upon the development of regionally integrated trade policies, and access to major seaports.

Recent increases in Central Asian exports in crude oil, metals and cotton fiber are a result of increased world prices, not growth of trade. Indeed, an ADB report agrees that barriers that delay transit, impede transit systems, and increase transport distances for Central Asian states and their trading partners, coupled with the lack of a regional trade policy, are creating unnecessary costs and delays.[34] It is believed that regional trade agreements and Pakistan's revitalized transport infrastructure via Afghanistan and the Karakuram region can boost the chances of WTO membership for Central Asian states.

Table 4 shows the value of Central Asian exports. A list of commodities traded is provided in the reference.[35]

---

[33] Ibid.

[34] Ibid.

[35] Merchandise commodities include animal and animal products, vegetable products, animal or vegetable fats, prepared foodstuff (including alcohol and non-alcohol beverages, tobacco, and substitutes), mineral products (including energy resources), plastics and rubber, chemical products (including pharmaceuticals, fertilizers, perfume, and detergents), hides and skins, wood and wood products, textile and textile articles,

Table 4: Merchandise Exports of Central Asian Republics, 1999-2004 (Millions $)[36]

	1999	2000	2001	2002	2003	2004
Azerbaijan	929.7	1,745.2	2314.2	2.167.4	2592.0	3,614.3
Kazakhstan	5,871.6	8812.2	8639.1	9709.0	12,926.7	20,096.2
Kyrgyzstan	453.8	504.5	476.2	485.5	581.7	718.8
Tajikistan	688.7	784.3	651.5	736.9	797.2	914.9
Uzbekistan	2,927.8	2,815.6	2,803.5	2,513.5	3,190.1	4,279.4

Table 5: Merchandise Imports of the Central Asian Republics, 1999-2004(Millions $)[37]

	1999	2000	2001	2002	2003	2004
Azerbaijan	1,035.9	1,172.1	1,431.1	1,665.3	2,626.2	3.504.3
Kazakhstan	3,665.1	5,040.0	6,446.0	6,584.0	8,408.9	12,781.2
Kyrgyzstan	599.7	554.1	467.2	586.8	717.0	941.0
Tajikistan	663.1	675.0	687.5	720.5	880.8	1,375.2
Uzbekistan	2,841.0	2,696.5	2,814.7	2,425.8	2,663.4	3,391.5

Possible Pakistan-Central Asia Cotton and Textile Cartel

Pakistan and Central Asia are major cotton producers and officials have suggested that both regions would benefit by initiating joint projects in cotton and textiles. Facilitating transportation inside Pakistan and

---

footwear and headgear, articles of stone, plaster, cement, and asbestos, pearls, precious or semi-precious stones, and metals, base metals and articles thereof, machinery, mechanical appliances, and electrical equipment, transportation equipment, instruments (both measuring and musical), arms and ammunition, miscellaneous manufactured articles, works of art and other materials (list drawn from the ADB report).

36 Source: Central Asia: Increasing Gains from Trade Through Regional Cooperation in Trade Policy, Transport and Customs Transit (Manila: Asian Development Bank, 2006), p.97

37 Source: Central Asia: Increasing Gains from Trade Through Regional Cooperation in Trade Policy, Transport and Customs Transit (Manila: Asian Development Bank, 2006) p. 98,

Afghanistan may eventually encourage Pakistan, Kazakhstan, the Kyrgyz Republic, Tajikistan, Turkmenistan and Uzbekistan to establish a world cotton cartel, either bilaterally or under ECO or all other frameworks.[38] The cartel would be based in the port city of Karachi with satellite offices in regional capitals, and would likely increase regional and cross-continental trade volumes. India could also join the cartel at a later stage, after the India-Pakistan détente leads to agreements on transit. A cotton and textile cartel could expand regional trade by billions of dollars, generating economic cooperation in other mutually beneficial areas, such as natural gas and oil, minerals, jewelry, hydroelectric power, education and institutional cooperation, software technology, regional agriculture, and tourism. Indeed a cotton cartel and related developments could become a cornerstone of the Central Asian prosperity.

Impediments

The major impediment to continental trade is the tense relationships between India and Pakistan and between Afghanistan and Pakistan. The end of the Soviet era and independence of the Central Asian states led to speculation that the new regional geopolitics would lead India and Pakistan to resolve their differences. But the gradually developing India-Pakistan détente needs time to mature before fundamental differences over Kashmir, Sir Creek and other issues can be resolved.

Despite increased trade and tourism, security concerns persist in both India-Pakistan and Pakistan-Afghanistan relations. Some factions in Afghanistan appear to support the insurgency in Baluchistan, and tensions between India and Pakistan persist. Several military training camps in Baluchistan—allegedly supported by the Indian consulates in Kandahar, Jalalabad and Zahidan—have been found and are being destroyed by the Pakistani Frontier Corps. Indian financial support of Sindhi and other anti-Pakistan groups based overseas is a major concern for Pakistan. Operating under the auspices of human rights and social organizations, these groups have spread propaganda hostile to Pakistan in the United States, Canada and the United

---

[38] Conversations at the Ministry of Foreign Affairs in 1996 and in February 2006.

Kingdom, working to continue negative stereotypes that do not reflect the sociopolitical and cultural realities of contemporary Pakistan. Thus, despite official rhetoric and joint statements, mistrust between India-Pakistan and Afghanistan-Pakistan appears to be increasing.

To develop infrastructure adequately, the following points must be considered:

1. Delays in developing road and rail infrastructure in Afghanistan could hamper effective communication throughout the region, leading donor agencies and countries to emphasize, at least temporarily, immediately available alternative transit routes, most likely via the Karakuram Mountains, rather than through Afghanistan.

2. Officials in the United States have expressed an interest in Pakistan providing direct transit for Indian products destined for Afghanistan and Central Asia.[39] However, according to Pakistani officials, the lack of trust between India and Pakistan, and Pakistan's still-developing trade and communication infrastructure prevent direct transit for the time being. In time and with improved relations, however, India may be granted this access. Currently, Central Asian states have no problems with trade through the Karakuram Mountains using the rail and road communication infrastructure of western China. In the meantime, India must rely upon the indirect transit facilities provided by Pakistan. If such transit is to be improved, Afghanistan will have to recognize and address Pakistani concerns.[40]

3. Many in India and the West attribute Pakistani interest in Afghanistan to strategic concerns. This may be true, but strategic issues are of concern to all of Pakistan's neighbors as well. Landlocked Afghanistan and the Central Asian countries are all dependent in part on Pakistan for access to world trade via maritime transport. Transit routes demand reciprocity in all key bilateral interests—geopolitical, economic, security and strategic — whether between Pakistan, Afghanistan and the states of Central Asia or China and India.

---

[39] Conversation with officials at the U.S. Department of Commerce, Washington, DC, January 2006.
[40] Conversations at the Ministry of Foreign Affairs, Islamabad, February 28, 2006.

4. Most South Asian states fear India, believing that its view of its role in the world is still based upon Lord Curzon's imperial worldview.[41] It is still remembered that in the 1950s K.M. Pannikar argued that India's zone of influence should extend over the entire Indian Ocean and the surrounding regions. India's presence in the Indian Ocean could eventually lead to a conflict of interests with the United States and with regional powers. One of India's leading political groups, the Bharatiya Janata Party, considers Southeast Asia, rather than Central Asia as India's proper sphere of influence. But if Southeast Asia may have been within India's sphere of influence during ancient and medieval times, the economies of this region have recently strengthened considerably, rendering it difficult for India to find suitable markets there. India's long-term competition with China and Russia in Central Asia and the Caucasus might become problematic, since China and Russia are located within Eurasia, while India is reliant upon China and Pakistan for access to the Central Asian heartland.

5. The Chinese government has reportedly been hesitant to grant Pakistan trade transit rights through Kashgar. India has the same problem with respect to both China and Pakistan. India, China, Russia, and Turkey are active in long-distance continental trade with the European Union (EU) and the United States. China and Russia both enjoy a favorable geographical location for trade with Central Asia, while India's lack of direct access to the region makes it unlikely that it can compete with these two regional powers for economic and political influence there. Indian exports to the United States, Australia and the EU are likely to be restricted by quotas, and it will be difficult for India to find suitable markets in Southeast Asia. India may seek markets in Africa but will face competition from the United States, the EU, China and Russia. If China has been hesitant to allow Pakistan, a long-time friend, transit trade rights through Xinjiang, it is likely that India, a long-time foe of Pakistan and China, will have even more difficulty attaining such rights, even if it seeks membership in the Shanghai Cooperation Organization (SCO).

---

[41] This worldview is thoroughly discussed the following work: Mohan, Raja, *Crossing the Rubicon: The Shaping of India's New Foreign Policy* (New Delhi: Penguin Books India, 2003).

Conclusions

The United States is trying to remove the various impediments to continental trade and has been advising both India and Pakistan in an effort to normalize relations between them.[42] Yet the success of the peace process will depend upon the leadership in India and Pakistan. The United States government should propose reciprocal confidence building measures to both governments. The prevailing distrust between Afghanistan and Pakistan will demand similar attention. Central and South Asia's complex ethno-political situation complicates matters. Regional state-building processes must include means of fostering interethnic communication, in addition to measures to establish rule of law, civil society, and constitutionalism. This is also true for Pakistan. New transit routes via Pakistan and subsequent economic developments will help stabilize political processes throughout Central and South Asia; but for the time being balance between economic and political development has yet to be achieved. In Pakistan, a democratic federal administration would greatly advance this cause. The essential administrative structures are already in place. If these are effective, democratization will inevitably occur over the long term. It will be important to recognize the multi-generational nature of democratization; attempts to hasten the process will cause more harm than good. Contrary to common opinion, Central Asia is a relatively stable region, thanks mainly to the efforts of Central Asian countries themselves. They have solved the vast majority of boundary issues through bi-lateral negotiations.

The U.S. State Department's new Bureau of South and Central Asian Affairs can facilitate the realization of the Greater Central Asian concept of regional and continental trade, which is based on geopolitical realism and solid historical experience. Improved transportation infrastructures and the reopening of Central Asia's traditional southern communication routes are likely to encourage foreign direct investment, contributing to peace and stability in Afghanistan, Pakistan, and throughout the region. The United States can also offer new incentives to encourage bilateral and multilateral confidence-building measures among Central and South Asian countries.

---

[42] Conversation at the U.S. Department of Commerce, Washington, DC, January 2006.

Region-wide corruption may cause problems in the short-term but a balanced economic and political development strategy will gradually overcome this problem, or at least keep it at manageable levels; the same development strategies can also curb terrorism. It is high time that Central and Southwest Asia's problems of underdevelopment are addressed. Alternative trade and transit routes through Pakistan could help pave the way toward region-wide integration and development.

The new transportation routes discussed here will likely forge new forms of regional interdependence, which will in turn, allow the major powers to balance their interests in Central and South Asia. Such interdependence will also help stabilize U.S.-China relations in the long term. Trade will therefore play a central role, just as it did in the region's long past, and can hasten economic and political stabilization throughout the region.

Tariff systems in Central Asia must correspond to those in the key transit countries, i.e. Afghanistan and Pakistan. Regional trade negotiations between Central Asian states must include Afghanistan and Pakistan, and all regional trade agreements must consider the tariff policies of SCO members and observers.

India's foreign policy must change over time to reflect its evolving relationship with the United States and the changing geopolitical realities in Central and Southwest Asia. It is understandable that India should want to tap into emerging Central and Southwest Asian markets, but restrictions on trade between regional powers can even today lead to unpredictable consequences.

Tajikistan

Khojamakhmad Umarov

Central Asian countries are still disentangling themselves from the former Soviet Union. Border conflicts in the region are increasing, with new restrictions preventing the movement of goods, services, and people. Industrial cooperation among these countries has almost completely stopped, and visa restrictions are becoming more stringent. Cultural and scientific bonds between the countries are breaking, with academic diplomas from one country no longer being recognized in another. It is not clear that Central Asian countries acknowledge the necessity and effectiveness of regional cooperation. They are focusing instead more on processes of economic globalization than on regional cooperation. Uzbekistan has signed a bilateral free-trade agreement with five members of the Commonwealth of Independent States (CIS), only one of which is a Central Asian state; Tajikistan signed such an agreement with four CIS members, only one of which is in Central Asia. Turkmenistan's recent agreement included a non-Central Asian country but none with a neighbor. Kazakhstan and Kyrgyzstan signed agreements with eight and six CIS members, respectively, both of which included only two Central Asian countries. None of Kazakhstan's main export partners are Central Asian countries. Kyrgyzstan's main trade partners include only Kazakhstan from the Central Asian region, while Uzbekistan has no significant trade with any countries in the region.

In spite of this, economic cooperation in the region is expanding. The volumes of inter-regional trade between 1994 and 2004 increased from US$1.6 to US$3.4 billion. However, the rates of trade growth among the countries themselves are low compared with those of other CIS members and nonmembers. As a result, the specific weight of the Central Asian region as a part of the total volume of foreign trade turnover decreased from 8.4 to 6.6 percent.

In 2004 Uzbekistan suggested establishing a Central Asian general market under the framework of the Organization of Central Asian Cooperation (OCAC). This suggestion called for the stage-by-stage implementation of the following measures:

- establishment of a free-trade zone;
- establishment of a customs union five years after the creation of the free-trade zone; and
- establishment of a regional general market five to seven years after the creation of the custom union.

Other OCAC-member countries supported this suggestion, and Uzbekistan took the lead in drafting the framework. However, without formal support from the OCAC itself, preparatory work on the establishment of such a market ceased. A new program to develop trade, transportation, and transit procedures is in the works, and another focuses on strengthening cooperation among Afghanistan, Kazakhstan, Kyrgyzstan, Tajikistan, Turkmenistan, and Uzbekistan. TRACECA, a European project to develop transport infrastructure, was begun in 1993 and has proceeded only haltingly since then.

The main problems facing the development of regional trade are as follows:

- unequal approaches to the issues of regional trade with no solid evaluation of the potential benefits of deepening cooperation;
- varying levels of socio-economic development among neighboring countries;
- structural imbalances of trade between neighboring countries. For example, Tajikistan relies more heavily on imports from Uzbekistan than Uzbekistan does on Tajikistan. A similar scenario exists between Kyrgyzstan and Kazakhstan.

The most serious obstacles to regional trade include the following:

- corruption among border officials, customs agents, and transport sector personnel;

- the prevalence of drug trafficking;
- inefficient banking systems;
- poor transportation infrastructure;
- poorly maintained transportation services, for example, old trucks and shortages of railway cars, passenger cars, passenger planes and helicopters, and poorly developed expediting services; and; the blockade of transit through Uzbekistan and Kazakhstan, which forces North-South transit through China rather than Afghanistan.

Borders are a serious obstacle to regional trade in Central Asia. More than 50 percent of respondents to surveys mentioned that difficulties in crossing borders have a negative impact on economic cooperation. These difficulties are more serious and time-consuming for regional transit firms than for those from more distant lands.

Border checkpoints are excessively strict and corruption is rampant. Eighty to 100 percent of goods crossing borders are checked by hand while in Europe only 5 percent of such loads are checked this way. It is no wonder that only five to seven trucks cross most borders in one day. At the Khargos crossing on the Kazakh-Chinese border, 50–70 trucks are allowed to pass daily - a regional record. In addition, between seven and nine different agencies must check each load, and no coordination exist among them.

High customs tariffs and other bureaucratic impediments lead to the widespread trade in contraband. The practice of understating the cost of declared goods is also widespread and accepted by customs officials and customers. This practice severely reduces the state's revenues.

The most productive steps toward increasing regional trade would be the following:

- simplifying border functions, visa processes, and civilians crossing;
- supporting step-by-step widening of the free-trade areas;
- development of a supportive political climate; and,
- state assistance of the private sector in the sphere of international trade.

Potential Role of the United States in the Development of Trade in Greater Central Asia

The United States is playing a decisive role in solving a number of issues hindering economic integration, including aiding in the development of trade links within Central Asia.

The United States routed the Taliban and Al-Qaeda, which has led to more favorable conditions for the coordination of large-scale trade between Afghanistan and the countries of former Soviet Central Asia. Examples of U.S. support include its participation in the construction of the road-transport infrastructure within Afghanistan and between Afghanistan and other Central Asian countries, notably the construction of the bridge across the Panj River between Tajikistan and Afghanistan.

The United States could render further assistance to the region on the following issues:

- assist in developing the road-transport infrastructure, especially with construction of bridges, tunnels, anti-mudslide galleries, and in providing machinery for road construction;
- assist in financing and construction of power lines to export electrical energy from Tajikistan, Turkmenistan, and other countries to Afghanistan;
- facilitate the construction of a further hydro-power station on the Panj River, which would expand trade between Afghanistan and Tajikistan;
- support the current efforts of Central Asian countries to join the World Trade Organization (WTO) and make their membership conditional on reducing the number of barriers to trade;
- supply Central Asian countries with the equipment necessary to raise handling capacity at border check points;
- assist in finishing the construction of international transport corridors crossing the Central Asia countries and in financing the construction of motels, camping sites, service stations, petrol stations, and phone stations; and,

- assist in establishing a trans-border area of free trade in the Panj River valley, which would reduce illegal trafficking in drugs.

Tajikistan and the Development of Regional Trade

The Republic of Tajikistan is well aware that international trade is an effective means of promoting socio-economic development and is aware that current trade levels are far below their potential. Goods imported from Kazakhstan amount to 12.2 percent of Tajik imports, a number that could increase to 40 percent if the full potential were realized. Imports from Kyrgyzstan amount to only 1.1 percent of Tajik imports but could reach as high as 17 percent. Currently, Tajik exports to Kazakhstan and Kyrgyzstan make up only 1 and 0.1 percent, respectively, of Tajik exports. However, studies suggest that trade between these countries could be as high as 3 and 5 percent, respectively.

Extending regional and continental trade would allow Tajikistan to do the following:

- increase GDP. Estimates suggest that had Central Asia had a single customs area since 2000, the average annual rate of growth in each country would be 12.9 percent, and in 2004 the GDP per capita would have been 35.7 percent more than it actually was.
- reduce poverty;
- foster new industrial cooperation among neighboring countries;
- change the geography of foreign-economic links, thereby rendering domestic production more effective; and
- ensure sustainable power sources.

The main motor roads connecting Tajikistan with the external world pass through Uzbekistan. All current methods of transporting goods and people along these corridors involve serious obstacles. The normalization of economic and political relations with Uzbekistan will therefore increase significantly Tajikistan's trade and economic links with other Central Asian countries, CIS members, and non-CIS members.

In addition, Tajikistan's small- and medium-sized businesses have a particular interest in the Uzbek market, especially in agriculture. Eliminating obstacles to the transport of Tajik goods will allow the increased production of vegetables, fresh and dried fruits, and non-perishables, and the demand for these goods will significantly increase in Uzbekistan. A similar scenario would occur in both Kyrgyzstan and Kazakhstan.

Trade between Tajikistan and other Central Asian Countries

Among Central Asian countries, Tajikistan's biggest trading partners are Uzbekistan and Kazakhstan. However, trade relations with these countries are not developing evenly. Exports to Uzbekistan were $4.2 million in 1991, $7.7 million in 1993, $190.7 million in 1996, and $65.9 million in 2004. Exports to Kazakhstan were $7.2 million in 1991, $12.5 million in 1993, $24.3 million in 1996, and $3.5 million in 2004. Exports to Kazakhstan fluctuate considerably.

The rapid growth of trade between Tajikistan and Asian countries is the result of dynamic economic relations with Iran and, in particular, with Turkey. In 2004, exports to these two countries made up 89.2 percent of Tajikistan's total exports to Asia. Between 1998 and 2003 exports to Iran quadrupled from $13.6 million to $51.4 million, (in 2004 this number dropped to $29.6 million), and to Turkey they grew from $0.4 million to $193.2 million, i.e., by 483 times (in 2004, exports dropped to $139.7 million).

Tajik exports to China are growing, albeit slowly. Over the last three years exports to Afghanistan have grown considerably ($0.6 million in 1998, $3.1 million in 2001, $6.3 million in 2002, and $7.7 million in 2004). The volume of exports to Afghanistan could be increased from $80 million to $100 million within the next few years.

From 1991 to 2004 Tajik imports from Uzbekistan increased 26.8 times but the volume has fluctuated greatly. The total was $6.3 million in 1991, $65.4 million in 1993, $261 million in 1997, and then $150.7 million in 2001, and $168.8 million in 2004. The primary cause of such drastic fluctuations remains the volatile political climate between the two countries.

Tajik imports from Kazakhstan have also fluctuated, but not by as much as those from Uzbekistan. Imports from Kazakhstan amounted to $5.5 million in 1991, $26.5 million in 1995, $95.8 million in 2003, and $152.8 million in 2004.

The volume of imports from Kazakhstan nearly doubled in the first half-decade of the new millennium. The largest single purchaser of Tajik products is China at $57.0 million annually. China is followed by Turkey, at $37.9 million; Iran, with $26.3 million; the UAE at $16.2 million; and India with $3.3 million.

There is a considerable gap in Tajikistan's balance of trade. Exports to Turkey exceed imports by a factor of 37. For Uzbekistan the ratio is 2.6, for China it is 9.3, and for Kazakhstan the ratio is 43.6.

Tajikistan's trade with neighboring countries in 2004 was as follows: it imported from Kazakhstan 280,100 tons of wheat and wheat flour, 80,200 tons of coke, 64,600 tons of oil products, and 48,400 tons of chemical fertilizers.[1] In the future, the import of wheat could be reduced if Tajikistan's government remains committed to increasing domestic production. If a coke plant is put into operation in the Zerafshan valley, then the import of coke for aluminum production will no longer be necessary. Conversely, the import of oil products and chemical fertilizers (phosphatic manure) from Kazakhstan would need to be increased proportionally if the goal is the development of the above-mentioned industries.

Meanwhile, Tajikistan exported to Kazakhstan 8,400 tons of fruit juice and 298 tons of aluminum and transformers. Tajikistan could expand the export of dried fruits and canned fruits and vegetables, aluminum, fresh flowers, fermented tobacco, cotton fiber, and cotton and silk yarn. Proper diversification of trade through these products could improve the balance of trade between these countries.

Tajikistan by 2005 was annually importing from Kyrgyzstan printed materials worth $14.1 million, 66,400 tons of asbestos products, and electric bulbs. More recently, the Tajik government has encouraged the rapid development of its own printing industry and the rehabilitation of the construction materials industry. If these projects are implemented, Tajikistan will not need to import asbestos or such printed materials, as texbooks. Meanwhile, through diversification Kyrgyzstan will be able to increase its exports.

---

[1] Tajikistan: 15th year of independence. Statistical Report. Dushanbe, 2006, p.p. 370-386.

There is much potential for greatly increasing Tajik trade with Turkmenistan. Tajikistan needs sulfur from Turkmenistan while Turkmenistan needs chemicals, construction materials, marble and granite, transformers, vegetables and fruit juices from Tajikistan. Future growth of Tajik imports of all products from Turkmenistan is all but guaranteed, although this could be impeded by Uzbekistan's obstructionist policy of inhibiting transport and not allowing pipelines from other countries to cross its territory.

By 2005 Tajikistan was exporting to Uzbekistan 2,200 tons of aluminum hydroxide, 4,700 tons of cotton fiber, and power. In addition 1.5 billion kwt/h of electric power, as well as aluminum, and medicines are smuggled from Tajikistan to Uzbekistan. Moreover, illegally exported Chinese consumer goods flow from Tajikistan to the neighboring Uzbek provinces of Surkhandarya and Kashkadarya. A recent survey shows that over 40 percent of goods, imported illegally from China to Tajikistan are re-exported illegally to Uzbekistan. The volume of smuggled goods from Tajikistan to Uzbekistan far exceeds the officially declared figure.

Tajikistan and Uzbekistan have great potential for a rapid increase in their mutual trade. If Uzbekistan were to remove its undeclared economic blockade on Tajikistan, and if visa restrictions were abolished between the two countries, as well as landmines cleared along the shared border, then the potential for growth would be impressive.

Evolution of Tajikistan's Foreign Trade Policy

The President of Tajikistan determines the main lines of the country's foreign trade policy. The government of Tajikistan, through the Ministry of Foreign Affairs and other ministries, carries out that vision. The Ministry of Economy and Trade, the Ministry on State Revenues and Dues, and the National Bank of Tajikistan are in charge of executing foreign trade policy.

Since independence Tajikistan's trade regime has made progress towards liberalizing the internal market. The state's monopoly over foreign trade was abolished in 1991. Customs tariffs changed frequently, though the external economic policy did not undergo any noticeable changes. Between 1994 and 2003 customs tariffs changed three times. The unrestricted liberalization of foreign trade had already forced the closure of some leading industries, some of them major employers.

Rates of Custom Duties—from 1997 to 2003[2]

	September 1997	June 1998	January 1999	April 2000	October 2001	April 2002	November 2003
Average arithmetical rate of customs tariff	16.0	16.0	25.5	16.4	11.2	2.3	7.5
Maximum level of tariff	30.0	30.0	60.0	60.0	30.0	5.0	15.0
Quantity of tariff corridors	2	10	8	3	4	4	4

The table shows the drastic fluctuations between customs tariffs, their average percentage, and the maximum levels. Such fluctuation shows the lack of understanding of the aims and tasks of customs and of foreign economic policy generally.

The most recent custom tariff of 23 November 2003, includes revisions made to correct past mistakes. It prioritizes export-oriented industries, even when such industries are not subsidized by the Tajik government. The present customs tariff is the result of a more complete consideration of interests of the society and of the leading traders and associations. It is genuine instrument for regulating trade policy in both internal and external markets.

The Tajik legislation sets down registration requirements for those involved in foreign trade. Registration cards are issued by the Ministry of Economy and Trade and carry an expiration date. In addition, exporters are obliged to have a taxpayer's identification number (TIN) to ensure proper tax collection in accordance with the tax code.

Tajikistan has no tariffs on exports but the customs legislation stipulates quantitative restrictions on exports, which have yet to be specified. The legislation also sets quotas on ethyl alcohol, and alcohol and tobacco products. Minimum export prices, voluntary restrictions on exports, and

---

[2] Calculation on the base of official statistical dates.

other market regulations are also stipulated by the legislation but have not been applied in practice. At the same time, the Republic of Tajikistan does nothing to encourage exports. The legislation to date provides no specific measures for encouraging the export by individuals.

Presidential decrees of 27 June 1995 and 10 February 1996 require that raw materials must be sold at prices fixed by the Republic Commodity and Raw Materials Exchange, taking into account world market prices. This requirement affects products as diverse as cotton fiber, aluminum, ores, precious metals and stones, scrap-iron, tobacco, leather, chemical fertilizers, geranium oil, natural honey, medicinal herbs, and snake venom. Such requirements dramatically confine Tajikistan's foreign trade. Moreover, the country offers no export credits and prohibits barter transactions. Tariffs of 0 percent, 5-10 percent, and 10-15 percent are currently in effect, amounting to about 6.7 percent of the value of total exports.

Barriers to Intraregional Trade

High border taxes including value-added tax (VAT), excise-duties, customs duties, and collections for customs service, are a serious barrier to trade. Taken together, they make up between 35 and 45 percent of the cost of goods. This heavy tax burden, forces importers to seek ways of concealing data. Importers and customs officers deliberately collude in order to understate costs. Estimates put the resulting lost revenue at between $250 and $300 million each year.

Another barrier to export/import operations is the amount of paperwork that producers face. They must produce sixteen documents for trade officials. As corruption is widespread in the country, an importer/exporter has to pay bribes to obtain almost all these documents, with the informal fees far exceeding the formal ones. One example of this inefficiency is the required certificate on quality issued by Tajikgosstandart, for all goods not manufactured in Tajikistan. Organizations, in charge of issuing the various certificates, create obstacles to importers/exporters for the purpose of generating bribe revenue. High taxes and formal and informal fees increase the market price of goods, and cause numerous bankruptcies.

Another significant barrier to regional trade is the range of customs duties charged by each country. This is particularly significant for trade between Tajikistan and Uzbekistan. Until recently, the official rate of customs duties for goods imported to Tajikistan was 5 percent, i.e., a unified customs tariff was in effect. But Uzbekistan did not apply this principle, and the maximum duty reached 19 percent. According to the recently revised customs tariff, the maximum rate of customs duties in Tajikistan can be 15 percent, while the maximum rate of customs duties in Uzbekistan can now reach 70 percent, thanks to Uzbekistan's strategy of import substitution. Obviously, this is much more beneficial to Uzbek entrepreneurs doing business in Tajikistan than to their Tajik counterparts in Uzbekistan. This helps account for the trade imbalance between the two countries.

As a result of these unilateral actions by Uzbekistan, some industries in Tajikistan are incurring great losses. For example, Uzbekistan has for ten years demanded pre-payment for the cost of transporting alcohol and alcohol products across that country. Alcohol exporters must deposit the sum in an Uzbek bank and do not receive it back until the shipment crosses another border.

Tajik vintners suffer badly from this procedure. No deposits have been returned during the five years since the procedure was adopted. Uzbek authorities simply keep the money, citing the need to pay off Tajikistan's debt. This situation has led to the extinction of winemaking in Tajikistan. Hundreds of thousands of hectares of vineyards in the Hisor, Vakhsh, Yavan and Obi Kiik valleys have been converted into dry lands for growing crops, which are up to a twentieth as productive financially.

A similar situation exists with the Isfara Chemical Plant, which manufactures explosive materials used in the construction of mines, roads, railways, irrigation canals and other structures. Following independence, Uzbekistan outlawed the export of these explosives through its territory, which is the only possible route for exporting this product to the North. The plant used to manufacture up to 300,000 tons of explosive material prior to the break up of the USSR, and the price ranged from $745,000 to $810,000 per ton. For transiting such consignments through Uzbekistan, the Uzbek customs and railway services require more than 20 documents and even if all necessary documents are submitted, they may still refuse transit. Exporters of perishable fresh vegetables, fruits, and citrus also incur great losses when their goods cross the Tajik-Uzbek border.

The total losses incurred by Tajikistan between 1992 and 2004 as a result of all such actions by Uzbekistan exceed $15 billion.

These many barriers have resulted in trade deficits with all Tajikistan's main trading partners, including Uzbekistan, Kyrgyzstan, Kazakhstan, Turkmenistan, and Russia. In addition to the above-mentioned barriers, the amount of contraband crossing Tajik borders has increased, costing Tajikistan an additional $5 billion annually. If the government could find a way to eliminate these barriers, it could reduce poverty by 35 to 40 percent.

Between 1992 and 2004, Tajikistan and Turkmenistan concluded seventeen agreements. The most important of which concern trade and economic cooperation, and long-term economic cooperation. They envisage the expansion of mutual trade, increased delivery of oil products, joint control over the flow of the Amudarya River, and the diversification of trade. However, these agreements have not been successful, as is evident from the constant decline in trade in recent years. The commodity circulation between the two countries fell from $73.3 million in 2001, to $41.3 million in 2004.

Bilateral relations between Tajikistan and Uzbekistan were secured in an agreement on eternal friendship, signed on 15 June 2000. The real relationship between them, however, is such that the agreement has become the subject of caustic jokes. Between 1992 and 2004, Tajikistan and Uzbekistan signed forty-seven documents on trade and economic cooperation. These documents remain a dead letter, however, and Uzbekistan maintains its economic blockade of Tajikistan. Almost all border passages have been mined, leading to the death of hundreds and the injury of thousands.

Between 1999 and 2004, commodity circulation between Tajikistan and Uzbekistan fell by 1.9 times, exports to Uzbekistan dropped by 2.7 times, and imports from Uzbekistan fell by 1.6 times.

Thirty one bilateral agreements regulating trade and cooperation exist between Tajikistan and Kyrgyzstan. A Tajik-Kyrgyz Intergovernmental committee on the construction and improvement of highways between the two countries and on the diversification of trade was set up in 1994. However, concrete results are all but nonexistent. Trade turnover between Tajikistan and Kyrgyzstan fell by half between 1996 and 2002; Tajik exports to Kyrgyzstan fell 2.9 times, and imports were reduced 1.4 times. Between 2002 and 2003 the situation briefly changed, with commodity circulation increasing by 3.5 times and imports from Kyrgyzstan increasing by 5.2 times. Exports to Kyrgyzstan remained at the same level, however. Notwithstanding these problems, there is evidence that the potential for trade between Tajikistan and Kyrgyzstan is great.

Tajikistan and Kazakhstan have signed twenty-nine documents touching on various aspects of trade and economic cooperation, but most of these have not been implemented. The further development of trade and economic cooperation will depend on long-term deliveries of aluminum from Kazakhstan's Pavlodar Aluminum Plant to the Tajik Aluminum Plant, as well as deliveries of uranium-rich raw materials to the Vostokredmet Company located in Khujand.

Unlike other countries in the region, commodity circulation between Tajikistan and Kazakhstan is growing, having increased 1.85 times since 1997. This progress sharply aggravated Tajikistan trade deficit however and worsened Tajik-Kazakh trade balance. Since 1997, the export volume from Tajikistan to Kazakhstan declined 3.5 times, while the import volume from Kazakhstan increased 1.7 times. The rate of exports from Tajikistan was 22.4 percent of the total trade turnover between the two countries in 1997, but fell to 4.6 percent in 2004. The rate of imports from Kazakhstan increased from 77.6 percent to 95.4 percent during the same period. Such trends are alarming and harmful to Tajikistan. Tajikistan is capable of balancing its trade relations with Kazakhstan, but for now all efforts to do so have been insufficient.

Transportation Problems

During Soviet times the annual volume of cargo crossing the Tajik/Uzbek border in the Zeravshan Valley reached 175,000 tons. No less than 75,000 tons of the concentrate coming out of the Varzob ore mine were transported for processing to the Kadomhaiski facilities in Kyrgyzstan. In addition, 200–

250,000 tons of ammonal (explosive material) produced by the Isfara Chemical Plant were transported through Uzbek territories, to be used for mine, tunnel, road, and railway construction. Today, this trade has ceased, at a cost to Tajikistan of $1.5 billion annually.

Truck transport from Uzbekistan to Kyrgyzstan has also ceased. Concentrates of antimony and mercury are now transported from Khudjand by railway, increasing the cost of processing. Uzbek authorities have also put an end to cargo transit from Khudjand to Tajikistan's Badakhshan region via the Fergana Valley.

During Soviet times there was also an extensive private trade relationship between Kazakhstan, Kyrgyzstan, Turkmenistan, and Tajikistan. Tajik traders, especially from the northern regions of the republic, sold fresh and dried fruits in all regions of Kyrgyzstan and Kazakhstan and also in the southern and eastern regions of Russia. The volume of such deliveries was huge. According to available statistics, traders from the Zeravshan Valley sold up to 45,000 tons of apples and pears and 3,500 tons of dried fruit annually. These numbers are for production in a single valley. Restrictions on the export of lemons, pomegranates, figs, pears, dried fruits, fresh flowers, vegetables, and wine cause huge losses for Tajikistan. Today hundreds of tons of fresh flowers, lemons, and fresh stone-fruits wait at inefficient border crossings, a process which can take several days. After the slow so-called antinarcotics check, many of these products are worthless and have to be sold at below-market prices. According to preliminary data, estimates of the deterioration of fresh production owing to unreasonable border delays cost Tajikistan $28–31 million annually.

Goods transported from Tajikistan to Kazakhstan must pass through Uzbekistan. The basic transit routes are as follows: Sari-Osiya – Denau – Kitob – Shahrisabz – Samarkand – Djizak – Guliston. The transit route to Turkmenistan is via Sari-Osiya – Baysun – Bukhara – Chardzhou. At present the basic transit route to China is via Aibek – Toshkoz – Chernovka – Dzhambul – Alma-Ata – Khorgos. It is possible that next year, this road will be replaced by a new one that will lie entirely within Tajikistanvia Kulyab – Darvoz – Khorog – Murghab – Kulma – Kashgar. For the southern areas of the country the transit route via Sari-Osiya – Denau – Samarkand –

Dzhizak – Guliston – Chernovka still functions. However, the economic value of these transit routes has been reduced due to the introduction of restrictive measures on the import of consumer goods to Uzbekistan.

For the last two and a half years, the flow of imported goods from Kazakhstan, Kyrgyzstan, and China has grown thanks to the restoration and expansion of the Osh – Bishkek road. This highway reaches the pass that connects Kzil-Art – Saritosh – Dzhirgatal – Garm – Nurobod – Obi-Garm – Faizobod – Dushanbe. The construction of this higway has not yet been completed but it is being used nonetheless, sometimes with tragic consequences. In 2002, 34 Tajik women returning from Almaty died in a bus crash on this road.

It would be possible to avoid this dangerous highway if the roads through the Ferghana Valley of Uzbekistan were open to the Kyrgyz and Tajik traders. Similarly, accidents could be avoided if the road between Chernovka – Oibek and Chernovka – Sir-Darya was opened.

The transport of goods by trucks tends to be very expensive. Secret surveys of Tajik truckers reveal that Tajik vehicles must pay at least $100 at each check-point in Uzbekistan. There are four such checkpoints en route between Sari-Asiya and Charjou and eleven en route between Sari-Asiya and Cherneevka. If they refuse to pay, drivers and accompanying persons are subject to physical beating as well as the seizure of their goods and vehicle.

Goods transported out of Tajikistan by trucks are subject to a number of non-official fees demanded by police and criminals. The author of this report found that the following payments demanded are standard: en route through Kazakhstan between Chimkent, Karaganda, and Almaty, traffic police require each vehicle carrying less than 20 tons to pay $200, while the ecological service demands $30, with no receipt provided. En route between Jambul and Karaganda drivers are stopped at nine separate check-points at each of which vehicles must pay between $75 and $100. The most complicated case is the so-called "vehicle escorts" that are unofficially “required” in Kazakhstan. One driver was charged $350 for an unwanted and illegal escort on the highway between Jambul and Almaty.

Kyrgyz motor transport can operate within Tajikistan without restriction or fees, while Tajik vehicles can do the same in Kyrgyzstan. But Tajik trucks are subject to high official and non-official fees on the territory of Turkmenistan. For entrance into the country, a fee of $250 is required and an additional fee of $35 is charged for a so-called "transit visa." There are four police check-points between Sarakhs and Charjon, each of which demands bribes of $50 to $70/per vehicle.

Such an approach to trucking in Central Asian countries is a result of near-total ignorance of norms of international transport communications. Political linkages, imperial ambitions, and the psychology of the "stronger power" also play roles in creating this problem. Uzbekistan's transit policy is designed to protect domestic agriculture and directly undermines Tajik agriculture in that part of Tajikistan where 75 percent of population lives. Tajik agriculture cannot develop without the use of mineral fertilizers. In 2002 the government of Uzbekistan issued a decree banning the export and import of nitric fertilizers on grounds that they could be used in the production of explosives.

Under the pretext of resisting drug trafficking, Uzbek customs officers do everything in their power to prevent Tajik trucks carrying large volumes from entering Uzbekistan. From 1993 to 1999 goods crossing from Tajikistan to Uzbekistan were unloaded at checkpoints and then reloaded onto Uzbek trucks. Under pressure from Tajik entrepreneurs, Tajik border guards and customs officers make concessions to Uzbek truckers, which allowed them to enter Tajikistan with few complications. Such approaches can work but they must be reciprocal.

Problems of Transit Mechanisms

Non-official fees account for between 2 and 3 percent of the entire value of Tajikistan's foreign trade . A partial list of such fees would include the following:

- payments for phyto-sanitary conditions;
- payment for bilateral road sanctions;
- border payments involving taxes and fees;
- fees for the issuance of declaration forms;

- fees for bridge crossings;
- insurance fees;
- payments for escorting goods or passengers;
- payments for guards;
- payments for the issuance of approvals by standardization authorities;
- payments to customs dealers on borders;
- payments for the traveling speed of vehicles;
- payments for axel taxes;
- payments for ecological services;
- payments for car inspectors; and,
- payments for police check-points.

Such fees dampen the entrepreneurial spirit in Tajikistan. As a result of the heavy burden of transit fees, the number of bankruptcies in Tajikistan increases every year, and the black market continues to develop and grow.

Professor L. Ojalla has analyzed the long waiting times at border points. He concluded that if trucks were checked in three hours or less, the annual financial savings would amount to approximately $30 million. Widespread corruption ensures that long waiting times continue and prevents any sort of reform. A major obstacle to the transit of Tajik goods are the "mortgage" requirements for the transport of tobacco, ethyl alcohol, wine and vodka introduced by Kazakhstan and Uzbekistan. Such arrangements do nothing to promote a liberal economy. After Uzbekistan introduced mortgage requirements, the Tajik wine industry collapsed as it relied on exporting to wineries in Kazakhstan and the Russian Federation where the wine was bottled and sold.

Trade with Afghanistan

Tajikistan's longest border (1030 km long) is with Afghanistan. Until recently, this border was closed on both sides. Now the situation has changed, and trade and economic relations between Afghanistan and Tajikistan are developing quickly. As the statistics indicate, the total volume of turnovers between the two countries in 1993 was $10.7 million, but by 2004 this figure had increased to $63.1 million. In the same time period the volume of exports from Tajikistan increased from $0.1 to $6.1 million, and imports increased from $10.6 to $57.0 million.[3] This shows that despite high rates of turnover, the trade balance for Tajikistan is negative. The turnover of goods between these two countries is marked by sharp fluctuations and is not sustainable.

Trade and economic relations between Tajikistan and its southern neighbor are below normal levels, thanks to civil wars both in Tajikistan and Afghanistan. Drug trafficking also has a negative impact on normal trade and economic relations. Prolonged peace and reduced drug trafficking along the borders will go a long way towards improving trade relations between the two countries.

Assistance from the U.S. government and from the Aga Khan Foundation has contributed to the creation of five bridges, connecting the left and right banks of the Panj River. The U.S. government and a number of other countries have provided assistance for the rehabilitation of road infrastructure in Afghanistan. These highways will all become organic parts of international transport corridors, that will connect former Soviet Central Asia with several ports on the Persian Gulf, as well as with industrial cities in Pakistan and northern India.

International transport corridors will connect the countries of the region with major continental economies by the shortest routes possible. At present, 52 such corridors are being constructed within the region. Kazakhstan's president Nazarbaev noted that the most important of these is the "North-South" corridor, which will connect Almaty, Bishkek, Osh, Dushanbe, and Kabul, and on to Pakistan's new port at Gwadar, as well as to India and will become the main transport and trade artery of the region.

When the present author was on a mission in Afghanistan, he was surprised to find that the Afghan portion of this transport corridor is already operational and is functioning successfully. The highway between Sherhon, Bandar, Kunduz, Baglan, Puli, Khumri, passage Salang, and Kabul is now up

---

[3] Tajikistan: 15 th years of independence. Statistical Report. Dushanbe, 2006, p.p. 339, 345, 363.

to the highest international standards. Due to U.S. financial support, this highway, constructed by Chinese and Turkish companies, was finished ahead of schedule. The corresponding infrastructures, including wayside restaurants, snack bars, motels, and service stations, function along this highway. Another transport corridor connecting the Uzbek city of Termez with Mazar-I-Sharif and Puli Khumri is also near completion.

The prospects for future trade between Tajikistan and Afghanistan are great. It is possible that by 2015 Afghanistan will be able to meet all of Tajikistan's natural gas requirements and a share of Tajikistan's electrical power needs as well, especially once Afghanistan brings to completion the hydro-electric stations at Sangtuda and Rogun.

The challenge of constructing transcontinental pipelines for the transport of oil and gas is a problem not only for Central Asia but for the rest of the world as well. The problem is particularly acute with regards to the construction of a gas pipeline between Turkmenistan and Turkey, and between Turkmenistan, Pakistan and India via Afghanistan, as well as a pipeline across the Caspian from Kazakhstan to Baku and the BTC route.

Beyond these projects, special emphasis should be put on the production and transmission of hydroelectric power. Hydro-electric power, unlike hydrocarbons, is renewable. The productivity of capital invested in hydro-electric development is higher than for oil and gas pipelines. Hydropower is also "greener" than petroleum-based energy. It is worth noting that a large percentage of oil and gas exported from Central Asia is transformed into electric power.

One potential obstacle to harnessing hydroelectric power in the region concerns rights to the water itself. Afghanistan is fencing off part of the Panj River for irrigation purposes. Turkmenistan and Uzbekistan must acknowledge this action and at the same time start utilizing more advanced irrigation technologies. More than 17 thousand cubic meters of water are used to irrigate each hectare of cotton in Uzbekistan, and as as much as 19 and 20 thousand cubic meters in Turkmenistan. By contrast, Israel uses only six thousand cubic meters of water to achieve the same results.

Afghanistan possesses the land resources necessary for self-sufficiency in food. It is possible to increase the area of irrigated land to 5.3 million hectares from the current level of no more than 2.1 million hectares. Doubling the amount of irrigated land and the improvement of agricultural methods could lead to the increase of crops production by a factor of no less than four. This would enable Afghanistan to meet domestic food needs and at the same time become a large exporter of agricultural produce. Afghanistan also needs a large-scale program designed to expand its irrigation capacity, as well as a concerted effort to identify and develop additional farm land.

Tajikistan could become Afghanistan's largest supplier of coal and coke, aluminum and reinforced-concrete construction materials, cement, and bitumen. In addition, Tajikistan is poised to provide Afghanistan with nitrogen fertilizers, crushed stone, gravel, gypsum, paints, decorative stones, and pavement slabs. Afghanistan, for its part, has the capacity to provide Tajikistan with wool for its carpet production, as well as oranges and tangerines, early vegetables, and potatoes and dried fruit. In the long-term, Tajikistan can become a permanent provider of electric power, building machinery, chemical products and household equipment. Afghanistan and Tajikistan can work together to construct hydroelectric stations on the Panj River, to secure stable supply of natural gas for Tajikistan, to construct joint irrigation projects in the northern provinces of Afghanistan and cultivate virgin lands in Tajikistan. An export-oriented free economic zone between Afghanistan and Tajikistan should also be developed through a joint effort by both countries. All this is more readily possible because the two countries share a common language, culture, history, and psychology. Thanks to this, too, Tajikistan is well positioned to assist in the education and cultural development of Afghanistan's people, thereby building up human capital and political stability. Such assistance will be particularly important in areas that affect Afghanistan's future role in trade. Tajikistan's agricultural and technical institutions of higher education can train competent agronomists, agrochemists, engineers of different profiles, as well as business leaders, economists, and public administrators in the field of international trade and finance. At present, Tajikistan has no financial resources for assisting Afghanistan in achieving these goals. However, with the help of international donors it can use its existing knowledge resources to remove impediments to regional and continental trade.

The most serious challenge facing Afghan-Tajik relations is the continued drug trafficking, which not only harms people of these and many other counties but also severely damages the credibility of regional states as partners in legal trade and commerce. Economic incentives must be devised in order to provide people with viable alternatives to the growing, selling, and transporting of drugs. Particular attention should be placed on improving the livelihoods of people on both sides of the Panj River, so that they can become a reliable barrier to the drug trade. This can be accomplished in part through the development of legal trade on the regional and continental basis.

Trade and Economic Cooperation

Overcoming trade barriers is particularly difficult in the case of states that were formerly part of the USSR. No gains in regional and continental trade will be possible until existing levels of corruption are reduced. All cases of illegal interference with cargo and transportation should be the object of special attention from security forces. All governments in Central Asia should have unified customs regimes that treat truckers from other countries with respect as their citizens. This means collecting duties only at check points and defining all demands for payments made elsewhere as crimes. Uzbekistan, in particular must apply these simple principles.

More integrated approaches to the management of transport will help all countries in the region. Special attention should be paid to highways, since they will be the principal means of transporting goods both in the regions and on a continental basis. Roads should be maintained in such a way that they meet international standards. Emergency technical assistance and telephone outlets should be available along all motor routes. In addition, general services, such as filling stations, motels, and rest stops must be developed. Above all, it is very important that truck transport systems in all countries function under the TIR regulations and standards. All barriers to this regimen should be removed.

In addition, the region should work toward adopting common insurance standards and unified banking practices to ensure smoother business transactions. Likewise, the collection of border taxes should work similarly at all borders, which in turn calls for unified tariff policies and procedures for collecting excise and value-added taxes.

Modern equipment can reduce the time needed to check cargo and passengers at border crossings. Check point staff must also be reeducated in order to reduce current levels of contraband. Greater transparency of the entire system is also needed, both of procedures and of personnel.

To prevent the flight of money from export operations, repayment schedules should be clear. The non-repayment of bonded money from the export of goods and services should be considered a crime. A better system for reporting such non-repayment by governments is also needed.

To foster both regional and continental trade Tajikistan should focus on reducing the cost of transport across its border with Afghanistan. A trans-Afghan railway could benefit not only Afghanistan but Tajikistan, Kyrgyzstan, and Uzbekistan as well. International financial organizations should work to make such projects a reality.

As noted above, the creation of free economic areas and border industrial zones could be of special importance to this region. In Tajikistan the Badakhshan area has particular potential in this regard.

For all this to happen, it will be essential to create inter-ministerial bodies among trading countries in order to monitor and assist the development of trade, transit, tax free zones, and other forms of cooperation among Central Asian countries. Such bodies should be charged with removing barriers to trade in accordance with WTO norms, rules, and standards.

It is the deep hope of Tajikistan, and other neighboring countries as well, that by joining the WTO it will be possible to remove nearly all above-mentioned barriers to trade. Such hopes also are focused on Uzbekistan's membership to EURASEC and the creation of a Central-Asian common market. To be sure, the transformation in recent years of Central Asia Economic Union into EURASEC will completely change certain dynamics. Will prices be based on the Central Asian region alone or continent-wide realities? How will other geographic parts of Central Asia such as Afghanistan or Mongolia, find their place in such an expanded market? These and other "global" issues will all have to be addressed in due course. However, the urgent first step is for Tajikistan to adopt a strategy of economic and social development that is based on the rational use of natural and human resources in the context of a region- and continent – wide market economy.

Appendix 1: Tajikistan: Foreign Trade Turnover (In millions of U.S. dollars)[1]

	1991	1992	1993	1994	1995	1996	1997	1998	1999	2000	2001	2002	2003	2004
Only, including	131..3	353.2	881.9	1038.9	1558.5	1438.2	1496.0	1307.6	1351.8	1453.3	1339.0	1457.4	1678.0	2106.2
Kazakhstan	12..7	27.6	81.8	42.9	33.5	76.7	52.1	61.9	81.4	88.1	92.2	75.7	100.4	156.1
Kyrgyzstan	5.1	4.5	6.2	2.9	5.3	17.7	14.4	11.1	11.1	10.2	7.7	8.9	31.2	22.0
Turkmenistan	5.1	21.7	29.5	41.2	59.6	34.8	39.8	40.0	16.5	34.0	72.0	57.1	33.8	41.3
Uzbekistan	10.5	21.3	85.7	105.9	384.3	389.6	434.0	353.0	445.4	285.4	237.9	205.3	199.8	234.7
Mongolia	-	-	0.4	0.3	-	-	-	-	-	0.1	0.0	-	-	0.1
XUAR	-	-	10.7	6.2	6.0	7.5	15.3	5.8	5.1	15.3	7.4	9.7	32.4	63.1
Afghanistan	-	-	1.0	2.0	0.3	4.2	4.5	1.1	2.3	2.7	3.2	6.6	7.4	11.7
On region GCA	33.4	75.7	215.3	201.4	489.0	530.1	557.2	472.9	562.8	420.4	420.4	363.3	405.0	529.0
percent	25.4	21.4	24.4	19.4	31.4	36.8	37.2	36.2	41.6	28.8	31.4	24.9	24.1	25.1

[1] Annual Report of Republic of the Tajikistan, Dushanbe, 2001, p.p.244, 245, Annual Report of Republic of the Tajikistan, Dushanbe, 2005, p.p.255, 256.

Appendix 2: Tajikistan: Exports (In millions of U.S. dollars)[1]

	1991	1992	1993	1994	1995	1996	1997	1998	1999	2000	2001	2002	2003	2004
Only, including	67.9	192.5	349.8	491.9	748.6	770.1	745.7	596.5	688.7	784.3	651.3	739.9	797.2	914.9
Kazakhstan	7.2	12.5	16.3	10.1	7.0	24.3	10.0	10.0	3.6	5.7	3.1	3.5	4.6	3.5
Kyrgyzstan	1.0	2.0	4.1	1.9	2.6	10.5	9.0	5.8	3.9	2.7	2.0	3.7	3.7	4.4
Turkmenistan	1.7	3.7	3.5	1.8	2.2	8.5	10.2	8.7	1.3	4.7	9.7	10.0	2.2	7.6
Uzbekistan	4.2	7.6	20.3	22.7	132.0	190.7	172.5	125.7	181.0	97.8	87.2	72.9	67.1	65.9
Mongolia	-	-	0.4	0.3	-	-	-	-	-	0.1	0.0	-	-	-
XUAR	-	-	0.8	0.8	0.3	1.3	0.8	0.6	2.2	2.6	3.1	6.3	5.8	7.7
Afghanistan	-	-	0.1	1.4	5.6	6.2	13.4	4.9	2.6	3.4	1.4	2.1	5.7	6.1
On region GCA	14.1	25.8	45.5	39.0	149.7	284.8	215.9	155.7	194.6	117.0	106.5	98.5	89.7	95.2
percent	20.7	13.4	13.0	7.9	20.0	37.0	28.9	26.1	28.2	14.9	16.3	13.4	11.2	10.4

[1] Annual Report of Republic of the Tajikistan, Dushanbe, 2001, p,p. 247,248; Annual Report of Republic of the Tajikistan, Dushanbe, 2005, p.p. 258,259.

Appendix 3: Tajikistan: Imports (In millions of U.S. dollars)[1]

	1991	1992	1993	1994	1995	1996	1997	1998	1999	2000	2001	2002	2003	2004
Only, including	63.3	160.7	532.1	547.0	809.9	668.1	750.3	711.0	663.1	675.0	687.5	720.5	880.3	1191.3
Kazakhstan	5.5	15.1	65.5	32.8	26.3	52.4	42.1	51.9	78.8	82.4	89.1	72.2	95.8	152.6
Kyrgyzstan	4.1	2.5	2.1	1.0	2.7	7.2	5.4	5.3	7.2	7.3	5.7	5.2	27.5	17.6
Turkmenistan	3.4	18.0	26.0	39.4	57.4	26.3	29.6	31.3	15.2	29.3	32.3	47.1	31.6	33.7
Uzbekistan	6.3	13.7	65.4	83.2	251.4	198.9	261.5	227.3	264.4	185.6	150.7	132.4	132.7	168.8
Mongolia	-	0.0	-	-	-	-	-	-	-	-	-	-	-	0.1
XUAR	-	-	0.2	1.2	0.0	2.9	0.8	0.5	0.1	0.1	0.1	0.3	1.6	4.0
Afghanistan	-	-	10.6	4.8	0.4	1.3	1.9	0.9	2.5	11.9	6.0	7.6	26.7	57.0
On region GCA	24.8	49.3	169.8	162.4	338.2	288.4	341.3	317.2	368.2	316.6	333.9	264.8	315.9	433.8
percent	39.2	30.7	31.9	29.7	41.7	43.2	45.5	44.6	55.5	46.9	48.6	36.7	35.9	36.4

[1] Annual Report of Republic of the Tajikistan, Dushanbe, 2001, p.p. 250, 251.
Annual Report of Republic of the Tajikistan, Dushanbe, 2005, p.p. 261, 263.

Appendix 4: Tajikistan: Imports from countries of Greater Central Asia

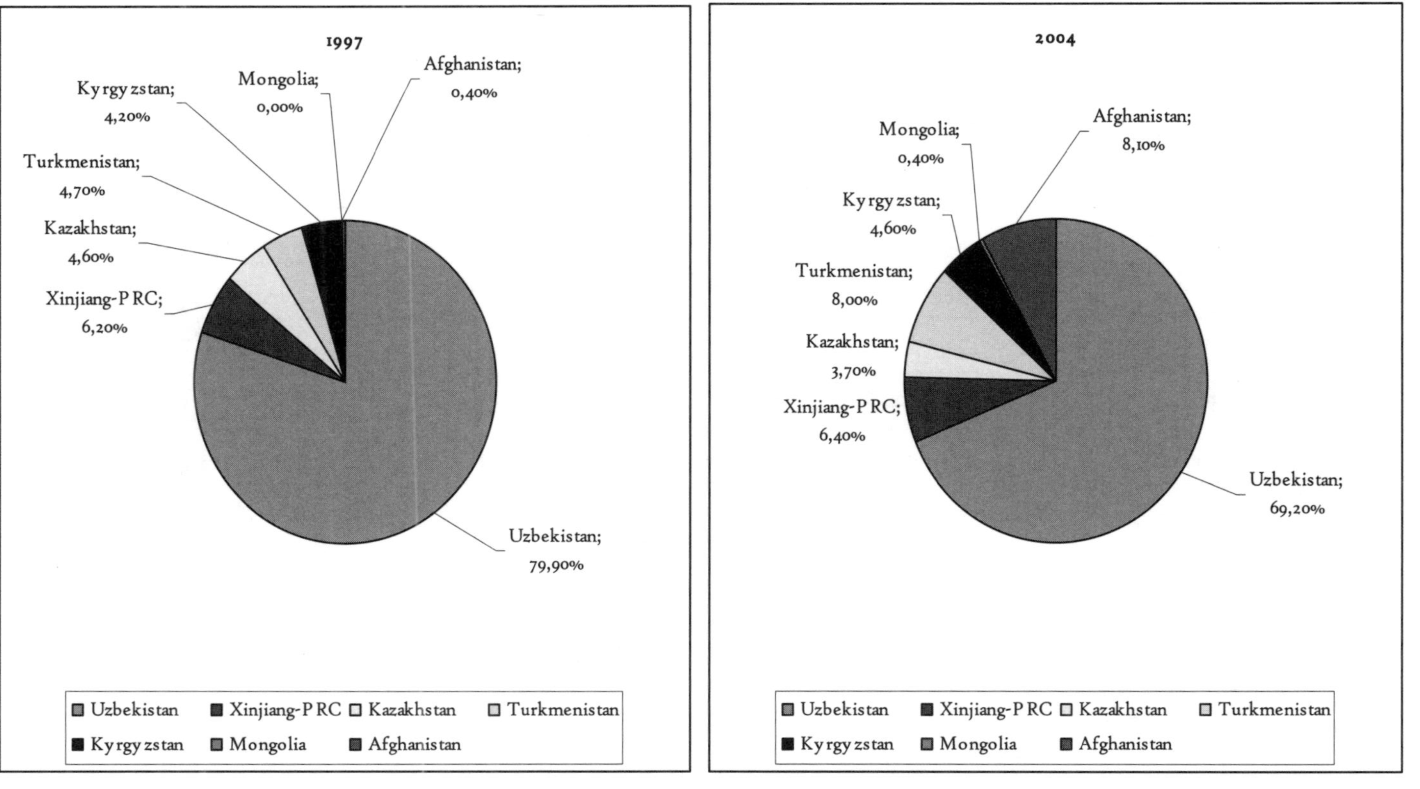

Calculation on the base of official statistics.

Appendix 7: Export International Service from Tajikistan [1]

	1997	1998	1999	2000	2001	2002	2003	2004
Only, including	10688.0	58099.0	49698.2	53353.7	66219.6	68933.6	58297.3	96025.3
Kazakhstan	2640.0	1979.2	1582.5	1700.2	1879.0	2659.6	2483.0	2144.2
Kyrgyzstan	111.6	101.6	1126.2	133.8	162.3	351.1	378.0	426.1
Turkmenistan	296.9	1073.9	168.6	198.8	758.8	1537.6	725.6	683.4
Uzbekistan	685.9	34724.4	31860.3	39131.3	45240.0	34105.8	20880.0	38454.3
Mongolia	-	-	0.03	0.0	0.1	0.6	0.3	0.0
XUAR	3.7	5.0	35.1	14.6	29.0	645.5	1081.4	374.5
Afghanistan	-	23.2	28.8	14.8	5.9	14.3	40.9	56.8
On region GCA	3738.1	31907.3	34809.9	41203.5	48075.1	39374.5	26589.2	42339.3
percent	35.0	65.2	70.0	77.2	72.6	57.1	45.6	44.1

[1] Annual Report of Republic of the Tajikistan, Dushanbe, 2001, p.p. 266,267. Annual Report of Republic of the Tajikistan, Dushanbe, 2005, p.p. 282,283.

Appendix 8: Tajikistan: Import of International Services (In thousands of U.S. dollars)[1]

	1997	1998	1999	2000	2001	2002	2003	2004
Only, including	39488.8	46019.0	58485.2	63963.5	51659.9	76265.6	70409.3	97076.2
Kazakhstan	1504.1	2084.5	1815.2	1566.3	891.0	4870.5	2210.03149.	690.0
Kyrgyzstan	6.4	680.2	364.8	414.3	206.8	1042.8	680.0	611.9
Turkmenistan	4804.8	4923.2	22656.6	24244.9	1501.6	8375.0	2275.9	4472.4
Uzbekistan	-	-	-	-	-	-	-	-
Mongolia	2.0	-	22.0	0.0	1.1	233.5	497.8	318.7
XUAR	-	-	-	-	-	-	13.1	-
On region GCA	6321.6	7872.2	24991.5	26413.3	2868.9	14718.9	5950.9	9292.1
B percent	16.0	17.1	42.7	41.3	5.6	19.3	8.4	9.6

[1] Annual Report of Republic of the Tajikistan, 2001, p.268.

Appendix 9

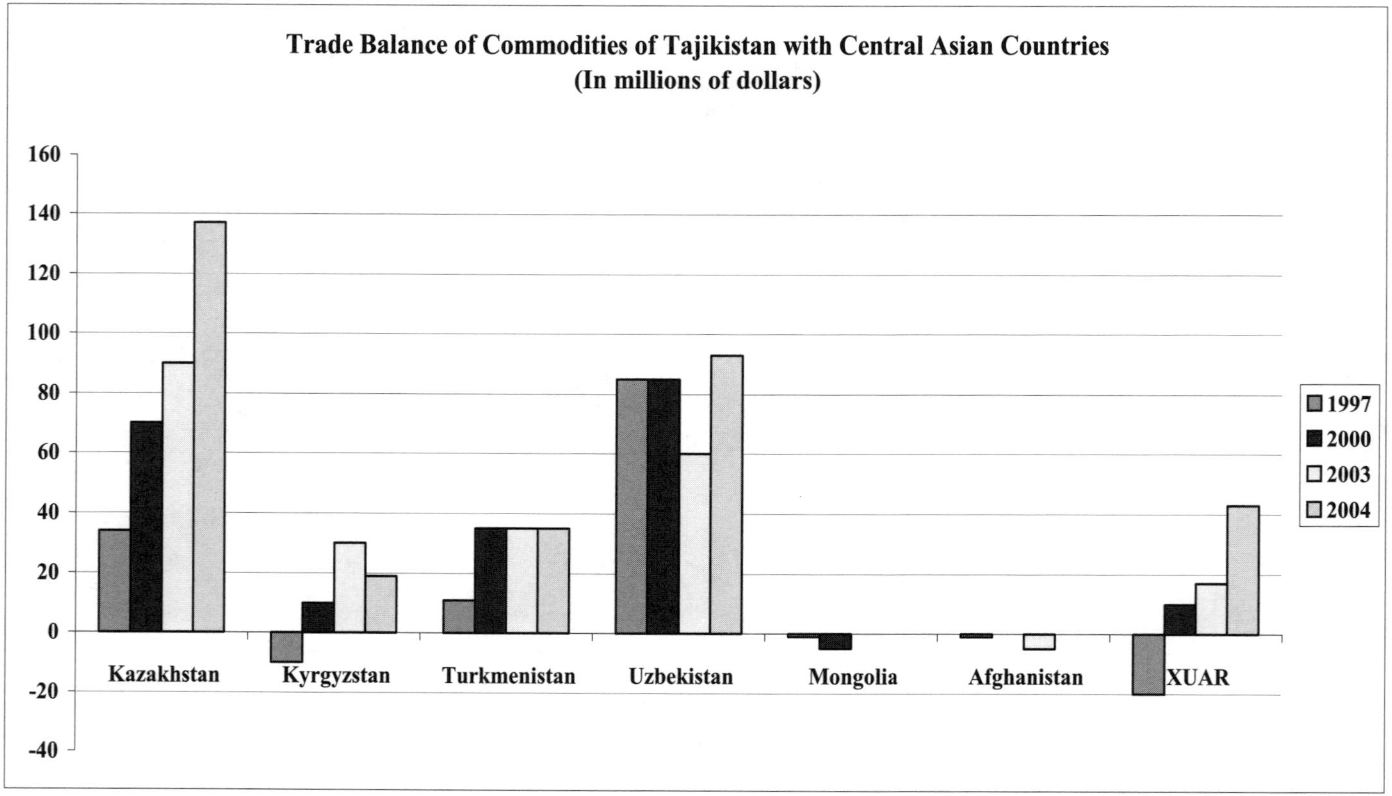

Trade Balance of Commodities of Tajikistan with Central Asian Countries
(In millions of dollars)

160
140
120
100
80
60
40
20
0
-20
-40

Kazakhstan
Kyrgyzstan
Turkmenistan
Uzbekistan
Mongolia
Afghanistan
XUAR

1997
2000
2003
2004

Appendix 10: Tajikistan: Import of Some Food Products (In thousands of U.S. dollars)[1]

	1997	1998	1999	2000	2001	2002	2003	2004
Sunflower oil	8,216	4,186	3,715	6,079	6,784	3,308	7,286	8,128
Only, including Uzbekistan	1,726	2,565	3,463	4,424	3,584	385	-	161
Azerbaijan	2,504	745	164	248	1,279	1,358	1,204	1,634
Kazakhstan	-	-	-	712	158	444	1,884	2,248
Iran	458	-	66	87	459	944	3,006	3,011
Sugar, only	21,062	13,802	11,363	10,759	5,160	12,517	79,018	22,985
including Kazakhstan	-	-	-	110	-	0	261	1,241
Uzbekistan	-	-	-	39	75	482	210	492
Flour, only	11,398	12,642	13,167	8,490	7,530	12,543	19,887	34,184
Including Kazakhstan	7822	9063	10769	7266	4989	11525	17531	27620
Uzbekistan	-	-	-	288	263	39	1317	3972
XUAR	-	-	-	-	-	-	-	22
Afghanistan	-	-	-	-	-	-	-	7
Wheat, only	13,249	29,978	32,797	36,332	30,156	23,332	12,401	15,049
Including Kazakhstan	12,578	27,786	32,237	36,272	29,596	22,783	12,082	10,437
Uzbekistan	-	-	143	60	510	418	164	24
Afghanistan	-	216	-	-	-	-	56	5
Tea, only	1,432	490	1,072.5	751	1,097	1,181	1,404	1,534
Including Kyrgyzstan	32	404	35	43	50	32	72	150
XUAR	-	28	84	19	90	129	96	198
Iran	140	314	340	459	680	787	952	866

[1]Annual Report of Republic of the Tajikistan, Dushanbe, 2001, p. 280. Annual Report of Republic of the Tajikistan, Dushanbe, 2005, p.281.

Appendix 11: Export of RT to Separate Countries (In millions of U.S. dollars) [1]

	1997	1998	1999	2000	2001	2002	2003	2004
In total export	745.7	596.5	688.7	784.3	651.5	736.9	797.2	914.9
Russia	63.5	47.9	115.1	258.8	104.7	87.5	52.2	60.5
India	0.0	0.0	–	0.0	–	–	0.0	0.2
Iran	3.5	13.6	13.5	12.5	29.9	28.4	51.4	29.6
The Incorporated Arab Emirates	0.9	6.0	2.2	0.4	0.3	1.2	0.7	0.3
Pakistan	1.3	0.3	0.1	0.1	0.2	0.0	0.1	0.2
Turkey	8.2	0.4	1.0	58.4	75.1	118.5	193.2	139.7

[1] Annual Report of Republic of the Tajikistan, Dushanbe, 2001, p.p. 247,248. International Activity of the Republic of Tajikistan, Dushanbe, 2005, p.p. 24,26.

Appendix 12: Import of RT from Separate Countries (In millions of U.S. dollars)[2]

	1997	1998	1999	2000	2001	2002	2003	2004
In total export	750.3	711.0	663.1	675.0	687.5	720.5	880.8	1191.3
Russia	115.1	102.1	92.4	105.1	129.4	163.5	178.1	240.8
India	1.0	0.8	1.0	0.1	34.4	31.5	3.2	3.3
Iran	12.0	11.3	10.4	7.6	10.0	15.6	23.7	26.3
The Incorporated Arab Emirates	7.1	4.9	4.0	2.8	4.9	6.9	13.8	16.2
Pakistan	1.1	0.2	0.2	0.1	0.1	0.1	0.0	0.3
Turkey	5.0	3.9	1.4	4.0	9.3	10.5	29.5	37.9

[2] Annual Report of Republic of the Tajikistan, Dushanbe, 2001, p.p. 250,251. International activity of the Republic of Tajikistan, Dushanbe, 2005, p.p. 28,30.

Appendix 13: Share of Foreign Trade Turnover, Export and Import of Tajikistan with Greater Central Asia (In total size of respective indicators)

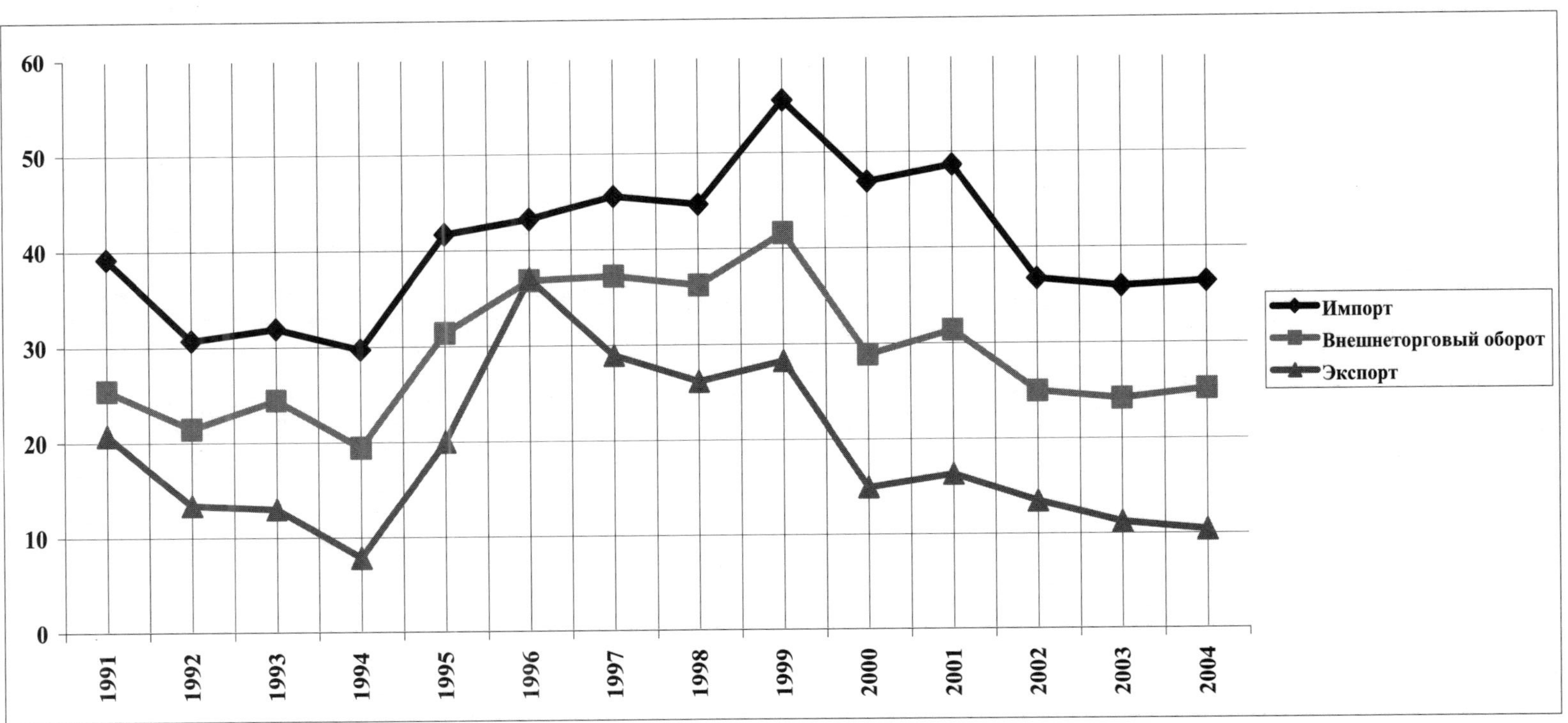

Appendix 14: Change of Share of Turnover, Export and Import of Tajikistan (In total size of respective indicators--Greater Central Asia)[1]

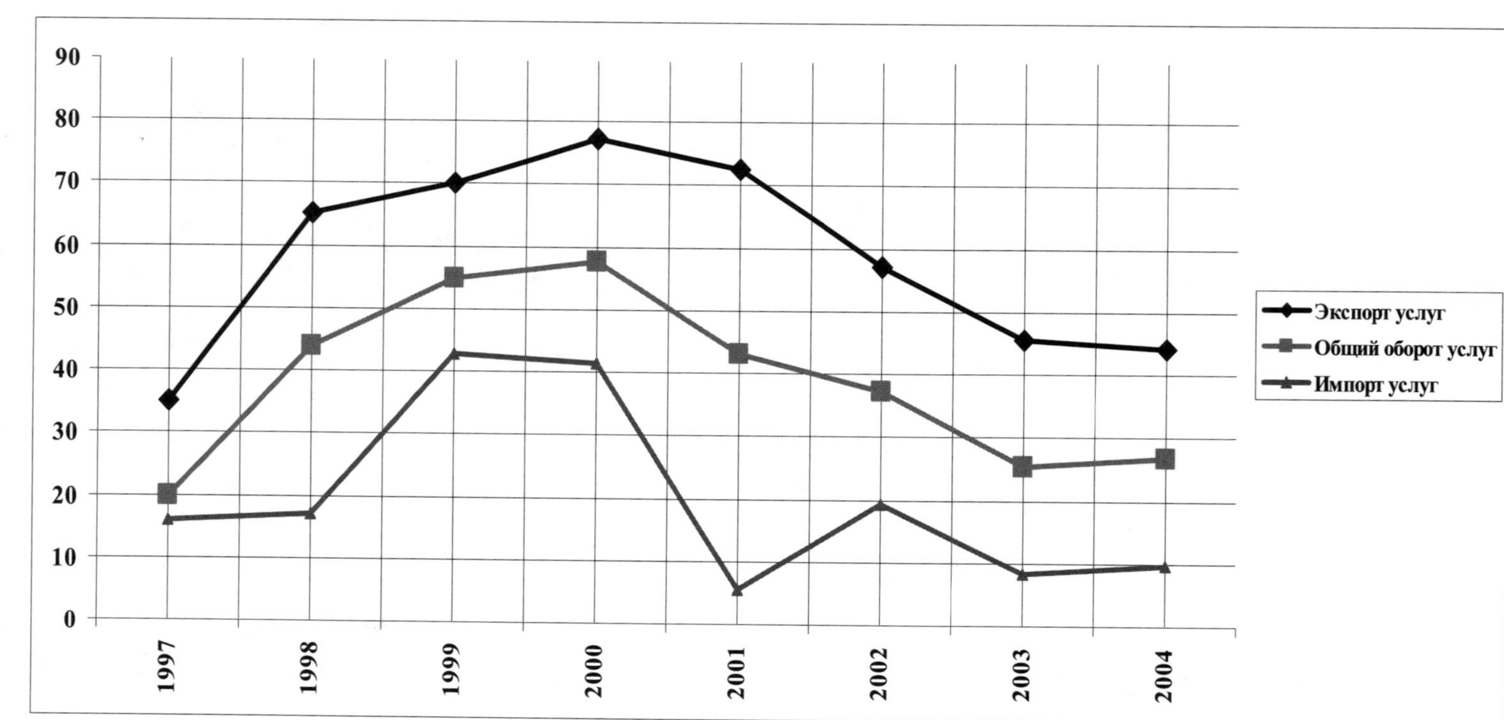

Turkmenistan

Firat Yildiz

By virtue of its geographical location, history, and economic circumstances within the region of Greater Central Asia, Turkmenistan should be a major crossing point for both regional and continental transport. Since independence Turkmenistan has done much to seize this opportunity and establish itself as an entrepot along major railroad and highway arteries. It has also labored heroically to break out of the Russo-centric and monopolistic system for the export of its rich deposits of natural gas that was built up during Soviet times and is now perpetuated by Russia's Gazprom.[1] Yet in the end these labors have fallen far short of their potential. Notwithstanding impressive achievements that have been largely underestimated abroad, Turkmenistan at the start of the twenty-first century lags behind many of its neighbors in transport and trade and shows few signs of breaking out of the isolation that results from this situation.[2]

Geography greatly favors Turkmenistan. True, the large Karakum desert that covers much of the country and all of its center is an impediment to transport. Yet the long route extending from the port of Turkmenbashi in the northwest to the borders of Afghanistan and Uzbekistan in the east and

---

[1] See article by Sergei Blagov, "Russia Looks to Protect Economic Interests in Turkmenistan amid political uncertainty." *Eurasia Insight*, December 22, 2006. Available online at http://www.eurasianet.org/departments/insight/articles/eav122206a.shtml

[2] See the World Bank Working Paper "Transport and trade facilitation issues in the CIS7, Kazakhstan and Turkmenistan" by Eva Molnar and Lauri Ojala, prepared for the Lucerne Conference of the CIS-7 Initiative, 20th-22nd January 2003. Available online at http://www.libertas-institut.com/uk/ECTIS/Transport%20and%20Trade%20Facilitation%20Issues.pdf

southeast is one of the major potential transport corridors of the entire region. This corridor is roughly defined by the Karakum Canal (later the Lenin Canal and, today, the Niyazov Canal). The mountains which define Turkmenistan's southern border with Iran have always been easy to cross, which makes it a simple matter to link this corridor directly to Iran and on to the Middle East and Turkey. The same corridor links with Afghanistan and Uzbekistan, which in turn opens access to Pakistan and India to the southeast, and to China in the east. By the same token, the flat terrain makes it easy to link this corridor northward to Kazakhstan, while the recently expanded port of Turkmenbashi can facilitate the trans-shipment of goods from India and Southeast Asia via Baku to the Caucasus and on to Europe, or to the Volga and then hence to Russia and northern Europe. Like Kazakhstan, Turkmenistan sits astride both land and sea (Caspian) corridors. But if Kazakhstan can easily serve as a main east-west corridor extending from Europe to China, geography allows Turkmenistan potentially to fill the same function while at the same time playing a central role in north-south transport and especially trade linking Turkey, the Middle East, and Southeast Asia.

Rich archaeological evidence from across Turkmenistan confirms that several powerful and highly developed civilizations on its territory prospered precisely because of their ability to exploit for transport and trade the advantages with which geography endowed them. At Nissa, Kunya Urgench, and especially Merv one finds a rich record of intense interaction with all the major economic and cultural centers of Eurasia extending over the course of two millennia.[3] Sitting aside the major continental trade routes of the so-called Silk Road, the territory of Turkmenistan seems destined by fate for a brilliant role in the currently emerging content-wide trade of Eurasia.

However, a contradictory tendency has always asserted itself in Turkmen history and is present today. During the fifteenth century the Silk Roads began to collapse due to the proliferation along their routes of rent-seeking khanates that could not match the high transit taxes they charged with a secure environment for traders. As this happened, nomadism spread across

---

[3] Denis Sinor, The Cambridge History of Early Inner Asia (Cambridge) 1990 (2nd Edition). ISBN 0-521-24304-1

the territory of what is now Turkmenistan. Over the following four centuries the Turkmen tribes played the role of spoilers, sacking both regional and continental caravans and pursuing a kind of perverse non-alignment by maintaining bad relations with all their principal neighbors, including the Safavids in Iran, the Shaybanid Uzbeks in Bukhara and the Uzbek Khivans. These practices in turn isolated the Turkmen tribes within the region. Turkmen foreign relations in this period are epitomized by a well-known British print from nineteenth century Khiva (now in Uzbekistan), which shows the local military being paid on the basis of the number of severed Turkmen heads they could produce.[4]

The Russian/Soviet period did little to improve the Turkmens' relations in the world. Having decimated a Russian army before being themselves slaughtered at the battle of Goek Tepe (1881), the Turkmen generated a distrust among the tsarist officer corps that eventually spread to the government and was transmitted to the Soviet regime. The fruit of this distrust was the Turkistan trunk railroad line from present-day Ashgabat to Tashkent. Built with incredible speed in the 1890s, this rail line served military, not economic, needs. Not surprisingly, it was built and maintained by the Ministry of War, with no input from the economic ministries. Other transport initiatives in Soviet times followed this same pattern. The Soviet pipeline system transmitted gas to Russia but not to neighboring Iran, while the road and railroad system linked Turkmenistan ever more closely with the North while isolating it from its natural trading partners to the South, West, and Southeast. Down to the end of the U.S.S.R. the only transport investment that made sense from the perspective of the regional and continental economies was the port of Krasnovodsk (now Turkmenbashi), which linked Ashgabat for the first time with Baku, and the Volga Basin.

The collapse of the U.S.S.R. should have ushered in the renewal of the continental trade links across Turkmenistan that had thrived over several millennia. But the end of Russian rule found Turkmenistan woefully unprepared for independence. Due perhaps to the Russians' century-old resentment towards the Turkmens, the Turkmen republic arrived at

[4] Armenius Vambery Travels in Central Asia. London: John Murry. 1864. Reprinted with an introduction by Denis Sinor. New York: Praeger Publishers. 1970.

statehood with less infrastructure in the spheres of transport, trade, and communications than any other republic. With fewer universities and technical institutes per capital than any other republic, Turkmenistan also lacked the human capital necessary to rectify these shortcomings and to capitalize on its new position in the world.[5] In short, the country lacked both an identity and the reality of skills and institutions that could give that identity reality in the modern world.

Turkmenistan's president to his death in December 2006, Saparmurat Niyazov, was well aware of these problems and understood the urgent need to rectify them. Some of his initiatives of those years warrant positive comment,[6] the more so since they have been largely forgotten as the more repressive and idiosyncratic aspects of his rule have gained strength and visibility. In many of these projects Niyazov depended on the capable leadership of his Foreign Minister, Boris Shikhmuradov,[7] but in others he himself took a prominent part.

The cornerstone of Turkmenistan's transport policy in the first seven years of independence was to open up contacts with both Iran and Afghanistan. Iran, with its 1200 km border with Turkmenistan, four road crossings and the railroad crossing at Sarakhs-Tejan, not to mention a Turkmen population of nearly a million within its borders, was a natural concern of Asghabat.[8] Land

---

[5] Pomfret, Richard, "Turkmenistan: From Communism to Nationalism by Gradual Economic Reform." in MOCT-MOST: Economic Policy in Transitional Economies, Vol. 11, No. 2: pp. 165-176 June 2001.

[6] See the United States Department of State "Turkmenistan Economic Policy and Trade Practices." February 1994. Available online at http://dosfan.lib.uic.edu/ERC/economics/trade_reports/1993/Turkmenistan

[7] Shortly after independence Boris Shikhmuradov became Deputy Prime Minister of Turkmenistan in 1992 and Foreign Minister in January 1993. In July 2000 he was appointed as Turkmenistan's special representative on Caspian affairs, and later served as ambassador to China. He resigned his posts in October 2001, and formed an opposition party the National Democratic Movement of Turkmenistan. In 2002 he was arrested and imprisoned in Turkmenistan. Biography available online at http://www.rferl.org/specials/turkmenelections/bios/shikhmur.asp

[8] Daly, John C.K., "Turkmenistan Pushes for New Offshore Oil Development." The Jamestown Foundation, Eurasia Daily Monitor Vol 1 Issue 11, May 17, 2004. Available online at http://www.jamestown.org/publications_details.php?volume_id=401&issue_id=2954&article_id=236715

trade with Europe and the Middle East all had to pass through Iran, which required good relations between Asghabat and Teheran. However, the U.S.-led sanctions against Iran fell more heavily on Turkmenistan than any other state except Azerbaijan.[9] And unlike Azerbaijan, to which the U.S. offered generous compensation in the form of support for the Baku-Ceyhan pipeline, there was no compensation package forthcoming for Turkmenistan.

Meanwhile, Iran had moved towards what Abbas Maleki in the chapter above, terms a "new regionalism." Under President Akbar Hashemi Rafsanjani (1989–97) Iran abandoned earlier hopes of extending its revolution to its northern neighbors in Central Asia and adopted a pragmatic and trade-based approach more akin to its pre-Soviet relations there. For his part, Niyazov reached an understanding with Rafsanjani that he would not champion the rights of Iran's Turkmen citizens if Teheran treated them decently and if it maintained stable relations with Turkmenistan. The new relationship was supported by Turkmenistan's decision to join the Economic Cooperation Organization[10] in which Iran played a prominent role.[11] When all the other Central Asian countries also joined ECO trade across the Turkmen-Iranian border immediately jumped, with Turkmen-Iranian trade exceeding that of all other Central Asian states.

For similar reasons Turkmenistan moved quickly to establish good relations with the fragile government in Kabul that was installed following the Soviet departure. Throughout the ensuing civil war period and through the entire Taliban era in Afghanistan Ashgabat not only maintained an embassy in Kabul but consulates elsewhere in the country.

---

[9] Torbat, Akbar E., "Impacts of the US Trade and Financial Sanctions on Iran." The World Economy 28 (3), 407-434.

[10] The Economic Cooperation Organization was expanded to include Azerbaijan and eventually all five Central Asian States, who joined Turkey, Afghanistan, Iran, and Pakistan in this organization. More information available online at http://www.ecosecretariat.org/

[11] See Speech by Saparmurat Niyazov, President of Turkmenistan, at ECO Summit Meeting, Tehran, 10 June 2000. Available online at http://www.turkmenistanembassy.org/turkmen/news/speech.html

Both of these were important strategic moves for Turkmenistan but both required follow-on measures. In the case of Iran several important steps followed. Afghanistan, wracked by bloody insurrection, lacked the capacity to deliver on its assurances to Ashgabat, with serious consequences. The immediate effect of the rapprochement with Iran was that a massive volume of goods, mainly construction materials but also consumer goods, began moving from Turkey to the new capitals of Central Asia via Iranian and Turkmen highways.

The U.S., eager to support the economies of the new states, welcomed this development. Because of the unrest in Afghanistan, the closed border between Afghanistan and Pakistan, and the absence of infrastructure connecting Turkmenistan with Afghanistan, no analogous opening occurred to the southeast, Pakistan and beyond.

Traceca[12]

Meanwhile, in 1993 the European Union instituted a Transport Corridor Europe-Caucasus-Asia as a means of extending the European transport links across the southern belt of the former U.S.S.R. to China.[13] Significantly from the standpoint of Turkmenistan, the EU failed to anticipate at this time the possibility that such a corridor might eventually extend across Afghanistan to India and southeast Asia. Turkmenistan joined this project, which came to include a sea connection from Baku across the Caspian to Turkmenbashi and thence by road and railroad across Turkmenistan and Uzbekistan to Kyrgyzstan and on to China.

Unacknowledged in the planning for Traceca was the competition between a northern route via Kazakhstan and a northern route via Turkmenistan and Uzbekistan. Even had political conditions in Turkmenistan remained favorable, which they did not, this competition would have worked against the southern route, first, because the main road crossing and the only railroad

---

[12] For more information visit http://www.traceca-org.org

[13] ibid.

crossing to China was via Dostykh (formerly Druszhba) in Kazakhstan and, second, because the advantages of a southern route crossing Turkmenistan depended mainly on the possibility of a future link to southeast Asia, which the founders of Traceca did not recognize in their calculations. This is perhaps understandable in light of the chaos that still prevailed in Afghanistan at the time, but since Traceca was a long-term and strategic project, the failure is all the more glaring.

Further complicating Turkmenistan's situation were the beginnings of Russia's planning for a major north-south route to connect Russia and northern Europe to India via Iran. Given conditions in the 1990s in Afghanistan, it was mere realism for Russia, with India's help, to favor an Iranian route through the proposed expanded Iranian port on the Persian Gulf, Chahbakar.[14] Yet this scheme also contained a strong geopolitical element. By crossing Azerbaijan to Iran, Russia hoped to counter the impact of the Euro-American-sponsored Baku-Ceyhan pipeline on that country, and also to do nothing to increase the possibility of Turkmenistan's gaining a "window" to the south through which it might eventually seek to export to Asia its gas, which Russia's gas monopoly Gazprom greatly coveted.[15]

Confronted by these realities, Turkmenistan pushed for the alternative east-west route that would traverse its territory. At 6861 kilometers, the Turkmenbashi-Ashgabat-Tashkent-Almaty-Dostykh route from the Caspian to the Chinese border is slightly longer than the route via Kazakhstan but has the advantage of being shorter than the other projected trans-Asian highway traversing Iran. In the end, strained relations between Askhabat and Tashkent prevented Turkmenistan and Uzbekistan from presenting a united front on this project and undermined the effectiveness of their advocacy.

---

[14] See "Indo-Iranian Energy Cooperation" and "Indo-Russian Energy Cooperation." Available online at http://www.progress.org/2005/energy42.htm

[15] Gazprom was reorganized as an independent entity under a presidential decree on November 5, 1992. It became a Russian Share-Issuing Company "RAO Gazprom." A condition of privatization was that the government retains a 40 percent share in the company. Gazprom managers received 15 percent of share and 28 percent went to people living in Russia's gas-producing regions. See Victor, David G. and Nadejda Makarova Victor. "Diversifying Russian Gas Export to Europe." Paper Draft for Geopolitics and the Emergence of a Global Natural Gas Market, 2004. Available online at http://pesd.stanford.edu/gasdrafts.html

Turkmenistan therefore concentrated its efforts on railroads rather than highways.

The key task at the outset was to effect a connection between the Turkmen/Central Asian railroad network and that of Iran. Without this, direct transport from Turkey to Central Asia would be impossible. The project was rendered far more attractive when, in 1995, Iran completed a rail link between Bafq and its Persian Gulf port at Bandar Abbas, which finally linked the eastern Iranian city of Meshed with the Gulf. The next year Iran completed the 300 kilometer link between this line and the Turkmen city of Tejen, which adjoins the Iranian town of Sarakhs. In a spirit of celebration, Turkmenistan and Iran constructed a railroad station at Sarakhs worthy of a world capital, even though for the time being no trains ran there from either direction. In a similar forward-looking spirit, Iran and Turkmenistan established a Sarakhs Free Trade Zone along the border at this point,[16] hoping to lure businesses to what they hoped would become a trade zone of continental importance. Parallel with this, Turkmenistan lent its support to the ECO's effort to develop the Almaty-Tashkent-Ashgabat-Teheran rail line as a means of moving goods more easily from both Turkey and Iran to the formerly Soviet parts of Central Asia.[17]

While all this was proceeding, Turkmenistan undertook to expand the capacity of its Caspian port at Turkmenbashi. Compared to both the four Iranian ports on the Caspian and to Baku Turkmenbashi's facilities were limited. The question was whether the Kazakh port of Aktau or Turkmenistan's port of Turkmenbashi would become the main cargo entrepot on the eastern shore of the Caspian. In spite of Turkmenistan's efforts, Aktau prevailed, and for time being dominates the east-west movement of goods. Turkmenbashi could even the balance, however, if the Turkmen government fully embraces the cause of transport across its

---

[16] See "Free zone planned in northeast" in Middle East Economic Digest, 7 February 1997:17.

[17] For an Overview of the Economic Cooperation Organization during this period, "The Economic Cooperation Organization: Current Status and Future Prospects." by Pomfret, Richard, Europe-Asia Studies, Vol 49. No. 4, June 1997, pp. 657-667.

territory to and from Turkmenbashi from Afghanistan and the Indian subcontinent.

Parallel with Turkmenistan's partial success in the sphere of roads and railroads, Ashgabat moved to transform its aged airport into a modern facility capable of handling the transfer of goods on a continental scale.[18] It scored a success with the new facility but failed to follow up with Asian airlines to assure that the new airport became a fueling stop. By contrast, Uzbekistan was slow to redevelop its terminal at Tashkent but moved effectively to capture east-west cargo shipments from Korea to Europe. Nor did Turkmenistan's national airline compete effectively against Uzbek Air, which established direct links with western Europe and India via Tashkent and reaped considerable profits thereby.

Viewing Turkmenistan's transport initiatives in the 1990s as a whole, it is impossible not to acknowledge their shortcomings. In spite of these, considerable progress was achieved during these years. When the Central Asia-Caucasus Institute organized a region-wide conference on trade and transport in Ashgabat in 1997 the government of Turkmenistan was fully justified in presenting the country as an emerging link in continental transport.[19]

The real test of Ashgabat's policy, however, lay in its effectiveness in breaking Russian Gazprom's monopoly on the export of Turkmenistan's most valuable product, natural gas. For the time being, Turkmenistan failed the test, even though it made prodigious efforts to defend its economic interests. The obvious solution was to open a gas pipeline across Iran to the Persian Gulf. But gas-rich Iran is a competitor to Turkmenistan in the export of natural gas, and was under Russian pressure not to allow the construction of a "back door" export route for Turkmen gas. Moreover, such a pipeline was at odds with Washington's policy, which favored the export of Turkmen gas across the Caspian to Baku and a proposed gas pipeline to the Mediterranean.

---

[18] See endnote #2.

[19] See "Turkmenistan Hosts Caspian Summit" in the Central Asia Caucus Institute Analyst, April 23, 2002, Available online at http://www.cacianalyst.org/

Well aware of these possibilities, Niyazov resolved to extract from Gazprom a more favorable sale price of Turkmen gas to Russia. He knew that the Russians were using Turkmen gas for their domestic customers and selling their own gas to Europe for up to three times more than they were paying the Turkmens.[20] When Niyazov demanded more, Russia's prime minister, Chernomyrdin, a former head of Gazprom, simply cut off Turkmenistan's gas exports, immediately causing a crushing 25% drop in Turkmenistan's GDP.[21] Niyazov went personally to Moscow to complain. When Chernomyrdin lectured him to the effect that "Europe does not want your gas" Niyazov went directly to Europe and arranged substantial contracts for Turkmen gas.[22] So successfully and publicly did he defy Chernomyrdin that within six weeks Yeltsin had removed Chernomyrdin from office.

Niyazov won the battle but lost the war. Azerbaijan and Georgia were already using the proposed Baku-Ceyhan pipeline as a means of aligning themselves more closely with Europe, the U.S., and NATO. Having declared his country's non-alignment, it was impossible for Niyazov to follow this route, which under any circumstances would have elicited further reprisals from Moscow. Beyond this, Niyazov's relations with Azerbaijan's president Gaidar Aliyev were so poor that the two countries came nearly to open conflict over a disputed gas field in the Caspian. As a result, Niyazov had no choice but to swallow his pride and arrange a deal with Moscow. With this, all talk of a trans-Caspian pipeline from Turkmenistan to Azerbaijan was suspended in favor of a pipeline from Kazakhstan to Azerbaijan. As a kind of consolation prize, Russia allowed Turkmenistan to sign swap deals with Iran and to participate in the construction of a gas pipeline between Korbeje in Turkmenistan and Kordkuy in Iran to convey 8 billion cubic meters of gas to Iran.

---

[20] Turkmenistan stopped all gas shipments to Russia at the end of March 1997 and unilaterally abrogated their association with Turkmenrosgaz in June 1997. See "Turkmenistan Recent Developments." IMF Staff Country Report No. 99/140, December 10, 1999.

[21] See "Turkmenistan The Economic Base" in APS Review Downstream Trends, Sep 20, 2004. Available online at http://www.highbeam.com/doc/1G1-152080733.html

[22] Ottaway, David B. and Morgan, Dan "Gas Pipeline Bounces Between Agendas." Washington Post, October 5, 1998; Page A1. Available online at http://www.washingtonpost.com/wp-srv/inat/europe/caspian100598.htm

In the face of these developments, Turkmenistan had only one further card to play, namely a gas pipeline across Afghanistan to Pakistan and, if possible, onward to India. Such a project would not only break Gazprom's monopoly on the export of Turkmen gas to world markets but deftly avoid Iran as well.

The story of Ashgabat's efforts to develop this pipeline with the help of America's Unocal and the Argentine firm Bridas is by now well known and need not be repeated here.[23] Suffice it to say that Turkmenistan had laid its plan carefully, to the point of opening a constructive dialogue with the fragile Afghan government in Kabul and also with the chief warlords along the proposed route. Kabul was persuaded that Turkmenistan harbored no designs on the large Turkmen population in northwest Afghanistan and therefore welcomed the establishment of several Turkmen consulates in cities relevant to the pipeline's route. Direct talks among all the relevant parties were held in Asghgabat and Houston. But in the end the essential personal relations between Niyazov and his key partners descended into acrimony. As this was occurring, the Taliban rose to power in Afghanistan, which enormously increased the project's already high risk and cooled all American interest in it. This slammed shut Turkmenistan's last possible "back door" export route for gas.

Thus, by 2000 a many-sided effort by Turkmenistan to open itself to regional and continental trade in goods and energy had been substantially hobbled. An unlikely coalition consisting of Russia, the U.S., Iran, and (by its passivity) the E.U. had trimmed back Ashgabat's hopes. Traceca had turned its attention to the east-west transport route across Kazakhstan, Russia's projected north-south transit corridor assigned Turkmenistan only a secondary role, Gazprom's monopoly over the export of Turkmen gas had been confirmed for the time being, and Iran, while supporting various openings to Turkmenistan, helped thwart its aspirations vis a vis Afghanistan. Further undermining Turkmen hopes was the steady erosion of its relations with Azerbaijan and neighboring Uzbekistan.

---

[23] For an account of Unocal and Bridas' claims see article by Pope, Hugh. "Pipeline Dreams: How Two Firms Fight for Turkmenistan Gas Landed in Texas Court," Wall Street Journal, January 19, 1998. Gopul, Philip and Pavel Ivanov. "Learning the Rules of Central Asia's Energy Game." Asia Times, April 29, 1997.

Added to all this was the growing cult of personality that Niyazov engendered within Turkmenistan and the suppression of human rights that accompanied its development.[24] The kernel of justification for this cult can be found in Niyazov's realization that the absence of any strong national feeling among the diverse Turkmen tribes demanded special efforts on his part. His choice of populist economic policies patterned after those of Iran (free gas and electricity, etc.)[25] and of grandiose expenditures on national monuments at the expense of education and social welfare – not to mention the increasingly bizarre elements of the cult that came to surround his person – all combined to undermine Turkmenistan's efforts in the sphere of transport and trade and to isolate the country from many of its key regional and continental neighbors. True, there remained important links with Iran and the ECO, with its ambitious but ill-funded transport schemes, but these by no means counterbalanced the negative factors that had come into play by 2000.

Turkmenistan's Role in Transport and Trade Today

The new century witnessed important changes both within Turkmenistan and in Turkmenistan's relationship to issues of transport and trade. The arrest in December 2002 of former Minister of Foreign Affairs Boris Shikhmuradov on the charge that he was seeking to foment a revolution against President Niyazov[26] signaled a dramatic further increase in the concentration of power in the hands of the president. During the same period the government took a series of measures affecting religious minorities, education, and welfare that elicited strong criticism from both European countries and the U.S. The perception that the regard for human rights in Turkmenistan was steadily deteriorating caused the European Union and the

---

[24] Olcott, Martha, "International Gas Trade in Central Asia: Turkmenistan, Iran, Russia and Afghanistan." Program on Energy and Sustainable Development Working Paper #28, May 2004. Available online at http://iis-db.stanford.edu/pubs/20605/Turkmenistan_final.pdf

[25] See RFE/RL Central Asia Report, 22 August 2003.

[26] See RFE/RL Central Asia Report. Available online at http://www.rferl.org/specials/turkmenelections/bios/shikhmur.asp

United States to distance themselves from the Niyazov government.[27] By September, 2006, the European Parliament's Committee for International Trade put on holds its ratification of a provisional trade accord between the EU and Turkmenistan.[28] In announcing its decision, the Parliament declared it would approve the treaty "only when Ashgabat has made "apparent, discernible, and consistent progress in the sphere of human rights."[29]

As this climate coalesced in the years before 2006 it adversely affected investment in Turkmenistan. True, the Turkmen government had decided to allow foreign investment only in off-shore energy initiatives, on the unstated grounds that the presence of international investors might discourage other states (e.g. Russia) from taking action against such projects. The yields on gas sales assured steady economic growth, although the rate of expansion in the period 2001-2006 was surely much lower than the 17% claimed by the government. This in turn provided a kind of insurance policy for the government, protecting it from the worst affects of some of its more questionable policies.

It is tempting to suggest that Turkmenistan's actions were leading to the country's steadily deepening isolation. Yet as we will see, this is actually a period of realignment, in which at first Turkmenistan adopted a more "Asian" approach to trade and transport, as exemplified by its various openings to China and the renewal of its trans-Afghan pipeline project (Turkmenistan-Afghanistan-Pakistan-India, or TAPI),[30] and then, during 2006, began to revive its flagging transport relations with the West. Amidst this shifting picture, the three points of absolute consistency have been the country's steady engagement with ECO transport schemes, its consistent

---

[27] See U.S. Embassy in Ashgabat, 2002 Investment Climate Statement. Available online at http://www.bisnis.doc.gov/bisnis/isa/020819txics.htm

[28] See European Union's Relations with Turkmenistan various documents. Available online at http://ec.europa.eu/comm/external_relations/turkmenistan/intro/index.htm

[29] 09.10.2006 14:55 msk.

[30] The Trans-Afghanistan Pipeline (TAP or TAPI) is a proposed natural gas pipeline being developed by the Asian Development Bank. The pipeline will transport Caspian Sea natural gas from Turkmenistan through Afghanistan into Pakistan and then to India. For update on TAPI see Alexander's Gas & Oil, 21 November and 26 November 2006. Available online at http://www.gasandoil.com/goc/news/ntc64919.htm

efforts to improve transportation across the border with Iran, and its critically important relations with Russia's Gazprom.

Highways and Railroads

Having long been preoccupied with finding means of reaching reliable and high-priced markets for its gas, Turkmenistan has now returned to its earlier focus on roads and railroads. In the autumn of 2006 it announced its intention to redouble its efforts to integrate its highway and railroad systems more closely with continental east-west routes across Iran, and to begin by upgrading its main roads to both Afghanistan and Iran.[31]

Even though the main corridor for the Russian and Indian-sponsored north-south corridor traverses Azerbaijan rather than Turkmenistan, Ashgabat is now an active participant in that project and hopes to reap benefits from the secondary route that crosses its territory. It is also helping to upgrade the Afghan highway that extends from the Turkmen border to Diloram via the regional Afghan center of Herat. This initiative is part of Turkmenistan's participation in the six-country (Afghanistan, Iran, Pakistan, Tajikistan, Turkmenistan and Uzbekistan) Central-South Asian Transport and Trade Forum (CSATTF).[32] This undertaking is expected to reopen a series of road corridors centering on northwestern Afghanistan at a cost of $5.7 billion which, it is hoped, will come mainly from international donors.

Productive relations between Turkmenistan and Japan are reflected in Ashgabat's more active involvement with the Asia Development Bank and its many initiatives to improve continental transport in Greater Central Asia. In addition to financing road corridor projects in the country, ADB has

---

[31] See "Ministry of motor transportation of Turkmenistan to act as customer in modernization of country's main road" August 14, 2006. Available online at http://www.turkmenistan.ru/?page_id=3&lang_id=en&elem_id=8475&type=event&sort=date_desc

[32] See Asian Development Bank document "Central and South Asia Transport and Trade Forum (CSATTF): Toward Harmonization and Modernization of Transit Transport Agreements among the CSATTF countries." Available online at http://www.afghanistan-mfa.net/RECC/CSATTF_PADECO_Transit_Report.pdf

proposed a Central-South Asian Transport Corridor Fund,[33] which is seeking donors from beyond the region.

Given Turkmenistan's cooperation with ADB, it is the more surprising that Ashgabat is not yet a participant in ADB's six-member (Azerbaijan, Kazakhstan, Kyrgyzstan, Mongolia, Tajikistan, Uzbekistan) Trade Facilitation Program, which is part of the Central Asia Regional Economic Cooperation (CAREC) Program.[34] This program is designed to promote a common customs regimen among all the countries of Greater Central Asia, and also to bring participating countries under the TIR (Transport International Routière) transit system.[35] Whether Turkmenistan will become part of this system remains unclear. Given the specific impediments to land transport that exist as a result of Turkmen border policies and procedures, it would be highly desirable for this to happen.

For all its demonstrated interest in improving its continental road and railroad links, Turkmenistan's border regimen is still plagued by the same impediments that hamper most of its neighbors. As detailed in the chapter on Tajikistan in this volume, Turkmenistan's border procedures are very time-consuming, with delays caused by the need for signatures from multiple agencies on all documents and slow inspection procedures. Moreover, Turkmenistan's border crossings are hampered by the poor enforcement of existing legislation, the absence of an industry capable of providing low cost and effective insurance to shippers, and the absence of coordination between the customs services of Turkmenistan and its neighbors.

Beyond this, border stations and related trade offices in the capital are understaffed and manned by personnel who are underpaid and under-trained.

---

[33] See Asian Development Report "Interim Comprehensive Action Plan" Southern Transport Corridor Road. Available online at www.adb.org/Documents/Events/2005/CAREC/4th-Conference/icap-executive-summary.pdf

[34] See Asian Development Report "The Central Asia Regional Economic Cooperation (CAREC), Recent initiatives under CAREC's Trade Facilitation Program." Available online at www.adb.org/Documents/CSPs/CAREC/2006/CSPU-CAREC-2006.pdf

[35] The TIR (Transport InternationalRoutière) procedures ensure that customs in a transit country will receive proper payment for dues and duties. Also see, Central Asia: Increasing Gains from Trade Through Regional Ties." More information is available online at www.adb.org/Documents/Reports/CA-Trade-Policy/prelims.pdf

This leads inevitably to graft and corruption, which are widespread. Irregular inspections and unsanctioned demands that shipments be accompanied by Turkmen officials can be avoided only through bribes to local officials. Until these conditions are alleviated, Turkmenistan's own land transport, as well as continental trade crossing Turkmenistan, will be laboring under debilitating handicaps. As long as such handicaps remain, Turkmenistan will suffer a competitive disadvantage as compared with Kazakhstan, Azerbaijan, and other key north-south and east-west transport alternatives.

The Port of Turkmenbashi

Competition with neighboring states is even more keen in the area of shipping on the Caspian. The capacity of Baku's port is being greatly augmented, as is that of Kazakhstan's port of Aktau, through the addition of new berths and facilities. Iran is investing far more in each of its several Caspian ports than is Turkmenistan at its one port at Turkmenbashi. Moreover, seaport fees at Turkmenbashi are higher than those at Baku and Aktau, and also the Iranian ports. As a result, Turkmenistan is gradually losing out in the competition for both north-south and east-west transport across the Caspian.

It is unclear whether this problem traces to a lack of money or of political will. Whatever the case, even though the route through Turkmenbashi is shorter than the one through Iran, Turkmenistan is in danger of losing out to Iran in the competition for handling trans-Caspian traffic originating in southeast Asia, India, Pakistan, and Afghanistan. The practical consequence of this is that Turkmenistan will lose millions in port, tariff and transit fees, while international shippers along key routes will suffer under the burden imposed by longer routes.

Airports and Airlines

Compared with its neighbors Kazakhstan and Uzbekistan, Turkmenistan has so far been a passive presence in the field of air transport. True, the airport at Ashgabat was handsomely reconstructed and equipped with up-to-date equipment for monitoring the contents of even large shipments and containers. But few follow-up measures have occurred, with the result that the country is best served by foreign (mainly Turkish) airlines and has failed to establish itself as a regional hub or even a significant fueling stop for continental air transit. Worse, there have been several apparently-well-based accusations that the airport at Ashgabat has become a hub for the drug cartels, frequented by traffickers as far away as Nigeria and even Colombia.

The Export of Electricity

The same Moscow-centric transport links that tied Turkmenistan's gas to Gazprom tied its electricity to the all-Soviet grid. However, in this sphere Turkmenistan has broken out of the former Soviet system and built the necessary transmission lines to establish direct exports of electricity to both Iran and Afghanistan. Both U.S.'s General Electric and Power Machines of Russia have been engaged modernizing the vast thermonuclear facility at Mary, which is the key to this export. By 2006 Iran was importing 400 megawatts during the first half of each year, only to sell back a similar amount during the second half, thus satisfying the annual cycle of energy needs in both countries.

The Transport of Gas

For understandable reasons, a major strategic goal of Turkmenistan's transport program has been to find ways of marketing its most valuable product, natural gas, at the highest possible price and with the least exposure to sudden shifts.

The construction of a 200 kilometer pipeline between the Turkmenistan town of Korpedzhe and Kord-Kuy in Iran assured the export of 8 billion cubic meters of gas each year into Iran's network. With Iranian financing, this pipeline is expected to become part of a larger system for exporting Turkmen gas to Turkey. The steady improvement of Turkmenistan's relations with Iran in the sphere of gas transport was symbolized by the joint decision in the summer of 2006 to increase Turkmenistan's annual export to the Iranian grid to 14 billion cubic meters.

Besides this important link, Turkmenistan has actively pursued three important new markets for its gas, and is exploring the feasibility of three new export routes for gas, any or all of which will have the strategically crucial effect of breaking the near-absolute monopoly exercised by Russia's Gazprom over Turkmen energy exports. If this stranglehold is broken, it will become a critically important step towards the redefinition of Greater Central Asia as a whole. Beyond this, it will remove a crucial impediment to the development of Turkmenistan's economy. The low capacity of the main Gazprom pipeline running north to Russia and the absence of alternatives constrains the development of Turkmenistan's gas industry and will continue to do so until one of the following three alternatives is realized.

The Turkmenistan-Afghanistan-Pakistan-India pipeline (TAPI)[36]

No transport project in Central Asia has generated greater expectations and met with more frustrations in practice than the proposed gas pipeline from Turkmenistan to Pakistan and beyond via Afghanistan. Originally conceived by the Turkmenistan government as early as 1992, it soon attracted both the American firm Unocal and the Argentinean firm Bridas as partners.[37] The rise of the Taliban and deteriorating relations between Ashgabat and its foreign partners led to the suspension of the project in 1997. Only after the U.S. crushed the Taliban government in Kabul in 2002 did the project revive. In that year the Asian Development Bank launched a feasibility study that would eventually result in a promising report.[38] In May of the same year the heads of state of Turkmenistan, Afghanistan and Pakistan met in Islamabad and set up a ministerial level steering committee to give fresh impetus to the project.

Plans called for the construction over five years of a 1,700 kilometer pipeline from Turkmenistan's Dauletabad gas field to Multan in Pakistan via Herat

[36] See endnote #30.

[37] See endnote #23

[38] The Asian Development Bank conducted a feasibility study on building a gas pipeline connecting Turkmenistan, Afghanistan, and Pakistan. The framework agreement for the development of the project was signed by the heads of the three governments in December 2002 and the feasibility study was presented to the heads of state in 2005. For a Power Point presentation on feasibility study see http://meaindia.nic.in/srec/internalpages/tapi.pdf and for more information on the project see www.adb.org

and Khandahar at a cost of $3.3 billion.[39] A more northerly route through Kabul and Peshawar was also considered. Far shorter than the Khandahar route, this advantage was more than offset by the need to route the pipeline through the Uzbek border town of Termez, thus giving Tashkent a veto over the project, and by the need to traverse more densely populated areas of Afghanistan.

Indications that the ADB study would reach a positive conclusion encouraged India to join. Earlier, India, Pakistan and Iran had been negotiating a direct pipeline across the Baluchistan provinces of Iran and Pakistan to India. However, both Iran and India were well aware of the mounting political unrest in Pakistan-ruled Baluchistan. Moreover, the U.S. made clear that it would not support such an alternative that would bypass Afghanistan, let alone one that would reinforce India's dependence on Iranian gas. When Delhi understood that funding for this variant would be nearly impossible to arrange it asked to join the trans-Afghan project, proposing at a 2005 meeting in Ashgabat that the project be expanded to include the transport of both gas and oil.

It was at this point that doubts were raised concerning the size of the Dauletabad reserves. Turkmenistan blamed these on disinformation being disseminated by Russia's Gazprom and engaged a U.S. exploration firm to provide an authoritative estimate of the actual reserves available. According to the Turkmenistan government, the resulting estimates far exceeded Ashgabat's own claims. But since the report itself has yet to be released, the doubts remain, and have so far served as a brake on financing. A meeting held in Delhi in November, 2006, heard reports of progress on the financing but to date no firm package is in hand. Equally serious, Pakistan remains reluctant to become a guarantor of gas deliveries to India until the two countries have achieved some sort of settlement in their dispute over Kashmir.

---

39 See article "Gas pipeline project Turkmenistan-Afghanistan-Pakistan-India approved." Available online at http://www.turkmenistan.ru

An Export Pipeline for Turkmen Gas to China?

In the midst of these negotiations, nearly the entire government of Turkmenistan headed to Beijing in April 2006, to hear proposals for large-scale purchases by China of Turkmen gas.[40] Former Foreign Minister Shikmuradov had launched this project while serving as Turkmen ambassador to China and before his arrest by President Niyazov. The resulting agreement committed Turkmenistan to long-term sales of gas to China, but at the time it had neither a pipeline to transport gas eastward nor the gas to fill it. The former problem was solved, in theory at least, when in August 2006 President Niyazov announced Turkmenistan's intention of building a gas pipeline to China by 2009, through which it would supply China with 30 billion cubic meters of natural gas annually for 30 years. The second problem took on an entirely new face in November 2006, when Turkmenistan announced the discovery of a "super giant" gas field at Yolotan containing a purported seven trillion cubic meters of gas.[41] Ashgabat accordingly awarded the Chinese National Petroleum Company a $151-million exploration contract to drill in the gas deposits in Yolotan.

A Trans-Caspian Pipeline to Baku?

The autumn of 2006 transformed the entire issue concerning the transport of Turkmenistan's gas to world markets. Ashgabat had signed its commitment to China and at the same time was pursuing the more intricate issue of a pipeline to India via Afghanistan. In an attempt to clarify the situation, in October 2006, Niyazov declared that the two priority markets for Turkmen gas were China and Russia.

---

[40] Hancock, Kathleen J., "Escaping Russia, Looking to 'China: Turkmenistan Pins Hopes on China's Thirst for Natural Gas" China and Eurasia Forum Quarterly, volume 4, No 3 (2006) p. 67-87, Central Asia-Caucus Institute & Silk Road Studies Program. Available online at http://www.silkroadstudies.org/new/docs/CEF/Quarterly/August_2006/Hancock.pdf Also see, Pannier, Bruce and O'Rourke, Breffni, "Turkmenistan: President Seeks Economic, Political Links With China" April 3, 2006. Available online at http://www.rferl.org/featuresarticle/2006/04/6a60e94b-6f54-4dd7-a4bb-664475d53d03.html

[41] See "Turkmenistan: Potential 'Super-Giant" Emerges on Energy Scene." *RFE/RL Central Asia Report*, 13 November 2006.

Besides sowing doubts about his government's commitment to the Afghan project and to India, this announcement seems deliberately to have obfuscated the fact that Turkmenistan had entered into a series of new discussions with both the European Union and the United States regarding the possibility of a trans-Caspian gas pipeline that would tie into the rapidly emerging east-west energy corridor via Azerbaijan.

This project dated to the mid-1990s when plans were being laid for the Baku-Ceyhan oil pipeline. It had foundered, however, over three specific issues. First, a cash-starved Turkmenistan had demanded large up-front payments that the BTC consortium was unwilling to consider. Second, Russia and Iran were actively contesting the legal status of the Caspian seabed. Third, Russia had already announced it would raise environmental arguments against the construction of such a pipeline. Fourth, personal relations between President Niyazov and President Geidar Aliev of Azerbaijan had deteriorated disastrously, culminating in an active conflict over a Caspian gas field. And, fifth, Russia's Gazprom indicated a willingness to raise somewhat the very low price it had been offering for Turkmenistan's gas.

Several equally germane factors in 2005-2006 changed this picture. First, the successful completion of the BTC project made the development of trans-Caspian links to the Baku-Ceyhan east-west energy corridor a realistic possibility. Second, Kazakhstan's declaration that it would build a pipeline from its port of Aktau to Baku raised the stakes for Ashgabat. Most important, the surge in world energy prices, combined with Gazprom's politically-charged pressure on both Ukraine and the EU, brought the Europeans to Ashgabat in search of a source of gas that would be free of Gazprom's direct control.

The dynamics of this new state of affairs are ably reviewed in the chapter on Azerbaijan in this volume. Prior to this new situation, Europe had been extremely cool towards Turkmenistan, sharply criticizing its record in the area of human rights and the rule of law. The United States had shared this critical stance, suspending nearly all contact with Ashgabat over a trans-Caspian pipeline over a period of half a decade.

The rise in gas prices, Gazprom's ham-handed moves in Europe, and the completion of the BTC project caused both to reconsider. Visits by

Germany's Foreign Minister, by the EU's special representative for central Asia, and by the U.S. Deputy Assistant Secretary of State for the Caucasus region signaled a willingness to revive discussions of the dormant project to link the port of Turkmenbashi to Baku via a seabed gas pipeline.[42] Indeed, Pierre Morel, the EU's special representative and himself a former French ambassador to Ashgabat, declared to President Niyazov in a meeting broadcast on Turkmenistan's national television that "The European Union is highly interested in bolstering and expanding full-scale cooperation with Turkmenistan; the EU views the country as a reliable and responsible partner."[43] At the same a further element in the strengthening of demand to Turkmenistan's west was an agreement struck between Ashgabat and Turkey, according to which Turkmenistan would provide 10 bcm of gas to Turkey by a trans-Caspian pipeline that had yet to be planned, let alone constructed. In an effort to keep alive this project without entering into further commitments regarding a trans-Caspian pipeline, Niyazov in November 2006, engaged the Turkish Çalik Energy Company to work along with the Chinese in exploring and developing the Yolotan gas field.[44]

Russia's Response and Ashgabat's Uncertainties

Singly or together, Turkmenistan's three potential projects for developing gas/oil transport between Turkmenistan, Europe, and Asia represent a fundamental change in the overall transportation map of Eurasia. By reopening direct transport in energy between Turkmenistan and India/Pakistan, China, and Europe, respectively, each would return to the territory of Turkmenistan that central role in the overall movement of valuable commodities between Europe and Asia that it had enjoyed over the millennia prior to the sixteenth century.

However, it is important to note that these projects would accomplish this at the expense of the monopoly over the international transport of Turkmen

---

[42] Socor, Vladimir, "Interest Rebounds in a Trans-Caspian Pipeline for Turkmen Gas," *Eurasia Daily Monitor*, 24 January 2006.

[43] See Ziyadov, Taleh, "Europe Hopes To Revive Trans-Caspian Energy Pipelines," *Eurasia Daily Monitor*, Vol. 3, Issue 38, February 24, 2006.

[44] "Weekly News Brief on Turkmenistan," December 8-14, 2006, The Turkmenistan Project.

gas that Gazprom had imposed during the Soviet era and which is one of the USSR's chief legacies to post-Soviet Russia.

How, then, has Russia expanded to these potential projects? Regarding the trans-Afghan pipeline Russia has long made its staunch opposition perfectly clear. By breaking Gazprom's monopoly on the export of Turkmen gas this pipeline would enable Ashgabat to drive a harder bargain on prices that Gazprom would have to offer. Moreover, it would go far towards confirming the success of the new government in Kabul, which enjoys a strategic partnership with the United States and close ties with the EU. For these reasons Russia strongly backed Iran and India in their unsuccessful effort to create a direct Iran-Pakistan-India pipeline. The fact that India, upon the collapse of this project, moved immediately to join the trans-Afghan TAPI project, signaled clearly the new realities with which Russia has to contend.[45] In this instance Russia's voice was neutralized by the Afghan Foreign Minister Dadfar Spanta, who, at the New Delhi conference, urged Islamabad to allow his country a transport corridor to India. Pakistan acceded, or so it seems.

Russia did not end the year 2006 empty-handed with respect to Turkmenistan's gas. In September Gazprom and Turkmenistan announced a further agreement on the transport of gas to Russia. But since this required Russia to offer a substantial greater payment than heretofore, and since the agreement is only for three years, it can hardly be seen as a victory for Gazprom. Against this background, and in the context of Ashgabat's agreement with China and its revived interest in the EU/US project for a trans-Caspian pipeline, President Niyazov's announcement that Turkmenistan views Russia and China as the priority markets for its gas is at best a pyrrhic victory for Gazprom.

The End of the Niyazov Era and Turkmenistan's Future as an East-West and North-South Transport Hub

Just as these diverse developments in road, railroad, electricity, gas, and oil transport were reaching a crescendo, President Niyazov died on 21 November

[45] Yunanov, Boris, "Gas Pipeline to India may become problem for India-Russian relations," *Novye izvestiia*, 21 November 2006.

2006. It is too early even to do more than speculate on Turkmenistan's future as an east-west and north-south hub for continental transport across Eurasia. However, a few factors that will affect the long-term evolution of Turkmenistan's policies can be enumerated.

First, it should be noted that the east-west corridor poses problems for Turkmenistan's strategic posture of non-alignment. Initially, the US and European sponsors of the Baku-Ceyhan pipeline viewed it as a means of undergirding the sovereignty of the new and fragile states of Azerbaijan and Georgia. As noted in the chapter on Azerbaijan, however, these two states see the project and its possible further extensions to Kazakhstan and Turkmenistan as a means of linking their overall security more closely with the West, specifically with NATO and the EU. Over time their perspective has gained credibility in both Washington and Brussels. Besides eliciting fears in Moscow, this poses a challenge to Ashgabat to find a path for engaging with western gas markets without sacrificing its non-aligned status. Should a post-Niyazov government in Ashgabat decide to modify that strategy, it will require a fundamental rethinking of the country's national security strategy and feasible tactics for implementing it. Given Gazprom's huge stake in its Turkmenistan pipeline, and Russia's overall strategy of neo-imperial assertiveness, this will not be easy, to say the least.

This said, it is also important to acknowledge the extent to which the new realities affecting Turkmenistan are driven not merely by political calculations but by fundamental economic forces that will make themselves feel independent of Ashgabat's calculations. China, India, and Europe all need Turkmenistan's gas and will not readily accede to arrangements in which any third party can exercise a veto over its export to their territory. Whether the situation is considered from the basis of free global market principles or of Marxist calculations on the primacy of economic forces, it would appear that Turkmenistan is fated once more to assume the geo-economic role its territory played over the millennia.

All of this would by now have produced "facts on the ground" were it not for the ambitious effort of the Putin government in Moscow to reassert the controlling influence that Russia exercised over Turkmenistan since the battle of Goek Tepe more than a century ago. This review has shown that this effort has extended to Turkmenistan's plans for roads, railroads, and pipelines, and that in all of these areas it has been countered by other major powers, including not only the United States but also China, India, Turkey, and the European Union. The urgency of the energy needs of these last countries is such that it is hard to imagine that in the end they will not prevail.

There are solid grounds for thinking that Russia will eventually make its peace with the powerful global forces that are at play in Turkmenistan. It has moved a long way in this direction in its relations with Kazakhstan, where many of the same forces are at work. Not only has it accepted Kazakhstan's assertion of its right to export oil and gas directly to China, but it is fighting a rear-guard action against that country's desire to export energy directly to the West. Moreover, Kazakhstan is proceeding with its plans with Traceca to open an east-west transport corridor to China, even though these compete directly with Russia's aspirations to create and control a more northern corridor through its territory.

All this has been possible because Kazakhstan has developed a security strategy based on strategic partnerships with China, the U.S., and, of course, Russia itself.[46] The key to this strategy is the concept of "balance." It is quite possible that the new government in Ashgabat will move towards such an arrangement, with the balance in Turkmenistan's case including Iran, Russia, China, India, and the E.U. and U.S. Such a policy could not only preserve the principle of non-alignment but give it a new reality in the post-Niyazov era.

---

[46] Starr, S. Frederick, "Kazakhstan's Security Strategy: A Model for Central Asia?", forthcoming.

Iran

Abbas Maleki

Iran's security is affected by a broad region that includes the Caspian Basin, Central Asia, Afghanistan, the Persian Gulf states, Pakistan, Turkey, and the Middle East. However, an increased focus on the countries of the Economic Cooperation Organization (ECO), as well as Iraq, on the one hand, and with members of the Gulf Cooperation Council (GCC) (including Yemen) on the other, provides a natural starting point in the search for building blocks of a future regional security mechanism.

Historical Background

Throughout history, except for the two most recent centuries, Afghanistan was part of various Iranian empires. The British Empire in India forced Iran to withdraw from the eastern part of Afghanistan and Herat. To recapture the city, the British Navy attacked the port of Bushehr in the Persian Gulf. Iranian troops withdrew from Herat. Afghanistan then served as a buffer between the British and Russian empires until it won independence from British control in 1919. Following Afghan independence Iran and Afghanistan maintained good relations. Iran sponsored cultural activities in various cities of Afghanistan and built a pipeline for sending petroleum from Mashad to Afghanistan's Herat. A brief experiment in democracy ended in a 1973 coup and a 1978 Communist counter-coup. The Soviet Union invaded in 1979 to support the tottering Afghan Communist regime and Iran hosted millions of Afghan refugees for decades. The Taliban, a hard-line movement sponsored by Pakistan that emerged in 1994, seized Kabul and most of Afghanistan except for the Northern Alliance's strongholds by 1998.

There was a serious risk that Iran might be drawn directly into the conflict, especially following the murder of ten Iranian diplomats when the Taliban took Mazar-i-Sharif in August, 1998. Even aside from this danger the conflict was costly to Iran, which gave expensive but covert support to Shi'ia and other anti-Taliban groups, coped with a large number of refugees, and found itself in the front line of the difficult struggle against drug trafficking. Such trafficking caused the spread of drug abuse within Iran itself.[1]

The tragic event of 11 September 2001 and the US military campaign against the Taliban regime in Afghanistan relieved Iran of the Taliban threat but did not improve its security overall.[2] U.S. forces and the Northern Alliance that benefited from Iranian military support, eventually toppled the Taliban. Iran supported the state-building process defined by the United Nations Bonn Conference. On 9 October 2004 Hamid Karzai became the first elected president of Afghanistan, while a National Assembly was inaugurated on 19 December 2005. Iran pledged $580 million for Afghan reconstruction.

Regionalism as a Priority in Iran's Foreign Policy

The combination of strategic location and rich energy resources made Iran a focus of great power competition throughout the modern period. This fact has profoundly affected Iranians' perceptions of the world and of international relations.[3] Iran is situated at the heart of the world's most important petroleum hub and also controls crucial transportation routes entering the landlocked countries of Central Asia with the high seas[4]. Its geographic diversity, skilled and semi-skilled workforce, and domination

---

[1] Herzig, Edmund, "Regionalism, Iran and Central Asia"; *International Affairs*; vol. 80 no. 3, 2004, 503-517.

[2] Hunter, Shireen, "Iran's Pragmatic Regional Policy"; *Journal of International Affairs*, vol. 56 no. 2, spring 2003.

[3] Fuller, Graham, *the Centre of the Universe: the Geopolitics of Iran;* Boulder, CO: Westview Press, 1990,pp. 17-23.

[4] Acemuglu, Murat, "Iran key state in Caucasian and Central Asia", *Armenian Reporter International;* vol. 32 no. 19, 1999.

of strategic and communication routes all contribute to this country's central role in regional affairs.[5]

Since the end of the war with Iraq (1988) and the death of Ayatollah Khomeini (1989), the Islamic Republic of Iran has accorded regional relations and coalition building an increasingly important place in its foreign policy. The prospects for regional cooperation, whether with Saudi Arabia, Turkey or Pakistan, or with the small and vulnerable states of the Persian Gulf coast were limited. Prospects for Iranian engagement in multilateral regional cooperation with its new northern neighbors following the dissolution of the USSR in 1991 were hardly more promising.

Regionalism first began to assume prominence in Iranian foreign policy during the presidency of Akbar Hashemi Rafsanjani (1989–97). Following the Iranian war with Iraq, the urgent need for reconstruction and, more generally, for social and economic development to meet the needs of a young population, forced policy-makers to focus on material needs in all areas.In foreign relations this was expressed in an emphasis on expanding trade and attracting investment through the development of mutually beneficial state-to-state relations and through closer integration into the global economy.

In time the change in emphasis led to improvements in Iran's relations with a number of countries but not, crucially, with the United States. In spite of a number of tentative moves towards rapprochement, this relationship deteriorated further. By the end of the Iran–Iraq War the significantly reinforced U.S. Navy in the Persian Gulf was involved in direct confrontations with Iranian forces, exposing the latter's weakness and vulnerability. Following the 1990–91 Persian Gulf War, Washington adopted a policy of 'dual containment' towards Iraq and Iran, which it branded as the region's two 'rogue' states. The collapse of the Soviet Union coincided with this shift, depriving the Islamic Republic of its

---

[5] Meshkini, Qadir Nasri, "Challenges and Imperatives of the Iranian Policy in Central Asia", *Amu Darya: The Iranian Journal of Central Asian studies*, vol. 4 no. 5, 2000; pp. 73-101.

main potential counterbalance to the threat posed by US global pre-eminence.[6]

To counter Washington's efforts to isolate Iran became an important objective for Tehran in its own right. In search of ways to frustrate Washington's policy of containment Tehran looked towards cooperation with nearby and Muslim states and with possible alternative major centers of power (Russia, China, Europe, India). It also sought to use those regional and international organizations that were not susceptible to western domination - for example, the Non-Aligned Movement, the Organization of Islamic Conference (OIC), and the Organization of Petroleum Exporting Countries (OPEC)-for the same purpose. More recently Tehran has gained observer status in the Shanghai Cooperation Organization. The constant themes of Iranian statements on regionalism have been self-reliance among regional states and the exclusion of extra-regional powers, specifically the United States.

Iran's geographical position, size, economic stature, and military muscle give it the potential to play a leading or pivotal role in the Persian Gulf, Greater Central Asia and the Caspian Basin. The collapse of the Soviet Union gave rise to a new awareness in Iran of the possibilities presented by the country's strength relative to other regional states and its geographical location at the heart of the Eurasian continent. The perception of Iran's natural role as a major regional power has increased not only in government but across a wide spectrum of elite and popular opinion. Participation in groupings that exclude extra-regional powers enables Iran to fulfill its proper role in a way that it cannot currently do within the international system, given the nature of its relations with the United States.

Iran's conversion to regionalism can best be understood as the response of a relatively weak state to the external challenge posed by the strong, in circumstances when the balancing option was taken out of play by the end of the Cold War. President Rafsanjani and his successors,

---

[6] Herzig, Edmund, "Regionalism, Iran and Central Asia"; *International Affairs*, vol. 80 no. 3, 2004, 503-517.

Muhammad Khatami, and President Ahmadi Nejad, have all placed a strong emphasis on regional relations. Khatami's foreign minister, Kamal Kharrazi, stated in his first address to the UN General Assembly in 1997 that "Iran's highest foreign policy priority ... is to strengthen trust and confidence and peace in our immediate neighborhood." The present Foreign Minister of Iran, Manouchehr Mottaki, has stated that the priority of Iran's foreign policy is to strengthen its Asian identity as opposed to its Middle Eastern identity.

This debate derives from a conception of the world as a set of interlinked and overlapping regions. The emergence and reinforcement of these regions and their internal and mutual linkages is held to be a part of a benign globalization process that will limit the capacity of any single power to dominate the system. Iranian conceptions of regionalism attach great importance to culture, both as a defining feature and as a basis for cooperation.[7]

Iran's Economy

Over the past ten years Iran's annual economic growth averaged 4.3 percent, while the unemployment rate – which has been the basic headache for every Iranian president – remained above 10 percent. During this time, the growth rate was as high as 7.5 percent (in 2002), while the unemployment rate peaked at 14.2 percent (in 2001). In U.S. dollar terms, GDP increased from $100 billion to $150 billion during Mr. Khatami's presidency.[8] The other headache – the inflation rate – averaged 15.8 percent, partly reflecting the high growth of bank liquidity, itself due to large government budget deficits.

Iranians' per capita income increased during these eight years, thanks to economic expansion and declining rates of population growth. Domestic and foreign investment also increased. Domestic investment's annual growth rate averaged 8.8 percent. Foreign direct investment was nil in

---

[7] Herzig, Edmund, "Regionalism, Iran and Central Asia", *International Affairs,* vol. 80 no. 3, 2004, 503-517.
[8] Pourian, Heydar, Iran Economics: from Mr. Khatami to Mr. Ahmadi Nejad, *Iran Economics,* Dec. 2005.

1997 but increased to $1.5 billion by 2004, above all in energy. The oil sector's share of the gross domestic product (GDP) increased from 9.26 to 13.2 percent. Had oil prices remained at 1997-98 levels, Iran's economic development would have ceased.

During 1997-2005 the growth rate of exports (including oil, gas and petrochemicals) was 12.5 percent, while non-oil exports averaged 12.3 percent. Imports grew at 12.5 percent annually. There are pockets of critics who argue that excessive imports during this period damaged Iranian industries and increased the unemployment rate. And since some of the imports were consumer goods, it is claimed that the country wasted its potential savings. In the meantime, the smuggling of commercial goods into Iran has exacerbated the situation.

Other accomplishments during this time include the expansion of road networks and agricultural improvements (including levels of wheat production that transformed Iran from the largest importer of wheat in the world to self-sufficiency). Meanwhile, a new tax law lowered corporate rates from 64 percent to 25 percent. Revisions in the law on foreign direct investment, modern securities law, lowered tariffs, the establishment of an Oil Stabilization Fund (OSF), exchange rate unification, and discipline in foreign debt have all helped strengthen the Iranian economy.

Nonetheless, the ratio of the governmental budget (including state-owned enterprises and state-sponsored entities) to GDP increased from 67 percent to 88 percent, reflecting the growing governmental share of the economy, despite government plans to promote privatization.

Finally, in 2001, for the first time since 1989, banking licenses were issued to private groups. In spite of some progress and development, Iran's status in the region has lagged. During 1997-2005, a total of $170 billion was earned as oil revenues. Critics argue that this amount (more than one-year's GDP) could have renewed the engine of industry had it been spent wisely. Observers also point out that foreign boycotts are continually hurting Iran and increasing the cost of doing business.

In the social sphere, while the number of marriages has increased from 512,000 to 680,000, (a 32 percent increase) during this period, the number of divorces has increased by more than 70 percent, from 42,000 to 72,000.

Cooperation in the Framework of ECO

The Economic Cooperation Organization (ECO) is the only major regional grouping of which Iran is a member. The ECO is a regional intergovernmental organization consisting of Pakistan, Iran, Turkey, Afghanistan, Azerbaijan, Turkmenistan, Uzbekistan, Tajikistan, Kyrgyzstan, and Kazakhstan. ECO may not be able to develop a soft security dimension for some time, but the organization can promote cooperation in trade liberalization, energy, migration issues and other "soft" security issues.

ECO is the successor organization to the Regional Cooperation for Development (RCD), which was established in 1964 by the triumvirate of Iran, Turkey, and Pakistan as an agent against Soviet Communism. Abandoned by Iran after the 1979 revolution, RCD was nonetheless revived and transformed into the present SCO.

The first ECO summit in Tehran and a subsequence extraordinary meeting of the ECO Council of Ministers in Islamabad (November 1992) culminated in the accession to ECO of five Central Asian republics as well as Azerbaijan and Afghanistan.[9] ECO member states work to promote intra-regional trade and took significant steps to improve regulatory frameworks and remove tariff and non-tariff barriers. The regional trade situation, however, is far from satisfactory when compared to earlier years and prospects of an imminent change do not seem likely unless private initiatives, backed by the political will of the member states, are given momentum. So far, the scope and depth of trade linkages served as the main channel for the transmission of external shocks between the member states. The total intra-regional trade volume of

---

[9] Afrasiabi, K & Pour Jalali, Y. The Economic Cooperation Organization: Regionalization in a competitive Context; *Mediterranean Quarterly*, Fall 2001.

the ECO region increased to $16.7 billion in 2004 (excluding Afghanistan) compared to $10.2 billion in 2002.[10]

According to 2004 statistics, the share of Iran's intra-regional exports was just 2.7 percent, with Kazakhstan at 5.7 percent, and Pakistan and Turkey at 6.7 percent and 3.5 percent, respectively; Azerbaijan amounted to 15 percent of the total, Kyrgyzstan to 22.0 percent, Tajikistan for 13.3 percent, and Turkmenistan and Uzbekistan for 23.7 percent and 15.8 percent, respectively. In most ECO countries the governments are moving ahead to reduce or remove trade barriers, deregulate internal markets, and privatize and liberalize investment flows. In some cases liberalization has been extended to such service industries as telecommunications, transportation and power generation and distribution, previously closed to foreign investors. Most of the countries have concluded bilateral treaties to protect FDI and avoid double taxation. Despite a global decline in FDI, several transition economies of ECO continued to see strong capital inflows. The resource inflows were uneven, however, with the oil and gas sectors in Azerbaijan, Kazakhstan, and Turkmenistan remaining the most attractive areas for FDI.

The short-term outlook remains favorable for countries of the region. ECO countries as a group are growing faster than the global economy, as well as some other groups of countries. This progress is providing greater stability in exchange rates and a more stable environment for investment, both domestic and foreign. However, institutional progress has been slower and more uneven, especially in the financial sector.

The region's short- and medium-term prospects depend critically on the implementation of structural reforms. The recent improvement in the region's growth performance has not made a significant dent in unemployment or brought about a sizable reduction in poverty. Yet the good macroeconomic performance of the last few years provides an opportunity to address these longstanding problems in the ECO region. And the favorable current economic outlook will present a timely

---

[10] www.ecosecretariat.org, as March 15, 2006.

opportunity to strengthen policies aimed at resolving macroeconomic imbalances, addressing the fragility of banking and financial systems, and implementing structural reforms.

Assuming robust growth in ECO countries over the next years, and in the absence of major unforeseen shocks, aggregate GDP growth for the ECO region should have been 6.4 percent in 2006. Although economic growth in ECO region is projected to settle to more sustainable rates after 2006, the oil and gas sector and intraregional trade and strong consumer demand will remain a major driver of growth in the ECO region over the coming years. Such regional trade promises to benefit the entire region.

Iran and Greater Central Asia

Iran has 8731 kilometers of territorial and maritime borders with fifteen countries. Links between Iran and the countries of Greater Central Asia include territorial border with Afghanistan and Turkmenistan and with Kazakhstan via the Caspian Sea. The Iran-Afghanistan border includes 945 kilometers of mountainous terrain that greatly assists drug traffickers.[11] Iran should be playing a major role in Central Asia and Afghanistan. Geography favors Iran's relations with the Greater Central Asian states, since all these states are landlocked, and some of them (Uzbekistan) double-landlocked. Their shortest and most natural route to the open seas is through Iran[12].

Iran's approach to Greater Central Asia is remarkably free of ideological influences.[13] The best example is the role of Iran during the civil war in Tajikistan (1992-1997) when it mediated between the Tajik government and the Tajik Islamic Renaissance Party. No Greater Central Asian country has ever complained of support by Iran for Islamic groups in the

---

[11] Nasri, Ghadir, "Iran, Challenges in Persian Gulf", *Nameh Defaae,* Strategic Center for Defense Studies, No. 3, 2002.

[12] Dannreuther, Roland, "Bridging the Gulf? Iran, Central Asia and the Persian Gulf"; *The Review of International Affairs,* vol. 2 no. 4, Summer 2003, pp. 32-46.

[13] Hunter, Shireen, "Iran's Pragmatic Regional Policy", *Journal of International Affairs,* vol. 56 no. 2, spring 2003.

region. Iran highest priority in regard to Greater Central Asia is to safeguard its security and its territorial integrity.[14]

The functional dimension of Iran's orientation towards the Central Asian region has been well received by neighboring states, forming the basis for the development of both bilateral and multilateral regional relations. Iran easily finds partners for the construction of roads, railways, pipelines and power grids to link its infrastructure with that of the countries of Central Asia and Afghanistan, for programs to remove barriers to trade, and for environmental protection in the Caspian Sea. So far, the new regionalism of Greater Central Asia has not reached the point at which states are required to pool sovereignty to any significant degree, and has therefore been more or less cost-free in political terms, but even this amount of regionalism implies the existence of a level of interaction and governance that lies between the global and the national.

Iran is a key player in the development of the new Afghanistan. Many prefer to consider Iran a Middle-Eastern country because of its role in oil production, as well as its tendentious relations with Iraq and Lebanon. Yet in reality Iran is preeminently a part of Greater Central Asia. Although its identity as the largest Shi'ia Muslim nation is important to Iran, and its first interest in Afghanistan is to protect Shi'ia (Hazara) groups there, when it comes to its relations with Central Asia Iran tends to define its policies in terms of the long-term intents of a Nation-State (Iran or Persia) rather than the short term interest of the current government. Iran sees itself as having been part of the Greater Central Asia for a millennium and as having always played a leadership role in the region.

In Afghanistan, Iran has multiple goals. In addition to ensuring that Hazara interests are accommodated, Iran wants an Afghanistan that is stable enough to permit the two million refugees now in Iran to return home. A longer-term goal is to prevent Russia, Pakistan, or Turkey from dominating the region and its resources. Iran's perspective is complicated

---

[14] Atal, Subdoh, "Central Asian Geopolitics and US policy in the Region: The Post-11 September Era", *Mediterranean Quarterly*, Spring 2003.

by the fact that Central Asian energy producers are competitors to Iran. The Iranians have plans to build oil and gas pipelines to Pakistan and India via Baluchistan that will compete directly with proposed pipelines from Turkmenistan. Finally, Iran, like Russia, wants to ensure that the United States is not a dominant player in whatever new order emerges in the region.

Iran sought and attained observer status of the Shanghai Cooperation Organization (SCO) in an effort to escape from the dilemma of military and security threats from both East and West, as well as from the threats of Al Qaida and the Taleban. The SCO also seeks to reduce America's military pressure in the region.

Iran has for centuries considered itself the first neighbor of Central Asia and Afghanistan. Its strategic objectives there include:

- Developing positive political relations with the states of the region, including expanded trade and investment, particularly with Turkmenistan, Kazakhstan, Kyrgyzstan, Tajikistan and Afghanistan. Its relations with Uzbekistan are likely to remain correct but strained.
- Protecting open access to energy supplies, including the development of energy-based industries that complement rather than compete with Iran's domestic industry.
- Building relationships that helps it escape from international isolation, which it sees as enforced by US global hegemony.
- Maintaining close and professional, if not necessarily cordial, relations with Russia.[15]

In the economic sphere Iran aims to accomplish the following in Central Asia:

- Expand its infrastructure, especially its railway network;

[15] Charles Fairbanks, Frederick Starr, Richard Nelson, and Kenneth Weisbrode, *Strategic Assessment of Central Eurasia;* Washington: The Atlantic Council of US & SAIS, Johns Hopkins University, Jan. 2001, pp. 73-77.

- Gain political and economic influence in Greater Central Asia through the Economic Cooperation Organization (ECO);
- Acquire shares in a number of Caspian oil and gas development and export ventures.

Iran seeks Central Asian and Afghan markets for its non-oil exports. It is also actively interested in developing transport infrastructure in Central Asia that will enable it to take advantage of its strategic location between Turkey and the Arab states in the west and South Asia in the east, and between the Caucasus, Caspian and Central Asia region to the north and the Persian Gulf to its south.

Iran has participated in the establishment of several free trade zones intended to stimulate regional trade. In Greater Central Asia it established the Sarakhs Free Zone between Iran and Turkmenistan, the Anzali Special Zone on the Caspian Sea, and the Dogharoon special Customs Zone with Afghanistan. For the first time in modern Iranian history, it has delegated to provincial authorities the power to establish relations with their regional counterparts in other states. As a result, the Province of Khorasan Razavi is working closely with Afghanistan, Golistan Province with Kazakhstan, and Mazandaran Province with Turkmenistan. It is hoped that the development of interdependent economic, social and cultural relations with other countries in the region will contribute to peace and stability by generating shared interests, mutual understanding, and trust.

Bilateral Relations

Iran's closest relationship in Greater Central Asia is with Turkmenistan. This is due to geographic proximity and their mutual interests in the exploitation and export of Turkmenistan's oil and gas resources. The Iran-Turkmenistan border extends 1200 kilometers and includes four highway border crossing points and a railroad border crossing at Sarakhs-Tejan. An important project was the construction of the 200-kilometer pipeline between Korpedzhe in Turkmenistan and Kord-Kuy in Iran, allowing the export of 8 billion cubic meters of Turkmen gas annually into the Iranian gas network. Iran financed the $160 million project, which is envisaged as the first step towards the export of Turkmen gas to Turkey and Europe via Iran. A connection between the Iranian and Turkmen electricity grids was completed in 2000.

Iran has recently been engaged in road-building projects in north-west Afghanistan, providing new routes to Uzbekistan and Tajikistan. These highways will eventually be of significant economic value, even though they have yet to be exploited to full capacity. Their symbolic significance in linking Iran to the Greater Central Asian states has been emphasized by politicians and commentators alike.

Railroads are an important element of Iran's transportation strategy. When eleven regional heads of state gathered at the opening of the Mashhad to Tejen rail link, they heard Iran's President Rafsanjani extol the wider significance of the project: 'The world is moving towards greater regional cooperation. Sustained and regionally-coordinated economic growth and development will consolidate peace and stability and pave the way for the enhancement of international relations.'[16] This 300-kilometer rail link from Mashhad, the capital of Iran's Khorasan province, to Tejen in Turkmenistan was opened in May 1996, providing the first direct connection between the Iranian and Central Asian rail networks. More recently, efforts to extend and integrate the ECO rail network have continued, with the first journeys of both passenger and goods trains along the route from Almaty via Tashkent, Ashgabat and Tehran to Istanbul taking place in 2002. This rail link was developed after the United States' 1997 sanctions preventing the construction of international oil and natural gas pipeline projects that pass through Iranian territory from the Caspian region. Iran has also strongly supported the construction of the Turkmenistan-Iran-Turkey-Europe gas pipeline project, and signed oil swap agreements with both Turkmenistan

[16] http://international.rai.ir/Site.aspx.

and Kazakhstan.[17] Iran also has close energy sector relations with Turkmenistan. A pipeline between Korbeje in Turkmenistan and Kordkuy in Iran sends annually 8 billion cubic meters of gas to Iran. In July 2006, Iran's Minister of Petroleum Kazem Vaziri Hamaneh and Turkmenistan's Gas Minister Qurban Atayov agreed to increase gas exports to Iran to 14 billion cubic meters per annum.

Iran's ethnic and cultural ties to Tajikistan are strong and now extend to energy and transportation issues. On a September 2004 trip to Tajikistan former President Khatami pledged to cover half of the $500 million cost of a hydroelectric plant on the Vakhsh River and promised investment of more than $700 million into the impoverished Tajik economy over the next five years. A road link from Tajikistan to Iran via Herat in Afghanistan also features prominently in Iran's plans for boosting trade.

The World Bank has acknowledged Iran's significant role in stabilizing and strengthening Tajikistan's economy:[18] "The construction of Tajikistan's Sang-Toudeh II and Raqoun power plants relying on Iranian and Russian capital depends on the atmosphere that the projects' managers provide, which also lowers risk for investors." Iran has also invested in the Anzab hydro tunnel. Tajikistan's Sang-Toudeh I and Raqoun power stations will be constructed by Russia, but Iran will construct its Sang-Toudeh II Power Plant. The construction of the 220 megawatt Sang-Toudeh II Power Plant is scheduled to take around four years at an estimated cost of $300 million.

Relations with Kazakhstan are also developing well, particularly in the oil sector. Uzbekistan, too, has recently opened its door to economic and commercial relations with Tehran. Iranian heavy trucks now use Uzbek roads to reach Kazakhstan, Tajikistan and also the north of Afghanistan.

---

[17] Efegil, E. & Stone, L., "Iran and Turkey in Central Asia: Opportunities for Rapprochement in the post-cold war era", *Journal of Third World Studies,* vol. 20 no. 1, 2003, pp.58-62.

[18] World Bank's Economic Affairs Expert in Tajikistan Utker Omarev, March 2005, http://payvand.com/news/06/mar/1063.html.

Despite their differing views on political and security issues in the region, Iranian traders are working actively with their Uzbek counterparts. Uzbek roads are essential if Iran is to have access to other Central Asian states and northern Afghanistan. In the energy sector Iran's Oil Exploration Operations Company (OEOC) has signed an agreement with Malaysia's Petronas to carry out seismic operations in Uzbekistan at a costly $30 million.[19]

Iran's Private Sector in Greater Central Asia

Iranian products are well known across Central Asia thanks to the historical ties between Iran and the region. They are relatively cheap since the transportation costs are the lowest in the region. Also, Iranian products are less complex than those from the West.

Several studies by Iranian and other specialists have identified the main barriers to Iran's exports to Greater Central Asian countries.[20]

One of the main issues in this regard is the huge demand inside of Iran for goods and products, which discourages Iranian firms from exporting. They are also inhibited by the lack of staff who are familiar with exporting and by weak governmental programs for encouraging export policies. There also exist external barriers to export from Iran. These consist largely of tariffs, but also to an inadequate knowledge in some countries of existing commercial agreements, and so forth.

Continental Trade

Iran is carefully shifting its economic strategies to affirm its Asian identity. This has already led to closer relations with Asian countries. For instance, the trade volume between Iran and its major partners over the first four months of 2006 hit $6.25 billion. Iran's main trading partner is China, then Japan, which together have replaced Europe; France, Germany, Britain, and Italy have fallen to third to fifth place, with

---

[19] Mehr News Agency, May 18, 2006.

[20] For example, Ghazi Zadeh, Mostafa, Analysis of attractiveness of Central Asian region for Iranian Companies, presented at Third Management Conference, Tehran, Dec. 2005.

Russia, and South Korea a low sixth and seventh. Iran's revenue from the export of crude oil, oil products, and condensates surpassed $18 billion during the second quarter of 2006, most of it from sales to Asian countries like China, Japan, Turkey and India.[21]

For the countries of Greater Central Asia, Iran is the major link to international markets. All the states of the region have requested Iran to expand its links to the rail system of Turkmenistan, so that the other countries in the region can gain access to Iran's railways to the Persian Gulf. In March, 1995, the Iranian and Central Asian presidents opened the 700 km railroad connecting the Iranian city of Bafq to the Iranian Persian Gulf port of Bandar Abbas. The construction of this line completed the rail link between the Iranian city of Mashad and the Persian Gulf. The line that connects Iran with Turkmenistan (the Tejen-Sarakhs-Mashad line) was completed in March, 1996. It is 140 km long and enables the countries of Greater Central Asia and Russia to access Europe via Turkey and also to reach the Persian Gulf, Pakistan, and India by a shorter and more time-efficient route than formerly. This transport link also provides an alternative rail link to the Russian railway system.

Another major project under way is the Trans-Asian Railway (TAR), which will connect Singapore with Istanbul. The United Nations Economic and Social Commission for Asia and the Pacific (ESCAP) initiated the TAR in the 1960s. The main direct route will have a length of 14,000 km. Currently the total length of unbuilt sector is 1550 km, of which 1400 km extends between Bangladesh and Thailand. Iran strongly supports the completion of this project.

Oil and gas are keys to the economic prosperity of the region but they must first be delivered to high-income importing countries. Iran plays an important role in both the exploitation and export of these resources. It has the world's second largest proven oil and natural gas reserves,[22] and an extensive pipeline network to which pipelines from the Greater

---

[21] *Jahaane Sanat*, August 4, 2006.

[22] http://www.gasandoil.com/GOC/marketintelligence/primevistas/iran_oil_report.

Central Asia could be connected. In contrast to the east-west pipelines which the US supports, Iran, Russia and China are looking to other routes to the north, east and south. A Kazakhstan-Turkmenistan-Iran pipeline is already under study. The swapping of oil via the Caspian Sea is growing steadily and the capacity of the Neka-Ray pipeline inside Iran has been expanded to 170 000 b/d.

Iran supports also the following possible pipelines:

- A Tabriz-Ankara pipeline from Tabriz (Iran) to Ankara (Turkey);
- A Baku-Tabriz pipeline from Baku (Azerbaijan) to Tabriz (Iran);
- A Tehran-Kharg Island pipeline from Tehran (Iran) to Kharg Island (Persian Gulf);
- An Iran-Pakistan-India gas pipeline via Baluchistan.

Impediments

Despite the many opportunities for expanding continental trade across Eurasia and beyond, there are several impediments that are equally formidable.

Not the least of these is the absence of a clear conception of the opportunities that continental trade presents. The long-term Soviet domination of Central Asia, prolonged warfare in Afghanistan, and the United States' sanctions against Iran combine to prevent a full appreciation of the potential benefits of commerce and trade on a continental scale.

Beyond this, the existing infrastructure is inadequate for continental trade. Most of the road and rail networks in Central Asia and Afghanistan are badly deteriorated as a result of poor construction and the lack of maintenance. Existing networks must be upgraded and expanded to meet the demands of future economic growth and activity.

Financial constraints on investment in infrastructure are also important, the more so because private investors usually are reluctant to invest in transportation infrastructure projects. Similarly, taxes, tariffs, and regulations affecting border posts are archaic and poorly coordinated among the countries.

Recently the ECO secretariat has been trying to deregulate commerce among its members but so far with modest results.

Beyond this, corruption is a major impediment to trade. Local officials and governmental personnel in customs, transport and banking are poorly paid and unfamiliar with the modern business practices in the rest of the world, leaving them more prone to corruption. Other problematic issues include unscheduled closures of border crossings, inadequate border crossing facilities and procedures, capricious charges, and poor control by police and other authorities along principal transit corridors.

o The Regional Economic Outlook

The economies of Iran and Greater Central Asia, despite many unfavorable elements, have displayed impressive resilience. After the downturn of 2001, GDP growth in the region picked up, thanks mainly to Iran and Kazakhstan, where the improved outlook was supported by substantial FDI in the oil and gas sector.

With a total population of 157,726,994 million (almost 2.45 percent of the world population), the aggregate GDP of the countries of Greater Central Asia amounted to $ 805 billion in 2005. This made up only 1.36 percent of the world GDP. The economic recovery achieved by Iran and Great Central Asian countries as a group in 2005, with average real GDP growth at 6.5 percent, compared very favorably to the level of 1.1 percent in 2001. To be sure, this strong performance has been underpinned by robust global growth, high commodity prices, low international interest rates, and generally accommodative monetary and fiscal policies. Recognizing this, ECO countries nonetheless have achieved average GDP growth of 6.2 percent annually, compared to 4.1 percent for all developing countries. Moreover, ECO countries have outpaced global growth since 2000.[23]

The core development challenge within the region is to ensure sustainable economic growth, macroeconomic balance and price stability by the countries of Greater Central Asia and Iran. These are essential steps to achieving a much better quality of life for a population of almost 158 million. But while the countries have achieved notable progress in resolving fiscal, monetary, structural and other systemic difficulties, the remaining agenda for reform and restructuring is formidable.

o North-South Corridor

Back in the 17th century Peter the Great had an ambition to establish trade contacts with India.[24]

The Astrakhan Local Lore Museum provides information on Caspian navigation and fishing, and also shows how Iranian and Indian merchants crossed the sea to settle in Astrakhan. The isolationism that came with Soviet power in 1917 closed this important route from Asia to Europe across the sea and along the Volga. Until the early 1990s the only international freight on the Caspian amounted to about 2 million tons crossing the sea to Baku from Iran.

The new north-south corridor as the International North South Transport Corridor (INSTC), which was initiated by between Russia, Iran, and India reduces the cost of freight from Southeast Asia to Greater Central Asia to one third, eliminating the need to use the Suez Canal and thus omitting the Mediterranean. Multilateral forwarding systems will allow goods to be sent from India to Bandar Abbas, the Iranian port on the Persian Gulf, then by rail to Central Asia, or by ship from the Caspian Sea to Russia, or by highways to Afghanistan. Iran also intends

---

[23] World Bank, 2005.
http://web.worldbank.org/WBSITE/EXTERNAL/EXTABOUTUS/EXTANNREP/EXTANNREP2K5/0,,menuPK:1397361~pagePK:64168427~piPK:64168435~theSitePK:1397343,00.html.

[24] Mukhin, A. & V. Mesamed, "The North-South International Transportation Corridor: Problems and Prospects, *Central Asia Journal*, 2001, p.341.

to build a 511 km railway along Iran's Caspian Sea coast, as part of the North-South rail corridor being promoted by Russian Railways. The line would start at Astara, the southern part of Azerbaijan, near the Azerbaijan/Iran border and follow the coast to the port of Bandar-e-Anzali, turning south to the city of Rasht before joining the existing Tehran-Tabriz main line, which is part of the East-West route at Qazvin. The new route will restart the rail traffic between Russia and Iran that was broken fourteen years ago. At present, the traffic along the North-South corridor moves by train ferry between Olya and Bandar-e-Torkeman near the Turkmenistan-Iran border.

Other countries, including Belarus, Kazakhstan, Tajikistan, Oman, Armenia, Azerbaijan, Syria, Bulgaria, Ukraine, Turkey, and Kyrgyzstan have joined the project. This corridor links northern European countries and Russia with the Indian Ocean, the Persian Gulf and Southeast Asian countries. Goods will travel through the ports of Amsterdam, Hamburg, Copenhagen, Stockholm and Helsinki in Europe to St. Petersburg and Moscow in Russia. From here they can reach the Caspian Sea ports of Anzali and Amirabad, Central Asia, and the Persian Gulf and Southeast Asia.[25]

At the same time Afghanistan has moved closer to its goal of becoming a major trade hub between Europe, the Middle East and Central Asia after signing favorable trade agreements with its neighbors. Commerce Minister Seyyed Mustafa Kazemi signed a deal with Iran that will give Afghan import-export merchants the right to use the port of Chabahar on the Indian Ocean with a 90% discount on customs and port fees for non-oil goods and a 50% discount on warehouse charges. India is participating in the development of a new port complex at Chahbahar on the Iranian coast of Iran, which is linked by a highway with Afghanistan.

Afghan-registered vehicles, moreover, will be allowed full transit rights on the Iranian road system. Consumer goods and construction materials

---

[25] www.instc.org, http://www.instc.org/EArchive/EArchiveE/Item.asp?ParentID=47&ItemID=104&Doc=1.

are likely to make up the bulk of the trade headed toward Afghanistan.In January 2006, India, Iran and Afghanistan signed an agreement to give Indian goods destined for Central Asia and Afghanistan similar preferential treatment and tariff reductions at Chabahar. New Delhi, which is barred from trading with Afghanistan through Pakistan, agreed to finance the upgrading of the road linking the port with the southwest Afghan town of Dilaram via the border post of Zaranj. India is also building the Afghan sector of the 22 km Zaranj- Milak road. Existing road networks link Dilaram to Turkmenistan, via the western Afghan city of Herat, and to both Uzbekistan and Tajikistan via Kabul. The road through Zaranj will also open up one of the poorest and most isolated regions of Afghanistan. India, in a memorandum of understanding with Iran, also agreed to build a rail line linking Chabahar to the main Iranian railway network. Iran will then extend its railway to the western Afghan border town of Islam Qaleh. Afghanistan's growing ties with Iran have prompted the U.S. to designate Afghanistan as a preferential trading partner. Kabul is also moving swiftly to open trading routes and receive concessions from neighboring Central Asian republics.

The East-West Transit Corridor

The rapid economic development of the East and Southeast Asian countries in the last quarter of the twentieth century increased trade turnover with Europe and required new faster and cheaper trade routes. Early in the 1990s trade turnover between the two ends of the Eurasian landmass accounted for over a third of the world's total. This coincided with the radical political changes in Eastern Europe, Russia, Central Asia, and Afghanistan, which produced new independent states and new markets. In view of this, the U.N. and international financial institutions drew up several projects for possible transportation corridors between Asia and Europe.

A report from the Asian Development Bank identifies 50 potential road corridors through Afghanistan connecting Tajikistan, Uzbekistan, and Turkmenistan with the five sea ports in Pakistan and Iran. Thirty-one of these roads would link to Pakistani ports and the other twenty-one would connect the region through Iranian ports. Most Afghan trading centers are located along the east-west corridor to Iran. The benefits from developing the Central Asia transport corridors are significant for the Greater Central Asian countries, as well as for the neighboring regions. However, the benefits will only materialize with engaged and close coordination and effectively integrated polices among the participant countries.

In assessing the potential impact of the road corridors, the ADB found, that for example, once the corridors are built in 2010, total regional trade will increase by 160% and combined transit trade will be greater by 113%. Total exports among the participating countries will increase by 14% (or $5.8 billion) and total imports will grow by 16% (or $6.7 billion) over the period 2005 to 2010.

The potential impact of trade on overall GDP as a result of trade via the corridors is also noteworthy. The ADB estimates that the combined GDP of the participant countries in the region will increase by over 5% per year during the 5 year horizon amounting to a total increase of $5.9 billion. Based on the ADB's estimates, these benefits come at a relatively low cost as the corridors require a total investment of about $5 billion for the entire region, but that this level of investment represents only less than 5% of the combined projected total national investments for the participating countries over the period.[26]

The Central-South Asian Transport and Trade Forum (CSATTF) is an initiative to establish the road transport corridors discussed above. The aim is to promote economic growth and social development and to reduce poverty in the six participating countries—Afghanistan, Iran, Pakistan, Tajikistan, Turkmenistan and Uzbekistan. This will be done by strengthening regional transport and trade links and by opening up alternative routes for third country trade. The corridor initiative is expected to cost about US $5.7 billion. It is expected that the funding will be a joint effort of the countries concerned, with assistance from the multilateral institutions and the international community.

---

[26] www.adb.org http://www.adb.org/Documents/Books/CAREC-Comprehensive-Action-Plan/default.asp.

Iran's infrastructure in the transportation sector is the central axis of the East-West route. The highways which link Iran to Turkey in the West and Afghanistan in the East, and Azerbaijan and Turkmenistan on both sides of Caspian, are known as "RCD Roads." These national highways along with Iranian railroads, give Iran the capability of playing a major role in the transit of goods, products, and people to or from GCA states.

The link between Iran's railroads and Herat in Afghanistan is under construction. Ali Saeed Lou and Ahmad Zia Masoud, Vice presidents of Iran and Afghanistan, inaugurated the construction of the 191 km sector of railroad between Khawaf in Iran and Herat. With this project, Afghanistan's first railroad will be linked to the Persian Gulf and to European, Russian, and Central Asian railroad networks. Iran has also finished construction of a 60 km road between Herat and Faryab province in the north of Afghanistan.[27] Earlier, in January 2005, Hamid Karzai and Mohammad Khatami inaugurated the Dogharoun-Herat highway. The 122 km road was constructed by Iran with $60 million from the Iranian Support Fund for Afghan Reconstruction.

A shared language (Persian), ethnic, and cultural features bind Iran closely with both Afghanistan and Tajikistan. At a July 2006 summit in the Tajik capital of Dushanbe, leaders of the three states signed several economic agreements, among them one establishing a "cultural cooperation commission" to promote closer economic and security ties. According to Iranian President Mahmoud Ahmadinejad, the commission will convene twice annually with the inaugural gathering in the fall of 2006 in the Afghan capital. In addition, the Iranian president advocated the creation of a television network that would "broadcast the Persian language and culture to the world," and promote the expansion of educational exchanges.

Conclusions

Iran's strategic geographical position allows it to be considered a country in the Middle East, Greater Central Asia, and the Caspian region. Iran's

---

[27] BBC Persian, July 28, 2006, http://www.bbc.co.uk/persian/afghanistan/story/2006/06/040819_v-heratsepanta .shtml.

foreign policy is therefore regionalist and takes advantage of its location at the crossroads of these three areas. A major change took place in this regionalist policy after the breakup of the Soviet Union. During the Cold War, Iran did not have relations with half of its neighbors.

Despite the great potential for cooperation in trade, Iran is not a dominant player in the region. Its internal economic and political problems, which are made worse by the U.S's effort to isolate Iran, hamper investment in the region as a whole.

Now, for the first time since 1979, Iran is positioning itself to be a regional economic power. Facing continued dependence on petroleum exports, corruption, and a brain drain, Iran believes that in order to survive it has to become a regional power. Iran has constructed a network of highways on its border with Afghanistan and Turkmenistan linking it to other Central Asian states. It conducts trade with Kazakhstan via the Caspian Sea, and has linked its power grid with the rest of Central Asia. Iran has also constructed a hydroelectric plant in Tajikistan to obtain energy from that country.

Iran is moving from an inward-oriented economy to a more liberalized and open market structure that welcomes interacting with the rest of the world. In fact, the Third Five-Year Plan was the first policy document since the 1979 Revolution to declare an "outward orientation" as a main policy objective. Challenges in Iran's domestic politics, as well as tensions caused by regional confrontations, suggest that some time will be required to implement this goal. It should also be stressed that the process of democratization and its related phenomena will create short-term complications in Iran's business environment, even though sustainable democratization will have positive long-term effects on the economy.

Iran's domestic dynamics will determine the success or failure of its policy toward trade and overall relations with Central Asia and Afghanistan. While Iran's role in the economic and political developments there should not be exaggerated, it is nevertheless fair to say that it has contributed to the economic development and political stability of the region and is likely to continue to do so in the future. On the economic level, though, Iran's activity and success have been modest.

This is partly because of the weakness of its own economy and also to the inexperience of Iranian firms in investing in foreign projects.

Tehran seems to be opting for continued ad-hoc cooperation with the states of Central Asia, avoiding collisions of interests with them. This follows the course of Iranian foreign policy in the region since the 1990s. Despite remaining differences, Tehran has managed to find its own niche of political and economic engagement with the Greater Central Asian states. Iran's policy is one of economic pragmatism and positive political engagement. But U.S. policy in Iraq and Afghanistan raises the question of how long Tehran will be able to sustain this course.

Since 1991, Iran has attempted to establish economic relations with the countries of Greater Central Asia, especially in trade, transport, and the construction of pipelines. It has also tried to strengthen cultural and scientific links with the region, emphasizing the historical Persian background of the common culture of the region. Despite this, Iran's economic involvement in Greater Central Asia is still limited, with the exception of its expanding ties with Turkmenistan. Iran's problematic relations with the West, especially the United States, pose an obstacle to its ambitions in Greater Central Asia. As Iran becomes more isolated because of its nuclear activities, Iran is turning its eyes more to the East, i.e. to Asian countries.

Given the international and domestic problems Iran faces in dealing with the Greater Central Asian countries, the record of Iran's performance has been relatively good. Iran should increasingly become a key bridge between Central Asia/Afghanistan and the Persian Gulf, facilitating the two regions' social, economic and cultural interconnection. Developing transport routes through Iran will be the most effective and efficient way to enable the countries of Central Asia and Afghanistan to break away from the Soviet legacy of dependence on transport corridors through Russia's territory.

One of the Iran's advantages in Greater Central Asia is its close relationship with Russia in several strategic and political aspects, while its chief failure is its lack of contact with Washington. Despite their historic rivalry, following the disintegration of the USSR Iran and Russia realized that their interests in Greater Central Asia were similar. The

Russo-Iranian alliance may turn into an important regional geopolitical fact in the post-Cold War era.

Regional economic integration between Greater Central Asia and Iran has been limited. The overall direction of Iran's economy is different from the economies of Central Asian countries. Economic ties between Central Asia and its eastern neighbor are growing, with Xinjiang province's cheap goods being very attractive to Central Asian traders. Thanks to this, Iran's bilateral relations with Afghanistan are far stronger than with the Central Asian countries.

Two pipeline projects involving Afghanistan will connect Central Asian energy exporters and South Asian markets. One is the projected Iran-Pakistan-India line (IPI) and the other is a Turkmenistan-Afghanistan-Pakistan-India line (TAPI). Naturally, these plans have spurred geopolitical maneuvering in the region. Given the U.S.'s goal of thwarting Iran's energy exports wherever possible, Washington opposes the IPI line and supports TAPI. The latter also could enhance Washington's new strategy of reorienting Central Asian energy to South Asian markets in order to steer Central Asian states away from Russia. Meanwhile it should be recalled that Iran is also trying to have access to China's energy market through a pipeline traversing Afghanistan and Tajikistan. It also looks increasingly on Afghanistan as a corridor to China's Northwest (Xingjian), and is eager to build a pipeline between the Caspian region and China. China, for its part, appears to welcome such a move as a means of decreasing its dependence on oil imported via maritime routes through the Indian Ocean.

Greatly facilitating Iran's position in the Greater Central Asia is the fact that its policy there is based not on ideology but on transport, trade, and cultural links between them. In short, Iran has not acted as a dragon breathing ideological fire across the region, but rather as a traditional entrepreneur and reliable trader.

Uzbekistan

Martin Reiser and Dennis DeTray

Uzbekistan: On the Slow Lane of the New Silk Roads?

In the broad sweep of history, Uzbekistan's current stance on trade is an anomaly. From the days of the famed Silk Road beginning in Roman times, the area that is now Uzbekistan has been an important transit route for trade and itself an active trader. More recently, Russian trade with the region grew rapidly through the eighteenth and nineteenth centuries, so much so that Russia thought it necessary to secure the region by occupying Tashkent in 1865. The Great Game, so aptly described in Peter Hopkirk's classic of the same name, was about trade or the prospects for trade. Greater Central Asia, Uzbekistan in particular, was and is the land bridge between many of the world's great cultures and trading partners: Russia to the north, China to the east, India to the South, Iran and then Europe to the west.

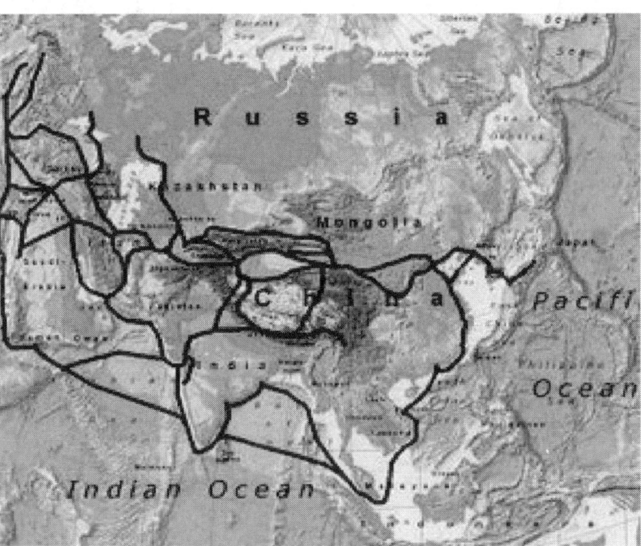

Even today the Uzbeks' trading heritage is evident to anyone visiting the Uzbek portion of the Ferghana Valley. Following the breakup of the Soviet Union Uzbekistan lost its protected markets in the Soviet Union.

Almost overnight huge ceramics factories went from producing for the massive Soviet market to producing for no one. Yet the instinctive entrepreneurial spirit of the Uzbek people found ways of using the abandoned factories and, more importantly, discarded skills and expertise to produce tradable goods. Today it is policy, not motivation or culture, that keeps the Uzbek people from assuming their place among the world's great trading nations.

With its illustrious trading history, why is Uzbekistan today a major barrier in the efforts to increase trade across the Greater Central Asia? The reasons lie in what changed and what did not change following independence on 1 September 1991. Change came in the form of a series of programs launched by President Karimov to reduce, if not eliminate, Uzbekistan's dependence on others. Self-sufficiency was the touchstone of Uzbek economic policy and import substitution its key instrument. But experience in many other countries and regions shows that inward-looking policies tend to produce economies that are distorted and inefficient, making it ever more difficult for those economies to open up. This is the position in which Uzbekistan finds itself today.

What did not change following independence were Uzbekistan's location and its population. Uzbekistan remains an important bridge for transport from south to north and from east to west, just as it was in the days of the Silk Road. However, the infamous Central Asia borders drawn in 1924– the jigsaw that carved up the Ferghana Valley, for example – impeded the flow of transport routes, roads, rail, rivers, ignore national boundaries. What this means is that getting around Uzbekistan is expensive. Uzbekistan is also the most populous of the Central Asian states, making it a potentially important internal market for the region.

As Uzbekistan's neighbors have begun to embrace the opportunities brought by opening up to the world and as the world's major trading powers discover Central Asia's potential for trade and transit, the opportunity costs of maintaining Uzbekistan's position have visibly increased. At the same time, the situation may be slowly improving, which creates opportunities for Uzbekistan and for the region.

The New Caravan Sarais: Trade and Transit Opportunities for Uzbekistan in the Greater Central Asia

Some of the ancient world's most glorious and rich cities lie on the territory of today's Uzbekistan: Bukhara, Samarkand, Khiva. These were major oases along the Silk Roads, and their rulers grew rich by offering protection to traders, providing storage facilities, and hosting important bazaars. The wealth of ancient Central Asia was built on trade. Can today's Central Asia become again a major element along the new Silk Roads?

There are different ways of estimating the potential benefits of greater international trade and integration for the countries of greater Central Asia. The existing literature has tended to focus on the following three potential benefits:

- An increase in the overall level of exports and imports as a result of the opening up of the economy, providing for greater foreign exchange revenues and at the same time greater access to foreign technologies and know-how.
- A re-orientation of trade flows away from traditional trading partners (i.e., the former USSR), increasing access to the more dynamic and competitive markets of Europe and Asia.
- An increase in trans-continental transit trade through Central Asia as the ancient silk routes are revived and cargo transit from China to Europe and from Russia to South Asia is routed through the reemerging East-West and North-South trade routes.

Greater Openness Overall

In general, the past 15 years have seen a significant opening up of the region, when measured in total trade volumes. Chart 1 shows that Uzbekistan was initially an exception to this trend, but since 2002 the country has started to catch up in terms of total export and import levels.

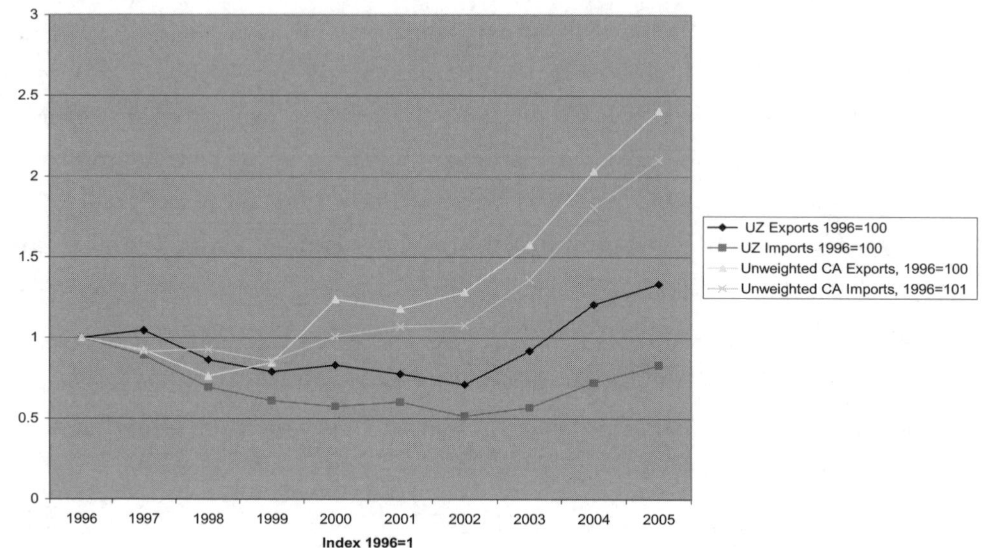

Source: World Bank Development Indicators Database

Today, Uzbekistan's total trade stands at around 70% of GDP at market exchange rates, a little below the CIS average but well up from the low of just 50% recorded in 2002.

Nonetheless, it appears that Uzbekistan is still not fully utilizing its potential to trade both regionally and with the global economy. Those living on or near its borders would attest to this. Various attempts have been made to estimate Uzbekistan's predicted level of openness.[1] According to IMF calculations, the ratio of actual to potential trade (using imports + exports) was around 0.6 in 2003.[2] Estimates of the same magnitude are reported in the EBRD Transition Report.[3] Broadman[4]

---

[1] This is done by regressing the share of exports or the combined share of exports and imports in GDP against the size of a country (population), it's income level (GDP per capita), and some other controls (country dummies and in some cases estimates for the distance to the major foreign markets).

[2] IMF Staff Report, Uzbekistan, May 2005, Washington DC, Selected Issues, p. 15 (unpublished).

[3] Transition Report: Transition and International Integration. EBRD, November 2003, London, p.87.

runs a similar calculation, but does not present actual to potential trade ratios because of concerns over measurement errors in the Uzbek data.[5] The IMF calculations are particularly interesting because they suggest that one of the main reasons for Uzbekistan's "under-trading" relative to potential may lie in its own restrictive trade policies, and that with trade policies as liberal as those in the rest of the CIS, Uzbekistan could increase its overall trade by at least $ 2 billion.

Taking statistical under-reporting into account, and with the recent significant rise in exports and imports, it is safe to assume that Uzbekistan's total level of openness still falls around 10-20% short of its potential. Over the period to 2015, for instance, this implies potential increases in Uzbekistan's exports and imports from $ 9 billion today to around $ 15 billion if GDP continues to grow at the historical average (1998-2005) of 5 percent. One may assume that a large share of the increase in openness in the future will come from growth in trade with non-traditional trading partners, including Uzbekistan's neighbors to the south.

Geographic Reorientation of Trade

For Uzbekistan, as a former part of the Soviet Union, the geographic reorientation of trade away from other former Soviet republics towards market economies in Western Europe, South and East Asia, and beyond has significant potential benefits. Greater trade with market economies, whether in the industrialized or developing world, entails access to modern technologies and the greater exposure to competition and innovative business practices. Growth in trade with non-traditional partners could help increase Uzbekistan's share in world markets and may allow consecutively for the deepening of economic relations and

---

[4] Broadman, Harry. From Disintegration to Reintegration: Eastern Europe and the Former Soviet Union in International Trade. The World Bank, 2005. Washington DC, p.103, footnote b.

[5] Indeed, the IMF's Direction of Trade Statistics on which all of the above calculations are based seem to suffer from significant under-reporting of Uzbekistan's foreign trade. It recorded exports of just US$2405 million in 2003, against actual exports of US$ 3725 million as per Uzbekistan's balance of payments.

Uzbekistan's gradual movement up the value chain. The experience of eastern European countries suggests that such a transition is possible, and the geographic reorientation of trade has played a key role in this regard.[6]

Yet, reality hasn't met these positive expectations. As pointed out by Broadman, most of the countries of the former Soviet Union remain highly dependent on trade with Russia. Indeed, according to Broadman, a Russia-centered trade block seems to be re-emerging in the former Soviet Union and trade dependence on Russia has grown in recent years. Table 1 below presents the latest data on the direction of trade for Uzbekistan obtained from the IMF Direction of Trade Statistics.

This suggests that dependency on Russia has indeed remained significant, with around 22% of reported exports and 27% of reported imports respectively going to and coming from the Russian Federation. Both shares have increased in recent years and are now close to what they were in the mid 1990s.

By contrast, there seem to be huge unexploited trade opportunities, particularly with South and East Asia. As can be seen from Table 1, Uzbekistan's trade with India was around one tenth of its trade with China, and less than 5% of its trade with Russia, although India is closer than the main commercial centers of Russia and has a similarly dynamic economy. The numbers for Pakistan are also disappointing. For Afghanistan official numbers do not exist; unofficial numbers indicate growing trade mostly as exports from Uzbekistan, but still at levels well below Uzbek trade with its post-Soviet neighbors.

---

[6] Broadman, Harry. *From Disintegration to Reintegration: Eastern Europe and the Former Soviet Union in International Trade*. The World Bank, 2005. Washington DC.

Table 1a: Geographic orientation of imports (CIF, US$ millions), Afghanistan and Central Asia, 2004

Imports from:	AFG	KAZ	KGZ	TJK	TKM	UZB	CA
Afghanistan	0	0	0	4	0	0	4
Kazakhstan	71	0	230	153	101	199	754
Kyrgyz Republic	8	73	0	18	8	24	129
Tajikistan	8	4	4	0	8	73	97
Turkmenistan	107	64	1	34	0	16	221
Uzbekistan	0	118	51	169	60	0	398
Total Imports from CA	**194**	**259**	**286**	**377**	**177**	**311**	**1,604**
Imports from CA as % of the total imports	**10%**	**2%**	**21%**	**32%**	**6%**	**10%**	**6%**
Iran	0	17	9	26	123	0	175
Pakistan	511	10	6	0	1	3	531
Russia	84	5,113	300	241	267	844	6,847
Total imports from WCA	**789**	**5,398**	**600**	**644**	**568**	**1,158**	9,157
as % of the total imports	**39%**	**37%**	**45%**	**54%**	**21%**	**37%**	**36%**
China	64	2,269	352	57	94	183	3,019
India	170	86	39	3	17	20	336
Turkey	78	391	72	38	236	160	975
United Arab Emirates	5	33	9	16	252	0	317
Total imports from WCA plus neighbors	**1,106**	**8,178**	**1,072**	**759**	**1,168**	**1,521**	**13,803**
as % of the total imports	**55%**	**55%**	**80%**	**64%**	**43%**	**48%**	**55%**
Total Imports (World)	**2,002**	**14,776**	**1,341**	**1,191**	**2,737**	**3,144**	**25,190**

Source: IMF Directions of Trade Statistics, International Monetary Fund, Washington DC, 2004.

* **Exports.** The exports for Wider CA are as reported by exporters (see table B5). Consequently discrepancies may be due to under-reporting of exports as well as to transport costs accounting for differences between fob export and cif import values.

Table 1b: Geographical orientation of exports (FOB, $US millions), Afghanistan and Central Asia, 2004

Exports to:	AFG	KAZ	KGZ	TJK	TKM	UZB	CA
Afghanistan		65	7	8	97	0	176
Kazakhstan	0		78	4	4	107	193
Kyrgyz Republic	0	191		4	1	46	242
Tajikistan	4	139	17		31	153	343
Turkmenistan	0	49	3	8		55	115
Uzbekistan	0	181	22	66	14		283
Total exports to CA	**4**	**624**	**127**	**89**	**147**	**362**	**1353**
as % of the total exports	**2%**	**3%**	**18%**	**10%**	**4%**	**14%**	**5%**
Iran	0	535	3	30	661	75	1303
Pakistan	45	1	0	0	8	6	60
Russia	4	3143	134	61	39	556	3937
Total exports to WCA	**52**	**4303**	**264**	**179**	**855**	**999**	**6652**
as % of the total exports	**28%**	**21%**	**38%**	**20%**	**22%**	**40%**	**23%**
China	1	2066	84	0	13	371	2535
India	39	13	1	0	9	26	88
Turkey	6	401	12	140	160	162	881
United Arab Emirates	4	280	198	0	124	0	606
Total Exports to WCA plus main neighbors	**103**	**7061**	**559**	**320**	**1161**	**1559**	**10763**
as % of the total exports	**55%**	**34%**	**80%**	**35%**	**30%**	**62%**	**37%**
Total Exports (World)	**185**	**20814**	**703**	**915**	**3810**	**2524**	**28951**

Source: IMF Directions of Trade Statistics, International Monetary Fund, Washington DC, 2004.

One way to assess the potential for increased trade with other regions is to use a so-called gravity model to predict bilateral trade flows between Uzbekistan and a range of other trading partners.[7] These predicted levels of trade can then be compared to actual trade; the difference represents the unexploited trade potential or, in the case of Russia, for instance, the extent of "over-trading."

Table 2 presents the ratio of predicted over actual trade for selected trading partners of Uzbekistan based on such a gravity model.[8]

---

[7] The simple idea of the gravity model is that trade between two countries is higher the closer they are geographically and the bigger their respective economies. This model can be modified to include bilateral or multilateral trade barriers, both natural and policy induced. See Anderson, J.E. and E. van Wincoop (2003), "Gravity with gravitas: a solution to the border puzzle", American Economic Review, Vol. 93, No. 1, pp. 170-192 for a recent influential theoretical derivation.

[8] The model was calculated using data from 84 countries from 1997-2004. Unlike much of the extensive existing literature it includes all the transition economies, allowing us to make predictions for Uzbekistan without resorting to out of sample estimates. Moreover, the gravity model used here controls for a whole range of factors that may limit bilateral trade, such as borders, the extensiveness of infrastructure, the openness of the trade regime, and the quality of domestic institutions. The resulting ratios are thus estimates of the "pure" trade potential that remains unrealized even taking current policy conditions into account. Assuming changes in any of the policy variables that present obstacles to trade would increase the predicted level of trade even further, and thus enhance the trade potential. Details of the data and the estimation used can be found in: Babetskii, Ian, Oxana Babetksaya-Kukhartchuk and Martin Raiser, "Gravity and integration: determinants of international trade in South-Eastern Europe and the former Soviet Union". Substantially revised version of EBRD Working Paper, No. 83, mimeographed.

Table 2: Potential trade as a percent of actual trade, Kazakhstan and Uzbekistan and selected trading partners

Kazakhstan

Geo	iso	Export	Import	Total
Eastern Asia	CHN	113.4	91.6	102.1
Eastern Asia	JPN	648.5	662.0	654.6
Eastern Asia	KOR	176.5	96.9	126.4
South Asia	BGD	194.8	1438.4	294.7
South Asia	IDN	1171.2	3696.5	1720.0
South Asia	NPL	N/A	N/A	N/A
South Asia	PAK	4392.5	377.1	868.9
South Eastern Asia	IND	2400.1	225.6	526.6
South Eastern Asia	MYS	1695.9	867.7	1171.4
South Eastern Asia	PHL	22551.9	93972.5	35081.8
South Eastern Asia	SGP	82582.2	1406.2	3128.0
South Eastern Asia	THA	224.3	1326.4	373.4
South Eastern Asia	VNM	86.6	4089.2	172.8
Russia	RUS	36.9	23.8	29.1

Uzbekistan

Geo	iso	Export	Import	Total
Eastern Asia	CHN	79.4	127.5	94.8
Eastern Asia	JPN	549.1	621.1	577.7
Eastern Asia	KOR	135.2	21.5	40.1
South Asia	BGD	9.3	516.2	14.5
South Asia	IDN	1757.2	5386.6	2485.5
South Asia	NPL	N/A	N/A	N/A
South Asia	PAK	348.4	355.9	351.0
South Eastern Asia	IND	366.9	268.4	326.2
South Eastern Asia	MYS	14543.9	472.6	1037.6
South Eastern Asia	PHL	N/A	8340.7	19042.2
South Eastern Asia	SGP	N/A	N/A	N/A
South Eastern Asia	THA	2592.8	1874.0	2212.1
South Eastern Asia	VNM	105.2	2725.3	194.5
Russia	RUS	29.4	17.9	22.7

While the estimates in Table 2 should be taken with a degree of caution, they confirm the impression obtained from a casual observation of current trade flows that Uzbekistan is under-trading with South and East Asia by a factor of 10-15 times, with the notable exception of China, which has greatly increased its economic presence all over Central Asia in recent years, and South Korea, which has historically played an important role in Uzbekistan's economy. In monetary terms, and using the estimates of total trade of $15 billion in 2015 derived above, Uzbekistan's trade with the Greater Central Asia region could amount to over $10 billion in that year. Trade with India may grow to $1.5 billion; trade with China could by that time exceed trade with Russia; and Iran, Pakistan and Afghanistan could together account for up to $1 billion in Uzbekistan's external trade. This conclusion is independent of Uzbekistan's particular trade policies, as the reference data in the Table provided for Kazakhstan clearly reveal. Kazakhstan has the same under-exploited trade potential with South and East Asia, with China and South Korea again being the exceptions.

From a product and sector perspective, geographic diversification presents a further potential advantage. On the export side, the opening of new export routes competing with present outlets through Russia may reduce transport costs and thus increase producer netbacks in Central Asia. This is most obvious for oil and gas exports, but in Uzbekistan's case it also applies to cotton exports and, increasingly, to manufacturing. The opening of the Sarakhs-Meshed rail-link in 1997 has led to a gradual re-routing of Uzbek cotton exports to Bandar-Abbas.[9]

The Uzbekistan product composition of trade is dominated by commodities due to the low competitiveness of Uzbek manufacturing and services (Table 3).

---

[9] It is estimated that around two thirds of the 2004 harvest was shipped through Bandar-Abbas. Recent geopolitical tensions with Iran have however increased the risk premium on shipments through Iranian ports and Russia has taken advantage of this situation (and Uzbekistan's misguided cotton marketing campaign in 2005) to attempt to re-capture lost market share by offering long-term off-take contracts from Russian textile companies.

Table 3: Geographic and Product Composition of Uzbekistan's exports, 2003

HS product code		Total trade flow (million US$)	Cumulative total (per cent)	Share of CIS countries (percent)
Exports				
5201	Cotton, not carded or combed	592	33.9	17.2
5205	Cotton yarn (not sewing thread) 85% or more cotton, not retail	128	41.2	8.7
7403	Refined copper and copper alloys, unwrought	113	47.7	0.0
7108	Gold unwrought or in semi-manuf forms	106	53.7	0.0
8703	Cars (incl. station wagon)	93	59.0	99.9
2711	Petroleum gases	86	64.0	100.0
5208	Woven cotton fabrics, 85% or more cotton, weight less than 200 g/m2	46	66.6	9.3
2844	Radioactive chem elements&isotopes, their compounds, mixtures&res	38	68.8	48.1
806	Grapes, fresh or dried	27	70.3	95.6
2612	Uranium or thorium ores and concentrates	26	71.8	0.0
7901	Unwrought zinc	23	73.1	12.0
7112	Waste & scrap of precious metal	20	74.3	0.0
2710	Petroleum oils, not crude	19	75.3	23.5
3102	Mineral or chemical fertilizers, nitrogenous	18	76.4	9.9
702	Tomatoes	18	77.4	100.0
7106	Silver,unwrght or in semi-manuf. form	17	78.4	0.0
7214	Bars&rods of iron/non-al/s, nfw than forged, hr, hd,/hot-extruded	16	79.4	44.0
5209	Woven cotton fabrics, 85% or more cotton,weight over 200 g/m2	13	80.1	5.5
703	Onions, garlic and leeks, fresh or chilled	13	80.8	95.1
5601	Wadding of tex mat&art thereof;tex fib	12	81.5	97.4
3901	Polymers of ethylene, in primary forms	12	82.2	29.8
807	Melons (including watermelons) & papayas, fresh	12	82.9	99.7
2002	Tomatoes prepared or preserved	10	83.5	99.9
809	Apricots, cherries, peaches, nectarines, plums & sloes, fresh	10	84.1	100.0
6204	Women's suits, jackets,dresses skirts etc&shorts	9	84.5	0.0
5202	Cotton waste (including yarn waste and garnetted stock)	8	85.0	35.3
6110	Jerseys, pullovers, cardigans, etc, knitted or crocheted	8	85.5	0.3
6002	Knitted or crocheted fabrics, nes	8	86.0	1.4
713	Dried vegetables, shelled	8	86.4	33.8
6203	Men's suits, jackets, trousers etc & shorts	7	86.8	5.6
Imports				
8708	Parts & access of motor vehicles	165	8.0	2.2
8802	Aircraft, (helicopter,aeroplanes) & spacecraft (satellites)	136	14.7	4.0
3004	Medicament mixtures (not 3002, 3005, 3006), put in dosage	65	17.8	42.6
8411	Turbo-jets, turbo-propellers and other gas turbines	38	19.7	89.6
8471	Automatic data processing machines;optical reader, etc	38	21.5	2.1
8525	Television camera, transmissn app for radio-telephony	38	23.3	2.0
8413	Pumps for liquids; liquid elevators	37	25.1	16.8
2709	Crude petroleum oils	35	26.9	100.0
8433	Harvesting/threshing machinery,hay mower,etc	31	28.4	1.9
8430	Moving/grading/scraping/boring machinery for earth	29	29.8	11.6
4011	New pneumatic tires, of rubber	28	31.2	59.1
8703	Cars (incl. station wagon)	27	32.5	18.0
1101	Wheat or meslin flour	25	33.7	96.5
2608	Zinc ores and concentrates	24	34.8	93.4
8431	Machinery part (hd 84.25 to 84.30)	23	36.0	17.3
8429	Self-propelld bulldozer, angledozer, grader, excavator,etc	22	37.0	15.0

Source: Data collected from mirror statistics as reported in the UN-Comtrade Database, electronic release, Geneva, 2005.

This reflects in part the skewed nature of transportation costs, which strongly favor rail shipments over road transport, due to Russia railway discounts, infrastructure weaknesses, and to the burden of informal payments that make road transport uncompetitive.[10] What manufacturing exports exist are largely concentrated on the Russian market and are supported by historically established technological and business links that have been revived in recent years.[11] Against this background, geographic diversification, and in particular the improvement in road links towards the Persian Gulf and the Indian Ocean, represent an opportunity to create new businesses linkages, import cheaper capital goods that allow the technological modernization of production, and find cheaper outlets for higher value added goods. For Uzbekistan, with Central Asia's largest population and hence its greatest manufacturing potential, these are particularly important opportunities.

Continental Transit Trade

Even greater than Central Asia's potential for trade with the wider region and its integration into the global economy is Central Asia's potential as a new land bridge on the Eurasian continent. The idea of reviving the ancient Silk Roads that once traversed Central Asia's oases and which brought great wealth thanks to caravan traders has captured the imagination of politicians both in and outside the region since the breakdown of the Soviet Union. Other chapters in this book attest to the vitality of this vision, even if precise estimates of the potential economic significance of transit trade through Central Asia are hard to come by.

The key to realizing the vision of a new land bridge between Europe, China and India across the greater Central Asia is the construction of new transport links. Investments in the twentieth century were almost exclusively directed towards integration with Russia. Presently, almost

---

[10] Raballand, Gael "The Determinants of the Negative Impact of Land-Lockedness on Trade: An Empirical Investigation through the Central Asian Case". Comparative Economic Studies 45: 520-536, 2003.

[11] Luecke, Matthias and Jacek Roberts. "Comparative Advantage in International Trade for Central Asia", Kiel Working Paper forthcoming. Institute of World Economics, 2007, Kiel.

all roads still lead to Moscow. Today most of the attention is concentrated on unlocking the roads south from Central Asia, and providing access through the region to the new deep water port currently being built at Gwadar in Pakistan, as well as to the existing port of Bandar Abbas in Iran. In addition, Iran is developing a port to the east from Bandar Abbas at Chabahar, while Karachi remains Pakistan's main port and its commercial capital. Perhaps the greatest prize in developing the Southern routes lies in access to the vast Indian market. Yet, as noted elsewhere in this volume, this will depend on a lasting political settlement of the Kashmir issue. The available calculations on which we draw in this chapter do not factor in the possibility of direct access to India through Pakistan (see the chapter on India in this volume for initial estimates).

In its Report 2005 the Asian Development Bank[12] identified a total of 52 potential routes along the major North-South corridors to the above-mentioned ports (including also Port Qasim just east of Karachi), and provided cost estimates for the construction and rehabilitation of these routes (ADB did not look at the parallel north-south route through Azerbaijan and Iran and the direct Russia-Iran-Persian Gulf link through the Caspian Sea, which are discussed in other chapters of this volume). In making an estimate of investment costs and resulting reductions in vehicle operating costs ADB also took into account the quality of road conditions along each corridor in order to obtain more precise estimates of the returns on these investments. The results of this study are summarized in Table 4.

---

[12] "Report on the Economic Impact of Central-South Asian Road Corridors". Prepared for the Transport Committee of CAREC. Asian Development Bank (ADB), March 2005.

Table 4: Key Impact of Central-South Asian Road Corridor under Various Scenarios

Note: Impact is due to corridor over without corridor.

Item	Base Case (So)	20% Reduction in Traffic Flow (S1)	20% Reduction in Voc Savings (S2)	20% Reduction in Average truck load (S3)	20% Reduction in Traffic Flow, Voc Savings and Average Truck load (S4)
Combined incremental regional trade growth 2002-2010 (%)	160	129	155	113	90
Combined incremental regional transit trade growth 2002-2010 %	111	93	111	89	75
Corridor investment cost ($ million)	5639	5639	5639	5639	5639
Corridor investment as % of total investment	4.55	4.66	4.56	4.67	4.75
Annual travel cost saving/$ of investment 2010 ($)	0.31	0.25	0.25	0.31	0.20
Incremental annual GDP growth rate 2005-2010 (%)	0.43	0.35	0.42	0.34	0.28
Incremental annual GDP/$ of investment 2010 ($)	1.05	0.85	1.04	0.83	0.68
Incremental annual full time employment in 2010 (million)	1.86	1.50	1.85	1.48	1.20
Total incremental export growth 2002-2010 (%)	14	13	14	13	12
Total incremental import growth 2002-2010 (%)	16	15	16	15	14
Incremental revenue in 2010 ($ million)	910	863	908	863	827

Source: "Report on the Economic Impact of Central-South Asian Road Corridors". Prepared for the Transport Committee of CAREC. Asian Development Bank (ADB), March 2005, p.3. Voc = vehicle operating cost

These suggest that the benefits of investing in new road corridors through Central Asia would be very significant indeed. Investments totaling an estimated $ 5.6 billion would raise total trade by some 15% compared with the no-investment case, or by some $ 12 billion, by 2010. Of these, more than half are assumed to be gains in transit trade alone, with the remainder being increased trade from and to Central Asia as it expands relations with new trading partners. An illustration of the same argument is provided in Chart 2, which shows that the southern rail link to Bandar-Abbas and the road link to Karachi would be highly competitive with northern and western routes to the Baltics and the Black Sea, if infrastructure and policy obstacles to using these routes could be overcome.

Chart 2: Trade-Transport Costs in Some Central Asian Republics

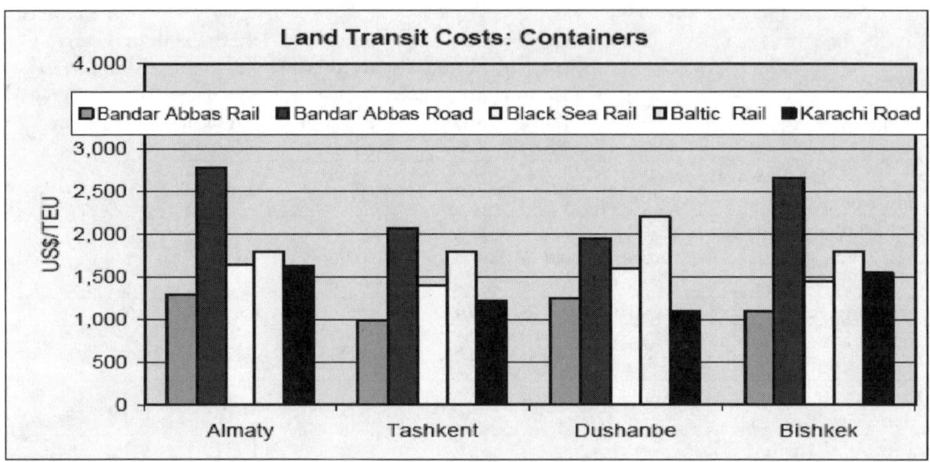

Source: "Trade and Regional Cooperation between Afghanistan and Its Neighbors." World Bank, Washington DC, February 2004, p. 39.

There are further significant transit trade opportunities related to the construction of a new East-West corridor from China across Central Asia, the Caspian, the South Caucasus and the Black Sea to Europe. Indeed, it is the East-West axis that was at the heart of such early concepts to revive the Silk Roads as the European Union's TRACECA initiative. Uzbekistan is one possible transit country along a new East-West route, which would progress along the Ferghana valley and connect to the Caspian port at Turkmenbashi in Turkmenistan. A rival proposal, and at this writing the most promising alternative, runs further North across Kazakhstan and on towards the port of Aktau. A railway link through Central Asia to rival both maritime transport and the Trans-Siberian railway through Russia would, in time, carry volumes of cargo from China to Europe valued at several billion dollars per annum.

For Uzbekistan, these calculations present both an opportunity and a challenge. The opportunity is that Uzbekistan sits at the center of Central Asia. With a less mountainous topography than that of the

Kyrgyz Republic or Tajikistan, it is a priori a preferred transit corridor for inter-continental North-South transit routes.[13] This is further supported by the existing infrastructure, which provides railway access all the way from Moscow to Hairatan on the Afghan border (a new Japanese funded railway spur will by-pass Turkmenistan along this route, thereby reducing delays and potentially saving transit costs), an existing railway link through Turkmenistan to Bandar Abbas, as well as Central Asia's best road network (although in need of repairs, particularly en route from Karshi to Termez). It should be noted in further support of this point that Uzbekistan is already utilizing the southern route to Iran to a far greater extent than is Kazakhstan or the Kyrgyz Republic, which have both diversified their trade routes primarily in the direction of China.[14]

The challenge is that to the extent that Uzbekistan becomes a major transit route its present restrictive trade regime will come under increasing threat. The combination of tariffs and import excises raises the effective import tax level for some consumer goods in the Uzbek market to three digit levels. Such levels of taxation present extremely attractive arbitrage gains for traders, who may violate transit rules and offload non-declared cargo en route in Uzbekistan. Increasing transit trade would tend to increase the competition for rents in this lucrative business – a difficult political challenge, even if most Uzbek consumers would welcome such a change.

Energy Rransit and Trade

There is significant additional potential in new energy transportroutes from and through the region. The Greater Central Asia region has substantial energy resources, although there are variations across

[13] This geographical advantage is not so clear East-West, where Kazakhstan offers a link from China to the Caspian with just one border as opposed to three on the route through the Ferghana and Turkmenistan.

[14] Ojala, Lauri. "Review of Inter-Regional Trade and Transport Facilitation in Europe and Central Asia Region, South Asia Region and East Asia and Pacific Region". Mimeographed, June 2005.

countries in the amounts and types of their energy endowments (see Table 5).

Table 5: Primary Energy Resources in Wider Central Asia (WCA) and Main Neighbors

Type of Reserves	**Crude Oil**	**Natural Gas**	**Coal**	**Total****		**Hydro Potential**	
Countries \ Units	MTOE*	MTOE	MTOE	MTOE	% of Total	TWh/ year	% of Total
Afghanistan	-	-	-	-	-	-	-
Kazakhstan	5404	2700	19810	27914	77%	62	12%
Kyrgyz Republic	6	5	580	591	2%	99	19%
Tajikistan	2	5	500	507	1%	317	62%
Turkmenistan	74	2610	Insignificant	2684	7%	5	1%
Uzbekistan	81	1674	2851	4606	13%	27	5%
Subtotal Central Asian countries:	**5567**	**6994**	**23741**	**36302**	**100%**	**510**	**100%**
Iran	18068	24750	-	42818	21%	88	4%
Pakistan	-	718	1017	1735	1%	130	5%
Russia	9859	43200	68699	121758	60%	1670	70%
Subtotal WCA:	**33494**	**75662**	**93457**	**202613**	**100%**	**2398**	**100%**
China	2328	2006	58900	63,234	18%	1920	37%
India	759	831	60843	62,433	18%	660	13%
Turkey	-	-	1488	1,488	0%	216	4%
UAE	13340	5454	-	18,794	5%	-	-
Total for WCA plus main neighbors:	**49921**	**83953**	**214688**	**348562**	**100%**	**5194**	**100%**

Source: Central Asia: Regional Electricity Export Potential Study. World Bank, Working Paper, 33877, Vol. 1, Washington DC, 2004, p.1..

* *Million Tons of Oil Equivalents.*

** *Does not include hydropower generation potential*

There is great potential for regional energy development and trade which can benefit all of the countries of the region. Specifically, there would appear to be good prospects for development of hydroelectric resources in the countries with large potential, much of whose output could be exported to electricity-deficient countries to the south, notably Pakistan, as well as to Iran. Similarly, there are opportunities for natural gas trade from gas-surplus countries like Turkmenistan and Iran to gas-deficit countries like Pakistan and India. New gas pipelines and electric transmission lines, while costly could generate hundreds of millions of dollars in transit revenues for the countries through which they pass.

Uzbekistan could play a critical intermediary role in the emerging continental energy trade. The country is self-sufficient in energy, thanks to its considerable natural gas reserves. Moreover, it is the center of the existing South Central Asian energy grid, with its central dispatch center in Tashkent. Uzbekistan's central position and availability of domestic thermal energy resources would allow it to draw on hydroelelectric power imports in summer as well as for its own peak consumption[15] while saving thermal resources for base load exports to the power-deficient countries further south. Moreover, Uzbekistan could earn considerable transit revenues from transiting Tajik and possibly Kyrgyz hydro-power once their hydro-capacity is fully developed. The main existing gas export pipeline also crosses Uzbekistan, giving the country additional leverage. If a southern gas export route from Turkmenistan is built, Uzbekistan could inexpensively connect its own gas reserves to such a project. One implication of these various opportunities is that Uzbekistan's own thermal resources are at a premium over the medium to long run. Energy saving in Uzbekistan is profitable business and would greatly increase the country's capacity to exploit export opportunities.[16]

Timing and Sequencing

The potential economic benefits of greater integration of the countries of post-Soviet Central Asia with Afghanistan and through it with South and East Asia are clearly significant. Yet, progress so far has been limited, and it seems for the moment that the forces championing

[15] Because hydro power can be quickly turned on and off and marginal costs are essentially flat, it is generally the preferred power source for peak loads, as marginal costs of thermal generation increase steeply as capacity utilization increases.

[16] See "Central Asia: Regional Electricity Export Potential Study." World Bank, Washington DC, 2004.

reintegration with Russia are stronger than the forces that support diversifying trade routes and economic opportunities. But in the long run the benefits of opening up are simply too big to be ignored. The message of many chapters in this book is that the time is ripe for bold policy moves to make the strategic vision a reality. In an effort to clarify why things may be moving more slowly than many would desire, we offer the following three caveats:

- Reintegration with Russia may entail important economic benefits.[17] To the extent that Uzbekistan faces the need to prioritize investments and policy measures, looking north may have higher returns in the short run than looking south. The flip side of this argument is that the southern trade routes are hostage to the security situation in Afghanistan. Strategic vision requires low discount rates, which most Central Asian politicians do not have. The distribution of benefits over time is thus a weighty argument in timing and sequencing policy measures.
- In the short-term at least, there may not be room for more than one major new North-South and East-West corridor. Central Asian countries are engaged in a competition over whose territory the route will cross. Realizing these new routes requires country-to-country collaboration and enforcement mechanisms to prevent transit countries from attempting to capture all the transit rents once the investment has been made. In principle, competition should spur each country to offer the best conditions and the most reliable partnership. But intense regional rivalries have delayed the necessary cooperation. It behooves the major regional powers (China, Russia, and more recently Japan, Europe and the USA) and the multilateral organizations to play a coordinating role. To make the strategic vision a reality thus requires astute statesmanship and a benign international policy environment. Neither is assured.

---

[17] Linn, Johannes and David Tiomkin. "Economic Integration of Eurasia: Opportunities and Challenges of Global Significance". CASE Center for Social and Economic Research paper, Warsaw, April 2005.

- The potential benefits of greater integration depend on the adoption of supportive policy measures. While the overall welfare effects of policy reform are positive, the distributional implications are usually not, raising significant political challenges that still need to be overcome – especially in Uzbekistan.

Against these caveats, the reintegration with Russia and the other former Soviet Republics represents a number of short-term advantages. First, links are well established along supply chains, with a high degree of asset specificity and concomitant costs of switching to alternative suppliers and customers. A good example in Uzbekistan is the Chkalov Aircraft factory in Tashkent, which builds planes using Russian intermediate inputs and markets these planes under the Ilyushin Russian brand. Such links are reinforced by a common working language, similar education systems, joint technical standards and, significantly, a common sense of pride for the technical achievements of the Soviet Union.

Second, for Uzbekistan, which has one of the most restrictive trade regimes in the region, re-integration with Russia may be a politically more expedient avenue towards opening up its domestic market and might thus represent a welcome intermediate step, its implementation aided by the greater short-term returns that re-integration with Russia may offer. From the perspective of Uzbekistan's leadership, in this direction the present geopolitical constellation would appear further to tilt the balance of benefits.

It would be wrong to see reintegration with Russia as an alternative to greater integration with South and East Asia. The two are clearly complementary rather than alternatives. Indeed, the first best option for Uzbekistan would be a policy of unilateral liberalization of trade with all its partners. However, political choices involve compromises and sequenced steps. Importantly, the relative weight of the associated economic costs and benefits does influence the sequencing of policy measures. International actors wishing to leverage the realization of the Greater Central Asia vision need to bear in mind these considerations.

Obstacles to Uzbekistan's Greater Integration with Continental Trade Routes

As the ancient traders gathered around their fires in the evening, tales abounded of obstacles they had encountered, bandits they had avoided or fought, desert storms they had braved, and water holes that had disappeared. Hundreds of years later there are still many tales to be told about obstacles along land-transport and transit routes through Central Asia, obstacles that stand in the way of realizing the potential we reviewed above.

In discussing the impediments to regional and transit trade in Greater Central Asia, we return to the gravity literature for helpful guidance. Gravity models can be specified, for instance, to include a host of barriers to trade induced by infrastructure, geography, culture, and policies.

One consistent result of recent gravity studies is that so-called "behind-the-border" obstacles to trade (such as the quality of a country's institutions) are at least as important, if not more important, in determining both the level and direction of trade flows than are physical or policy obstacles related to the movement of goods across borders.[18] In other words, countries that provide business-friendly environments, have well-functioning financial sectors, modest levels of corruption, legal system that make possible the enforcement of contracts, and educational systems that promote outward orientation and the easy absorption of new ideas and technologies, are likely to do well as exporters, and are more likely to be attractive as trading partners. This should come as no surprise. But from the point of view of Central Asia, and of Uzbekistan in particular, it serves as a cautionary reminder of the comprehensive developmental challenges faced by the region.

The results of the gravity model presented earlier suggest that trade policies and the "border" effect tend to exceed the quantitative importance of the density of infrastructure.[19] Moreover, they suggest that

---

[18] Broadman, Harry. *From Disintegration to Reintegration: Eastern Europe and the Former Soviet Union in International Trade.* The World Bank, 2005. Washington DC.

[19] Babetskii, Ian, Oxana Babetksaya-Kukhartchuk and Martin Raiser, "Gravity and integration: determinants of international trade in South-Eastern Europe and the

WTO membership has only a marginal impact on trade volumes once the openness of the trade regime is accounted for. This is consistent with the analysis by Subramanian and Wei[20] which suggests that WTO membership has been effective in promoting liberalized trade in the industrial countries. However, WTO accession has not led to the liberalization of economies of developing countries and has had only a limited impact on trade levels. The conclusion again seems to be that for countries such as Uzbekistan to fully exploit the opportunities provided by greater integration into the world economy, complementary policy reforms are a prerequisite.

Table 6: Estimated Freight Costs for the Countries of Central Asia

Country	GDP	Exports	X as % of GDP	Imports	M as % of GDP	Freight Costs	Freight Costs
	(US$ billion)	(US$ billion)	%	(US$ billion)	%	(US$ billion)	% of GDP
Kazakhstan	41	18	45%	16	40%	5.7	14%
Uzbekistan	12	5	39%	4	31%	1.4	12%
Turkmenistan	6	4	62%	3	54%	1.2	19%
Afghanistan	5	0.6	12%	3	69%	0.6	13%
Kyrgyz Rep	2	1	42%	1	51%	0.3	15%
Tajikistan	2	1	55%	1	65%	0.4	20%
Total:	68	29	44%	29	42%	9.6	14%

Source: World Bank staff calculations based data provided by national statistical agencies.

Transport costs: an overview

A large literature confirms the importance of transport costs for economic growth and trade performance.[21] For Central Asia land transport costs matter, since all countries in the region are landlocked.

---

former Soviet Union". Substantially revised version of EBRD Working Paper, No. 83, mimeographed.

[20] Subramanian, Arvind and Shang-Jin Wei. "The WTO Promotes Trade, Strongly but Unevenly". International Monetary Fund, Working Paper No. 03/185, 2003.

[21] For a review in the context of Central Asia, see Byrd, William and Martin Raiser (with Alex Kitain and Anton Dobronogov) (2006), "Prospects for Economic Development and Cooperation in the Wider Central Asia Region". World Bank Working Papers No. 75, April 2006.

For Uzbekistan this issue is even more severe as it is one of only two double-landlocked countries in the world, the other being Liechtenstein. Table 6 provides a snapshot summary of estimated transportation costs, obtained from a comparison of cif and fob prices for exports and imports. For Uzbekistan, freight costs in 2004 amounted to around 17% of total trade values, in line with average estimates for landlocked countries but much higher than the 5-9% typical for countries with direct access to a shipping port.

Table 7: Estimated Transport Costs from Europe to Central Asia and other CIS Capitals

	Dushanbe (TAJ)	Khujan (TAJ)	Tashkent (UZB)	Almaty (KAZ)	Bishkek (KGZ)	Ashgabat (TKM)	Baku (AZE)	Tbilisi (GEO)	Yerevan (ARM)
40' Container by Road Transport									
Typical Transit Time	**15**	**14**	**12**	**13**	**14**	**14**	**13**	**12**	**14**
Ojala Spring 2004	9200	9000	7000	8000		8000	7000	6000	7000
Raballand 2004*			4000						
Ojala Spring 2005	7500	7000	5500	5500	6500	n.a.	6000	5000	6500
40' Container by Rail									
Typical Transit Time	**28**	**26**	**23**	**21**	**24**	**28**	**24**	**24**	**30**
Ojala Spring 2004	3400	3000	2800	3000		3300	2700	2500	2800
Raballand 2004*			4000						
Ojala Spring 2005	3400	3200	3000	3000	3100	2900	3000	3000	3300
A Small Shipper Exporting 1 ton by Road Freight									
Typical Transit Time	**19**	**19**	**14**	**14**	**16**	**17**	**15**	**14**	**18**
Ojala Spring 2004	500	480	300	300		400	280	300	420
Ojala Spring 2005	430	400	320	300	350	n.a.	300	300	360
1 ton by Air Freight									
Typical Transit Time	**6**	**6**	**4**	**4**	**5**	**6**	**5**	**5**	**6**
Ojala Spring 2004	2400	2200	2000	2100		2300	2100	2000	2300
Ojala Spring 2005	2100	2000	1800	1800	2000	2300	2000	2000	2300

Source: Lauri Ojala,"Review of Inter-Regional Trade and Transport Facilitation in Europe and Central Asia Region, South Asia Region and East Asia and Pacific Region". Mimeographed, June 2005, p. 27; Ojala's data are from Belgium/Netherlands and include unofficial payments. Raballand's data are to Paris. Both sources are based on surveys of freight forwarders.

Ojala provides a comparison of transport costs both in dollars and also in transit time for transport by road, rail, and air from different locations in post-Soviet Central Asia to Europe via Russia (see Table 7).

This comparison shows that the cheapest form of land transport is by rail. Road and airfreight are more expensive but are much faster. The choice of transport mode is hence a function of the nature of the goods being shipped. For the standard commodities which still comprise the greatest share of Central Asia or Uzbek exports, the railway dominates. However, for perishable goods, or intermediates traded as part of a global value chain, time is of the essence. Table 7 also reveals the considerable cost added by border crossings: e.g., $1000-1500 for road transport nd around 3 extra days for rail transport.

Compared to the European routes analyzed in Table 7, southern routes to the Persian Gulf or the Indian Ocean are much shorter and thus potentially highly competitive. Added to this is the present imbalance in most road shipments, with trucks entering Central Asia loaded but leaving empty. Truckers from Iran and Turkey potentially could offer very competitive rates. In an ideal world, a typical 40 ton truckload could reach Teheran for $ 3,000 round trip and Bandar-Abbas for about $4,000. In practice, the round trip to Teheran costs $ 5,000 and to Bandar-Abbas around $6,000, with most of the extra cost attributable to informal payments. Based on current freight rates in Pakistan and assuming these were recognized by the Central Asian countries, the land route to Karachi would be even more competitive. However transit cargo takes on average around two weeks from Karachi to Tashkent compared to 7-9 days from Bandar-Abbas and around 15 days from Europe. So far, therefore, neither of the two southern routes is much utilized.

The picture is similar for transportation by rail, as shown on Table 8. The railway to Bandar-Abbas is considerably shorter than any of the western or northern routes. Because of long delays at the Turkmenistan border and further delays during transhipment at the Iranian border due to a change in gauges, this route remains under-utilized, although its use has been increasing recently.[22]

Table 8: Existing Railway Links Between Central Asia and Major Ports

Origin	Destination seaport	Distance
Almaty	Aktau-Baku-Poti (Black Sea)	4600
	Novorossiysk (Black Sea)	4630
	Bandar Abbas (Persian Gulf)	4800 (3770*)
	Riga (Baltic Sea)	5350
	Druzhba-Shanghai (Pacific)	5370
	Mersin (Mediterranean Sea)	5421
	Vladivastok (Pacific)	7850
Tashkent	Bandar Abbas (Persian Gulf)	3800 (2770*)
	Aktau-Baku-Poti (Black Sea)	3900
	Novorossiysk (Black Sea)	3950
	Mersin (Mediterranean Sea)	4421
	Riga (Baltic Sea)	5500
	Druzhba-Shanghai (Pacific)	6320
	Vladivastok (Pacific)	8800

Source: "Transit Transport Issues in Landlocked and Transit Developing Countries". United Nations, Oxford University Press, New York, 2003.
* After the completion of Mashad-Bafq railway section in Iran.

The construction of the Bafq-Mashhad rail link will further reduce the distance on this route and may make it competitive with European routes in the future. But the key constraint appears to be the time required to cross borders.

Evidence on the costs of official and unofficial barriers to trade and transit from Afghanistan through Iran and Pakistan is scantier than for post-Soviet Central Asia. For a 40 ft container from Karachi, costs to Kabul or Kandahar are around $3,000. Two-thirds of this is pure transport costs, the remainder being expenditures on port charges, customs, unloading and reloading charges, and road tolls. To this must be added informal payments to customs and road security forces, for which no precise estimates are available. The most important costs incurred are due

---

[22] More than half of Uzbekistan's cotton exports are now estimated to be shipped by rail through Bandar- Abbas.

to time delays, with transit through Pakistan to Kabul taking around 20 days by road and rail or 14 days by road alone, of which four days is in Afghanistan. Transit by road from Iran is more expensive but saves around eight days on the journey. Increasing the speed of transit through Afghanistan is therefore a key to developing trade and transit on the North-South corridors.[23]

The estimates of transport costs can also be read as the reverse side of future potential. With faster processing times and reduced informal payments, the two southern routes to Gwadar and Bandar Abbas (and in the future Chahbahar) would be the preferred outlet for Uzbekistan.[24] The emerging competition has already led Russia to lower its railway tariffs for Uzbek exports and prompted greater attention to the cost of road transport along existing northern routes.

Physical Barriers to Transport on Southern Routes

In the railway sector, the main physical barrier is the absence of a link from Termez through Afghanistan to Pakistan. Existing studies are cautious about the economic returns on an investment in this project, which would cost billions of dollars and traverse difficult terrain. As Afghanistan develops it may still be built, but probably not for quite a few years.

The low quality of road networks, particularly in Afghanistan and Pakistan, prevent greater road transport . While around 90% of roads in formerly Soviet Central Asia are paved, the share in Afghanistan and Pakistan is a fraction of this level. However, it should be noted that road

---

[23] Existing studies of the costs of different transportation corridors are largely based on surveys of freight forwarders. For routes that are in regular use, these provide reasonably robust estimates and show some interesting changes over time. However, on the North-South routes through Afghanistan trade is estimated at less than US$170 million (against US$0.5 billion on the route to Iran, US$ 1 billion on the route to China, and much higher numbers on all Northern routes). Additional analytical work will be required to obtain more robust comparisons.

[24] And at present, the Iranian route would appear to have the upper hand over the route to Gwadar from Uzbekistan's perspective. This may change, if tensions over Iran do not subside, and alternatively, if Pakistan and Afghanistan find ways to cooperate and reduce transit times and costs through Afghan territory.

reconstruction efforts have progressed well in Afghanistan, and major transit links are now in good condition, security obstacles not withstanding.

The ADB Report[25] estimates that needed investments in road rehabilitation and modernization along 52 transport corridors through Central Asia at $ 5.6 billion.

Differing axle load requirements for trucks also hinder road transport. In the five formerly Soviet republics of Central Asia, axle load limits are 7-8 tons, reflecting the norms for road construction in the Soviet Union. Russia itself is moving to the EU norm of 11.5 tons in a move that may spread to Central Asia over time. By contrast, axle loads limits in Afghanistan and Pakistan are 12 and 14 tons respectively. Different axle load requirements present a physical barrier to competition among truck operators, made worse by the fact that axle load limits are rarely enforced for domestic truckers but used as a pretext to keep foreign trucks out. The estimated investment needed to bring Central Asia's road network consistent with the European 11.5 ton standard are around $ 5-6 billion, of which around $ 800 million would be needed in Uzbekistan.[26]

The low quality of transport fleets and the lack of investment in them further hinders road transport. In the formerly Soviet Central Asian countries, private ownership and investment in the transport fleet remain low. Ojala in his work[27] estimates that in Uzbekistan the trucking sector remains 50% state owned. While private ownership in the other countries is higher, private transport operators are typically small, with little access to credit. Hence transport fleet is gradually depreciating. Regional truckers are thus non-competitive internationally, which in turn makes

---

[25] *"Report on the Economic Impact of Central-South Asian Road Corridors"*. Prepared for the Transport Committee of CAREC. Asian Development Bank (ADB), Manila, March 2005, p. 1.

[26] Estimates provided by Henry Kerali, senior transport specialist of World Bank. It is likely that these investments are not entirely additive to the ADB estimates of road rehabilitation costs along different North South corridors; at least for Uzbekistan they should overlap to a considerable extent.

[27] Ojala, Lauri. "Review of Inter-Regional Trade and Transport Facilitation in Europe and Central Asia Region, South Asia Region and East Asia and Pacific Region". Mimeographed, June 2005, p. 34.

them reluctant to reduce some of the policy barriers to competition discussed further below.

Lack of transshipment and logistics infrastructure is a further impediment. Because of varying axle loads as well as different railway gauges, transshipment is often necessary for cargo crossing borders in Greater Central Asia. There is a corresponding need for modern logistics and transshipment centers. In best practice models, these centers simultaneously offer customs clearance, storage, and transshipment, as well as competitive freight forwarders. This lowers costs and adds to the speed of continental container trade, which will be essential if Greater Central Asia is to become a continental trade corridor. However, at present we have no information concerning the costs of investment in such logistic centers.

Trade Policy and Trade and Transport Facilitation

There are many policy obstacles to trade and transit within and across the region, which are summarized in Table 9. They are grouped into obstacles related to trade policy, border management and customs harmonization, and regulation of the transportation sector.

Table 9: Major Policy Related Trade and Transit Obstacles

Trade Policy	Differences in tariff rates Different stages in the WTO accession process Overlapping, sometimes inconsistent regional trade preferences Non-tariff tax barriers such as excise taxes on imports, labeling requirements, import licenses
Border Management	Lack of harmonized customs procedures, leading to detailed checks on both sides of the border Numerous and cumbersome documentation requirements Lack of recognition of TIR seals and high cost of transit convoys High levels of corruption of customs officials and other inspection agencies
Transport Sector	Visa restrictions on entry of foreign truckers Truck entry fees Trucking cartels to guarantee safe passage

In addition to the physical barriers mentioned above, competition in road transportation is hampered by policy obstacles such as the difficulties for truckers to obtain entry visas and the high fees charged to foreign trucks entering a country. Uzbekistan, mainly for security reasons, prohibits the entry of trucks from Afghanistan, and non-CIS drivers pay high costs for entry visas (Table 10).

Table 10: Cost of Visas in Central Asian Republics, 2005

(In US dollars)

Country	For CIS Nationals		For Non-CIS Nationals	
	Single Entry	Multiple Entry	Single Entry	Multiple Entry
Azerbaijan	0	0	40	250
Kazakhstan	Varies	Varies	70	210
Kyrgyz Republic	4	20	35	125
Tajikistan	7–8	60	30–60	150–350
Uzbekistan	4–6	30	60	250

Source: "Central Asia regional cooperation in trade, transport and transit". Paper prepared for the Trade Policy Committee of CAREC Asian Development Bank, Manila, March 2005, p.14.

Uzbekistan's policies are mirrored by those of its neighbors in a pattern characterized until recently by retaliatory escalation. It remains to be seen whether in the context of Uzbekistan's joining EurASEC these and other issues will begin to be tackled.[28] However, EurASEC does not

[28] Interestingly, in two successive meetings in late summer 2006, Uzbek officials have called for visa free travel with both Kyrgyz Republic and Tajikistan. There may still be a gap between political rhetoric and practical reality, but it is one among a number of signals that point towards a gradual rapprochement.

include Afghanistan and Turkmenistan and thus progress within EurASEC will tend to reinforce rather than reduce the trade dependence on Russia.

At the heart of many of the obstacles hindering trade and transit are the significant variations in trade policy regimes across the region (see Chart 4).

Chart 4: Trade Restrictiveness Indexes in Central Asia and their Northern and Southern Counterparts

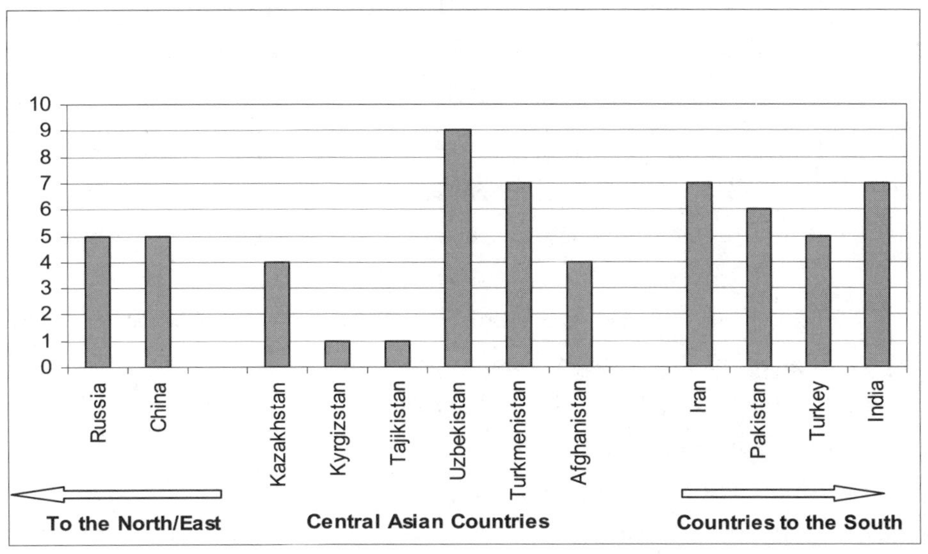

Source: International Monetary Fund data, taken from Byrd, William and Martin Raiser (with Alex Kitain and Anton Dobronogov) (2006), "Prospects for Economic Development and Cooperation in the Wider Central Asia Region". World Bank Working Papers No. 75, April 2006, p.68.

These differences in trade policies are reflected in policy-induced variations in the prices of goods in the different national markets, in turn creating incentives for shuttle traders to exploit these differences. [29]

---

[29] See Grafe, Clemens, Martin Raiser, and Toshiaki Sakatsume (2006), "Beyond the Border: Reconsidering Regional Trade in Central Asia". EBRD Working Paper

Shuttle imports into Uzbekistan from China, Iran and Turkey may account for close to $1 billion (25% of the total) and smuggled exports of cotton, energy products, agricultural goods and precious metals (all subject to high excises and/or domestic price controls) are also significant. Anecdotal evidence suggests that shuttle trade between southern Uzbekistan and Mazar-i-Sherif is also increasing. Land-based shuttle trade is likely to increase significantly with the opening of the new bridge across the Panj River between Afghanistan and Tajikistan and with the completion of the Anzob tunnel connecting southern Tajikistan with the Ferghana valley. If Uzbekistan wants to avoid further tensions in the Ferghana valley it will need to re-think its trade policies and adopt a more relaxed attitude towards shuttle traders. We offer some proposals on this issue.

While informal trade generates important employment opportunities, in particular for poor people, it undermines revenue collection and creates significant difficulties for domestic producers, who face competition from informal imports which pay neither import duties nor domestic taxes.[30] The Uzbek government therefore seeks to suppress informal trade by making it more difficult to cross borders and by placing restrictions on domestic wholesale and retail trade. But these policies affect not only small informal traders but formal traders as well. The fear of informal trade evading customs and other duties is also one of the main reasons for the high costs of transit trade, manifested in the requirement for escort services, failure to implement the TIR convention, etc. Harmonization of trade policies will be needed if progress in other areas of trade and transit facilitation is to be sustained.

No. 95. For Uzbekistan, excise taxes levied discriminatorily on imports in reflection of "domestic market conditions" are in fact a much more important element of trade policy than tariffs per se (which are relatively moderate, with three bands up to 30% for MVN partners, twice the rate for all others). Yet in practice it seems that final goods prices are essentially limited by arbitrage as well as low consumer spending power in Uzbekistan. The complex trade regime thus serves primarily as an instrument in reallocating rather than increasing the absolute level of arbitrage rents. This suggests welfare losses well in excess of the dead weight loss resulting from higher domestic prices.

[30] Such complaints are heard frequently, for instance, from Uzbek businessmen.

Crossing borders anywhere in the world is costly. Commercial traffic often faces cumbersome formal documentation and registration requirements and lengthy delays before receiving clearance. Table 11 illustrates some of the obstacles faced by traders wishing to clear goods through customs in Central Asia.

Table 11: Trading Across Borders

Region Or Economy	**Documents for export (number)**	**Signatures for export (number)**	**Time for export (days)**	**Documents for import (number)**	**Signatures for import (number)**	**Time for import (days)**
Europe & Central Asia	7	10	31	11	15	42
OECD: High income	5	3	12	6	3	14
South Asia	8	12	33	12	24	46
Uzbekistan	..	..	..	18	32	139
Kyrgyz Republic	..	..	..	18	27	127
Afghanistan	..	..	..	10	57	97
Kazakhstan	14	15	93	18	17	87
Iran	11	30	45	11	45	51
India	10	22	36	15	27	43
Pakistan	8	10	33	12	15	39
Russian Federation	8	8	29	8	10	35
Turkey	9	10	20	13	20	25
China	6	7	20	11	8	24
United Arab Emirates	6	3	18	6	3	18

Source: Doing Business Report, World Bank, Washington DC, 2005.

Compared with its regional neighbors, Uzbekistan has some of the most time-consuming border procedures, as the number of signatures and documents required for import clearance demonstrates.[31]

A notable issue in all countries of Greater Central Asia is the presence of several inspection and enforcement agencies at the border, who often act in an uncoordinated and highly discretionary manner. A culture of control and red tape prevails among most enforcement agencies, leading to duplication and harassment. While customs codes are being reformed throughout the region (indeed, Uzbekistan made the reform of the customs code a priority for 2006), implementation may lag behind changes in primary legislation, leading to legal and procedural inconsistencies. This can occur even though Central Asian customs have comparatively low case loads, which indicates the need for improved customs efficiency.

A large part of the estimated economic returns from new transportation routes come from increased transit trade. Of particular importance in this respect are improvements in the regulation of transit by road. Because of concerns over the evasion of import duties, governments often require trucks in transit to be escorted. Private escort services are expensive, costing between $1,000-1,500 per truck for a crossing through Kazakhstan, and up to $2,000 through Uzbekistan (these numbers include informal payments to the road police). Truckers usually prefer convoy systems rather than "escort service" for the following reasons: (i) greater security, (ii) no need to make a deposit for the duties which is always difficult and takes a long time to get back, and (iii) the absence of road police or other harassment. Convoys are escorted by customs officers. Normally, there is

---

[31] Some very interesting new results come from a survey of transport operators on the route Bishkek-Almaty. These results, part of a Central Asia wide initiative to measure performance along selected transit corridors, suggests that the delays due to road blocks and customs clearance on this journey of usually 4 hours, make up an additional 10 hours on average, with much of this time spent in customs facilities in land rather than at the border. Moreover, informal payments exceed official costs by a factor of 10 and total US$450 for a stretch of less than 400km. Unpublished survey results as part of the Central Asia trade and transit facilitation initiative of the World Bank.

one convoy per day, except in Tajikistan where it is not uncommon for 2-3 days to be lost waiting for convoys to form.

The TIR convention, to which all post-Soviet countries are signatories but which does not apply in Afghanistan, allows sealed trucks to transit unchecked to their final destination. In practice this is not enforced. The number of TIR carnets issued is minimal (21,500 for the whole of Central Asia in 2003), and alternative insurance bonds are not available. The application of TIR is also hampered by the lack of modern trucks that would meet TIR requirements, except in Iran and Kazakhstan, where reasonably modern fleets exist.

The above obstacles create entry barriers to private trucking companies that lack connections with the customs officials and road police who try to extract further rents along the way through checkpoints, etc. These problems are compounded in Afghanistan by levies by illegitimate authorities akin to "protection money". These differ little in their impact on transporters from police checkpoints in some other countries of the region.

The Transport of Energy

Energy is the sector in which Uzbekistan could reap the greatest gains from more cooperation with its neighbors and the international community without requiring a fundamental change in domestic policies. Still there are important constraints and impediments to coordinated development and the trade of energy resources in the Greater Central Asia region and in Uzbekistan in particular.

Afghanistan and some other countries of the region suffer from insecurity in certain geographical areas, which could adversely affect the construction and operation of transmission lines and natural gas pipelines. Current plans are to provide populations along main transmission lines with social benefits to create an incentive to protect the line. Implementing and enforcing such a regime will pose a huge challenge.

There is a lack of trans-regional electricity transmission lines and gas pipelines, and the national energy networks in a number of the countries are limited, most notably in Afghanistan. Major investments in electricity generation and gas production capacity will also be required to exploit regional potentials.

Reliable supply and demand are important for energy trading, which often involves high up-front investments in transmission infrastructure. Uzbekistan, like its Central Asian neighbors, has followed a policy of energy self-sufficiency and so far seems reluctant to agree to long-term power trading arrangements that will be essential if opportunities in this sector are to be realized.

Energy transmission networks often have "network monopoly" characteristics, which means that there are discrete "either-or" choices of transmission routes. Such choices can easily become the subject of destructive geopolitical competition, with the risk of technically and financially attractive routes being blocked and of inferior routes being chosen due to geopolitical factors.[32]

The regulatory framework for regional energy planning, financing, and investment protection, contract enforcement, and policy and commercial risk mitigation is notably weak in Uzbekistan and elsewhere.

Energy prices in several countries remain below cost recovery and regulation is weak, putting investments at risk. It should be noted, however, that the increase in energy prices, and gas prices in particular, has increased the opportunity costs of not reforming the domestic energy sector. Revising this Uzbekistan has moved rapidly in this area.

---

[32] For Uzbekistan, there is a risk that given the country's reluctance to sign-up to longer term power trading with its neighbors, alternative transmission routes by-passing the country may be built. One such route would link Toktogul in Kyrgyz Republic with Tajikistan and on towards Afghanistan (a 110KV link between the two countries has already been completed). Putting such an alternative route in use would, however, require the recalibration of the Central Asian energy grid, which requires either the agreement of UDC Energia, or the establishment of a new regional dispatch center. Evidently, by-pass solutions would be expensive, but Uzbekistan should be aware that such solutions will be pursued unless it shows more willingness to cooperate.

In the case of hydropower, which can serve as the production base for substantial regional electricity trading, there are are many riparian issues which would need to be resolved for major investments to go forward.

These constraints require both investments in physical infrastructure and complementary policy measures. Investments in infrastructure in Afghanistan are proceeding. From the Uzbek perspective the most important investments concern the completion of the Kabul-Puli Khumri-Termez 220KV transmission line, scheduled for 2008 (see Chart 5).

Chart 5: Priority Transmission Lines

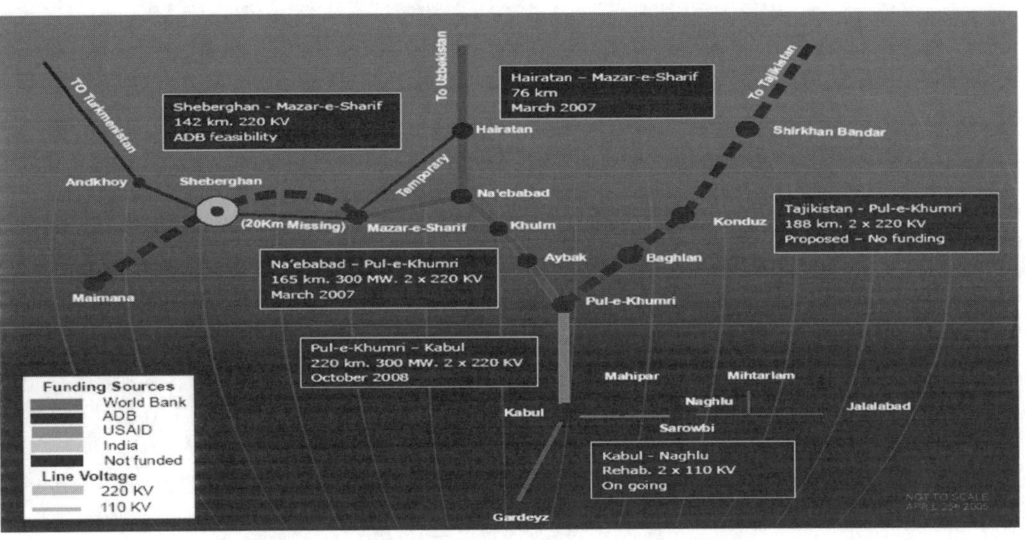

Source: World Bank staff. Taken from Byrd, William and Martin Raiser (with Alex Kitain and Anton Dobronogov) (2006), "Prospects for Economic Development and Cooperation in the Wider Central Asia Region". World Bank Working Papers No. 75, April 2006, p.43.

The current 110KV transmission line from Hairatan directly to Mazar is not fully utilized because of the lack of a local distribution network in Mazar. Uzbekenergo has conducted feasibility studies for the required investments in the Mazaar area to allow the existing 150MW export capacity to be more fully utilized and would be prepared to complete this work if financing is obtained. An upgrade of the Mazar-i-Sharif distribution network is included in the World Bank's upcoming power sector loan to Afghanistan, and Uzbekenergo may have an opportunity to bid for the resulting contracts, although it is likely that they would have to do so as partners in a consortium.

Turning to policy, until recently, Uzbekistan charged 2.3 cts per kwh for power exported to Afghanistan, which is below the estimated long run marginal cost of around 3.5 cts. and also below the domestic price of more than 3cts. In 2006 Uzbekistan announced that it will seek to increase prices, but the status of negotiations with the Afghan government is uncertain. For now contracts are concluded annually between the two countries. This does not provide a solid basis for investments to realize the medium-term power trading potential. Multi-year power purchase agreements would be one way to go but this would require Afghanistan to be able to commit to purchases over a medium term timeframe, which would under current circumstances be impossible without donor guarantees. It will also require Uzbekistan to be able to commit to reliable power supplies over the medium-term, something which the country has so far been reluctant to do.[33]

Proposals to Overcome Obstacles in Uzbekistan

For Uzbekistan to move from the slow to the fast lane in regional cooperation and integration is first and foremost a question of leadership and political will. This chapter argues strongly for the potential economic benefits of opening up. Uzbekistan's leadership has instead chosen to emphasize the risks of doing so. Unless Uzbekistan's political leadership embraces change and the opportunities it brings, the country will risk being left behind.

Still, the number and size and multitude of the obstacles identified above requires careful thought on how best to sequence policy measures and

---

[33] Uzbekenergo insists that this is not because of uncertainties over domestic energy needs and availability of resources, but rather reflects the desire to be able to adjust pricing as market conditions change. If this were to be the case, a contractual solution allowing for some variation in price is likely to be possible, as for instance with the gas pricing formula for Russian gas exports in the European market.

investments. Moreover, the required policy measures are typically not distributionally neutral. For a country like Uzbekistan, where distributional issues are at the core of the political economy, this is not a trivial consideration. Designing ideal policy options is easy; implementing them in the Uzbek policy environment is not.

We therefore concentrate on short-term measures that we believe may offer high returns and pose relatively few political risks for the present leadership. These measures are unlikely to be sufficient. Clearly, it would be desirable both for Uzbekistan and its neighbors that the country accelerate its market-oriented reforms, not just in the area of trade policy but also in improving the business environment, promoting private entrepreneurship and market-based financing. Uzbekistan should also increase its international competitiveness by being more open to the flow of ideas and more willing to debate policy alternatives. We advocate our short-term policy proposals as a possible way of overcoming the skepticism that still prevails in Tashkent about a policy of greater openness and liberalization. As the international environment changes and the opportunity costs of standing still become ever greater, more ambitious measures may become feasible. But since the catalogue of desirable reforms in Uzbekistan is both long and well rehearsed, we do not list it here.

In the short term, the following proposals deserve closer consideration:

1. Create border zone markets.

These are being developed already in Kara-Su area and would represent a first step on the way towards greater trade liberalization. The basic idea would be to create markets in border zones which are accessible to residents from these border zones and within which duty- free trade is possible. Non-residents would continue to have to pay customs and other duties. An extension of this model would allow for the creation of free trade zones in border areas for storage and re-export as is presently under consideration along the Chinese and Kazakh borders. By providing opportunities for residents of border areas to trade across borders as well as visit relatives, this proposal would be a step towards separating trade and security issues, since residents are relatively easy to identify. This could in turn be a step towards confidence-building particularly in the Ferghana valley. It would also allow border guards to concentrate on real security risks, including illegal border crossings, rather than losing time chasing after the numerous shuttle traders (and attempting to extract private gains in the process).

2. *Rebuild Uzbekistan as a wholesale trade center for Central Asia.*

Uzbekistan's location makes it the first choice for wholesalers wishing to penetrate the Central Asian market. Indeed, this is the role Tashkent played until Uzbekistan's trade policies turned inwards. As a result of these policies, Uzbekistan has lost the greatest benefit from trade in Central Asia, which comes from controlling wholesale trade into the region.[34] Uzbek wholesalers are forced to use a complicated system of "mules" – small traders that bring in goods from the Kyrgyz Republic, Kazakhstan, Moscow and Dubai and sell them to Uzbek wholesalers for resale inside the country. These wholesalers control the domestic market, but they are price takers on the international market, with the "mules" evading Uzbek trade restriction in order to reduce import costs.[35] As a pilot project the Uzbek government might consider allowing competitive access of import wholesalers to wholesale market in Uzbekistan at Andijan and observe whether a relocation of trading activities from Kara Su occurs. This would include a reduction in shuttle trade, since residents would now be able to buy legally imported goods in their own country. This could set the stage for a broader liberalization of wholesaling in the import market. An important side benefit would be the reduction of production costs in Uzbekistan because of easier and more reliable access to imports. Such policies would therefore also promote domestic

---

[34] This argument is based on the notion of economies of agglomeration in wholesale trade, which would need to be further investigated. But given the very high transport costs into the region, high transshipment costs, and weak trade logistics, the existence of agglomeration economies would seem likely.

[35] Because of shuttle trade, the wholesalers are effectively also price takers on the domestic market. The only rents available are obtained through discretionary reduction of official trade levies, either by under-invoicing or outright avoidance of customs and taxes through "connections". These are small amounts compared to the potential gains of being the wholesale center for Central Asia as a whole.

production, as suggested by the successful experience of similar schemes in China, Vietnam, Thailand and Laos.

3. Concentrate support for trade and transit along a few selected transit routes.

From Uzbekistan's perspective there would be much merit in providing assistance to Afghan security services, border management and customs officers along a few selected border posts, including Hairatan. This would reduce Uzbek concerns about allowing greater movement of goods and people across the "friendship bridge", and thus produce greater value from the modern equipment and training that has already been provided to Uzbek border guards at Termez. Such a concentrated approach could extend to the roads and raillinks along continental corridors, so that transport investments and trade facilitation measures are fully coordinated. This is not presently the case. From Uzbekistan's perspective, two routes deserve particular attention: (i) Termez – Mazar – Kabul – Jalalabad and (ii) Bukhara – Charzhou – Mary – Meshed – Teheran. Whichever routes are chosen, Uzbekistan should actively participate in multilateral forums discussing trade and transit facilitation in the region. Uzbekistan's current bilateral approach to diplomacy in the region and particularly with its southern neighbors is in this context bound to be sub-optimal.

4. A donor initiative on trucking and road transportation.

Such an initiative is needed to deal with the problem of differing axle load requirements that result from regulations and ageing infrastructure. For example, Uzbek truckers could be given access to donor-funded credit facilities subject to certain conditions on convoys, entry fees, visas etc. This initiative could be motivated by a more detailed corridor performance measurement, which is already being developed.

5. Uzbekistan could serve as an energy clearing house.

Uzbekistan can achieve this through the import of hydro-generated power in summer and the sale of thermal-generated power in winter. Donor strategies would need to concentrate on giving Uzbekistan a stake in the rehabilitation of the power sector in Afghanistan and on delivering parallel transmission solutions from Toktogul and Sanctuda to break up

Uzbekistan's hold over Kyrgyzstan's and Tajikistan's power exports. We believe that a combination of such carrots and sticks is vital if the Uzbek authorities are to be convinced of the value of a more cooperative approach in this area. Conversely, solutions aimed merely at by-passing Uzbekistan are likely to be expensive and unsustainable and will cause political difficulties to those they are intended to help.

6. Technical assistance to help Uzbek suppliers compete in Afghan rebuilding efforts.

Aside from energy, options in this area include road building, the sale of construction materials, and the promotion of qualified personnel. Uzbek companies are often unable to meet international procurement requirements such as bank guarantees and relevant international experience. Moreover, they are often inept at complying with bidding procedures. Technical assistance to overcome some of these barriers should be considered, as well as efforts to create partnerships with successful western bidders. While to outside observers there is no doubt that Uzbekistan should open up in its own interest and should need no additional prodding to do so, the political realities require a more subtle approach. Afghanistan's reconstruction is an area where both Afghanistan and Uzbekistan could benefit from working together and thus build greater mutual confidence and a basis for sustainable regional cooperation in the future.

Conclusions

We have argued that there are significant benefits from increasing Uzbekistan's openness to trade and significant barriers to its realization. At a technical level, the conditions seem right for Uzbekistan to move on a new trade agenda. Yet the external environment in which Uzbekistan increasingly finds itself may send it in the other direction, toward closing up, toward increased reliance on old trading partners. In a region already struggling to find its footing, this would be a shame. Bringing Uzbekistan back into the continental trading fold depends in part on bringing it into the global fold. This, in turn, depends on finding ways to reverse Uzbekistan's growing isolation from the West. How to rebuild Uzbekistan's trust in the West and thereby reopen dialogue on the issues discussed in this paper is a topic for another study. Under any circumstances, this remains a critical challenge.

The Kyrgyz Republic

Joomart Otorbaev
Rafkat Hasanov
Gulzhan Ermekbaeva
Dinara Rakhmanova
Sergey Slepchenko
Murat Suyunbaev

Problem in Historical Perspectives

Greater Central Asia is home to 1.15 percent of the world's population and covers 3.3 percent of the world's landmass, yet the countries' combined gross domestic product (GDP) is only 0.12 percent of the world's total. The region's population and GDP are smaller than those of Iran or Turkey.

During the Soviet era, Greater Central Asia was called "Middle Asia and Kazakhstan" reflecting the physical and geographical differences within the area. Southern Kazakhstan was often referred to as "Middle Asia" and northern Kazakhstan as "Southern Siberia." The climate and terrain of northern Afghanistan resembles those of Middle Asia. The region was labeled "Central Asia" in the post-Soviet period, a moniker that is not geographically justified. "Middle Asia" is a geographically appropriate term, since Asia extends from latitude 40º North at the western part of Asia Minor peninsula (in longitude 26º East) to the eastern part of Hokkaido island in Japan (in longitude 146º East). The region's six countries are wholly or partially encompassed by Middle Asia, making "Greater Central Asia" the most accurate name for the region with the center of Eurasia located in Kyrgyzstan. The region is extremely remote from sea ports, being at the center of the world's largest continent.

The difficulty of accessing world markets and trade protectionism in other countries will likely cause Greater Central Asia to trend toward centripetal trade relations. While this tendency is curtailed by the high quantity and low cost of raw minerals in regional markets, the region is inclined toward running a trade deficit due to low commodity saturation shaped by geopolitical factors, and by the fact that its export goods are largely uncompetitive in world markets. Greater Central Asia remains the weakest link within the transcontinental system of cooperation.

The development of trade across Greater Central Asia is hindered by:

- Formidable physical barriers, such as mountains and deserts, and lack of access to sea and river ports.
- Problematic or unstable political regimes and instability that create geopolitical barriers.
- Transport barriers created by poor ground-based transportation and pipeline infrastructures, and a lack of goods that can be shipped by air.
- Inconsistent customs, trade, tax, tariff and non-tariff regimes throughout the region that block free trade.
- Increasing bureaucratic impediments, which have now become the principal barriers to integration and trade.

These physical and political obstacles impede the development of trade and threaten regional economic growth and stability. They can be overcome only through joint effort and assistance from donor countries.

Geographical and Physical Characteristics

Greater Central Asia's primary physical characteristics are its central location within the globe's largest continent and its remoteness to countries with developed market economies. The Kyzylkum, Aralkum, and Moyun-Kum deserts are located in the center of Greater Central Asia, inhibiting relations between the region's states. The eastern and southern borders follow mountain ranges that inhibit the region's relations with neighboring countries. Kyrgyzstan, Afghanistan and Tajikistan are particularly mountainous; Uzbekistan, Kazakhstan and

Turkmenistan are less so. The region is open only to the north, i.e towards the Arctic Ocean.

Greater Central Asia is extremely arid, due to the surrounding mountains and its distance from oceans. The region is open to masses of cold air from the Arctic Ocean and its mountain ranges block weather systems, such as monsoons, that originate in the Indian Ocean. The result is a harsh, dry climate. The sharp variation in altitudes contributes to the marked contrast among local climates in the region. At high altitudes the climate is arctic and sub-arctic; in the deserts, summer temperatures can reach 50ºC in the shade and 70ºC in direct sunlight. During the winter, the temperature in high, mountainous regions can dip to -60ºC. Such extreme minimum and maximum temperatures can be found in only a few of the world's regions.

The mountainous areas are hemmed by deserts, and the lack of topsoil and summertime precipitation leads to low agricultural productivity. The wide variation in regional climate also contributes to agricultural problems. For example, Central Asian riverheads, the areas best supplied with water are topographically unsuitable for farming.

Mountain communities depend heavily on agriculture, with limited employment opportunities outside the agricultural sector. Farming yields are three to ten times lower than in other countries of the world. The efficiency of animal husbandry is also low. The regions' climatic extremes and low biological productivity have led to the widespread development of a nomadic way of life. Today, up to 20 percent of Afghanistan's population is nomadic or semi-nomadic.

Prior to the Soviet war in Afghanistan, the majority of its population practiced subsistence farming. Their integration with and even awareness of, the outside world was very low. Paradoxically, a generation of war introduced Afghanis to globalization, heightening their awareness of events outside the region via the modern infrastructure of military information, the Internet, foreign military instructors and military training camps in Pakistan and other countries. People became aware of modern living standards and began to earn money, allowing the pursuit of a modern lifestyle. But it is difficult to achieve this standard of living while practicing traditional agriculture, especially under the region's harsh conditions.

Afghanistan cannot restore agriculture without increasing water diversion from the Amu Darya river. It is unavoidable that all further water resource management initiatives in the region will have to consider the potential demands of Afghanistan. The best way to meet future needs is to have all countries along the Amu Darya participate in negotiations to determine mutually appropriate solutions. The United States can assist in solving this issue by providing the requisite technical assistance.

Among the Greater Central Asian countries persists a myth about the richness of their mineral and other natural resources, and the benefits to be realized through their exploitation. The prevailing view is that these resources are in great demand abroad and that feeding this demand will enable the region's states to leap forward in economic development. In reality, the mountains indeed contain a variety of minerals, but not in great quantity.

Afghanistan, Tajikistan and Kyrgyzstan are small, landlocked, mountainous countries with weak resource bases. This creates difficulties for the maintenance of statehood and sovereignty. Countries that are 75 to 100 percent mountainous are usually poor and typically suffer from a range of associated problems. For instance, mountainous territories and peoples that have never attained sovereignty due to lack of resources include Tibet, Kurdistan and several nations in the Caucasus.

Arable land in mountainous regions is delimited by two lines of altitude: the snow line and a second line separating mountainous zones from deserts and alkaline soils. Only a narrow area, where soil moisture is liquid during the growing season, is suitable for efficient agricultural production. Thus, only about 7 percent of Kyrgyzstan's territory is farmed. The World Food Organization considers half of the Greater Central Asian countries—Afghanistan, Tajikistan, Uzbekistan—to be insufficiently nourished, although two-thirds of their populations work in agriculture.

The region's countries also have small populations and low labor productivity. Most people are trapped in a vicious cycle of poverty, intensifying social tensions that facilitate the development of extremist movements. The vicious circle of poverty is supplemented by a vicious cycle of safety: the threat posed by extremism and international terrorism decreases the region's ability to attract investment, creating yet another obstacle to social and economic development. Investment in the region is low due to lack of infrastructure, including roads to bring in equipment and materials, and ship out the goods produced.

Low economic density due to mountainous terrain reduces the value of infrastructure investments as well as broader economic investments. Mountains make development difficult by demanding greater capital and current investments, significantly increasing the cost of imported and exported goods.

International trade in Greater Central Asia requires transporting goods long distances through the neighboring countries, but the large number of mountain ranges and their exceptional height lead to a naturally low regional transit capacity. Large capital investments are required to overcome the transit resistance of the region's mountains, yet this investment is not locally available. It is difficult to build roads on mountainous terrain, and even more difficult to build tunnels through mountains. Transportation issues and climatic conditions are prime contributors to the economic underdevelopment of the region.

Regional Geopolitical and Geo-economic Status

The U.S. State Department long grouped Kazakhstan, the five Central Asia republics and Russia into the Eurasian region, while Afghanistan was considered to be a part of Southwestern Asia. Only in 2006 did it move the five former Soviet states into a new Central and South Asia bureau. The U.S. Department of Defense has always considered these six countries to be one region. But regional integration is not a pre-requisite to being considered a region by political institutions moreover and military planning, with its reliance on air transport, considers different factors than the logic of economic integration, which emphasizes ground transport. And the possibility of conducting trade does not make integration necessary or inevitable. It is important to note that international organizations working in the region do not have a coherent approach to the issue.

The Interests of Greater Central Asia and its Neighbors

Pakistan is interested in developing transport communications to open a route to the southern part of the Commonwealth of Independent States (CIS), which could yield significant economic benefits. But conflicts in Afghanistan have prevented Pakistan from realizing this goal, and the increasing instability in the Pakistani province of Baluchistan could block access to Gwadar harbor. Friction with India and tense relations with Iran further complicate Pakistan's security situation.

Civil discord in Afghanistan has distracted the Pushtun people from reuniting with Pushtuns living in adjacent areas of Pakistan. Pushtuns constitute 14 percent of Pakistan's population and they do not recognize the border established by the Durand line; nor does Afghanistan with its large Pushtun population. The Pushtun's desire for their own nation-state could lead to a lengthy conflict between Pakistan and Afghanistan. Pakistan's protectionist policies have led Afghanistan to lean toward cooperation with its western neighbor, Iran.

Iran needs a regional market. Tehran's recent anti-Israel statements and the unresolved issues regarding Iran's nuclear program undermine its foreign policy positions. Nevertheless, Iran should be given an opportunity to find its place in implementing the Greater Central Asia (GCA) project. Iran is flanked by Iraq and Afghanistan; excluding it from the project would likely drive Tehran into a corner, with unpredictable consequences.

India fears that the spread of Islamism from Afghanistan to Central Asia could create a pro-Pakistani coalition of Islamic states. Such a coalition would threaten India's security interests.

Turkmenistan's position toward Afghanistan is primarily defined by its gas export interests. Its doctrine of positive neutrality does not allow for joining any integration unions.

Uzbekistan is keen on gaining access to the sea. However, after the events in Andijan and the subsequent chill in relations with the United

States, Uzbekistan has become alert to any projects with purported "democratic" backing.

The gradually forming Kabul-Dushanbe-Moscow axis causes discontent in Tashkent, which has responded by forming a Pakistan-Uzbekistan axis. This partnership is supported by the economic rationale of building transport and communications between the two states through the territory of Afghanistan. The Tajik-Uzbek conflict seriously impacts regional stability.

Kazakhstan, along with Iran and Turkmenistan, is one of the region's largest hydrocarbons producers. Kazakhstan is the only country in Greater Central Asia that sent troops to support the current war in Iraq.

Kyrgyzstan is the only country that hosts both U.S. and Russian military bases. Kyrgyzstan and Kazakhstan are not members of 6+2 group formed under UN auspices in 1998, which includes the six countries bordering Afghanistan, Russia and the United States.

Russia is interested in maintaining a stable buffer area to limit the spread of Islamic extremism.

China is concerned about growing separatism and Islamism in the Xinjiang Uyghur Autonomous Region. China's rapid economic growth has boosted competition for natural resources, especially energy, throughout Central Asia. Goods from all over the world enter Greater Central Asia's markets, but these must cross several borders en route, making them expensive and unaffordable to most consumers. Chinese goods, which are competitive in U.S. and European markets, cross only one border and have almost no competition in Central Asian markets. China's involvement in the region is shaped in part by its interest in procuring energy assets, and is thus considered to be a serious competitor by other countries.

Regional integration processes will seek to consolidate local control over regional energy carriers and could limit economic links between Russia, China and Iran, and between these states and the other states in Central Asia. But if Russia, China, or Iran were to impede integration instead of facilitating it, prospects for success would be low.

The United States and other Western countries are concerned over possible political and social destabilization in Greater Central Asia. Destabilization would erode their influence and increase the spread of international terrorism, while strengthening Russia's position in the region. The West is keen on maintaining moderate Muslim regimes and developing economic relations within the region. Maximal economic involvement of European countries is highly important for the GCA project.

Central Asian security concerns could be addressed by the German initiative to create a "Group of Three" comprised of Russia, the United States and Germany as the European Union (EU) representative. The prospective group would work with the Organization for Security and Cooperation in Europe (OSCE) to develop measures aimed at stabilizing Kyrgyzstan and the surrounding region. Germany is a member of the anti-terrorist coalition and has an airbase at Termez in Uzbekistan.

Regional Integration Processes

The prospects for Greater Central Asia integration are not strong, since the area lacks economic integration, which typically defines the integrity of a region. During the Soviet era, the volume of foreign trade within Greater Central Asia did not exceed 10 percent of the region's total aggregate goods turnover, and the absolute values of trade decreased. For example, Tajikistan's share of Kyrgyzstan's foreign trade is several times less that that of China and the United States.

But integration is possible after partner countries have reached a threshold level of economic density. Each country's economic activity will focus abroad only when domestic saturation has been reached. To determine the trajectory of economic development, Greater Central Asia's economic density is compared below with that of the EU, a successfully integrated union.

The economic density of Kyrgyzstan's territory is, on average, 102.2 times less than that of a small EU country, while Afghanistan's density is 1037 times less. Regional integration processes will be difficult to implement in an area with such low economic density.

Table A: Economic Density of Countries

Country	GDP, in billon USD on PPP* (2002)	Area, thousand km2	Economic density, GDP/S, in million USD/ km2
Belgium	295.8	30.5	9.7
The Netherlands	432.8	40.8	10.6
Portugal	182	92.0	1.98
Switzerland	228	41.3	5.5
Average			**6.95**
Kyrgyzstan	13.6	199.5	0.068
Afghanistan	4.4	652	0.0067

* Purchasing Power Parity

A natural geo-economic region can be created by territories (either countries or regions within countries) between which trade and economic links can be established with minimal transport resistance. Transport resistance is not always related to geographical distance, yet it can be measured simply: by the amount of time spent on the road to reach a destination. Subsequent sections of this paper will show that transport resistance is quite high between Afghanistan and the region's former Soviet republics.

Tajikistan, Uzbekistan and Afghanistan border each other along underdeveloped areas, further hampering larger regional integration. This underdevelopment has caused the vectors of major economic activity to focus in diverse directions. Kazakhstan and Uzbekistan aim at the West, while Tajikistan, Turkmenistan and Kyrgyzstan orient northward. In the next five to ten years, China may become the major trading partner for Greater Central Asia, redirecting the vectors of economic activity eastward. Minimal standards of internal integration are necessary before regional integration processes can occur. For example, until local leaders in Afghanistan recognize Kabul's central authority it is unlikely that they would recognize any supra-national structures.

Economic internationalization—the process of economic interaction with surrounding trading partners—is another necessary development. But economic internationalization and integration are not the same. For instance, in the beginning of the 1990s, strong internationalization occurred with the activity of "shuttle traders" between China's Xinjiang Uyghur Autonomous Region and Greater Central Asia; this type of integration was not directed by state policy.

The low growth of trade indicators is linked to political barriers. Some Greater Central Asian states have not participated in removing transport barriers. The West's penetration within the framework of the Transport Corridor Europe Caucasus Asia (TRACECA) and Greater Silk Road (GSR) projects can have a broad impact since the removal of transport barriers has the potential of opening, decompressing and eventually destabilizing non-democratic political regimes.

Afghanistan's current regime isolates certain Afghani regions from each other and from the rest of the country. This practice directly opposes integration and the need to maximize openness. Major trunk highways are being restored by U.S.-funded development projects, but for the most part the internal road system remains in disrepair. Developing the internal road system is a key to integration, and must be addressed.

Relations between Greater Central Asia states can be internationalized, but it is unlikely that this will be accomplished in the foreseeable future, as demonstrated by the failures of the Turkish "Greater Turkic World" project in the early 1990s, of the CAC/CAEU/CAF/OCAC[1] projects that ran from 1993 to 2005, and the waning of the "Greater Middle East" and GUUAM[2] projects that were sponsored by neighboring countries beginning in 2005.

These failures created a high level of wariness in the region regarding similar integration efforts. The GCA project launched in 2006 must continue for at least 15 to 20 years; the long-term nature of the project could cause it to lose its urgency. It is critical to maintain and forecast progress—failure of yet another integration project could further increase resistance to integration and exacerbate anti-American sentiment.

---

[1] CAC – Central-Asia Cooperation
CAEC – Central Asia Economic Union
CAF – Central Asia Forum
OCAR – Organization of Central Asia Cooperation

[2] GUUAM – Georgia, Ukraine, Uzbekistan, Azerbaijan, Moldavia

Table B examines whether Greater Central Asia (excluding Afghanistan) or Pakistan and Iran are the more preferred partners for Afghanistan.

Table B: Criteria for Partnership with Afghanistan

Criteria for Partnership	**Pakistan and Iran**	**GCA (excluding Afghanistan)**
Share of Afghanistan borders, %	58.5	40
Share of the volume of the nearest market (excluding China), %	80.0	20.0
Share in the foreign trade of Afghanistan, %	Pakistani exports - 27.0	No data available
Cultural/Civilizational identity	+	-

The Iranian market is the second largest, with 65 million people, and the first in purchasing power (per capita gross national income is $1720), yet the Pakistani market, with 162 million people, is by far the largest in the area and the sixth largest in the world. The combined market of Greater Central Asia is smaller than that of Iran; excluding the Chinese market, it is only a fourth of the combined markets of Pakistan and Iran. In 2003, the foreign trade turnover between Kyrgyzstan and Afghanistan was less than 0.5 percent of total turnover for the region. It should be noted that the economic and social significance of trade for Iran is much smaller than its for Afghanistan.

The Economic Cooperation Organization (ECO), which includes Greater Central Asian countries, Pakistan and Iran, best meets Afghanistan's needs. Afghanistan also now benefits from membership in the South Asia Association for Regional Cooperation (SAARC), which includes Pakistan.

The creation of a "significant economic zone with its center in Afghanistan"[3] would be beneficial, but would also be highly difficult. It is easy for an economic powerhouse to become the center of an integrated economic zone, but weaker economies cannot assume the same role. The development of the EU demonstrated that there is no need to force

---

[3] S. Frederick Starr Partnership in Central Asia. New Big Game in Central Asia: Myth and Reality – Bishkek, 2005, p. 14.

regional economic expansion, and that the regional economic structure must prove its viability.

The minimum task is to strengthen internationalization. It is necessary to formulate a strategy for regional development and to create an international development fund for Greater Central Asia.

Issues of Identity

Greater Central Asia may be the only region in the Islamic world that does not exhibit anti-American sentiment. This may be the result of its European-style education system. However, in the process of globalization, the region has experienced the growing pains of "sovereignization": rising nationalism, political extremism and ideological crises, and "socio-cultural intervention" including westernization and the penetration of extremist religious practices.

Sovereignization has fueled nationalism and cultivated national myths, creating micro-civilizations and nationalistic ideologies that erode regional cohesion and directly impede integration. Integration and the ensuing openness may lead to conflict between these micro-civilizations. The region's political regimes are in part preserved by these national myths, and are eager to strengthen them, despite the economic costs incurred.

The low level of regional identity throughout Greater Central Asia has hindered the process of regional integration. However, ethnic Turkmen, Uzbeks and Tajiks living on both sides of national borders are establishing cooperative relations across state boundaries, helping to overcome trade barriers.

Regional identity criteria, including historical elements and the current political situation, are summarized in Table C.1. By all criteria, Kyrgyzstan is the closest to the regional mean, while Afghanistan falls outside of the regional mean according to most of the criteria. It can be concluded that the regional economy is divided because of the split betwee[illegible]ion's governments and peoples.

Table C1 Criteria for Regional Identity

Criteria for Identity	Countries of the Region						Typical within region
	Kazakhstan	Kyrgystan	Tajikistan	Turkmenistan	Uzbekistan	Afghanistan	
Regime type	Weakly liberal	Weakly liberal	Weakly liberal	Authoritarian	Authoritarian	Weakly occupational	Weak democracy
External orientation	RF	RF	RF	RF, Neutrality	RF	U.S.	RF
History over past 150 years	Kokand khanate,* Russian empire, USSR	Kokand khanate, Russian empire, USSR	Bukhara emirate,* Kokand khanate,* Russian empire, USSR	Bukhara emirate,* Khiva khanate,* Russian empire, USSR	Bukhara emirate, Khiva, Kokand khanate, Russian empire, USSR	Buffer zone of British and Russian empire; Interventions, civil wars	Bukhara, Kokand khanate, Russian empire, USSR
Language group/ sub-group	Turkic/ Kypchaksky	Turkic/ Kypchaksky	Iranian/ Tajik	Turkic/ Oguzskaya	Turkic/ Karlukskaya	Iranian /Pushtu	Turkic
Change in alphabet over past century	Arabic, Latin, Cyrillic	Arabic, Latin, Cyrillic	Arabic, Latin, Cyrillic	Arabic, Latin, Cyrillic, Latin	Arabic, Latin, Cyrillic, Latin	Arabic	Cyrillic
Percentage belonging to titular nationality	50.6	60.6	62.3	77	75	50	64.2
Consolidated status of titular nation	Regionalism (3 zhuz)	Regionalism, tribalism	Regionalism, badakhshan people	Tribalism	Clan-based relationship	Tribalism	Regionalism
Titular national tradition	nomadic	nomadic	settled	nomadic	settled	nomadic	nomadic
Major religions, percentages	Sunni, orthodox 60/40	Sunni, orthodox 80/20	Sunni, Ismailite, 95/2	Sunni, orthodox 90/10	Sunni, orthodox 92/8	Sunni, Shiite 80/20	Sunni, orthodox 82/13
Regional integration status**	SOC, EuraAsEC, CEA	SOC, EuraAsEC	SOC, EuraAsEC	-	SOC, EuraAsEC	-	SOC

*Partially **Excludes CIS, Economic Cooperation Organization, and Islamic Conference Organization affiliations.

Trade

Absolute trade indicators have grown while specific gravity has declined as demonstrated by a 8.4 percent drop in Kyrgyz exports since 2000. Regional imports have increased by 2.1 percent since 2003.

Figure A. Trade Balance of Kyrgyzstan's Regional Trade, 2000-2004 (Central Asian countries and Afghanistan)

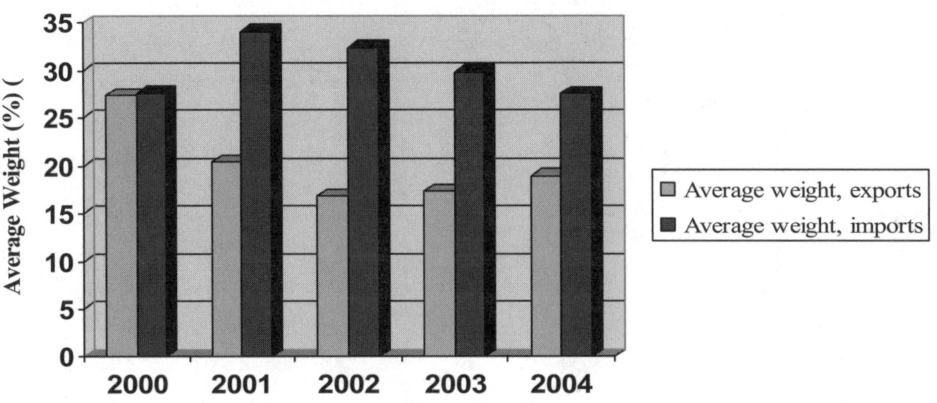

Table D: Kyrgyzstan's Goods Turnover, within large international organizations[4] *(million USD, %)*

Year	Goods turnover	ECO		CIS		Outside CIS	
		USD	%	USD	%	USD	%
1992	737.7			590.7	80.1	147.0	19.9
1993	787.4	264.4	33.6	583.9	74.2	203.5	25.8
1994	657.9	288.9	44.0	432.5	65.7	225.4	34.3
1995	931.2	410.2	44.0	622.8	66.8	308.4	33.2
1996	1343.0	592.4	44.1	880.3	65.5	462.8	34.5
1997	1313.1	506.8	38.6	755.0	57.5	558.0	42.5
1998	1355.1	418.1	30.9	671.3	49.5	683.9	50.5
1999	1053.7	290.1	27.4	442.5	42.0	611.1	58.0
2000	1058.6	346.1	32.7	505.9	47.8	552.7	52.2
2001	943.3	303.2	32.1	425.5	45.1	517.8	54.9
2002	1072.2	338.8	31.6	491.2	45.8	581.0	54.2
2003	1298.2	345.3	26.6	611.4	47.1	686.8	52.9

Table E: Kyrgyzstan's Goods Turnover, within small international organizations (million USD, %)

Year	Goods Turnover	CAEC/OCAR		EuroAsEC/CU		SOC	
		USD	%	USD	%	USD	%
1993	787.4	246.1	31.3	430.3	54.6	-	-
1994	657.1	264.8	40.3	291.8	44.4	-	-
1995	931.2	351.4	37.7	421.7	45.3	-	-
1996	1343.0	513.9	38.3	587.4	43.7	-	-
1997	1313.1	409.5	31.2	465.2	35.4	-	-
1998	1355.1	336.3	24.8	463.5	34.2	-	-
1999	1053.7	227.6	21.6	321.5	30.5	-	-
2000	1058.6	264.2	25.0	304.8	28.8	-	-
2001	943.3	243.2	25.8	287.8	30.5	376.8	39.9
2002	1072.2	284.1	26.5	369.9	34.5	544.7	50.8
2003	1298.2	293.4	22.6	518.0	39.9	658.2	50.7

Kyrgyzstan's goods turnover with ECO countries amounts to 70 percent of its total goods turnover. The next step is to develop trade relations with Iran, Pakistan and Turkey, with whom current goods turnover averages just over

[4] Data from the National Statistical Committee and the Center for Economic and Social Reforms are used here and throughout this paper.

13 percent. The importance of these countries in foreign trade, except for Turkey and Iran, is insignificant and less than 1 percent.

Figure B

Dynamics of Exports from Kyrgyzstan to Afghanistan, 2002 -2005

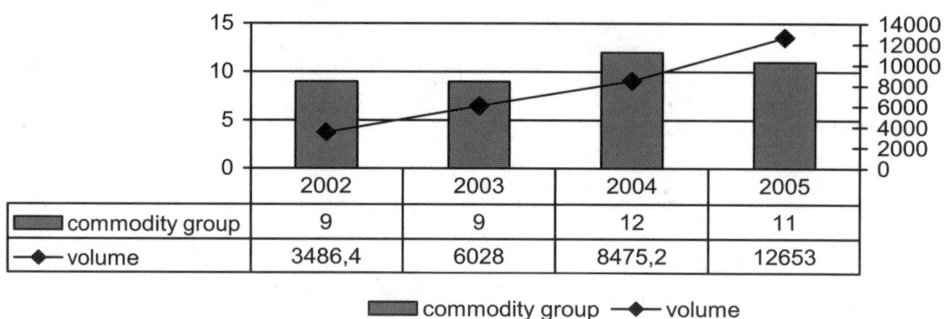

	2002	2003	2004	2005
commodity group	9	9	12	11
volume	3486,4	6028	8475,2	12653

Figure B indicates that the export of Kyrgyz commodities to Afghanistan has experienced consistent growth in recent years. Export volume in 2005 had increased 3.55 times since 2002, when annual growth was over 50 percent. The specific gravity of supply to Afghanistan was valued at 2 percent of total Kyrgyz exports, while the specific gravity of exports to Afghanistan, excluding gold, was valued at 3 percent. In 2002, these specific gravities were approximately 0.7 percent and 1 percent, respectively.

The dynamics of export growth was supplemented by extension of the list of exported goods by 22 percent. Six commodity groups, or about 50 percent of all assortments, had stable indices. This indicates that Kyrgyzstan has a stable external economic position in the Afghan market that relates to high-quality foodstuffs, construction materials (including glass), ferrous metals, machinery and equipment.

Analysis shows simultaneous significant changes in the composition of Kyrgyz exports to Afghanistan. Sugar and confectioneries topped the list of exported goods in 2002, while mineral oil and distilled products were top exports in 2005. On the whole, the tendency has been toward export concentration. The commodities group accounted for 18 percent of all exports in 2002, 33 percent in 2003, 32 percent in 2004, and 73 percent in 2005.

The following six commodity groups accounted for 94 percent of Kyrgyz exports to Afghanistan in 2005:

1. fuel, oil and distillated products	$9.2378 million
2. ferrous metal products	$1.1618 million
3. glass	$0.5082 million
4. transport	$0.4934 million
5. dairy products, eggs and others	$0.2828 million
6. ferrous metals	$0.2432 million

The development of Kyrgyz exports to Afghanistan has been dynamic in recent years, the volume of exports to Afghanistan having increased 3.5 times. The existing trade dynamic suggests that the volume of exports to Afghanistan will continue to increase. A portion of the exports were re-exports—Kyrgyzstan is a straight exporter as well as a transit exporter for Afghanistan.

Impediments to Kyrgyzstan's Active Involvement in Continental Trade

Security

Regional political instability, which creates a political barrier to transit, is an important issue for investors. Drug trafficking and terrorism ties between Afghanistan and other Greater Central Asian countries could expand. However, security issues in northern Afghanistan are not as acute as those in the central, southern or southeastern parts of the country. Mosques are the only legal infrastructure the opposition has access to, which is one reason why the opposition has fomented religious extremism in the region. Poverty, coupled with rapidly increased Islamism, has the potential to destabilize the region.

Trade volume between Afghanistan and other Greater Central Asian countries surged after the Taliban regime was overthrown, proving that security is key to trade development.

In Afghanistan, geographical decentralization due to rugged terrain and increased political centralization has resulted in conflicts between central and local elites. Kabul's control over certain parts of Afghanistan—the eastern and southern areas in particular—is minimal. The country remains organized by the principle of *tanzim*, the simple aggregation of various independent military and political groups. On a practical level, local Afghani administrators and leaders lacking formal power are capable of guaranteeing the security of economic activity, communications and cargo transport, as well as insuring that customs procedures are observed and financial settlements are legitimate. But these local officials can be replaced without warning.

Close ties between Afghanistan and Tajikistan and Uzbekistan may intensify irredentism, with calls for creation of a "Greater Tajikistan" or a "Greater Uzbekistan."

Impact of Environmental Factors on Regional Stability

Traditional agriculture may not be able to feed the Greater Central Asian population due to a lack of arable land, low harvest yields and high population growth. The only crops capable of supporting the population are cash crops that are later processed into illegal drugs, such as marijuana or opium poppies. Hemp grows wild on tens of thousands of square kilometers of semiarid and arid plains not used for farming, and those profiting from illegal drugs seek the destabilization of the regions where they operate.

By some estimates, illegal drug production now amounts to 60 percent of Afghanistan's gross national product. Over 90 percent of heroin in the world market is from Afghanistan, which is becoming a "narco state" dependent on illegal drug production. Over 350,000 Afghani families—about 10 percent of the population—rely on opium cultivation or trading for their livelihood.

Isolation is a major contributor to regional poverty causing the notion of "alpine poverty" to become fixed in the literature. The Himalayas have helped to create an "arch of instability" since it is relatively easy to wage guerilla warfare in mountains, and to create and sustain terrorist groups. Historically, mountain territories have been plagued by instability, struggles for resources and armed conflicts. But the primary reason for conflicts remains the shortage of the key resources for agriculture—land and water.

There is little arable land in the region, biological productivity is low and population growth rates are high. Lack of resources deepens poverty and exacerbates social inequality, increasingly the likelihood of armed conflict.

According to American ecologist U. Odum, each person requires an average of two hectares: 0.6 hectares for food production, 0.2 hectares for settling and industrial needs and 1.2 hectares that should remain virgin.[5] The figure of two hectares per person is relevant for Western Europe and North America, these being territories with potential productivity several times greater than that typical for Greater Central Asia.

This cause and effect between scarce natural resources and conflict is especially significant in mountainous regions. Mountains are extremely prone to wars and conflicts due to their high ecological, social and economic vulnerability. Poor mountain regions supply scarce water to richer plains territories, creating yet another source of conflict. Mountainous ecological systems are typically less capable than plains of recovering from such damage as large-scale soil erosion or destruction of flora.

Due to their relative inaccessibility and harsh conditions, mountainous regions tend to lag behind the general process of development, remaining marginalized and isolated economically and politically. Because mountain zones lack resources needed to solve ecological problems, political crises can quickly develop there, particularly if they are destabilized by population growth or external pressures.

Infrastructure and Energy

Cargo shipped from Pakistan to Tajikistan must pass through the Suez Canal to Black Sea ports, and is then hauled by rail through several countries before arriving in Tajikistan. Yet only the thin Vakhan corridor divides these two countries. The situation is similar for Kyrgyzstan and Kazakhstan. For all three countries, it is critical that north-south transport connections be created, which requires transport across Afghanistan.

Due to its geographical location, Afghanistan could play an important role in developing trade and economic relations between Greater Central Asia and countries to the south. The shortest route to ports on the Indian Ocean is via Afghanistan and Pakistan, which is also a potential path for oil and gas pipelines. But instability in Afghanistan remains a serious obstacle.

---

[5] Odum, Y., “Ecology fundamentals”. Moscow: Mir, 1975, p. 740.

This region's location at the center of Asia means that it lacks access to sea or lake transport routes, except in the thinly inhabited desert regions along the east shore of the Caspian Sea. Due to mountains and the harsh climate, there are virtually no navigable rivers in the region. The only navigable river is the Amu Darya. Even, here there is little water in winter, while water flows are violent during the spring and summer.

Cargo transport by ship is the most economical form of transport, and is used to move 60 percent of world trade. Rail transport costs four times as much as ship transport, and road transport costs 15 times as much. Exacerbating the cost of land transport is the rarefied air at high altitudes, which degrades truck performance: engine power output is reduced by 8 percent at an altitude of 1000 meters, by 12 percent at 1500 meters, and decreases 20 percent at altitudes over 3200 meters.[6] Thus, the cost of truck transportation in mountainous regions can be expected to be 20 times as much as transport by ship. Rail transport may not be a viable option, and transportation costs in Greater Central Asia can be expected to exceed significantly the cost of transportation elsewhere.

Since trains cannot run on a grade steeper than 4 percent, significant investment in tunnels, bridges, and overpasses would have to be made to build a railway along mountainous routes where camel caravans once passed. Prior to the Soviet era, a single east-west railway through Eurasia was impossible due to the difficulty if traversing colossal Altai-Himalayan mountain range.

Following the conflicts between Pakistan and India over Kashmir in the 1970s, the high altitude Karakorum highway was built in the Pakistani-controlled zone of Kashmir. This highway now connects Xinjiang and Pakistan.

By the end of the twentieth century, railroads from the Pacific Ocean extend to Kashgar in western China to the border with Kazakhstan. In Iran, railroads that start at the distant Bosporus terminate in Mashhad. Uzbekistan has connected Afghanistan with the region via the railway and auto bridge across the Amu Darya between Termez and the Afghani river port of

---

[6] N. A. Gvozdetskyi, Yu.N.Golubchikov, Moscow, Mysl', 1987.- 399 p.

Khairaton. Kazakhstan plans to build the Druzhba-Atyrau railroad with a European (and Chinese) track gauge. There are also plans to construct a high-altitude Kashgar-Torugart-Jalalabad railroad—it will be important for this railroad, too to be constructed with the European gauge.

Three principal regional corridors exist. The western corridor runs along the Caspian Sea through Iran to the Bender-Abbas and Bender-Chahbahar ports in the Persian Gulf. The middle corridor runs through Afghanistan and Pakistan to the Indian Ocean. And the eastern corridor runs from Turksib to Torugart, crossing the Khundjerab and Karakorum mountains to the Indian Ocean.

There are virtually no railroads in Afghanistan. Motor roads are seasonally passable and mountain passes are closed in winter. In August 2002, the construction of the first bridge across the Panj began; a total of five bridges are to be built between Afghanistan and neighboring countries within the framework of the Program for Restoration of Transport Traffic. Construction of small bridge in Khorog area has been completed. In July 2004, another small bridge in Ruzvay, a village in the Darvaz region of the Badakhshan Autonomous Region, was put into operation, funded by the Agha Khan Development Network. But these bridges do not solve the major transportation problems in these areas, due to their small size, lack of infrastructure on the Afghani side and the weakness of Tajik infrastructure.

At present, there are three routes by which motor traffic can pass from Pakistan through Afghanistan. The first is through Chitral to Tajikistan; the second is through Torkham, Jalalabad, Mazar-e-Sharif and Termez to Uzbekistan; and the third is through Quetta and Chaman, Afghani Kandahar and Herat to Kushka and onto Turkmenistan. It is also possible to construct a railroad connecting Quetta and Kushka.

A highway between Faizabad-Shugnan-Khorog would also play an important role and would use the new bridge over Panj. A highway route connecting Osh-Irkeshtam-Karakorum is also possible in the near future.

The tunnel through the Salang Pass in Afghanistan was reopened at the end of November, 2003, and in May 2004 an auto border-crossing between

Tajikistan and China was opened in Tajikistan at the Kulma Pass, and will operate during the summer months.

Reconstruction of the only year-round road via the Pamirs, the Osh-Khorog-Faizabad road, was completed in 2002 with emergency humanitarian aid funding from Russia, Kyrgyzstan and Tajikistan. The railroad at Osh (Kara-Suu station) defines the potential high capacity of the Pamir highway.

A 68-kilometer railroad line from Khairaton to Mazar-e-Sharif is planned, and Uzbekistan has inked contracts for the repair of existing bridges and the construction of new bridges along the Kabul-Khairaton motor road.

The objective of the TRACECA project is to transfer the bridging function between Asia and Europe from Russia to Central Asia and the Caucasus. This politicized plan envisioning routes bypassing Russia and Iran is not favorable for the region's countries, their neighbors or for Russia. The creation of a transport corridor through the Caspian Sea and the Black Sea requires the organization of an equivalent counter-flow of goods from Europe via ferries, which is problematic. Meanwhile, Turkey plans to construct a transport tunnel under the Bosporus.

There is no key reason to create an independent route with two ferries through the Caspian and Black Seas; indeed, there was no need for two ferries during the Great Silk Road's two thousand years of operation.

The Barogil Pass, the most accessible pass through the Hindu Kush mountain range, is located in Vakhan, the most peaceful region of Afghanistan. The Barogil Pass is at an altitude of 3777 meters, while the Kulma Pass is at 4352 meters. The Barogil Pass is open year-round and runs through a five-kilometer-wide saddle in the mountain range. This pass provides the easiest access to the northern Indian plains at all times of year.

An energy bridge is possible within this transport bridge, exploiting the Toktogul Cascade running from Osh to Sary-Tash to Lyangar to Barogil to Chitral. It is critical to note that the development of communication links provides a fundamental basis for the sustainable development in Afghanistan. Highway and railway construction in the mountain terrain of Afghanistan is very expensive and time-consuming.

In addition to developing telecommunications, there is a need to build power transmission lines in the immediate future. Only 5 percent of Afghanistan's demand for electricity is currently being met, and only 6 percent of Afghan citizens have access to electricity—most of them being urban residents. Lack of electricity hampers industrial development and the growth of other sectors, leaving most of the population with no alternative to the agricultural employment. Yet all neighboring countries, except China and Pakistan have well-developed electric power systems and can supply electricity to Afghanistan. Furthermore, all post-Soviet countries, regardless of whether or not they border Afghanistan, could also supply Afghanistan with electricity. This is possible via an interconnected power system built during the Soviet era.

The idea of the TRACECA project has existed for 13 years, and the idea of reestablishing the Great Silk Road has been around for nine years. During this time, the transportation volume has increased 25 percent, an annual growth of about 2 percent. If such low growth rates remain, the larger project will be a long time in coming.

During the past fifty years, the thickness of the ice over the northern seas has halved and is decreasing 3 percent every ten years; regular trade navigation along the North Pole may be possible by 2010. This northern seaway would reduce the sea route from Europe to Japan and China by half and would be 1.6 times less expensive than other modes and routes of transport.

It will be a long time before Afghanistan has the infrastructure needed to make it an alternative route connecting Russia, China and Iran. Transport via Iran is the optimal route for Caspian oil. In any case, transport communications must pass through Pakistan in order to reach the Indian Ocean; thus, it is unrealistic to exclude Pakistan and Iran from any proposed Partnership on Cooperation and Development in Greater Central Asia.

According to many authors, maintaining the integrity of a polycentric integration union is possible only when the development of integrative infrastructure has priority over economic development.[7] Infrastructure supporting transport is key to developing social infrastructure, and thus is critical for improving stability and fighting poverty in Afghanistan and throughout the region.

Legal and Institutional Issues

The Regional Trade Facilitation and Customs Cooperation Program (RTFCCP) started in 2002 aims to facilitate the reform of customs bodies. It is developing member countries in East and Central Asia. The RTFCCP has a three-part strategy to facilitate trade: modernization of customs infrastructure, including legal and material elements; development of auxiliary customs infrastructure by involving private customs brokers in trade facilitation; and solving common member problems and assisting with country-specific issues.

A project proposed under the RTFCCP is a regional effort to develop the infrastructure of customs border checkpoints in Kyrgyzstan and Tajikistan, with financial support from the ADB. The project's objectives are to improve customs processing at primary border checkpoints, to donate equipment for customs operations and the prevention of smuggling, and to facilitate training and encourage cooperation between border agencies.

Joint customs control and handling of cargoes at borders is acknowledged to be a key means of facilitating trade. But the joint handling of cargoes at border crossings requires a high degree of harmonization between customs entities, and might require the expansion of jurisdiction to the territories of adjacent countries, which must usually be ratified by legislatures of the countries involved.

International and Bilateral Treaties

Kyrgyzstan acceded to the World Trade Organization (WTO) on November 20, 1998 and grants most-favored nation status (MFN) to other WTO

---

[7] V.N. Knyaginin. Report for organizational and activity game "Projecting of institutions and technologies of strategic management of the Republic of Armenia", Yerevan, 2002, p.9

member-countries. By joining the WTO, Kyrgyzstan established a stable and predictable tariff regime. This includes two types of service restrictions: nationally based restrictions and restrictions on market access. However, no restrictions on the services area were instituted. Kyrgyzstan applies the most liberal foreign trade regime among CIS states and has eliminated restrictions on the participation of foreign capital in insurance companies. There are no restrictions on the import or export of currency and enterprises are free to trade. State and private enterprises can engage in import and export operations without special registration or restrictions, except for cases involving goods subject to import or export licensing in accordance with world practice.

Trade with Tajikistan and Uzbekistan occurs under the framework of bilateral Free Trade Agreements (FTAs). The basis for all bilateral FTAs was established by the Agreement on the Creation of Free Trade Areas, signed by the heads of CIS countries on 15 April 1994, and by the Protocol on Amending and Adding the Agreement, signed on 2 April 1999. These agreements stipulate that trade is not subject to customs duties, taxes or fees, or quantitative restrictions. The FTAs created a regional trade regime without customs duties or quantitative restrictions *de jure*. However, Uzbekistan is an exception. It applies exemptions from free trade treatment on goods produced in Kyrgyzstan under a free trade regime exemptions protocol enacted on 25 December 1996. These exemptions, approved by resolutions of the Cabinet of Ministers of Uzbekistan, provide for export duties on a number of goods and entail various non-tariff regulations on exports and imports.

Joint Intergovernmental Commissions, chaired by governmental members, were formed to increase foreign trade. Problems and possible solutions to problems of cooperation are considered during commission meetings.

Barriers to Trade Development

Kyrgyzstan has signed a number of agreements within CIS, ECO and the East Asia Economic Caucus (EAEC) that stipulate common principles and terms of transit across the territories of the signatory states.

Article 8 of the Agreement on Transit Via Territories of CIS Member-Countries of 4 June 1997 states that means to ensure the transit of goods shall be granted to exporters, importers or carriers in a country of transit under conditions no worse than those available to national exporters, importers or carriers.

The 1998 Agreement between countries that signed the Agreement on Formation of the Transport Union on International Motor Traffic was established within the framework of the EAEC. Article 6 of the agreement stipulates that goods transported by motor vehicle between the territories of signatory countries or within the Transport Union shall be exempt from permits.

Under Article 11 of the agreement passengers and cargo, as well as transport vehicles, shall be exempt from taxes and fees for the use or maintenance of roads, except for toll fees, and then only if toll-free roads are available. This agreement has not yet been ratified by Kazakhstan.

The agreement between the customs bodies of Kyrgyzstan and Uzbekistan "On Further Development of Cooperation in Mutual Aid in Customs Affairs" of 26 May 1998 envisages that in transit traffic only excisable goods will be subject to customs. Obviously the levying of additional fees on motor carriers would curtail the development of regional trade and economic relations.

Various issues regarding joint water supplies and regional energy resources can impact electric power supply. Issues related to economic relations and the use of water and fuel-energy resources are regularly considered by the heads of state in Central Asia and the Caucasus countries.

In addition to a visa regime that restricts trade and economic relations, Uzbekistan unilaterally imposed high excise tariffs and non-tariff barriers on a range of Kyrgyz goods—clearly the FTA is not always implemented properly. For instance, beginning in 2000 Uzbekistan unilaterally suspended observance of the Agreement on International Road Traffic enacted on 4 September 1996, and started levying a $300 fee for passage through Uzbek territory and a 200 Euro fee for customs escorting of Kyrgyz motor carriers. This action was taken despite the agreement signed between the customs bodies of Kazakhstan, Kyrgyzstan and Uzbekistan on 26 May 1998 and has negatively affected Kyrgyz exports to Uzbekistan.

These problems were addressed during joint meetings of the Intergovernmental Kyrgyz-Uzbek Commission on Bilateral Cooperation. The Uzbekistan cabinet adopted Resolution #247 on 15 May 2001 ending the levying of temporary excise rates on goods imported from the Kyrgyz Republic. This decision partially resolved the issue of Kyrgyz motor carrier transit through Uzbekistan.

Bureaucratic barriers are increasingly prevalent, however, and have become principal obstacles to trade. Current non-physical barriers fall into three categories: barriers related to border crossings; barriers of a fiscal and bureaucratic nature; and barriers created by officials with the aim of personal profit.

The first category of barriers include:

- Permits for entry and exit, transit, and transport from and to third countries;
- Visas requirements;
- Requirements for paid parking during customs formalities, for instance, if a person is detained for a customs violation, a parking fee is levied on the carrier;
- Prohibition on the transit of particular cargoes;
- Examination of transit cargoes;
- Customs deposit and customs formalities of goods, not subject to excise rate;
- Repeated weighing of cargoes.

The second category of barriers includes:

- Insurance of transport vehicles and crew;
- Ecological and sanitary fees;
- Services of various brokers;
- Various fees established by local government bodies.

The third category of barriers includes actions of officials of law enforcement and fiscal bodies for the purpose of personal enrichment, i.e corruption.

The immediate outcomes of such barriers include:

- Financial costs: Transport operators must pay numerous fees and duties, and raise transport fees accordingly. This reduces the amount of imported goods that the population and national enterprises can purchase, while domestic goods also become less competitive in world markets.
- Protectionism of national transport operators may lead trade partners to take punitive measures and create transport blockades.
- Maximal and bureaucratically enforced safety measures decrease movement across borders, thereby reducing the exchange of goods and lowering overall trade.
- When intensive control of documentation is maintained in the interests of ensuring traffic safety, the effect can be the opposite of that intended, due to higher traffic density and long waiting times in queues.

The long-term effects of these measures include:

- A drop in foreign investments, increasing economic isolation as potential trading partners are dissuaded by a country's bureaucratic trade barriers;
- A reduction in international trade, and the lowering of state tax revenue, leading to budget deficits;
- Unfulfilled commitments undertaken as conditions of WTO membership.

Together, these bureaucratic barriers form a dense obstacle to the development of motor transport and pose a serious threat to overall economic development.

The cost of eliminating these barriers is difficult to assess, although a recent initiative has defined the necessary level of financing. The World Bank implemented a Governance Structural Adjustment Credit (GSAC) in

Kyrgyzstan over three years at a cost of $10 million. The initiative was carried out within the framework of the proposal on "Formation of Good Governance in Kyrgyzstan," and other programs. The GSAC enabled Kyrgyzstan to boost its rating in the Transparency International's corruption index rating by ten points.

Projected Benefits to Kyrgyzstan from the Removal of Regional Trade Barriers

There have been various evaluations of the economic benefits that Kyrgyzstan would realize from the removal of trade barriers. A group of International Monetary Fund economists determined that trade barriers imposed by Kyrgyzstan's neighbors have had a highly negative impact on its export industry.[8] Another report states that a 50 percent reduction of tariffs and trade margins in Kazakhstan and Kyrgyzstan would increase Kyrgyzstan's real GDP of by 55 percent.[9]

This paper evaluates the impact that the transport barriers of neighboring countries have on Kyrgyzstan's economic development.[10] Despite the efficiency of rail transport, it is not heavily used due to Kyrgyzstan's small export volume. Hence, 95 percent of exports are shipped by trucks.[11] Several road transport companies were surveyed regarding the costs they incur when transporting goods into countries neighboring Kyrgyzstan. These expenses are summarized in Tables F.

---

[8] http://www.akipress.kg/ Accessed on AKIpress May 5 2006.

[9] Johannes Linn, et al. Central Asia Human Development Report: Bringing Down Barriers, Bratislava: UNDP Regional Bureau for Europe and the Commonwealth of Independent States, 2005, p. 4.

[10] This section also considers trade flows into Russia; trading with Russia causes Kyrgyz exporters to incur major costs in Kazakh territory.

[11] Ministry of Transport and Communication of the Kyrgyz Republic, " Draft of the Concept of Kyrgyzstan Development as a Transit Country for the Period up to 2020.", Bishkek, 2006.

Table F: Goods Transportation Costs (per one 80 cubic meter van)*

	Bishkek-Dushanbe	**Bishkek-Tashkent**	**Bishkek-Ashgabat**	**Bishkek-Kabul**	**Bishkek-Ekaterinburg**	**Bishkek-Almaty**
Transportation services, total	2900	1000	3300	3500	2200	700
Escort and storage (customs terminal services) 5%	145	50	165	175	110	35
Expenses for gasoline	145	50	165	175	110	35
Depreciation (0.0833 per day)	817	233	1167	1167	233	233
Customs fees (5%)	145	50	165	175	110	35
Wage of a driver	100	50	100	150	100	30
Profit of a transportation company (30%)	870	300	990	1050	660	210
Estimate						
Direct transportation expenses	1932	633	2422	2542	1103	508
Customs expenses	290	100	330	350	220	70
Non-compulsory payments (bribes)	678	267	548	608	877	122
Decrease of tariffs of transportation companies due to the strengthening of the competition	290	100	330	350	220	70
Possible decrease: tariffs in USD	1548	567	1538	1658	1537	332
Percentage of total expenses	53.4%	56.7 %	46.6%	47.4%	69.8 %	47.4%

***Data from survey of transportation companies. Interviews were conducted by IRT employees.**

Bribes and fees make up the largest share of non-compulsory expenses. Depending on the route, these expenses reach 16 to 40 percent of the cost of goods delivered. The next largest expense is customs escorting and goods storage, including customs terminal services and customs fees; this expense amounts to 10 percent of the cost of goods.[12] Another important yet often overlooked trade barrier arises from the restrictions on competition and imperfect market mechanisms in a given sector; this inflates transport tariffs. The exclusion of non-compulsory transport expenses would lower costs 46 to 70 percent, depending upon the route. This decrease in tariffs would facilitate economic development in Kyrgyzstan, where roads are the major trade routes.

Projected benefits resulting from the removal of these barriers are based on an evaluation of the transport compound of export and import trade flows was made using "input-output" models.[13] Data on the growth of export inflows and the reduction in the cost of imports for major Kyrgyz industries are presented in Tables F and G.

It is estimated that the removal of barriers to motor vehicle transport would boost export earnings by 1.7 percent of the export cost and by 2.5 percent for Greater Central Asian countries and Russia. As the share of gold in Kyrgyzstan's exports reaches 40 percent, removing the barriers will have an even greater economic impact. The removal of barriers will have also have more influence on certain priority industries, including textile.

Table G: Increase of Export Earnings due to Barriers' Removal 2002 case study, in thousand USD

Industries	By all countries		By five countries	
	Growth rate	Export structure	Growth rate	Export structure
Textile and apparel industry, leather manufacture and articles thereof;	1.5	5.9%	0.2	23.5%
Production of charred coal, oil refining, chemical industry and manufacturing of rubber and plastic articles	6.3	9.0%	5.2	5.1%
Manufacturing of non-metal mineral products	5.3	7.3%	5.3	29.4%
Machinery and equipment manufacturing	1.8	6.0%	1.7	14.3%
Total in the economy	1.7	100.0%	2.5	100.0%

---

[12] Tax payments are not included; taxes are not considered to be barriers, although they complicate trade.

[13] It is assumed that barriers have a symmetric character, i.e. specific costs are applicable to both exports and imports. Simulation calculations were made using 2002 data, which is the most recent available information for the "costs-production" model.

The removal of trade barriers is projected to have an overall impact equal to 2.7 percent of total Kyrgyz imports and 3.7 percent for Greater Central Asia and Russia. Furthermore, the elimination of barriers will greatly improve regional trade relations, intensifying the process of integration.

Table H. Import Cost Reduction Due to Barrier Removal 2002 Case Study, in Thousand US$

	By all countries		**By five countries**	
Industries	Growth rate	Export structure	Growth rate	Export structure
Exploitation of coal, raw oil and natural gas	-2.0	8.0%	-2.0	18.5%
Textile and apparel industries, leather manufacturing and products	-1.4	6.1%	-1.4	1.0%
Production of charred coal, oil refining, chemical industry and rubber and plastic manufacturing	-5.9	24.7%	-5.8	48.6%
Manufacturing of other non-metal mineral products	-4.9	1.3%	-4.9	3.1%
Machinery and equipment manufacturing	-1.8	17.9%	-1.9	7.2%
Total in the economy	-1.0	100%	-3.7	100%

The benefits from the removal of trade barriers will be evenly distributed throughout Kyrgyzstan's economy (see Table I), resulting in a projected GDP growth rate of 2.3 percent.[14] The dominant industries will be able to increase GDP by 0.5 to 4.4 percent. Industries with currently insignificant statistical impacts on the economy will receive a greater stimulus for development, with growth ranging from 8.8 to 92.5 percent. This is due to the small scale of these industries at present, and the fact that their development is highly dependant on transport costs. The removal of barriers will stimulate less developed industries, in turn diversifying and strengthening Kyrgyzstan's economy as a whole.

---

[14] Estimates are based on 2002 data, the increase for 2006 will be greater due to increased production volumes.

Table I. Projected GDP Growth due to Barrier Removal

Dominant Kyrgyz industries	**Industry Growth**
Agriculture, hunting and forestry	0.5
Production of food stuff and tobacco	1.2
Metallurgic industry	0.7
Production and distribution of electrical power	4.4
Industries with insignificant average weight	
Coal, raw oil and natural gas production	92.5
Other mining industries	62.3
Production of wood and wooden articles	16.5
Production of paper and carton, printing industry	9.5
Production of charred coal, oil refining, chemical industry and production of rubber and plastic articles	52.5
Manufacturing of non-metal mineral products	8.8
Manufacturing of ready-made metal articles	13.3
Manufacturing of machinery and equipment	9.7
Total GDP growth	2.3

Table J: Projected Kyrgyzstan Tax Revenue Growth

Indicator	**Tax base change**	**Tax rate**	**2002**	**Growth**	
	Thous.Som	%		Thous.Som	%
VAT on export-import operations	-1390689	20	3262902.7	-278138	-8.5
VAT on domestic products	1772597	20	1530776.1	354519	23.2
Profit tax	941060	10	967614.3	94106	9.7
Road tax	3555992	0,8	336654.4	28448	8.5
Emergencies tax	3555992	1.5	651344.4	53340	8.2
Tax from turnover of retail trade and services for the population	123750	5	410388.8	6188	1.5
Total, by tax group			7159680.7	258463	3.6

The above analysis suggests that the removal of barriers to trade will boost tax revenue growth to 3.6 percent (see Table J), while income from export-import operations due to the improvement of trade balance will also grow. The growth of export volumes will in turn increase tax revenue, specifically from profit and income taxes. However, it is difficult to evaluate this impact due to the difficulty of building elasticity curves.

In summary, the removal of trade barriers will result in:

- Growth of the domestic economy and of taxable income;
- Strengthening of integration tendencies within Greater Central Asia;
- Greater balance in economic growth and improved economic diversification through the stimulation of weak sectors;
- Greater export volumes from priority industries.

Means and Costs of Removing Trade Impediments

The following recommendations derive from the above analysis of barriers to trade in Greater Central Asia.

1. Security Recommendations

Regional trade development is impossible until the main security issues are resolved. The OSCE, SCO, Pakistan and Iran should participate in this process, and Afghanistan should join the OSCE.

2. Recommendations on Infrastructure

- The most effective way to boost trade is to improve transportation.
- The possibility of developing a regional transit system should be considered.
- The direction of transportation development should be determined: i.e. whether to focus on developing hubs or service corridors, or of upgrading existing infrastructure.
- A strategy for integration of various types of transport hubsand sea ports should be developed.
- New trunk highways designed to meet international standards should be constructed.
- New gas and oil pipelines and high-voltage electrical lines should be installed to increase the volume of energy resources transiting throughthe region.
- Communication lines should be expanded, and a regional fiber-optic network should be developed.

- Cargo and passenger air equipment and facilities should be upgraded, and new airline companies created.
- The computerized transit systems of various countries should be studied to determine optimal solutions for Greater Central Asia.

3. Recommendations on Legal and Institutional Issues

- Countries of Greater Central Asia should join the Transport International Routière (TIR) Transit System.
- The transit agreement signed between Kazakhstan and the Kyrgyz Republic on 26 March 2004 was a significant step towards implementing transit initiatives. Accession to this bilateral transit agreement by other regional countries should be encouraged as an initial step toward creating a new system of regional transit.
- Insurance and banking systems should be mobilized to encourage the use of national vehicle stock in regional transport.
- Accession to major international conventions, and training to facilitate accession, is necessary for all the countries of the region.
- A common legal system should be developed to harmonize customs codes and procedures.
- Modern customs services methods, including risk management, should be encouraged.
- A unified transit system should be developed.
- Customs procedures should become more transparent and information technologies introduced to facilitate the exchange of data.
- For border trade, there should be inter-governmental agreements to identify settlements considered to be within a border territory, and to specify which goods produced in these territories shall be considered duty-free. This is particularly important to increase Kyrgyz trade with Uzbekistan.
- Customs bodies should not charge duties for border trade; this will be facilitated by a pre-approved list of allowed goods.

- When borders significantly increase the cost of trade, simplified customs procedures, agreed upon documentation, introduction of electronic processing of documentation, and the creation of favorable conditions for progress should all be instituted.
- To intensify border trade and the opening of border trade centers, area governors could reach agreement within the framework of currently applicable agreements.
- Mechanisms for implementing decisions should be determined when signing inter-governmental agreements are signed, as should joint follow-on activities.
- To attract foreign investment and wider public support, policies and procedures should be clarified, streamlined and publicized.
- Consider extending the Convention on Preferences in Trade for Island States to intra-continental landlocked countries.

4. Recommendations on Bureaucratic Barriers

- Identify the roots causes of each barrier in order to develop targeted mechanisms for removing it.
- Since international conventions and agreements usually take precedence over the domestic legislation of member countries, it is recommended that regional governments address barriers that contradict pre-existing bi- and multi-lateral agreements, as well as international agreements and conventions.
- Consider making a joint appeal to regional governments for the reduction of fees.
- Implement a step-by-step approach to eliminate existing barriers and to limit the creation of rules and regulations that could create future barriers to motor transport development.
- In order to reduce transport demurrage, it is recommended to synchronize work schedules on both sides of a border crossing, and to create a centralized location at each crossing for the different services that issue border crossing documentation.

The above recommendations should be implemented by:

- Informing organizations responsible for barriers about their unfavorable impact, and demanding either the abolition or amendment of the corresponding laws, rules and instructions. Short- and long-term consequences should be evaluated before making any changes to regulations.
- Creating a position for a single officer to serve border passes at crossings with high volumes of international auto traffic; the officer would be responsible for addressing citizens' complaints about civil servants and could referee disputes on-the-spot. Disputing parties should be able to receive instructions on acts mandatory for immediate decision making and have the right to appeal.
- Establishing joint committees within the frameworks of international agreements to consider every new law, rule or instruction that might influence motor transport. Committee approval would be required prior to document ratification.

Conclusions

Geopolitical factors—the issues of strategic partnership and balance, state preservation and national security—take precedence over such economic factors as trade balances or tariff regimes, when assessing the long-term prospects for the development of foreign economic links. Geopolitical factors are key to selecting integration partners and vectors. Economic considerations influence political relations and foreign economic ties often represent a continuation of geopolitical links.

The geopolitical peculiarities of Greater Central Asia define its geo-economic situation: risky and low-productivity agriculture, lagging economic development and high population density in areas with arable land create conflicts over scarce resources, land and especially water. These conditions can give rise to cycles of instability.

The countries of Greater Central Asia support stability and development in Afghanistan, since regional problems are often re-exported Afghan problems. Afghanistan's development serves the interests of Afghanistan and the rest of Greater Central Asia, while the means of achieving it are of secondary importance.

Afghanistan requires a three-prong strategy that simultaneously addresses security, development and culture. Modernization without the cultural component caused a reverse effect in Iran. Both Pakistan and Iran should participate in solving Afghanistan's problems. Regional trade promotion in Central Asia should start with the stabilization of Afghanistan—this will lead to the free movement of goods, people and services, in turn facilitating development.

The development of trade across Afghanistan and the rest of the region will contribute to the greater commerce between both north and south, and west and east. If this is to be achieved, decisive steps must be taken toward removing regional trade impediments..

Kyrgyzstan stands to benefit considerably from the removal of existing trade impediments. Even though, the removal of trade barriers will have the greatest positive impact on more developed countries, yet more importantly, their elimination will enhance the integration of Greater Central Asia as a whole.

Kazakhstan

Sanat Kushkumbayev

Introduction

An important means of advancing Kazakhstan's economic and political independence is the development of internal and external transport corridors. The country's relative remoteness from major global transport corridors and its comparative isolation from southern and eastern neighbours (the result of under-developed communications) continue to be important factors limiting factors to the development of full-scale economic and political relations with potential new trading partners.

Central Asia's weak transport sector contributes to the region's economic instability. The issue is not just about oil and gas pipelines but extends also to railway transportation, highway networks, and port terminals.

The implications of these issues extend beyond economics. The continuing political conflicts along regional borders carry geopolitical significance. Historically, all the countries of this region have, at one time or another, been under imperial control from beyond their borders. Because of their vulnerability, these landlocked countries perceive all attempts to use transport communications as geopolitical instruments with deep suspicion. At the same time, smaller countries in the region have to accept the "rules of the game" (in most cases imposed), which in effect links geo-economical interests and geopolitical concerns.

Since the time of Alexander the Great, transcontinental trading routes have played an important role in the development of the Eurasian continent. The Silk Roads provided routes for the movement of goods, the exchange of ideas, the spread of religions, and the movement of armed forces. The Roman, Byzantine, Chinese, Turkic, Mongolian, and Ottoman empires, as well as the

Muslim caliphate, were, in many respects, dependent on the transport arteries of this trade route. Further, the success of these empires relied on their ability to coordinate and govern from a central location, allowing complex trade and economic interaction between cities and provinces. In order to promote successful trade, each country observed strict rules. Infringement on either a trader's safety or his property was met with severe punishment.[1]

In the end, such enfringements occured but with some frequency, causing the decline of trade, which led to the isolation of the entire region. By the the sixteenth century improvements in sea transport leveled the playing field for sea trade between Central Asia and Europe and killed East-West land transport.

Countries with access to the sea experienced a boom in trade, while their landlocked neighbors struggled to keep up. Finding themselves cut off once again from trade, these lands developed in isolation. By the nineteenth century, the Central Eurasian region had become a source of geopolitical importance as a strengthened Russian Empire created safe transport and as both China and Russia expanded into Central Asia. It was this at this time that Russia began to be more attracted to the markets of eastern and southern countries such as China, India, and Iran. Europe's dominant geopolitical position with respect to sea routes and especially, most of all Britain's sea power, pushed Russia to search for alternative routes to Asian markets.

Central Asia's fractured nature can be traced to geopolitical shifts in the second half of the nineteenth and the beginning of the twentieth centuries, when European states and Russia created definitive borders that resulted in the creation of such notions as "Central Asia," "Russian Turkestan," "East Turkestan," and "Afghani Turkestan." From this time on, development in the region became inconsistent and uneven.

The above historical review of Central Eurasia helps us appreciate the importance of the current problems facing the region. In the near future,

---

[1] Characteristic example: medieval Mongols consistently tried to observe these norms. In XIII century, the formal reason of war between Mongols and the state of Horezmshah's, was destruction of ambassadors and merchants of Chinghiz-khan.

solutions to the challenge of creating efficient international transport corridors will become of the utmost geo-strategic importance for the region as a whole.

Advantages of Expanding International Trade in Central Asia

In light of the many factors surrounding the transport sector in Central Asia, it is certain that the future development of new routes to the north, south, east, and west will be shaped through a process of geopolitical struggle. Ethnic, territorial, religious, and interstate conflicts, as well as feelings of rivalry, mistrust, and fear all stand in the way of effective interaction. At the same time, competition and cooperation are not always regarded in the region as mutually exclusive processes.

The following five Eurasian transport corridors were all established within the framework of the European Economic Commission of the United Nations (EECUN) and the Economic and Social Commission of the United Nations for Asian and Pacific Countries (ESCAPUN), established in Bangkok in June, 2000:

1. from Western Europe to Russia to the Korean peninsula and on to Kazakhstan and China, or to Mongolia and China;
2. from Europe to southern and southeast Asia and on to Turkey and Iran;
3. from Europe to Turkey to Iran to Central Asia and on to China;
4. from Europe to the Caucasus and on to Asia (TRACECA); and
1. from northern Europe and Russia to Central Asia to the Persian Gulf (with an alternative route through Turkey to Iran).[2]

Territorial expansion is not only way a state can strengthen its geopolitical positions. Large empires have gained power through participation in various coalitions and integrated groups or unions. In this process one or two countries can act like locomotives.

---

[2]Karibzhanov, Khayrat; Tuleugaliev, Gaziz, *Economic and legal basis of the transit*, Petropavlovsk (Kazakhstan), 2002, p.22.

Initiatives geared toward regional and international cooperation are often dictated by geo-political and geo-economical intentions. For international organizations the goals tend to be regional and international security, mutually advantageous trade, and harmonious economic relations. The involvement of a country in interstate organizations can neutralize some negative geopolitical factors, expand international transport and communication infrastructures, and increase stability and safety.

The success of Central Asian integration with the global community depends on the strength and focus of those international organizations involved in the region. Such organizations include, among others, the Eurasian Economic Community, the Shanghai Cooperation Organization, and the Organization of Economic Cooperation. Despite varying levels of participation in these organizations, it is possible to assume that not all these structures will be viable, which may give rise to yet more transnational groupings. Central Asia has always been of geopolitical importance as a trade hub linking Asia with Europe. Yet the integration of Central Asia with the global economy has been slow. Weak transport and communication infrastructures, at both the national and regional levels, have hampered Central Asia's integration with the global economy.

The development of functioning structures for interstate transport is a major task for this region. Central Asia's ability to meet this challenge will shape the region's relative competitiveness, economic attractiveness, and ability to build strong relationships with the international community.

Trade between the Republic of Kazakhstan and the Countries of Central Asia from 2000 to 2005

Trade between Kazakhstan and its Central Asian neighbors is insignificant, a mere 2–2.5 percent of the country's total. These data, however, highlight the potential for greater mutual trade among regional states (Figure 1). Statistics show that trade between Kazakhstan and Kyrgyzstan, Tajikistan, Turkmenistan, and Uzbekistan for the period 2000 to 2005 reached $3.7 – 5.7 billion, with Kazakh exports to these states at at $2.6 billion and import at $4.8 billion (Table 2-4).

Figure 1: Ratio of Various States Trade with the Republic of Kazakhstan, January September, 2005 (In percent)

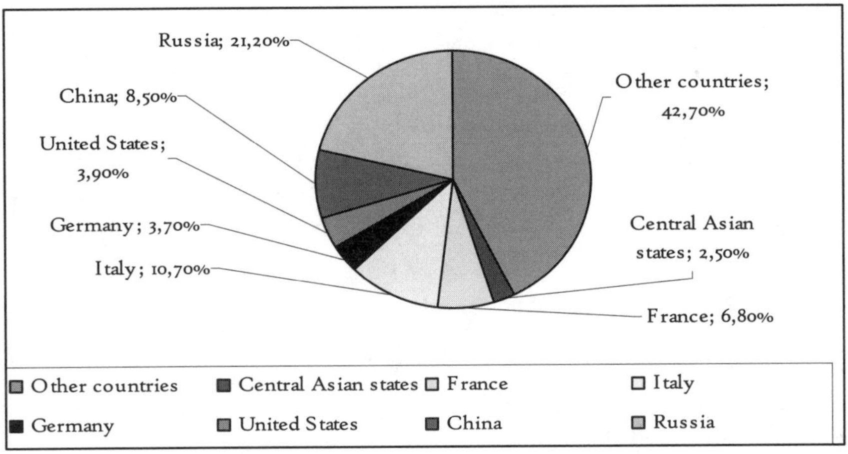

Russia; 21,20%
China; 8,50%
United States; 3,90%
Germany; 3,70%
Italy; 10,70%
Other countries; 42,70%
Central Asian states; 2,50%
France; 6,80%

Other countries, Central Asian states, France, Italy, Germany, United States, China, Russia

Source: Customs Control Committee of the Ministry of Finance, Republic of Kazakhstan.

Kazakhstan's trade with its neighbors is as follows: Uzbekistan $16,7 billion (44.2 percent); Kyrgyzstan $11 billion (29.7 percent); Tajikistan 5 billion (13.4 percent); and Turkmenistan $4,8 billion (12.7 percent) See Table 2, Figure 2.

Table 2: Turnover of Goods: Republic of Kazakhstan with Central Asian Countries (In thousands of U.S. dollars)

	2000	2001	2002	2003	2004	2005 *	Total for the period
Kyrgyzstan	900,852	1,195,983	1,395,180	2,050,742	3,132,038	2,511,858	**11,186,653**
Tajikistan	577,596	635,718	488,207	827,391	1,396,132	1,109,856	**5,034,902**
Turkmenistan	515,241	915,577	898,351	868,384	1,016,490	543,403	**4,757,446**
Uzbekistan	2,124,887	2,290,449	1,884,155	2,187,215	4,293,006	3,847,019	**16,626,731**
Total by year	**4,118,576**	**5,037,727**	**4,665,893**	**5,933,732**	**9,837,666**	**8,012,136**	**37,605,732**

***Jan.–Sept., 2005**

Source: Statistical Agency of the Republic of Kazakhstan.

Figure 2: Ratio of Central Asian Countries in Foreign Trade with the Republic of Kazakhstan (In percent)

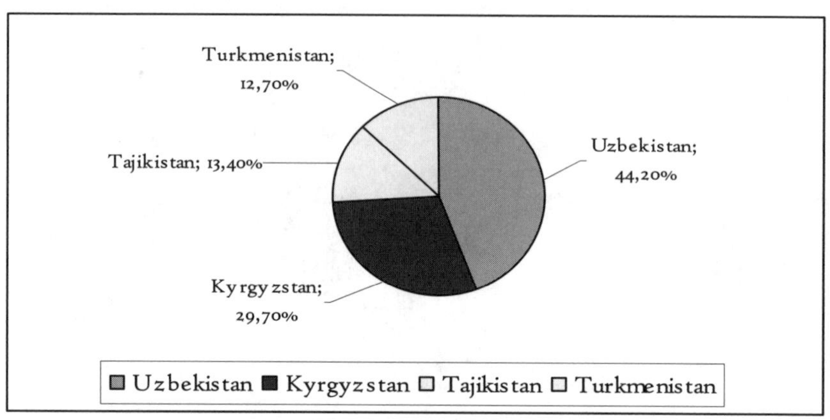

Source: Statistical Agency of the Republic of Kazakhstan.

Export

The main regional importers of Kazakh products are Uzbekistan and Kyrgyzstan, with export volumes of $8 billion (39.3 percent) and $7,9 billion (34.9 percent), respectively. Export levels to Tajikistan and Turkmenistan have reached $4,76 billion (20.9 percent) and US$1 billion (4.9 percent), respectively (Table 3 and Figure 3).

Table 3: Export from Kazakhstan to Central Asian countries (In thousands of U.S. dollars)

	2000	2001	2002	2003	2004	2005 *	Total for the period
Kyrgyzstan	584,942	870,534	1,075,832	1,525,492	2,219,646	1,673,632	**7,950,078**
Tajikistan	522,815	613,253	460,080	755,295	1,361,352	1,046,335	**4,759,130**
Turkmenistan	74,492	140,807	152,363	369,970	260,912	116,590	**1,115,134**
Uzbekistan	13,92,331	1,488,410	1,035,475	1,291,061	2,016,924	1,737,970	**8,962,171**
Total by year	**2,574,580**	**3,113,004**	**2,723,750**	**3,941,818**	**5,858,834**	**4,574,527**	

***Jan.-Sept., 2005**

Source: Statistical Agency of the Republic of Kazakhstan.

Figure 3: Export Ratio of Central Asian Countries in External Trade with the Republic of Kazakhstan (In percent)

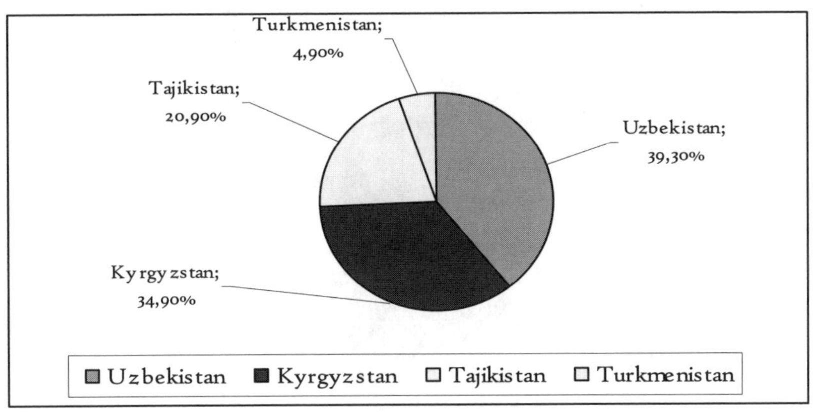

Source: Statistical Agency of the Republic of Kazakhstan.

Import

Kazakhstan's neighbors import from Kazakhstan the following: Uzbekistan $7 billion (51.7percent) Turkmenistan $3.6 billion (24.6 percent); Kyrgyzstan $3.2 billion (21.8 percent); Tajikistan $2.76 billion (1.9 percent); (Table 4 and Figure 4).

Table 4: Imports to Kazakhstan from Central Asian Countries

(In thousands of U.S. dollars)

	2000	2001	2002	2003	2004	2005 *	Total for the period
Kyrgyzstan	315,910	325,449	319,348	525,250	912,392	838,226	**3,236,575**
Tajikistan	54,781	22,465	28,127	72,096	34,780	63,521	**275,770**
Turkmenistan	440,749	774,770	745,988	498,414	755,578	426,813	**3,642,312**
Uzbekistan	732,556	802,039	848,680	896,154	2,276,082	2,109,049	**7,664,560**
Total by year	**1,543,996**	**1,924,723**	**1,942,143**	**1,991,914**	**3,978,832**	**3,437,609**	

***Jan.-Sept., 2005**

Source: Sstatistical Agency of the Republic of Kazakhstan.

Figure 4: Ratio of Imports among Central Asian Countries from Kazakhstan (In percent)

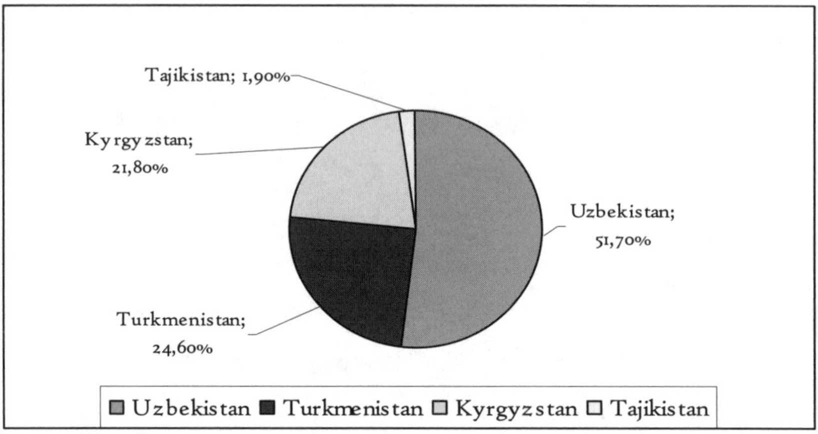

Tajikistan; 1,90%
Kyrgyzstan; 21,80%
Uzbekistan; 51,70%
Turkmenistan; 24,60%

Uzbekistan ■ Turkmenistan □ Kyrgyzstan □ Tajikistan

Source: Statistical Agency of the Republic of Kazakhstan.

Growth of GDP (2000–2005)

With the exception of Turkmenistan, the average gross domestic product figures for the countries of Central Asia increased by 7.48 percent between 2000 and 2005. Annual growth rates in 2000 were 6.83 percent and about 6.07 percent for 2005 (Table 5).

Table 5:GDP (In percent compared with the previous year)

	2000	2001	2002	2003	2004	2005 *
Kazakhstan	109,8	113,5	109,8	109,3	109,4	109,2
Kyrgyzstan	105,4	105,3	100,0	107,0	107,1	99,4
Tajikistan	108,3	109,6	110,8	111,0	115,0	108,5
Uzbekistan	103,8	104,2	104,0	104,2	107,7	107,2*

***Jan.-Sept., 2005**

Source: Statistical Agency of the Republic of Kazakhstan.

Between 2000 and 2005 Kazakhstan's annual GDP grew by 10.16 percent (9.8 percent in 2000 and 9.2 percent in 2005). The implementation of economic reforms and the active development of small- and medium-size businesses have fostered the development of industry, agriculture, transport, and external trade, among other sectors. By 2004 Kazakhstan's GDP had the following structure: services sector: 39 percent; industry: 33 percent; transport and communication: 13 percent; agriculture: 9 percent; and construction: 6 percent. It should be noted that some international estimates of GDP growth in this same period are lower, reflecting the minimal diversification of production and inefficiencies in bank taxation, and law-enforcement.

Between 2000 and 2005 average Tajikistan's annual GDP growth in Tajikistan reached 10.53 percent (8.3 percent in 2000 and 8.5 percent in 2005). In an effort to counter the effects of economic and social shocks during the earlier civil war, Tajikistan has implemented certain internal stabilizers. The inflation rate has been kept under control, the exchange rate is stable, and poverty has been reduced from 83 percent in 1999 to less than 60 percent in 2005.

From 2000 to September 2005, average GDP growth in Uzbekistan reached 5.18 percent (3.8 percent in 2000 and 7.2 percent in 2005). This traces to developments in agricultural, industry, and the transport and communication sectors. At the same time, growth in general increased through sales in rare metals, gas, and oil. In terms of GDP structure, the ratio of industry and construction was only 16 percent and 7 percent, respectively, and transport and communication made up only 8.5 percent of the total. The majority of Uzbekistan's GDP consists of the service sector (34.5 percent) and agriculture (34.0 percent).

In Kyrgyzstan, average GDP growth reached 4.03 percent (5.4 percent in 2000 and 0.6 percent in 2005). The significant decrease in growth at the end of the period resulted from the political events of 2005 and the absence of a coordinated governmental action program for destabilizing the economy. Kyrgyzstan's GDP structure is as follows: the industrial sector: 25 percent; the construction sector: 4 percent; with transport and communication making up only 1.3 percent. The dominant agricultural and service sectors make up 37 percent and 32.7 percent, respectively.

Down to 2005 there was no significant change in the geographical structure of Central Asia's external trade. Kazakh main trading partners (i.e., China, Italy, and Switzerland,) remained unchanged. The case is similar for Kyrgyzstan, whose trading partners included China, Switzerland, and the United Arab Emirates; for Tajikistan, whose partners include the Netherlands and Turkey; and for Turkmenistan, whose partners include Iran, Italy, Turkey, and the United Arab Emirates.[3]

Restrictions on International Trade between Kazakhstan and Other Countries of Central Asia

Trade between Central Asian states assumes the existence of generally cooperative relations among them, especially in such critical areas as the use of hydroelectric and hydrocarbon resources. However a number of problems specific to the transport sector impede trade and cooperation. Experts point out that inadequate transport and support infrastructure characterize even the most capital-intensive components of Central Asian production. High railroad tariffs especially have limited trade and economic relations. Over the last decade the countries of Central Asia sought to address such obstacles, but the implementation of agreements among them has been slow. For example, an International Transport Consortium that should lead to the creation of a common transport policy for Central Asian states has yet to become operational. Yet programs of individual countries to achieve self-sufficiebcy in such areas as food been effective. Conditions for growing grain in Uzbekistan are far from idea and the goal of self-sufficiency in food has not been achieved. The only way to do so would be on a regional basis, which would utilize Kazakhstan's excellent conditions for growing grain.

These trends testify to the complex problems facing increased cooperation among Central Asian states. Other obstacles to cooperation and trade include the different structures of their economies and their very diverse progress towards market systems. This latter difference is most clearly illustrated in GDP per capita, which in Kazakhstan in 2005 reached $3,620. Other Central Asian states have achieved far lower rates of growth. In some states geographical isolation has had a significant impact on GDP per capita.

[3] The data of Interstate Statistical Committee of the CIS, 2005.

Tajikistan, for example, where more than 90 percent of the country is mountainous and transport and communications poor, GDP is only $236 per capita, a regional low.

Kazakhstan's transition to a market economy has succeeded because it adopted reforms that increased the country's competitiveness. By contrast strict controls over internal market in Uzbekistan and administrative and legal pressure on businesses there , have significantly constrained industrial production in that country. The absence of transparency in political and economic decisions making and the closed nature of commerce hamper governmental measures aimed at improving the situation.

The low level of economic cooperation within Central Asia decreases significantly the development of trade. The withdrawal of specific items from free trade (as both Kazakhstan and Uzbekistan have done) has inhibited trade turnover. States have set high customs duties and excise taxes and blocked the export of some goods. As a result, their mutual economic relations are limited mainly to energy supplies and the transit of goods. Both the export and import of industrial goods and food items are insignificant throughout the region. Central Asian nations have considerable potential to lift their mutual commodity turnover to higher levels but have failed to do so.

The level of intra-regional investment is also low. This is particularly evident in Uzbekistan, where some fifty enterprises with Kazakh capital make up only 1.5 percent of the economy. The number of Kazakh enterprises owned in Kyrgyzstan (which fell as a result of the political events in that country in the first half of 2005) and Tajikistan is low. Thus, the potential for trade and economic cooperation among Central Asian countries has yet to be realized, despite a number of intergovernmental agreements in the area

In summary, the following factors are impeding the development of international and transit trade among Central Asian countries:

- Infrastructure needed to support efficient transport has yet to be created. The further expansion of transport routes is necessary, both within national borders and within the region, as are better systems of telecommunication and information management for interacting with international commodity markets.

- The differential rates at which Central Asian countries are transforming themselves into market economies create serious impediment to trade. Macroeconomic policies are not harmonized, nor have the governments adopted coordinated actions for carrying out economic reforms. Kazakhstan, for example, has made efforts to reform its economy and increase competitiveness; as a result, it became the first CIS state recognized by the European Union and the United States as a market economy. Yet because no other state has followed this path, few of the potential benefits for the region have been realized.
- Uzbekistan's economy is increasingly closed to international trade and foreign investments. International financial institutions have pressed the Uzbek leadership to carry out market reforms and liberalize foreign trade but the government has responded with half-measures that have left the situation no better than before.

Balancing these are such positive factors as the following: the stable growth of the world economy at 3.3 percent per annum; high global demand for Central Asian energy; favorable oil prices that promise to remain above $45 per barrel; and China's accelerated economic growth and its influence as an international center of development.

In view of these specific factors, the overall prospects for development in the region are positive. Indeed, as early as 2010, it should be possible for all the countries of the region to be considered developed nations (Table 6).

Table 6:Forecast of Some Parameters of Economic Development of the Central Asian Republics by 2010

Economic Parameters	GDP Growth, percent within year	GDP, per capita, in U.S. dollars	Population, in millions	Poverty Rate as a percent of Total Population	Export of Manufacturing, per capita, in U.S. dollars
Central Asia as a whole	up to 7	up to 2,000	up to 75	21–23	141

Source: "Overcoming of Crisis: Economic Revival of Central Asia," Policy Studies, Center of Analysis of Public Problems, June, 2005.

Of course, the associated risks must also be assessed before reaching definitive conclusions on the future. Possible risks include the following:

a collapse in oil prices during the period before 2010; a decrease in demand for such key Central Asian exports as cotton, aluminum, and gold; an increase in the number of externally generated issues that could affect the security of the region; destabilization of the internal political situation in one or more of the Central Asian countries; and a failure by one or more regional governments to observe international agreements on economic cooperation.

Central Asian countries have taken some important steps towards creating a free trade regime, including the harmonization of customs, tariff and non-tariff regulations on inter-regional trade, and measures to promote of advancing the free transit of exports and imports.

We recommend that further concrete measures be taken to increase the tempo of market reforms that will create essential commodity markets. In addition, we recommend that the free flow of capital be encouraged, that favorable coordination be created for the development of enterprises, and that the creation of financial-industrial groups receive the highest priority. Further efforts should be made to solidify Kyrgyzstan's membership in the World Trade Organization (WTO) and to hasten the membership of Kazakhstan and Uzbekistan. Customs duties must be further reduced. Finally, normal environmental and ecological standards should be rigorously and equitably applied across the region.

The North-South Meridian Transport Corridor

A core issue at the heart of relations among Central Asian countries and between them all, China, India, and Russia, is the further development of transport routes in Eurasia. In August, 2000, the governments of Russia, India, and Iran decided to develop a strategic transport corridor connecting the countries of the Persian Gulf, India, and Pakistan to Iranian and Russian ports on the Caspian Sea. The proposed corridor would also stretch through Russian water routes, railways, and highways to east and central Europe and to Scandinavia. In total, the corridor would encompass areas of Northern Europe, the Russian Federation, Central Asia, the Caucasus, and the Persian Gulf.

On 12 September, 2000 at the second Eurasian Transport Conference in St. Petersburg, transport authorities of the three countries signed an agreement to proceed with the project.[4] That same month delegations from Russia, India, Iran, and Oman signed corresponding documents. In April 2001 India ratified the agreement on the Transport Corridor; in October 2001 Iran and Oman ratified it; and the Russian Federation followed in February, 2002. Russian Deputy Minister of Transport Smirnov claims that Russia stands to gain between $8 and $9 billion annually through freight traffic between Asia and Europe. He asserted that up to $2 billion could be made from transport along the "North-South" corridor alone.[5]

In April 2003 Kazakhstan joined this North-South corridor agreement, which should increase considerably the amount of transit in and out of the country. Special attention along this route is given to the Kazakh ports of Aktau, Bautino, and Khuryk. Use of the ice-free port of Aktau during winter reduces considerably both the time and transport expenses, increases the capacity of the northern Caspian sections of the route, and enables further development

---

[4] Karibzhanov, Khayrat; Tuleugaliev, Gaziz, *Economic and legal basis of the transit*. – Petropavlovsk (Kazakhstan), 2002, p. 322-329.

[5] Interview of deputy minister of foreign affairs of Russia, N. Smirnov, *www.strana.ru*, August 14, 2001.

of transportation in the region.[6] However, if new export-import and freight traffic is to be attracted, these ports must be modernized.

The Kazakh portion of the route will include railways and highways, as well as a sea route through Aktauthat will provide an oulet through the Caspian Sea to international sea routes.The volume of cargo traffic through Aktau has increased steadily from 1999 to the present. In 2001-2002 alone the growth was 19 percent. The benefits to Kazakhstan from the development of this route are obvious. Estimates suggest that transportation costs will fall by 15–20 percent. It is expected this East-West route could be up to twice as fast as the existing route, which passes through the Suez Canal.

Kazakhstan has carefully examined all potential merits and demerits of each route before entering into international committments.[7] The importance of appropriate trade routes to Kazakhstan's overall development cannot be overstated. The scale of these economic and geopolitical benefits to the country was highlighted at a 2003 session of Kazakhstan's Security Council, when it was affirmed that he development of transport is a major component of any strategy to promote. Kazakhstan's security and overall national interests.[8] Azerbaijan also hopes that the "North–South" corridor will strengthen its involvement in world trade by targeting a significant part of the freight traffic between the countries of the European Union and Southern Asia.

On 28 August, 2003, a conference organized by the United Nations convened in Almaty, with ministers from landlocked developing countries, emerging transit countries, donors, and representatives from international financial and development institutions. Experts from 75 countries agreed on the so-called "Almaty Action Program," which underscores five basic priorities: (i) policy, (ii) infrastructure, (iii) international trade and measures for its

---

[6] Ratification was proposed (official chronicle), *Kazakhstanskaya pravda* (Kazakhstan), June 26, 2003.

[7] Kasenov, Farkhad. The prospects of interaction are widening, *Kazakhstanskaya pravda* (Kazakhstan), June 14, 2003.

[8] Security Council session (official chronicle), *Kazakhstanskaya pravda* (Kazakhstan), October 17, 2003.

simplification, (iv) international technical assistance, and (v) monitoring of the program's implementation.

In Kazakhstan, the share of transport costs for cargo now reaches 50 percent. Marine transport remains the most profitable and effective method of transport, which gives the North-South corridors to the Persian Gulf and Arabian Sea particular importance.[9] Thus Iran requires between 3 and 5 million tons of grain per yearwhich it imports from Australia rather then from nearby Kazakhstan. The reason for this is simple: marine transportation from Australia is cheaper than overland transport from Kazakhstan, which is as high as $7–10 per ton. Indeed, 15-20 percent of the final price comes from the cost of transportation. The most important transit countries for Kazakhstan at present are Azerbaijan, China, Georgia, Russia, and Ukraine. Kazakh experts believe that it is impossible to achieve improved trade through bilateral agreements alone.[10] According to Mr. Mamin, Kazakhstan's Minister of transport, transport's share in the final cost of production reaches 20 percent, which greatly reduces the competitiveness of the economy.[11]

The North-South corridor in Kazakhstan is already outfitted with the necessary infrastructure. The following railway lines will be part this corridor:

1. Shengeldy (Uzbek border)-Arys-Kyzylorda-Aktobe- Uralsk-(Russian border with an outlet to Samara);
2. Arys-Lugovaya (Kyrgyzstan border)-Chui-Karaganda-Astana-Petropavlovsk-(Russian border with the outlet to Ural and Western Siberian regions); and
3. Chu-Almaty-Aktogai-Semipalatinsk (Russian border with outlet to Altai and central Siberia).

---

[9] *Donskikh, Alevtina.* Seven feet under keel, *Kazakhstanskaya pravda*_(Kazakhstan), August 28, 2003.

[10] Ibid.

[11] Speech of minister of transport and communication of Kazakhstan A. Mamin, *Panorama* (Kazakhstan), October 7, 2005.

In the south there are two junctions with Uzbek railways (Shengeldy station) and Kyrgyzstan (Lugovaya station). In the north, there are eleven junctions with the Russian railway system, some of which do not currently operate. Railway transport coming out of Kazakhstan makes up 85 percent of regional transit (in 2001 this was 5.6 million tons).

The main regional automobile transit routes coincide with the railway routes and are supplemented in western Kazakhstan by the following: from Karakalpakstan (Uzbekistan) through Bozoi-Karabutak with an outlet to the Russian borders (Urals and western Siberia regions); from Turkmenistan through Bekdash, Jana-Uzen-Beineu-Jety-bai with an outlet to European Russia and the Urals. Motor transit across these routes is carried out mostly by Kyrgyz, Russian, and Uzbek operators.[12]

Due to inconsistent economic policies and political disagreements among the countries of Central Asia, many international transport agreements have yet to be implemented there. Due to cooling of intra-regional relations and periodic boundary disputes, the Kazakh Parliament has gone so far as to consider canceling two of its agreements with Uzbekistan.[13]

Experts from the region agree that the large-scale development of transport corridors running from north to south should occur along the following routes:

1. a route through Kyrgyzstan and Tajikistan, assuming that a multi-purpose transport and economic corridor can be developed along the Surkhob Valley through Kyzyl-Su (i.e. the Alay Valley in Kyrgyzstan) with an outlet to Sary-Tash (Tajikistan) and proceeding then to the Chinese city of Kashgar, which in turns provides a route to the Karakorum highway, i.e., an outlet to Pakistan, northern India, and the western regions of China (the Karategin-Alai Transport Corridor).

---

[12] Karibzhanov, Khayrat; Tuleugaliev, Gaziz, *Economic and legal basis of the transit.* – Petropavlovsk (Kazakhstan), 2002, p. 16-17.
[13] Report by "Khabar" agency (Kazakhstan), October 9, 2003.

2. a route through Uzbekistan, Turkmenistan, and Iran to the Persian Gulf, using the Tedzhen-Serax-Meshkhed (Turkmenistan-Iran) railway line.

3. a route across the territories via Uzbekistan (Tashkent), Tajikistan (Dushanbe), Afghanistan (Barogil pass, at the Afghani and Pakistani border), and Pakistan (to the port of Karachi, or alternatively to the newer port of Gwadar).

4. a route through the territories of Kyrgyzstan (Osh), Uzbekistan (Tashkent), Irkeshtam pass (Chinese and Kyrgyzstani border) to the Karakorum highway in Pakistan.[14]

China, India, Iran, Pakistan, and Russia have also shown interest in developing continental transport routes. However, these countries face some of the same challenges as the Central Asian states There is a limited number of commodities they might trade; their customs regulations are incompatible with one another; serious political differences prevent cooperation; and security problems are in some cases prohibitively grave, notable on Pakistan's eastern border with India and along its western border with Afghanistan.

Countries to the southeast of Central Asia have repeatedly declared their strategic interest in opening transport links among the states. Yashvang Singh, India's Minister of Foreign Affairs, stated on 17 October 2005 that one of the main components of Indian foreign policy is its intention "to construct a new "Silk Road" which will open a direct connection with the states of the Central Asia." In his view, a new stage of cooperation with the states of Central Asia has already begun for India, providing huge opportunities for trade and economic relations. [15]

China's interests are focused on the Karakorum Highway, one of the largest transport projects in Asia. China has been the financial backer and designer of the project, which began in 1967. The route traverses very complicated

---

[14] Grigoriev, Sergey; Zabello, Jakov; Chakeeva Marina, *Motorway of Tashkent - Karachi: New Routes for the Russian exporters // New markets* (Russia), № 4 (August), 2002, p. 14-15.

[15] Report by "Kabar" agency (Kyrgyzstan), October 17, 2003.

terrain, including a narrow mountain corridor. The highway, opened in 1986, connects the Chinese road network directly with Islamabad and the port of Karachi, passing through the disputed territories of Jammu and Kashmir. The Karakorum Highway provides easy access to South Asia. For political reasons neither Kazakh, Russian nor Uzbek transport firms use the alternative route through Dushanbe. Instead they route traffic along a land detour through the Kyrgyz city of Osh and thence to the customs port at Irkeshtan. The Karakorum Highway marks an important step in the restoration of the Silk Road and is a symbol of unity among Central Asian states that is of great strategic importance. The route enables China to engage in effective cooperation with its neighbors, while also providing an alternate to the sea in the case of rened conflict in Afghanistan.[16] The system of which it is a part runs in two directions: a North–South corridor, that includes western China, Kazakhstan, Pakistan, Russia, and Uzbekistan; and an East-West corridor that includes all of China, Central Asia, and Russia to Europe.

Pakistan has also shown great interest in making the Karakorum Highway fully operational. Though the highway today carries only 20 percent of that country's export-import trade, it is valuable as the only major land link between Pakistan and the external world, affecting Pakistani transit to the north and northeast. Pakistan's new port at Gwadar will greatly enhance the value of the Karakorum Highway and also of all emerging trade routes from Central Asia via Afghanistan.

East – West Arteries

Several east-west corridors connect Europe, the Caucasus, the Middle East, Central Asia, and the Asian Pacific region by networks of roads, railways, pipelines, and sea and air freight. The Euro-Asian Transport and Communication Corridor (EATCC) embraces several such transport routes, including the Eurasian Highway and the Eurasian Land Bridge. The Eurasian Land Bridge includes all transport modes, including pipelines, which are

---

[16] Grigoriev, Sergey; Zabello, Jakov; Chakeeva Marina, *Motorway of Tashkent*, p. 16.

lucrative instruments for export both for Central Asian and South Caucasus countries.[17]

The EATCC, based on an agreement signed in Turkmenistan in 1996, coordinates railway activity between Azerbaijan, Georgia, Turkmenistan, and Uzbekistan. The agreement also provides for interrelationships with the Eurasian Highway, the Pan-European Transport Area (PETA), and the transport systems of Southeast and East Asia.

At the third Pan-European transport conference held in Helsinki in 1998 , the TRACECA (the Eurasian transport corridor) was adopted as Europe's priority transport system to the East.[18] The TRACECA Program was created in 1993 in an effort to develop a transport corridor between Europe and Asia via the countries of the South Caucasus and Central Asia. Since then, the geography of the TRACECA program has broadened to include Bulgaria, Moldova, Mongolia, Romania, Turkey, and Ukraine.[19]

Kazakhstan has a strategic interest in the TRACECA program, which includes railways, highways, and ports of the Black Sea and Caspian Sea.[20] The European Union, within the framework of the TACIS program, has proposed another regional program, the Interstate Oil and Gas Transport to Europe (INOGATE), which focuses on the rehabilitation of existing oil and gas transport corridors and the construction of new ones. According to Ukrainian experts, TRACECA can compete with traditional sea routes in providing safe, inexpensive and flexible continental transport.

Meanwhile, Russia has responded to this potential competition by increasing the competitiveness of the Tran-Siberian Highway. Efforts have been made to improve train schedules, simplify the declaration of goods, and accelerate the registration of freight ships at borders. In April 1998 a trial container train

---

[17] Gegeshidze, Archil, "Once again about the Great Silk Way", *Central Asia and Caucasus*, № 3, 1999, p. 172.
[18] Ibid., p. 174.
[19] Ibid., p. 173.
[20] Tokaev, Kasimzhomart, *Kazakhstan's foreign policy in terms of globalization*, Almaty, 2000, p 292.

using the route between port Vostochny and Brest took 8.5 days, twice as fast as cargo delivered to Europe by sea.[21]

Some experts relate TRACECA with the GUAM, the organization of Georgia, Ukraine, Azerbaijan and Moldova. Supported by the United States, GUAM calls for the expansion of ties with NATO's "Partnership for Peace" and for the development of a Europe-Caucasus transport corridor.

Despite strong support from Washington, however, GUAM does not have the capacity or even the strong intention to support large projects. Hence, GUAM should not be considered as part of the EU's TRACECA project, a position the United States is in agreement.[22]

Since the GUAM summit in July, 2003, in Yalta, there has been a decline in interest in the organization.[23] Ukraine has strengthened cooperation with its Eurasian neighbors Belarus, Kazakhstan, and Russia. In September, 2003, during the summit in Ukraine, the leaders of the Commonwealth for Independent States signed an agreement to create yet another new organization for regional integration. Since 2001, Uzbekistan has been a member of SOC and, in January, 2006, joined the EAEC, an organization actively supported by Russia.

The development of new transport corridors began in 1990 with the restructuring of the railroad line across the Kazakh-Chinese border was and has been expanded thereafter.[24] During this same period, the Tedzhen-Serakhs-Meshed railroad was constructed between Turkmenistan and Iran with freight traffic beginning after 1996. According to Iranian experts, this rail link is expected to increase capacity by up to 8 million tons of cargo and one million passengers annually.[25]

---

[21] Preiger, David; Malyarchuk Irina; Novikova, Alla, "Economic interests of GUUAM in labyrinths of the Great Silk way", *Central Asia and Caucasus*, № 3, 2001, p. 18-20.
[22] Gorovoi, Valeriy; Omelyanchik, Natalya, "*GUUAM: Problems and Perspectives*"// *Central Asia and Caucasus*, № 3, 2001, p. 82-83.
[23] Gamova, Svetlana. Not all flags are guests of GUUAM, *Nezavisimaya gazeta*, July 4, 2003.
[24] Isingarin, Nigmatzhan, *Problem of integration into the CIS*, Almaty, 1998, p. 57.
[25] Abdullayeva, Tamila, "State and prospects for development of transport highways in Central Asia", *Central Asia and Caucasus*, № 3, 2001, p. 173-174.

With the opening of these new railway lines the development of two trans-continental highways will have been completed. In addition to the Trans-Siberian Highway, the following routes have been launched:

- The Eurasian trunk railroad connecting Belarus, China, Kazakhstan, Southeast Asia, Russia, Ukraine, and Western Europe, and the northern corridor Trans- Asian railroad line; and
- The Trans-Asian Highway connecting Bejing, Almaty, Chardzhou, Istanbul, Tashkent, and Tehran, and the southern corridor Trans-Asian railroad line.[26]

Routes going south are as yet in a primitive state but represent potential for Russian and Chinese cargo, and for the export of goods from the Central Asian countries. The outlet to the Persian Gulf through the southern corridor via the Trans-Asian railway, under the coordinated policy of Central Asian states, could become highly profitable, as could the outlet to the Arabian Sea at Gwadar in Pakistan.

At the same time there are some serious drawbacks to the routes headed in both directions. Due to topographical and climatic conditions, transport costs along them will always remain high. Other possible routes might also be considered, but these will have to fit the political as well as the geographical landscape.

New Pipeline Projects

The expansion of pipelines is a key element in transport infrastructure in Central Eurasia. Kazakhstan, as well as others Caspian countries, has deftly tested the political conditions for such an expansion. At the annual KIOGE-2003 exhibition (Oil and Gas, 2003), Kairgeldy Kabyldin, Executive Director of the Kazakh oil and gas company KazMunaiGaz called a proposed pipeline to China a number one priority, and called also for a plan to connect Kazakhstan to the Baku-Tbilisi-Ceyhan (BTC) project.[27] Washington has

---

[26] Tokaev, Kasimzhomart, *Kazakhstan's foreign policy in terms of globalization,* Almaty, 2000, p. 139.

[27] Donskih, Alevtina. Extraction curve that peaks, *Kazakhstanskaya Pravda* (Kazakhstan), October, 10, 2003.

also insisted on this. During a 2006 visit, A. S. Bodman, the U.S. Secretary of Energy, expressed strong interest in the export of Kazakh oil through BTC.[28]

Not all Kazakh experts share this point of view. Some believe that the link to BTC has too many economic drawbacks that other projects lack. Some object to a Caspian pipeline on environmental grounds.[29] Meanwhile Russia is keen to prevent "outside players" from becoming involved in Caspian affairs. Victor Kalyuzhny, Special Representative to the Russian president regarding the status of the Caspian Sea, has stated that Russia opposes a Kazakhstan-Azerbaijan pipeline that does not involve third parties, and also opposes Ukraine's proposed Odessa-Brody project as an oil "pipeline to nowhere." [30]

Russia sees such pipeline projects of others as important to its own security. Hence its participation is needed to assume stable relations among countries in the region. Moscow would not only interfere with the pipeline projects coming through its territory, but would also actively engage in its own alternative pipeline projects near the Caspian Sea.

Another important project is the completion of the Western Kazakhstan-China pipeline. The pipeline will serve the growing needs of China, which now uses over 70 million tons of oil per year and by 2010 will need to buy 130 million tons annually. The first section of this pipeline, Atyrau-Kenkiyak in the northwest of Kazakhstan, is already operational. Financing for the construction of the second section, Atasu-Alashankou (China), which covers a distance of about 1,300 km, was undertaken by China. Construction of the pipeline on the Atasu-Alashankou segment was completed in December 2005. The initial capacity of the project is 20 million tons of oil per year but the designed capacity is up to 50 million tons.[31] The first barrels of oil are expected to be transported over this pipeline during 2006.

Between 2000 and 2003 China and Russia negotiated a pipeline that will run from the Siberian city of Angarsk to the Chinese city of Datsin. Delays on a

---

[28] Report by "Kazakhstan-today" Agency, March 15, 2006.

[29] See *Perspective routes for transportation of Kazakh oil*, Oil-and-gas resources of Kazakhstan in the system of global and regional relations, Almaty, 2002, p. 134-137.

[30] Donskikh, Alevtina. Not united by oil. *Kazakhstanskaya Pravda*, October 10, 2003.

[31] Ibid.

decision from the Russian side pushed Beijing to begin construction of the pipeline in Kazakhstan. Meanwhile, trade in power resources between China on the one hand and Kazakhstan and Russia on the other hand has increased annually through the use of the railway network.

According to the managing director of KazMunaiGas, the new pipeline will be used by CNPC to transport 8 million tons of oil a year from western Kazakhstan. Added to this will be oil deposits from the south of the country developed by the Russian firm LUKOIL and PetroKazakhstan (10–12 million tons one year). In 2005 these assets were bought by the Chinese CNPC. Such tonnage will be sufficient to make the pipeline profitable. In the long term, production can grow to 50 million tons per year.[32]

It is important to state that Kazakhstan sees all the single-buyer markets as entailing high risk. It is, therefore, attempting to work out conditions that will insure stable pricing.

The third potentially important direction for Kazakh oil exports is to the south via the Caspian Sea. The majority of Kazakh experts consider this direction to be very promising both from the economic and geopolitical standpoints. At meetings held in Tehran in 2003, the ministers of transport for Kazakhstan and Iran addressed the issue of increasing Kazakh oil exports through Iran. In view of the potential growth of hydrocarbon production in Kazakhstan, Tehran has declared its readiness to allow up to 120 thousand barrels of oil per day to be exported through its borders. Iranians argue that the potential of Iran as an export route will become evident as soon as Kazakhstan begins the commercial development of hydrocarbons from the shelf of the Caspian Sea. By the end of 2006 it will be possible to pump up to 40 million tons of oil annually to world markets via Iran, and a significant part of this could be delivered from Kazakhstan.

Based on this forecast, officials in Tehran have developed a staged scheme for receiving and exporting "big" Kazakh oil. Iran began modernizing and expanding its processing capacities in Tehran and Tabriz oil refineries, which in 2000 could already handle 400 thousand barrels per day. The

---

[32] Skorniakova, Anna, "Nazarbayev is pushing Moscow out of Chinese pipeline", *Nezavisimaya gazeta*, October 14, 2003.

National Iranian Oil Company (NIOC), the State Oil Company of China (CNPC), Hong Kong Sinopec Group, and Swiss Vitol have started construction of a new bulk-oil terminal and bulk-oil ramp in the Neka port. Additional pumping stations have been created in order to increase the capacity of the oil pipeline Neka-Tehran-Tabriz to up to 370 thousand barrels per day. By 2006, production is expected to grow to 540 thousand barrels per day.

By creating the necessary transport infrastructure, Tehran will be in the position to increase oil processing at its refineries. Tehran plans to increase oil imports from Kazakhstan and Russia from four to five-fold. Currently, Kazakhstan delivers up to 20 thousand barrels per day to northern Iran but a swapping process will greatly increase this figure.[33]

Iran's influence on the transport of energy resources vividly attests to the geopolitical basis of the problem. The main constraint on the further development of trade in energy resources between the Central Asian countries and Iran is the position of Washington vis-à-vis Iran.

Conclusion

The development and implementation of international projects such as TRACECA, EATKK, the North-South route, ASEM, and country associations such as GUAM, EAEC, the Organization of Economic Cooperation (OEC), are all dependent on the successful implementation of transport agreements that, strengthen cooperation in trade.

In many respects, these diverse organizations reflect the wide spectrum of economic and geopolitical interests affecting the newly independent states of the region. An important factor is the geo-economical attractiveness of the region to the highly industrialized countries, with their large markets and vast export-import potential. For North-South transport, the centers of attraction are India, Iran, Pakistan, Russia, and the countries of Northern Europe. For East-West transport arteries, these centers include the European Union, Eastern Europe, Turkey, Southeast Asia, China, Japan, and South

---

[33] Lukyanchikov, Victor, "Expectation of a lot of oil", *Novoe pokolenie* (Kazakhstan), September 26, 2003.

Korea. The development of North-South and East-West corridors are not mutually exclusive and are in many ways complimentary. The combination and crossing of the two will benefit all transit countries and improve regional economic prospects overall.

The expansion of trade and economic relations among the states of Central Asia must be continued. This should be accomplished by creating functioning free trade zones; facilitating cooperation in business and investment; implementing coordinated customs systems, tax and tariff policies; harmonizing monetary, credit, and currency relations; and coordinating relevant national legislation.

In order to move free trade area forward among the states of Central Asia, the following steps must be undertaken:

- remove customs taxes and duties, as well as other restrictions to mutual trade;
- harmonize customs legislation, and also tariff and non-tariff mechanisms for the regulation of trade; and
- generally, to accept and observe the core principles of free trade.

Central Asian countries need to pursue harmonized macroeconomic policies and work to coordinate their individual economic reforms. Kazakh experts believe concrete measures are needed in order to create conditions for common commodity and service markets. Priority should be given to strengthening cooperation in the financial sector, providing for the free movement of capital, creating favorable conditions for business development, co-production arrangements, and financial and industrial groups. The development of the main transport corridors will improve cooperation among Central Asian states and create common markets for power, transport services and agricultural products.

The International Transport Consortium should help define measures for developing railway and road routes, the transit potential of the Central Asian states, and civil engineering principles for transport. Coordinated principles for customs, tax, and tariff policies are needed. In particular, countries must adhere to signed contracts and agreements (including those within the framework of EAEC) that will simplify customs registration and control over internal borders, enable the free transport of cargo between these countries and transit through their territories, and implement the principle of "two borders-one stop." In the field of tax policy, a system of flexible taxation for transport enterprises among Central Asian countries is badly needed.

Special attention should be given to measures to align internal and international railroad tariffs. Differences in tariffs complicate the development of interstate transportation and raise the cost of transport. In the long term, the Central Asian States must develop a united tariff policy and take measures to unify and harmonize transport legislation and laws.

The implementation of a Transport Consortium would facilitate the expansion of transport and trade, and economic relations among Central Asian states and between them and their major trading partners. It will promote the modernization of transport infrastructures and the development of related industries, a rise in employment rate in the regions along transport corridors, and, in the long term, help create a joint transport space.

Thus, the creation of a functioning free trade zone is a critical step toward the long-term goal of a common commodity and services market. Such a market would promote the stable development of the Central Asian states and their successful integration into the world community, as well as increase standards of living and promote stability and security in the region. As Asia and the Pacific region assume the role of the world's main economic center, strong relations between the countries of Europe and East Asia will become increasingly important, and Central Asia can serve as the geographical and transport link between them.

Achieving the 2025 targets of "creating a global zone and joint development that will facilitate the free movement of goods and services" should be a main focus of policy across the region. A Seoul Asia-Europe summit in 2000 called for liberalization of trade through the expansion of water, railway, highway, and air transport between Asia and Europe. The post-Soviet countries should play a big role in the creation of connecting bridges between the economically influential regions of Eurasia. Some of the countries of Central Asia are expected to join the CIS as well as the WTO. This will affect development of transport infrastructure in a positive way, as these countries adopt world standards for the passage of goods and services across borders.

Azerbaijan

Taleh Ziyadov*

The tradition of highly regionalized trade is becoming old-fashioned as the world becomes increasingly interdependent and globalized. International commerce is moving toward a globalized system in which continental trade between Europe and Asia is bound to gain significance.

In 2000, Eurasian trade turnover embraced some 300 million tons of goods, consisting of 72 million tons of European exports into Asia and 228 million tons of Asian exports into Europe.[1] By 2015 this trade turnover is expected to reach 460 million tons. Energy products from Middle Eastern and Persian Gulf countries remain the primary Asian import to Europe—making up approximately 60 percent of total imports—yet East Asia's trade share of 20 percent will continue to grow in the coming years.

The volume of inland transportation, especially container trade, is expected to double from 65 million tons in 2002 to 135 million tons in 2015.[2] The number of goods and products shipped by container will increase as well, reaching 40 percent of total exchanged cargo by 2015. Today, almost all containers moving between Europe and Asia—95 percent—are transported by sea via the Suez Canal and the Mediterranean Sea. In 2005, the estimated number of containers shipped by sea from East Asia to Europe totaled over three million

---

* Some segments of this chapter were previously published in *CACI Analyst* (April 19, 2006) and *CESR Review* (Summer 2006).

[1] See the remarks from the discussion table held during the 3rd Annual Eurasian Conference on Transport in Saint-Petersburg, September 11-12, 2003. Also available online at http://www.eatu.ru/eatu.ru.page(DOC).doc(4859).folder(64).html

[2] Ibid.

units. By 2015, this figure is expected to triple, reaching 10 million containers per year.[3]

Eurasian land corridors are far shorter than the maritime routes, prompting European experts and government officials to suggest the development of new inland transportation corridors to carry the growing volume of maritime shipments between Europe and Asia. This will complement sea transport while enabling the transit countries to develop their infrastructure and become involved in continental trade.

Azerbaijan is a natural crossroads for the growing continental land - based trade and its geostrategic location is key to connecting the transportation networks and markets of Europe, Asia, the Middle East and the Mediterranean region. As a strategic intersection, Azerbaijan will accommodate the rapidly growing transit traffic from China and Central Asia to Europe, and from India and Iran to Russia.

There are two potential inland alternatives to the current Europe-Asia maritime transportation routes and both involve Azerbaijan: the East-West transport corridor and the North-South transport corridor. The former consists of a China-India-Central Asia-Caucasus-Europe route, while the latter would link the routes of the Asian continent, the Caspian region and Europe via an India-Iran-Russia axis. Both corridors have great potential for reviving the traditional Silk Road with container trade (see appendix 1).

The construction of the Baku-Tbilisi-Ceyhan oil and the Baku-Tbilisi-Erzurum natural gas pipelines through Azerbaijan will, in the next 20 years, bring over $100 billion into the state budget,[4] while enabling additional oil and gas from Kazakhstan and Turkmenistan to be shipped to Europe via trans-Caspian pipelines.

---

[3] See report by European Conference of Ministers of Transport's "Globalisation: Europe-Asia Links Synthesis Report and Political Decision Required," April 26, 2005. Also available online at http://www.cemt.org/online/council/2005/CM200501e.pdf

[4] According to *BP Azerbaijan Sustainability Report 2004*, potential Azerbaijan State revenues from the country's major oil and gas fields are estimated at $107 billion (price of oil based on $30 per barrel rate). The report is available online at http://www.bp.com/

This paper examines Azerbaijan's role in continental trade by means of the East-West and North-South transport corridors, with a focus on Azerbaijan's road, rail, maritime and energy networks, and customs system. It will assess current and potential projects in each of these sectors, as well as the impediments that hinder facilitation of Europe-Asia trade. In addition, it will consider the economic and strategic implications of specific projects for Azerbaijan and the Caspian region.

Road Networks and Customs Transit System

Connecting the separate countries' transit networks is critical if Azerbaijan is to become open to European, Middle Eastern and South Asian markets. Azerbaijan has an 18,800 km-long road network (excluding Nakhchivan), which consists of 52 percent paved road, 47 percent gravel road, and 1 percent dirt track.[5] Roads carry 78 percent of all passengers and 28 percent of goods traffic. In general, the roads that run from Baku to Georgia are a part of the East-West "Silk-Road" highway corridor, and the roads that run along the Caspian Sea to connect Russia and Iran are a part of the North-South transportation corridor. Both road networks are part of the Asian Highway Network (see appendix 3).

Azerbaijan signed the "Main Multilateral Agreement on International Transport for the development of Transport Corridor Europe-Caucasus, Asia" (TRACECA) during the International Conference "TRACECA – Rehabilitation of the Historical Silk Route" in Baku in September, 1998. It also joined the North-South Transport Corridor in September 2005.

Launched in May 1993, TRACECA is a European Union initiative that aims at deepening regional and inter-regional cooperation between TRACECA member states and at integrating the TRACECA transport corridor into the Trans-European Transport Networks (TEN). Since 1993, the EU has

[5] See the ADB Technical Assistance Report, "Republic of Azerbaijan: Preparing for Southern Road Corridor Improvement Project (Alat-Astara Road)," Project No. 39176, November 2005

invested more than €110 million for the realization of 53 technical and investment projects.[6]

According to Azerbaijan's State Statistics Committee, the volume of cargo transported through the TRACECA corridor increased by 34.2 percent between 2001 and 2003, reaching 40.9 million tons. This includes cargo shipped by all transportation modes: 46.7 percent (primarily oil and oil related products) was moved by rail, 28.2 percent was moved by road, and 25 percent was shipped by sea.[7]

Within the TRACECA project, East-West highways are being built to European standards. Construction and renovation work is supported by grants and loans from the World Bank, the European Bank for Reconstruction and Development (EBRD), the Islamic Development Bank (IDB) and the Kuwait Fund.[8] A 40 km-long section of the Alat-Gazi-Mammed highway has been completed and the remaining segments of the Baku-Georgian border highway are under construction. This will mean that the entire Azerbaijani section of the Europe-Caucasus-Central Asia corridor, from Baku to the Georgian border, will meet European technical standards.

Before the Azerbaijani Ministry of Transport was established in 2003, national road maintenance was the responsibility of a state-owned company, Azeravtoyol. Since the early 1990s, roads in Azerbaijan have been poorly maintained and most still need significant modernization. According to the Asian Development Bank's (ADB) Technical Assistance Report:

[A]bout 75% of the network is in poor condition. Based on the road condition data available, 61% of the [East-West] and [North-South] highways, 76% of other republic roads, 66% of secondary roads, and 76% of rural roads require rehabilitation. In addition, projections of increased traffic

---

[6] For more information visit http://www.traceca-org.org

[7] This data is from the annual report "Development of Transport Infrastructure and International Transport Linkages in Azerbaijan Republic" prepared by the Azerbaijani Government for the UNECE and UNESCAP joint project "Developing Euro-Asian Transport Linkages (2002-2006)."

[8] See TRACECA website, TA Project No 37, Rehabilitation of Caucasian Highways, Jacobs Gibb, November 2002.

indicate that the current capacity of the [North-South] highway will be insufficient and that widening and upgrading is needed.[9]

The Azerbaijani government spent $14.4 million on road maintenance in 2004, a sizable increase over the $6.7 million spent in 2001.[10] Yet this falls short of the estimated $260 million required to maintain roads country-wide. The government acknowledges this gap and is developing a ten-year program to achieve this needed investment.

Sixty percent of trucks crossing the Azerbaijani-Georgian border are transit traffic.[11] Most cargo transport between Europe and Asia via Azerbaijan is performed by automobiles from some 40 countries. About 20,000 Iranian vehicles, 8,000 Turkish vehicles and 3,500 Russian vehicles pass through every year.[12]

A similar situation exists for the North-South corridor, where daily traffic volume is around 8,100 vehicles (an estimated 62 percent being freight vehicles).[13] Traffic is expected to increase significantly once the work on Alat-Astara road to the Iranian border and the northern portion of the North-South corridor (connecting Baku to the Russian border) is completed.

In the view of the projected high traffic volumes on the [North-South] corridor, the [Road Transport Services Department] intends to upgrade this road to Category I with dual carriageway and four lanes. Based on initial feasibility work, the proposed road will be constructed on over 80% new and improved alignment in order to avoid major resettlement along the original corridor and to reduce the length (to about 200 km).[14]

---

[9] ADB Technical Assistance Report, op cit, note 5.

[10] Ibid.

[11] See the World Bank study "Trade, Transport and Telecommunications in the South Caucasus: Current Obstacles to Regional Cooperation." Available online at http://www.worldbank.org

[12] See "Azerbaijan Transport Sector, Sector Development, Review and Update,"- a part of the review of
Transit and International Multi-Modal Transport Integrated Border Management Corridor Transport and Trade Information by the TRACECA National Secretary, A. Mustafayev, July 2004. Available online at http://www.worldbank.org

[13] See annual report, op cit, note 7. Annex 1

[14] ADB Technical Assistance Report, op cit, note 5.

The Iranian government agreed to sponsor a feasibility study for the 243 km-long Alat-Astara connection that links Azerbaijan's costal roads with roads in Iran. The main purpose of this project is to "construct a part of the road from Alat [a town near Baku] to Astara [a town near the Azerbaijan-Iran border], develop the cross-border facility at Astara, improve local roads to provide accessibility to poor areas in the South, and enhance the road network's sustainability by supporting policy and institutional reforms in the [Road Transport Services Department]."[15]

This road is key to the North-South transport corridor linking the road networks of Russia, Azerbaijan and Iran. The northern section of the North-South corridor that stretches from Baku to the Azerbaijan-Russia border is operational, but needs modernization. The total length of the route from the Azerbaijan-Russia border to the Azerbaijan-Iran border is 521 km,[16] and the road link is part of the Asian Highway project, a 140,000 km network of standardized roadways promoted by the United Nations Economic and Social Commission for Asia and the Pacific (UNESCAP). 1,500 km of the Asian Highway route is located in Azerbaijan, 17,000 km is in Russia, and 11,000 km is in Iran.[17]

One of the major challenges to facilitating trade between states is the issue of improved integration of national customs services. The Trade Facilitation Program sponsored by the ADB within the Central Asia Regional Economic Cooperation (CAREC) Program is one of the few initiatives that seeks to develop a common customs transit system throughout Greater Central Asia. The six CAREC member countries—Azerbaijan, Kazakhstan, Kyrgyzstan, Mongolia, Tajikistan, Uzbekistan, with the addition of China, a TIR Convention member—have tried to accelerate continental trade and economic growth by facilitating international transit of goods under the TIR Transit System.[18] Participating countries have signed bilateral and

[15] Ibid.
[16] See annual report, op cit, note 7.
[17] UNESCAP Press Release No: G/13/2004. Available online at http://www.unescap.org/unis/press/2004/may/g13.asp
[18] "TIR Carnet is a Customs transit document permitting facilitation of international trade and international road transport, under cover of which transport of goods from

multinational agreements to standardize and harmonize their custom services.

The TIR Transit System is used by 55 states around the world and is the only international customs transit system that provides "a single procedure from the point of departure to the point of destination, with an international guarantee chain."[19] In addition to SafeTIR procedures that involve international electronic data interchange (EDI) control system for TIR Carnets, the TIR Transit System has five principles: secure vehicles or containers; international guarantees; TIR Carnet; mutual recognition of custom controls; and controlled access.[20]

Azerbaijan became a signatory to the TIR Convention in 1996; the Azerbaijan International Road Carriers Association (ABADA) is the national association responsible for oversight and operation of TIR procedures. Supporting and advancing the TIR Transit System is a priority of Azerbaijan, the SafeTIR system having already been implemented on its territory. Azerbaijan issued 600 TIR Carnets in 1998 and 3,900 in 2004,[21] with strong increases likely in the years to come.

A joint initiative started in 1999 by the United Nations Development Program (UNDP) and the State Customs Committee led to the creation of the Data Transmission Network, which improves coordination between various custom checkpoints around the country. Thanks to this system, the

---

(a) Customs office(s) of departure to (a) Customs office(s) of destination is carried out under the procedure called "TIR procedure" laid down in the 1975 Convention on the International Transport of Goods under Cover of TIR Carnets (TIR Convention)." For further information visit http://www.adb.org/Projects/TradeFacilitation/

[19] See the paper by Jeffrey Liang and Dorothea Lazaro "TIR Customs Transit System: Experiences and Initiatives of CAREC Participating Countries," *Asian Development Bank*, January 2006. Available online at http://www.adb.org/Projects/TradeFacilitation/

[20] Ibid.

[21] Ibid.

State Customs Committee, and the Baku Chief Customs Department, most regional customs checkpoints can effectively coordinate with each other.[22]

There are 18 regional custom bodies and 58 custom posts (28 are border posts) in Azerbaijan. The country's custom administration oversees and screens about 19.2 million tons of imported and exported freight, valued at over $5 billion.[23] In 2003, custom duties accounted for $215 million, most of which (67.4 percent) were collected as a Value Added Tax (VAT), followed by import taxes (24.1 percent) and excise taxes (4 percent).[24]

Azerbaijan seaport fees are the lowest along the TRACECA corridor and three to four times lower than the fees charged at the Caspian ports of Aktau (Kazakhstan) and Turkmenbashi (Turkmenistan). (For other tariff schemes, see appendix 4).[25]

The East-West Railway Networks

The Aktau-Baku-Tbilisi-Poti/Batumi Railway System (TRACECA)

One of the East-West projects within the TRACECA transport corridor is the Aktau-Baku-Tbilisi-Poti/Batumi railway network. Azerbaijan, Georgia and Kazakhstan are working to advance the TRACECA route from Aktau to Baku and onward to Poti or Batumi (the distance from Aktau to Baku is 468 km; the Azerbaijani rail section measures 503 km and the Georgian rail section measures 360 km) (see appendix 3). The railway system between Baku and the Georgian port cities of Poti and Batumi has been equipped with fiber optic cable; the European Commission financed the laying of fiber-optic cable along the Azerbaijani section of the railway.[26]

Oil is the primary export product delivered along the Baku-Tbilisi-Poti route. In 1995, the export of oil and oil products via this route was about 335,000

---

[22] See http://www.scc-undp.org/eng/

[23] See Asian Development Bank's Azerbaijan Country Report, April 2004. Available online at http://www.adb.org/Projects/TradeFacilitation/ictcountryreports.asp

[24] Ibid.

[25] See review by A. Mustafayev, op cit, note 12.

[26] See annual report, op cit, note 7.

tons; this grew to 5.2 million tons between 2000 and 2002, and reached roughly 13 million tons in 2003.[27]

The Aktau-Baku-Tbilisi-Poti/Batumi rail network is part of the planned China-Central Asia-Caucasus-Europe railways transport corridor promoted by the United Nations and supported by participating states. One of the routes of this railway network is a 7077 km-long corridor that will link the rail lines of four countries—China, Kazakhstan, Azerbaijan, Georgia and Turkey—directly to European transportation networks. The operational Kazakh portion of the rail system is 3850 km long and starts in the city of Dostik (Druzhba) near the Kazakh-Chinese border, passes through Astana, Orsk, Kandagach, and ends in the Kazakh seaport of Aktau.[28]

An alternative route from Europe to China branches off in Baku and goes through Turkmenistan, across Uzbekistan, and terminates in Dostik (the Turkmenbashi-Ashgabat-Tashkent-Almaty-Dostik route is 6861 km) (see appendix 2). This route is 415 km shorter than the Trans-Asian railway route that passes through Iran, although the latter promises access to India.[29]

The transport cost from Western Europe to Baku in 1999 was $3,000 for a 40-foot container and $2,000 for a 60-ton wagon, according to a 2000 World Bank study.[30] To lower costs and expand the rail network to Central Asia and China, ministers from Azerbaijan, Georgia and Kazakhstan signed a trilateral protocol on October 28, 2005 in Aktau, Kazakhstan. The protocol set tariffs for container shipments via the Poti-Baku-Aktau-Almaty railway: tariffs for import shipments into Kazakhstan were set at $0.28 per container/km, while export container tariffs were set at $0.22 per container/km. Similar charges will apply in Azerbaijan and Georgia, where tariff for transit cargo was set at $0.28 per container/km.[31] Signatories also

---

[27] See review by A. Mustafayev, op cit, note 12.
[28] Ibid.
[29] This data is from the background report by the Azerbaijan's Ministry of Transport dated September 29, 2005.
[30] See paper by Evgeny Polyakov, "Changing Trade Patterns after Conflict Resolution in the South Caucasus," *the World Bank*, Washington DC, 2000.
[31] This Protocol was signed by Minister of Transport of Azerbaijan, Minister of Economic Development of Georgia and Minister of Transport and Communication of

started a pilot program by running a container track along the route on December 25, 2005. In the future, cargo from China will be shipped to Aktau, where it will travel 468 km by railway ferries to Baku, and then will be shipped directly to Istanbul and onward to Europe either by sea from Georgia or by rail via the potential Baku-Tbilisi-Akhalkalaki-Kars-Istanbul railway system.

The Baku-Tbilisi-Akhalkalaki-Kars Railway Connection

(UNECE/UNESCAP)

The Baku-Tbilisi-Akhalkalaki-Kars (BTAK) railway is a section of the Trans-European Railway networks that will connect Azerbaijani, Georgian and Turkish railroads. The route is a strategic project for Azerbaijan, although it is a UNECE/UNESCAP-sponsored initiative and is not yet part of TRACECA (see appendix 3).

Azerbaijan views the BTAK as a missing link—a link that will eventually connect the railway systems of China-Central Asia-South Caucasus-Turkey and the EU. The realization of this project depends on the construction of a 98 km-long rail segment from Kars in Turkey to Tbilisi in Georgia (68 km in Turkey, 30 km in Georgia). The project is estimated to cost around $400 million.

The length of the BTAK and the Kars-Istanbul rail sections are 826 km and 1933 km, respectively. Once completed, cargo from the EU can be shipped directly by rail to China through Turkey, Georgia, Azerbaijan and Central Asia, increasing the volume of container traffic through Azerbaijan and providing a more secure and shorter route to China. (The distance from Istanbul to Dostik could be further shortened to 6297 km if Kazakhstan constructs its Trans-Kazakhstan route, the Aktau-Beineu-Aktogay-Dostik railway.)[32]

Kazakhstan on October 28, 2005 in Aktau, Kazakhstan. A copy of this document was provided by Azerbaijan's Ministry of Transport.

[32] Data provided by the Ministry of Transport of Azerbaijan.

The idea of connecting Azerbaijani, Georgian and Turkish railways was first discussed during the Joint Transport Commission meeting in July, 1993. The initiative was later integrated into the UNECE sponsored Master Plan on the Trans-European Railway (TER) networks. In July 2002, the Ministers of Transport of Azerbaijan, Georgia and Turkey signed a protocol confirming the route and agreed to conduct a feasibility study at a February, 2005 meeting.[33] UNECE lists this route as a Priority I project, indicating that it could be funded and implemented by 2010. Stakeholders hope to begin construction late in 2007. Most forecasts suggest that during the first two years of operation, transport will reach 2 million tons, and will then grow to 8 to 10 million tons over the following three years.[34]

The construction of the BTAK railway will also open markets in the Mediterranean region. Goods and products could be shipped directly to Mersin, a costal Turkish port at the Mediterranean Sea; from there they could be transported by sea to the United States, Israel, Egypt or other North African and South European states.

The project also has a geopolitical significance. It bypasses Armenia, with which Azerbaijan is still at war. Armenia has voiced disapproval of the BTAK route and proposed instead the use of the century-old Russian-built Kars-Gyumri (Armenia)-Tbilisi railway. Azerbaijan argued that this rail link has not been used since the collapse of the Soviet Union and that its renovation may cost more than the construction of the new line.[35]

It is unlikely that Azerbaijan will consider using the Kars-Gyumri rail link as an alternative to the Kars-Akhaklakali railway. Due to the "no peace, no

---

[33] Ibid.

[34] This data is from the Information Paper prepared by the Azerbaijani, Georgian, Turkish delegates for the 1st Meeting of the EU-Black Sea-Caspian Basin Expert Working Group on Transport Infrastructure on December 13, 2005 in Kiev, Ukraine.

[35] According to the information provided by the Ministry of Transport of Azerbaijan, the Armenia-proposed Kars-Gyumri-Tbilisi railway passes though a mountainous terrain and the railway has not been used for more than a decade. During this time the route's condition worsened and it needs extensive repair. Thus, its rehabilitation cost could exceed the construction cost of the Tbilisi-Akhalkalaki-Kars link.

war" situation on the ground and Armenia's refusal to withdraw troops from occupied Azerbaijani lands in return for re-establishment of communications between Baku and Yerevan, Azerbaijan has no other option but to move ahead with the Kars-Akhaklakali project. Azerbaijani officials have repeatedly stated that they cannot delay strategic and economic projects until the Karabakh conflict is resolved. Thus, construction of this project is likely to advance even if the Karabakh peace process does not.

Caspian Sea Ports and the North-South Railway System

There are eleven seaports on the Caspian Sea, including five that belong to Iran, three to Russia, and one each to Azerbaijan, Turkmenistan and Kazakhstan.[36] The capacity of the four main Iranian ports on the Caspian exceeds the total combined capacity of the six ports in Azerbaijan, Kazakhstan, Turkmenistan and Russia.[37] Even with such a disparity, the Baku port utilizes only 13 percent of its total capacity.[38]

Baku's International Sea Port is one of the three TRACECA seaports, the other two beeing Aktau port in Kazakhstan and Turkmenbashi port in Turkmenistan. The Baku seaport has four main revenue-generating divisions: the Main Cargo Terminal, the Ferry Terminal, the Oil Terminal and Shipping Services.[39]

Port traffic has grown 19 percent a year since 1993. An ongoing $16.2 million project sponsored by the EBRD will expand the port's freight cargo handling capacity to 30 million tons a year[40] and allow Azerbaijan to increase the number of cargo and ferry services to and from Aktau and Turkmenbashi, as well as potential shipments from Iran and Russia as a part of the North-South Transport Corridor.

---

[36] See Allister Maunk, "International Transport Corridor South – North," *AIA News*, April 24, 2005. Also available online at http://www.axisglobe.com/article.asp?article=48

[37] See Alekander Sobyanin, "North-South: Will it work? (*MTK «Sever-Yug»: budet li tolk?*)," *Journal Container Business* (*Jurnal Konteynerniy Biznes*), No. 1, January 2006.

[38] See the World Bank study, op cit, note 11.

[39] See Azerbaijan Export and Investment Promotion Foundation's website at http://www.azerinvest.com/eng/

[40] Ibid.

According to the Ministry of Transport of the Russian Federation, the volume of transport via the North-South corridor, excluding oil and oil related products, could reach 30 to 40 million tons by 2008.[41] In 2001, the transport volume was 5.4 million tons and reached 8 - 9 million tons in 2003.[42] Russia hopes to add some $15 billion to its state budget from transit shipment, with an average 15 million tons of cargo.[43] This is precisely why Azerbaijan is interested in the North-South corridor and in transporting some of this increased future cargo volume through its national railways, roads and seaport.

The initial agreement on the North-South corridor was signed between Russia, Iran, India and Oman in Saint Petersburg, Russia in September 2000. The agreement proposes the shipment of goods and containers from India to Russia via Iran and the Caspian Sea. Azerbaijan officially joined the corridor project on 10 September, 2005, when President Ilham Aliyev signed a bill approving Azerbaijan's decision to join the North-South project.

Russian experts estimate that, when compared to routes from South Asia to Northern European and Baltic ports via the Mediterranean and the Suez Canal, the North-South route through the Caspian Sea will shorten delivery periods by 10 to 20 days and reduce shipment costs by $400 to $500.[44] For example, if shipping a container from Germany to India via the Suez Canal costs about $3,500 and takes 40 days, it will cost $2,500 and take 15 to 20 days if shipped through the North-South corridor.[45]

Russia is improving its internal infrastructure in the Astrakhan region, with a focus on the transportation capacity and networks of Russia's Caspian ports, including Astrakhan, Olya and Makhachkala. Between 1999 and 2002

---

41 *Rossiyskaya Gazeta*, September 16, 2003.
42 Rossiyskaya Gazeta, May 13, 2003.
43 *Izvestia.ru*, July 28, 2004
44 See Regine A. Spector, "The North-South Transport Corridor," The Analyst, July 03, 2002
45 See Daniel Shipkov, "Russian Transport Today (*Rossiyskiy Transport Segodna*)," July 2, 2004. Also available online at http://www.novopol.ru/article172.html

Russia spent $29 million[46] on improving its three ports and plans to spend another $250 million within ten years on Astrakhan's regional ports.[47] Iran, on the other hand, devoted $40 million to upgrades in its Amirabad port alone.[48] On 28 July, 2004 Russian officials inaugurated a 47 km railway that connected Yandiki to Olya.[49] It is predicted that Olya's port will handle about 8 million tons of cargo by 2010.[50]

In February 2005, Baku, Moscow, and Tehran endorsed the construction of a 375 km railway—the Kazvin-Rasht-Astara connection—to join the railways of the three countries (see appendix 3). According to the Azerbaijani state railway administration, the North-South railway network could transfer 5 million tons of cargo during its first year of operation, gradually increasing shipment volume to 20 million tons annually.[51] Some experts have argued that the shipment by rail will improve delivery time by an additional five to seven days when compared to ferry shipment via the Caspian Sea.[52]

Most construction will take place in Iran, with an approximately 15 km-long segment to be built in Azerbaijan. The estimated cost of the entire project is about $600 million.[53] Tehran hopes to finish its segment of the railway in four years.[54] The northern part of the North-South railway network that runs from Baku to the Russian border is already in place, but needs renovation. Azerbaijan requires additional investment to modernize and upgrade its roads and railways to accommodate increased transit cargo volumes.[55]

---

[46] See Andrei Milovrozov, "Baku and Yerevan Couldn't Share the Corridor (*Baku i Yerevan ne podelili koridor*)," *Utro.ru*, March 3, 2005. Also available at http://www.utro.ru/articles/2005/03/03/413489.shtml

[47] Maunk, op cit, note 35.

[48] Milovrozov, op cit, note 45.

[49] See National Container Company's Press Release: Opening of the port Olya railway station, July 28, 2004. Available online at http://www.container.ru/English/Company/News/20040728.html

[50] *Nezavisimaya Gazeta*, January 26, 2004

[51] Data provided by the Ministry of Transport of Azerbaijan.

[52] Ibid.

[53] *RIA Novosti*, May 3, 2005

[54] Milovrozov, op cit, note 45.

[55] See interview with Head of the Azerbaijani State Railway Administration, Arif Askerov, on *Trend.az*, December 20, 2005

The East-West Energy Pipelines

The Baku-Tbilisi-Ceyhan Oil Pipeline

The East-West energy projects are the main economic, political and strategic components of Azerbaijan's foreign and transportation policy. The intertwined, complex relationship between energy, security and economic issues in the Caspian region is the major reason for which existing and potential energy pipelines are so important for Azerbaijan.

The recently constructed Baku-Tbilisi-Ceyhan (BTC) oil pipeline and the Baku-Tbilisi-Erzurum (BTE) natural gas pipeline epitomize the close relationship between the pipeline politics and regional security. These pipelines and their routes, which bypass Russia and Iran, were widely discussed throughout the 1990s; both are considered part of the East-West Energy Transport Corridor. These pipelines have allowed Azerbaijan to export energy to Western markets independently of Russia, and created an opportunity to incorporate potential trans-Caspian pipelines from Kazakhstan and Turkmenistan into this corridor.

The construction of the 985 km-long Baku-Supsa oil pipeline in 1998 marked a significant shift in Azerbaijan's energy policy and was a milestone in developing the East-West energy corridor. The Baku-Supsa pipeline was the first pipeline that bypassed Russia. Although the pipeline has a limited capacity (115,000 barrels per day[56] or 5 million tons of oil annually[57]) and its initial purpose was to transport "early Azeri oil," its completion was a remarkable achievement for Azerbaijan, Georgia and international energy companies. Not only did the Baku-Supsa lessen the Yeltsin administration's political pressure on Baku, it also helped Azerbaijan and its partners to progress on the BTC project.

---

[56] Jennifer DeLay, "The Caspian Oil Pipeline Tangle: A Steel Web of Confusion" in Oil and Geopolitics in the Caspian Sea Region," in Michael P.Croissant and Bulent Aras, eds., *Oil and Geopolitics in the Caspian Sea Region.* (Connecticut: Praeger Publishers, 1999), p. 73

[57] Nassib Nassibli, "Azerbaijan: Oil and Politics in the Country's Future" in Michael P.Croissant and Bulent Aras, eds., *Oil and Geopolitics in the Caspian Sea Region.* (Connecticut: Praeger Publishers, 1999), p. 116

There was only one available energy transport route to the West before the construction of Baku-Supsa in 1998 and the BTC pipeline in 2005. That route, the Baku-Novorossiysk pipeline, was constructed during the Soviet era and passes through Russia on its way from Baku to Russia's Black Sea port of Novorossiysk. The 1996 bilateral agreement signed between Baku and Moscow permitted 5 million tons of Azerbaijani oil to be shipped per year via this pipeline, giving Russia considerable leverage over Azerbaijan's internal politics and economy.

By 2004 Azerbaijan was shipping only 2.6 million tons of oil through the Baku-Novorossiysk pipeline. This route became even less appealing after the BTC pipeline opened, since the tariffs for oil shipments using Baku-Novorossiysk are four times higher than tariffs for oil transports via the Baku-Supsa pipeline ($15.67 versus $3.40 per ton).[58] The fate of Baku-Novorossiysk remains unclear—it may stop functioning in the near future or could be reversed to pump Russian and Kazakh oil to Azerbaijan.

The major breakthrough came in 1994 when the Azerbaijani government and a consortium of international energy companies signed the production sharing agreement to develop the Azeri-Chirag-Guneshli (ACG) offshore field (with an estimated 4 to 6 billion barrels of oil reserves). The agreement proposed $8 billion invested over 30 years for exploitation of the ACG field alone. In November 1999, Azerbaijan, Georgia and Turkey agreed on the route for the Baku-Tbilisi-Ceyhan pipeline that would carry oil from the ACG field. The construction of the 1,730 km BTC pipeline began in 2002, and was completed in 2005. This pipeline marked a major turning point in Azerbaijan's recent history.

Thanks to revenues from the BTC project, Azerbaijan is expected to double its economy by 2008. Oil export revenues in 2003 were nearly 50 percent of the total state budget and accounted for over 86 percent of Azerbaijan's total exports.[59] In 2005, state income from energy exports was projected to increase

---

[58] See *Interfax-Azerbaijan* interview with First Deputy Prime Minister of Azerbaijan, Abbas Abbasov on August 2, 2005.
[59] *EAI*, Azerbaijan Brief, June 2005.

by about 65 percent, and an average of over 128 percent from 2006 to 2009.[60] In 2005, the Azerbaijan's State Oil Fund (SOFAZ) added some 660 million manats-AZN to its assets in 2005.[61] As of January 1, 2006, SOFAZ's funds stood at about AZN 1.3 billion or roughly $1.4 billion.[62]

President Ilham Aliyev has approved a long-term oil and gas revenue management strategy that aims to ensure balanced economic development of the non-oil sector by investing a portion of oil and gas revenues generated in SOFAZ.[63] The strategy also calls for reducing the country's need for external borrowing and also the current external debt, which is 20.7 percent of GDP or 47.6 percent of exports.[64] By 2010, these numbers are projected to be 15 percent and 24 percent respectively. SOFAZ revenues are expected to grow from 11 percent of GDP in 2002, to 80 percent of GDP in 2010, improving Azerbaijan's net asset position.[65]

The Baku-Tbilisi-Erzurum Natural Gas Pipeline

The Shah-Deniz offshore field is the major source of natural gas in Azerbaijan. The field holds 600 billion cubic meters (bcm)[66] of natural gas and 101 million tons of condensate, with potential to contain up to 1 trillion cubic meters of gas and 400 million tons of condensate.[67]

Turkey in 2001 has agreed to buy 6.6 bcm of Azerbaijani natural gas annually. The current delivery schedule calls for 2 bcm is to be delivered in 2006, which will slowly ramp up to an average of 6.3 bcm per year by 2009.[68] With additional infrastructure upgrades, the Shah-Deniz field will be able to

---

[60] Ibid.
[61] See "SOFAZ's Revenue and Expenditure Statement for 2005." Available online at http://www.oilfund.az/
[62] Ibid.
[63] Decree of the President of the Azerbaijan Republic on the Approval of "The Long-Term Strategy on the Management of Oil and Gas Revenues," from September 27, 2004. Available online at http://www.oilfund.az/doc/neft_str_en.pdf
[64] Azerbaijan Country Assistance Strategy, *World Bank Report* No. 25790-AA, April 29, 2005
[65] Ibid.
[66] *EIA*, 'Azerbaijan: Production-Sharing Agreements', June 2002
[67] *Interfax*, 'Shah-Deniz consortium, GIOC sign gas export deals', October 31, 2003
[68] Ibid.

produce 8.4 bcm of natural gas and 40,000 bpd of condensate in the short term.[69]

Azerbaijani natural gas will be shipped to Turkey and onward to Europe via the South Caucasus Pipeline, also known as the BTE natural gas pipeline. The $4 billion BTE pipeline project runs parallel to the BTC pipeline; starting in Baku, it passes through Georgia and ends at the Turkish city of Erzurum. The BTE pipeline is 680 km long with an annual transfer capacity of 6.6 bcm[70] that could be expanded. The BTE is the first pipeline to carry Caspian gas to Europe that will bypass Russia and Iran (see appendix 4)

Turkey and Greece will be the main consumers of the exported Azerbaijani natural gas in the initial stage of the BTE project. Both countries' demand for natural gas has increased dramatically in the recent years; Turkish gas demand is expected to triple by 2010 and the Turkish Natural Gas company BOTAS estimates that by 2020, the country will demand 43 bcm of natural gas yet supplies will only be about 41 bcm.[71] Likewise, Greece's natural gas demand had grown from 0.03 bcm in 1996 to 2.2 bcm in 2001.[72]

New opportunities for boosting Caspian natural gas exports to Europe are being created by ongoing projects between Turkey, Greece and Italy. A subsea pipeline between Greece and Italy with a 11.3 bcm capacity will allow Greece to transfer roughly 10 bcm of natural gas to Italy per year.[73] Another 285 km natural gas pipeline from Turkey to Greece[74] will make it possible to ship natural gas from Azerbaijan, and potentially from Turkmenistan, to Greece and other South European states.

Ankara and Ashgabat have signed an agreement to deliver 10 bcm of Turkmen gas to Turkey per year.[75] The agreement with Turkmenistan called

---

[69] *EIA*, Country Analysis Brief: Azerbaijan, June 2005

[70] Ibid.

[71] See natural gas supply and demand scenarios from BOTAS (Petroleum Pipeline Corporation) web site. Available online at http://www.botas.gov.tr/

[72] *EIA*, Country Analysis Brief: Greece, July 2003

[73] *Baku Today*, September 15, 2005

[74] A Memorandum of Understanding was signed between DEPA and the Turkish company BOTAS, providing for the interconnection of the Turkish and Greek gas networks. Available online on DEPA Official Web site at http://www.depa.gr/

[75] *IEA*, 'Flexibility in Natural Gas Supply and Demand', 2002

for a sub-sea trans-Caspian pipeline across Azerbaijan and Georgia, but the project remains stalled. The recent Russia-Ukraine gas dispute that caused panic among many European states may have the effect of reviving this project, which could be implemented in the mid-term.

Trans-Caspian Sub-Sea Pipelines

Azerbaijan's oil production has increased over the years and yet is still not enough to utilize fully the BTC pipeline. The annual capacity of the BTC pipeline is 50 million tons or 1 million bpd, but Azerbaijan's oil production has not yet reached 1 million bpd. 23.7 million tons of oil is expected to be exported in 2006, followed by 40.2 million tons in 2007 and 54.8 million tons in 2008.[76] Without new field discoveries, oil production will top out at 65 million tons per year around 2011; by 2018 production is expected to be half that amount and a quarter of the peak level by 2024.[77]

This creates an opportunity for Kazakhstan and international energy companies—and a strategic necessity for Azerbaijan—to export Kazakh crude oil via the BTC pipeline, initially by oil tankers and eventually via a potential Aktau-Baku trans-Caspian sub-sea pipeline. Although Azerbaijan and Kazakhstan have yet to finalize an agreement on transporting Kazakh oil via the BTC, Azerbaijani and Kazakh officials have declared that Kazakhstan will join the BTC project and export as much as 30 million tons of oil each year through its pipeline.[78]

The shipment of Kazakh oil to Azerbaijan will develop in three stages that coincide with the development of schedule of Kazakhstan's huge Kashagan field, with its estimated reserve of 13 billion barrels. Initially, some 7.5 million tons of Kazakh oil will be shipped to Baku by oil tankers, followed by 20 million tons around 2010, and 30 million after that.[79] In the meantime, oil

---

[76] 525ci *Newspaper*, November 2, 2004.

[77] Azerbaijan Country Assistance Strategy, *World Bank Report* No. 25790-AA, April 29, 2005.

[78] *The News Bulletin of the Embassy of the Republic of Kazakhstan*, August 10, 2005. Available online at http://www.kazakhembus.com/081005.html

[79] Vladimir Socor, "Trans-Caspian Export Option Now Available To CPC Companies in Kazakhstan," *Eurasia Daily Monitor*, Vol. 3, No. 52, March 16, 2006.

production from Kashagan will reach 21 million tons annually before 2010, 42 million tons between 2010 and 2013 and 56 million tons by 2016.[80]

Four international energy companies—Eni, Conoco Philips, INPEX and TotalFinaElf—involved in the construction of BTC are also stakeholders in the Agip Consortium that is developing the Kashagan field. Other companies, including BP, Chevron, ExxonMobil, and Shell, also operate in Azerbaijan. The decisions of international energy companies will influence the future of the trans-Caspian sub-sea pipelines. Transit tariffs to the Caspian Pipeline Consortium pipeline running from Kazakhstan to Russia's Novorossiysk port have already reached $30.83 per ton, which will increase in the absence of alternative routes in the region.[81]

Some experts have suggested that the shipment of around 20 million tons of Kazakh oil would make the trans-Caspian sub-sea pipeline from Aktau to Baku commercially viable.[82] This is the same amount that Kazakhstan is projected to be delivering to Azerbaijan by 2010-2011. Hence, it is likely that the decision on building a trans-Caspian sub-sea pipeline could come during the Kashagan field's second stage of development (2011-2013), when Azerbaijan's production will start to decline. Construction of the trans-Caspian natural gas pipeline from Turkmenistan to Azerbaijan will depend on several factors, including the resolution of disputes between Baku and Ashgabat, the availability of foreign direct investment, political will, support from the EU and the United States, of the existence of relevant infrastructure, and market demand in Turkey and Southeast Europe.

Impediments and Challenges

The realization of East-West and North-South transportation projects that cross Azerbaijan requires effective intergovernmental collaboration, infrastructure building, foreign direct investments, and the resolution of political obstacles.

---

80 *Zerkalo*, February 26, 2004.
81 Socor, op cit, note 78.
82 Ibid.

The Karabakh Conflict: The Karabakh conflict between Armenia and Azerbaijan is the major impediment to long-term peace, cooperation and stability in the region. Because of this conflict Armenia and Azerbaijan have no economic or political ties. Azerbaijan cannot transport its goods and products to the Nakhchivan Autonomous Republic, an Azerbaijani exclave separated from Azerbaijan proper by Armenian territory. Armenia, for its part, is isolated and has no access to either Eastern or Western markets through Azerbaijan and Turkey. All roads and railways that connect Armenia, Azerbaijan and Turkey are currently closed; instead, both Armenia and Azerbaijan use Georgian and Iranian transportation networks to ship goods and products to world markets.

A significant portion of the Soviet-era railway from Azerbaijan to Turkey via Armenia (Baku-Alat-Julfa-Masis-Qumri-Kars) passes through Armenian-occupied Azerbaijani territory. Some 240 km of Azerbaijan's railway and about 4498 km of road networks lie in the occupied territories.[83] Moreover, 132 km of the Azerbaijani-Iranian border is also currently occupied and out of the control of the Azerbaijan government. This creates a security threat, since much of the occupied territory is a haven for the trafficking in drugs and illicit materials.

According to a 2000 World Bank study, the economic benefit of potential peace would be greater for Armenia than Azerbaijan. Yet, a peace agreement could reduce the cost of trade between Azerbaijan and Turkey by 10 percent and could boost overall exports by $100 million and possibly increase GDP by about 5 percent.[84] Nonetheless, Baku and Yerevan have failed to agree on a framework agreement in 2006, which made the resolution of the Karabakh conflict less likely in the next two- three years and raised the possibility of a military conflict between Armenia and Azerbaijan in the mid-term.

Infrastructure and Lack of Investment: Roads and railways in Azerbaijan require serious investment and improvement. The TRACECA highway will significantly improve the quality of roads in Azerbaijan, yet road maintenance will require additional resources; some sections of the newly

---

[83] Data provided by the Azerbaijan's Ministry of Transport.

[84] See the World Bank study, op cit, note 11.

built highway have already begun to crack. The government is now developing short- and mid-term maintenance plans and assembly necessary capital for keeping the roads in good condition.

A similar situation exists with the railway system. Antiquated tariffs and a lack of essential maintenance on rail lines hamper efficient use of the country's railway networks.[85] And the realization of international projects, such as the trans-Caspian sub-sea pipelines, will require international political and financial assistance. To achieve this, Azerbaijan's government will have to collaborate with international donor organizations and create better conditions for foreign direct investment.

Corruption and Standardization: Rent seeking and corruption are endemic in all South Caucasus and Central Asian states, Azerbaijan being no exception. Bureaucratic obstacles created by public or recently privatized agencies contribute to the creation of local monopolies, reduce competitiveness and increase transit costs. According to a World Bank report, it takes ten to twelve days and $700-$800 to ship a container by road from Bandar Abbas (on the southern coast of Iran) to Baku; moving the same container from Baku to Poti in Georgia takes only three to five days, yet costs $2,200.[86] In addition, a portion of the collected payments go as "an ex ante 'facilitation payment'" which can vary between $500 and $1500 per shipment.[87]

The harmonization of regional quality management systems with the International Standards Systems (ISS) is another important issue for all regional parties involved in the Trans-European and the Trans-Asian transport corridors. Standardization is needed in all areas of transport operations, including law, procedures, infrastructure, tariff regulations, and security oversight.

To facilitate trade and the efficient shipment of goods along the TRACECA and North-South corridors all participating countries will have to form similar policies on trade and corruption. Continental trade makes transit countries interdependent, so that procedural failures or delays in one state

---

[85] Ibid.
[86] Ibid.
[87] Ibid.

will impact others, disrupting international shipments and extending delivery times.

Security: Providing security for inland container transport, track transit, or oil and gas export pipelines remains the most significant challenge. During the 2004 European Conference of Ministers of Transport held at Ljubljana the participants discussed transport security, counter-terrorism measures and risk assessments involving international trade.[88] In particular, two container scenarios "hijacked" and "Trojan horse" were debated. The "hijacked" scenario involved insertion of an illegal or harmful consignment into a container during its voyage, while the "Trojan horse" scenario envisioned a legitimate trading company with a good reputation transporting illegal shipments. The participants concluded that by enhancing security and screening mechanisms, local transport authorities can counter "hijacked" containers, but they have "considerably less scope for action in thwarting a "Trojan horse" shipment. In the latter case, effective customs control is of paramount importance."[89]

Azerbaijan uses X-ray devices and other equipment to monitor the shipment of large-size freight at the Baku international airport,[90] but border crossings around the country lack these technologies. One method to better monitor transit cargo was initiated by the ADB's CAREC program, and involves developing a regional system that allows participating states to share intelligence and customs data. Such an intelligence sharing mechanism would help national customs enforcement agencies fight drug trafficking and illicit trade.[91]

To improve the security of the BTC and BTE pipelines, Azerbaijan, Georgia and Turkey signed a trilateral security agreement in 2001. This initiative will

---

[88] See European Conference of Ministers of Transport Annual Report 2004, *Joint OECD/ECMT Transport Research Centre*, p. 55. For more information visit http://www.cemt.org

[89] Ibid.

[90] See Asian Development Bank's Azerbaijan Country Report, op cit, note 22.

[91] See Discussion Paper "Regional Trade Facilitation and Customs Cooperation Program: Progress and Future Directions," *Asian Development Bank*, April 2004. Available online at http://www.adb.org/Projects/TradeFacilitation/.

have to be expanded to cover other transportation areas, such as interstate highway and railway projects.

The legal status of the Caspian Sea is probably the most challenging issue impacting the future sub-sea pipeline projects from Kazakhstan and Turkmenistan to Azerbaijan. Russia and Iran will oppose the construction of trans-Caspian pipelines without their consent. Sovereignty over the Caspian's surface remains unresolved despite the trilateral agreement signed by Russia, Kazakhstan and Azerbaijan that determined the seabed boundaries on the basis of the median line approach. Russia has proposed 24 km national sectors, while Azerbaijan and Kazakhstan suggest that the division of the sea surface should be similarly to the seabed divisions. Iran does not recognize the trilateral agreement between Baku, Moscow and Astana and proposes that each state should be allocated an equal 20 percent share. And, as has been noted, Azerbaijan and Turkmenistan have unresolved disputes regarding the ownership of several oil fields in the middle of the Caspian Sea.

Some Russian officials have recently stated that Moscow will oppose the construction of a trans-Caspian Aktau-Baku sub-sea pipeline as long as the legal status of the Caspian Sea remains unsettled.[92] Similarly, Iran will oppose the construction of trans-Caspian sub-sea pipeline from Turkmenistan to Azerbaijan. But it is naïve to expect a full resolution of the legal status issue in the near future, as Iran's recalcitrance will surely delay the permanent settlement for many years. Nonetheless, the major obstacle for a potential trans-Caspian oil pipeline from Kazakhstan to Azerbaijan would be removed if Baku, Moscow and Astana agreed on the partitioning of the sea surface. Hence, cooperation and collaboration with Russia could speed the resolution of issues impacting the Aktau-Baku sub-sea pipeline.

Engagement by regional powers, the EU and the United States will speed the development of certain projects, while interrupting and delaying others. For example, the converging American and European interest on the need for trans-Caspian sub-sea pipelines could attract investment and political support for these projects. At the same time, Iran's nuclear program—and

---

[92] See Taleh Ziyadov, "Europe Hopes To Revive Trans-Caspian Energy Pipelines," *Eurasia Daily Monitor*, Vol. 3, Issue 38, February 24, 2006.

potential sanctions or military action against Iran—could delay some projects along the North-South direction. Likewise, while Moscow strongly supports the North-South projects, it is likely to try to impede East-West projects that bypass Russia.

Conclusions and Implications

The significance of the East-West and the North-South corridors is increasing as the Trans-European and Trans-Asian transportation networks become more integrated. There is no question that Azerbaijan will play an important role in both the East-West and the North-South transport corridors. Compared to its neighbors, Azerbaijan's relatively stronger economy and mid-term cash flow potential will make the country capable of accommodating all international projects involving the South Caucasus. Suffice it to note that over the next 20 years Azerbaijan will receive over $100 billion in revenues from the two major oil and gas pipelines.

The East-West TRACECA highway project will upgrade road standards to international levels. Renovation projects will initially be subsidized by international donors, who view these projects as a part of a global road network. As transit traffic grows and the state budget begins receiving transit revenue, the Azerbaijan government will be able to maintain and upgrade road networks without outside assistance. Between 2006 and 2009 the Azerbaijani government intends to spend half a billion dollars to modernize and rehabilitate its national highways and railways.

Likewise, the seaports and railway networks need funding to increase capacity. The modernization of the Baku International Sea Port is critical—with upgrades, the port's freight cargo handling capacity could be boosted to 30 million tons a year, enough to accommodate the transit cargo from Kazakhstan and Turkmenistan in the short-term. While the cargo deliveries from Aktau to Baku will likely increase and make the China-Kazakhstan-Azerbaijan-Georgia-Europe route more efficient, the development of the complementary route through Tukmenbashi port will require political will from Turkmenistan that is now lacking.

The Baku-Tbilisi-Poti/Batumi and the Baku-Tbilisi-Akhalkalaki-Kars railways will play a strategic role in the Asia-Europe transportation corridor.

While the Baku-Poti/Batumi link could accommodate cargo for Central and North European countries, the Baku-Tbilisi-Akhalkalaki-Kars connection could be used for shipments of goods towards South-East and Western Europe. Moreover, these railways will strengthen the transportation routes of Azerbaijan, Georgia and Turkey, leading to further integration of their transportation, customs and security systems.

Azerbaijan is likely to continue building and renovating its North-South transportation links between Russia and Iran. This corridor is one of the few areas where the interests of Azerbaijan, Iran and Russia converge. Azerbaijan is interested in moving some of the transit cargo shipments from Iran or India towards Russia through its highways and railways—failure to do so would be costly. And holding both ends of this strategic transportation corridor connecting two regional powers will give Azerbaijan leverage over Iran and Russia, leverage which Azerbaijan currently lacks. Yet these projects have some potential risks, such as possible delays in the construction of the Kazvin-Rasht-Astara railway connection or the disruption of shipping in the event of economic embargo or a military attack against Iran.

Although Azerbaijan will profit economically from container transit via the Europe-Asia corridor, it is the strategic aspect of these projects that will be the most beneficial for Baku. By linking transportation networks with Europe, modernizing and standardizing infrastructure to European standards and adapting to legal and procedural requirements of continental trade, Azerbaijan will move closer to the Euro-Atlantic community. Interstate highways and railways will raise the issue of common security threats, while providing the opportunity to work jointly to overcome them. Azerbaijan, Georgia and Turkey will further integrate their security agencies as Azerbaijan and Georgia pursue membership in the North Atlantic Treaty Organization.

Azerbaijan will garner the most economic and strategic benefits from the current and potential energy pipelines in the region. The completion of the BTC and the BTE projects creates a suitable ground for the construction of trans-Caspian pipelines from Kazakhstan and Turkmenistan. The trans-Caspian projects are feasible, but require substantial political and financial international backing. As noted earlier, the Aktau-Baku sub-sea oil pipeline is likely to be realized after 2010, when the production from the Kashagan field exceeds 20 million bpd and Azerbaijan's oil production will be peaking. This pipeline will resolve the full capacity utilization problem for the BTC in the long run and guarantee the westward flow of Caspian oil. Similar to the BTC pipeline, construction of the trans-Caspian pipelines will stipulate further security cooperation between Azerbaijan and Kazakhstan. Both states are involved in the U.S.-sponsored Caspian Guard initiative, which will likely lay the foundation for future pipeline security structures.

APPENDIX -1

Potential volume of container trade in the East-West direction

Year	Total Volume of Trade, mln/ton	Export of European countries into Asia, mln/ton	Export of Asian countries into Europe, mln/ton
2002	8,5	4,3	4,2
2010	13,9	6,5	7,4
2015	17,9	8,0	9,9

Potential volume of container trade in the North-South direction

Year	Total Volume of Trade, mln/ton	Export of European countries into Asia, mln/ton	Export of Asian countries into Europe, mln/ton
2002	3,5	2,4	1,2
2010	5,7	4,0	1,7
2015	7,3	5,2	2,1

Source: http://www.eatu.ru

APPENDIX – 2:

Alternative Transport Routes from Istanbul (Turkey) to Dostik (Kazakhstan), a city near Kazakhstan-China Border

Route Name	Distance/km
Istanbul-Kars-Akhalkalaki-Tbilisi-Baku-Caspian Sea (ferry)-Turkmenbashi-Ashgabat-Tashkent-Almaty-Dostik	6873
Istanbul-Kars-Akhalkalaki-Tbilisi-Baku-Caspian Sea (ferry)-Aktau-Kandagach-Orsk-Akmola-Dostik	7089
*Istanbul-Kars-Dogukapi-Masis-Yervan-Barkhundarli-Baku-Caspian Sea (ferry)-Turkmenbashi-Ashgabat-Tashkent-Almaty-Dostik **	6913
*Istanbul-Kars-Dogukapi-Masis-Nakhchivan-Julfa-Baku- Caspian Sea (ferry)-Turkmenbashi-Ashgabat-Tashkent-Almaty-Dostik **	6936
Istanbul-Van Lake (ferry)-Kapikoy-Tehran-Mashad-Sarakhs-Tashkent-Almaty-Dostik	7286
*Istanbul-Van Lake (by rail)-Kapikoy-Tehran-Mashad-Sarakhs-Tashkent-Almaty-Dostik ***	7545

*** This route cannot be currently used as they pass through Armenia and Armenian occupied territories of Azerbaijan. Armenia and Azerbaijan do not have communications due to the Karabakh conflict.**

**** This route requires the construction of 259 km-long railway to the north of Van Lake.**

APPENDIX – 3 - MAPS

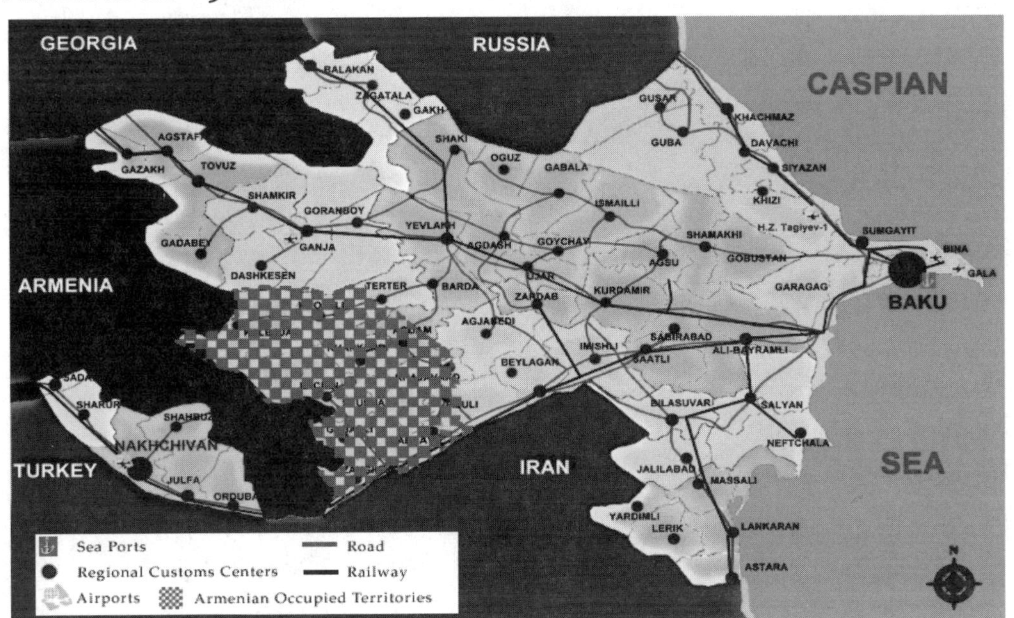

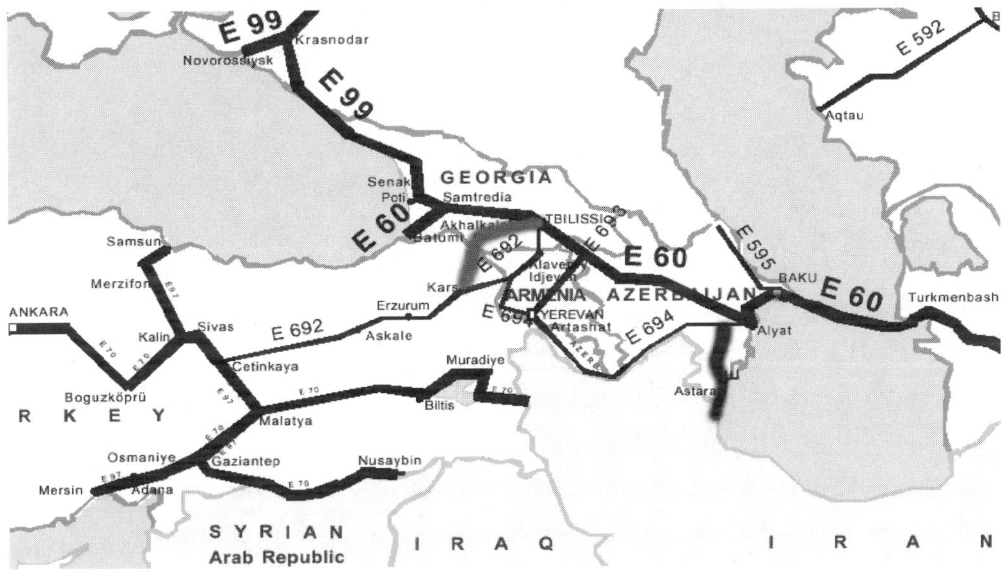

Source: UN

APPENDIX – 4 – Tariffs in Azerbaijan

Source: The following data is from "Azerbaijan Transport Sector, Sector Development, Review and Update" for the year 2003. Available online at http://www.worldbank.org

Regular Tariffs

CASPIAN SEA

I. Ferry transit

Baku – Aktau

Per line meter of loaded car $35.0

Per line meter of empty car $30.0

Baku – □ur□m□nbashi

Per line meter of car $30.0

II. Transit of oil in tankers

Aktau – Baku

Per 1 ton of oil $6.0 – $6.5

Turkmenbashi – Baku

Per 1 ton of oil $7.0 – $7.5

Baku – Ports of Iran

Per 1 ton of oil $10.0 – $12.0

BLACK SEA

III. Ferry Transit

Konstance (Romania) – Batumi

Per 1 line meter of car $36.5 – $44.0

Konstance – Derinje (Turkey)

Per 1 line meter of car $18.25 – $22.0

Special Rates (with 50% discount in accordance with MMA) on Transit through Railways of Azerbaijan and Georgia of Oil, Oil Products and General Cargo For 2004 (in US Dollars per 1 ton)

Through Georgia

	Oil	Oil Products	Gen. Cargo
Ghardhabani – Batumi (342 km)	6.0	8.0	-
Poti – Ghardhabani (360 km)	-	-	8.64

Through Azerbaijan

	Oil	Oil Products	Gen. Cargo
Baku-dock-Georgian border(503 km)	5.5	6.78	9.8

Special Rates on Transit of 20 ton Containers (in US Dollars per 1 Container)

Through Georgia

Poti – Ghardhabani (360 km)

100.0

Through Azerbaijan

Baku-dock – B/Kesik (503km)

213.0

Tariffs for Permits on International Transit through the Territory of Azerbaijan Republic by Foreign Road Transport Carriers

Entry to country or transit	**Amount of duty (in US dollars)**
By auto carriers from countries having the bilateral Agreement	100.0
By auto carriers from countries lacking the bilateral Agreement	150.0
Return shipment from Azerbaijan	100.0
Transit to/from third countries (one way)	600.0
Entry without car	350.0

Notes:

1. border, permits are obtained by auto-carriers lacking the transit permit (received in accordance with the bilateral agreements).

2. For Iranian auto-carriers the amount of duty for permit is $160.

3. Duty is not levied for the transit of empty trucks.

Road Tax, levied based on provisions of the Tax Code of Azerbaijan Republic (in US dollars)

Type of Transport Means	For entry to the Republic (for the first day)	from 2 t□ 7 days 20%	For each day from 8 to 30 days 30%	More than 30 days 40 %
Passengers vehicle	15	-	-	-
Bus up to 12 seats	30	6	9	12
Bus from 13 to 30 seats	40	8	12	16
Bus more than 30 seats	50	10	15	20
Trucks and trailers b/c to 10 tons	40	8	12	16
Trucks and trailers b/c from 10 to 24 tons	70	14	21	28
Trucks and trailers b/c more than 24 tons	100	20	30	40

India

Gulshan Sachdeva

Political Economy & Security in GCA: Background

The strategic location and abundance of natural resources were reason enough for many analysts to create theories of a "*New Great Game*" akin of the nineteenth century Great Game between Tsarist Russia and the British Empire. This new game centers on the competition among companies to develop energy resources as well as among nations to determine export routes. Recently the role of the military and "regime change" experiments through "color revolutions" have added a new dimension to the game.

Since the early 1990s the economic and political systems of the countries in the region have been transformed. Despite a very complex legacy (of central planning, dissolution of the former Soviet Union, distorted economic structures, and ethnic problems) most of the countries of Greater Central Asia (GCA) have made significant progress in market reforms, but this progress on democratic reforms falls far below expectations. Due to such features as natural resources, strategic location, political systems, and the background of the political elite, countries of the region has used both standard as well as non-conventional strategies for economic transformation.

In the political arena, the authoritarian leaders who came to power in the late Soviet era with little or no competition have tried to promote economic stability while securing their own dominance in the new political system. They have learned lessons from the Chinese model of development as well as from the East and Southeast Asian "tiger" economies. As they did in Central and Eastern Europe, Western countries and multilateral institutions have promoted democracy and the development of market economies, sponsored peace through cooperation within and among the countries of the region, and supported the integration of these countries with the larger international community.

In terms of geo-strategy, the events in Afghanistan, both before and after September 11, 2001, have had a significant impact on the region. This impact led many nations within the region and beyond to a re-evaluate their strategic priorities. The 2001 Bonn Conference established a new process of political reconstruction in Afghanistan. The adoption of a new constitution in 2003, a presidential election in 2004, and the election of the National Assembly in 2005 have fostered a more democratic political environment across the GCA region.

Despite the varied players, the real competition in the region has been between the United States and Russia. Although Russia had the advantage of history and geography in it's so called " near abroad," the United States consolidated its position both before and after September, 2001. It was further enhanced with the opening of Baku-Tbilisi-Ceyhan (BTC) pipeline in 2005. Recently, China has joined the race by investing in transport, pipelines, and trade diplomacy.

In the strategic field, the West tried in the 1990s to influence the region through the North Atlantic Treaty Organization's (NATO) Partnership for Peace and through the Organization for Security and Cooperation in Europe (OSCE). Other important security mechanisms revolve around the Russian-dominated Collective Security Treaty Organization (CSTO), and the Shanghai Cooperative Organization (SCO), in which China's influence predominates. The establishment of military bases by the United States, Russia and India in Uzbekistan, Tajikistan, and Kyrgyzstan has also added to the strategic dynamic.

In recent years, the major issue for the United States has been to balance two of its major foreign policy goals in the region — democratization and counterterrorism, which together have left the United States overstretched in West and Central Asia. Aware of this U.S. preoccupation, China and Russia have, in an effort of cooperation, consolidated their positions in the region. Central Asian Republics, after witnessing the Rose revolution in Georgia, the Orange revolution in Ukraine, the Tulip revolution in Kyrgyzstan, and the violent protests in Uzbekistan, have moved clearly to seek support for their regimes from Russia. The SCO statement calling on the United States to set a deadline for the removal of its military bases in the region, as well as Uzbekistan's decision to close the U.S. base, indicate a new geopolitical scenario. Some analysts have blamed the U.S. "regime change" experiments in Georgia, Ukraine, and Kyrgyzstan for this. Others, however, argue that as a result of the "war on terror," the United States actually focused less on building democratic institutions in the region than it had intended. However, the very real popular discontent against the regimes cannot be ignored for long. These factors suggest the likelihood of political instability among most of the countries of GCA in the near future.

After the fall of the Soviet bloc, countries in the region started the transition toward market economies. Even countries which still consider themselves socialist or communist, like China and Vietnam, shifted, to a great extent, from bureaucratic coordination of resources to market-based allocations.[1] Most of the earlier reform deliberations within these countries were confined to improving "market socialism." From the vast literature on transition, however a consensus on a new paradigm emerged. Though it may be nearly impossible to capture the complex analytical framework of transformation, it is not that difficult to cobble together from a few key writings a workable "model" of this transformation.

Kornai[2] highlights two changes: 1) forcing a move from a seller's market to a buyer's market by means of price liberalization, and 2) enforcing hard budget constraints through privatization and by ending various government-supported mechanisms. Blanchard[3] defines this process of change as comprising two elements: 1) reallocation of resources from old to new enterprises, through closures and bankruptcies and the establishment of new enterprises, and 2) restructuring within surviving firms by means of labor rationalization, product line change, and new investment. The policy actions

---

[1] Grzegorz Kolodoko, *Ten Years of Post-Socialist Transition: The Lessons for Policy Reforms* .Policy Research Working Paper No. 2095 (Washington DC: The World Bank, 1999).

[2] Janos Kornai " Transformation Recession: The Main Causes" *Journal of Comparative Economics*, Vol. 19, No.1, 1994, pp.33-63.

[3] Oliver Jean Blanchard *The Economics of Post-Communist Transition* (Oxford, Clarendon Press, 1997).

needed to put these ideas in place have been outlined in many works[4] well exemplified by Fischer and Gelb.[5] The key measures of reforms are (1) macroeconomic stabilization; (2) price and market liberalization; (3) liberalization of exchange and trade system; (4) privatization; (5) establishment of a competitive environment with few obstacles to market entry and exit; and (6) redefinition of the role of the state.[6]

The *1996 World Development Report*[7] argued that building on early gains of transition would require major consolidating reforms, strong market supporting institutions, a skilled and adaptable work force, and full integration with the global economy. It also recognized that while initial conditions were critical, decisive and sustained reforms were important for recovery of growth and social policies designed to protect the most vulnerable. It emphasized that investing in people is the key to growth. After a decade of reforms, the World Bank[8] highlighted the key role in generating economic growth and employment of the entry of new firms, particularly small- and medium-sized enterprises. It called for an "encouragement strategy," which was to be accompanied by a "strategy of discipline." It also called for the strengthening of legal and regulatory institutions to oversee the management and governance of enterprises, both those in the private sector and those remaining in the state sector. It recognized that winners from the early stages of reforms may oppose subsequent reforms when these reduce their benefits or rents.

---

[4] Oliver Blanchard, Kenneth A Froot and Jeffery D Sachs (eds.) *The Transition in Eastern Europe*, 2 Volumes (Chicago: University of Chicago Press ,1994); Paul Marer & Salvatore Zecchini (eds) *The Transition to a Market Economy*, 2 Volumes, (Paris:OECD,1991).

[5] Stanley Fischer & Alan Gelb " The Process of Socialist Economic Transformation" *Journal of Economic Perspectives*, Vol.5, No.4, 1991, pp.91-105

[6] Some of this literature survey has been taken from Oleh Havrylyshyn, Thomas Wolf, Julian Berengaut, Marta Castello-Branco, Ron van Rooden, and Valerie Mercer-Blackman, *Growth Experience in transition Countries, 1990-98*, Occasional Paper No.184, (Washington DC: IMF, 1999).

[7] The World Bank *From Plan to Market: World Development Report 1996*, (New York: Oxford University Press ,1996).

[8] The World Bank ,Transition: The First Ten Years: Analysis and Lessons for Eastern Europe and Former Soviet Union, (Washington DC: The World Bank, 2002).

As a result of these policy prescriptions and later empirical findings,[9] most of the multilateral institutions devised a new approach for the economies, which it called the "economics of transformation,". Most recently, research on transition economies has moved from purely economic issues to political economy as a whole. Central Asian economic transition has, however, other dimensions. Apart from managing the challenges of transition, the region simultaneously faces challenges in development.[10]

Despite a common historical and cultural background, including more than seven decades of Soviet rule, the five former Soviet countries of the Greater Central Asia have demonstrated different abilities for coping with the challenges of transformation. The transition strategies adopted by these countries have also been influenced greatly by the political environment of the region and of that in their particular countries. Discussion of possible "models of development" in the region has dominated intellectual discourse since the early 1990s. Discussion ranged from the Turkish secular political model to the Iranian theocratic model, the Chinese model of gradual economic reform, and to Russia's shock therapy approach. There has been very little attempt in the region to define the exact implications of any of these models for the domestic and foreign policies of the countries in the region. Still, the reference to a "model of development" has become an important part of these countries' attempt to create a new national/regional identity within the international community.[11]

From the beginning, Central Asian leaders understood that western investment and assistance would come only after political and economic

---

[9] Stanley Fischer and Ratna Sahay , *The Transition Economies After Ten Years*, IMF Working Paper 00/30 (Washington:IMF, 2000); *UN Economic Survry of Europe* (From 1990-91 To 2001) (Geneva;UNECE).

[10] This point was discussed first by Joseph E Stiglitz in the context of Chinese economic transformation, . See Joseph E Stilitz, "Whither Reform? Ten Years of the Transition" *Annual World Bank Conference on Development Economics 1999*, 2000, pp.27-56.; Also see Laszlo Csaba, *The New Political Economy of Emerging Europe* (Budapest: Akademiai Kiado, 2005).

[11] See Rafis Abazov, "Central Asian Republics' Search For a "Model of Development" in *Central Asia in Transition*, SRC Occasional Paper No. 61 (Hokkaido University: Slavic Research Center, 1998) [Online web]http://src-h.slav.hokudai.ac.jp/publictn/CentralAsia/rafis/rafis.html

reforms. Most countries in the region shifted to a state-controlled economic system, mixed with nationalist revivalism and regional cooperation. Each president in the region formulated his own economic and social strategy.

Major dilemmas faced by the regional elite in the former Soviet republics of the Greater Central Asia are still not fully resolved. They are still discovering the national economic models appropriate to their complex identities. After being part of a Eurasian power for so long, many also continue to identify themselves more with Europe than Asia. But the deficit in market reforms and democratic processes push them to search for solutions within their Asian surroundings.

Progress with Economic Reforms in GCA

In the early years, the break-up of the Soviet Union hit the region very badly for many reasons. The creation of new borders caused interruptions in trade and transit, the costs of transportation increased, and illegal checkpoints emerged while traditional markets collapsed. Industrial and agricultural production was disrupted by inaccessibility to inputs and markets. Enterprises and households lost social subsidies. Administrative structures collapsed and the pool of skilled labor shrank, as many Russians left the region. Reduced access to secure water and energy resources was also a regional problem, greatly affecting agriculture, industry, and household economies. Countries in the region were left with large environmental burdens (including the Aral Sea ecological disaster, as well as industrial, nuclear, and biological waste). Above all, the prevalence of ethnic tensions and civil war (in Tajikistan) inhibited economic reform.[12] All these were added complications to the 'normal' transformational problems faced by any country moving from a centrally planned economy to a market system.

After fifteen years of reform, the countries of the region display some common trends and some significant variations. One commonality in all the countries of the region is a very deep and long decline in output. The greatest loss of output occurred in Kyrgyzstan and the least in Uzbekistan. According

---

[12] See Johannes Linn, "Central Asia: Ten Years of Transition", Talking points for Central Asia Donors' Consultation Meeting, Berlin, Germany, March 1, 2002.

to World Bank data, Central Asia had an average of seven years of decline, resulting in the loss of almost 41 percent of the initial measured output. Measured by the base year of 1990, even at the end of the decade Central Asia had recovered only 75 percent of its starting GDP values. Recovery in some of the countries was further derailed by the 1998 fiscal crisis in the Russian Federation.

This "transformation recession" is now over. Some of the countries in the region are now on a strong path to recovery. There is, however, a serious problem with data regarding the countries of the Greater Central Asia. Data from the International Monetary Fund (IMF), European Bank for Reconstruction and Development (EBRD), and the Asian Development Bank (ADB) do not agree with one another. In the following tables the ADB data is used as it is closest to official statistics from the countries in the region. These data show that the countries are fairly stable, with low inflation and exchange rate stability. They are all growing briskly and have very low rate of unemployment.

Table 1: Growth Rate of GDP in GCA (in % per year)

	2001	**2002**	**2003**	**2004**	**2005**	**2006***	**2007***
Afghanistan	-	28.6	15.7	8.0	13.8	11.7	10.6
Kazakhstan	13.5	9.8	9.2	9.4	9.4	8.5	8.5
Kyrgyz Rep.	5.3	0.0	7.0	7.0	-0.6	5.0	5.5
Tajikistan	10.2	9.5	10.1	10.6	6.7	8.0	6.0
Turkmenistan	20.4	19.8	23.0	21.0	10.0	6.5	6.5
Uzbekistan	4.2	4.2	4.4	7.7	7.0	6.2	6.0

* projections

Source: Asian Development Bank Outlook 2006 (ADB, 2006), p.311.

Table 2: Inflation in GCA (in % per year)

	2001	2002	2003	2004	2005	2006*	2007*
Afghanistan	-	-	10.2	16.3	10.0	8.0	5.0
Kazakhstan	8.4	5.9	6.6	6.9	7.6	7.3	7.0
Kyrgyz Rep.	6.9	2.0	3.0	4.0	4.4	4.5	4.3
Tajikistan	38.6	10.2	17.1	7.1	7.1	7.0	5.0
Turkmenistan	11.6	8.8	5.6	5.9	-	-	-
Uzbekistan	27.4	27.6	10.3	1.6	7.8	9.2	6.0

* projections

Source: Asian Development Bank Outlook 2006 (ADB, 2006), p.318

Table 3: Unemployment Rates in GCA (in %)

	2001	2002	2003	2004	2005
Afghanistan	3.9	3.9	3.8	3.8	-
Kazakhstan	10.4	9.4	8.8	8.4	7.8
Kyrgyzstan	7.8	8.6	9.0	9.0	9.0
Tajikistan	2.3	2.2	2.2	1.8	-
Turkmenistan	2.6	2.5	2.5	-	-
Uzbekistan	0.3	0.3	0.2	0.2	-

Source: Asian Development Bank Outlook 2006 (ABD, 2006), p.316

Table 4: National Currencies: Exchange Rate to the US dollar (annual average)

	Currency	Symbol	2000	2001	2002	2003	2004	2005
Afghanistan	Afghani	AF	67.3	54.4	44.8	49.0	47.7	49.8
Kazakhstan	Tenge	T	142.3	146.9	153.5	149.5	136.7	132.9
Kyrgyzstan	Som	Som	47.7	48.4	46.9	43.7	42.7	41.0
Tajikistan	Somoni	TJS	1.8	2.4	2.8	3.1	2.9	3.1
Turkmenistan	Manat	TMM	5200	5200	5200	5200	5200	5200
Uzbekistan	Sum	SUM	237.3	423.3	772.0	971.0	1020.0	1115

Source: Asian Development Bank Outlook 2005 (ADB, 2005), p.321 and Asian Development Bank Outlook 2006, (ADB, 2006) p.329.

Other economic analysis, however, suggest that successes in market-oriented structural and institutional reforms are resulting in mixed progress throughout the region. According to different methodologies developed by major multilateral organizations and independent agencies to measure the progress of reform in transition economies, Kazakhstan and Kyrgyzstan have progressed much faster. By contrast, Uzbekistan and Turkmenistan have been classified as countries that have achieved less progress in establishing market institutions. According to EBRD indicators, reforms of prices, enterprises (privatization), the banking sector, foreign exchange and external trade, privatization, enterprise reforms, and the banking sector are high in Kazakhstan and the Kyrgyz Republic, with progress in some areas that is comparable to Russia and Poland. Tajikistan also has made significant progress in price reforms, external sector reforms and the privatization of small firms. The level of reforms in Uzbekistan and Turkmenistan is low, particularly in the external, enterprise, and banking sector.

External economic reforms in the region touch on five areas: liberalization of foreign trade prices, reform of the system of trade, market diversification, phasing out of barter trade, and currency reforms. Progress on these reforms has varied across the region.[13] The earlier trend of diversification towards non-CIS countries has partly reversed in recent years and, with the exception of Afghanistan, these economies are still linked more closely with European (Russia) than Asian partners (Tables 6 and 7).

---

[13] For details see Jimmy McHugh and Emine Gurgen "External Sector Policies" in Emine Gurgen et.al, *Economic Reforms in Kazakhstan, Kyrgyz Republic, Tajikistan, Turkmenistan and Uzbekistan,* IMF Occasional paper No. 183 (Washington: International Monetary Fund, 1999), pp. 35-47.

Table 5: Progress with Transition: EBRD 2005 Indicators

(Average transition Score from 1 to 4)

Enterprises					**Markets & Trade**			**Financial Institutors & Infrastructure**		
Country	Private Sector Share (% of GDP Mid-2005)	Large Privati-zation	Small Privati-zation	Enter-prise Restruc-turing	Price Liberali-zation	Trade & Foreign exchange system	Compe tition Policy	Banking Reform and Interest Rate Liberali-zation	Security market & Non-Bank FIs	Infra-structure Reforms
Kazakhstan	65	3.00	4.00	2.00	4.00	3.33	2.00	3.00	2.33	2.33
Kyrgyz Rep.	75	3.67	4.00	2.00	4.33	4.33	2.00	2.33	2.00	1.67
Tajikistan	50	2.33	4.00	1.67	3.67	3.33	1.67	2.00	1.00	1.33
Turkmenistan	25	1.00	2.00	1.00	2.67	1.00	1.00	1.00	1.00	1.00
Uzbekistan	45	2.67	3.00	1.67	2.67	2.00	1.67	1.67	2.00	1.67

Source: Transition Report 2005, EBRD.

Table 6: Direction of Exports in GCA in 2004

(percent of total merchandise exports)

	Asia	Europe	North & Central America	Middle East	South America	Africa	Oceania	Rest of the World
Afghanistan	53.0	25.0	13.2	3.0	2.3	3.3	0.2	0.0
Kazakhstan	18.3	57.9	16.1	3.8	0.0	0.2	0.0	3.7
Kyrgyzstan	29.6	43.6	2.6	24.2	0.0	0.0	0.0	0.0
Tajikistan	26.6	64.2	1.1	8.0	0.0	0.1	0.0	0.0
Turkmenistan	10.4	62.9	4.3	20.4	0.0	0.0	0.0	2.0
Uzbekistan	46.6	45.4	4.5	2.6	0.2	0.1	0.0	0.6

Source: Key Indicators of Developing Asia and Pacific Countries (ADB, 2005), p.168

Table 7: Direction of Imports in GCA in 2004

(In percent of total merchandise imports)

	Asia	Europe	North & Central America	Middle East	South America	Africa	Oceania	Rest of the World
Afghanistan	62.0	23.1	9.2	1.5	0.1	3.9	0.3	0.0
Kazakhstan	22.5	72.2	3.4	0.8	0.8	0.2	0.1	0.1
Kyrgyzstan	57.0	36.4	4.6	1.8	0.1	0.1	0.0	0.0
Tajikistan	44.0	37.4	7.2	7.7	2.8	0.8	0.0	0.0
Turkmenistan	22.5	52.3	11.8	13.3	0.1	0.0	0.0	0.0
Uzbekistan	39.1	55.8	4.0	0.5	0.2	0.1	0.1	0.3

Source: Key Indicators of Developing Asia and Pacific Countries (ADB, 2005), p.169

World Energy Trends and the Importance of GCA to India

Global energy consumption is projected to increase by 57 percent from 2002 to 2025. According to the U.S. Energy Information Administration, the world's marketed energy consumption is projected to increase on average by 2.0 percent per year until 2025—slightly lower than the 2.2 percent average annual growth rate from 1970 to 2002.[14] Emerging economies are going to account for much of this projected growth.

---

[14] *International Energy Outlook 2005*, (Washington DC: Energy Information Administration, 2005), p.1.

Among the emerging economies, the highest demand is expected to occur in Asia, particularly China and India. During this period, the use of all energy sources is going to increase. Fossil fuels will continue to supply much of the energy, while oil will remain the dominant energy source. World oil use is expected to grow from 78 million barrels per day in 2002 to 103 million barrels per day in 2015 and 119 million barrels per day in 2025. The projected increment in worldwide oil use will require an increment in world oil production capacity of 42 million barrels per day over 2002 levels. As Table 8 shows, the area of the former Soviet Union will play an important role in supplying this energy. In addition, countries of the Central Asian region (including Azerbaijan) will account for about 6 percent of the global oil capacity by 2025.

Table 8: World Marketed Energy Consumption by Region, 1990–2025

(in Quadrillion Btu)

					Average Annual % Change	
Region	**1990**	**2002**	**2015**	**2025**	**1990-2002**	**2002-2025**
Mature Market Economies	183.6	213.5	247.3	271.8	1.3	1.1
Transitional Economies	76.2	53.6	68.4	77.7	-2.9	1.6
Emerging Economies	88.4	144.3	237.8	295.1	4.2	3.2
Asia	51.5	88.4	155.8	196.7	4.6	3.5
Middle East	13.1	22.0	32.0	38.9	4.4	2.5
Africa	9.3	12.7	19.3	23.4	2.7	2.7
C & South America	14.5	21.2	30.4	36.1	3.2	2.3
Total World	348.2	411.5	553.5	644.6	1.4	2.0

Source: International Energy Outlook 2005, (Washington DC: EIA, 2005), p.7.

Table 9: World Oil Production Capacity by Region, Reference Case, 1990–2025

	History (Estimates)		**Projections**			
	1990	2002	2010	2015	2020	2025
OPEC	27.2	30.6	39.9	43.7	49.7	56.0
Persian Gulf	18.7	20.7	28.3	30.8	35.2	39.3
Non OPEC Mature Market Economies (US, Canada, Mexico, North Sea, Australia, NZ, etc)	20.1	23.7	25.2	26.1	25.8	25.4
Former Soviet Union	11.4	11.2	13.6	15.3	16.5	17.6
Russia	11.3	9.6	10.3	10.8	11.1	11.3
Total World	69.4	80.0	96.5	105.4	113.6	122.2

Source: International Energy Outlook 2005, (Washington DC: EIA, 2005), pp. 157, 160.

Estimates suggest that the region could be sitting on the world's third largest oil and natural gas reserve (after the Middle East and Russia).

Kazakhstan is the only country in the region with proven onshore and offshore hydrocarbon reserves, which are estimated to be between 9 and 29 billion barrels. During the first half of 2005, it exported on average 1.1 million barrels of oil per day (bbl/d.) It exported in three directions: northward (via the Russian pipeline system and rail network); westward (via the Caspian Pipeline Consortium Project and barge to Azerbaijan); and southward (via swaps with Iran). It also exported about 30,000 bbl/d eastward to China via the Alashankoy rail crossing.

Turkmenistan's proven oil reserves are estimated to be between 546 million and 1.7 billion barrels. Oil production has increased from 110,000 bbl/d in 1992 to about 260,000 bbl/d in 2004, when exports reached approximately 170,000 bbl/d. The country plans to boost oil extraction to 2 million bbl/d by 2020. It has proven natural gas reserves of approximately 71 trillion cubic feet (Tcf).

Uzbekistan is also one of the top ten natural gas-producing countries in the world, with estimated reserves of 66.2 Tcf.[15]

To reduce the region's dependence on Russia, a few massive projects like the Caspian Pipeline Consortium Project (CPC), the Baku-Tiblisi-Ceyhan oil pipeline (BTC), and the South Caucasus Pipeline (SCP) have been outlined. These will redirect the region's energy flows from the existing northern routes toward Russia, to western, eastern and southern routes toward Europe and Asia. In recent years, Asian demand (particularly in China and India) has been expected to grow much faster than European demand, and eastward routes towards China and southern routes (through Iran) or southwest routes via Afghanistan were looked upon as economically lucrative options.

Unfortunately, all routes from the region face serious political, security, and financial constraints. Moreover, due to asymmetric investments as a consequence of different economic policies, the north Caspian states of Kazakhstan and Azerbaijan have emerged as major oil producers and exporters. In fact, Kazakhstan's production accounts for about two-thirds of the roughly 1.8 millions bbl/d currently being produced in the region. As a result of new investments, its production level is expected to increase to about 3.5 million bbl/d by 2015.

On the energy front, India is facing a huge challenge. Primary commercial energy demand grew almost three-fold at an annual rate of 6 percent between 1981 and 2001.[16] In an effort to catch up with the rest of Asia and to reduce poverty, it is essential for India to continue growing at about 8 percent or more over the next 25 years. According to the Indian government's recently released draft energy policy, even a conservative projection of India's energy needs to fuel this kind of growth will require that basis capacities in the energy sector and related physical infrastructure such as rail, roads, highways, and ports will have to grow by factors of 3 to 6 times by 2031, with nuclear and renewable resources rising to over 20 times their current

---

[15] Figures in this paragraph are taken from various country pages of Energy Information Administration of the United States [Online web http://www.eia.doe.gov]

[16] *Tenth Five Year Plan 2002-2007*, (New Delhi: Planning Commission, 2002) p. 759.

capacities. According to estimates, energy consumption is expected to grow from a low of 5.5 percent per annum to high 6.2 percent per annum.[17]

Currently, India's primary energy source is fossil fuels imported from about 25 countries. Nearly two-thirds of this total comes from just four countries: Iran, Kuwait, Nigeria, and Saudi Arabia. With this current scenario, India's oil import dependency is likely to grow beyond the current level of 70 percent.[18]

Table 10: Sources of India's Oil Imports 2004–05

Middle East			**Other Regions**		
Country	**Oil Imports (mmt)**	**% of Total imports**	**Country**	**Oil Imports (mmt)**	**% of Total imports**
Iran	9.61	10.03	Angola	2.44	2.55
Iraq	8.33	8.69	Brazil	0.29	0.30
Kuwait	11.46	11.85	Brunei	0.81	0.84
Neutral Zone	0.15	0.15	Cameroon	0.35	0.36
Oman	0.14	0.14	Congo	0.14	0.14
Qatar	1.19	1.24	Egypt	2.12	2.21
Saudi Arabia	23.93	24.96	Equator	0.15	0.16
UAE	6.43	6.71	Equatorial Guinea	1.66	1.73
Yemen	3.51	3.66	Gabon	0.28	0.29
			Libya	1.47	1.53
			Malaysia	3.43	3.58
			Mexico	2.28	2.38
			Nigeria	15.08	15.73
			Russia	0.16	0.16
			Sudan	0.33	0.34
			Thailand	0.27	0.28
Sub Total	64.64	67.43	Sub Total	31.23	32.57

Source: Draft Report of the Energy Committee on Integrated Energy Policy (New Delhi: Planning Commission, 2005), p. 63.

[17] Draft Report of the Energy Committee on Integrated Energy Policy (New Delhi: Planning Commission, 2005), p. 72.
[18] *Tenth Five Year Plan 2002-2007*, (New Delhi: Planning Commission, 2002) p. 765.

India believes that energy security can be increased both by diversifying its energy mix as well as diversifying sources of energy imports. As a result, India is seriously perusing nuclear energy options, as well as other import possibility from beyond the Middle East. New energy sources from the Greater Central Asia will play an important role in Indian energy strategy in the coming years.

In the last ten years, there has been lot of discussion on the Turkmenistan-Afghanistan-Pakistan-India (TAPI) gas pipeline.[19] ADB has brokered the 1,700 km pipeline project since 2002. It has already proposed various structures of the pipeline for attracting investors, contractors, and financial institutions. Turkmenistan has informed members that an independent firm — De Golyer and McNaughton — had confirmed reserves of over 2.3 trillion cubic meters (TCM) of gas at Daulatabad field. Additional reserves of about 1.2TCM are expected after drilling of the adjacent area. The gas production capacity of the field could be increased to about 125 million cubic meter per day (mmcmd) from the current 80 mmcmd. Turkmenistan is committed to providing sovereign guarantees for long-term uninterrupted supplies to Pakistan and India.[20] On 15 February, 2006, India was invited to join the $5 billion pipeline project.[21] In May 2006, the Indian government officially approved its participation in the TAPI project and authorized the Petroleum and Natural Gas Ministry to make a formal request to join.[22]

Major challenges to this project exist: there are remaining uncertainties about the volume of gas reserves in Turkmenistan, still unstable security situation in Afghanistan, and serious difficulties in India-Pakistan relations. Yet, despite these, all parties are considering the proposal very seriously.

In another serious attempt to enter the central Asian energy sector, India's international branch of the Oil and Natural Gas Corporation (ONGC Videsh) recently lost a close bid of about $4 billion to China National

---

[19] Happymon Jacob "India and the Trans-Afghan Gas pipeline" http://www.observerindia.com/ analysis/A020.htm
[20] "Delhi Invited to Join TAP Project" http://www.dawn.com/2006/03/16/top10.htm
[21] "India Invited to Join TAP Project", *The Hindu*, 17 March 2006.
[22] Union Cabinet decision press release May 18, 2006, http://pib.nic.in/release/release.asp?relid=17859&kwd=

Petroleum Corporation (CNPC). The competition was over the acquisition of Petrokazakhstan, which accounts for about 12 percent of oil production in Kazakhstan and is that country's third largest oil producer. Recently, the Indian Petroleum Ministry and public sector gas company GAIL India have signed a memorandum of understanding (MOU) with Uzbekistan's Uzbekneftegaz for oil and gas exploration and production. It is also reported that GAIL and an Uzbek company have jointly agreed to build a few liquefied petroleum gas plants in western Uzbekistan. Each plant will have US$50 to US$60 million invested to produce 100,000 ton per annum capacity, and will produce liquefied petroleum gas mostly for the Uzbek domestic market.[23]

Regional Economic Initiatives in the Greater Central Asia and India

In an effort to counter the disadvantages of their landlocked locations and relative remoteness from major world markets, the GCA countries have participated in many initiatives to foster regional and international trade. It is argued that regional cooperation can help the region to liberalize trade policies at low costs, reduce the risks of protectionist measures with trading partners, create new trade, and improve social welfare.[24] According to some estimates, slashing trade costs by 50 percent would increase GDP in Kazakhstan by 20 percent and 55 percent in Kyrgyzstan over 10 years. The poor would be the biggest benefactor of this boost in trade .[25]

Historically, it has proven difficult to develop regional cooperation among all the countries. States such as Kazakhstan and Uzbekistan have jockeyed for the role of regional leader, while Turkmenistan has consistently declared a policy of neutrality. Afghanistan, meanwhile, has yet to become a key player due to its unstable political and security situation.

Four Central Asian countries are important members of the Commonwealth of the Independent States (CIS). This organization has not implemented a customs union or a free trade area covering all member states, but in

---

[23] http://www.upi.com/Energy/view.php?StoryID=20060508-113000-5315r

[24] Central Asia: Increasing Gains from Trade through Regional Cooperation in Trade Policy, Transport, and Custom Transit, (ADB, 2006).

[25] Central Asia Human Development Report (UNDP, 2005), p.4

September, 2003, the idea of Single Economic Space (SES) (sometimes called the "Common Economic Space" or "Common Economic Area") was introduced during a CIS Summit in Yalta. Among the states of a Greater Central Asia, only Kazakhstan is the member of the SES.[26] The problem with the SES is that almost every member is pursuing a different goal. Russia and Belarus sought to create a customs union and a monetary union based on the ruble. Kazakhstan preferred a monetary union based on a new currency called the "Altyn." Ukraine feels that the Union conflicts with its European objective, and hence would like to see it as a free trade area. Despite these inherent problems, member states are trying hard to make it a meaningful organization.

In 1995 Kazakhstan and Kyrgyzstan formed a customs union with Belarus and Russia, with Tajikistan joining in 1999. In October 2000, the customs union became the Eurasian Economic Community (EAEC). Ukraine, Moldova, and Armenia have also been granted observer status in the EAEC. As a result of the merger between EAEC and CACO, Uzbekistan gained membership in 2006. Its main objective is "to create the necessary conditions for cooperation between the member countries in the trade, economic, social, humanitarian and legal spheres with an optimal balance of national and common interests." Its stated long-term objective is to promote the creation of a customs union and the Common Economic Space, as well as to ensure the effective execution of other objectives defined in the Customs Union Agreement of January,1995, and related agreements of 1996 and 1999.

In 1994, Kazakhstan, Kyrgyzstan, and Uzbekistan formed the Central Asian Union (CAU). The aim was to create a single economic space with improvements in payment arrangements and reduction in tariffs among member countries. In 1995, CAU members approved the principle of free trade. A Central Asian Bank for Cooperation and Development was also created. In 1998, Tajikistan joined the group. During the same year the organization was renamed the Central Asian Economic Community (CAEC). In 2001, the CAEC became the Central Asian Cooperation Organization (CACO) and Russia joined the organization in May 2004.

---

[26] Belarus, Russia, and Ukraine make up the other three members.

Ukraine, Georgia, and Turkey were given observer status. In 2005, the member states of EAEC and CACO agreed to allow Uzbekistan to join the EAEC and to merge both organizations.

This merger could lead to improved opportunities for meaningful regional cooperation. It also raises serious issues regarding harmonizing Uzbekistan's restrictive trade policies in line with other countries.

The Economic Cooperation Organization (ECO) was created by Iran, Pakistan, and Turkey in 1985 to promote what it called Regional Cooperation for Development (RCD). The main objectives of the organization is to "promote conditions for sustainable economic development and to raise the standard of living and the quality of life in the member states" through regional economic cooperation, and the "progressive removal of trade barriers within the ECO region and expansion of intra and inter-regional trade" The organisation has signed a number of agreements with various multilateral agencies like the UNDP, ASEAN, FAO, and the Islamic Development Bank (IDB).However, the dozen agreements and MOUs signed by the ECO members, only four agreements have become operational. Immediately after the disintegration of the former Soviet Union, six new members (Afghanistan, Azerbaijan, Kazakhstan, Kyrgyzstan, Tajikistan, Turkmenistan and Uzbekistan) were admitted in the organization. All GCA countries have joined the ECO.

All GCA countries have also joined the Organization of Islamic Conference (OIC), an intergovernmental organization with 56 members, established in 1971 in Saudi Arabia. Its aim is to promote Islamic solidarity by improving cooperation in the political, economic, social and cultural, and scientific fields.

Along with China and Russia, Kazakhstan, Kyrgyzstan, Tajikistan and Uzbekistan are also members of the Shanghai Cooperation Organization (SCO). The SCO was founded in 2001 on the basis of its predecessor, the Shanghai Five grouping. It began as a forum for discussing border delineation issues, but as a result of the threat of terrorism in the region, it now focuses more on security issues. Economic cooperation among its members is also envisaged.

The Central-South Asian Transport and Trade Forum (CSATTF) is an initiative to establish transport corridors in Central and South Asian. It began with ADB assistance in 2003 with the aim of promoting economic growth and social development and reducing poverty in the six participating countries—Afghanistan, Iran, Pakistan, Tajikistan, Turkmenistan, and Uzbekistan. This will be done by strengthening regional transport and trade links and by opening up alternative routes for third country trade. The corridor initiative is expected to cost about US$5.7 billion. Iran also participates in its meetings as an observer and uses its own resources for infrastructural and customs improvement. China, India, Kazakhstan, and Kyrgyz Republic participated in its second meeting in March, 2005.[27] It is expected that funding will be a joint effort of the countries concerned and assistance will be provided by multilateral institutions and the international community.

Kyrgyzstan has become a member of the WTO and the other regional states have also shown interest in becoming members. The European Union (EU) has granted Central Asian countries access to the Generalized System of Preferences (GSP). It allows tariff reductions on manufactured products and certain agricultural goods. To encourage regional cooperation, the ADB initiated a program called Central Asia Regional Economic Cooperation (CAREC). The operational strategy of CAREC is to finance infrastructural projects and improve the policy environment for promoting cross-border activities in the areas of trade, energy, and transportation.

The United Nations also started a Special Program for the Economies of Central Asia (SPECA) in 1997. The objective of the program is to strengthen regional cooperation in order to stimulate economic development and facilitate integration into Europe and Asia.

Another international initiative, known as the CIS 7 Initiative, promotes poverty reduction, growth, and debt sustainability in the following seven low-income CIS countries: Armenia, Azerbaijan, Georgia, the Kyrgyz Republic, Moldova, Uzbekistan and Tajikistan. The initiative is sponsored by the following organizations: ADB, EBRD, IMF and IDA (part of the World Bank), and a group of bilateral creditors/donors. Currently 24 countries participate in the CIS 7 Initiative and an additional six organizations/countries act as observers. These include Canada, China, the

---

[27] www.adb.org/Documents/Conference/in 120-05.pdf

European Union, the Organization for Economic Cooperation and Development (OECD), the IDB, France, Germany, Italy, Japan, Russia, Turkey, the United Kingdom, and the United States.

Other regional initiatives, including the Inter-governmental Commission on Central Asian Sustainable Development, the Inter-State Water Commission, the Central Asian Energy Advisory Group, and Regional Electricity Grid, focus on technical issues.

Afghanistan's membership into the South Asian Association for Regional Cooperation (SAARC) in late 2005 created a new dimension in the economic integration of Greater Central Asia. Afghanistan's membership to SAARC has the potential to fundamentally change and rejuvenate regional economic linkages between the South and Central Asian regions.

An Agreement on the South Asia Free Trade Area (SAFTA) was signed by member countries in January, 2004. Negotiations on all aspects of SAFTA were concluded recently and the implementation of the tariff liberalization program was begun in July/August 2006.

The following table summarizes major regional economic cooperation initiatives in the GCA:

Table 11: Some Important Regional Economic Initiatives in GCA and India

	CIS	EAEC	CACO	ECO	OIC	CAREC	SCO	CIS-7 Initiative	SAARC	SPECA	INSTC	CSATTF
Afghanistan				X	X	X			X*			X
Kazakhstan	X	X	X	X	X	X	X			X	X	P
Kyrgyzstan	X	X	X	X	X	X	X	X		X	X	P
Tajikistan	X	X	X	X	X	X	X	X		X	X	X
Turkmenistan	A			X	X					X		X
Uzbekistan	X	X	X	X	X	X	X	X		X		X
India							O		X		X	P

X – Member A – Associate member O - Observer P – participated in meetings. * membership approved, subject to completion of formalities

CIS- Commonwealth of Independent states (with Armenia, Azerbaijan Belarus, Georgia, Moldova, Russia, Ukraine).

EAEC – Eurasian Economic Community, ex Customs Union (with Russia and Belarus + Moldova, Ukraine and Armenia observers)

CACO – Central Asian Cooperation Organization (with Russia since May 2004 + Georgia, Turkey and Ukraine Observers), ex Central Asian Economic Community), merged with EAEC in 2006

ECO - Economic Cooperation Organization (with Iran, Pakistan, Turkey and Azerbaijan)

OIC- Organization of Islamic Conference (total 56 members, established in 1971)

CAREC (ADB) - Central Asia Regional Economic Cooperation (with Azerbaijan, Mongolia and Xinjiang Autonomous Region of China and Russia)

SCO - Shanghai Cooperation Organization (with Russia and China + Iran, Mongolia, Pakistan as other observes)

CIS-7- An International initiative to promote poverty reduction, growth and debt sustainability in seven low-income CIS countries: Armenia, Azerbaijan, Georgia, Kyrgyz Republic, Moldova, Uzbekistan, Tajikistan

SAARC: South Asian Association for Regional Cooperation (with Bangladesh, Bhutan, Pakistan, Nepal, Sri Lanka and Maldives).

SPECA: Special Program for the Economies of Central Asia

INSTC: International North South Transport Corridor (with Iran, Russia Belarus, Oman, Armenia, Azerbaijan, Syria, Bulgaria, Ukraine and Turkey)

CSATTF -Central and South Asia Transport and Trade Forum (with Pakistan as member and Iran as observer, China, India Kazakhstan and Kyrgyz Republic also participating in meetings)

As a result of these initiatives, the countries in the region have made some modest gains in regional cooperation. Although a limited amount of regional trade has developed in Central Asia, its growth has been uneven at best. These countries started with roughly similar trade policies, but trade policy regimes today vary from very liberal in the Kyrgyz Republic to quite restrictive in Uzbekistan and Turkmenistan. Despite the common interest of increasing trade, all the countries in the region have trade-restricting policies and practices such as tariffs, restrictive procedures and regulations, and weak financial systems. Other policy-related constraints to trade include import quotas, export licensing requirements, and transport restrictions. Arbitrary and often corrupt bureaucracies throughout the region administer regulations that are archaic and frequently conflicting. Slow and difficult border procedures, multiple cargo inspections within a single country, and prohibitions that prevent vehicles from transporting goods between countries alsohinder further gains in cooperation. Other barriers to trade include high transit fees and the costs of dealing with corrupt border officials and local police. Trade is also restricted by such practices as requiring importers to register contracts and restrictions on currency conversion. Due to the lack of a healthy financial system, a large part of trade is still conducted through inefficient cash transfers or barter.[28]

The above analysis demonstrates that most of the regional initiatives in Central Asia are either groupings to recreate lost linkages among the former Soviet republics or initiatives by multilateral organizations to strengthen regional linkages in the areas of trade, energy, water resources, infrastructure, and communications. These are largely affairs within the former Soviet space. Other countries like China, Iran, Turkey, and Pakistan have also been able to create some formal structures for closer interactions, some of which may become useful in the long run.

It is clear that as far as regional economic initiatives are concerned, India has integrated into the region only recently through INSTC, its observer status in the SCO, participation in CSATTF meetings and through Afghanistan's membership to the SAARC. However, considering its indirect access to the GCA region and its difficult relations with Pakistan, India's major initiative in the region so far has been cooperation in building up the North-South trade corridor.

Russia, Iran, and India are founding members of the International North South Transport Corridor (INSTC), consisting also of Belarus, Kazakhstan, Tajikistan, Oman, Armenia, Azerbaijan, Syria, Bulgaria, Ukraine, Turkey, and Kyrgyzstan. This corridor establishes a transit link between Scandinavian countries and Russia to the Indian Ocean, the Persian Gulf, and Southeast Asia. This transit route connects European countries and

---

[28] See Chapter 3, Central Asia Human Development Report (UNDP, 2005).

Russia through the ports of Amsterdam, Copenhagen, Hamburg, Helsinki, and Stockholm to St. Petersburg and Moscow and can extend to the southern ports of the Caspian Sea (for example, Anzali and Amirabad). It also connects Central Asia through Russian ports north of the Caspian Sea and can extend to Iran via the southern ports to the Persian Gulf and countries on the Indian Ocean to Southeast Asia. Compared with the current long and costly sea transport routes (Suez Canal), this route will be faster and cheaper. The route links the Indian port of Mumbai with Bandar Abbas in southern Iran through maritime transport. From there, goods will be shipped to northern Iranian ports on the Caspian Sea (Bandar Anzali and Bandar Amirabad) through roads and railway and then finally will be dispatched to Astrakhan and Lagan ports in Russia.[29]

Chahbahar on the coast of Iran is the only example of an Indian-supported transport project in the GCA to use this program. India will build a 235 km link from Zaranj on the Iran-Afghan border to Delaram, from where all major cities in Afghanistan and further north Central Asian republics are connected. India is also building on the Afghan side of the 22 km Zaranj-Milak road. Another road transport project involves the linking of the ChahBahar port to the Iranian rail network which is connected to Central Asia and Europe (Figures 1 and 2).[30] When completed, this initiative will make possible faster flows of goods, especially energy, from greater Central Asia to Iran and to India. Once these linkages are operational, the Indian economy could be meaningfully linked with the GCA region. Still, the shortest route from India to the GCA is through Pakistan.

---

[29] For details about the INSTC see www.instc.org

[30] For details see *Report on the Economic Impact of Central-South Asian Road Corridors* (ADB, 2005); C Raja Mohan, "India, Iran Unveil Road Diplomacy" *The Hindu*, 26 January 2003; Sudha Ramachandran, "India, Iran, Russia Map out Trade Route" *The Asia Times*, 29 June 2002 and Stephan Blank, The India-Iranian Connection and its Importance for Central Asia, Eurasianet.org, 3/12/03

Figure 1: Transport Corridors: Greater Central Asia

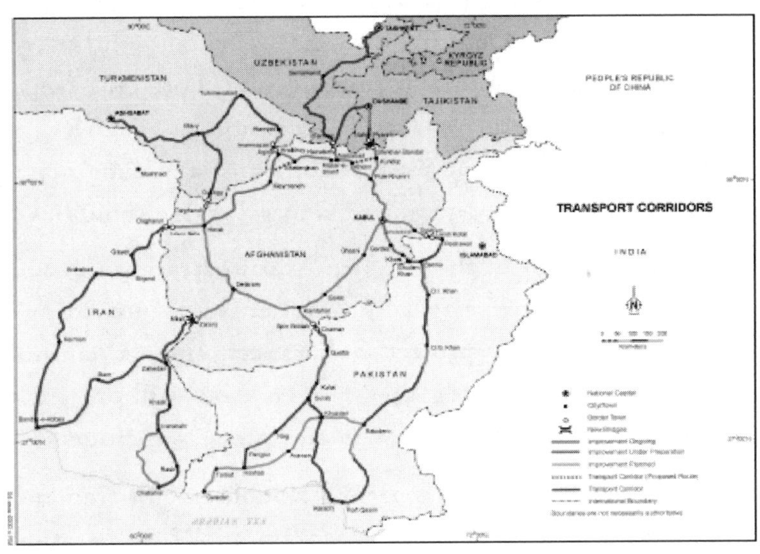

Source: Report on the Economic Impact of Central-South Asian Road Corridors (ADB, 2005), p. 8.

Figure 2: International North South Transport Corridor

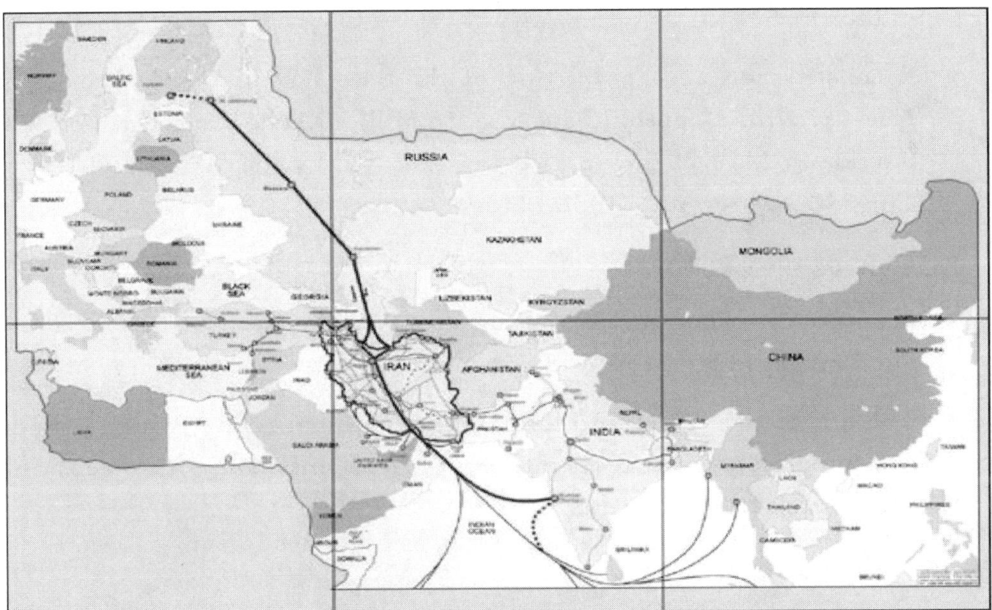

Source: International North South Transport Corridor Secretariat website www.instc.org

Other economies in the region could also become partners of SAARC. China and Japan already have observer status and the United States and South Korea have formally requested it. Iran has also shown interest in the grouping. During his visit to India, former Iranian Foreign Minister, Kamal Kharrazi, said that "the issue of Iran's accession to SAARC was under discussion."[31] He also spoke about the possibility of a West Asian Economic bloc comprising Iran, Pakistan, India, and Central Asian republics.[32]

Following the establishment of the Interim Administration in 2001, India has supported the reconstruction effort in Afghanistan, providing extensive humanitarian, financial, and project assistance. India's commitment to Afghanistan's reconstruction adds up to over $600 million, including one million tons of wheat as food assistance. Major projects include:

- Funding and construction of a 220KV double circuit transmission Line from Pul-e-Khumri to Kabul and a 220/110/20KV Sub-station at Kabul. The project is to be implemented by the Power Grid Corporation of India;
- Reconstruction of the Zaranj-Delaram road (approximate cost $84 million);
- Reconstruction and completion of the Salma Dam Power Project in Herat province (approximate cost $80 million). The project, which will provide 42 MW of power, is being executed by the Water and Power Consultancy Services (India) Ltd;
- Funding the construction of a new parliament building in Afghanistan;
- $200,000 contribution per annum to Afghan Reconstruction Trust Fund managed by the World Bank; and
- The gift of 300 vehicles to the Afghan National Army, which include one hundred 2.5-ton troop carriers, 15 field ambulances, 120 jeeps and fifty 4.5-ton troop carriers.

---

[31] "Iran is not Averse to Joining SAARC", *The Hindu_*, February 23, 2004.

[32] "Pay for Iran Gas on Arrival" *Hindustan Times*, February 23, 2005.

A further $100 million worth of financial assistance were announced at the Tokyo conference in 2002:

- 400 buses for public transport system;
- 3 Airbus aircrafts transferred from Air India to Ariana Airlines;
- Indian Medical Missions were opened in Kabul, Mazar-e-Sharif, Herat, and Kandahar;
- Rehabilitation of Habibia School and Indira Gandhi Hospital;
- Common facility and tool center set up at the Industrial Park in Kabul;
- Emergency restoration of basic telecommunication networks in 11 provincial capitals;
- Setting up power transmission lines and substations in Farhad province;
- 105 utility vehicles/equipment (water tankers, rear drop tippers, dump trucks, bulldozers, motor graders and garbage tippers) provided to the Kabul Municipality;
- Revamping an augmentation of TV hardware in Jalalabad and Niagara Province; and
- Training has been provided in India to more than 800 Afghans in different fields.[33]

The aim of the SAFTA agreement is to eliminate trade barriers and facilitate the cross-border movement of goods between contracting states; to promote conditions of fair competition; and to establish a framework for further regional cooperation. It also provides for the creation of two institutions to oversee implementation: the SAFTA Ministerial Council (consisting of ministers of commerce or trade of the member states, meeting at least once a year) and the Committee of Experts (meeting at least once every six months). Qualifying for SAFTA preferences has some additional requirements regarding rules of origin, sensitivity lists, balance of payments,

---

[33] The details of different programs are taken from Indian Ministry of External Affairs website http://meaindia.nic.in/

and safeguard measures. Concerns over the fate of less developed countries have also been considered, as shown by planned tariff cuts under SAFTA:

Table 12: Planned Phased Tariff Cuts on Intra-SAFTA Trade

SAARC Countries	**First Phase (two years)** 1/1/2006–1/1/2008***	**Second Phase** 1/1/2008–1/1/2013**	**1/1/2008–1/1/2016**
Least Developed Countries (LDCs) — Bangladesh, Nepal, Bhutan, and Maldives	Reduce maximum tariff to 30 percent		Reduce tariffs to the 0–5 percent range in 8 years (equal annual reductions recommended, but not less than 10 percent).
Non-LDCs-- India, Pakistan, and Sri Lanka	Reduce maximum tariff rate to 20 percent	Reduce tariffs to theo–5 percent range in 5 years (Sri Lanka: in 6 years) NOTE: It is recom-mended that reductions be done in equal install-lments at least 15 percent reduction per year Reduce tariffs to 0–5 percent for products of the LDCs within a timeframe of 3 years	

* This phase was delayed for six months.

** These phased tariff cuts for intra-SAFTA trade may not apply to items on each country's 'Sensitive Lists'

Source: Reproduced from South Asian Free Trade Area: Opportunities and Challenges (USAID, 2005), p. 23.

The South Asian region also shows that regional economic cooperation is sometimes influenced more politics than by the principles of economics. In addition, various rounds of Preferential Trading Arrangements have not been able to produce the desired results. Despite all the talk of regional economic cooperation, intra-regional trade is still less than five percent and most products of the South Asian region actually go to rich countries such as Europe and the United States.[34]

Historically, India adopted a very cautious approach to regionalism, and was engaged in only a few bilateral or regional initiatives, mainly through Preferential Trade Agreements (PTAs) or through open regionalism.[35] In recent years it has entered into Comprehensive Economic Cooperation Agreements (CECAs) with many countries. These CECAs cover FTA in goods, services, investment, and other specified areas of economic cooperation. These include SAFTA; the India-ASEAN agreement; the framework agreement for India and Bangladesh; the India, Myanmar, Sri Lanka and Thailand Economic Cooperation (BIMSTEC) FTA; the India-Thailand FTA; and the India-Singapore CECA. India already has FTAs with Sri Lanka and Nepal. India-China, India-Japan, and India-South Korea joint study groups have also been set up. Indian Prime Minister Dr. Manmohan Singh asserted recently that "this web of engagements may herald an eventual free trade area in Asia, possibly extending to Australia and New Zealand. This pan-Asian FTA could be the future of Asia and, I am certain, could open up new growth avenues for our own economy."[36] Hence, these kinds of FTA/CECA agreements with the GCA countries fit very well within India's vision for Asia. Other examples of cooperation include: agreements with MERCOSUR and Chile, the Gulf Cooperation Council (GCC), Mauritius for FTA/CECA, and joint study groups with Israel, Brazil, South Africa (IBSA).

In order for regional cooperation to be successful, a regional economic initiative consisting of all GCA countries, China, India, Iran, Japan, Russia, Pakistan, Turkey and the United States is needed, an idea consistent with S. Frederick Starr's "Greater Central Asia Partnership for Cooperation and

---

[34] See South Asian Free Trade Area: Opportunities and Challenges (USAID, 2005).

[35] For details see Gulshan Sachdeva 'Indian Experience with Regional Economic Integration" in Charan Wadhva and Vatroslav Vekaric (eds) *India & Serbia & Montenegro Reengagement: Regional and Bilateral Dimensions*,(New Delhi: APH Publishing Corp, 2005)

[36] "Capital Account Convertibility in Full will Help India: Manmohan" *The Hindu*, March 19, 2006.

Development" proposal.[37] It is only by the joint endeavor of all these countries that regional economic cooperation is going to be truly successful. Pakistan and India have a common interest in unlocking the energy resources of the region. If economic opportunities are created, Russia's economic ties may not decrease but it is likely that their relative importance will. Meanwhile, China's aggressive economic strategies and the US-Iranian stand-off create complications for India in its economic engagements with GCA.

In addition, regional economic cooperation in the short and long run will be limited if the countries of GCA do not pursue policies that continue to open them politically and economically and which, lead, eventually, to WTO membership. In the meanwhile, India should be concentrating more on relations with Afghanistan and Kazakhstan for energy and trade cooperation.

Air Corridors

In regional integration, air transportation will play an extremely important role in the coming years. Since land and rail corridors are going to take time to develop, air services at reasonable rates with reliable services could greatly improve cooperation in the GCA region. However, air traffic in and out of the region may not be enough to sustain daily reliable services at economic rates. Hence, air traffic control must be linked with the main traffic routes. India has had success with this, with about 29 direct weekly flights from India to all important destinations in Greater Central Asia. These flights are operated on low-cost Central Asian airlines to and from Delhi and Amritsar to Europe via such Central Asian cities as Tashkent and Ashgabat. In the coming years, an Afghan airline could follow suit. In this way, Delhi and Amritsar could become the central air corridor for the entire region. This is the more likely because the airports of Delhi and Mumbai have the potential to become world class in the next two to three years.

---

[37] S Frederick Starr " A Partnership for Central Asia , *Foreign Affairs*, Vol. 84, No.4, 2005 and S. Frederick Starr A *'Greater Central Asia Partnership' for Afghanistan and Its Neighbors*, (Washington DC: Central Asia-Caucasus Institute & Silk Road Studies Program, 2005)

Table 13: India-Greater Central Asia Direct Air Connections

Airlines	**Route**	**Flights Per Week**
Uzbekistan Airways	Delhi-Tashkent	4
Uzbekistan Airways	Amritsar-Tashkent	6
Turkmenistan Airlines	Delhi-Ashgabat	2
Turkmenistan Airlines	Amritsar-Ashgabat	4
Indian Airlines	Delhi-Kabul	4
Ariana Afghan Airlines	Delhi-Kabul	2
Kam Air	Delhi-Kabul	3
Air Astana	Delhi-Almaty	2
Tajik Air	Delhi- Dushanbe	1
Kyrgyzstan Airlines	Delhi- Bishkek	1
Total		29

Sources: Compiled from Airline websites and with information from travel agents.

India-Greater Central Asia Trade

During the Soviet period, all contacts with the republics of the USSR were through Moscow only. In the post-socialist period, India's economic relationship with the Central Asian region declined considerably. Today, official two-way annual trade between India and the region is less than $ 500 million. Apart from trade with Afghanistan and Kazakhstan, which is restricted to traditional items, economic relations with other countries are minimal. The main commodities being exported from India are pharmaceuticals, tea, ready-made garments, leather goods, jute manufacturers, cosmetics, cotton yarn, machinery, machine tools, rice, plastic products, machinery and instruments, electronic goods, and chemicals. Imports from the CAR are restricted to raw cotton, iron and steel, and zinc (Tables 14–19).

Table 14: Trade between India and Greater Central Asia, 1996–97 to 2004–05*

(In US$ millions)

	1996–97	1997–98	1998–99	1999–00	2000–01	2001–02	2002–03	2003–04	2004–05
Afghanistan	25.79	31.95	40.93	54.26	52.45	41.89	79.23	185.98	204.05
Kazakhstan	16.96	51.16	50.43	40.65	64.12	53.09	59.61	84.07	94.75
Kyrgyzstan	0.98	10.8	8.81	15.61	22.02	11.52	15.13	38.74	49.72
Tajikistan	1.53	1.12	3.04	4.72	4.10	2.56	8.73	8.42	10.23
Turkmenistan	1.65	1.70	2.03	6.03	3.83	6.30	15.70	28.55	25.32
Uzbekistan	10.74	20.3	14.50	22.91	19.98	23.80	25.62	42.84	49.09
Total Central Asia	57.65	117.03	119.74	144.18	166.50	139.16	204.02	388.60	433.16
Total Indian Trade	72602	76490	75608	86493	95096	95240	114131	141992	189713
Percent of Total Indian Trade	0.079	0.153	0.158	0.166	0.175	0.146	0.178	0.273	0.228

* The Indian Financial Year is from April to March.

Sources: Directorate General of Foreign Trade, Government of India.

Table 15: Indian Exports to Greater Central Asia, from 1996–97 to 2004–05

(In $ millions)

	1996–97	1997–98	1998–99	1999–00	2000–01	2001–02	2002–03	2003–04	2004–05
Afghanistan	22.74	21.25	12.81	33.20	25.86	24.37	60.77	145.47	157.73
Kazakhstan	4.39	15.13	38.0	27.19	50.08	45.70	46.88	74.81	79.40
Kyrgyzstan	0.98	10.79	8.70	13.80	17.59	10.95	14.67	38.20	49.10
Tajikistan	0.73	1.12	0.51	2.38	3.55	1.22	8.65	4.47	6.25
Turkmenistan	1.38	1.68	1.93	5.64	2.71	4.35	10.29	19.21	14.63
Uzbekistan	8.14	17.59	12.83	9.94	9.39	6.53	5.08	15.14	19.66
Total Central Asia	38.36	67.56	74.78	92.15	109.19	93.15	146.34	297.30	326.77
Total Indian Exports	33470	35006	33219	36822	44560	43827	52719	63843	80540
Percent of Total Indian Exports	0.114	0.192	0.225	0.250	0.245	0.212	0.277	0.465	0.405

Sources: Directorate General of Foreign Trade, Government of India.

Table 16: Indian Imports from Greater Central Asia, from 1996–97 to 2004–05

(In $ millions)

	1996–97	1997–98	1998–99	1999–00	2000–01	2001–02	2002–03	2003–04	2004–05
Afghanistan	3.05	10.70	28.12	21.06	26.59	17.52	18.46	40.51	46.32
Kazakhstan	12.57	36.03	12.43	13.45	14.04	7.39	12.73	9.26	15.35
Kyrgyzstan	--	0.01	0.10	1.82	4.43	0.56	0.47	0.54	0.62
Tajikistan	0.80	--	2.53	2.33	0.54	1.34	0.08	3.95	3.98
Turkmenistan	0.27	0.02	0.11	0.38	1.12	1.95	5.40	9.34	10.69
Uzbekistan	2.60	2.71	1.67	12.97	10.58	17.27	20.54	27.70	29.43
Total Central Asia	19.29	49.47	44.95	52.02	56.91	46.02	57.68	91.30	106.39
Total Indian Imports	39132	41484	42389	49671	50536	51413	61412	78149	109173
Percent of Total Indian Imports	0.049	0.119	0.106	0.104	0.112	0.089	0.093	0.116	0.097

Sources: Directorate General of Foreign Trade, Government of India.

Table 17: Trade Balance between India and Greater Central Asia

(In $ Millions)

	1996–97	**1997–98**	**1998–99**	**1999–00**	**2000–01**	**2001–02**	**2002–03**	**2003–04**	**2004–05**
Exports to GCA	38.36	67.56	74.78	92.15	109.19	93.15	146.34	297.30	326.77
Imports from GCA	19.29	49.47	44.95	52.02	56.91	46.02	57.68	91.30	106.39
Balance	19.07	18.09	29.83	40.13	52.28	47.13	88.66	206.00	220.38

Sources: Directorate General of Foreign Trade, Government of India.

Table 18: Indian Exports to Greater Central Asia, from 2002–03 to 2004–05

(In $ millions. Only items more than $ 1 million are included)

Afghanistan

	2002–03	2003–04	2004–05
Meat and edible meat offal	0.05	0.30	1.74
Coffee, tea, mate, and spices	1.01	3.37	2.05
Sugars and sugar confectionery	2.93	4.57	0.09
Ingredients of cereals: flour, starch or milk; pastry ingredients.	0.05	0.09	2.80
Edible preparations	0.06	0.76	1.42
Tobacco and manufactured tobacco substitutes	2.62	2.90	3.30
Organic chemicals	0.49	2.60	2.22
Pharmaceutical products	4.20	22.80	23.32
Perfumery and cosmetic, ingredients	1.03	0.90	0.74
Rubber and articles thereof	13.69	7.09	8.29
Cotton	2.43	7.73	9.58
Man-made filaments	0.92	6.54	19.11
Man-made staple fibers	3.08	4.65	10.19
Special woven fabrics; tufted textile fabrics; lace; tapestries; trimmings; and embroidery	1.88	0.42	2.78
Knitted or crocheted apparel and clothing accessories	0.91	26.50	1.54
Non knitted or crocheted apparel and clothing accessories	4.74	16.20	23.49
Other made-up textile articles; sets; worn clothing and worn textile articles; rags	1.19	4.90	2.69
Iron and steel	2.89	4.56	2.02
Articles of iron or steel	1.47	4.98	3.99
Machinery and mechanical appliances	2.08	6.77	7.54
Electrical machinery and equipments	0.33	0.96	7.11
Vehicles	7.15	8.41	10.30
Total	60.77	145.97	157.73

Kazakhstan

Commodity	2002–03	2003–04	2004–05
Coffee, tea, mate, and spices	14.50	31.91	28.37
Tobacco and manufactured tobacco substitutes	0.20	1.25	1.95
Organic chemicals	5.24	0.08	0.57
Pharmaceutical products	6.46	10.77	14.61
Perfumery and cosmetic ingredients	1.29	1.33	0.33
Articles of leather, travel goods, handbags and similar articles of animal gut (other than silk-worm).	4.96	5.02	7.22
Articles of apparel and clothing accessories, knitted or crocheted	1.58	1.71	6.12
Articles of apparel and clothing accessories, not knitted or crocheted	0.77	5.96	3.68
Iron and steel	0.73	2.89	3.46
Articles of iron or steel	1.91	1.47	0.11
Nuclear reactors, boilers, machinery and mechanical appliances and parts thereof	4.25	7.80	6.55
Total	46.88	74.81	79.40

Kyrgyzstan

Commodity	2002–03	2003–04	2004–05
Pharmaceutical products	0.12	0.66	2.78
Soap, crocheted preparations etc.	0.01		1.75
Articles of leather, tack; travel goods, handbags and similar articles of animal gut(other than silk-worm)	1.01	1.66	0.64
Articles of apparel and clothing accessories knitted or crocheted.	8.74	11.93	16.88
Articles of apparel and clothing accessories not knitted or crocheted.	2.72	19.71	24.11
Total	14.67	38.20	49.10

Tajikistan

Commodity	2002–03	2003–04	2004–05
Inorganic chemicals	3.63	0.02	0.00
Pharmaceutical products	0.89	0.93	0.59
Articles of apparel and clothing accessories, knitted or crocheted	0.12	1.33	2.39
Articles of apparel and clothing accessories, not knitted or crocheted	0.61	0.81	0.99
Machinery and mechanical appliances; parts	0.03	0.34	0.90
Total	8.65	4.57	6.25

Turkmenistan

Commodity	2002–03	2003–04	2004–05
Pharmaceutical products	1.32	1.44	2.89
Perfumery and cosmetic ingredients			
Articles of apparel and clothing accessories knitted or crocheted.	1.75	2.44	1.13
Articles of apparel and clothing accessories not knitted or crocheted.	1.29	1.14	1.89
Machinery and mechanical appliances; parts	1.97	6.06	1.66
Electrical machinery and equipments	1.65	4.61	5.10
Total	10.29	19.21	14.63

Uzbekistan

	2002–03	2003–04	2004–,05
Meat and edible meat offal	0.20	0.72	4.03
Ores, slag, and ash		4.10	
Pharmaceutical products	1.76	3.71	5.71
Machinery and mechanical appliances	0.58	3.32	1.54
Total	5.08	15.14	19.66

Sources: Directorate General of Foreign Trade, Government of India.

Table 19: Indian Imports from Greater Central Asia

(In US$ million. Only items that are more than US$ 1 million are included)

Afghanistan

	2002–03	2003–04	2004–05
Edible fruit and nuts; peel or citrus fruit or melons	16.33	30.44	33.31
Coffee, tea, mate, and spices	0.72	2.28	1.77
Lac; gums, resins and other vegetable saps and extracts.	0.62	5.98	10.22
Pulp of wood or of other fibrous cellulosic material; waste and scrap of paper or paperboard		1.14	0.08
Total	18.46	40.51	46.32

Kyrgyz Republic

	2002–03	2003–04	2004–05
Total	0.47	0.54	0.62

Kazakhstan

	2002–03	2003–04	2004–05
Salt, sulphur, earths and stone; Plastering materials, lime and cement	4.03	4.98	5.91
Iron and steel	3.73	2.35	7.99
Machinery and mechanical appliances		0.03	1.13
Natural or cultured pearls, precious or semiprecious stones, precious metals, clad with precious metal and articles thereof ; imitated jewelry, coin	2.22		
Zinc and articles thereof	1.93	0.23	0.12
Total	12.73	9.26	15.35

Tajikistan

	2002–03	2003–04	2004–05
Cotton		3.90	1.96
Aluminum And Articles Thereof.			2.00
Total	0.08	3.95	3.98

Turkmenistan

	2002–03	2003–04	2004–05
Cotton	2.60	7.83	9.69
Inorganic chemicals	2.46	1.43	0.87
Total	5.40	9.34	10.69

Uzbekistan

	2002–03	2003–04	2004–05
Cotton	3.87	6.95	4.44
Edible vegetables and certain roots and tubers	3.13	4.15	0.81
Natural or cultured pearls, precious or semiprecious stones, precious metals, clad with precious metal and articles thereof, imitated jewelry, coin		3.27	
Zinc and articles thereof	12.52	13.82	19.93
Aircraft, spacecraft, and parts thereof		1.92	0.06
Total	20.54	27.70	29.43

Sources: Directorate General of Foreign Trade, Government of India.

To give impetus to bilateral trade, economic, and scientific cooperation, bilateral inter-governmental Joint Commissions have been set up with the countries of the region. A number of high level visits have also taken place as well as ministerial visits. India has also extended lines of credit ranging from $5 million to $10 million, and signed multiple agreements for technical economic cooperation under the International Technical and Economic Cooperation (ITEC). So far more than 1,000 candidates from the region have come to India from various disciplines, such as diplomacy, banking, finance, trade, management, and small industry promotion. ONGC Videsh has also been active in Kazakhstan.

Despite all these developments, economic connections between India and the region have yet to reach their potential. The main reasons are lack of information and connectivity. The absence of economic and financial reforms in the region have also discouraged many Indian companies.

Indian policy makers and think tanks have identified potential areas for cooperation, including energy, tourism, information technology, consultancy services, petrochemicals, and construction.[38] Another area of major interest to Indian businesses is the continuing privatization of state sector enterprises. Indian companies, such as Ispat International, are acquiring some of these newly - privatized entities. Ispat International bought the 6.5 million ton capacity steel plant in Karaganda, an active power plant, and 15 coal mines in Kazakhstan. Ispat could turn this loss-making enterprise into a profit-making venture with a work-force of 67,000 local workers.

Other Indian companies, such as Punj Lyyod, have participated in oil pipeline projects in Kazakhstan. India and Afghanistan signed a Preferential Trade Agreement in 2003, providing for substantial duty concessions for such Afghan items as dry fruits. Similarly, Afghanistan has allowed reciprocal concessions to Indian products, including tea, sugar, cement, and pharmaceuticals. Trade between the two countries continues to improve.

At present, Indian trade within the Greater Central Asian region is too insignificant (just 0.23 percent of total Indian trade) to build a model. Indeed, the "gravity" models of international trade, which assesses distance heavily influences the destination of trade, have not worked, even in the case of South Asia. In the case of India-Central Asian countries, the application of the gravity model is of little use due to limitations of data.[39] Even if there is a significant increase in regional trade it will still be less than 1 percent of total India trade.

Importance of Greater Central Asia for Continental Trade

The importance of the Greater Central Asia to India, however, should not be limited to the modest amount of regional trade. With the right initiatives,

---

[38] Ramgopal Agarwala, *Towards Comprehensive Economic Co-operation between India and Central Asian Republics*, Discussion Paper No. 108 (New Delhi: RIS, 2006) http://www.ris.org.in//dp108_pap.pdf; *Central Asia and Indian Business: Emerging Trends and Opportunities*, Seminar Proceedings, (New Delhi: Confederation of Indian Industry, May 2003).

[39] See presentation by Ram Upendra Das Prospects and Constraints for Trade Cooperation between India and Central Asian Republics: Some Issues, http://www.ris.org.in/ramupendradas_cii.pdf

this region has the potential to alter the nature and character of India's *continental* trade. Thus far, the majority of Indian trade is conducted by sea. Land-based border trade with China ceased after the India-China war in 1962; similarly, very little trade with Bangladesh, Myanmar, and Pakistan takes place via roads.

Despite some positive developments in border trade, policy initiatives have been limited to a few border points with a small number of commodities exchanged by local communities living on either side of the borders. These initiatives are targeted to stop large "unauthorized trade," which is already taking place through these borders.

Looking beyond the Greater Central Asia region, it is important to note that India trades a great deal with other CIS countries, Iran, and Europe. In 2004–05, India's total trade with these countries amounted to about $50 billion (Table 20). In the last three years, India's total trade, as well as trade with this part of the world, has grown at about 26 percent per year. There are indications that it may grow even at a higher rate in the coming years. Under an assumed growth of 26 percent per year, simple calculations show that India's trade with Europe, CIS, Iran, Afghanistan, and Pakistan would be in the range of $ 500 billion by 2014–15 (Table 21). Because of positive political and economic developments in the GCA region, even if 20 percent of this trade is conducted along highways, $100 billion worth of Indian trade will pass through the region within a decade.

Table 20: India's Trade with Greater Central Asian Countries plus the rest of CIS and Europe (In US$ Millions)

Exports			
	2002–03	**2003–04**	**2004-05**
EU-25	11,847.87	14,443.58	17,329.05
Rest of Europe	891.56	1,223.41	1,495.09
CIS countries	921.69	1,036.54	1,050.93
Afghanistan, Iran, Pakistan	921.66	1,350.52	1,880.70
Total Exports	14,582.78	18,054.05	21,755.77
Imports			
EU-25	12,780.42	14,991.80	18,715.89
Rest of Europe	2,500.08	3,794.90	6,373.04
CIS countries	8,44.30	1,261.47	1,807.58
Afghanistan, Iran, Pakistan	321.61	3,64.99	5,36.05
Total	16,446.41	20,413.16	27,432.56
Exports + Imports			
EU-25	24,628.29	29,435.38	36,044.94
Rest of Europe	3,391.64	5,018.31	7,868.94
CIS countries	1,765.99	2,298.01	2,858.51
Afghanistan, Iran, Pakistan	1,243.27	1,715.51	2,416.75
Total Trade	31,029.19	38,467.21	49,188.33
Percent growth		23.97	27.87
Percent growth of total Indian trade	19.84	24.41	33.61

Sources: Directorate General of Foreign Trade, Government of India.

Table 21: India's Trade Projections up to 2015 with Greater Central Asian Countries plus Rest of CIS and Europe (Based on current trends, in billion of US dollars)

Year	Total trade
2004–05 (actual)	49,188.33
2005–06	61,977.29
2006–07	78,091.38
2007–08	98,395.14
2008–09	123,977.88
2009–10	156,212.13
2010–11	196,827.28
2011–12	248,002.37
2012–13	312,482.99
2013–14	393,728.57
2014–15	496,098.00

Sources: author's calculations based on current data and trends from the Ministry of Commerce and Industry data sources.

For this to happen, a massive effort is needed to rebuild Afghanistan's transport network and economy. To date, commitments from the international community and multilateral institutions are contingent on political stability in the country. Already there are plans to improve institutions and coordination as well as infrastructural in the region through the ADB's CAREC and CSATTF programs. India should start thinking seriously about participating in these programs as an active member with its own plans for linking Indian rail and road network to the GCA region. It could offer to support new plans through SAARC or some newly created organization. Within a decade, this region is going to offer the quickest and cheapest route for hundreds of billions worth of Indian merchandise, particularly from the northern Indian states of Delhi, Haryana, Jammu and Kashmir, and Punjab. This would also justify billions of dollars of infrastructural investment in the GCA. Similarly, with serious Indian participation, huge economic opportunities for all participating countries could result, particularly in Afghanistan.

The major obstacle to realizing this potential is the difficult relationship between India and Pakistan. In the last few years, however, there have been some positive developments. The changing mood is reflected in the Lahore Declaration of February 1999 and various other joint statements (6 January, 2004, 18 February, 2004, 8 September, 2004, 24 September, 2004, 28 December , 2004, and 18 April , 2005). 2004 marked a new beginning when Indian Prime Minister Vajpayee visited Pakistan for the SAARC Summit. Through a joint statement, Pakistan gave a clear commitment that no territory under its control would be used to support terrorism in any manner. Both countries also agreed to resume a "composite dialogue" process. Under this both sides have agreed to discuss "peace and security, including confidence building measures" and "Jammu and Kashmir," along with other issues.[40] This process has been strengthened by further bilateral meetings and peopleto people-contacts. In April 2005, President Musharraf and Dr. Manmohan Singh declared the peace process irreversible.

---

[40] For details of all agreements and statements see Ministry of External Affairs India website http://meaindia.nic.in/

Despite all these developments, India continues to have serious concerns about Pakistani terrorists targeting India. Pakistan has still not extended most-favored nation (MFN) status to India, although India granted MFN status to Pakistan in 1995–96. Things have not changed, even after SAFTA became operational; Pakistan has refused to implement the free trade agreement with India.[41]

It is clear that both countries pay huge economic costs for not cooperating in the GCA. If road and other infrastructural projects end in Pakistan, many of them will never become viable due to low volumes. Similarly, India may never be able to shift its continental trade through the north-south corridor, a linkage that could give a huge boost to Central Asian economies. Policy makers in both countries need to be sensitive to the rising opportunities in the Greater Central Asia region. Overall, the political economy of trade and improvements in physical connections (both air and road) will determine India's economic relations with the Greater Central Asia in the coming years.

Conclusions and Recommendations

Despite having a very complex legacy, the Greater Central Asia region has made significant progress in market reforms. The region has used both standard as well as non-conventional strategies to advance economic transformation. Greater Central Asia countries had to face political transformation and economic reorganization at the same time. While the regional countries have advanced a degree of economic stability its record in structural and institutional reforms is mixed. In some countries, the reforms have not been consolidated and the region as a whole is still vulnerable to external shocks.

Although countries of the region face many common challenges, the force of these challenges impact each country differently. Many of their economic strategies depend on further political reform in the region. Positive outcomes will depend on natural resources, stability in Afghanistan, good human

---

[41] "Mfn Status, Safta Not Linked" *The Dawn*, http://www.dawn.com/2006/07/08/top3.htm

resources, and the willingness of leaders to push economic reforms and regional cooperation. The Greater Central Asia region faces enormous difficulties in actual realization of its potential. Negative tendencies will arise from the weak institutional capacities and investment climate in the region, limited commitment to economic (and political) reforms, the lack of concrete progress in regional co-operation and inadequate resources for public investments and social spending. Most of the regional economic arrangements have yet to prove their utility.

Due to Asia's increased demand for energy, the Greater Central Asia region will play an important role in the global energy scene over the next ten years with Kazakhstan emerging as a major oil producer and exporter. Although energy supplies from Turkmenistan to Asian markets will be less significant due to Ashghabat's restrictive economic policies, the Turkmenistan-Afghanistan-Pakistan-India (TAPI) gas pipeline could nonetheless become a reality.

Due to social discontent and the play of external interests, the region will continue to experience instability in the coming years. The economies of energy-rich countries like Kazakhstan and Turkmenistan will grow much faster than the others. Booming oil prices will help them buy some political stability through state subsidies. Country's like Uzbekistan will face much harder economic choices.

Policy makers as well as analysts in India believe that GCA is important for India because of its strategic location (Tajikistan is just 20 km from Greater Kashmir) and because of its energy resources. Except for a very small military presence in Tajikistan, India has not been able to make a major impact in the region. It is not a major partner in any meaningful economic or security arrangement there. Excluding Afghanistan, two-way trade with the entire region is less than $200 million. Still, as long as regimes in this region do not become hotbeds for religious-inspired terrorism, India will feel comfortable pursuing cooperative relations. However projected oil and gas pipelines could lose all viability because of instability moments in Afghanistan or if Pakistan's stand-off with its neighbors continues. Although things are beginning to change for the better, a clear and long-term policy from New Delhi is lacking.

India will be further integrated more with the region through its observer status in the SCO and through Afghanistan's membership in the SAARC group. Due to the lack of direct access to the Greater Central Asia, and its difficult relations with Pakistan, India has chosen to focus its major initiative on the International North South Transport Corridor. Soon this will be operational throughout the region. The extension of SAFTA to the Greater Central Asia could also be useful to India. However, Central Asian regimes have shown little interest in the organization.

It is becoming clear that Soviet-era leaders in Central Asia are going to face tough domestic challenges in the coming years. These leaders have played an important role in providing stability in the post Soviet vacuum. In spite of this , these societies may face instability and further economic pains in their transition to democratic pluralism and market economies. Because this region is part of India's extended neighborhood, India should be ready to play an important role during this difficult period. India is playing a very constructive role in the reconstruction efforts of Afghanistan and has already emerged as an important donor there. The likelihood is strong that in the coming years India will also emerge as an important energy investor in Kazakhstan as well as an important partner in the TAPI gas pipeline project.

In the rapidly changing scenario, India can look at the Greater Central Asia region with fresh thinking within the following framework:

- The importance of the Greater Central Asia region for Indian trade should not be seen merely in the context of the very modest regional trade;
- Within ten years, India's trade with Europe, CIS, Iran, Afghanistan, and Pakistan will be in the range of $ 500 billion annually;
- Even if only 20 percent of this trade is conducted by continental land routes, $ 100 billion worth of Indian trade will pass through the region;
- For this to happen, a massive effort is needed to rebuild Afghanistan's transport network and economy. An immediate first step is for India's efforts in Afghanistan's reconstruction to be greatly expanded;

- To eradicate duplication, there is need to coordinate INTEC, CSATTF, and TRACECA. India should present its own design for linking its rail and road network with the Afghan economy and beyond;
- The difficult relationship between India and Pakistan is a major impediment to continental trade across Eurasia.
- The impressive emerging possibilities in the Greater Central Asia region suggest that the cost of conflict between India and Pakistan is going to be much bigger in terms of lost "opportunity cost" for both countries than was thought earlier;
- Ideally, the Greater Central Asia area needs a regional economic initiative consisting of all GCA countries, China, India, Iran, Japan, Pakistan, Russia, Turkey, and the United States. These countries should in their interaction cooperate on an *a la carte* basis. Unless all these players are accommodated, suspicions and tensions will continue; and
- All important players in the region have good relations with India. It maintains "strategic partnership" agreements with the United States, Russia, and China and has good relations with Iran. In cooperation with all these countries, India could work seriously for an entirely new regional economic organization for the GCA.

With well conceived initiatives, the GCA region has the potential to alter the nature and character of India's continental trade. India, in turn, is ideally positioned to expand greatly the volume and directions of land-based trade across Greater Central Asia, and also to become a regional hub for the GCA region as well.

China

Niklas Swanström

Nicklas Norling

Zhang Li

There are presently two forces at play in China's engagement with Greater Central Asia that will fundamentally shape the concept of trade on the Eurasian continent: China is strengthening bilateral trade ties with all of its Greater Central Asian neighbors; and the continental transport corridor running from China to Europe is developing at a rapid pace. In light of the geographical proximity between Greater Central Asia and China and the historical connection between Asia and Europe on the Silk Road, it is not surprising that these developments have gathered such momentum. The damage caused by the Soviet legacy on the economies of Greater Central Asia is slowly disappearing and short- as well as long-distance trade is taking root. Growing ties between China, South Asia, and the Middle East put Greater Central Asia at the cross-roads of the Eurasian continental trade corridors, opening alternatives to the Central Asian states. For the first time in a century the Greater Central Asian states can trade freely with their friends in the south, east, and west. Provided that governments in Greater Central Asia and China pursue favourable trade policies and reduce border inefficiencies, they have the potential to raise GDP, increase state income, and make full use of the complementarities that exist among their economies.

The dynamics here should not be mistaken. Trade between China and the post-Soviet states in Central Asia has greatly increased from virtually zero since the collapse of the former Soviet Union in 1991.[1] Today, according to

---

[1] For other assessments of this development see for example, John W. Garver, "Development of China's Overland Transportation Links with Central, South-west

Chinese Customs Statistics the total trade volume between China and Central Asia has increased from approximately $465 million in 1992 to $7.7 billion in 2005. In 2002, for instance, total trade volume reached a modest $2.4 billion, while 2003 saw an increase to $4.1 billion. The 2004 figure of $5.8 billion then increased by 72.5 percent to an all-time high of $7.7 billion (see Appendix 1).[2]

At the same time, the so-called "second Euroasian land-bridge" running from China's coast in Lianyungang to Rotterdam via Xinjiang and Greater Central Asia, has attracted increasing interest. This will result in great savings in transport time that will be possible thanks to infrastructural developments in Greater Central Asia and China. For example, the sea journey from China to Europe takes twenty to forty days, whereas cargo transported by railway from Lianyungang to Rotterdam via the second Eurasian land-bridge promises to cut transport time down to just eleven days.[3]

Despite these ties, bilateral trade with Central Asia is still in its infancy, and continental land trade with the West could stall unless substantial efforts are devoted to facilitate it. To put things in perspective, only 1 percent of China's total foreign trade is with Greater Central Asia, despite significant complementatives among the economies, and China's trade relationship with other neighboring regions is stronger than those with Greater Central Asia. Without necessary infrastructural investments, bilateral trade is unlikely to

---

and South Asia," *China Quarterly* 2006; Vladimir Paramonov, "China and Central Asia: Present and Future Economic Relations," Conflict and Studies Research Centre, Central Asian Series 05/25 (E), May 2005; Martin Spechler, "Crouching Dragon, Hungry Tiger: China and Central Asia," *Contemporary Economic Policy* 21, 2 (2003); P. H. Loughlin & C. W. Pannell, "Growing Economic Links and Regional Development in the Central Asian Republics and Xinjiang," *Eurasian Geography and Economics*, 42, 7 (2001): 207-217; Hsiu-Ling Wu & Chien-Hsun Chen, "The Prospects for Regional Economic Integration between China and the Five Central Asian Countries," *Europe-Asia Studies* 56, 7 (November 2004); ADB, Xinjiang Autonomous Region, PRC: Trade Facilitation and Customs Cooperation Project, Draft Technical Assistance Consultant's Report, November 2005.

[2] The 2005 figure is based on the period from January to November, which means that the figure reached over $8 billion.

[3] Xinjiang Autonomous Region, PRC: Trade Facilitation and Customs Cooperation Project, Draft Technical Assistance Consultant's Report, November 2005.
, , p.30.

reach its full potential, and transport along the second Eurasian land bridge will continue to be limited. Despite potential time and cost savings of transport by land across Central Asia, more than 95 percent of Chinese goods destined for Europe are currently transported via sea or by much more complicated systems using Russia.[4] For example, seaborne transport from Asia to Europe via the Suez Canal, or on the first Eurasian land bridge via Russia on the trans-Siberian railway (Nakhodka-Moscow). Impediments in informal charges, border delays, and capacity constraints on the route reduce potential gains.[5] Prices, costs, and transit times are often highly arbitrary, which affect Central Asia's competitiveness. While some of these factors could be ascribed to the topography of the region, the majority are man-made: customs rules change frequently, border crossings are inefficient, and customs declarations are not standardized.[6]

The transactional costs imposed by these impediments are unfortunate for all states involved. Natural specialization could be achieved by opening old trade routes and encouraging greater inter-state cooperation. For example China is now tapping into Central Asian energy resources and Kyrgyzstan has taken steps to supply Afghanistan with building materials. Beyond this, cotton from Tajikistan could be exported to Turkey, China, and Pakistan, and Pakistani producers could compete with Chinese and Indian manufacturers.[7] Electricity from Tajikistan and Kyrgyzstan could alleviate the critical situation in the Afghan and Pakistani power supply, and China could provide Greater Central Asia with technology and manufactures. Trade policies should reflect these larger emerging forces and avoid regimes solely focused on intra-regional trade, especially those designed by Russia to maintain influence over its former dependents. This chapter aims to explore these

---

[4] Xinjiang Autonomous Region, PRC: Trade Facilitation and Customs Cooperation Project, Draft Technical Assistance Consultant's Report, November 2005. p.3.

[5] Ibid, p. 32.

[6] Sena Eken, Presentation to the CAREC Trade Policy Coordinating Committee' pp.11, http://adb.org/Carec/documents/tpcc.pdf (accessed on 30 January 2007)

[7] Frederick Starr, "Central Asia's Reemerging Transport Network: Promise and Perils for Mountainous Regions," Paper for the International Workshop Strategies for Development and Food Security in Mountainous Areas of Central Asia, Dushanbe June 6-10, 2005, p.6.

prospects and problems by estimating the potential gains in continental and regional trade, by establishing what the regional trade patterns look like, what bottlenecks exist, how these bottlenecks can be alleviated, and what costs are involved. We will start with a brief overview of China's trade with Greater Central Asia and its significance.

China's Trade and Interests in Greater Central Asia and Beyond

Since World War II there have been four main phases in China's border trade with its western neighbours in Central Asia: 1949--85; 1986–90; 1991–2000 and 2001–to the present. In 1949 an agreement was signed with the Soviet Union on cross-border trade between Soviet and Chinese state companies. This was followed with the opening of four border trading zones in Horgos, Turugart, Jimnay, and Baktu, but these were subsequently closed between 1963 and1967 due to political factors. As a result, all border trade ceased. Trade resumed in 1982, but was not formally recognized until 1986, when China began to reform its foreign trade policies. On September 12, 1990, the railways of China and the Soviet Union were connected at the Druzhba-Ala Pass in Xinjiang, laying the groundwork for the second Eurasian land bridge. The disintegration of the Soviet Union led to greater trade with Central Asia, reflected in cross-border trade figures topping $464 million in 1992—a growth of 65 times the value of 1986. In the early 1990s, several agreements were signed between Xinjiang Transport Cargo Bureau and its Kazakh counterpart resulting in the opening of five land routes for passenger transport and cargo freight.[8] This laid the foundation for the massive expansion of border trade that has occurred during the fourth phase since 2000.

---

[8] Xinjiang Autonomous Region, PRC: Trade Facilitation and Customs Cooperation Project, Draft Technical Assistance Consultant's Report, November 2005. pp.12–18.

Graph 1. China's Trade with Central Asia 1992-2005

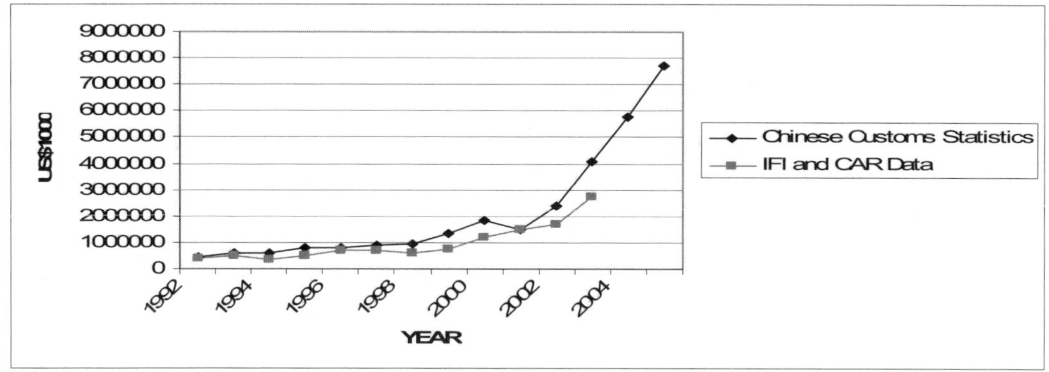

As illustrated in Graph 1, China's trade with Central Asia grew steadily from 2001 through the end of 2005.[9] Interestingly, accounts of bilateral trade differ widely depending on the source, which can help in discerning the extent of the shuttle trade.[10] While Chinese Customs Statistics include shuttle trade in their estimates, the IMF does not.[11] Even though estimates using this method should be treated with caution, it is possible to get an idea of the extent of both official trade and shuttle trade. The extent of the shuttle trade also reveals foregone state income and, as shuttle trade to a large degree is an effect of trade barriers, it gives an indication of the potential gains that governments could reap by reducing these barriers.[12] Neither of these methods includes illegal trade, which is substantial in all states. Indeed, and today both legally and illegally Chinese goods are now flooding the bazaars of Central Asia at the cost of Russian and internally produced goods.

---

[9] This growing trend is confirmed by data from International Financial Institutions (IFI) and the Central Asian Republics (CARs) national statistics (pink graph).

[10] Shuttle trade is defined as the activity of individual persons and entrepreneurs purchase goods across the border which they import for resale in bazaars and street markets. These goods are often imported without full declaration to escape from import duties, see *Measuring the Non-Observed Economy: A Handbook*, (Paris: OECD, 2002) OECD, IMF, ILO, Interstate Statistical Committee of the Commonwealth of Independent States, 2002, Annex 2, Glossary.

[11] Vladimir Paramonov, "China and Central Asia: Present and Future Economic Relations," Conflict and Studies Research Centre, Central Asian Series 05/25 (E), May 2005, p.3.

[12] Increasing Gains from Trade Through Regional Cooperation in Trade and Policy and Customs Transit, Asian Development Bank, Manila, April 2006, p.32.

China is not the only power that has expanded its economic ties with the Central Asian states, however. Russia's overall trade volume with Kazakhstan, for example, has grown steadily from approximately $3.8 billion in 1998, to $4.8 billion in 2001, to top $8.1 billion in 2004.[13] Yet China's total trade volume with Kazakhstan has expanded even faster, from a modest $635.5 million in 1998to almost $4.5 billion in 2004, according to Chinese Customs Statistics (see Appendix 1). Even though China has some way to go before it surpasses Russia's trade volume with Kazakhstan, Beijing has demonstrated its intention to make full use of the completitiveness that exist between the economies of China and Central Asia.

China is particularly interested in Central Asian energy resources, while Central Asia needs consumer and manufactured goods. Apart from the logic of the market and the mutual benefits that both parties could reap by trading, regional economic cooperation brings comprehensive gains for China in the political, security, and economic spheres.

The northwest region of Xinjiang is the main Chinese beneficiary of economic cooperation with Central Asia. Indeed talking about bilateral China-Central Asian trade is somewhat misleading as the Xinjiang region accounts for over 80 percent of the total Chinese trade volume with Central Asia.[14] Moreover, Chinese trade is heavily directed towards one trading partner, Kazakhstan. China's trade with Kazakhstan was close to 80 percent of total trade with Central Asia in 2005, while trade with Turkmenistan was just over 1 percent of the total bilateral trade with the region.[15] Though one may speak of Sino-Central Asian trade, the very large majority of this trade takes place around the border regions of Xinjiang and Kazakhstan and to a lesser degree around Kyrgyzstan.[16] This is especially important for

[13] IMF Country Report No. 05/378, Russian Federation: Statistical Appendix, October 2005, see Table 26. Russian Federation: Origin of Imports, 1998-2004 and Table 24. Russian Federation: Destination of Exports, 1998-2004.

[14] Wang Haiyan, "Xinjiang's Position in China's Economic and Trade Relations with Central Asia," *Markets of Russia, Central Asia and Eastern Europe* 2 (2006),p.33.

[15] Based on figures for 2004, see, "Yearbooks of China's Customs Statistics", 2004, China's Customs Press, Beijing.

[16] Explanations for this concentration of trade to the border regions can partly be explained by the Chinese border trade policy. This policy entails a promotion of border

Afghanistan and Tajikistan, both of which could be prominent trading partners for China.

The Rationale Underlying Chinese Engagement

Five motives drive Chinese engagement in Central Asia: the economic development of Xinjiang; domestic political stability; regional stability; energy security; and the creation of an alternative transport corridor to Europe.

Through China's "develop the west" program, launched by Chinese President Jiang Zemin in 1999, China has sought to integrate the western region of China into the booming Chinese economy, and make it more competitive. Though the western development program includes Tibet, Qinghai, Gansu, Sichuan, Yunnan, Shaanxi and Guizhou provinces in addition to Xinjiang, Xinjiang has been the main area of focus. Sharing a 3,500 km long border with the Central Asian republics, Xinjiang's economic integration is of crucial importance for its development. As such, development of Xinjiang's infrastructure has been a prime concern. Today, the infrastructure of Xinjiang is comparatively well developed with 11 airports, 3,361 km of railway, 80,900 km of road network, a highway running across the Taklimakan desert, and modern telecommunications.

A precondition for this development, however, has been a massive resource transfer from Beijing for the development of infrastructure, including road and rail ties between China's east and west. For example, the 4,395 km national highway from Lianyungang to the Horgos customs point in Xinjiang, which opened in 2004, cuts cross-country transport time from 15

---

trade with neighbouring regions and use increased economic interaction to promote stability and growth. Specifically, it aims to facilitate exchange between inhabitants living within 20km of the Chinese border and neighbouring countries; to ease restriction on small-scale border trade; reducing tariffs and import turnover taxes by half for border trade; as well as reducing restrictions on goods brought into the country for the purpose of economic or technology collaboration projects, see Hsiu-Ling Wu & Chien-Hsun Chen, 2004, p.1071.

days to 50 hours.[17] The real impact of the Chinese "develop the west" policy, however, is still to be seen, as crucial bottlenecks remain.[18]

By deepening economic cooperation between China (especially Xinjiang) and Central Asia, China seeks to diminish the influences of those groups that promote ethno-religious extremism and separatism.[19] China fears that these influences will spill over into Xinjiang, due to the historical trans-border interactions between these peoples. China's policy is fairly straightforward: to increase incentives to Central Asian governments that assist in repressing "East Turkestan" secessionist forces, and not to let Central Asia become a base from which secessionists can operate.[20] This promotion of China's territorial integrity has been promoted both on a bilateral and multilateral level through the SCO.

Second, as repeatedly demonstrated in the past, drastic shifts in Central Asia tend to create problems for China. From the Manchu's establishment of the northwest province of Xinjiang in the 1860s to the Republic Revolution in 1911, this region has seen several major revolts, most of which are believed to have been instigated and supported by those with an anti-Chinese agenda. Mass ethnic upheavals a in the 1940s and emigration to the Soviet territory in the 1960s were unwelcomed external influences from Soviet Central Asia.[21]

China's present concern over possible turmoil in this region is clearly demonstrated in its very nervous reaction to the March 2005 Tulip Revolution in Kyrgyzstan. In addition to fear of a domino effect and growing

---

[18] Hongyi Harry Lai, "China's Western Development Program: Its Rationale, Implementation, and Prospects", *Modern China* 28, 4 (2002): 451-453.
[19] "China, Russia, CIS nations to fight terrorism", *Daily Excelsior*, Jammu, India, June 16, 2001
[20] Hsiu-Ling Wu & Chien-Hsun Chen, 2004; For an early assessment of this see, Lilian Craig Harris, "Xinjiang, Central Asia, and the Implications for China's Policy in the Islamic World," *The China Quarterly* 133 (1993), pp. 111-129.
[21] Zhao Changqing, "China's Strategic Interests in Central Asia", *Central and West Asia Studies*, No. 2, 2005

regional instability, China's support of the Uzbek government following the Andijan events of 2005 further confirmed its dedication to the status quo.[22]

Third, China hopes for a relatively secure energy supply from Central Asia and especially Kazakhstan. Such energy links would benefit the cooperative political structures that have been initiated in the region, but which have encountered problems. Economically it would benefit the states in the region by decreasing costs and securing long-term energy security. China needs to diversify its energy supplies. By relying on oil transported by sea lanes through the Malacca Straits China places itself in an insecure position since those straits are often closed to Chinese transports.[23] Currently, there is also a premium of US$1–2 per barrel on the oil that is imported to Northeast Asia due to world demand on Middle-Eastern oil, and to the simple reality of distance.

To reduce dependence on the Malacca Straits China has shown a keen interest in the alternative route via the port of Gwadar in Pakistan, in which China has invested over $200 million.[24] To transport energy supplies from the Gwadar port, China has made efforts in rehabilitating the 616 km Karakorum highway linking Pakistan with Xinjiang, although this is unlikely to carry more than a little oil. Plans are also underway to build a highway linking Gwadar with Kandahar and Islamabad, as well as to the east-west trunk railroad from Urumchi to Kashgar.[25]

Fourth, the construction of the second Eurasian land bridge via Central Asia and Xinjiang will reduce the over-load at Chinese ports on the east coast. Development of the corridor will also increase access by China's underdeveloped western regions to world markets and balance the wealth gaps within China. Large oil deposits in Kazakhstan and Azerbaijan and gas deposits in Turkmenistan are already drawing Chinese attention, leading to

---

[22] Stephen Blank, "Islam Karimov and the Heirs of Tiananmen", *Eurasia Daily Monitor*, Vol. 2, No.115, June 14, 2005

[23] Niklas Swanström, "An Asian Oil and Gas Union: Prospects and Problems," *CEF Quarterly* 3, 3 (2005), p.88.

[24] Tarique Niazi, "Gwadar: China's Naval Outpost on the Indian Ocean," *China Brief*, January 16 2005.

[25] Frederick Starr, "Central Asia'a Reemerging Transport Network", 2005 p.2.

expanded political interaction. In the case of Azerbaijan alone this has led to the Chinese showing interest in developing the Baku-Tbilisi-Kars railway corridor, as well as to further multiple production-sharing agreements with the Azerbaijan State Oil Company following a 2004 grant by China's Shengli Oil Company to develop the Garachukhur oil field.[26]

Assessment of Possible Gains and Benefits from Continental and Regional Trade Involving China and Greater Central Asia

What are the potential gains to China from continental and regional trade? Today, trade between the Asia-Pacific region and Europe exceeds $300 million per year, and stifling congestions at Chinese ports, combined with increasing freight rates for maritime shipments, have led Chinese producers to look for alternative overland trade routes. In comparison to the sea-routes via Asia and Europe, whose freight costs can reach as much as $167 per ton and take 45 days, the second Eurasian land-bridge could cut transport time by more than half and cost only $110 per ton[27]. Instead of the 26,000 km detour to Europe by sea, the second Eurasian land-bridge reduces distance to 6,379 km, translating into a cost saving of 30 percent for forwarders[28] promising significant transit fees and greater market access for Greater Central Asia not to mention the environmental benefits. Beyond this, of course is the opportunity cost to China if it decides not to participate.

The few estimates of potential benefits to Chinas of continental trade tend to be highly speculative.[29] For example, the Institute of Spatial Planning & Regional Economy State Development Planning Commission of the People's

---

[26] Fariz Ismailzade, "Azerbaijan and China Move to Increase Security and Economic Cooperation," *Eurasia Daily Monitor* 2, 56 22 March, 2005.

[27] Xinjiang Autonomous Region, PRC: Trade Facilitation and Customs Cooperation Project, Draft Technical Assistance Consultant's Report, November 2005, p.31

[28] Ibid, p. 31.

[29] There is to the authors awareness no such study to date. The ADB, Xinjiang Autonomous Region, PRC: Trade Facilitation and Customs Cooperation Project, Draft Technical Assistance Consultant's Report, November 2005 bring up potential gains and impediments on the route but does not quantify them. With regard to Central Asia there are a few more quantitative studies made on potential gains with trade facilitation. For a literature review on quantitative studies on trade facilitation see, "Quantitative Assessment of the Benefits for Trade Facilitation", OECD TD/TC/WP, (2003)31, Paris, 2003. (Unclassified).

Republic of China estimates that trade barriers on the second Eurasian land bridge reduced Chinese GDP by 13 percent in 2000,[30] which places the opportunity cost at roughly $130 billion.[31] This is certainly an overly optimistic forecast. An Organization for Economic Cooperation and Development (OECD) report suggests that gains from trade facilitation will be between 0.04 percent and 2.3 percent of GDP.[32] Land-locked countries with protectionism, inadequate infrastructure, and slow borders have most to gain, and could raise their GDP by as much as 2.3 percent. Moreover, a recent Asia Development Bank (ADB) report, "Central Asia: Mapping Future Prospects to 2015," echoes these figures and forecasts GDP growth of about 2 percent, depending on the trade facilitation measures implemented.[33] In contrast, recent United Nations Development Program (UNDP) estimates suggest that GDP could be 50-100 percent higher in a 10 year-period Central Asia if impediments to transport and trade were removed and a program of regional cooperation implemented.[34] On the basis of these projections it seems that potential gains for Xinjiang and Greater Central Asia would involve at least a yearly 2% GDP raise.[35]

It would seem likely that Xinjiang's GDP - starting from a higher base - would increase by less than that of Central Asia. This would be due to its

---

[30] Institute of Spatial Planning & Regional Economy State Development Planning Commission P.R.China, Study on the Development and Opening-up of the New Asian-Europe Continental Bridge Area (China`s Side), <http://www.ecdc.net.cn/events/asian_europe/> (accessed on 15 May, 2006)

[31] In the same year China's total logistics costs represented 17,7 percent of GDP which should be compared to the U.S. average of 10 percent, see "Going Intermodal," *The China Business Review*, August 10, 2005.

[32] "Quantitative Assessment of the Benefits for Trade Facilitation", OECD TD/TC/WP, (2003)31, Paris, 2003. (Unclassified), Table 5, p.16.

[33] Malcolm Dowling and Ganeshan Wignaraja, Central Asia: Mapping Future Prospects to 2015, Asian Development Bank, Manila, April 2006, p.2.

[34] See Malcolm Dowling and Ganeshan Wignaraja, *Central Asia After Fifteen Years of Transition*, ADB Working Paper Series on Regional Economic Integration (July 2006), p. 17, <http://aric.adb.org/pdf/workingpaper/WP3%20CARS%20230706.pdf> (accessed 30 January, 2007).

[35] This difference is probably a result of how many factors that are included in the model. The OECD trade facilitation estimates seem to be more limited focusing mostly on increasing border-efficiency and infrastructure and logistics impediments, while the ADB and UNDP estimates appears to be more comprehensive.

more developed infrastructure, China's membership in the World Trade Organization (WTO) and its more favourable trade policies. Because the current foreign trade as share of GDP is higher in Central Asia than in Xinjiang, the latter has comparatively more unrealized foreign trade potential. While total foreign trade (exports plus imports) in Xinjiang amounted to $5.6 billion in 2004 and represented 20 percent of total GDP, the Chinese average was 75 percent. This suggests that there is considerable potential for Xinjiang's foreign trade to raise GDP significantly should access to western markets be improved.[36]

The role of Xinjiang as a transit region will also increase significantly in the coming years, although the volume of transit-trade through Xinjiang today already is much larger than actual import and exports to and from the region. The current total value of transit is estimated to be about $8 to $10 billion with annual growth reaching at 15 percent.[37] Although the contribution of the transport sector to GDP in Central Asia (and Xinjiang) is in itself relatively small, accounting for 3–8 percent of GDP and aggregate output, the transport sector is crucial for integration and growth in terms of participation in the second Eurasian land bridge and international trade in general. [38]

As with forecasts on GDP increases, quantifiable assessments on the potential magnitude of trade volume on the second Eurasian land bridge are uncertain at best. One assessment suggests that annual income for participating countries could reach "hundreds of millions of dollars" in increased container transit.[39] Yet the second Eurasia land bridge faces fierce competition from alternative routes, primarily from sea transport but also from the first Eurasian land bridge through Russia. Currently, only a sixth of exports from Japan and Korea to Europe are transported via the second

---

[36] See ADB, *Xinjiang Autonomous Region*, p. 51 and authors own calculations. This discrepancy could partly be explained by the high share of energy resource extraction in the region and soaring domestic demand.

[37] Description of ADB Technical Assistance Project for Xinjiang, 2006. Provided to authors upon request from CAREC.

[38] ADB, "Increasing Gains From Trade Through Regional Cooperation in Trade Policy and Customs Transit," April 2006, p. 49.

[39] Mikhail Mostovoy, deputy director general of Ukranian State Rail Administration in "Railways revive the Silk Road," *Transport Weekly* (?).

Eurasia land bridge. Russia has shown concern over this competitive trunk route, and has made considerable efforts in enhancing the competitiveness of its route via the trans-Siberian railway. Although the corridor through Russia is 1300 km longer than the second bridge, traders and forwarders still prefer this route due to its greater efficiency, Russian tax incentives, customs rebates, and better facilities.[40] It has been estimated that if China attains TIR status, the volume of transit goods on the second land bridge will reach 500 to 600 million tons per year.[41] In addition, when China becomes a member of TIR, Chinese goods also will be more competitive both in the Central Asian states as well as within the European market.

Potential benefits are not limited to China and Greater Central Asia. The recent linkage of the Kars-Akhalkalaki rail network linking Georgia and Turkey on the cross-Caucasus segment of the second Eurasia land bridge, will also boost trade. Cargo from China could be delivered to Aktau in Kazakhstan, sent onward by ferry to Baku, and then shipped to Istanbul and Europe via the railroad link. Estimates suggest that trade volume through this corridor will jump from 2 million tons in the first two years, to 8-10 million tons in the following three years.[42]

Access to ports for Xinjiang and Greater Central Asia will also provide substantial projected benefits. The joint Sino-Pakistani development of the Gwadar port and restoration of the Karakorum highway will lead to an increase in cargo trade volume at Gwadar from approximately 200,000 twenty-foot containers in 2005 to an estimated 295,000 in 2015.[43] This joint development entails that Gwadar will double the capacity of Pakistani oceanic trade and open a "window to the sea" for the landlocked countries in Central Eurasia.[44] Rehabilitation of roads to Afghanistan from the Gwadar

---

[40] ADB, November 2005, p. 54

[41] Ibid, p. 28.

[42] Taleh Ziyadov, "The Kars-Akhalkalaki Railroad: A Missing Link Between Europe and Asia," *Central Asia Caucasus Analyst*, April 19 2005.

[43] Aftab Kazi, Pakistan's Trade with Greater Central Asia, Pakistan Country Paper, Presented on First Kabul Conference on Continental Trade and Transport, Kabul, Afghanistan, April 1-2, 2006.

[44] John W. Garver, "Development of China's Overland Transportation Links," 2006, p. 8.

port will also give Afghan products greater export possibilities and shipping options. Gwadar is closer to Xinjiang than any other saltwater ports in China proper, and will reduce much of the transaction costs currently imposed on trade to and from Xinjiang. Central Asian states will benefit significantly as well, as the port opens the possibilities for promoting their oil trade globally, while Pakistan and Tajikistan are likely to reap new transit fees.

Bilateral Trade Patterns and Positions in the Eurasian Continental Trade Network

China and Kazakhstan

In 1998, China and Kazakhstan finally settled the border dispute that had plagued their relations since Kazakh independence. This laid the foundation for the strong bilateral trade relationship that exists today. Bilateral trade has increased from 37 to 54 percent annually. Trade turnover between Kazakhstan and Xinjiang alone reached $4,5 – 5 billion by 2004.[45]

The opening of the Atasu-Alashankou pipeline in late 2005 symbolizes the firm ties between China and Central Asia. Continued expansion of this pipeline connects Kumkol in central Kazakhstan with Kenkiyak in western Kazakhstan, providing a possible tap into energy resources flowing from the Caspian by the Atyrau and Chevron-operated Tengiz fields. This promises huge benefits. For example, in the beginning of 2005 Kazakhstan exported merely 25,000 barrels per day (bpd) to China. The Atasu-Alashankou pipeline will initially increase this to 200,000 bpd. When the link between Kenkiyak and Kumkol is completed, exports will likely reach about 1,000,000 bpd.[46]

Kazakhstan is a transit country in trade between China and Azerbaijan, as well as between Russia, Kyrgyzstan, Tajikistan, and Uzbekistan.[47] Thus the

---

[45] Kazakhstan mainly exports raw materials to Xinjiang, 58 percent of which are energy resources and 24 percent non-ferrous metals. Xinjiang's exports to Kazakhstan are mainly grain, edible oil, granulated sugar, ketchup, cotton, and textile. figures for 2003, see Vladimir Paramonov, "China and Central Asia: Present and Future Economic Relations," Conflict and Studies Research Centre, Central Asian Series 05/25 (E), May 2005.

[46] "Circumventing the Bear," *Stratfor*, December 16, 2005.

[47] ADB, "Increasing Gains From Trade Facilitation," April 2006, p. 49.

borders at Druzhba-Ala and Horgos have emerged as indispensable nodes in trade between China and Europe.

Shuttle trade between China and Kazakhstan is estimated by the Kazakh Customs Committee to be about $2–3.5 billion, making it comparable to the official bilateral trade.[48] Cross-border interaction will likely increase further with the opening of the Jeminay border trade zone in 2006.

China and Uzbekistan

Uzbekistan is particularly well-positioned to participate in a continental trade network and serve as a transit country between Kazakhstan and Iran, as well as between Afghanistan, Tajikistan and Kazakhstan. Unfortunately the Uzbek government has failed to capitalize on this position, and its restrictive trade policies have hampered both transit trade and bilateral trade with its neighbors. China is no exception to this. Bilateral trade between China and Uzbekistan has been limited by Uzbek protectionism and the uncertain investment climate since Uzbek independence.[49] Ill-connecting infrastructure with the other Central Asian states has further reduced the competitiveness of the Uzbek economy. As with Kazakhstan, the 1990s saw an incremental increase in total trade turnover except during the period from 1997 to 2001, when bilateral trade plummeted from approximately $203 million in 1997 to $40 million in 1999 (Appendix 1). This drop resulted from changing demand in Uzbekistan and China, as well as from the financial crisis in Russia.[50] Since 2002 there has been a steady increase to an all time high of around $628 million in 2005.[51]

---

[48] Vladimir Paramonov, May 2005, p.3.

[49] UNDP, "Bringing Down Barriers: Regional Cooperation for Human Development and Human Security," Central Asia Development Report, UNDP, Bratislava, 2005, p. 61.

[50] Hsiu-Ling Wu & Chien-Hsun Chen, "The Prospects for Regional Economic Integration," 2004, p.1066.

[51] Figures on goods exported from Uzbekistan to China vary substantially. Uzbek state statistics claim that cotton made up only 4 percent percent of total exports in 2003, whereas services accounted for 48 percent, foodstuffs 4,6 percent, machinery and equipment 19 percent, and non-ferrous metals 1.5 percent see Paramonov, "China and

Shuttle trade represents a significant share of the increase in the volume of bilateral trade, although this is less so than in bilateral trade between China and Kazakhstan. The harder border restrictions probably reduce the shuttle trade in Uzbekistan, but recent improvements in Sino-Uzbek relations will likely increase the percentage of official trade in the total.

In 2006 Uzbekistan and China signed many bilateral agreements on trade and energy cooperation, including the $600 million agreement between the China National Petroleum Corporation and the Uzbek state oil company. At the signing, Chinese President Hu Jintao and his Uzbek counterpart pledged further cooperation in trade, customs, high technology, and energy.[52]

China and Kyrgyzstan

Chinese Customs Statistics show that trade volume between China and Kyrgyzstan was relatively low during the 1990s, ranging from $100 to $200 million. On average, trade between China and Kyrgyzstan is similar in volume to Sino-Uzbek trade. However, considering that Kyrgyzstan population is a sixth of Uzbekistan's trade relations between China and Kyrgyzstan are significantly stronger than between China and Uzbekistan. Annual turnover stood at $202 million in 2002, but reached $840 million in 2005 (Appendix 1). IMF figures are slightly lower, but the upward trend in bilateral trade is confirmed by Kyrgyz authorities, which suggests trade strengthened from $74.8 million in 1995 to $101 million in 2003 (Table 1). Yet the Kyrgyz figures are markedly below those from Beijing.

Central Asia," 2005, p. 5. Chinese Customs Statistics assert however that cotton, cotton yarn, and cotton fabric made up 84,33 percent of China's imports from Uzbekistan, see "China's Customs Statistics," 2003, from Hsiu-Ling Wu & Chien-Hsun Chen, 2004. China's main exports to Uzbekistan included in 2003 engineering products (48 percent), chemical products (19 percent), and foodstuffs (9 percent), Paramonov, "China and Central Asia," 2005, p. 5.

52 "China, Uzbekistan sign $600 million oil agreement," *China Daily*, May 26 2005.

Table 1. Kyrgyz Republic: IMF Direction of Trade Statistics (w/ China)

(in millions of US dollars)

	1995	1996	1997	1998	1999	2000	2001	2002	2003	2004 Jan.—Jun.
Exports	68.5	36.4	31.6	15.7	25.3	44.1	19.4	41.1	23.3	19.6
Imports	6.3	7.8	32.5	44.4	36.9	36.9	48.5	59	77.7	37.2
Total	74.8	44.2	64.1	60.1	62.2	81	67.9	100.1	101	56.8

Source: IMF Country Report No. 05/31 Kyrgyz Republic: Statistical Appendix, February 2005.

The gap between the Kyrgyz and Chinese statistics implies the existence of shuttle trade with huge turnovers.[53] Nevertheless, there has also been growth in official trade turnover. The Intergovernmental Kyrgyz-Chinese Commission on Trade and Economic Cooperation in 1994 opened the way for trade across the Chinese-Kyrgyz border. However, it was not until 1998 and 1999 that the commission started to address the bottlenecks in cross-border trade and investments. In 1999, the parties agreed to rehabilitate roads, in particular the Osh-Sary-Tash-Irkeshtam road and such cargo and passenger routes as Osh-Kashgar-Osh and Osh-Artush-Osh.[54] At the sixth session of the commission in Beijing in 2004 it was agreed that Sinopec's subsidiary, Shenli Oil Company, would participate in developing Kyrgyzstan's Alai Hollow oil fields.[55] Due to a lack of investments, however, many planned projects have not been realized, among them $1 billion railroad line between Osh, Turugart and Kashgar.

Kyrgyzstan's WTO membership has resulted in a trade deficit with China. In 2002, China exported goods to a value of roughly $146 million and imported less than $55 million from Kyrgyzstan (Appendix 1). Kyrgyz authorities confirm the trade deficit but downscale it to $20 million (Table 1).[56] Compared with other players in the region, however, China's trade with

---

[53] For similar assertions see also, Paramonov, "China and Central Asia," 2005.

[54] Intergovernmental Kyrgyz-Chinese Commission on Trade and Economic Cooperation, Website: <http://www.mvtp.kg/main.php?lang=en&p=7.21> (accessed March 24, 2006).

[55] *UPI Energy Watch*, June 24 2004.

[56] In 2003 Chinese exports to Kyrgyzstan were primarily in textiles, staple fibres, footwear, plastic and machinery, while Kyrgyzstan exported primarily aluminium, iron, steel, copper, hides and skins.Chinese Customs Statistics, 2003, from Hsiu-Ling

Kyrgyzstan is however small: Kyrgyz-Russian trade stands at $273,1 million, while Kyrgyzstan – Kazakhstan trade is $228 million.[57]

China and Tajikistan

Civil war between 1992 and 1997, the weakness of the state, and drug trafficking have created a huge illicit economy in Tajikistan. By contrast, bilateral trade with China was modest down to 2003, where it increased a significant 206.8 percent, from $12,386 million to $38 million (Appendix 1).[58] These official Chinese figures, however, are about four times higher than IMF estimates.[59] The difference may be attributable to the extensive shuttle trade that arose with the opening of the Chinese-Tajik border in 2004.[60]

Xinjiang has built a new road to Tajikistan and Chinese specialists are participating in the rehabilitation of the Duhanbe-Nurobod-Jirgoatol-Kyrgyz border highway, as well as the construction of the Tajik highway tunnels "Sharshar" and "Shahriston."[61] The United States is financing and building a bridge over the Panj River, linking Tajikistan with Afghanistan, which will facilitate trade to the south. This will also give China an opportunity to transport goods through Afghanistan onward to destinations further south. Nevertheless, much work remains before the Tajik infrastructure is competitive. Typical is the still primitive Kulyab-Khorog highway section in

---

Wu & Chien-Hsun Chen, 2004, "The Prospects for Regional Economic Integration between China and the Five Central Asian Countries," *Europe-Asia Studies* 56, 7 (November 2004)

[57] IMF Country Report No. 05/31, February 2005, Kyrgyz Republic: Statistical Appendix, Table 21. Kyrgyz Republic: Direction of Trade, 1995-2004.

[58] The goods traded in the bilateral official economy in 2002 were primarily aluminium, iron, steel and cotton exported to China, while Tajikistan imported home appliances, electrical machinery, woven apparel, footwear, and food.Chinese Customs Statistics, 2003, from Hsiu-Ling Wu & Chien-Hsun Chen, 2004.

[59] Paramonov, 'China and Central Asia," May 2005, p. 6.

[60] Zafar Abdullaev and Lydia Isamova, "Tajikistan looks to the East," *RCA* No.303, July 27 2004.

[61] Welcoming address by Tajik Prime Minister Akil Akilov at the First Preparatory Conference to the Fourteenth OSCE Economic Forum, Dushanbe, Tajikistan, November 7-8, 2005.

the south of the country, which is an essential part of the route to China.[62] Nor is Chinese infrastructure ready for trade. The south-western region is the poorest in Xinjiang, which is forcing China to invest heavily in infrastructure development there.[63]

Although the Tajik economy is oriented mainly to Russia and Uzbekistan with a total trade turnover of $394 and $235, respectively,[64] the Sino-Tajik economic ties have strengthened significantly with the opening in 2004 of the Kulma Pass linking China and Tajikistan. China's and Tajikistan's interest in a functioning transport corridor has resulted in several further projects, including collaborations in telecommunication and communication services.

China and Turkmenistan

Until recently, economic ties between China and Turkmenistan were limited. According to Chinese Customs Statistics, the total trade turnover amounted to $32.7 million in 2001, but by 2005 had topped $100 million. The Turkmen trade deficit is substantial, until its exports to China accounted for no more than $735,000 as recently as 2002.[65]

Energy cooperation over the Turkmenistan-Afghanistan-Pakistan-Indian pipeline could, if realized, be a ground-breaking event. The April 2006 visit of President Niyazov to Beijing promises to change this situation radically. While details remain unclear as of this writing, China has signaled its interest to import gas from Turkmenistan via Kazakhstan. Chinese firms may also invest in the proposed TAP or TAPI (Turkmenistan-Afghanistan-Pakistan/India) pipeline from the Dauletabad-Donmez gas field in Turkmenistan through Afghanistan to the Pakistani port of Gwadar, with a

---

62 Ibid.; this section of the highway is presently being upgraded by Turkish companies, however it is estimated that rehabilitation will take years.

63 Yueyao Zhao, "Pivot or Periphery? Xinjiang's Regional Development," *Asian Ethnicity* 2, 2 (2001): 217.

64 IMF Country Report No. 05/31, February 2005, Kyrgyz Republic: Statistical Appendix, Table 21. Kyrgyz Republic: Direction of Trade, 1995-2004.

65 *Chinese Customs Statistics*, 2003. These exports were mainly made up of plastic, silk, and yarn.

possible extension to India.[66] Both China and Russia have been competing for influence and put themselves forward as possible funders.[67] Due to Turkmen President Niyazov's unfavorable reputation among foreign investors, the situation in Afghanistan, as well as the animosity between India and Pakistan, it long remained unclear whether and when the pipeline will be built. It remains to be seen if his death in December, 2006, will change the situation

China and Afghanistan

Since the fall of the Taliban regime, China has shown interest in the reconstruction of Afghanistan, even though Chinese assistance thus far has been extremely limited; a stable Afghanistan integrated into the regional economy is certainly in the interest of China.[68] At the recent Afghanistan Compact Conference in London, China promised a total of US$10 million in 2006, and agreed to abolish tariffs on Afghanistan exports to China.[69]

The increasing engagement of China in Afghanistan is also discernible in the volume of bilateral trade (Table 2). Beginning in 2003–04, China has established itself as the main exporter to Afghanistan. Afghan imports from China have increased from 2 percent in 2001–02, and 1 percent in 2002–03 to 18 percent of the total in 2005–06, according to IMF statistics provided by Afghan authorities. Afghan sources claim that this amount represented a total import of $385 million.[70] Chinese Customs Statistics estimate that the total trade volume was $58 million in 2004, which fell to $48 million in 2005.[71]

---

[66] "Poor prospects for Transafghan Gas Line," *Stratfor*, December 26 2002.
[67] Starr, "China's Reemerging Transport Network," 2005.
[68] "Special envoy of China on Afghanistan Reconstruction," *People's Daily,* January 23 2002.
[69] "China pledges nearly $10m in aid to Afghanistan in 2006," The Chinese Government's Official Web Portal, 1 February,2006,http://www.gov.cn.misc/2006-02/01/content_176548.htm, (accessed 30 January 2007).
[70] IMF Country Report No. 06/114 March 2006 Islamic Republic of Afghanistan: Selected Issues and Statistical Appendix Table 40. Islamic Republic of Afghanistan: Direction of Trade, 2001/02–2005/06, March 2006, www.imf.org/external/pubs/ft/scr/2006/cr06114.pdf (accessed 30 January 2007).
[71] Xinhua's China Economic Information Service, Feb 6 2006.

Table 2. Afghanistan: Direction of Trade 2001–02/2005–06

	2001–02	2002–03	2003-04	2004-05	2005-06
Exports	100	100	100	100	100
Pakistan	39	26	69	85	85
India	15	27	8	7	7
Other	46	47	23	8	8
Imports	100	100	100	100	100
Pakistan	9	8	9	15	15
Japan	35	41	14	16	16
China	2	1	18	18	18
Other	54	50	59	51	51

Source: IMF Country Report No. 06/114 March 2006 Islamic Republic of Afghanistan: Selected Issues and Statistical Appendix.

Chinese companies have also shown some interest in investing in Afghanistan, although there is significant undeveloped potential even here. In 2003, for instance, a Chinese trading firm China Merchandise Trade Center Ltd opened an office in Kabul, marketing approximately 1,000 Chinese wholesale products.[72] According to President Karzai, some 100 Afghan businessmen also went to China that same year.[73] Chinese companies ZTE and Huawei are partnering with the Afghan Ministry of Communications to implement digital telephone switches and are providing roughly 200,000 subscriber lines.[74] China has taken part in the reconstruction of Afghanistan's infrastructure by participating in the Parwan irrigation project, restoring water supply in Parwar province, as well as the reconstruction of the public hospital in Kabul.[75] The U.S. has also hired Chinese firms for various construction projects in Afghanistan.

Afghanistan and Pakistan

Pakistan is by far Afghanistan's most important trading partner in Greater Central Asia. Today, 85 percent of Afghanistan's exports are sent to

---

72 "First Chinese trade firm opens in Afghan Capital," *People's Daily*, 30 July, 2003.

73 "Karzai: Deem neighbourhood with China an Honour," *People's Daily*, 16 July, 2004.

74 Ministry of Communications, Islamic Republic of Afghanistan. website: <http://www.moc.gov.af/vendors.asp> (accessed 28 March,2006).

75 The Economic and Commercial Counsellor's Office of the Embassy of the PRC in Afghanistan, Communique of Vice President Zeng Qinghong's talks with Afghan Vice President Nimartullah Sharani, 28 November, 2004.

Pakistan, while Pakistani exports to Afghanistan represent 15 percent of Afghan total imports. This strong bilateral trade results primarily from the improved political situation in Afghanistan, macro-economic stabilization in Pakistan, and a surge of Pakistani investment in Afghanistan.[76]

Although this development is favorable for the Afghan economy, Afghanistan would be well advised to reduce its export dependency on Pakistan by forging stronger ties with other states in the region.[77] The current dependence on Pakistan leaves Afghanistan vulnerable to exogenous shocks.[78] By opening up its north/northwest corridors through improvements in infrastructure, Afghanistan has the potential to become the center of regional and continental trade and an important transit point on both the east/west and the north/south routes.[79]

Here, China could play an even more important role. The Chinese project of linking the Gwadar port in the Arabian Sea to Xinjiang via both Pakistan and Afghanistan/Tajikistan will intensify Afghanistan's trade, as will the proposed project of a highway from Gwadar to Kandahar and Islamabad.[80] These routes will make it possible for Chinese goods to transit Afghanistan on their way to Gwadar.

Impediments to China's Active Involvement with Continental Trade Involving Greater Central Asia

Despite these impressive developments in Sino-Greater Central Asian economic integration, several important impediments to further cooperation remain. These impediments could compromise the revival of the open economic space that once existed between the Central Asian states.

The single most important impediments are bureaucratic delays at borders and costs caused by demands for unofficial payments. Transport from

---

76 Starr, "Central Asia's Reemerging Transport Network,", 2005, p. 6.

77 IMF Country Report No. 06/114 March 2006 Islamic Republic of Afghanistan: Selected Issues and Statistical Appendix Table 40. Islamic Republic of Afghanistan: Direction of Trade, 2001/02–2005/06

78 Ibid.

79 Starr, "Central Asia's Reemerging Transport Network,", 2005, p.3.

80 Ibid, p.2.

Xinjiang through Central Asia entails delays, uncertainty, unofficial payments, legal perplexity, and a number of other problems.[81] A recent survey of continental truck drivers passing through the Greater Central Asia region was revealing: almost none cited security or corruption as a major concern, while only one-third cited poor roads as impediments to trade. However, 96 percent of them pointed to lengthy waits at customs as the main impediment to trade.[82] Reducing border inefficiency and slow waits is the sine qua non for expanding continental trade.

Xinjiang and Greater Central Asia will suffer from high transport costs to world markets due to their land-locked locations. But transport times are quite a different matter, however.[83] High transport costs to and from the region can be partly mitigated by low production costs, but long transport times cannot. As stated by Lucke and Rothert, "Long transport times are likely to be an obstacle to trade development quite apart from direct *transport costs* (...) As participation in production networks requires just-in-time deliveries of goods along the production chain, long (and presumably variable) transport times render it more difficult for Central Asian firms to initiate non-traditional exports by participating in production networks."[84] This has important implications for the formulation of a strategy on infrastructural problems in Central Asia. Haulers waiting at borders generate expense through wages and inoperative trucks. Arbitrary and unpredictable transport times can disrupt an entire production chain. A quantitative

---

[81] Martha Blaxall, presentation at Forum "China's Emergence in Central Asia; Security, Diplomacy and Economic Interests: Energy and Trade in China-Central Asian relations," Washington DC, CSIS, 22 April, 2003.

[82] See Nicklas Norling, "First Kabul Conference on Partnership, Trade and Development in Greater Central Asia," Central Asia-Caucasus Institute and Silk Road Studies Program, Washington, DC, 2006, p.6.

[83] It has been estimated that transport costs in Central Asia amount to as much as 60 percent of the value of manufactured imports. See Statement by H.E. Mrs. Madilna B. Jarbussynova, Ambassador Permanent Representative of Republic of Kazakhstan to the United Nations, Agenda item 92 (a), New York, 26 October, 2000, www.un.int/kazakhstan/s_261000.htm (accessed on 30 January 2007)

[84] Matthias Lucke and Jacek Rothert, "Comparative Advantage in International Trade for Central Asia," Paper commissioned for ADB, Kiel Institute of World Economics, January 2006, p. 11 < http://siteresources.worldbank.org/INTTRADERESEARCH/Resources/Luecke_Rothert-Comp_Adv_Central_Asia-Jan2006.pdf> (accessed on 31 January 2007).

assessment made by the OECD of the different effects of direct (e.g., extensive documentation requirements) and indirect (e.g., slow waits) trade transactional costs argues that reducing waiting times at borders has a more marked effect than the reduction of documentation requirements.[85] To boost competitiveness, the Greater Central Asia states and Xinjiang should attack this problem by developing a functioning logistics network and improving border efficiency, rather than by subsidizing transport operators in order to lower transport charges.

Rail Transport (China-Kazakhstan)

Presently, railroads carry 75 percent of all trade between China and the Central Asian republics. However, the Druzhba-Ala pass is increasingly becoming a bottleneck and the differences in gauge-width between China and Kazakhstan delay cargo significantly. The problem is worst on the Kazakh side, in Ala, where cargo has to be manually off-loaded and transferred to Chinese train cars. The situation on the Chinese side, in Druzhba, is markedly better where Chinese trains go through a retrofit of wheels that adjusts them to the Kazakh system.[86] Incoming goods from Kazakhstan now include raw materials and other bulky items, while Chinese exports are low- bulk manufactures. This results in shortage of Chinese railcars from the border to Urumchi and lengthy waits estimated to be 3–5 days for cargo at borders.[87] This of course is part of a broader problem caused by China's overall trade imbalance. This is especially so in sea-borne transports, where ships are forced to return empty on their back-haul from America and Europe.[88]

---

[85] OECD, Quantitative Assessment of the Benefits of Trade Facilitation, 2003, p.4.
[86] Ibid, p. 38.
[87] Ibid, p. 38.
[88] Thomas Fuller , "China trade unbalances shipping," *International Herald Tribune*, January 30, 2006.

Road Transport (China-Kazakhstan)

Due to bottlenecks in rail transport, road transport has become increasingly popular, not least because of the greater flexibility in distribution it allows. The road through Horgos is becoming a more viable option and will relieve pressure on the Druzhba-Ala pass. China has begun to rehabilitate the Jinhezhi-Yining-Horgos route, and this alternative route will reduce the distance between Urumchi and Almaty by 200km.[89] As with Druzhba-Ala, there is a significant trade-imbalance at Horgos with trucks rolling full en route to the Kazakh border but returning empty.[90] Overall, rail transport, if available, would be the preferred alternative as it is cheaper, safer, and more certain.[91] As China is not yet a signatory to the TIR convention, trucks from China and Xinjiang cannot enter Kazakhstan. Although an exemption is made for trucks accessing border trading zones in Kazakhstan, and though trucks may access Almaty from Xinjiang, they cannot go as far as Astana. Instead, trucks usually stop at the border, where goods are unloaded while waiting for permission to travel into foreign territory. This imposes high transaction costs, as cargo may be delayed up to half a month at the border.[92]

The impact of poor infrastructure is even more severe in the energy sector. The lack of a regional energy strategy not only prevents economies of scale through pooled investments but also increases costs in transporting energy outside of the region. For example, the export of gas-generated electricity from Turkmenistan and Uzbekistan to Herat and the north of Afghanistan is conducted over Soviet-era lines, while Kyrgyz electricity destined for Xinjiang is limited due to inadequate electric transmission lines.[93] In all the new Atasu-Alashankou pipeline connecting China with Kazakhstan is a major boost, but more work remains. Participating countries have to date depended on their own limited solutions, pursuing their few cooperative measures bilaterally only rather then multilaterally. Meanwhile, the business

---

89 ADB, *Xinjiang Autonoumos Region*, 2005, p. 33-34.
90 Ibid, p. 46.
91 Ibid, p. 33.
92 Eva Molnar and Lauri Ojala, Transport and Trade Facilitation Issues in the CIS-7, Kazakhtan, and Turkmenistan, The paper was prepared for the Lucerne Conference of the CIS-7 Initiative, 20th-22nd January 2003.
93 Starr, "Central Asia's Reemerging Transport Network," 2005, p.3.

sector has been developing cooperative energy projects without clear policy direction at the governmental level.[94] The obvious step towards improving energy cooperation between Tajikistan and Afghanistan is the restoration of the electricity exporting capacity to 100 kV from 35 kV, which the U.S. is now undertaking. But even this is a rare exception.

Infrastructure within Greater Central Asia

The failure of Central Asian states to integrate their infrastructures with neighbouring countries is due both to political mistrust and the lack of financing. Politics intervened when Kazakhstan built the Kuzylasker-Kirovskii road from the Chardara Reservoir in the south; it was not connected with Uzbekistan as would have made sense geographically. Similarly, Kyrgyzstan, made a $12 million upgrade of the Jalal-Abad to Uzgen road in order to avoid passing through Uzbekistan, and Turkmenistan has avoided linking Uzbekistan into its new rail line connecting Kerkishi snd the Amu Darya valley. Uzbekistan, in turn, has responded by excluding Turkmenistan from its $10 million Uchkuduk-Misken-Karauzak rail line connecting Bukhara with Nukus via Navoi. While these improvements of national infrastructure certainly have benefited domestic movement of goods and people, they hamper the possibilities of regional trade and entrench a system of continued border rigidity.[95]

The problem of poor infrastructure is exemplified by the link between Osh and Bishkek in Kyrgyzstan and Dushanbe and Khorog in Tajikistan. Other key infrastructure is simply non-existent. As stated by Kydykbek Isaev, Director General of the Kyrgyz Railways National Company, "The railway system of Kyrgyzstan is divided into two parts—northern and southern. The absence of reliable contacts between the two economically developed regions of the country creates a number of economic, social, and political problems."[96]

---

[94] Kim Hyun-Jae & Shim Sang-Yul, "Operation and Support of the SOM and Conference for Energy Cooperation in Northeast Asia," *KEEI* (March 2004): 3.

[95] UNDP, Central Asia Human Development Report, 2005, p. 61.

[96] "Numbers of Chinese companies are united and ready to participate in construction of railway China-Kyrgyzstan-Uzbekistan," *Kabar*, December 29 2005.

The mountainous nature of the region also affects prospects for a regional economy and the equal distribution of trade gains. To include remote mountain areas, there is a need to build costly secondary roads, communication systems, and access to new highway systems. Only then will rural and mountainous areas have a chance of survival as economic integration goes forward.[97] If not, backwardness and underdevelopment is a natural consequence, and that is why regional cooperation, the building of infrastructure, and the reduction of trade barriers is even more important in mountainous zones than in coastal areas.[98] Moreover, there are few trans-regional transportation systems such as buses and trains. This impacts the flow of merchandise and people to and from the region and reduces prospects of business interaction across regions. To be sure there has been some progress, for example, the new bus links between Tajikistan and Kashgar in western China and the new bus services between China and Pakistan, but much remains to be done.[99]

There is also a need to integrate Afghanistan into the regional network. The construction of the Dushanbe–Kurgonteppe–Kolkhozobod–Nizhny-Panj railway line with an exit to Afghanistan and the ADB-proposed rehabilitation of the Uzbek-Afghan rail link are two of many projects with obvious potential for such integration.[100]

There is also lack of cooperation between local banks and those foreign banks that could assist Central Asian traders in China.[101] By contrast, Chinese traders in Central Asia have received support from their national banking system and trade offices. Chinese trade offices have opened in all five Central Asian states, while the Bank of China and the Industrial and Commercial Bank of China have representatives in Kazakhstan.

---

97 Starr,"Central Asia's Reemerging Transport Network," 2005, p.10.

98 Paramonov, "China and Central Asia," 2005, p.10.

99 Zafar Abdullaev and Lydia Isamova, "Tajikistan looks to the East," *RCA*, No. 303, July 27 2004.

100 CAREC, Central Asia Regional Economic Cooperation Member Countries: Regional Cooperation Strategy and Program, 2005-2007.

101 Martin Spechler, 2003, p.278.

Security impediments to China's deeper engagement in Greater Central Asia and continental trade have two dimensions: first, the direct threats to Chinese citizens, entrepreneurs, and construction workers in Pakistan and Greater Central Asia; and the more overarching security threats of drug-trafficking, terrorism, and cross-border criminality. Although both of these may impede the expansion of regional and continental trade, they do not impede trade to the extent often claimed, nor do they put any significant brakes on Beijing's expansion into the region. In fact, the causation may be reversed, as increased economic interaction inadvertently gives rise to a safer and more stable security environment. Nonetheless, Chinese concern over separatism and over unstable socio-political climate in Central Asia have moderated Beijing's determination to boost trans-border trade and investment initiatives.

One of the foremost concerns for Beijing is the fear that the weak Central Asian states could provide safe-havens for various kinds of criminal groups. The Chinese point in particular to the Semirechye region in Kazakhstan, the Ferghana valley in Uzbekistan, Osh in Kyrgyzstan, and Khojent in Tajikistan. Worse, China believes that these areas are home to groups affiliated with Xinjiang's separatist movements.[102] The almost unchecked drug economy in Afghanistan, and Tajikistan also affects China's willingness to decrease border controls and increase cross-border trade.[103]

Attacks on Chinese workers in Pakistan and Afghanistan have to some extent also affected Chinese engagement in these countries. In February 2006, the Balochistan Liberation Army (BLA) killed three Chinese workers and their driver in southern Pakistan just prior to Pakistani President Musharraf's state visit to China.[104] Chinese workers in Gwadar have been targeted occasionally as well,[105] restoration work on the Karakorum Highway has also been negatively affected by terrorist activities and cross-border

[102] Xu Tao, "Central Asian Countries' Security Strategies and China's Western Border Security", *Strategy and Management*, No.5, 2006

[103] Xing Guangcheng, "Security Cooperation in Central Asia", *Contemporary World, Iss.* 282, 2005.

[104] "Pakistan: Chinese Workers Shot Dead," *Stratfor Situation Reports*, February 15 2006.

[105] See for instance B. Raman's account of "The Blast in Gwadar," *South Asia Analysis Group* paper No. 993, 8 May 2004.

crimes.[106] Further the slaying of eleven Chinese workers near the Northern Afghan city of Kunduz in 2004 provoked a strong Chinese reaction.[107] The recently proposed pipeline running from Gwadar to Xinjiang, as well as Iranian energy supplies transiting Baluchistan by road are both impeded by separatist activity in the Pakistani region province of Baluchistan.[108]

All in all, security concerns serve as a caution flag as Beijing expands trade with Greater Central Asia and Pakistan.[109] Yet of the impediments affecting trade, security should not be over-estimated as a factor determining trade policies, for Beijing realizes that increased trade with its neighbors will alleviate the security situation in the long term.

Even though some improvements have been seen in the political climate, especially in Kazakhstan and Afghanistan, further efforts are needed. Uzbekistan's strict control over foreign investments have all but killed major investments.[110] Corruption is a further reason cited by foreign investors for staying out of the region.[111] The weak legal frameworks of the Central Asian countries are another major impediment to investments and economic development. As countries become independent, judicial remedies become inaccessible in many situations. These factors made the Central Asian region less competitive and unattractive for foreign investors, while simultaneously fostering corruption and abuse of the legal system. Central Asia is still suffering from turbulence in its legal systems.[112]

Protectionism represents a further brake on cooperation and integration. This varies from high protective tariffs in Uzbekistan, with lower tariffs in

---

[106] "Sino-Pak. Energy Corridor: A Tentative Analysis of Feasibility", *Economic Times* (China), 2 March, 2006

[107] See for example, "Attack on Chinese Workers in Afghanistan Condemned," *People's Daily*, 11 June ,2004.

[108] B. Raman, "Chinese Presence in Balochistan & Northern Areas," *South Asia Analysis Group* Paper no. 1809, 2006.

[109] Ji Fangtong & Zhu Xinguang, "Central Asian Non-traditional Security Cooperation in Post-Cold War Scenario", *World Economics and Politics*, No. 5, 2004

[110] Hsiu-Ling Wu & Chien-Hsun Chen, "The Prospects for Regional Economic Integration," 2004, p. 1074.

[111] UNDP, Central Asia Human Development Report, 2005, p. 63.

[112] Hsiu-Ling Wu & Chien-Hsun Chen, "The Prospects for Regional Economic Integration," 2004, p.1076.

Kazakhstan, and lower ones still in Kyrgyzstan and Tajikistan. Protectionist trade policies have effectively prevented a return to the old intra-regional trade patterns that previously united the extended region. Wherever it exists, protectionism raises the real exchange rate, levying a heavy burden on companies, which they pass along in the form of higher prices.[113]

In addition, border disputes can interrupt water flows and energy supplies, sowing uncertainty among farmers and villagers who need predictable supplies of both.[114] The failure to meet these challenges is partly rooted in the lack of effective region-wide cooperative structures in Greater Central Asia. This is due tin part to fears that Uzbekistan aspires to become a potential regional hegemon.[115]

Unfortunately, some of the trading agreements that have been reached in the region have adversely affected the regional economy. Apart from the fact that the initiatives of the CIS, EURASEC, SES, and ECO remain toothless abstraction, their full implementation could have destructive consequences for some countries. A recent study by the ADB suggests that Kazakhstan, Kyrgyzstan, and Tajikistan are particularly vulnerable if the EURASEC customs union would be implemented, due to its effect on extra-regional trade. For Kazakhstan the cumulative shortfall would reach almost $10 billion, translating into a GDP that is 20.8 percent less by 2015, compared with the baseline scenario.[116] The report concludes: "We found that implementing the customs union, even with a reduction in Kazakhstan's external tariffs, would cause substantial trade diversion and slow down real GDP growth compared with the baseline scenario. Implementing the [EARASEC] customs union is likely to have even greater adverse

---

[113] Richard G. Lipsey, Peter O. Steiner, and Douglas D. Purvis, "The Gains From Trade," Chapter 40 in *Economics* 7 ed. (New York: Harper & Row Publishers, 1984).
[114] "Regional co-op key to Central Asian Integration," *China Daily*, 6 February, 2006.
[115] Richard Pomfret, "Trade policies in Central Asia after EU enlargement and before Russian WTO accession: regionalism and integration into the world economy", *Economic Systems* 29 (2005); Niklas L. P. Swanström, *Regional Cooperation and Conflict Management: Lessons from the Pacific Rim* (Department of Peace and Conflict Research: Uppsala University, 2002).
[116] Dowling and Wignaraja, "Mapping Future Prospects to 2015," p. 43.

macroeconomic effects on the Kyrgyz Republic and Tajikistan than in Kazakhstan."[117]

These various impediments will have adverse long -term effects on Central Asia's development in other sectors. If the present trend continues, with Central Asia serving mainly as a natural resource base for China and Russia, it will erode the region's processing industries and drain capital. China will supply cheap manufactures to the detriment of Central Asia's long-term human-resource and capacity development. This suggests that China will eventually have to actively promote the development of Central Asia's human resources if it truly seeks stability and prosperity for the region. This is not needed in Central Asia only, but also in Xinjiang, where massive amounts of investment have been devoted to infrastructure, but almost none to human capital, health, or education.[118] Considering the high transport costs incurred on goods, an expansion of local manufacturing industries will also reduce expenditures on transport.

An example of such encouragement, but which also proves the depreciation of human capital in parts of Central Asia, is the Lishida Yarn Factory in Tajikistan. The factory was established as a joint Sino-Tajik venture at a total capitalization of $9.74 million with the assistance of the Export-Import Bank of China. However, the firm has ceased production due to a lack of experienced Tajik managers, as well as a shortage of parts needed to repair production equipment.[119] Examples such as these will only increase until investments are made in Central Asian human capital.[120]

Means for Removing These Impediments and Their Estimated Costs

Security concerns, political impediments, and human-resource needs are crucial issues for facilitating regional and continental trade, the most

---

[117] Ibid, p. 44-45.

[118] OECD, *China in the Global Economy Challenges for China's Public Spending: Toward Greater Effectiveness and Equity*, March 2006, p.6, www.oecd.org/dataoecd/18/26/36228704.pdf (accessed 30 January 2007)

[119] Hsiu-Ling Wu & Chien-Hsun Chen, "The Prospects for Regional Economic Integration," 2004, p.1074.

[120] Paramonov, "China and Central Asia," May 2005, p. 12.; see also Hsiu-Ling Wu & Chien-Hsun Chen, "The Prospects for Regional Economic Integration," 2004, p. 1061.

important step to this end is reduction of long waits at borders and the streamlining of transport times and costs. Only then can Greater Central Asia take advantage of its location at the cross-roads of major transport corridors. This suggests that urgent efforts should be devoted to reduction of these barriers. Regional initiatives such as EURASEC, ECO and SCO should be commanded, yet many of these same initiatives have actually complicated trade (i.e., the spaghetti bowl effect).[121]

China is currently working to join the TIR convention that will bring its road transport system with international standards. Due to the increasing significance of the Horgos border crossing in continental truck trade, it is all the more important for standards to be harmonized between China and Central Asia, and that Chinese and Kazakh trucks can enter each others country. Further expansion of the Horgos border processing will also relieve Druzhba-Ala and help balance trade flows from Central Asia. The TIR convention will speed the flow of goods from China to Europe as goods transported under the TIR convention are exempted from customs inspections. The TIR convention will also require China to stop subsidizing the transport industry in Xinjiang. This significantly distorts competition and imbalances trade flows, as bulky high-volume items from Central Asia can be transported at prices far below market costs.[122]

The problem with the TIR convention is that it is costly for entrepreneurs to implement it. Trucks have to meet very demanding and expensive standards and truckers need to carry insurance to cover the potential loss of TIR-transported goods. Although the cost of insurance is costly it can be offset by potential profits. New trucks that meet the Euro-class 3/5 emission requirements cost between $70,000 and $100,000, making them unaffordable for Central Asian firms. Still, the implementation of the TIR system is crucial if overland continental trade is to develop. A possible solution is to temporarily exempt small-sized trucking firms from emission and vehicle requirements. As truckers benefit from increasing volumes, they should be

---

[121] See for example, UNDP, *Bringing Down Barriers*, 2005.

[122] ADB, *Xinjiang Autonomous Region*, November 2005, p.70.

able to afford new trucks that will fully meet TIR requirements, at which time the full TIR convention can be implemented.

For Afghanistan, Kazakhstan, Tajikistan and Uzbekistan, the most important potential trade framework is the World Trade Organization (WTO). The membership of China, India, Pakistan, and Kyrgyzstan, combined with Russia's expected accession, leaves the remaining Greater Central Asian states encircled by WTO states without preferential market access to these countries. WTO accession could expand bilateral trade significantly, while giving the benefits of most-favored nation (MFN) status. Beyond all of this, WTO membership will bring greater access to world markets.

All Greater Central Asia countries have started accession negotiations, but only Kazakhstan has made most progress. The costs of joining WTO are small and are mainly associated with the negotiation process e.g., building national institutions, preparing accession documents, as well as the actual negotiations. But WTO membership also limits policy options, such as relying on strategies of import substitution strategies. And while there should be no doubt about the potential benefits of WTO membership, without good governance these gains will go unrealized.[123]

China has shown interest in making infrastructure investments in Central Asia, primarily in the regions neighbouring Xinjiang and in countries with which they share major business interests. Some of the road construction projects are unlikely to be completed, like the Kashgar–Torugart–Jalalabad road, which is projected to cost over $1 billion due to the difficult terrain.[124] Even with the projected trade volume of 10 million tons on this route, the project will not be financially viable. Other projects, like the construction of a new Urumchi-Horgos-Almaty line, are relatively cheap ($300 million) and will reduce bottlenecks. Newly constructed roads or upgraded roads along the most heavily used corridors should also reduce impediments, especially on the Bishkek-Torugart and Tashkent-Bishkek-Almaty-Horgos-Urumchi

---

[123] OECD, OECD Regional Trade Forum on Economic and Trade Implications of the WTO Accession, Almaty, June 3-4 2004. TD/TC/WP(2004)19/FINAL.

[124] See for example John W. Garver, "China's Development of Overland Transport Links," 2006.

roads, as well as on the Andijan-Osh-Irkeshtan route.[125] These international transport corridors need in turn to be linked with national transport routes to disperse the benefits to all regions of each state.

Although new roads would be of great benefit, there is also an urgent need to develop further the logistics and customs sector. Expanded warehouses at Horgos and Druzhba-Ala would help to meet the growing volume of trade, and there is an urgent need to decrease the manual handling of goods.[126] To increase efficiency in the logistics sector, it will be important to create a more even flow of goods across the border by reducing trade imbalances. This is best accomplished through the further development of additional main border posts, the elimination of subsidies in the transport sector, and the promotion of manufacturing and processing in Central Asia so as to reduce the high volume/low value one-way trade in raw materials.

Overall, it will be necessary to increase the current combined annual spending of approximately $1 billion on Central Asian infrastructure. Some estimate that for Central Asia to sustain growth this figure must be raised to $2-$3 billion for each year down until 2010.[127] There is also a need to integrate Afghanistan more closely with former Soviet parts of Central Asia. These projects mainly involve the rehabilitation of existing roads, bridges, and tunnels such as the Freedom bridge linking Afghanistan at Termez in Uzbekistan and the Salang tunnel further south.[128]

Energy Cooperation

Considering the substantial complementarities in this sector, energy cooperation has great potential for the region. There have been several attempts at bilateral and trilateral energy cooperation, and even some cases of multilateral energy cooperation such as ASEAN+3, the Shanghai

---

[125] ADB, The 2020 Project: Policy Support in the People's Republic of China, Manila,2003, p. 133.

[126] ADB, Xinjiang Autonomous Region, November 2005, p.65.

[127] Dowling and Wignaraja, "Mapping Future Prospects to 2015,"p.36

[128] Frederick Starr, "Afghanistan: Free Trade and Regional Transformation," for the *Asia Society*, <http://www.cacianalyst.org/Publications/Starr_Asia_Society_Afghanistan.htm?SMSESSION=NO> (accessed 28 March , 2006).

Cooperation Organization, and the Northeast Asian Economic Forum. A serious problem with these programs to date is that they do not take into account the interests of all actors, including the national sources of natural resources, the refining points, and the transit countries for oil and gas. Successful integration needs to include all available actors in a truly multilateral forum. There have been several suggestions on how best to accomplish regional cooperation on energy issues.[129] But as yet there are very few actual mechanisms in the region to make such cooperation real. The geo-strategic aspect of energy greatly complicate matters, with Moscow, for example, keeping Beijing's proposals for a true "strategic partnership" in energy at arm's length.[130]

There are no organizations in Eurasia today that have the credibility needed to bring about such cooperation. Most states acknowledge the need for further cooperation. For example, China developed a strategy for energy security in the 1990s called the "Pan-Asian Continental Oil Bridge" that would link Japan with the Middle East by means of structures that would have been under Chinese control.[131] From a Chinese perspective this was seen as positive, since the regional economies would become tied with one another. Others in the region viewed this as a bold attempt by China to dominate regional markets. Doubtless, any state that controls the energy transit routes would have significant power in the region.

The picture is further complicated by the fact that major external actors would view strengthened energy cooperation on the Eurasian continent with suspicion since it would, over time, integrate participating states both economically and politically. Such a Eurasian energy bloc might decrease the political and economic influence of the European Union, Middle East states,

---

[129] Vladimir Ivanov, "Creating a Cohesive Multilateral Framework Through a New Energy Security Initiative for Northeast Asia," ERINA Report 55,December 2003. < www.erina.or.jp/En/Research/Energy/Ivanov55.pdf> (October 30, 2005)
Vladimir Ivanov, "An Energy Community for Northeast Asia: From a Dream to Strategy," *ERINA Report* 52. (June 2003) <www.erina.or.jp/Jp/Research/db/rep15/RS-EE/04070.pdf> (October 30, 2005)

[130] "China dissatisfied with energy cooperation with Russia," Interfax China, 3 March, 2006.

[131] Gaye Christoffersen, Problems & Prospects for Northeast Asian Energy Cooperation, Paper presented at IREX, 23 March, 2000.

and, most important, the United States. If such a grand project is to succeed, it needs strong external support similar to that which was received during the formative period of the European Coal and Steel Community (ECSC) project. This will also further the interest of the Euro-Atlantic community.

It all boils down to giving both consumers and producers as many options as possible. Energy cooperation and diversified export routes could increase confidence at all levels and reduce Russia's leverage over its former dependents. The construction of the Baku-Tbilisi-Ceyhan pipeline was a landmark in this regard. The trans-Afghan pipeline (Turkmenistan-Afghanistan-Pakistan-India) could open up similar vistas, as a confidence-building measure between India and Pakistan, a symbol of normalization in Afghanistan, and a window to the south for Turkmenistan—a state now strongly subject to control from Russia. Just as the BTC pipeline would have been financially impossible without Western backing, most of the planned pipelines on the Eurasian continent have similar conditions for realization, often requiring the involvement of China, Russia or both. Though all may not be fully cost-effective, they could all have huge political pay-offs in terms of strengthened sovereignties and better mutual relations.

Conclusions

The development of continental trade on the Eurasian landmass represents a true win-win situation. China is becoming an ever more important trading partner for states in the region and also for Azerbaijan, Russia, Pakistan, and Iran. If impediments are removed, China will realize its four aims in the region: the development of Xinjiang; political and regional stability; energy security; and an alternative transport corridor to Europe and South Asia. Trade facilitation would likely raise GDP in Xinjiang and the Greater Central Asian states from two to three percent, with the second Eurasian land bridge forming the backbone for this growth.

There is also unexplored bilateral trade potential between China and Greater Central Asia if a trading regime is set up with greater efficiency than the current muddle of agreements. Bilateral trade could triple in the case of Tajikistan, or double in the case of Kazakhstan. Already, the bourgeoning trade is bringing considerable benefits, although much state income is lost with the increase of shuttle trade between China and Greater Central Asia that is a result of continuing obstacles to trade. Further advances in both regional and continental trade will require that such issues as the impediments to road and rail transport at the Sino-Kazakh border and within Central Asia be addressed. Overall, the most urgent issues are the lengthy waits at borders and uncertain transport times and costs.

To remove these impediments it is recommended that China and various Central Asian countries sign and implement the TIR convention; that states of the Greater Central Asia receive help in the WTO accession process; that $2–3 billion are invested annually in infrastructure, with a sizeable portion of this devoted to the customs and logistics sectors; and that donor countries, the private sector, and international organizations realize the potential gains of energy cooperation in Eurasia and act on that realization.

In contrast to the empty talk of a "new Great Game" in Central Asia and its immediate surroundings, the reality is that the real "game" today is in the construction of infrastructure and the ability of "players" to be as well-connected as possible across region.[132] The monopoly that Russia held over Central Asian and Caucasian infrastructure is waning, promising greater market-access for these countries. Pipelines as well as transport routes are increasingly bypassing Russia - for example the Baku-Tbilisi-Ceyhan pipeline, the trans-Caspian pipeline, the second Eurasian land-bridge, the bridges of the Panj River linking Tajikistan and Afghanistan, and all the other hundreds of projects proposed for the region. All these are opening new transport routes and trade outlets for the former Soviet dependents.

Most existing regional trade agreements, including the Russia-dominated Eurasec, will harm rather than facilitate trade. This agreement will effectively maintain the Central Asian states within the Russian orbit and deny them market access beyond the former Soviet borders, which this is scarcely in the best interests of the Central Asian states, let alone of their emerging trading partners in Afghanistan, India, China, Pakistan, and Turkey. Instead, adherence to the most vital international regulatory

---

[132] Stephen Blank, "Infrastructural Policy and National Strategies in Central Asia: the Russian Example," *Central Asian Survey* 23, 3-4 (December 2004).

frameworks (e.g., the WTO and the TIR) would give both China and the Greater Central Asian states access to preferential trading terms on the world market, as well as the possibility of transport capacities sufficient to carry their products to these markets.

Appendix 1. Chinese Customs Statistics: Trade Between China and Central Asia (in $1,000)

		Kazakh-stan	Uzbek-istan	Kyrgyz-stan	Tajik-istan	Turk-menistan	Total
1992	Trade Volume	369,100	52,520	35,490	2,750	4,500	464,360
	China's Exports	227,930	38,890	18,850	1,950	4,090	291,710
	China's Imports	141,170	13,630	16,640	800	410	172,650
1993	Trade Volume	434,730	54,250	102,420	12,350	4,650	608,400
	China's Exports	171,690	42,800	36,550	6,480	3,850	261,370
	China's Imports	263,040	11,460	65,870	5,880	800	347,050
1994	Trade Volume	335,654	123,667	105,375	3,177	11,260	579,133
	China's Exports	138,689	51,458	29,925	675	3,669	224,416
	China's Imports	196,965	72,209	75,450	2,502	7,591	354,717
1995	Trade Volume	390,992	118,552	231,039	23,859	17,595	782,037
	China's Exports	75,447	47,566	107,498	14,617	11,267	256,395
	China's Imports	315,545	70,986	123,541	9,242	6,328	525,642
1996	Trade Volume	459,901	187,258	105,494	11,715	11,467	775,835
	China's Exports	95,306	38,154	68,678	7,640	8,452	218,230
	China's Imports	364,596	149,104	36,816	4,075	3,015	557,606
1997	Trade Volume	527,410	202,916	106,622	20,227	15,240	872,415
	China's Exports	94,628	61,528	70,601	11,045	11,633	249,435
	China's Imports	432,782	141,388	36,021	9,182	3,606	622,979
1998	Trade Volume	635,537	90,245	198,099	19,229	12,516	955,626
	China's Exports	204,681	57,833	172,406	11,042	10,293	456,305
	China's Imports	430,856	32,362	25,692	8,187	2,223	499,320
1999	Trade Volume	1,138,779	40,336	134,871	8,041	9,491	1,331,518
	China's Exports	494,375	27,388	102,899	2,298	7,468	634,428
	China's Imports	644,404	12,948	31,972	5,743	2,023	697,090
2000	Trade Volume	1,556,958	51,465	177,611	17,170	16,159	1,819,363
	China's Exports	598,749	39,432	110,174	6,793	12,102	767,250
	China's Imports	958,209	12,033	67,437	10,377	4,057	1,052,113
2001	Trade Volume	1,288,369	58,301	118,859	10,760	32,712	1,509,001
	China's Exports	327,719	50,684	76,639	5,308	31,488	491,838
	China's Imports	960,651	7,617	42,221	5,452	1,224	1,017,165
2002	Trade Volume	1,954,742	131,777	201,874	12,386	87,515	2,388,294
	China's Exports	600,097	104,374	146,156	6,501	86,780	943,908
	China's Imports	1,354,645	27,403	55,718	5,886	735	1,444,387
2003*	Trade Volume	3,300,000	346,000	317,000	38,000	99,000	4,100,000
2004**	Trade Volume	4,493,305	575,174	602,207	N/A	98,680	5,769,366
2005***	Trade Volume	6,117,294	627,899	838,692	N/A	100,863	7,684,748

Sources: 1992–2002 Chinese Customs Statistics, 2003 (corrected version from Hsiu-Ling Wu & Chien-Hsun Chen 2004; 2003* Xinhua (from Paramonov, 2005); 2004** Xinhua's China Economic Information Service, February 7, 2006, based on Chinese Customs Statistics; 2005*** Xinhua's China Economic Information Service, February 7, 2006, based on Chinese Customs Statistics (Note: only January-November 2005).

Turkey

Kemal Kaya

Historical Background

After the fall of the Soviet Union, both pessimistic and optimistic scenarios on the future of Central Asia emerged. Pessimistic views arose from the prediction of some Western analysts that Islamic fundamentalism would become the primary threat to the region's future, and from the Central Asian governments' inability to mitigate economic stagnation following the Soviet collapse. Typically, pessimists foresaw the emergence of radical Islamic nations, the proliferation of nuclear weapons, Chinese domination, wars among territorial states and clashes of civilizations. The optimists, by contrast, anticipated democratization, free market economies, integration with the West, improved economic welfare, and the total elimination of Soviet institutions and establishments. Consequent events revealed that both of these simplistic views were flawed.[1]

In the early 1990s the international community and international organizations noted that nearly all Central Asian States faced a difficult transition from the Soviet regime, including negative economic growth coupled with very high inflation rates. As the economies shrank, most people became poorer, governments lost power, the quality of public education decreased and public health worsened. Although the macroeconomic situation stabilized toward the end of the decade, the overall success of the transition process in the region was limited—it could even be argued that they have all failed.

---

[1] Eric W. Sievers, "Central Asia's Lost Capital Assets: Denial of Development or Curse of Globalization", The Geopolitical and Economic Transition in Eurasia: Problems and Prospects, Fatih University, Istanbul, May 2001, p.1

The bureaucratic establishment and centralized decision-making systems inherited from the Soviet Union played an important role in this failure. Starting at their inception in the early 1990s, republics of the former Soviet Union labored to replace central planning with price mechanisms, and market systems. But the Central Asian republics consistently lagged behind the transition in other countries formerly in the Soviet sphere —especially the South and East European states—in indicators of economic, social and economic competitiveness.[2]

The distance of the land-locked Central Asian republics to major markets and democratic states contributed to the slow and unsuccessful early transition process. Conversely, the countries of East and Central Europe and the Baltic states took advantage of their geographic proximity to the European Union (EU), gaining impetus for their reform processes. They efficiently liberalized prices and the banking sector, decreased inflation, and achieved a widespread privatization of state-owned enterprises.

The West's Attitude Toward Central Asia

Most western states have assumed a pragmatic but superficial attitude toward Central Asia. The United States and EU focused on the region's rich natural resources and, to a lesser extent, its security and stability. Western governments are often faced with the dilemma of weighing their strategic interests against other legitimate concerns that influence domestic public opinion, such as democratization and basic human rights.[3] Pragmatism overshadowed idealism as the West established and deepened relations with Central Asia. But, the 11 September, 2001 terrorist attacks caused security threats from the region to become a significant concern, which reshaped the West's perspectives and caused it to pay greater attention to Central Asia.

---

[2] Harry Broadman, World Bank Report, "From Disintegration to Reintegration: Eastern Europe and the Former Soviet Union in International Trade", Washington D.C., 2005, p.2, http://web.worldbank.org/WBSITE/EXTERNAL/COUNTRIES/ECAEXT/0,,contentMDK:20723133~pagePK:146736~piPK:146830~theSitePK:258599,00.html

[3] Vahit Erdem, "The Caucasus and Central Asia", NATO Parliamentary Assembly1995-2005, Brussel, 2005, p201

Security in the Euro-Atlantic area and beyond cannot be guaranteed as long as stability remains fragile in some areas, leaving them vulnerable to religious fundamentalism. After all, it was the fragility of government in Afghanistan that provided the fertile ground for the Taliban regime. In a post-September 11 era, Euro-Atlantic security has been closely linked to the situation in Central Asia. The social fabric in Central Asian states, and particularly in states neighboring Afghanistan, is not immune to fundamentalist trends: organized crime, porous borders and illegal migration are all endemic problems there. These issues cannot be resolved by anyone country acting alone and must instead be tackled through a process of international cooperation.[4] Part of the solution is to integrate Central Asian states into global commercial and financial institutions. By ensuring their economic stability and development they will be drawn into the international community. Economic instruments are key to this process for Central Asia. World Trade Organization membership for Uzbekistan, Tajikistan, Kazakhstan and Afghanistan should be a priority of the United States and the EU, since the accession process exerts a strong liberalizing pressure on the aspiring country and will facilitate economic growth.

Turkey's Relations with Central Asia

Turkey was the first nation to recognize the independence of the Central Asian republics, yet it was unprepared to deal with its new neighbors. Despite limited resources and conceptual conflicts at the state and public levels, however, the Turkish state, private sector and civil society have all put a great deal of effort into developing relations with these countries. As a result, Turkey today has a significant political and social presence in Central Asia—a presence independent of any strategic or cyclical political interest.

Turkey's political, economic and social interests in Central Asia are stronger than those of its Western allies. Official Turkish opinion from the outset saw that a constructive role in Central Asia would enhance Turkey's

---

[4]Vahit Erdem, "The Caucasus and Central Asia", NATO Parliamentary Assembly 1995-2005, Brussel, 2005, p.205

international image and provide an opportunity to show goodwill towards its Western allies, the EU and United States in particular.

Relations between Turkey and the new states of Central Asia have now been put on a solidly rational basis after an initial period of romanticism. Immediately after independence, the new republics, quite inexperienced in international affairs, were unprepared for, and confused by, Turkey's keen interest in the region. The Turkish Cooperation and Development Agency (TIKA) was from the outset a vital instrument for providing aid, institutionalizing government policies, and devising economic strategies for Central Asia. Through TIKA, Turkey supported the new governments' state-building efforts. Indeed, 36 percent of all TIKA projects and programs focus on Central Asia, which is not surprising since the objectives of the Central Asian states mesh with Turkey's priorities. Recognizing this, TIKA since 1992 has developed and implemented numerous economic, administrative, social and cultural projects in Central Asia. The main emphasis has been on developing human resources, specifically the training of government officials, which has been supported by relevant offices of the Turkish government.[5] There have also been joint Turkish-Western projects, such as the Private Sector Development Center in Istanbul, which is sponsored by TIKA and the Organization for Economic Cooperation and Development (OECD). This project provides a platform for officials from developed country to share experiences with counterparts from Central Asia. Another such initiative is the OECD-Turkish Ministry of Finance Tax Training Center for Transition Economies, where training activities focus on support for small and medium-sized enterprise (SME), improving the investment climate, and reforms in the financial sector.

Political and economic instability in Central Asia is one of the most important regional challenges facing Turkish authorities, investors and non-governmental organizations (NGOs) that deal with region. However, Turkish entrepreneurs have been able to work successfully under conditions of instability, especially in SME investment, especially as compared to Western companies.

---

[5] For more information about the TIKA projects visit www.tika.gov.tr.

The language barrier was another problem faced by officials and investors during the first period of Turkey's relations with the new states of Central Asia. Russian is still the *lingua franca* in these countries, especially for members of the social elite who retained political control. Yet the states' Turkic roots facilitated Turkey's penetration into different sectors of the regional economies. As a result of deepening economic, political and cultural relations, and the practical needs of Turkish investors, Turkey started a scholarship program allowing Central Asian students to receive secondary and higher education in Turkey. Thousands of Central Asian students have graduated from Turkish universities and now work in Turkey or their home country. Many have found jobs in governmental institutions and international NGOs that focus on regional development, as well as in Turkish companies.

Turkish-run universities and secondary schools have established an important presence throughout the region. Both use Western teaching methods and are supported by the Turkish government and NGOs. Many graduates of these institutions pursue further studies at Turkish universities. Over the past decade and half, Turkish high schools have become among the most prestigious in Central Asia. True, there has been some political resistance to the concept of private secondary schools, both in the region and in Turkey, yet this has not posed a serious problem[6]. Regardless of whether they receive public or private funding, these Turkish secondary schools serve the practical purpose of educating the region's future workforce and providing an important cultural bridge between Turkey and Central Asia.

Turkey's relations with the Central Asian states are affected by its economic and political relations with surrounding countries. China, India, Iran, Russia and Pakistan all have vital strategic and economic interests in the region of which Turkey must be cognizant. They all will play a major role in the reemergence of continental trade in Eurasia.

---

[6]For Turkish Private Schools in Central Asia see Jean –Christophe Peuch, "Turkey's Fethullahci School's: A Greenhouse for Central Asian Elites?", www.rferl.org/reports/turkmen-report/2004/06/0-140604.asp Radio Free Europe, June, 2004.

Following the Soviet collapse, Turkish private firms and NGOs became very active in Russia. Over time, these commercial and cultural relations alleviated the political animosity that had long existed between Turkey and the Soviet Union. But Russia grew anxious over Turkey's presence in Central Asia and the Caucasus and by its ties to the groups in North Caucasus that sought independence. Turkey has tried to reduce these tensions by cooperating with Russia on key strategic issues such as energy. Yet Russia still seeks to maintain its weakening influence in the Caucasus by intervening in the Abkhazia and Ossetia conflicts in Georgia, and in the Karabakh conflict between Armenia and Azerbaijan. Russia is also seeking to dominate Kazakhstan and Turkmenistan by controlling the transport routes for their most valuable commodities—oil and natural gas. Given this. It is all the more important to note that in spite of Russian opposition, the Baku-Tbilisi-Ceyhan pipeline was fully implemented, thanks to crucial support from the United States.

Turkey is a gateway for Central Asian trade and energy transit, and will become a regional transit corridor within the framework of TRACECA, the EU's transportation program. The soon-to-be-implemented integration of Turkish railways with those of the region, and with the Kars-Ahalkale connection, will alter the means and dimensions of commerce between Turkey, the Caucasus, and Central Asia.

Increased world oil prices have forced the major energy-consuming states to seek alternative energy sources and routes. This has generated great interest in alternative transport routes for oil and natural gas from the Caspian Sea region to world markets. But Russia grows nervous over every new pipeline project that it does not control — particularly the Trans-Caspian Pipeline Project. Tensions arising from pipeline issues have tremendous potential to disrupt Turkish-Russian relations.

Turkish-Chinese relations began developing after China emerged as a rising economic power in the 1980s. Turkish-Chinese trade has been increasing every year, with Turkey running a negative trade balance with China. But since the 1950s disputes over East Turkistan (China's Xinjiang Uyghur Autonomous Region) have been a source of friction between the two countries. China is anxious about the actions of members of the East

Turkistan diaspora (mainly Uyghurs) who live in Turkey, following their activities closely and lodging diplomatic protest with Turkey whenever "unacceptable" activity is detected. Despite growing trade, the Xinjiang issue remains a potential problem between the two countries in the mid- and long-term. However, expandingtrade and China's support for Turkish defense industry projects have softened tensions. Thus, defying pressure from the West, Turkey in 2001 briefly closed the Bosphorus Strait to allow passage of the *Varyag* aircraft carrier that China had purchased from Ukraine.

Turkey's relations with India are shaped by the close Turkish-Pakistan relationship. However, Turkey's trade with both India and Pakistan is much lower than with the other countries that surround Greater Central Asia.

Turkish-Iranian relations have moved through several phases. Until the beginning of the twentieth century, Turkic dynasties ruled Iran, and throughout this shared history Iranian Turks warred with Ottoman-Western Turks. The existing border between Iran and Turkey was created in 1639 by the Kasrı Şirin accord, yet after the agreement the two sides continued fighting.[7] After the Republic of Turkey was established, ties between the two countries were strengthened by the fact that both were members of the pro-Western Central Treaty Organization (CENTO) and the Economic Cooperation Organization (ECO). Relations remained smooth until the Iranian Islamic revolution in 1978. Secular Turkey feared that the Islamist movement would cross its borders, yet Iran's eventual abandonment of the policy of exporting religious ideology to Turkey calmed relations, allowing economic and business ties once more to develop.

Yet Iran's nuclear ambitions and the resulting tension with the United States has damaged Turkish-Iranian relations. Mindful of the chaos in neighboring Iraq, Turkey is keen to find a peaceful solution to the stand-off with Iran and wants to help mediate critical issues. Turkey has informed Iran that its nuclear activities must be kept within peaceful limits and be open to international inspection. Tensions persist, though, endangering Turkish-

---

[7] Soner Çağatay and DudenYegenoğlu, "Exposing the myth of Lasting Iranian-Turkish Amity", Daily Star (Lebanon), May, 2006, for more information www.washingtoninstitute.org/templateC06.php?CID=931

Iranian relations and other relations throughout the region. Recent activity of the Azeri Turkic minority in Iran has also strained ties.[8] Notwithstanding, these various obstacles, Turkey wishes to maintain good relations with Iran and seeks to strengthen ties by developing economic interactions.

Economic ties between neighboring countries can mitigate actual or latent or expected tensions. In the case of Turkey and Iran this has been demonstrated clearly over the past 15 years. Yet this process is threatened by recent activities of both countries and of the United States, Russia and other powers seeking influence in the Caspian Sea region.

Turkey's Trade with Greater Central Asia

A key element of Turkish foreign policy in the post-Cold War era is to develop economic relations with the newly independent states of Central Asia. Turkish businesses have gained visibility in Central Asia by signing several framework agreements in finance, customs, manufacturing, small business, energy, transportation, tourism, health and technical assistance. Ambitious governmental program of aid and credit oriented toward the region have also been initiated. Turkey has become an important regional investor, especially in SMEs, with other sectoral investments in construction, telecommunications, energy, banking, textile and retail. While current total trade volumes between Turkey and Central Asia do not reflect their full potential, both the potential and the means of achieving it are growing, thanks to high world oil prices and important structural improvements in Turkey's foreign trade regimen that promote exports, imports, and the competitiveness of domestic industries.

[8] See more detailed information about ethnic problems in Iran, "Stirring the Ethnic Pod" by Iason Athanasiadis, Asia Times, www.atimes.com/atimes/Middle_East/GD29Ak01.html, April, 2005

Turkey's growing economic presence is depicted on the following graph:

Figure I[9]*:*

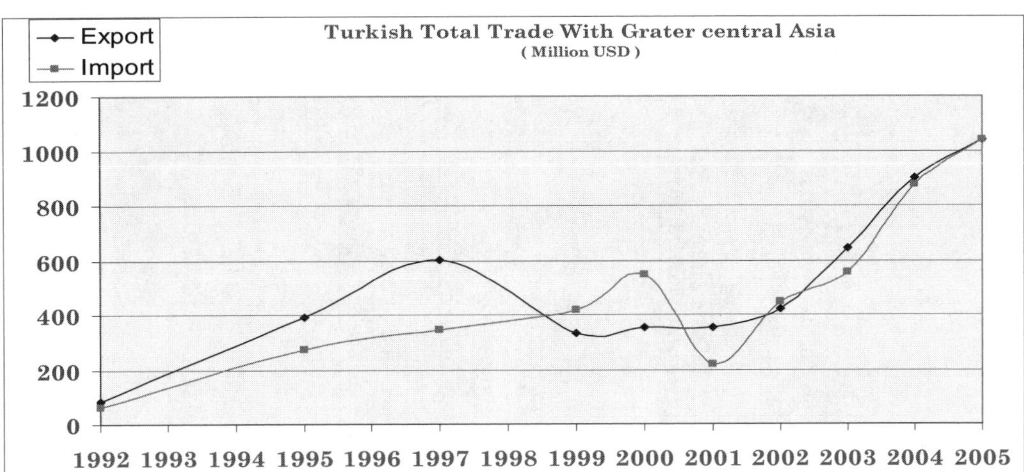

Figure I indicates that trade volume between Turkey and the Central Asia countries (Afghanistan, Kazakhstan, Kyrgyzstan, Tajikistan, Turkmenistan and Uzbekistan) was very low in 1992, amounted to only $145 million. As relations intensified after independence, trade volume grew until the Russian economic crisis in 1997. Trade exports declined from then through Turkey's economic crises in 2000 - 2001.

Since 2002 Turkey's trade volume with Central Asian countries has ramped up quickly, from $844 million in 2002 and to over $2 billion in 2005. Trade grew by 55 percent in 2004, and 16 percent in 2005. Kazakhstan is Turkey's largest Central Asian trading partner, followed by Uzbekistan and Turkmenistan. The value of trade with these three countries is about $1.76 billion, amounting to nearly 90 percent of all Turkish trade with Central Asian countries. It should be noted that the capital expenditures of small, unregistered businesses are not included in this data, although their role is by no means insignificant.

---

[9] Trade Statistics, Undersecretariat for Foreign Trade of Turkey, Ankara, 2006, and Country Reports of Turkish Foreign Economic Relations Board (DEIK), Istanbul, for more information see www.dtm.gov.tr/ead/ulkegos/ulkegos.htm and www.deik.org respectively

Table I: Turkey's Trade with Central Asian States[10]

Import From The Region (US$)

Countries	1992	1995	1997	1999	2000	2001	2002	2003	2004	2005
Afghanistan	204,000	65,000	691,000	698,000	497,000	420,000	1,053,000	2,684,000	6,776,000	8,300,000
Kazakhstan	10,510,516	86,631,496	165,285,250	295,911,002	346,375,953	90,342,703	203,851,624	265,953,233	439,864,000	556,979,000
Kyrgyzstan	1,442,084	5,512,746	7,555,800	2,779,482	2,349,517	6,307,053	17,622,564	10,577,908	13,097,000	9,156,000
Tajikistan	7,762,099	6,342,334	3,381,913	4,052,532	16,511,405	13,662,054	40,695,917	56,962,111	62,700,000	47,300,000
Turkmenistan	21,181,246	111,825,796	73,547,097	67,028,806	97,877,997	71,738,647	106,348,207	123,670,002	175,500,000	159,926,282
Uzbekistan	21,019,403	61,528,703	94,772,966	47,476,861	85,794,461	36,045,330	75,342,346	97,781,167	178,671,000	257,453,000

Export To The Region (US$)

Countries	1992	1995	1997	1999	2000	2001	2002	2003	2004	2005
Afghanistan	785,000	496,000	6,265,000	667,000	8,053,000	6,983,000	20,232,000	36,489,000	70,945,000	113,232,000
Kazakhstan	19,411,991	150,774,833	210,577,801	96,595,591	118,701,179	119,795,053	160,152,590	232,644,917	353,170,000	459,198,000
Kyrgyzstan	1,831,270	38,156,446	49,579,653	23,198,342	20,572,202	17,350,084	24,004,847	40,158,080	74,701,000	88,850,000
Tajikistan	687,522	6,085,684	7,199,647	5,250,375	4,467,496	15,552,540	10,915,302	28,571,501	41,500,000	46,500,000
Turkmenistan	7,288,957	56,290,482	117,533,514	106,627,694	120,155,152	105,277,888	110,020,805	168,972,782	214,500,000	180,414,916
Uzbekistan	54,438,607	138,541,654	210,588,163	99,139,301	82,647,409	89,725,260	93,735,468	138,300,003	145,225,000	151,014,099

---

10 Trade Statistics, Undersecretariat for Foreign Trade of Turkey, 2006, Ankara, and Country Reports of Turkish Foreign Economic Relations Board (DEIK) Istanbul, for more information see www.dtm.gov.tr/ead/ulkegos/ulkegos.htm and www.deik.org respectively

Turkey's exports to Central Asia consist mostly of chemicals, construction materials, textiles and food products. The major imports from the region are petroleum products and raw materials, mainly cotton.

Since the birth of the new states of Central Asia, approximately one thousand registered Turkish businesses, most of them SMEs, have invested in the region. Turkish companies are providing a diverse array of services across Central Asia. While small business activities in the region are not included in the official economic figures, their influence is as important as that of big businesses, not least because they encourage entrepreneurship among the general public in Central Asia, where individual initiative suffered under communist rule.

Turkey's entrepreneurial investments in the region are focused in energy, textiles, foodstuffs, banking and tourism sector, with total Turkish private investment standing at over $3.5 billion, not counting investments by the small, unregistered firms. Most Turkish investments have been made in Kazakhstan, Turkmenistan, and Uzbekistan.

Turkish construction companies are very active in the region and enjoy significant competitive advantages over their rivals. Turkish companies have completed a large amount of construction work there, including educational, governmental, medical and residential buildings, as well as transportation infrastructure.

In parallel with strengthening economic and commercial relations, Turkey has invested in the modernization of business practices in the region. $690 million out of a total of $1,295 million credits appropriated by the Turkish Eximbank have been in support of free market reforms in Central Asia.

Turkey's Economic Relations with Afghanistan

Relations between Afghanistan and Turkey entered a new phase after the fall of the Taliban regime in 2003. The Turkish public and private sector both evince a keen interest in Afghanistan, with the latter involved in construction and road projects in that country. Turkey's interest in Central Asia as a whole is paralleled by the growing commerce between it and Afghanistan. The volume of trade in 2001 was $7 million, which grew to over $100 million by 2006. Turkish enterprises are becoming the lead foreign businesses in Afghanistan, with Turkish investment now standing at approximately $115 million. Turkish firms have realized many important projects in that country, including the construction of residential complexes, business centers, and cement plants.[11]

Because of their extensive experience, Turkish construction firms that have carried out prestigious projects in Central Asia and the Caucasus have become major players in building critical infrastructure in Afghanistan. Such firms have moved materials, equipment, and employees to Afghanistan, taking on many projects as subcontractors. The World Bank and United States have financed most of these projects, which are valued at $1 billion.[12] Because Afghanistan lacks the capacity to produce the necessary volume of construction materials, Turkey has brought them from abroad. Security concerns still obstruct business and construction activities outside of Kabul, and while there have been no deliberate attempts to kill Turkish citizens, the situation requires that they be continuously protected.

Economic Relations with Kazakhstan

Kazakhstan's economic performance and political stability reflect its successful transition from a planned to a market-based economy. The volume of annual trade between Turkey and Kazakhstan has increased five-fold to $1 billion since 2001.[13] This promising trend, coupled with Kazakhstan's relatively successful economic reforms, suggests that there is good potential for the further expansion of Kazakh-Turkish economic relations.

---

[11] Country Profiles, Undersecretariat For Foreign Trade of Turkey, 2006, Ankara and Country Reports of Turkish Foreign Economic Relations Board (DEIK), Istanbıl, for more information see www.dtm.gov.tr/ead/ulkegos/ulkegos.htm and www.deik.org respectively

[12] Turkey's Role in the Reconstruction of Afghanistan, DEIK Document, Istanbul,August, 2005, for more information see www.deik.org

[13] Country Profiles, Undersecretariat For Foreign Trade of Turkey, Ankara, 2006, and Country Reports of Turkish Foreign Economic Relations Board (DEIK), Istanbul, for more information see www.dtm.gov.tr/ead/ulkegos/ulkegos.htm and www.deik.org respectively

Kazakhstan's hydrocarbons sector provides major opportunities for foreign investors. U.S. firms have the largest share of foreign direct investment (FDI) in Kazakhstan, and dominate this sector as well. Joint ventures are a common form of FDI in Kazakhstan, with the United States and western European countries, using them to tap into Kazakhstan's oil and gas reserves. Kazakh oil and gas are also important to Turkish investors, although they are more heavily invested in other sectors of the Kazakh economy.[14]

Approximately $435 million in Turkish FDI flows into Kazakhstan each year, with additional capital brought from third countries by Turkish companies bringing annual total to $1.3 billion.[15] Turkish investments lessened after the Russian economic crises of 1997-98, but Kazakhstan's rapidly developing economy caused Turkish investment to rebound quickly. Turkish investment has created over ten thousand jobs across Kazakhstan, mainly in telecommunications, logistics, energy, hotels, and banking. Turkish construction companies are also very active in Kazakhstan, garnering over $3.2 billion in contracts spread among 147 different projects. It is notable that Turkish firms are carrying out 70 percent of all construction in the new capital city of Astana.

Economic relations with the Kyrgyzstan

Kyrgyzstan is the only member of the Commonwealth of Independent States that is also a member of the World Trade Organization (WTO). WTO membership gives Kyrgyzstan the opportunity to be a balanced partner in the global economy, but institutional and structural problems continue to plague the development of its trade. Nonetheless, bilateral trade with Turkey reached $100 million in 2005, four times the 2001

---

[14] Vildan Serın, "The Impact of Foreign Direct Investment on the Socio-Economic Development of Kazakhstan", Paper Presented at the 4th Annual Central Eurasian Studies Society Conference, Cambridge, Mass, USA, October 2003, p.7

[15] Turkish- Kazakh Economic and Commercial Relations, www.deik.org/bilateral_eng.asp?code=KAZ

figures. Turkish exports constitute 90 percent of the bilateral trade volume, making it a key trade partner for Kyrgyzstan[16].

Turkish companies were among the first foreign firms to bring technology and investment to the new Kyrgyz economy. Turkish investments have focused on banking, foodstuffs, plastics, and construction materials. Turkish construction companies have completed nineteen projects in the Kyrgyz Republic at a total value of more then $330 million. Credits from the Turkish Eximbank have done much to stimulate trade and business links between the two countries.

Turkey invested over $100 million on supporting education in Kyrgyzstan. The Turkish education Ministry currently operates three schools and one language training centre in Kyrgyzstan. Moreover, Turkish businesses and charities have also set up 14 high schools and 1 university as well as other related institutes.[17]

Economic Relations with Tajikistan

Compared to trade with other Central Asian countries, Turkey's economic relations with Tajikistan remained limited until 2001. Civil war, political uncertainty and structural problems long suppressed the volume of trade down. But between 2001 and 2005 Turkish - Tajik trade grew from $29 million to $93 million. Carpets, plastic products, machinery and cleaning materials are the primary Turkish exports to Tajikistan, while aluminum and aluminum products are Tajikistan's main exports to Turkey.[18]

---

[16] Kyrgyzstan Country Profile, Undersecretariat for Foreign Trade of Turkey, Ankara, 2006, Country Reports of Turkish Foreign Economic Relations Board (DEIK), Istanbul, for more information see www.dtm.gov.tr/ead/ulkegos/ulkegos.htm and www.deik.org respectively. See more information at the website of Istanbul. Chamber of Commerce, www.ito.org.tr

[17] Yaşar Sarı, "Turkish Schools and Universities in Kyrgyzistan", The Times of Central Asia, June,2006, see www.turkishweekly.net/comments.php?id=2134 for further information.

[18] Tajikistan Country Profile, Undersecretariat for Foreign Trade of Turkey, Ankara, 2006 and Country Reports of Turkish Foreign Economic Relations Board

Turkish FDI in Tajikistan is very limited — a mere $30 million— placing Tajikistan last among the Central Asian states in that respect. Construction, textile, foodstuffs and cleaning materials are the main areas in which Turkish companies are active.

Economic Relations with Turkmenistan

After Kazakhstan and Uzbekistan, Turkmenistan is the region's third-largest Turkish trade partner. The volume of bilateral nearly doubled between 2001 and 2005, increasing from $175 million to $345 million. Turkish trade makes up about 5 percent of Turkmenistan's total trade.[19]

Turkmenistan receives the second largest amount of Turkish FDI in Central Asia. Most investment is via joint ventures established with Turkmenistan state-owned companies, since the privatization process has not advanced there. The most important sector for investment is textiles, as a result of which Turkmenistan has become a textile exporter. Turkish companies are also investing in agriculture, foodstuffs, banking and health care. Some 200 Turkish firms are active in Turkmenistan's construction, textile and food sectors.[20]

Turkmenistan is the biggest regional market for Turkish construction companies. As of 2005, Turkish firms had signed over 300 projects with an estimated value of $5.45 billion, making Turkey a key player in the reconstruction of Turkmenistan.

Cotton and energy are Turkmenistan's primary exports and technology products are the main items of imports from Turkey. Turkmenistan's natural gas resources are of key importance to Turkey, since they could provide an alternative to Russian and Iranian gas, and, hence improve

---

(DEIK), Istanbul, for more information see www.dtm.gov.tr/ead/ulkegos/ulkegos.htm and www.deik.org respectively.

[19] Turkmenistan Country Profile, Undersecretariat for Foreign Trade of Turkey, Ankara, 2006 and Country Reports of Turkish Foreign Economic Relations Board (DEIK), Istanbul, for more information see www.dtm.gov.tr/ead/ulkegos/ulkegos.htm and www.deik.org respectively. See more information at the website of Istanbul. Chamber of Commerce, www.ito.org.tr.

[20] Ian Gill, "Turkey Ties", , ADB Review, www.adb.org , Philippines, October 2005, p. 3.

Turkey's energy security. The much discussed but as yet unbuilt pipeline for Turkmen gas across the Caspian through Azerbaijan, Georgia and Turkey could provide Turkmenistan an alternative route to Western markets for its most valuable product.

Economic Relations with Uzbekistan

Due to a weak business and investment environment, inflation, and other structural problems the growth rate of the Uzbek economy is the smallest among the CIS countries . Significant free market reforms have not been implemented due to fear of social unrest. Nonetheless, Uzbekistan is Turkey's second-largest trade partner in Central Asia. Trade volume gradually increased between 2001 and 2005, peaking at $400 million. Turkey ran a trade surplus with Uzbekistan until 2003, but went into deficit thereafter. [21]

Uzbekistan's main exports are copper and energy, while technology products are the main items imported from Turkey. Turkish FDI in Uzbekistan began upon Uzbekistan's independence. Down to 1995 Turkish SMEs were most active in Uzbekistan, but thereafter, large companies began also to invest. Turkish businesses have invested in the textile, automotive, tourism, banking and foodstuff sectors. As in other Central Asian states, Turkish construction companies are very active in Uzbekistan, with over 50 projects.

---

[21] Uzbekistan Country Profile, Undersecretariat for Foreign Trade of Turkey, Ankara, 2006 and Country Reports of Turkish Foreign Economic Relations Board (DEIK), Istanbul, for more information see www.dtm.gov.tr/ead/ulkegos/ulkegos.htm and www.deik.org respectively. See more information at the website of Istanbul. Chamber of Commerce, www.ito.org.tr.

Figure II[22:]

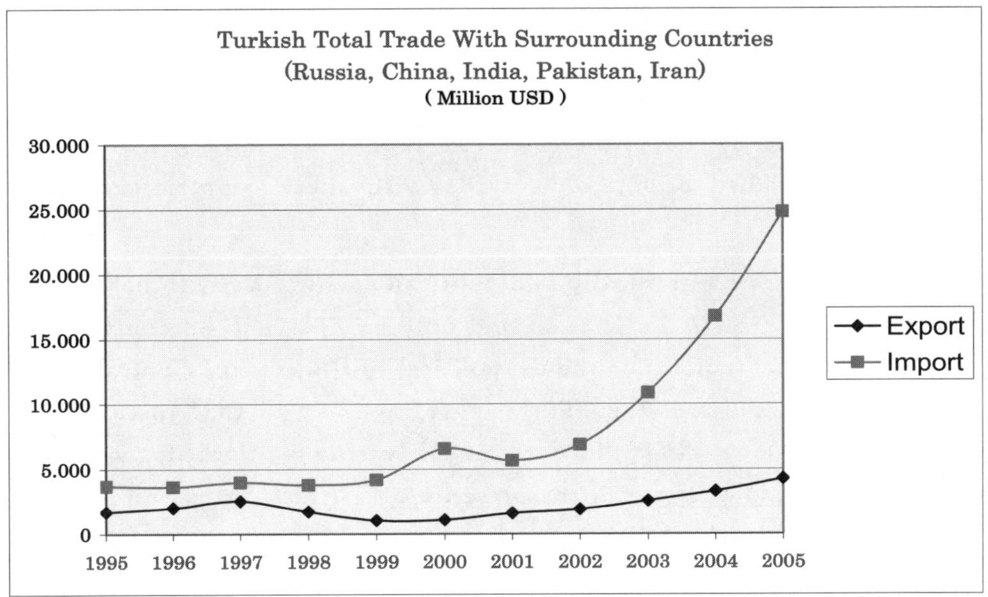

Turkey's Trade with Large Countries Neighboring Central Asia

Turkey's import (10.3%) and export (7.9%) figures with China, India, Russia, Pakistan and Iran were similar in 1995, but by 2005 the picture has changed dramatically. During the same period, these countries' role T in urkey's foreign trade grew. In 1995 their total share of Turkish imports reached 10.3 percent ($3.7 billion), and 7.3 percent ($1.7 billion) of Turkish exports. By 2005 21.3 percent ($24.8 billion) of Turkish imports came from these countries, and they received 5.8 percent of total Turkish exports. Although the share of Turkish exports had decreased, the value had grown to $4.2 billion.[23] There are several reasons for the disparity between these figures. The policies of neighboring countries and the EU accession

---

[22] Trade Statistics, Undersecretariat for Foreign Trade of Turkey, Ankara,2006, www.dtm.gov.tr/ead/ulkegos/ulkegos.htm

[23] Trade Statistics, Undersecretariat for Foreign Trade of Turkey, Ankara, 2006 and Country Reports of Turkish Foreign Economic Relations Board (DEIK), Istanbul, for more information see www.dtm.gov.tr/ead/ulkegos/ulkegos.htm and www.deik.org respectively. See more information at the website of Istanbul. Chamber of Commerce, www.ito.org.tr

process have directed the bulk of Turkish trade towards provided the EU, Black Sea, and Middle Eastern countries.

Meanwhile, Turkey's growing oil and natural gas needs have deepened its reliance on Russian and Iranian resources, and China and India exports to Turkey have increased as economies have grown. The resulting imbalance of Turkey's trade with these countries remains uncorrected.

Turkey competes economically and politically with China, India, Russia and Iran in Central Asia. It is second only to Russia in its commercial presence in the region. Turkey's political influence in Central Asia recently decreased as the Turkish ruling party, the Justice and Development Party (AKP), focused on cultivating realtionships with the EU and the Middle East. But the presence of Turkish firms and NGOs, and institutions such as TIKA, assure that Turkish commercial activity in Central Asia will continue to grow.

Over the past 15 years, Turkey's total trade volume with the CAS was over $2 billion dollars, while total trade volume with the sourrounding countries—Russia, China, India, Iran and Pakistan—reached $29 billion. Turkish trade volume with the region will continue to increase, despite Turkey's strategic considerations regarding EU accession, which have resulted in over 50 percent of Turkish trade being directed towards EU.

While most Turkish trade overall is shipped by sea, most of its commerce with Central Asian countries is conducted by road, and recently by rail. Turkey is becoming the transfer point for oil and natural gas from the Caspian basin for Western markets. This has been greatly faciliated by the opening of Bakü-Tbilisi-Ceyhan (BTC) pipeline in July 2006, the integration of Azeri gas into the Turkish pipeline system via Erzurum, and the transfer of Kazakh oil to Ceyhan via the BTC. Turkey's role as the EU's energy terminal will be assured by the NABUKO Project, currently under construction, which will transfer natural gas to Austria via Turkey, and by forthcoming projects to transfer natural gas to Italy via Greece. These projects support the transport of Kazakh petroleum and Turkmen natural gas to Europe via Transcaspian pipelines. Russia's use of natural gas pricing as a political tool, notably against Ukraine and Georgia, has pushed European countries, including Turkey, to find alternative energy resources and routes. And Iran's restriction of natural gas transferred to Turkey during winter of 2005 underscored the need for Turkey to find new hydrocarbon resources. Russian and Iranian behavior regarding their energy sales has garnered international support for new Transcaspian pipelines.

At the end of Turkey's ninth five-year development program in 2013, Turkish exports to countries neighboring the Central Asia will reach $13 billion dollars and imports will be around $60 billion.[24] Turkey will undoubtedly try to correct this imbalance. However, its consumption of Kazakh oil and Turkmenistan natural gas are expected to increase to $10 billion within the next seven years.

---

[24] Nineth Five-Year Development Program of Turkey, Ankara,2006, p.25, http://ekutup.dpt.gov.tr/plan/ix/9kalkinmaplani20061208.pdf

Table II: Turkish Trade With Surrounding Countries[25]

IMPORT ($)-%	1995	1996	1997	1998	1999	2000	2001	2002	2003	2004	2005
RUSSIA	2.082.352.354	1.921.139.118	2.174.258.117	2.155.006.116	2.374.132.817	3.886.583.276	3.435.672.619	3.891.721.401	5.451.315.438	9.033.138.484	12.869.945.272
IRAN	689.476.335	806.335.161	646.401.629	433.026.395	635.928.166	815.730.198	839.800.076	920.971.696	1.860.682.809	1.962.058.691	3.469.704.708
PAKISTAN	153.625.344	83.466.561	57.023.441	57.363.171	25.443.587	82.232.358	101.280.249	117.654.683	192.027.798	240.720.072	315.320.026
INDIA	222.872.231	258.173.689	300.892.377	276.474.271	243.006.381	449.307.322	354.875.121	564.463.264	722.855.219	1.046.398.380	1.278.999.653
CHINA	539.019.099	556.491.722	787.457.233	846.133.978	894.812.799	1.344.731.392	925.619.822	1.368.316.717	2.610.298.044	4.476.077.424	6.867.855.947
5 COUNTRY	3.687.345.363	3.625.606.251	3.966.032.797	3.768.003.931	4.173.323.750	6.578.584.546	5.657.247.887	6.863.127.761	10.837.179.308	16.758.393.051	24.801.825.606
TOTAL	35.707.519.776	43.626.690.167	48.558.720.673	45.921.392.207	40.671.272.031	54.502.820.560	41.399.082.953	51.553.797.329	69.339.692.058	97.539.765.968	116.562.532.073
EXPORT ($)-%	**1995**	**1996**	**1997**	**1998**	**1999**	**2000**	**2001**	**2002**	**2003**	**2004**	**2005**
RUSSIA	1.238.225.601	2.082.352.354	2.056.400.339	1.348.002.243	588.663.804	643.902.938	924.106.727	1.172.038.590	1.367.590.908	1.859.186.551	2.377.001.524
IRAN	268.433.937	297.521.435	307.007.494	194.696.358	157.814.999	235.784.797	360.535.772	333.962.009	533.786.239	813.031.280	912.753.627
PAKISTAN	90.870.476	77.875.104	58.160.735	63.585.006	128.527.155	52.856.796	31.186.426	57.457.227	70.353.952	86.399.691	187.554.234
INDIA	42.006.128	59.390.127	60.826.402	73.570.754	120.531.819	56.047.013	74.373.323	72.723.969	71.365.460	136.317.405	219.869.435
CHINA	66.961.101	65.114.673	44.375.287	38.446.860	36.648.986	96.010.398	199.372.814	268.229.485	504.625.797	391.585.394	549.763.633
5 COUNTRY	1.706.497.243	2.011.535.099	2.526.770.257	1.718.301.221	1.032.186.763	1.084.601.942	1.589.575.062	1.904.411.280	2.547.722.356	3.286.520.321	4.246.942.453
TOTAL	21.636.476.293	23.224.465.343	26.261.071.786	26.973.951.738	26.587.224.962	27.774.906.045	31.334.216.356	36.059.089.029	47.252.836.302	63.167.152.820	73.472.288.786

[25] Trade Statistics, Undersecretariat for Foreign Trade of Turkey, Ankara, 2006, www.dtm.gov.tr/ead/ulkegos/ulkegos.htm

Continental trade figures will increasingly affect on Turkey's GDP and its state income; even today Turkey is receiving $600 million annually from the customs duties paid by the Central Asian countries and China, India, Iran, Pakistan and Russia. Applying this rate to the projected $70 billion trade volume in 2013 yields a projected state income of $1.4 billion from customs duties deriving from regional and continental trade.

Economic Relations with Russia

Russia's share of Turkish imports grew from 5.8 percent ($2.08 billion) in 1995 to 11 percent ($12.86 billion) at the end of 2005. Over the same period, Russia's share of Turkish exports decreased from 5.7 percent ($1.24 billion) to 3.22 percent ($2.38 billion).[26] In 1984 the two countries agreed that 70 percent of the cost of Russian gas would be paid for with Turkish goods and services. Yet this was never applied and Turkey's growing energy needs increased the trade gap. In the 1990s the value of shuttle trade between Turkey and Russia reached $10 billion, but decreased to $2 billion in 2005. Turkey's primary exports to Russia are industrial products, while it imports fossil fuel, iron and steel products, and unrefined goods. By the end of 2004 Turkish firms had invested $1.5 billion in Russia, either directly or via third countries.

Turkey's Economic Relations with China

China's share of Turkish imports has grown from 1.5 percent ($539 billion) in 1995 to 5.9 percent ($6.87 billion) at the end of 2005. Over the same period, exports increased from 0.3 percent ($67 million) to 0.7 percent ($549 million).[27] By 2006 China had become Turkey's major

---

[26] Trade Statistics, Undersecretariat for Foreign Trade of Turkey, Ankara, 2006 and Country Reports of Turkish Foreign Economic Relations Board (DEIK), Istanbul, for more information see www.dtm.gov.tr/ead/ulkegos/ulkegos.htm and www.deik.org respectively. See more information at the website of Istanbul. Chamber of Commerce, www.ito.org.tr

[27] China Country Profile, Trade Statistics, Undersecretariat for Foreign Trade of Turkey, Ankara 2006 and Country Reports of Turkish Foreign Economic Relations Board (DEIK), for more information see www.dtm.gov.tr/ead/ulkegos/ulkegos.htm and www.deik.org respectively. See

trading partner in the Asia-Pacific region. Turkish exports to China have been limited to items like iron and steel, but export volumes decreased after Chinese production of these products grew. Conversely, China's exports to Turkey have been increasing both in volume and variety of goods, but there are as yet no significant Turkish investments in China.

Economic Relations with Pakistan

There appears to be an inverse relationship between the volume of Turkish-Pakistani commerce volume and the friendliness of Turkish-Pakistani political relations. Turkish imports decreased from 0.4 percent ($154 million) in 1995 to 0.3 percent ($315 million) in 2005. Turkish exports decreased from 0.4 percent ($90.8 million dollars) in 1995 to 0.3 percent ($187.5 million) in 2005.[28] Turkey's primary exports to Pakistan are industrial goods, while its main imports from Pakistan are cotton and apparel. Investment levels between the two countries are very low.

Economic Relations with India

Turkish commercial relations with India strengthened after India became a major exporter, but the bilateral trade volumes do not reflect the full capacity of either country. In 1995, Indian exports to Turkey were only $226 million, but they have grown to $1.28 billion by 2005. India imported only $42 million worth of goods from Turkey in 1995, and a decade later this figure had grown only $219 million.[29] Investment between the two countries remains very low.

Economic Relations With Iran

Iran remains the main transport corridor for Turkish goods entering Central Asia and Afganistan. In 1995, imports from Iran constituted 1.9 percent ($689 million) of Turkey's total imports, which grew to 3 percent

---

more information at the website of Istanbul. Chamber of Commerce, www.ito.org.tr

[28] Trade Statistics, Undersecratariat for Foreign Trade of Turkey, Ankara,2006, www.dtm.gov.tr/ead/ulkegos/ulkegos.htm

[29] Trade Statistics, Undersecratariat for Foreign Trade of Turkey, Ankara, 2006, www.dtm.gov.tr/ead/ulkegos/ulkegos.htm

($3.47 billion) in 2005. Turkish exports to Iran constituted 1.2 percent ($268 million) during the entire period 1995-2005. A trade gap has developed due to substantial Turkish purchases of Iranian oil and natural gas. While both countries are invested in each other, FDI is a small portion of total business volume.[30] Recently, Turkey has become an attractive tourism destination for Iranians.

Benefits to Turkey from Continental Trade

It has been noted that Turkey lacked a clear strategy toward Central Asian countries during the period immediately following their independence. Yet, over time, routine business activities brought about more intensive official and unofficial interactions, and enhanced mutual understanding. Turkey learned about Central Asia thanks to routine issues that Turkish businessmen grappled with there. Today, it appears that Turkey is well-acquainted with the region's problems, and has a good sense of how they might be overcome in the short- and mid-term.

Thousands of Turkish citizens living and work in the Central Asia, many people from these countries came to Turkey on business. Visits to turkey by Central Asian businessmen enable them to understand practical aspects of doing business in a free-market economy. This contact also provides them with impressions of a successful a Muslim-majority, secular, and democratic state. Most Central Asians fear Islamic extremism, have no interest in close relations with Islamic countries, preferring instead to remain open to the United States, Turkey and other outside secular powers.

Business activities have provided a sound basis for cultural contacts, leading private companies to support cultural programs organized in Turkey and across Central Asia. Turkey is the first tourist destination for Central Asians who can afford to travel.

---

[30] Iran Country Profile, Trade Statistics, Undersecretariat for Foreign Trade of Turkey, Ankara,2006 and Country Reports of Turkish Foreign Economic Relations Board (DEIK), Istanbul, for more information see www.dtm.gov.tr/ead/ulkegos/ulkegos.htm and www.deik.org respectively. See more information at the website of Istanbul. Chamber of Commerce, www.ito.org.tr

Eurasian countries became significant international arena for Turkish businessmen after the radical free-market reforms initiated by Turgut Özal's government in the 1980s. The experience gained by Turkish construction companies operating in the region facilitated penetration of the more challenging EU market.

Caspian Basin Strategic Assets: Oil and Gas

The natural resources of the Caspian Basin are attracting the interest of the big economical and political powers to the region. Oil and gas are the main assets have the potential to bring welfare (actually it is started) to the region and boosting factor to integrate region to outer world while creating intensive competition between big powers. The development of oil and gas resources in the Caspian region is particularly important for the development of the central Asian and Caucasian economies. Investment attracted to the oil and gas sector, including in the transportation infrastructure of neighboring countries, could provide significant revenue for the region's governments and stimulate investments in other economic sectors.[31]

Estimation of oil and gas reserves of Caspian basin and Central Asia varies. However figures represent 1.5% to 4% of world proven oil reserves and 6% of its gas reserves. Production levels are expected to reach 4 million barrels per day (bbl/d) in 2015 compared to 45 million bbl/d for the OPEC countries in that year. Central Asia is neither the world's largest source of oil and gas nor easily accessible; market access is hindered by political and geographic conditions, including continued Russian influence, limited access to waterways beyond the Caspian Sea, and limited export infrastructure.[32]

However, the region is clearly important geopolitically and geoeconomically. Russia controls the majority of oil export routes from reserves in Central Asia and the Caspian. Nevertheless, prior and

---

[31] Hans Kauch (team leader) Caspian Oil and Gas, IEA Report,Paris, 1998, p.34, www.iea.org/textbase/nppdf/free/1990/caspian_oil_gas98.pdf,

[32] Ariel Cohen, " U.S. Interest and Central Asia Energy Security", The Heritage Foundation, Backgrounder, Washington D.C.,November 2006

continuing efforts by major Western oil companies, particularly the Baku–Tbilisi–Ceyhan (BTC) pipeline, as well as current and planned investments in the Central Asian oil sector by India and China, have yielded more options for non-Russian export routes and diversification of the customer base. These developments may help to break the Russian energy-transit monopoly, but they also open the region to intensified competition over energy resources on the part of other energy-hungry economies[33].

The BTC pipeline - built by a consortium of 11 companies, including British Petroleum, the American firm Unocal, and Turkey's national oil corporation - is designed to bring a non-Middle Eastern source of oil to the West. This would loosen Russia's and Iran's grip on the transport of Caspian and Central Asian oil by creating a new route that is friendlier to the United States and Europe[34]. The realization of the BTC makes fundamental changes on the perception of in and out side of the region. Especially, in the Caucasian and the Central Asian republics, it diminishes the idea of the Russian domination over the region, and also accelerates the process of being a state[35].

The reality of Russian purchasing of the Kazak oil and the Turkmen natural gas under the market prices and selling them from the market price forces these countries to seek new routes. Indeed, BTC came online at exactly the time when Kazakhstan began debating how to export the resources of the Kashagan oil field, the largest oil field discovered globally in the past two decades. Kazakhstan's stated interest in exporting oil through BTC and ongoing negotiations with Consortium is an encouraging sign that Europe and US should take advantage of by supporting politically and financially, through export credits, the

---

[33] Ariel Cohen, " U.S. Interest and Central Asia Energy Security", The Heritage Foundation, Backgrounder, Washington D.C., November 2006

[34] Yigal Schleifer ," Pipeline Politics Give Turkey an Edge", Christian Science Monitor, 25 May 2005 Edition

[35] S. Frederick Starr , "School of Modernity", in Starr and Svante E. Cornell, eds., *The Baku - Tblisi Ceyhan Pipeline : Oil Window to the West*, Washington D.C.: CACI, 2005,., p.8, see www.silkroadstudies.org/BTC.htm for more information about BTC implications.

building of Trans-Caspian oil as well as gas pipelines[36]. As a matter of fact that US government efforts show that the regional and the international conditions are getting adequate in order to realize the Trans-Caspian pipe lines. These strategic materials are important not only for the producer countries but also for the countries that the pipelines are passing through. If we leave the dispute between Azerbaijan and Turkmenistan related to natural gas to one side, Azerbaijan and Georgia both are not hiding the ambitions of joining to the NATO and the EU, support transfer of oil and gas through their territories. Carrying the some of the Kazak oil via the BTC is a good example. The transformation, created by the BTC in the region, obviously strengthens the position of the supporters of this idea. However, it seems to gain new allies. Because of the Turkish Government's focus on the EU process and the unrest in Iraq, Turkey has lost some of its momentum in the Caucasus in the past few years.[37]

Due to the geographical vicinity to both the Caspian Sea and the Middle East oil and gas, Turkey frequently mentions that it is eager for being an energy corridor and a terminal for the west[38]. However decreasing interest to the Caucasus and Central Asia during the AKP government with different reasons this claim has not been supported sufficiently to become reality. Of course another factor that adversely affected pipeline politics passing through Turkey to western markets is the disagreement between Turkey and US about the Iraq war and in a certain extent different views about methodology of US in Greater Middle East Project and engagement to developments in Iraq particularly Northern Iraq.

However, dependency to the Russian and Iranian natural gas, 65% and 20% respectively, and the possibility of using energy as a weapon by these countries push Turkey to search for the alternative sources and strategies. Especially, problems experienced at the delivery of gas supply last winter with Iran and disturbance of shortage because of the so-called technical

---

[36] Svante E. Cornell, S. Frederick Starr , *The Caucasus: A Challenge for Europe*, Silk Road Paper, Washington D.C., June 2006, p.83, www.silkroadstudies.org
[37] Ibid., p.77,
[38] Zeyno Baran, "Implications for Turkey", in Starr and Cornell, eds., *The Baku - Tblisi Ceyhan Pipeline*, p.104.

excuses, Turkey accelerates its search for the alternatives. The claim being a transport corridor to west for the oil and gas transfer will not give only strategic importance to Turkey but as well Turkey will diversify its energy sources and break Russian and Iranian monopoly. With the impetus of BTC, need to diversify energy sources both for Turkey and Western Countries and relatively thawing relations with US are increasing the realization chance of pipelines all the way starting from eastward Caspian up to middle of Europe.

Some analysts project that by 2030 Europe will import more than 90% of its oil and oil products demand, about 84% of its gas demand (with 40% from Russia), and approximately 60% of its coal demand. This provides new arguments for improving energy efficiency and diversification. In addition, it suggests the need for a more stringent policy of oil and gas security storage and for actions in the field of foreign policy such as maintaining a constant dialogue with key energy suppliers such as Russian and Central Asian States, and with transit countries such as Poland, Ukraine and Turkey.[39]

Results of the studies, performed by various research institutions and energy companies, as well as the European Union itself, are giving signals of significant amounts to be transported via Turkey to the European countries in the near future. Within this context, studies were initiated for another route to reach the European market. This additional route is envisaged to carry the gas coming from Middle East and Caspian sources together with the route through Greece to Italy. Another route is planned to pass through Bulgaria, Romania, and Hungary to reach Austria and will reach Europe from another angle. The Greek pipeline is already contracted and will be operational in 2007. Presently, the pipeline projects related to natural gas, come from Egypt, Iraq, Turkmenistan and Kazakhstan and go to Europe (NABUCO), are on the agenda of Turkish authorities. The most important of the pipeline proposals are the

---

[39] Jean Marie Chevalier, "Does Europe Need a Common Energy Policy?", CERA Report, May, 2006, http://www.cera.com/aspx/cda/client/report/reportpreview.aspx?CID=8104&KID=

NABUCO Pipeline and the Trans-Caspian Pipeline. NABUCO, with strong Turkish support and official approval from the EU, is expected to be built in 2008. It will provide a direct link between Caspian natural gas fields and European markets without Russia as an intermediary, bringing Azerbaijani, Kazakh, Turkmen, and Iranian gas from Erzurum to Austria via Romania and Hungary even some Russian gas through Blue Stream pipeline if the related agreements realized. A Trans-Caspian pipeline would link the large gas supplies of the eastern Caspian to Baku, presumably feeding Kazakh and Turkmen gas into SCP (South Caucasus Pipeline) and subsequently to NABUCO[40]. On the other hand, Turkey is planning to build a bypass pipeline, at the feasibility phase, from the black sea port of Samsun to energy terminal at the Mediterranean Port Ceyhan. Considering the heavy tanker traffic at the straits and obvious threat to downtown Istanbul and increasing export potential of Caspian oil forcing the construction of new pipelines.

Just a brief look at the map of the broader Central Eurasian region shows how important corridor of BTC is for this mostly landlocked region. This pipeline is an integral part and most important pillar of the larger transportation network – also known as the new silk road- running all the way from western China and central Asia, through the Caspian and Caucasus, across the black sea, and then on to ports in Ukraine and Mediterranean. This transportation Superhighway is designed to complement existing transport roots from Asia to Europe, including the traditional and often heavily overloaded outlets via Russia. Eventually, the goal is to create a fully integrated transportation network- including upgraded highways, pipelines, railroads, ports, ferries, fiber-optic lines, electricity transmission lines- that will make it easier for the states of Central Asia and the Caucasus to trade not only with each other but also with Europe, the Middle East, and the rest of the world.[41]

---

40 Ariel Cohen, Conway Irvin ,Turkey: A Linchpin in Pipeline Politics, *Central Asia-Caucasus Analyst*, November 1, 2006.

41 Svante E. Cornell, Mamuka Tsereteli and Vladimir Socor, "Geostrategic Implications of the Baku-Tblisi-Ceyhan Pipeline", in Starr and Cornell, eds., *The Baku - Tblisi Ceyhan Pipeline*, p.20.

Impediments to Turkey's Active Involvement in Continental Trade

There are significant barriers to trade in Central Asia pertaining to trade policy, transport and transit systems in the CASs, their neighbors, and trading partners. The more significant trade barriers pertaining to trade policy in the CASs include a complex tariff schedule and relatively high tariffs (Kazakhstan and Uzbekistan); escalation of tariffs (all the CASs); frequent and unpredictable changes in the tariff schedule (Kazakhstan, Tajikistan, Turkmenistan and Uzbekistan); high implicit tariffs in the form of taxes that are levied on imported goods than domestically produced goods (Kazakhstan and Uzbekistan); explicit export taxes (Kazakhstan); and prohibition and licensing of exports and imports of certain commodities (all the CASs). Uzbekistan appears to continue using restrictions on access to foreign exchange in regulating imports and imposes relatively tight restrictions on cross border movements of people and transport equipment in an apparent effort to restrict imports from neighboring countries. Large agricultural subsidies that developed countries provide to their farmers also constitute significant barriers to trade in Central Asia[42].

Private Turkish firms operating in Central Asia have suffered from a variety of business-related problems. These impediments relate to security, infrastructure, legal and institutional matters, banking and fiscal systems, customs organizations, visas and employment permission, and transportation.[43,44]

Security

The Central Asian states face common security challenges from crime, corruption, terrorism, Islamic extremism, ethnic and civil conflict, border

---

[42]Adrian Ruthenberg and Bahodir Ganiev, "Central Asia: Increasing Gains from Trade Through regional cooperation in Trade Policy, Transport, and Customs Transit.", , Asian Development Bank, Philippines, 2006, pp 34-35, see more information at www.adb.org/Documents/Reports/CA-Trade-Policy /chap3.pdf

[43] Country reports issued by the Foreign Economic Relations Board of Turkey (DEIK), Istanbul, 2006,

[44] Hasan Selçuk, " Problems Faced by Turkish Companies at Turkic States", Investment Opportunities in Turkic Republics, Istanbul, 2004, pp.146-150

tensions, water and transport disputes, the proliferation of weapons of mass destruction (WMD), and illegal narcotics.

The problems of authoritarian regimes, crime, corruption, terrorism, and ethnic and civil strife and tensions jeopardize the security and independence of all CAS including Afghanistan, though to varying degrees. Kazakhstan has faced the potential of separatism in Northern Kazakhstan where ethnic Russians are dominant, although this threat appears to have diminished in recent years with the emigration of hundreds of thousands of ethnic Russians. Tajikistan faces the uncertain resolution of its civil war and possible separatism, particularly by its northern Soghd region. Kyrgyzstan has faced increasing demand by its southern regions for autonomy that it has tried to meet in part by promulgating a new constitution in 2003 that provides some local rights. Turkmenistan faces clan and regional tensions and declining social services that could exacerbate a succession crisis. Uzbekistan faces rising dissidence from those President Islam Kerimov labels as Islamic extremist, from a large ethnic Tajik population, and from an impoverished citizenry.[45]

Security is a critical pre-condition for the development of entrepreneurial activity. Although security issues threaten business ventures, Turkish businessmen, particularly in mid-sized ventures are bolder generally and have a higher tolerance for political risk than entrepreneurs from other countries. Political regimes in Central Asia are relatively unstable—despite security agreements and close ties to Western countries—creating a constantly changing strategic equilibrium. Weak regional governments, the ongoing state-building process and possibility of conflict in border regions are major factors discouraging foreign investment.

Like other countries, Turkish firms, entrepreneurs and citizens operating in Central Asia have experienced various security-related problems since independence. While the severity of these problems varies from one republic to another, security is always at the top of the business decision-making agenda. Recent attacks on Turkish citizens and their investments

[45] Jim Nichol, "Central Asia's Security : Issues and Implications for U.S. Interests, CIS report for Congress, Washington D.C., January 2005, p.6

during the political upheavals in Kyrgyzstan underscores the importance of security.

Among all the sectors affected by security, transportation may be the most important since it is key to trade activity. Yet the transportation sector, particularly road and rail transport, is plagued by serious and persistent security issues. Turkish truck drivers routinely encounter serious threats, including robbery and violence, as well as excessive fees levied by local officials.

Transportation

Transport related significant barriers to trade in Central Asia are high transport costs and long and unpredictable transport times for international shipments to and from CASs. This is not only landlocked and remote location of the CASs and their difficult topography, but also due to deficiencies in their transport networks, high costs and low quality of transport and logistic services in the region, and difficulties with movements of goods and transport equipment across borders and through the territories of the CASs and neighboring countries[46].

Many Central Asian countries have poor quality trade-related transportation services that are excessively expensive. Borders crossings typically cause endless difficulties for Turkish transport companies, while steep taxes on road use impose withering fiscal burdens on Turkish truckers. Distribution remains imperfect and problems continue despite a major reduction in free-pass paperwork for cross-country transit. Poorly organized transit gateways to Central Asia via Iran, Azerbaijan, and Georgia create significant problems for Turkish truck drivers. Road taxes and tolls in Azerbaijan cost up to $1,000 per Turkish truck, although these fees are often not levied on trucks from such neighboring counties as Iran. Nor is it uncommon for political instability to render a region impassable to cargo transport, further increasing the time and money spent required for continental trade.

---

[46] Adrian Ruthenberg and Bahodir Ganiev, "Central Asia: Increasing Gains from Trade Through regional cooperation in Trade Policy, Transport, and Customs Transit.", Asian Development Bank, Philippines, 2006, pp 34-35

Figure-III and Figure-IV compare the actual transport costs and transit times for shipments by road and by rail between CASs (Kazakhstan, Kyrgyz Republic, Tajikistan, and Uzbekistan) and selected countries outside the region with the corresponding transport costs and transit times in the "ideal world" (i.e., a world with balanced transport flows, competitive markets for transport services smooth border crossing, low transit fees, and no visa problems and unofficial payments)[47]. Although Turkey has comparatively advantageous position than the other European countries regarding transport costs and time, still figures from cost side 1.5-2 times higher than average ideal world practices and transit times 2-3 times longer than from normal practices.

Again excluding exports of primary commodities and imports of heavy machinery and equipment, for which transport costs are relatively low, transport costs comprised an estimated 11-16% and logistics costs accounted for more than 20% of the total value of exports and imports in the CASs. By comparison, transport costs made up 8.4% of the value of the imports in Asia as a whole and 6.1% of the value of imports in the world at large 2001[48].

Improving the transport infrastructure and logistic services within the Region and along the transit corridors has vital importance for the Regional countries, both for integration with world trade systems and in a way to their economic liberalization. However solving the regional transport problems often requires several inter related issues to be tackled simultaneously in more than one country.

There are several potentially important corridors across Central Asia:

1. East-West Corridors linking Asia and Europe along the former Silk Road either through Kazakhstan or through Kyrgyz Republic

---

[47]Adrian Ruthenberg and Bahodir Ganiev, "Central Asia: Increasing Gains from Trade Through regional cooperation in Trade Policy, Transport, and Customs Transit.", Asian Development Bank, Philippines, 2006, p 31

[48]Adrian Ruthenberg and Bahodir Ganiev, "Central Asia: Increasing Gains from Trade Through regional cooperation in Trade Policy, Transport, and Customs Transit.", Asian Development Bank, Philippines, 2006, p 31

2. North-South corridors between Siberia and South-West Asia and between the Urals and the Persian Gulf.[49]

The EU assists the transport sector in Central Asia through its TACIS (Technical Assistance for the Commonwealth of Independent States) program mainly through its TRACECA program[50] (Transport Corridor Europe, Caucasus, Asia). TRACECA is one of its network development programs and mainly gives through studies in a wide range transport fields[51]. Basic targets of the program are: to enable political and economic stability among the member nations and encourage the cooperation directed to increase commerce; to determine the problems of transportation systems in the region; to improve the regional cooperation by the contributions of international finance organizations and private investors; and to encourage integration of TRACECA and TENs (Trans European Networks).

From 1996 till 2006, the TRACECA program, having disbursed a total amount of about 160 m EURO, supported 61 technical assistance projects and 15 investment projects. TRACECA has helped to attract large investments from the development partners, that include the European Bank For reconstruction and Development (EBRD) that have committed funds for capital projects on ports, railways and roads along the TRACECA route, the World Bank (WB) that have financed new capital projects on roads in Armenia and Georgia, the Asian Development Bank (ADB) that have allocated substantial funds for road and railway

---

[49] Ian Jenkins, Paul Pezant, "Central Asia: Reassessment of the Regional Transport Sector strategy", Philippines, January 2003, p.44, for more information visit www.adb.org/documents

[50] TRACECA Program: The Transport Corridor Europe Caucasus Central Asia Program is a European Union funded technical assistance program that aims to develop a west-east transport corridor from Europe, across the Black Sea through the Caucasus and the Caspian Sea to central Asia. The Program launched at a conference in Brussels in May 1993, which brought together trade and transport ministers from the eight original TRACECA countries (Armenia, Azerbaijan, Georgia, Kazakhstan, Kyrgyz Republic, Tajikistan, Turkmenistan and Uzbekistan) . Turkey Joined to TRACECA program together with Bulgaria and Romania in Tashkent meeting in 2002.

[51] Ian Jenkins, Paul Pezant, "Central Asia: Reassessment of the Regional Transport Sector strategy", Philippines, January 2003, p.100

improvement and the Islamic Development Bank (IDB) that had invested into development of the transport sector in the TRACECA countries.[52]

Figure III[53]*:*

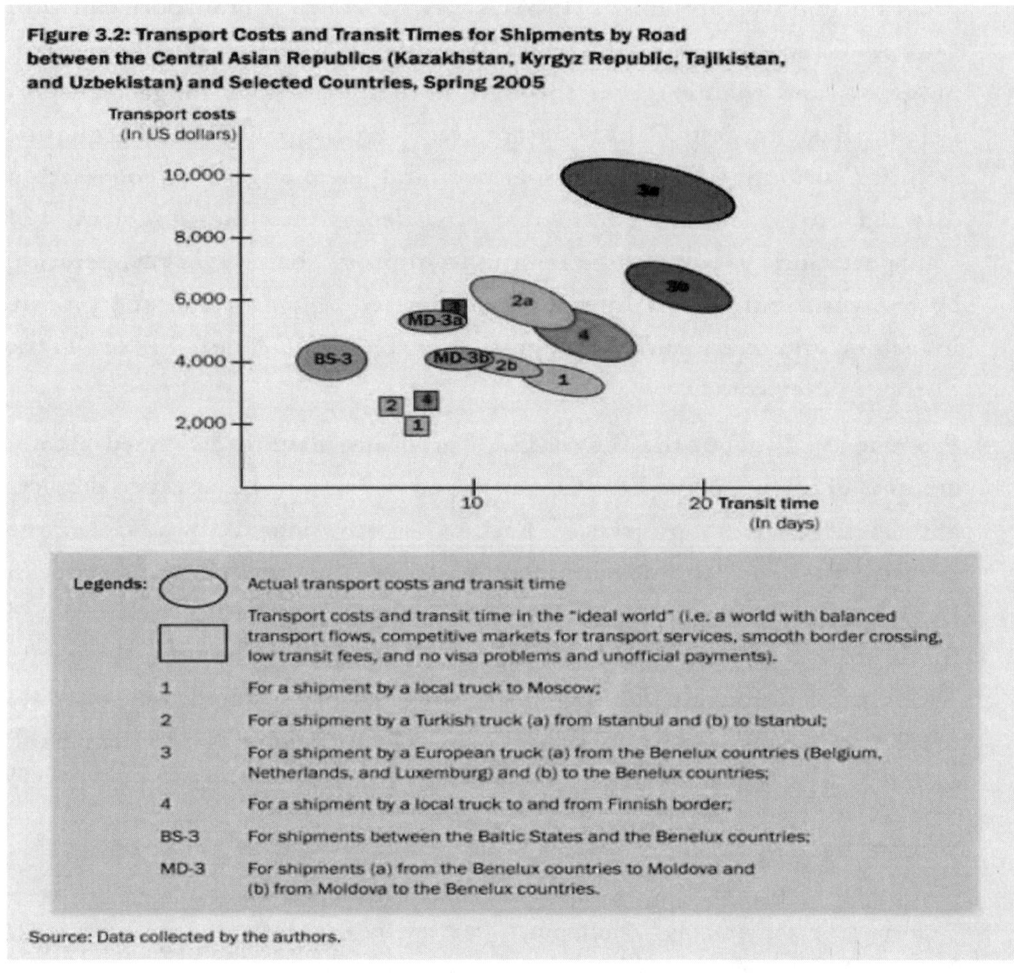

Figure 3.2: Transport Costs and Transit Times for Shipments by Road between the Central Asian Republics (Kazakhstan, Kyrgyz Republic, Tajikistan, and Uzbekistan) and Selected Countries, Spring 2005

Source: Data collected by the authors.

---

[52] Source: http://www.trecaca-org.org /

[53] Adrian Ruthenberg and Bahodir Ganiev, "Central Asia: Increasing Gains from Trade Through regional cooperation in Trade Policy, Transport, and Customs Transit.", Asian Development Bank, Philippines, 2006, p.29

Figure IV[54]

Figure 3.3: Transport Costs and Transit Times for Shipments by Rail between the Central Asian Republics (Kazakhstan, Kyrgyz Republic, Tajikistan, and Uzbekistan) and Selected Countries, Spring 2005

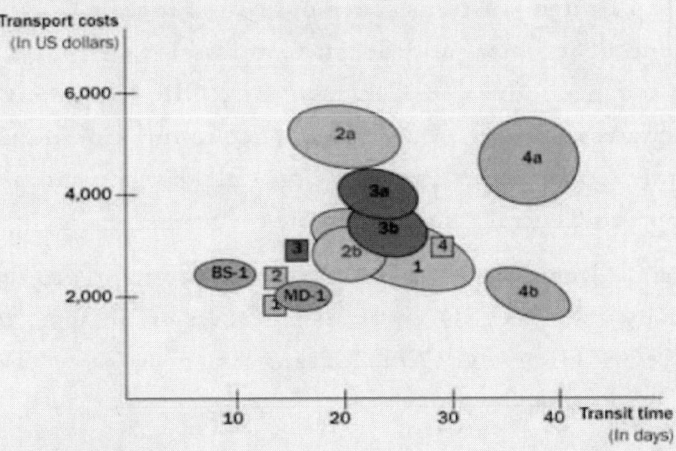

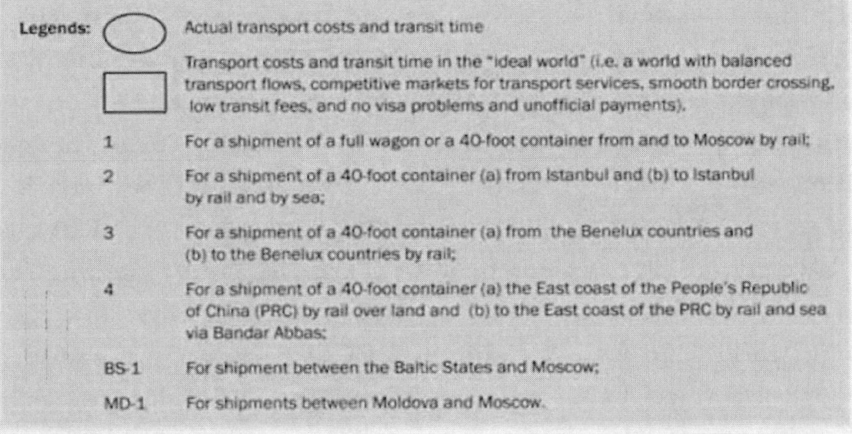

Source: Data collected by the authors.

[54] Adrian Ruthenberg and Bahodir Ganiev "Central Asia: Increasing Gains from Trade Through regional cooperation in Trade Policy, Transport, and Customs Transit.", Asian Development Bank, Philippines, 2006, p.30

Like the EU, many other regional and international organizations such as EBRD, IDB, JBIC (Japanese Bank for International Cooperation), USAID (United States Agency for International Development), World Bank, UNDP (United Nations development Program), UNESCAP (United Nations Economical and Social Commission), SPECA (Special Programs for the Economies in Central Asia), CIS (commonwealth of Independent States), EAEC (Euro Asian Economic Community) and ECO (Economic Cooperation Organization.) make technical assistance, financial support to Central Asian transport programs.

The Asian Land Transport Infrastructure Development project, which was endorsed by the UNESCAP at its 48th session in 1992, has three pillars: the Asian Highway (AH), Trans-Asian Railway TAR, and facilitation of land transport projects.[55]

The activities conducted within the context of ECO can be examined within five titles such as "Commerce and Investment", "Transportation and Communication", "Energy, Mining and Environment", and "Agriculture and Industry", However, during the past 15 years, transportation, transit routes and trade facilitation took the central position within the activities of ECO towards CASs. The Izmir Treaty (Sep. 14, 1996) which provided the basis for establishment of ECO, called for "accelerating the development of Transport and Communications infrastructures linking the member states with each other and with the outside world." To facilitate this, the ECO Secretariat annually plans eleven to fourteen ECO and non-ECO events. Besides, the member states in May 1998 adopted the Transit Transport Framework Agreement (TFA), heavily drawing on TIR convention. TTFA could become the key driver of all activities related to the removal of non-physical barriers, to the harmonization of operations and regulations, and the accession by member states to international transport conventions and standards[56].

---

[55] Source: htpp://www.unescap.org/

[56] ECO Prospects and Challenges in Transport and Communication Sectors, Tehran, 2002, p.8, http://www.ecosecretariat.org/

Turkey's only rail connection to Central Asia goes through Iran but not effectively working. Because of the problems with Armenia rail connection of Turkey to CIS countries is closed. Turkey, Georgia and Azerbaijan have been focused to join their rail networks through Kars-Ahalkala connection where feasibility study already performed and governmental negations are continuing and mainly focused on finance of the program. Estimated budget is slightly over 400 million USD. The capacity of the route estimated around 20 million ton/py, which will give a tremendous potential to regional countries.

Turkey's air connection to the CAS has been started immediately after dissolution of FSU. For the time being, national air carrier of Turkey-Turkish airlines has flight to all the capitals within the region (Astana, Tashkent, Dusanbe, Bishkek and Askahabat) and preferable connection for many westerners from Istanbul.

Infrastructure

Limited financing remains a key problem for Turkish firms seeing to make infrastructure investments in Central Asia. Financial bottlenecks, coupled with security issues, cause serious interruptions in many projects. Although institutions like the European Bank for Reconstruction and Development (EBRD) and the International Finance Corporation (IFC) provide private sector financing, both require significant credit conditions and international financial guarantees, both which are —this is difficult for Turkish entrepreneurs given their limited assets. The credit costs for Turkish investment are further increased by the relatively low credit ratings of Central Asia states, with the exception of Kazakhstan.[57]

In an attempt to rectify the situation, the Turkish government is working to provide levels of credit, including new investment credits and country risk insurance programs, via the Turkish Eximbank. In the meanwhile almost all of the Eximbank's current credits programs have been

---

[57] "Economic Relations Between Turkey and Turkic States", 8th Five Year Development Program, 2000, p127,see for more information www.ekutup.dpt.gov.tr/disekono/oik528.pdf

suspended due to lack of repayment by the Central Asians. Indeed, Uzbekistan is the only country in the region that does not have severe problems relating to credit payments.

Legal and Institutional Issues

Bureaucracy and administrative caprice are excessive in every country of Central Asia. Moreover, complex decision-making processes cause causing frequent delays in work. The interference of a seemingly endless number of various authorities on the grounds of technical, commercial, environmental, or fiscal issues imposes yet more delays.

Economic and commercial laws and regulations across Central Asia are underdeveloped. Gaps and differences in interpretation cause legal conflicts, while the mechanisms for resolving these conflicts are insufficient and entail complex and costly procedures. An effective arbitration authority is essential for the resolution of legal conflicts. To this end the Istanbul Chamber of Commerce and Chamber of Trade are establishing an internationally recognized arbitration center that can serve the region.

Problems with credit and banking often arise in Central Asia due to the underdeveloped systems of accounting, poor application of international standards for accounting, inadequate regulations for mortgages and bankruptcy, and other related concerns. Continuous changes in the regulations have created an unpredictable environment for foreign firms; indeed they might encounter different bureaucratic requirements within the same country.

Foreign firms are often subjected to repeated audits by various official agencies . Such excessive oversight chills relations with Turkish and other foreign investors. Laws concerning foreign investors and investments are often unclear, while inadequate commercial bankruptcy cause serious problems in collecting payments. In Kazakhstan, exemptions that had previously been granted were later abolished during a wave of economic nationalism. Such issues, repeated endlessly continue to raise difficulties and disadvantages for foreign investors.

The implementation of free-trade zones in Kazakhstan and the Kyrgyz Republic has been an important improvement. Yet discrepancies in the laws governing them are creating serious problems. For example, in Kazakhstan, a free trade zone that included exception from the value-added tax (VAT) has not applied the relevant laws properly, posing a serious problem to Turkish firms.

Across Central Asia foreign commerce and exchange have been subjected to rigid restriction. For example, quotas on cash transfers are still widespread, which is made worse by the general tendency not to allow the use of cash for payment. In Uzbekistan and Turkmenistan, the convertibility problem is especially serious, despite Uzbekistan's nominal decision to accept convertibility. The operations of foreign firms are further hindered by broad discrepancies between official and black market exchange rates.[58]

Outside of Kazakhstan, local banking services cannot meet the needs of foreign entrepreneurs. In fact, Turkish businessmen believe the region's banking concepts are incompatible with world practice. And the accreditation processes create additional problems. Other serious issues include slow transactions and processing, delays on the transfer of money orders into accounts, and the lack of cash for paying workers, even when e early notice of paydays has been given. In some of the Central Asian states, the required use of broker firms with very limited quotas further increases difficulties and raises the cost of operation.

Recent regulations in Turkmenistan, have ceased the foreign correspondent accounts of partnered banks, with all money orders now being handled by the brokerage arm of the Turkmenistan Central Bank. This increases the cost of transactions and reduces the competitive power and effectiveness of foreign-partnered banks. The Turkmen Turk Bank, which is partnered with the Turkish Ziraat Bank, has expressed grave concerns over these new regulations.

---

58 "Economic Relations Between Turkey and Turkic States", 8th Five Year Development Program,Ankara,2000, p130, see for more information www.ekutup.dpt.gov.tr/disekono/oik528. pdf

Customs Organizations

The imposition of unofficial fees on cargo crossing state borders is a particularly serious customs-related problem, and is endemic in all Central Asia, as well as in Afghanistan. These are compounded by the impediments created by officialdom such as lack of coordination between border agencies on neighboring states, complex procedures, unclear codes and regulations, and the low utilization of information technology in customs operations.[59]

Regional customs organizations do not meet the needs of international trade. Customs employees are underpaid, undereducated, and undertrained. Frequent changes in customs regulations and insufficient control of contraband lead to unfair competition. Some SMEs take advantage the situation, bringing cheap, poor quality goods to the market. Local commerce and trade is further damaged by high and frequently changing tariffs.

Several Central Asian States have unilaterally abrogated previously confirmed exemptions on importation of raw materials and semi-manufactured products. Tariffs on raw materials and depreciation on final products undermine the development of the local manufacturing sector.

Visas and Employment Permissions

Although the procedures for employing foreigners in Central Asian countries have recently been streamlined, problems persist. Visas are expensive and application process complex; these problems are particularly troublesome for temporary, specialized workers. Obtaining permanent visas is also difficult. The durations of work visas are often unacceptably short—only three months in Uzbekistan—leading to frequent re-application, which wastes both time and money.[60] In some

---

[59] World Bank Report, "From Disintegration to Reintegration: Eastern Europe and the Former Soviet Union in International Trade", Washington D.C., 2005, p. 16,
[60] "Economic Relations Between Turkey and Turkic States", 8th Five Year Development Program,Ankara 2000, p. 276, see for more information www.ekutup.dpt.gov.tr/disekono/oik528.pdf

countries, visa procedures have become even more ponderous. For instance, after the assassination attempt on the President of Turkmenistan, Saparmurat Niyazov, Turkmenistan's visa procedures became prohibitively onerous causing some firms simply to suspend operations.

Overcoming Trade Impediments

The following recommendations address the impediments to regional and continental trade enumerated above, and will help integrate Greater Central Asia into the global economy:

1. Improved regional cooperation in trade policy, transport and customs transit could help the CASs lover the trade barriers, expand trade, increase the gains from participation in international trade and reduce the associated risks.[61]
2. Improve transport infrastructure and logistic facilities through national, regional and international programs. Donor programs regarding with transportation and trade facilitation should also be coordinated through regular meetings.
3. Provide continues engagement of international banks and organizations for establishing a base for sustainable development. Try to escape in maximum extent from contradictory Bilateral Trade Agreements (BTA) and Regional Trade Agreements (RTA). However, RTA and BTAs are very important that reflecting individual experience of each country and related region.
4. Remove the transport monopoly of the traditional trade partners, sometimes used as political pressure over CASs, through international programs. Within this context revitalization of TRACECA, AH and TAR programs crucially important. A regional transportation strategy should be developed with the participation of all relevant international organizations. The

[61] Adrian Ruthenberg and Bahodir Ganiev, "Central Asia: Increasing Gains from Trade Through regional cooperation in Trade Policy, Transport, and Customs Transit.", Asian Development Bank, Philippines, 2006, p 36

strategy should focus on improving road, rail, and air transport. Current international programs in this area should be accelerated and receive increased fiscal support.

5. Construction of new pipelines through east, south and west corridors will provide to producer countries to get the market value of their oil and gas. Naturally increasing income will boost the regional economies as well as provide necessary financial sources to remove the structural problems adversely affecting trade within the region. Eventually, the goal is to create a fully integrated transportation network- including upgraded highways, pipelines, railroads, ports, ferries, fiber-optic lines, electricity transmission lines- that will make it easier for the states of Central Asia and the Caucasus to trade not only with each other but also with Europe, the Middle East, and the rest of the world.

6. WTO accession is a critical policy objective for the five regional countries that are not yet members. WTO membership will provide realistic mechanisms for each country to overcome its trade-related problems. Western countries and Turkey, having significant economic and security interests in the region, should support and accelerate the accession process by providing funding and technical assistance.

7. International economic institutions, such as the World Bank, IMF, WTO and OECD, should enhance their cooperation with the region, especially in the promotion of continental trade. The West and Turkey can collaborate to provide technical assistance and capacity-building to the countries of Central Asia, strengthening their trade-related institutions and helping them to implement and manage sound trade policies. Istanbul's OECD private sector development center can play a larger role by increasing and diversifying its training work, Turkey can also provide additional technical assistance, such as utilizing its WTO experience and establishing a WTO training center for the region under the umbrella of Turkish trade institutions.

8. Improving regional security will improve the climate for business and trade. Central Asian states should therefore be encouraged to deepen their relations with such Western institutions such as NATO and other specialized institutions that can facilitate regional military reform while at the same time encouraging the regional governments to focus on the development of democratic institutions.
9. International support and assistance aside, free market reform is largely dependent on the implementation efforts of the governments of the Central Asian states themselves. Necessary policy changes include tariff reductions, the termination of non-tariff barriers, and the elimination of export disincentives, active pursuit of WTO accession, vigorously working to attract foreign direct investment, and harmonizing existing regional trade agreements with one another.[62]
10. It will take time to eliminate barriers in the form of inefficient bureaucracies, customs gates, and other practices both intentional and unintentional. In the long-term, though, consistent progress in overall institutional helps eliminate these human-generated barriers as well. Among general reforms, a comprehensive strategy to eliminate poverty and social inequality is of the utmost importance.
11. In addition to the more comprehensive application of standard international policies on trade, intraregional bilateral economic relations should be institutionalized through periodic meetings and common policy mechanisms. While this institutionalization already exists between Turkey and each Central Asian country on bilateral basis, better region-wide policy mechanisms are still needed. Since many Turkish companies work in the region, they

[62] Harry Broadman, World Bank Report, "From Disintegration to Reintegration: Eastern Europe and the Former Soviet Union in International Trade", Washington D.C., p.44, 2005, http://web.worldbank.org/WBSITE/EXTERNAL/COUNTRIES/ECAEXT/0,,contentMDK:20723133~pagePK:146736~piPK:146830~theSitePK:258599,00.html

should maintain a forum for discussing, investigating and solving the problems they experience in Central Asia.

12. TIKA is the main Turkish body responsible for aid and development programs in Central Asia. Increasing TIKA's budget could directly improve these programs. TIKA has spent fifteen years working with the region, developing considerable expertise in the process. TIKA could become a focal point for implementing aid and technical assistance programs sponsored by other international organizations and NGOs, as well as those from Turkey only.

Conclusions

Despite the turbulent relations that exist from time to time, Turkey is a focus for the rulers and elites of other majority-Muslim countries as well as for the EU. It is inevitable, then, that Turkey's successful EU accession would deeply impact the Central Asian states and would in turn affect their strategic preferences.

Turkey has pursued economic, political, social and cultural relations with the countries of the Greater Central Asia since they gained independence in 1991-1992. The positive fruits of this interaction can be seen in the growth of trade, increases in the number of Turkish firms operating and investing in the region, and in the number of bilateral economic, social and cultural agreements and programs. Turkey has amassed considerable information on Central Asia, and Turkish public opinion surveys on the region are well developed. Moreover, Turkey has put considerable effort into evaluating regional issues and developing solutions, and on establishment and maintenance of regional cooperative institutions.

Stability in Central Asia is key to overcoming existing difficulties and increasing cooperation in trade. Radical reforms are still required for the full development of free market economies in the region, and international support fore reforms should therefore be enhanced and accelerated. Free market reforms will facilitate economic development and reinforce the process of democratization, which in turn will help to solve continuing political and social problems.

Once positive developments have been observed Western interest in Central Asia will be encouraged to seek further opportunities for renewal and reform. Accession to the WTO, and similar organizations, and requisite free market reforms will remove barriers to international trade. This, coupled with the improved business climate, will attract more Western firms to the region, while possibly creating serious competition for Turkish entrepreneurs, this development will be beneficial to the economic and social life of Central Asia itself. The further development of continental trade will improve all the key economic, social and political indicators of Central Asian countries. But transport-related problem across the region must be solved before trade can be developed, and these have as much, or more, to do with legislation or administrative factors (i.e: the human element) as with physical infrastructure, however inadequate that may be.

Russia

Vladimir Boyko

This paper examines the current and possible future role of Russia in continental trade and other kinds of cooperation within the space conditionally called Greater Central Asia.[1] In order to identify the main drivers of cooperation/linkages between Russia and Greater Central Asia, a multi-level (macro-regional/regional/sub-regional) approach has been chosen, focusing on Russia and post-Soviet Central Asia and other Asian states; Asiatic Russia (the Siberian Federal District) and the rest of Asia; the Russian Altai and the rest of Asia including other parts of Altai, China, Mongolia, and Kazakhstan. The analysis is based on relevant international and regional data, and on fieldwork undertaken by the author in the period 2000 – 2006.

---

[1] Although this book frames Greater Central Asia as constituted by five post-soviet republics and Afghanistan, assumed as a bridge for cooperation with South Asian countries and some other interested states, the author will follow the approach more justified from a scholarly (historical-civilizational) point of view and include also the Xinjiang in China, Mongolia, and some Russian borderlands (Altai and some other territories of South-Western Siberia, etc).
Kazakhstan's former minister of foreign affairs, K.Tokaev, in his talk at the international conference "Partnership, trade and cooperation in Greater Central Asia" (Kabul, April 2006) pointed out, that "... besides the territory of traditional Central consisting of Kazakhstan, Uzbekistan, Kyrgyzstan, Tajikistan, Turkmenistan and Afghanistan, it is sometimes complimented by parts of Pakistan and Iran, Azerbaijan, Xinjiang-Yughur autonomous region of China, the Urals and Western Siberia and Mongolia". - http://www.afghanistan.ru/doc/5494.html
This approach fits with R.Cutler's formula of Central Eurasia which "(like Greater Central Asia) includes swaths of
Russia and China, but not necessarily the whole of both countries". Cutler, Robert M. "Central Asia and the West after September 11," Originally published in *NATO and the European Union: New World, New Europe, New Threats,*
Hall Gardner ,ed., London: Ashgate, 2004, pp. 219–231.- http://www.robertcutler.org/download/html/ch03hg.html

Regional Integration as a Theoretical Framework

Regional cooperation and integration can be seen as an evolving processes rather than as a uni-directional movement towards a pre-determined outcome. Through the various regional integration arrangements across the globe, countries are seeking to find new cooperative solutions to existing problems and to improve collective decision-making to resolve issues that cannot be dealt with by national governments alone. Globalization has opened up a space between the national and global levels of decision-making and policy-formulation, within which states and non-state actors can develop the processes and institutions that guide and restrain the collective activities of groups. Governance is here understood as a multi-faceted process of regulation that is based upon laws, norms, institutions, policies, and voluntary codes of conduct. It thereby involves both "hard" and "soft" regulation. Economic integration has both historical and modern dimensions, and quite rightly attracts the attention of politicians and experts worldwide.[2] One of the responses to the challenges of the new century is to create networks of new infrastructural and trade linkages on both regional and macro-regional levels and to conceptualize them in new formulas that express the emergence of new geo-political and geo-economic forces and players.[3]

---

[2] Slocum, Nikki, and Langenhove, Luk Van, *The Meaning of Regional Integration: Introducing Positioning Theory in Regional Integration Studies.* UNU-CRIS: United Nations University, Comparative Regional Integration Studies. UNU-CRIS e-Working Papers W-2003/5; *Regional Integration and Security in Central Asia: Search for New Interaction Mechanisms for Analytical Community and Governments during Formulation and Promotion of Regional Initiatives.* CAG Working Paper Series, # 1. May 15, 2006. – http://www.cagateway.org ; Alchinov V.M., "Protsessi regionalnoy integratsii v Evrope I na post-sovetskom prostranstve: interesi Rossii," Summary of doctoral thesis). Diplomatic Academy of the Ministry of Foreign Affaies of the Russian Federation. Moscow, 2006; Rutland, Peter. "Russia's Economic Role in Asia: Toward Deeper Integration.," *Strategic Asia 2006-07: Trade, Interdependence, and Security*, Seattle: The National Bureau of Asian Research, 2006.

[3] Starr, S. Frederick, "A Greater Central Asia Partnership for Afghanistan and Its Neighbors", *Silk Road Paper*, March, 2005, p. 17; see also: Starr, S. Frederick, "A Partnership for Central Asia," *Foreign Affairs*, July-August 2005.

S. F. Starr publicized his idea of a Greater Central Asia (GCA) (which is not a new term) in the early 2000s, conceptualizing a vast zone of cooperation including post-soviet republics and adjacent countries in South and West Asia.[4] His GCA partnership scheme called upon cooperation of the five Central Asian republics plus Afghanistan. Their close connection with South Asia has been welcomed by the expert community with certain reservations. Many analysts, especially those in Russia and the CIS, perceive it as part of a continuing effort to reframe the Asiatic rim (including former Soviet republics) in accordance with US visions and strategies.[5] According to some CIS analysts (M. Laumulin, etc), the basic purpose of the GCA partnership is to connect Central Asia and Afghanistan to form a cohesive military-strategic and geopolitical entity and than to link it with the Greater Middle East which, at the time it was proposed, would supposedly be controlled by the West.[6] It is said, further, that this project aims to shift this extended region out from under the supposedly monopolistic influence of Russia and China.

---

[4] See, for instance: Canfield, Robert L., "Restructuring in Greater Central Asia: Changing Political Configuration", *Asian Survey*, vol. 32 no. 10, October 1992, pp. 875-887; Belokrenitsky V.Y., "Russia and Greater Central Asia," *Asian Survey*, vol. 33 no. 12, December 1993, pp. 1093-1108; Naumkin V.V. (ed.), *Tsentral'no-Aziatskii makroregion i Rossiia,* Moscow, 1993.
One of the first references to the subject is Starr, Frederick S., "Afghanistan: Trade and Regional Transformation,

http://www.asiasociety.org/publications/update_afghanreform.html#trade;
Alexei Voskressenski, one of the brightest Russian Orientalists with a strong methodological focus, frames the vast Eurasian space as consisted of several mega-zones, which in turn are constituted by regions, etc. The separate countries can be divided into different regions within two or even three different regional clusters according to various parameters, forming a "Eurasian Far East and Siberian Meso-Area". Voskressenski , Alexei D., "Regional Studies in "Russia and Current Methodological Approaches for the Social/Historical/Ideological Reconstruction of International Relations and Regional Interaction in Eastern Eurasia," *Reconstruction and Interaction of Slavic Eurasia and Its Neighboring Worlds.*, Ieda. Osamu and Uyama, Tomohiko, Slavic Research Center, 2006. - http://src-h.slav.hokudai.ac.jp/coe21/publish/no10_ses/contents.html.

[5] *Novaya bolshaia igra v bolshoi tsentralnoi Azii. Mifi i realnost*, Bishkek, 2005, 192 p.

[6] Laumulin M., "Bolshaya Tsentralnaya Aziia (BTsA): noviy megaproject SSA?", p. 29.

It appears that GCA follows a neo-Westfalian paradigm of international politics, organized around of nations-states. Assessments of the proposed GCA partnership range from "a big illusion" to «an idea ahead-of-its time». The Uzbek analyst F.Tolipov is right is stating that Central Asia and Afghanistan comprise a single "security complex". Tolipov calls Starr's idea of establishing a regional forum (Partnership on cooperation and development in Greater Central Asia) a "new Marshall plan" for Central Asia and suggests that it be multilateral rather than solely an American project.[7]

One of the loudest opponents of Starr's GCA formula is the Russian historian and journalist A. Knyazev, who is currently a professor at the Kyrgyz-Russian Slavonic University in Bishkek. He argues that the regional integration projects under discussion are nothing more than efforts to maintain US influence in this region, whether in "traditional" Central Asia or in the extended version that includes Afghanistan.[8]

Meanwhile, the Russian analyst A. Bogaturov found all recent US regional concepts for Central Asia to be nothing but an attempt to

---

[7] Ibid, p. 52

[8] Knyazev A., "Situatsiia v Afghanistane i Proyekt Bolshoi Tsentralnoi Azii," *Novaya Bolshaya Igra ...,* p. 85
A.Knyazev never question the historical Central Asia-Afghanistan interconnection in the spheres of economics, politics, ethno - confessional life, culture and mentality, but refers to the extended breakdown of ties and mutual isolation during the Soviet and post-Soviet periods. He says that any approach of Euro-Atlantic politics towards Afghanistan and Central/South Asia should be determined on a country-by-country and regional basis.
In 2003 A.Knyazev took part in a small research project with TACIS support, aimed to explore opportunities of border cooperation of Central Asian states and Afghanistan's northern provinces (Takhor, Kunduz, Baglan, Badakhshan). It was found that many local leaders involved in drugs business were seeking to legalize their capital and invest it in the legal economy. An example of these new activities is electric power supplies by Tajik company "Barqi Tajik", which are regularly paid from local (Afghan) sources.
Bilateral economic activities on the local level would aggravate the traditional Afghan regionalism, according to

Knyazev A., "Ekonomitcheskoe vzaimodeystvie Afghanistana i tsentralnoaziatskikh gosudarstv i problemi regionalnoi

bezopasnosti ," (http://www.afghanistan.ru/doc/6517.html

produce "flank stabilization" across what could become an alternative energy belt for the West. He argues that the US, whether unintentionally or by design, has successfully tied its worldwide anti-terrorist campaign with the goal of gaining access to new energy resources, which would be transported from the Eurasian heartland to the major sea ports. The resulting zone of Washington's geo-strategic interests would run from Russia's Siberian regions into the North Pakistani littoral on the South, and from the Caucasus/Caspian region on the West, to the Kazakhstan-Chinese border on the East. According to Bogaturov, American military and security experts are actively considering Afghanistan's role as a potential transport corridor for energy resources between Central Asia and the Indian Ocean. It is doubtful that these projects are feasible but they are nonetheless highly attractive, as they constitute alternative transport routes for energy. Fairly or not, the USA and EU have considered formerly Soviet Central Asia, above all Kazakhstan but also Turkmenistan, as a rich energy source and "Greater Central Asia" as the belt of territories across which these resources must be transported.[9]

Bogaturov from his side proposes to create a new transcontinental transport corridor that would extend to the Russian heartland and would export gas and oil to the USA. Today only a northern route via Murmansk is under discussion. But if US efforts to build the energy routes from Central Eurasian mainland southwards bear fruit, then Russia's inclusion in this corridor may be of real value. Indeed, a Siberian energy corridor to the South may be of benefit to all, and warrants serious consideration.[10]

Eurasian Alternative Plans for Integration: Chino-Centric Globalization?

When exploring Russia's possible role in trade and cooperation to the East, it should be taken into account that there already exist regional integration entities. An interesting vision of these phenomena is

---

[9] Bogaturov A., "Indo-Sibirskii corridor v strategii kontrterrorizma," http://www.ng.ru/courier/2005-10- 24/14_koridor.html

[10] Ibid

presented by the Russian analyst S. Louzianin of the Moscow Institute of International Relations. He states, first, that Central Asia is a "virgin land" in terms of integration. Despite the multiplicity of existing projects (United Economic Space, SCO, Eurasec, etc), the main direction of Central Asian integration in the coming decade is not clear, i.e whether it will be oriented towards the North through Kazakhstan and Russia, West via GUAM countries to the EU, South towards Pakistan and India, or eastward to China.

From a Russian perspective, the value of a northern orientation is obvious, for it would take advantage of old Soviet pipelines and infrastructure to Russia, Kazakhstan's growing prosperity, and Uzbekistan's recent decision to join the Eurasec integration. Evidence of such northward integration is to be found in the growth of trade between Russia and the countries of Central Asia (in 2005 - 2006 alone it expanded from $13.2 to $17 billion); growing investments in Central Asia by large Russian companies that now total $ 4.1 billion; the intensification of energy cooperation between Russia and Kazakhstan, Uzbekistan, and Turkmenistan and Russia's own growing prosperity.

However, the Central Asian countries themselves do not see this northward orientation as inevitable or even particularly desirable. Regional elites of both the old and new generation would like to reach out beyond the possibility of integration with Russia. One heady option is for a link to South Asia (India, Pakistan), which offers unlimited opportunities in the exchange of goods, energy resources, and services. The Indian giant is considered as more attractive than Russia as an integrative center, source of investments and of technologies. Turbulence in Afghanistan and Indo-Pakistani tensions present obstacles to this dream, however.

The weakness of the northern scenario lies in its connection with the prospects of the Commonwealth of the Independent States (CIS). Once a grand integration idea advanced by Kazakh president Nursultan Nazarbayev, this integration format is now reduced to Russia and Kazakhstan. The northward variant is weakened by the decay of the CIS, which has reached the point that even president Nazarbayev, a proponent of such ties, speaks mainly today of Kazakh-Russian links.

The southward-looking hopes of Central Asians are inspired by the trilateral Russian-Chinese-Indian partnership which, in terms of energy, transport and security, would revolve around Central Asia. However, the three major powers view Central Asia in this scenario as a subordinate transit zone, with all the benefits going to Russia, India and China. Also uncertain are the prospects of a Central Asia-South Caucasus-Black Sea orientation, as the South Caucasus countries have their own demanding local needs, i.e to maintain the hydrocarbon corridor of the Baku-Tbilisi-Ceyhan pipeline, to resist Russian pressures, and to strengthen ties with EU, NATO, and the USA.

The eastern scenario calls for China to lead in the integration of Central Asia using above all the SCO framework, and to maintain its own niches at the expense of Russia's interests in Central Asia. The implementation of the Chinese agenda in the framework of SCO may turn Eurasia into a new space, fully oriented towards China and absorbing Eurasec into SCO. This would create a new "post-Chinese" space that would fulfill China's ancient dream of uniting Central Asia with the Middle Kingdom. If one takes into account Beijing's integration plans in the Asian-Pacific rim (ASEAN+3 - Japan, South Korea, and China or ASEAN+China), this could lead to a form of Chinese-based globalization.

This scenario is against the interests of both Russia and of Central Asia. Russia's agenda can be advanced through Russian-Central Asian cooperation.[11] But Chinese investment, technology and trade are like a poison, which is beneficial in small portions but in larger portions can kill. Central Asian commerce with Russia could be balanced and mutually profitable, but with Chinese it is clearly not profitable for Central Asia, as Chinese goods are exchanged only for raw materials. This will eventually kill the region's light and heavy industries. For this

---

[11] Louzianin S. Globalizatsiya po-kitayski: Evrazoyskiye alternative neizbezhnoy integratsii (Chinese-like globalization; http://centrasia.org/newsA.php4?st=1163401260

reason, Russia, together with other SCO members, rejected China's idea of a regional "free trade zone". This is the reason, too, that Central Asian countries (except Kazakhstan) reject Chinese trade credits. Meanwhile, China convinced Kazakhstan to form several free trade zones on their common border. For now, these "windows" are not troublesome but it is easy to predict their future. China can be expected to form such free-trade zones also with Tajikistan and Kyrgyzstan.

Russia still has one more potential source of strength, namely to establish a SCO energy club. This would be equally beneficial to all participants, including SCO non-member Turkmenistan, and would upgrade the role of the energy exporters, i.e. Russia, Kazakhstan, Turkmenistan and Uzbekistan. This suggests that the prospects of China's integration into Eurasia, including Central Asia, are high, and the potential profitability great and more promising than the integration of Russia and Central Asia into some eastward-oriented "Chinese regimen."

Trans-continental or trans-Asian cooperation involves many paradoxes, among them Russia's non-participation to date in such leading international organizations as the powerful Eurasian network ASEM (Asia-Europe meeting). ASEM was formed in 1996 and now includes twenty-five European Union states and thirteen Asian states. Soon some sixty percent of the world's population will be involved in this Eurasian entity. Russia should become a full member of ASEM by 2008, which will strengthen its geopolitical voice and enhance the prospects for reorganizing Eurasian trade and transport in a manner consistent with Russia's methods.

Russia and India

The proposed GCA partnership project is certainly inclusive in that it involves the five former Soviet states of Central Asia, Afghanistan, and the main neighbor states including Russia and Iran. Yet its main focus is on Central Asia's links to Asia. Will this foster Russia's connection with the southern states of Asia as well?

Russian-Indian ties have a long history – Afanasii Nikitin's early journey led eventually to the growth of Russian interest in India under Peter the Great. Peter's goal was to establish a direct route to India via Central Asia's turbulent lands. The first military-reconnaissance expeditions to Central Asia (to Yarkand and Khiva; both failed) were organized in 1715 and 1717. Their aim was to explore possible water routes to India via the Caspian Sea and Amu Darya River. Russian attention later turned from India to Persia as a means of gaining a southern "window". In due course this project failed, but meanwhile Russia-India linkages were being facilitated by Indians themselves. From the seventeenth century a community of Indian traders in Astrakhan controlled the route from Russia to India. By the 1730s Indian turnover of textiles, silk, jewelry, etc. via this "terminal" exceeded all Russia's Eastern trade.[11] It is interesting to note that in the eighteenth century Indians preferred to send goods northbound via Afghanistan and Iran rather than through Central Asia, which was rendered insecure by the raids of Kazakh nomads.

Russian and then Soviet ties with India multiplied in the twentieth century, especially following World War II, even though there were many problems and tensions in what was in reality a marriage of convenience. The breakup of the USSR brought deep changes to the Russian-Indian partnership, and not all of these changes were comfortable for both sides. Commodity turnover between Russia and India fell by four-fifths in the early 1990s and annual bilateral trade (not counting military items) fell to less than $1 billion until 1994, as compared to $ 5.5 billion before 1991. By 1999 - 2000 the annual trade between the countries reached only $ 1.5 billion.

By this time India had become a dynamic Asian superpower, yet one that is dependent on energy resources and raw materials from abroad. Russia is one of India's most favorable sources for both. The export of Russian energy grew, and Moscow meanwhile is moving to diversify its commercial and economic relations with India. Both partners are

---

[11] Petrukhintsev, N.N., "Orenburgskaia ekspeditsiia i 'indiyskie' plani I.K.Kirillova," *Rossiia-India: perspectivy regionalnogo sotrudnichestva (Lipetskaia oblast)*, Moscow, 2000, , p. 206-207.

planning to reach and surpass the scale of trade of the Soviet era. India imports Russian fertilizers, iron and steel, scrap metal, paper and energy.

Nuclear power engineering, information and communication technologies, medical research and space exploration, and energy deliveries constitute the main areas of the emerging high-tech partnership. High-tech, transportation, and energy, according to the Indian analyst Allister Maunk, are the "Three Wedding Rings" of Russia-India cooperation, a view with which Russia concurs.[12] By 2003, commodity exchanges reached $3.3 billion with a peak of $5 billion being predicted soon. Recently the balance of trade started to lean again in Russia's favor, as it did during Soviet times. Russian exports exceed imports by five times ($2.7 billion against $584 million in 2003). But Russia's exports to India still lag behind its exports to the USA, China, Great Britain, Germany and Japan.

Russia's initiative in developing the "South-North" *international transport corridor (ITC)* from Europe to India and Southeast Asia marks a significant new phase of Russian-Indian cooperation.

Officially opened in 2000 by Russian, Iranian, and Indian representatives, this transport corridor connects EU countries via Russia, Iran, and India to the South and Southeast Asian states and the Middle East. ITC shortens the traveling distance from India to Russia from 16,000 km to 6,000, greatly reducing the transport time of Indian goods to Europe. Thanks to the "South-North" ITC, Russia is becoming the main intermediary of economic relations between the EU and India.

The Road from Central Asia: Ties with Russia and Pakistan

Pakistan's former, current and future role in the Greater Central Asia partnership is a key variable and will be determined by many domestic and external factors. This country is now internationally isolated due to its Cold War era heritage and recent controversies with both Afghanistan

---

12 "Economic Cooperation Between Russia and India," http://www.axisglobe.com/article.asp?article=1

and India. Nevertheless, Pakistan might come to play a central role in trans-Asiatic economic networking.

The USSR welcomed the emergence of Pakistan, but opposed its participation in SEATO and CENTO, which it saw as part of a US policy to contain Moscow. It also viewed with great concern Pakistan's close alliance with China. Against this background of suspicion engendered by Pakistan's partnerships and alliances, there were instances when both the Soviet Union and Pakistan took significant steps to improve their relations. President Ayub Khan's visit to Moscow in April, 1965, was the first direct personal contact between the top leaders of Pakistan and the USSR. The visit resulted in the signing of three agreements on trade, economic cooperation and cultural exchanges. April 1968 saw the visit of Soviet Premier Kosygin to Pakistan. As a consequence of that visit, Moscow announced a limited quantity of arms to be supplied to Pakistan. According to recently released Soviet archival documents, the Soviet leadership viewed Pakistan's domestic developments with tolerance. However, Moscow's decision to send military forces to Afghanistan in 1979 greatly worsened its relations with Islamabad.

Despite the ready availability of Russian arms, Pakistan has failed to secure arms sales from Moscow, mainly because the pro-Indian lobby in Russia is very strong and active. Another important point of tension between the countries is Islamabad's intention to build strategic ties with the Central Asian republics, which Russia interprets as an attempt to limit its own influence in that region.[13] However, it is in the long-term interest of Pakistan to establish mutually constructive relations with Russia. Russia already took steps to involve Pakistan in the SCO.

Henceforth, Russian leaders would do well to realize that Pakistan is marginalized internationally by the charge that it is clandestinely hosting the Taliban forces, and that it is overshadowed by its larger neighbor, India. Both Moscow and Islamabad could learn from the example of

---

[13] Ali Shah, Adnan. "Pakistan-Russia relations: and the Post-Cold War era," http://www.issi.org.pk/journal/2001_files/no_2/article/6a.htm

China and Russia, which were adversaries during the Cold War yet their relations have become highly prospective in the twenty first century.

There is much scope for trade and scientific cooperation between Pakistan and Russia. During former Prime Minister Nawaz Sharif's visit to Russia in April, 1999, the two sides signed an agreement to create an inter-governmental commission for trade and economic cooperation, replacing the bilateral accord of 1956. The Russians also showed interest in the construction of power plants, roads, and bridges in Pakistan and in supplying power, engineering, and road construction equipment. Russia also evinced its desire to modernize the steel plant in Karachi, built by the Soviet Union in 1975, with a credit of $525 million to purchase machinery and technology. More recently, the possibility of setting up joint ventures in Pakistan's free trade zones, as well as direct interaction between Pakistani exporters and Russian regions, has emerged. Russian engineers were already participating in the modernization of the Pakistan Steel Mill, and a tank production deal between Uralvagonzavod plant and Islamabad was signed in 2004, while KAMAZ, one of the Russia's biggest truck makers, has announced its intentions to begin production in Pakistan. Meanwhile, many items of future mutual trade between the two countries have been identified. To advance this relationship further it is important that Russia, Pakistan and the Central Asian states resolve their outstanding issues, and that they do so in a regional framework.[14] The decision to allow Pakistan to become an observer in SCO is therefore a meaningful step towards ending that country's international isolation.

Russia-Iranian Intimacy

Iran figures centrally in Russia's plans to link Greater Central Asia and the broader world. But despite its own geopolitical ambitions and economic growth, Iran today still suffers from the legacy of the political-religious reforms of late 1970s-1980s and is struggling with the challenges of globalization. Russian-Iranian bi-lateral and multilateral relations have

---

[14] Ibid

long been based on mutual accommodation and compromise. Unfortunately, Russia-Iran nuclear deals overshadow other aspects of their cooperation, which extends to many fields. Trade and economic cooperation is undertaken in accordance within the inter-government agreement of 14 April 1997. A main motor of Russian-Iranian ties is the Permanent Russo-Iranian Commission on Trade and Economic Cooperation, the Russian chair of which is Sergey Kirienko, the head of Rosatom. Currently the two countries are planning projects worth $ 8 billion total.

Table A: Russia-Iran trade turnover, according to data of the Federal Customs Service (mln USD)

	2000	2001	2002	2003	2004	January-November 2005
Total turnover	661,4	933,5	803,0	1390,5	2012,4	1,906
Export	607,8	899,1	753,5	1327,8	1910,2	1796,8
Import	53,6	34,4	50,0	62,7	102,2	109

Potential large-scale projects include the construction of a coal-driven power station "Tabas", with the simultaneous development of the "Mazino" coal field at an estimated cost of $ 1 billion; Iran's purchase of five Russian TU-204-100 airplanes; and the building of a 375 km railroad line from Qazvin via Resht and Enzeli to Astara within the framework of the North-South transport corridor. In November 2005 both countries signed memoranda to establish a Russian-Iranian business council.[15]

A major Russian-Iranian initiative is for "Gazprom" and its Iranian counterpart to construct a trans-continental gas pipeline from Iran via Pakistan to India, a distance of 2,700 km and at a cost of $ 4.1 billion. But

---

[15] http://www.mid.ru/ns-rasia.nsf/1083b7937ae580ae432569e7004199c2/f59eef21d4cb660043256a54002a62ae?OpenDocument

for now this project is stalled, with India shifting its main interest to a proposed project from Turkmenistan via Afghanistan and Pakistan. Separate from this, Gazprom is already getting dividends from its joint exploitation of Iran's important South Pars gas field, although it has yet to get the right to export gas from it. Russia's proposed pipeline could also be used to export Turkmenistan gas but Turkmenistan prefers instead an alternative gas pipeline to India via Afghanistan.[16]

There are fears in the West that if Russia and Iran were to combine forces, a "gas OPEC" will be born. Russia's gas reserves in 2005 were 48 trillion cubic meters, and Iran's 27.5 trillion, which together comprise 42% of world reserves. A Russian-Iranian consortium for gas production would differ from OPEC, however, in that it would monopolize not only the production of gas but also its transport to world markets.

Russia-Central Asia Relations: the Impact of History[17]

Analysts point out the "absence in Russian historical writings of a general conception of Central Asia that includes Kazakhstan and South Siberia".[18] Such a vision could not be developed by Soviet historiography, with its focus on only a few politicized topics and its artificial divisions among sub-disciplines. The current state of research has improved, but there exists no broad historical-geographic approach to the region as a whole. However, it is worth considering the idea of Harvard professor R. Frye who agreed that Central Asia constitutes a cultural unity, but one made up of the dichotomy of nomadic and sedentary peoples and states. Accordingly, constituent parts of Central Asia, such as Eastern Persia and Eastern (Chinese) or Altai Turkistan are nothing but "border" zones/cultures in between the main sedentary areas of Russia, China, India and the semitic Near East. Very specific patterns in such areas as

[16] "Gazprom" tianet trubu v Indiiu iz Iran," http://i-r-p.ru/page/stream-event/index-6009.html

[17] Kaushik, Devendra, "Russia and Central Asia relations: reassertion of Russia's Eurasian identity," *Contemporary Central Asia*, vol. 8 no. 1-2, 2003, pp. 1 – 31.

[18] Verkhoturov, D.T, "Osnovi sibirskoi kulturnoi samostoatelnost," http://www.dialog.kz/print.php?lan=russian&id=139&pub=1149

irrigation, trade, and commerce give meaning to the whole and assure its survival as an entity.[19]

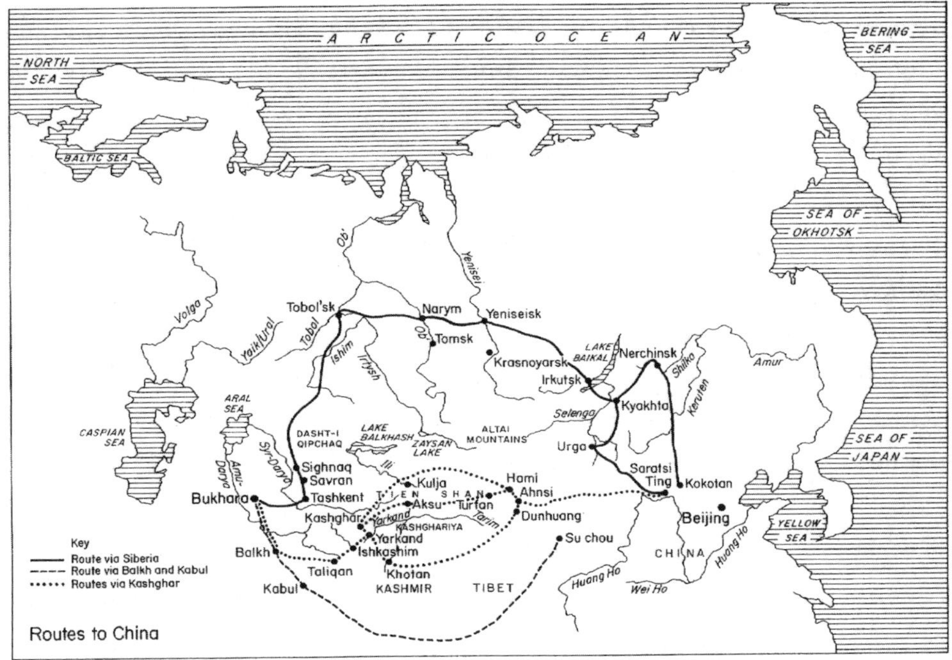

Map of trade routes from Siberia to Bukhara and China in XVI – XVIII. – Drawn from: Burton, Audrey. "Bukharan trade 1558 – 1718." Papers on Inner Asia # 23, Bloomington, Indiana, 1993

In accordance with this and some other frameworks, certain parts of Russia and Central Asia belong in many respects to the same civilizational, geopolitical and geo-economic space, e.g. Eurasia or Central Eurasia. This point may be proven historically as well as by the map.[20]

---

[19] Richard N.Frye, "The Meaning of Central Asia, in: Conference on the Study of Central Asia," March 10-11,
983, Woodrow Wilson International Center for Scholars, Washington, 1983, pp. 11 – 13; see also the the transcript
of his presentation "Pre-Islamic and Early Islamic Cultures in Greater Central Asia" at seminar "Central Asia as a Cultural Area", Papers of Richard Frye, Harvard University Archives, box 12933

[20] See appendix A (Central Asia in Eurasian context)

When the Russian state shifted eastwards and southwards in the XVI – XVIII centuries, it brought not only territorial expansion but also ethnic interactions and mixings, which in turn brought social, economic, and cultural interaction with Tatars, Bukharans, etc .[21]

The ninetienth century witnessed Russian expansion and colonization of the vast territories to the south, producing a cohesive yet socio-politically and ethno-culturally diverse system that endured in various forms for a century and a half. Today new forms of cooperation and integration within the area that was once the Soviet "hyper-state" are under discussion, even though it is recognized that parts of the Central Asian periphery have gained much from independence. Indeed, the bitter debates among scholars do not question the achievements of the Soviet model, even though it eventually failed.

Russia and Post-Soviet Central Asia

There is widespread but not universal agreement among analysts and scholars that Russia has the potential to become again a global pole in the economic, cultural and political spheres. The main object of criticism is the CIS, but others say that this body never aimed at real integration, but only for a peaceful divorce from the Soviet Union. Still others argue the need for a step-by-step reintegration, which is in fact occurring. For the moment, the ideological base of many of the new sovereign states is their independence from Russia, whereas integration is occurring on the basis of their geographical, political, economic commonalities with Russia. President Nazarbayev of Kazakhstan has offered the idea of Eurasianism as the mixture of Slavic, Byzantine, Turco-Mongolian, and European cultures. But this idea is too abstract to serve as a basis for integration. More relevant would be to find solutions to concrete issues faced by all countries in the region. But, again, there are many alternative national schemes for achieving this, not to mention pressures and attractions from the US and EU.

---

[21] Sherstova,L.I., *Turki i russkie v Yuzhnoi Sibiri: etnicheskie protsessy i etno-culturnaia dinamika v XVII – nachale XX vv*, Novosibirsk, 2005

International experience suggests that the success of integration projects is conditioned by the formation of a nucleus of states. In Europe, these were Germany, France and the UK. Lacking powerful businesses, integration efforts must be driven by governments, but state-run activities do not suffice for economic development. The most applicable model for CIS integration today is not the EU but the North American Free Trade Association (NAFTA), especially its umbrella organization under US leadership. Also relevant to CIS integration is the experience of the South-Eastern Asia area.

Russia-Uzbekistan

Russian-Uzbek trade and economic cooperation proceed on the basis of bilateral and multilateral (i.e., CIS) agreements. The main bilateral ones are 1the 992 and 1998 agreements on trade and economic cooperation. In the early 2000s trade fell by 20% for both sides, due mainly to falling cotton production in Uzbekistan, unfavorable weather, and falling world prices for cotton. Since 2003 a steady expansion of trade is evident. By now about 18% of Uzbekistan's external trade is with Russia. Russian exports focus on mechanical and electrical equipment, transport, finished metals, chemicals and pharmaceuticals. Besides cotton, Uzbekistan sells Russia machinery, small cars, and farm produce.

Table B: External trade of the Russian Federation with CIS (in real prices; mln $)

	Export							Import						
	1995	2000	2001	2002	2003	2004	2005	1995	2000	2001	2002	2003	2004	2005
Total	14530	13824	14617	15711	20498	29471	32594	13592	11604	11202	10163	13139	17713	18935
Including trade with EurAZes states[1)]	5815	7974	8278	8497	11172	16335	17257	5128	6236	6169	6063	7528	10140	9164
From total amount per country:														
Azerbaijan	85,6	136	133	277	410	621	858	107	135	81,1	86,8	93,1	139	206
Armenia	127	27,5	75,5	94,5	126	135	191	75,1	44,0	51,8	56,6	78,8	73,7	101
Byelorussia	2965	5568	5438	5922	7602	11219	10118[2)]	2185	3710	3963	3977	4880	6485	5716[2)]
Georgia	48,9	42,3	58,2	91,4	153	230	353	57,9	76,6	83,4	69,0	84,2	107	158
Kazakhstan	2555	2247	2778	2403	3281	4664	6526	2675	2200	2018	1946	2474	3429	3209
Kyrgyzstan	105	103	83,3	104	161	268	397	101	88,6	61,9	74,2	104	150	145
Moldova	413	210	240	269	306	372	448	636	325	347	281	404	496	548
Tajikistan	190	55,9	69,4	67,9	129	183	240	167	237	130	66,0	70,0	75,9	94,9
Turkmenistan	93,1	130	140	143	222	242	224	179	473	39,1	32,1	28,4	43,2	77,2
Uzbekistan	824	274	409	453	512	767	861	889	663	584	344	485	613	904
Ukraine	7149	5024	5282	5885	7598	10770	12403	6617	3651	3845	3230	4438	6100	7777

The data drawn from Russian Federal Statistical Service web-site: http://www.gks.ru/free_doc/2006/b06_13/24-08.htm

Table C: Foreign trade of Russian Federation with Asia (beyond CIS) (in real prices; mln$)

	1995	2000	2001	2002	2003	2004	2005
Asia							
Afghanistan	17,6	11,2	7,8	32,3	54,5	75,9	104
Vietnam	322	168	163	321	357	707	739
Hong Kong	311	136	153	184	322	318	349
Israel	624	1045	945	1095	1454	1437	1538
India	998	1082	1123	1630	2735	2502	2314
Iran, Islamic Republic	249	633	904	757	1312	1912	1927
China	3371	5248	5596	6837	8252	10105	13048
North Korea	70,1	38,4	61,8	68,7	111	205	228
Korean Republic	747	972	1108	1271	1324	1963	2361
Mongolia	197	182	216	232	284	363	443
United Arab Emirates	194	178	248	386	270	479	690
Pakistan	41,1	62,7	57,3	81,5	70,8	227	231
Singapore	490	477	575	522	158	190	309
Syria	75,4	95,5	131	143	209	321	440
Thailand	389	80,2	71,4	96,0	130	373	547
Taiwan	463	404	258	463	837	1987	1438
Turkey	1644	3098	3246	3358	4807	7440	10857
Japan	3173	2764	2427	1803	2421	3404	3743

Data drawn from Russian Federal Statistical Service web-site: http://www.gks.ru/free_doc/2006/b06_13/24-07.htm

Russia-Tajikistan

A 2006 the SCO summit document liberalized regime of road transport among member states. However, other SCO members, notably Tajikistan, were interested in curbing exports from China. At this same time Russian president Putin suggested establishing an SCO Energy club in order to unite energy producers, consumers and transit states. Russia declared its readiness to construct an energy network to buy hydro-electricity from Tajikistan and Kyrgyzstan and transit it to the rest of Central Asia and South Asia.[22] This energy club is focused heavily on Tajikistan.

Among its urgent projects were the construction of the Sangtudin power station and completing the Rogun station. The Russian aluminum firm Rusal invested $50 million in the Sagtudin project but the deal was fiercely disputed. Meanwhile, Lukoil approached Tajik authorities with an offer of cooperation in oil and gas, promising to construct a textile factory, supermarket, and business center in Dishanbe. The total of Lukoil's proposed investments could reach $1 billion. But the Rogun project, only recently called a symbol of Russia-Tajik strategic partnership, is now stopped, with the Tajik side accusing Rusal of breaking its agreement, and the World Bank upholding Tajikistan's charges. Instead, Tajikistan decided early in 2007 to complete the project on its own, seeking foreign investments elsewhere as necessary. Clearly, this breakdown has political as well as economic implications.[23]

Russia and Afghanistan: from allies to conflict, and now renewed cooperation.

The American idea of promoting Afghanistan as the connecting bridge between Central and South Asia is fully justified from both economic and other perspectives. Its role as a crossroads has continued over the millennia and seems a natural path forward today. Indeed, involvement in continental trade over the vast space of Central and South Asia presents Afghanistan options for resolving its social and political problems. Thus, the construction of a gas pipeline from Turkmenistan through Afghanistan to Pakistan and India would allow Afghanistan to serve as an energy bridge between Central and South Asia, garnering transit fees in the process. But some observers assess this project as part

---

[22] Aliakrinskaia, Natalia, "Soyuz razumnich egoistov. Rossiia rasschiriaet svoi ekonomicheskie sviazi v SOS," http://centrasia.org/newsA.php4?st=1158915000

[23] Kozhevnikova, E., "Rogunskii tupik. Kto postroit krupneyshuiu GES Tajkikistana?" http://centrasia.ru/newsA.php4?st=1170482160

of Western geopolitical scheme to move Turkmenistan from under Russian influence.

Meantime, the role of Afghanistan itself should be re-assesssed from a more positive and creative perspective. When Afghanistan regained its independence in 1919, the new Afghan king Amanullah-Khan failed to fulfill his ambitious reform scheme, yet he also aspired to unite major parts of Central Asia under a federative or confederative umbrella. This project of regional political integration under Afghan leadership eventually failed, too, as the Soviet forces established control over the formerly tsarist political space after 1920.[24] Yet, in spite of the numerous political failures of the Afghan elite in the twentieth century, Afghanistan has demonstrated an impressive national coherence and ability at self-governance and, also, significantly, the inclination and skills to cooperate at the national and regional levels.[25]

When speaking of the recent renewal of Russia's interest in Afghanistan, one should note that Russia could come to play a far more considerable role in Afghan affairs even then in the past. The so-called "Afghanistan syndrome" in Russian public life has been partially overcame, not least because the Afghans themselves have reassessed the Soviet presence in their country and recognized some positive elements in it . Few Russians today are inspired by neo-imperialist dreams of ruling others. Most illuminating in this respect is the nationalist A.Prokhanov's recent interview "Russians enjoy the Orient,"[26] in which even he distances

---

[24] Boyko, V., "Afghanistan na nachalnom etape nezavisimogo razvitiia (1920-e gg.): tsentralnoaziatskii kontekst vnutrennei i vneshnei politiki", *Afghanistan I Bezopasnost' Tsentralnoy Azii*,. Knyazev, A.A.. VYp. I, Bishkek, 2004 .

Boyko, V., *Separatizm I regionalism v Bolshoy Tsentralnoy Azii v XX – nachale XXI vv. – Etnicheski separatizm i regionalism v Tsentralnoi Azii i Sibiri: proshloe i nastaiashshee*. Barnaul, 2004.

[25] "Regionalizm v Afghanistane: "Heratskaia respublika," in Rahuima, Abdul, *Musulmanskie strany u granitsy SNG*, Institute of Oriental Studies, , Moscow, 2001.

[26] A.Prokhanov, the well-known nightingale of the Soviet presence in Afghanistan in the 1980s, is still the imperialistic Kipling-like poet of the East: "As every Russian, I am attracted by Asia as a whole. The Russian consciousness, especially that of a Russian military officer, is captured by the mystery and magic of the Orient – whether there are yurts of Kazakh steppe or camels going across jasper-

himself from neo-imperial designs. The dominant approach today is motivated by security concerns and by pragmatic economic intents, the former being aroused by the impact of Afghanistan's domestic situation (especially drugs) on Russia, and the latter by the desire to approach Afghanistan with an eye to mutual profits from trade and other forms of cooperation.

Russia was represented at the London donors' conference for the first time in February, 2006. Foreign Minister Lavrov noted that Russia had not made any commitments at the Tokyo donors' conference in 2000 or at the Berlin follow-up conference. Nevertheless, between 2002 and 2005 Russia rendered $30 million of assistance to Afghanistan in the form of humanitarian aid and sent $200 million worth of supplies for the Afghan national army. Russia, according to the minister, intended to continue rendering Afghanistan the assistance necessary to ensure security and develop mutually advantageous economic cooperation. Moscow also declared its intention to consider writing off Kabul's debt, which Russia estimates at $10 billion.[27]

Russian-Afghan trade turnover for the first ten months of 2005 was $83 million, equal to the whole of 2004. Russian exports heavily prevailed in this sum: $80 million of the total. These data do not include Russian goods sent to Afghanistan via Central Asian countries. Russian exports to Afghanistan consist mainly of machinery and spare parts, whereas Afghanistan exports to Russia dried fruits and furs. Russian-Afghan

---

colored Kara-kum canals, or the ardent air of Kyrgyz valleys. I have never forgotten my journey to Ust-yurt..., there was an old Kazakh graveyard and old crypts. I walked and felt myself surprisingly well. I was never sad since I felt at home and even had thoughts that perhaps Qipchaq blood is running in my veins. Russians inexplicably adore the Orient. ... I think that Anglo-Saxons, including Americans, coming to the Orient, experience the same magic. My Afghanistan experience showed me that American agents, working with the mojahedeen, similarly loved the Orient with a mysterious, Kipling-esque love. There is a kind of wish to embrace, for there is something that is very womanly, loving, mysterious, and ravishing in the Orient ..." Prokhanov ,A., "Russkie obozhaiut Vostok," http://www.cainfo.ru/article/actual-interview/886/?PHPSESSID=5b852020b65f590da1fa3952fa1188e3

[27] Korgun,, V., "Konferentsiia po Afghanistanu v Londone," http://www.afghanistan.ru

trade is far below its potential, due to the lack of information in both countries and the absence of banking institutions. The main prospects for future Russian investment are connected with the restoration and modernization of facilities built initially with Soviet assistance; which still constitute the core of Afghanistan's industrial base. There is also potential is for Russian-Afghan cooperation in the reconstruction of motor roads. Cooperation in the mining sector would also be favorable due to the rich experience and technical expertise at the disposal of Russian companies. Such qualitatively enriching relations must be supported by a new legal basis for bilateral ties, which is currently in preparation. Other agreements under consideration will protect investments and prevent double taxation.

Until recently the Russian-Afghan partnership was expressed only in military-technical assistance, since the scale of Afghanistan's debt to Russia prevented further economic agreements. By 2006 this issue was resolved thanks to the visit to Russia of the Afghan foreign minister, R.D. Spanta. Remaining issues will be resolved through the Club of Rome. Against all odds, trade turnover for 2005-2006 rose by 19% over the previous year, with Russian exports to Afghanistan still heavily dominating.

Two Russian companies have applied to take part in an international tender to develop the Ainak copper deposits. Seven other companies from India, China, the US, and Kazakhstan are also competing. The key issue will not be the actual mining but transportation, as the energy shortage requires that the copper-smelting works be built outside of Afghanistan. Hence, this project entails the whole infrastructural network, including power station, highways and railroads, a concentrating mill, etc.

Another relevant factor will be political, for Kabul is naturally interested in expanding the peace process. Russian diplomats, if involved could, provide useful support in this area.

Various uncertainties complicate Russian business activity in Afghanistan. Under the circumstances it is best not to start with large projects, as their failure would worsen the climate for cooperation. Russian businessmen should be able to compete effectively with Western companies there, although the effect of non-economic and overly political factors cannot be minimized.[28]

Russia brings experience (which is not always positive) and a thorough knowledge of Afghan realities due to its long-time involvements there. Russia is also closer to Afghanistan than most developed Western countries. India and China, which also have interests in Afghanistan, do not posess the specific technologies that Kabul needs. The new Afghan leadership and business community are showing themselves to be interested in cooperation with Russia in the fields of infrastructure and transport. Several schemes are under consideration: Chelyabinsk-made tractors are being sold in the northern Afghan provinces; ZIL and *Russkie Mashiny* hope to export light trailers, medical and passenger mini-buses. Infrastructural cooperation may be furthered if the Russian firm "EES" and the Afghan government agree to export electric power from the Tajik hydro-electric station «Santgudin-1» to Pakistan.[29] The US government strongly supports this project and the work may go instead to the American firm AES.

The Afghans themselves are also requesting Russia's involvement in the Afghan energy sector. Russia's "Ruselprom" firm is already exporting hydro-electric equipment for reconstructing the "Naglu" hydro-electric station, constructed in 1965 with the assistance of the USSR. This deal entails the provision of four sets of hydro-generators, modern digital systems, assembling of equipment, and the training of local staff. Further, in August, 2006, the Afghan Ministry of Energy and Water Resources signed a contract with the Russian company "Technompromexport" valued at $32 million. With funding from the World Bank, this project will reconstruct and modernize the "Naglu" hydro-electric station.[30]

---

[28] Verkhoturov, D., "Rossiisko-afghanskoe ekonomitcheskoe sotrudnichestvo doshlo do konkretnihh proyektov," http://www.afghanistan.ru/doc/7496

[29] Pakhomov, N., "Sotrudnichestvo s Rossiei mozhet pomoch Afghanistanu stat silnee," /3.1.2007. - http://www.afghanistan.ru/doc/7651.html

[30] "Nachalis postavki oborudovaniia dlia vosstanovleniia GES "Naglu," /26.1.2007 http://www.afghanistan.ru/doc/7828.html

Russian-Afghan cooperation from a regional perspective

Russia's regions were involved in international trade since early Soviet times, but the devastated post-civil war economy and Stalin's autocratic regime made difficult any cooperation with such similarly weak adjacent countries as Afghanistan. However, extraordinary opportunities for Soviet firms arose during the 1929 Afghan civil war as Afghanistan's breakup into several centers of power severed the northern regions from their traditional British-Indian markets. It was then that Soviet state-run agencies successfully penetrated the northern Afghan karakul wool and agricultural trade. This zone of influence was maintained during the post-WWII years when Afghanistan benefited from a short-lived USSR-US cooperation that extended to their relations in distant Afghanistan. During the 1980s Soviet-Afghan trade took place at the inter-state, inter-regional, and sometimes even inter-city levels. For example, Russia's Altai province maintained ties in various fields with the Afghan province of Baglan. In 1980s many cooperative agreements were signed. Thus, the "Altaistroy" state construction company operated for many years in Afghanistan's northern areas.

After the Soviet breakup new opportunities for inter-regional Russian-Afghan ties re-emerged. For instance, the Afghan community in Altai (in all about 300 people)[31] offered themselves as intermediaries for economic linkages between Asiatic Russia and Afghanistan, Pakistan, the UAE, etc. Some of the Afghan emigres had money at their disposal, so this would have been advantageous for all. But this sensible proposal was rejected by local Altai business circles. Primarily former Communist party activists or government officials, they preferred to make money on a family/corporate basis. This short-sightedness disappointed many entrepreneurial Afghans and prompted them to flee to the West.

---

[31] Boyko, V.S., "Vihodtsy iz Azii v torgovo-ekonomitcheskoi zhizni I vneshnikh sviazakh Zapadnoi Sibiri v XX .- Sibir v strukture transaziatskikh svyazei," *Problemy prigranichnoi torgovli i mezhregionalnogo vzaimodeistviia*, Barnaul, 2000; and also his "Afghanskaia obshshina na Altae: osnovnye cherty sotsio-kulturnogo profilia.,"

Etnographiia Altaia i sopredelnye territorii, Barnaul, 1998.

In spite of this recent history, Afghanistan is increasingly attractive to Russian businessmen in the Russian East. Even small firms with modest foreign exports are managing to export Altai limber by railway or truck to Afghanistan. This business requires good working relations with Central Asians and Afghans, and smooth custom procedures. There are many further prospects for Russian-Afghan trade -- agricultural machinery, domestic, flour, etc -- but these will not develop until the high transport tariffs are reduced.

Russia-Greater Central Asia Cooperation from a Regional/Sub-Regional (Siberia/Altai) Perspective

Since the middle of the first millennium Siberia was populated by Turkic peoples, who came there a century before Slavs settled in the upper Dnepr valley and established their state at Kiev. The state of Muscovy and the Siberian khanate were both the products of the disintegration of the Mongol-Turkic Golden Horde. Russians reached Siberia in the sixteenth and seventeenth centuries and peacefully merged with indigenous patterns of life. Far more complicated were the ethno-cultural relations over the landmass of Siberia. The Siberian ethnologist L. Sherstova came to the conclusion that over time Russified groups of Turco-Siberian origin developed a new "Asiatic" regional self-consciousness, a new Russian sub-ethnicity formed by diverse migrants.[32]

Thus, Western Siberia, earlier a peripheral part of the Turkic world, evolved into the main base for Russian influence in Asia, a bridge for the transfer of Russian goods to the nomadic Kazakhs, Mongols and other peoples of the western Chinese steppe. Conversively, Siberian towns became centers for the purchase and processing of steppe produce. Another Siberian researcher, V. Zinoviev, argues that it was this fact that caused some Siberian cities in the 1920s to seek to join the Republic of

---

[32] Sherstova, L.I., *Tyurki i Russkie v Iuzhnoi Sibiri*, p. 274.

Kazakhstan, since they constituted a single economical entity that included Kazakh nomads.[33]

Even though Siberia in Soviet times was heavily managed from above, it gained a certain experience with international trade and cross-border interaction that is of value today.[34]

Siberian Trade with CIS countries

In the early 2000s the Siberian Federal District (SFD) accounted for 8% of Russia-CIS trade. Siberia's main trading partners are Kazakhstan, Ukraine, Uzbekistan, and Belorus.

The level of Siberian-CIS trade expresses less the export potential of these territories than conscious decisions by regional authorities. As a result, CIS-oriented trade is 50% of all Siberian trade. The main Siberian export items are machinery and equipment, mineral products, chemical products and chemical equipment, with chemicals, minerals, food-stuffs, machinery and equipment being the chief imports.

---

[33] Zinoviev, V.P., Tovarooborot Sibiri I Tsentralnoy Azii v nachale XX veka," Sibir u Tsentralnaua Aziua: problemy regionalnikh sviazei XVIII - XX. Tomsk, 1999 , 119.

[34] On this phenomenon see the case study coverage by Abdusalamov, M.A., *Problemy ekonomicheskoi integratsii Tsentralnoi Azii i Sibiri*, Tashkent, 1982.

Table D. Siberia's external trade turnover trade with CIS countries in 2002 (in million USD)

	External turnover with CIS	Share in total external turnover	% to 2001	Country share, %
CIS countries in total	2001,8	15,7	91,9	100
Kazakhstan	1055,3	8,3	86,4	52,7
Ukraine	677,8	5,3	89,6	33,9
Uzbekistan	106,6	0,8	96,3	5,3
Belorussia	57,2	0,4		2,9
Kyrgyzstan	41,6	0,3	114	2,1
Tajikistan	23,7	0,2	90,8	1,2
Turkmenistan	18,5	0,1		0,9
Azerbajian	11,5	0,1	160,6	0,6
Armenia	4,1		80,9	0,2
Moldova	3,7		69,2	0,2
Georgia	1,8		90,7	0,1

(Data from the Siberian Customs Department)

Trade with Uzbekistan is particularly relevant to Southern Siberia, since the Siberian industrial complex was planned in Soviet times to supply Central Asia with equipment and machinery. Since the early 2000s Siberian enterprises have participated in Uzbek privatization. Siberian universities are training Uzbeks, and new trading houses and joint transport companies are being organized. Thus, in Samarkand a joint venture with the Novosibirsk Instrument Plant has been established to manufacture optical instruments; a joint-stock company with Yurga Machine-building Plant is purposed for making automobile cranes; and another joint stock company set up by Prodmash in Kemerovo province produces equipment for grain mills and elevators. The result of all this effort has been to increase Uzbek-Siberian trade turnover to $ 2 billion.[35]

These and other projects are being carried out in accordance with WTO requirements. These include liberalizing custom procedures, unifying indirect custom rules, etc. One more constructive change has been the mutual adaptation of improved custom codes by Russia, Kazakhstan, and Ukraine. The Russian code reduces custom procedures to a maximum of three days, and establishes trans-shipping points on transit states for onward deliveries to third countries.

Table E: Russia-Asia ties: Siberia's economic cooperation with more distant countries.

Turnover, thousands USD	2005 (January – November)	2004	2003	2002	2001
Iran	75468,7	20982,0	2117,8	201,1	175,4
Japan	30130,4	42841,7	10896,3	8368,4	-
Cyprus	23230,8	47927,0	103035	10487,5	0
India	21520,8	45905,0	18976,1	1769,7	4263,5
Mongolia	13134,6	14622,0	15472,2	10712,5	2703,9
Slovakia	9703,3	4400,8	8144,1	81,4	183,9
Germany	9459,5	14902,2	12343,7	1493,4	1415,1
China	9493,8	17134,4	15504,4	16599,9	18803,9
Italy	2261,5	3607,6	3674,5	-	2233,7

[35] Tikhomirov, S., "Siberia and Uzbekistan: the beginning of integration," *Siberia and East of Russia Quarterly*, 2002,
Nos. 1-2, pp. 14 – 15.

Table F: Siberia's country turnover, 2006

Country	Turnover, thousands USD	Share %	% to 2005
Total	36984549.3	100	133.0
Including (selectively):			
Distant abroad (selectively)	31858456.1	86.1	134.2
Afghanistan	53073.4	0.1	129.4
Vietnam	113771.4	0.3	60.0
Germany	1437069.8	3.9	139.0
Israel	53540.4	0.1	в 5.0р
India	671268.3	1.8	203.7
Iraq	7350.7		82.4
Iran, Islamic Republic	245865.5	0.7	79.8
China	8418865.4	22.8	145.5
Korea, Peoples-Democratic Republic	150871.7	0.4	178.8
OAE	13216.2		в 3.8р
Pakistan	20477.7	0.1	в 7.8р
United Kingdom	799746.2	2.2	111.6
USA	2122751.4	5.7	155.2
Japan	2148980.6	5.8	143.8
CIS	5126093.2	13.9	125.7
Azerbaijan	27551.0	0.1	138.0
Armenia	13678.4		218.7
Georgia	5585.9		133.6
Kazakhstan	2713369.6	7.3	135.6
Kyrgyzstan	301169.0	0.8	176.7
Tajikistan	117714.7	0.3	138.7
Turkmenistan	15400.2		54.7
Uzbekistan	391218.3	1.1	154.9
Ukraine	1537530.6	4.2	102.1

http://www.sibfo.ru/stu/stat.php?action=art&nart=3144

Table G: Cooperation with CIS countries

Turnover, thousands USD	2005 (January-November)	2004	2003	2002	2001
Kazakhstan	294822,1	305900,0	173837,1	107154,7	190146,3
Ukraine	161309,4	173733,9	100711,4	78438,1	30640,1
Uzbekistan	78283,5	75319,1	50722,9	29798,4	44920,9
Belarus	51317,9 (January-October)	43825,1	39939,9	44672,0	36204,3
Tajikistan	26898,0	19726,0	17659,7	8355,6	11024,7
Kyrgyzstan	23135,5	38376,2	17498,4	10717,3	12521,3

Altai-Kazakhstan

In September 1990 the legislature of the Russian Altai region established a free economic zone to link Altai province and what became the Altai Republic with the world economy. The goal was to develop mining and build up new industrial enterprises in close cooperation with external partners. However, legal and organizational uncertainty and a new Russian customs law in 1991 alienated foreign investors. Only in the late 1990s did a more progressive format for foreign trade emerge with a new department of foreign economic ties and new internationally oriented business, both looking mainly to Asia.[36] Kazakhstan is now the main trade partner of Russia's Altai province, with 30% of the total turnover.

---

[36] Distinctive patterns of external cooperation and integration are being introduced on the sub-regional level, within the so called Greater Altai area. See below.

Table H: Altai-Kazakhstan trade turnover, 2000-2005:

	Turnover, thousands USD	Export, Thousands USD	Import, Thousands USD	share % to previous time frame
2000	168109,4	129152,2	38957,2	193,4
2001	190146,3	145464,7	44681,6	113,1
2002	107154,7	80942,2	26212,5	56,3
2003	173837,1	110937,3	62212,5	162,2
2004	303442,1	189009,4	116890,6	176
2005 (Jan-Sep)	237763,3	171600	66163,3	104,6

Impediments to inter-regional cooperation

Altai's cross-border trade is impeded by the fact that automobile and railway border check-points are still poorly organized and not properly equipped. Many are even at a distance from the actual borders, resulting in delays at border crossings and reduced trade. Since January, 2001, the State Customs Committee of the Russian Federation heavily bureaucratized the rules on goods traffic from East and South-East Asia. In Altai province only one check-point was permitted for highways, and transport was re-directed to Moscow. As a result, Altai shuttle-traders were forced to buy goods in remote Eastern Siberia or in Moscow, which naturally reduced trade and increased smuggling.

The following steps are now essential if Altai is again to play a role in regional trade: establish industrial ties between Altai and Kazakhstan enterprises and organize industrial complexes as necessary to build on complementarities; seek investments from abroad for the Altai economy; develop border tourism; and organize trade links between China and Russia via the Altai sector of the Russia-Kazakhstan border.

Altai also has significant trade with Belarus, other CIS countries, and Asia. Top level visits of Altai and Belarussian delegations have resulted in many recent agreements. In the same spirit, a 2005 Uzbek delegation to

Altai charted out extensive possibilities for trade, ranging from cotton yarn and agricultural produce to wood and spare parts.

Altai-Tajikistan

Tajikistan is among the ten top trading partners of Russia's Altai province. Altai province leads Siberia in trade turnover with Tajikistan and stands third among Russia's regions in this regard.[37] This trade, however, is subject to abrupt changes. In 2004 alone the export of lumber doubled, flour grew by six times, while several other products fell sharply. The most stable and important Altai exports to the Tajiks are lumber, farm tractors (from the Alltrac factory), and electric power generators (including for the Dushanbe and Khojent airports).

Fruits and vegetables are the main export items from Tajikistan, although this trade is dominated by Novosibirsk-based intermediaries. Altai entrepreneurs and state agencies actively recruit Tajik labor for construction, the building trades, and agriculture. In nine months of 2005 more than 600 work permits were issued to Tajikistan citizens, with the actual number of migrant laborers being far larger.

Eurasian regionalism and the "Greater Altai" project[38]

The proposal to establish a "Greater Altai partnership" in the field of trade and transport offers an illuminating case-study of both opportunities and impediments for regional interaction in this larger zone of Asia.

---

[37] Nozhkin S., Report at presentation of economic, scientific, and cultural potential of Altai province in the framework of the Russia-Tajikistan economic forum (01.12.2005, Dushanbe)

[38] One of the first detailed coverage of this project was done by O. Barabanov, then senior researcher at the
Institute of Strategic Studies in Moscow, "Greater Altai: a proposed alliance of the regions bordering Central Asia and Siberia.,"
http://www.iiss.org/publications/russian-regional-perspectives-journal/volume-1--issue-2/greater-altai-a-proposed-alliance

The Russian Altai region, consisting of the Altai province and Altai Republic, lies in the strategically important borderof the Russian Federation and Kazakhstan.

The Russian Altai, together with Novosibirsk and Tomsk provinces, constitutes one of the main elements of the current Russian heartland. Altai's political situation is stable, but its economy remains stagnant. The Altai business community and many politicians consider China as the most promising international trade partner. Whether the region advances economically well depends on whether or not proposed highways and gas pipelines to China are actually constructed. However, serious environmental arguments against these projects may in the long run undermine their viability. Meanwhile, ties between the Russian and Mongolian Altai zones are weak and even decreasing, in spite of mutual demands for economic and cultural cooperation. At the same time, the delineation of the Russian-Kazakhstan state border is proving a challenging process, the outcome of which will also affect trade and security. Against this background, it is surprising that Tajikistan, northern Afghanistan, and even Pakistan and India present tremendous opportunities for the Russian Altai, thanks to the mutually complementary nature of their economies.

The Russian Altai belongs historically, culturally and economically to Central and Inner Asia and is in turn part of a larger Altai region that is sometimes called "Greater Altai," which includes also the East Kazakhstan province of Kazakhsntan, the Xinjiang-Uyghur autonomous Region of China, and the Bayan-Ulgy and Khovd *Aymaks* of Mongolia. This term was introduced long ago but is now gaining currency, thanks to the new spirit of regionalism that is developing there.

This unique Eurasian regionalism manifests some features of European integration, but is more reminiscent of the "soft" interrelationships that have developed in South-East and South Asia. The history of sub-regional cooperation among adjacent territories of Russia, Kazakhstan, China, and Mongolia is short, but encouraging. There were Chinese who in 1996 raised the idea of forming an East Central Asia economic zone uniting East Kazakhstan, Russia's Altai Republic and Altai province,

Bayan-Ulgy and Kobdo *Aymaks* of Mongolia, and China's Xinjiang region. This idea was furthered in 2000 when representatives of these six regions signed in Urumchi a Declaration on International Cooperation in the Altai Mountain Region. Since 1998 the Chinese-Russian initiative to build a transport corridor via Kanas pass (the so-called "Eurasian continental bridge" framework) has been under discussion. This project is complemented by the Mongolian initiative of 2000 to create a "Eurasian continental bridge."

Whereas proponents of Altai economic development have merely suggested certain ideas on international transport, environmentalists have already implemented some integrative ecological projects, among them the "Long-Term Protection of Bio-Diversity of the Altai-Sayan Ecoregion" (1997), and UNDP's "Development and Implementation of Local Strategies of Sustainable Development in the Altai Republic"(2001). At the moment researchers and government agencies from Mongolia, China, Kazakhstan, and Russia, with support from the German government and UNESCO are developing the concept of a trans-border bio-sphere territory for sustainable development in Altai. The authors of this project suggest that it might eventually mesh with such economic projects such as the "Eurasian trans-continental bridge."

In September, 2002, Russia, Kazakstan, and Mongolia, and China established a joint committee, called "Altai: Our Common Home," to develop the resources of the Alta mountain range and link them with the broader world. The signatories agreed to focus on trade, transport, tourism, environmental protection, and education. The goal is to develop the entire region as an eco-tourism destination with world-class agriculture and a base for new technologies.

This quadripartite project of regional cooperation has now become an institutionalized network involving the academic communities and legislators, with the support also of the business communities and governments. The expert who has contributed the most and also to this idea since the late 1990s is S. Nozhkin, currently the vice-head of the Department of International Cooperation in the government of Altai Province. It was he who energetically encouraged not only the process itself, but its informational support by starting the web-site http://www.altaiinter.info, one of the best and most dynamic websites in the field.

Map A: Western Siberia and Central Asia

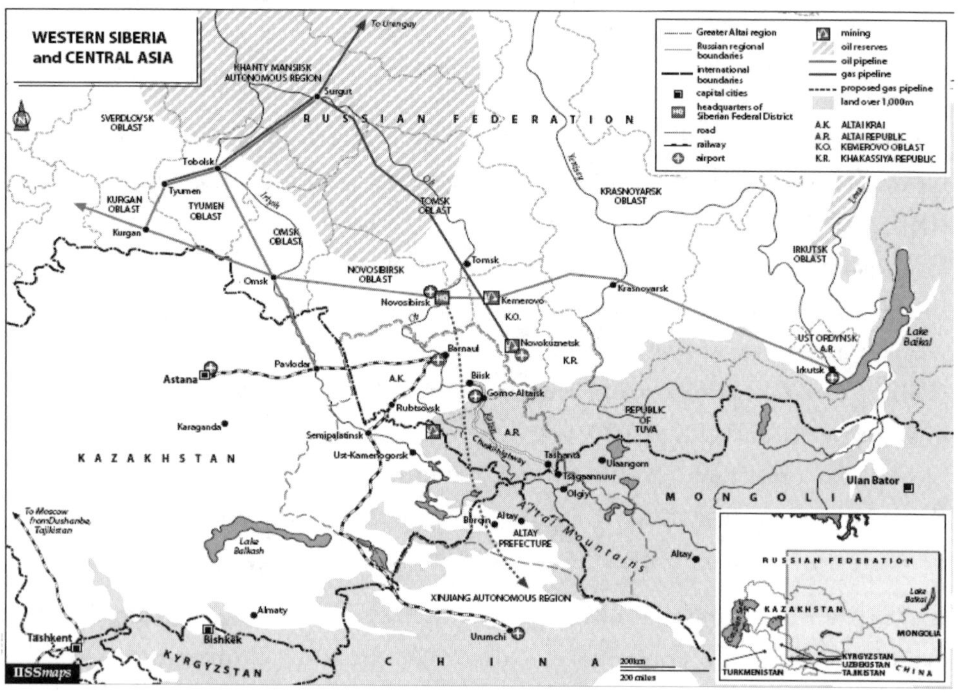

Source: Russia's New Southern Border: Western Siberia–Central Asia. The IISS Russian Regional Perspectives Journal for Foreign and Security Policy, Issue no. 2. London, 2003, http://www.iiss.org/showdocument.php?docID=165 (accessed 6 February 2006).

The Altai-Altai project for roads and gas pipelines

One of the most controversial aspects of the development of the Altai region is the proposed construction of a highway from Barnaul, the administrative center of Altai province, to Urumchi, the capital of the Xinjiang Uyghur Automomous Region of China. The project to build a road connecting Russia and China through the Altai was developed by Russia and China and is supported by Western development organizations. However, it has foundered on the massive opposition mobilized by local Russian environmentalists and nationalists. The length of this new trans-national transport line will be 260 km, of which 140 km is already constructed. The Xinjiang government is ready to allocate funds to build the remaining 120 km.[39] There is still no checkpoint on the 55 km, western border sector between China and Russia, and all cargos are going instead through Kazakhstan, leading to increased costs.

The proposed highway connecting China and Russia will go via the Ukok plateau and will cross the border at the Kanas pass. Opponents point out that the Ukok plateau is included among UNESCO's World Heritage Sites because of its many archeological sites. For example, it is here that the archeologist N. Polosmak found the famed "Altai princess" mummy. Many ethnic Altaians consider the region to be holy and explain the earthquake of 2003 as being the consequence of the "princess's" spirit having been disturbed. Altai Republic authorities are also opposed to the idea of road construction and are offering to build a link to China via Mongolia, using the alternative route Tashanta-Ulgiy (Mongolia)-Kobdo (Mongolia)-Taikishken in China.

Nor is the highway the sole bone of contention. In March, 2006, President Putin announced in China Russia's plans to construct two pipelines from Siberia to China. Russia hopes to export to China 60-80 billion cubic meters of gas annually by this route. The Chairman of Gazprom, Aleksei Miller, stated that the cost of this new gas pipeline could reach $10 billion and that it might be completed by 2011. Greens strongly oppose this project. In April, 2006, the matter was discussed by Russian Prime Minister Fradkov, the presidential representative in Siberia, Kvashnin, and the governor of the Altai province, Karlin. While the Prime Minister cautioned that all relevant data must be taken into

---

39 "V blizhayshie 1 – 2 goda Kitai postroit dorogu k Altaiu, "http://www.altaiinter.org/news/?id=10396

account, including relevant ecological issues,[40] Altai's Governor Karlin told the media that the project will definitely go forward with direct financing and will cross 450 km of Altai territory.[41]

Conclusions

Since the breakup of the Communist system in the early 1990s Russia has become a dynamically developing state and society, where democratic norms and patterns of economic and political life are steadily gaining strength. Due to historical factors and to its geographic location, Russia is a Eurasian power, with a substantial part of its territory located socially and economically in Asia, and with certain southern border-belt regions falling within Central Asia proper. Russia's Asianness (or Central Asianness) while shifting over time, has always been a factor in its domestic and external politics. This fact, as well as geo-political and geo-economic factors, assures the permanence of Russia's interest in the East and her cooperation with its Asian neighbors, whether China, Kazakhstan, India, or Japan, etc. Integrative projects in the strategic and economic sphere are important for Russia. Of particular importance are the states of Central Asia – the vast landmass that includes five former Soviet republics and other states with similar ethno-cultural roots including China's Xinjiang region, the Turco-Tajik north of Afghanistan, the Turkic north ofIran, and India and Pakistan, with their Central Asian territories of Kashmir. [42]

Any partnership framework for Greater Central Asia should involve Russia fully and give it a key role. This includes the exploitation of North- and Western Siberian energy resources and related pipelines between Siberia, Central Asia, and South Asia (the Siberian-Indian corridor). It should not be forgotten that Russia, while burdened by her

---

[40] Interview with M.Fradkov on 14 April 2006 see at: http://www.altaiinter.org/news/?id=10463

[41] http://www.altaiinter.org/news/?id=15117 1 December 2006

[43] Schneider-Deters, W. , "Bezopasnost I ekonomika: neobkhodimost regionalnogo sotrudnichestva v Tsentralnoy Azii. – Tsentralnaya Aziya v XXI: sotrudnichestvo, partnerstvo i dialog," Proceedings of the international conference on this theme, Tashkent, 2004, p. 6

own domestic problems, has not yet begun to play its full role in the region, which constituted the borderlands of both the Russian imperial and post-imperial states. In the future Russia will surely play a bigger role in reframing the broader geo-political and geo-economic space than it has for the past fifteen years and, in doing so, will demonstrate its capacity for cooperation with its culturally and economically akin neighbors. One of the most illuminating proofs of this cooperation on a regional and sub-regional level is the Greater Altai partnership project, which is an expression of a trans-national Asiatic regionalism.

Returning to the chief concept and program under discussion, that is the Greater Central Asia partnership (GCAP), one may conclude the following: it obviously offers a viable alternative to existing and emerging patterns of regional integration. Acknowledging this, the GCAP plan should include a decisive roles for out-of-region players, first of all the USA. This important regional partnership is justified by the stagnating economy, which requires extraordinary initiatives from out-of-region investors.

Even though it would achieve them through technological means (transport and trade), GCAP's goals are bold, even radical. It would bring about the fundamental alteration of archaic and in some cases deliberately preserved socio-political institutions at the local and regional levels. Such traditional forms as nomadism and tribalism, and various autonomous or semi-autonomous ethno-political structures such as those which exist on the Afghan-Pakistan border, and even the world-wide drug smuggling networks, would all be eliminated by the technological force of trade.

Perhaps GCAP's goal is too radical, a romantic notion that is ahead of its time. In proposing to modernize economic and social patterns it lays bare too many "blank spots" that endure in the complex world of Central Asia.

Viewed from a purely scholarly perspective, one can say that the GCA project partially ignores or comes into frontal conflict with earlier theoretical ideas regarding the regions and countries that might be termed Central Asia proper. Above all, it would significantly impact the territories on Russia's southern flank, China's western province of Xinjiang, Kashmir, and other areas.

The notion of a Greater central Asia assumes that Afghanistan should be included as part of Central Asia, even as it is simultaneously to be incorporated into South Asia by means of its Pashtun population. The point is not that Afghanistan, with its ongoing conflicts, is alien either to Central or South Asia. But for a century very different conditions prevailed there, which included its status as a tribal state which a reforming monarchy had formed into a kind of federation, a quasi-republic, etc, etc. The GCAP concept proposes to correct all this through a scheme based on mutual collaboration.

There is a basis for this. The Afghan clergy, for example which includes knowledgeable and authoritative personalities and groups, was educated not only at Al Azhar in Egypt and at the Deobandi schools of Pakistan, but at Bukhara, Tashkent, and other Central Asian centers of Islamic education and learning. The ties of these Afghans with their counterparts in Central Asia endured even through the Soviet era. Beyond this, the northern areas of Afghanistan belong to Turkic Central Asia, and their population includes many descendents of people who emigrated from the southern USSR during the 1920s.

It cannot be denied that the potential for cooperation and integration between the Central Asian republics and Afghanistan is severely reduced by the differences between them today and by political instability. All the same, the imperatives of world economic developments and the growth of new linkages within Asia and globally render closer ties between Central Asia and Afghanistan inevitable. An opening to the Indian Ocean of great significance to the future of all Central Asia. It is therefore in the interest of all Central Asia to re-establish economic links with Afghanistan and the Indian sub-continent, as well as with Iran. Given this, the extension of Central Asia's regional cooperation southwards would appear to be the first commandment of the twenty-first century.

Biographical Sketches of Participating Authors

Masood Aziz

Masood Aziz is a Counsellor at the Afghanistan Embassy in Washington. He is the founder and acting Executive Director of the Afghanistan Policy Council, a think tank providing a distinct voice to challenging policy issues pertaining to Afghanistan. Mr. Aziz has over 19 years of experience in executive management, international management consulting, banking and institutional investment management. He holds the French Baccalaureat, a Bachelor of Science degree and an MBA from the United States and is a frequent speaker and writer on economic and political matters related to Afghanistan and the greater Central Asia.

Vladimir Boyko

Dr. Vladimir Boyko is Director of the Center for Regional Studies and Associate Professor of Asian Studies at Barnaul State Pedagogical University in Barnaul, Russia. He obtained PhD from the Institute of Oriental Studies, USSR Academy of Sciences (Moscow), and has held fellowships at Harvard University, Ruhr University, and the London School of Economics. Dr Boyko is the author/co-author or editor of ten books on Afghanistan and Central Eurasia.

Dennis de Tray

Dennis de Tray serves as Vice President at the Center for Global Development (CGD). Before joining CGD, de Tray directed the World Bank's Mission for the five Central Asian republics from Almaty, Kazakhstan. Previously, he served as IMF senior representative to Vietnam in Hanoi, and as the World Bank's Director, Resident Staff and then Country Director in Jakarta, Indonesia. He earned his Ph.D. in economics from the University of Chicago in 1972.

Guljan Ermekbaeva

Guljan Ermekbaeva is a graduate of Kyrgyz State University and received an MBA from the International Academy of Management, Law, Finance, and Business. An expert on regulatory reform, Ms. Ermekbaeva is executive director of the Junior Achievement Kyrgyzstan Foundation.

Rafkat Hasanov

Rafkat Hasanov is executive director of "The Investment Round Table," which gained renown for its contribution to economic reform in the Kyrgyz Republic. He carries out applied and policy-relevant research in the areas of fiscal reform, tax legislation, budgetary issues, macro-economic modeling, revenue forecasting, foreign investment, deregulation, and poverty reduction.

Kemal Kaya

Dr. Kemal Kaya is co-founder of the East and West Institute in Ankara. An aeronautical engineer by training and with a Ph. D. from Istanbul Technical University, he has a decade-long experience in the Turkish defense industry and has coordinated numerous international defense projects for the Turkish government. Currently, he is a senior administrator/ manager in the Turkish Parliament.

Aftab Kazi

Dr. Aftab Kazi is professor of International and Comparative Politics, American University of Central Asia, Bishkek, the Kyrgyz Republic. He completed his doctoral degree in International Studies at the University of Pittsburgh. He is the founder and first editor-in-chief of the Journal of Asian & African Affairs (1988-94), and his publications include the monographs Ethnicity and Education in Nation-Building: the Case of Pakistan and The Politics of Civil-Military Relations in Pakistan.

Sanat Kushkumbayev

Dr. Sanat Kushkumbayev is First Deputy Director at the Kazakhstan Institute of Strategic Studies. He holds a Doctorate degree from al-Farabi Kazakh State University and specializes in political studies. His publications include a monograph Central Asia on the Way of Integration: Geopolitics, Ethnicity and Security (2002), and more than 70 articles in Kazakhstan and foreign research-analytical journals.

Abbas Maleki

Abbas Maleki completed his undergraduate and master's degrees at the Sharif University of Technology in Tehran, where he holds the post of assistant professor. With a PhD in strategic management, he has taught courses on Iranian foreign policy, the Islamic revolution, and Iran and its neighbors. In 1985-89 he was Director General of the Institute for Political and International Studies at the Foreign Ministry of the Islamic Republic of Iran, and then Deputy Foreign Minister for Research and Education, in Iran's Foreign Ministry, to 1997. Since 1997 he has served as Director General of the Institute for Caspian Studies in Teheran and in other senior advisory capacities.

Djoomart Otorbaev

After working in various Kyrgyz research institutes, Djoomart Otorbaev became a visiting professor at Eindhoven University, The Netherlands, 1992-1996. In 2001 he was appointed as a special representative of the President of the Kyrgyz Republic for foreign investments, and at the same time he founded the Investment Round Table. Between 2002 and

2005 he served as a Vice-Prime-Minister of the Kyrgyz Republic with responsibility for economic development. From April 2006 Djoomart Otorbaev has served at the EBRD's London headquarters as Senior Advisor for the Caucasus and Central Asia.

Martin Raiser

Martin Raiser holds a PhD in Economics from the University of Kiel, Germany, and a master's degree in Economics and Development Studies from the London School of Economics. Until 2003 he worked at the European Bank for Reconstruction and Development as lead economist for Central Asia. He then served as country manager for the World Bank in Tashkent, Uzbekistan, before being named to the World Bank's regional office for Belarus, Moldova and Ukraine in Kiev. Mr. Raiser is on the editorial board of the Journal of Comparative Economics.

Dinara Rakhmanova

Dinara Rakhmanova heads the International Relations Unit of the Kyrgyz Republic's National Agency on Corruption Prevention. Holding a master's degree in public administration, she earlier worked in international development organizations, mainly in the area of good governance and public administration reform. She also served with the United Nations development Program in Afghanistan and in her native Kyrgyzstan.

Gulshan Sachdeva

Dr. Gulshan Sachdeva, who holds a PhD degree from the Hungarian Academy of Sciences, is Associate Professor at the School of International Studies, Jawaharlal Nehru University in New Delhi. His expertise includes transition economies, European economic integration, regional economic cooperation and India's Northeast. Presently he is in Kabul working in the ADB-funded capacity building project on regional cooperation at the Afghanistan Ministry of Foreign Affairs. He is the author of The Economy of North-East: Policy, Present Conditions and Future Possibilities (2000) and many articles, and is on the editorial board of the journal International Studies.

Sergey Slepchenko

Sergey Slepchenko directs the analytical consortium "Perspective" in Bishkek, the Kyrgyz Republic, having participated earlier in research for the United Nations Development Program and various World Bank projects. Working in Kazakhstan, Russia, France, and Tajikistan, as well as Kyrgyzstan, he specializes on regional development and trade, technologies of communication, and processes of decision making.

S. Frederick Starr

S. Frederick Starr is Chairman of the Central Asia-Caucasus Institute and Silk Road Studies Program. Starr holds a Ph.D. in History from Princeton University, an MA from King's College, Cambridge University, and a BA from Yale University.

Niklas Swanström

Niklas Swanström is Program Director of the Central Asia-Caucasus Institute and Silk Road Studies Program. He is Editor of the *China and Eurasia Forum Quarterly*. He holds a Ph.D. from Uppsala University, and a MALD degree from the Fletcher School of Law and Diplomacy, Tufts University.

Murat Suyunbaev

Dr. Murat Suyunbaev is Vice-Principal of the Diplomacy Academy under the Ministry of Foreign Affairs of Kazakhstan. After completing his doctorate he worked for fifteen years he in various research organizations, where he specialized in strategic planning, development, and geopolitics. In this capacity he drafted concept papers for the government of Kazakhstan on cultural policy, foreign policy, national security, and sustainable human development.

Khojamahmad Umarov

Professor Khojamahmad Umarov is head of the Macroeconomic Studies Department of the Institute of Economic Studies, Ministry of Economy and Trade, in Dushanbe, Tajikistan. The author of thirty books, his areas of expertise include regional and continental trade, infrastructure, logistics, and transit; strategies of economic and social development; and social issues. A Tajik by nationality, he hails from the Aini district of Tajikistan.

Zhang Li

Zhang Li is Research Professor of International Relations at the Centre for Asian Studies, Sichuan University, in China. He is has been a visiting scholar at Oxford University, Jawaharlal Nehru University, and the University of Hong Kong.

Taleh Ziyadov

Taleh Ziyadov is Deputy Executive Director of the U.S.-Azerbaijan Chamber of Commerce in Washington. He holds a Master's degree in Eurasian, Russian, and East European Studies from the School of Foreign Service at Georgetown University. His analytical articles appeared in *Analysis of Current Events*, the *Central Asia-Caucasus Analyst*, the *Turkish Policy Quarterly*, the *Moscow Times* and the *Eurasia Daily Monitor*.